www.wileyplus.com

D1473340

WileyPLUS is a research-based online environment for effective teaching and learning.

WileyPLUS builds students' confidence because it takes the guesswork out of studying by providing students with a clear roadmap:

- **what to do**
- **how to do it**
- **if they did it right**

It offers interactive resources along with a complete digital textbook that help students learn more. With *WileyPLUS*, students take more initiative so you'll have greater impact on their achievement in the classroom and beyond.

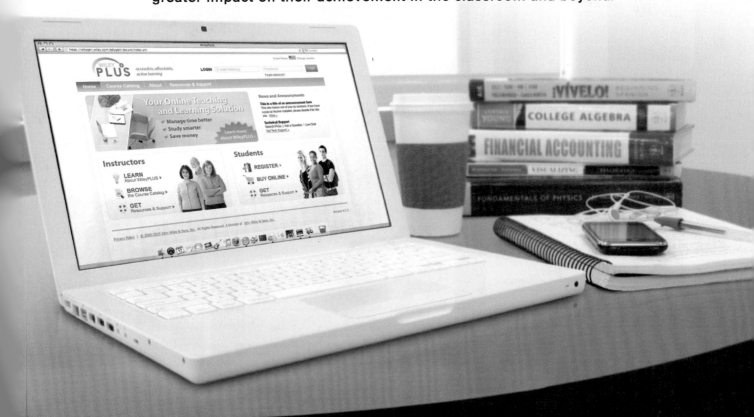

For more information, visit www.wileyplus.com

introduction to business
INFORMATION SYSTEMS

THIRD CANADIAN EDITION

JAMES L. NORRIE
Ryerson University

MICHELLE NANJAD
Nanjad Project Services

MARK W. HUBER
University of Georgia

WILEY

John Wiley & Sons Canada, Ltd.

DEDICATION

To our students, present and past, who have guided us both in the classroom and while writing this book; to our many colleagues and friends who encouraged us along the way; and most importantly to our family, whose indulgence and tolerance made this book possible. You are all awesome!

Library and Archives Canada Cataloguing in Publication

Introduction to business information systems / James Norrie . . . [et al.].—3rd Canadian ed.

Includes index.
ISBN 978-1-11-829979-1

1. Information technology—Management—Textbooks.
2. Management information systems—Textbooks.   I. Norrie, James, 1965-

HD30.2.I58   2012   658.4'038011   C2012-902155-5

Production Credits

VICE-PRESIDENT AND PUBLISHER	Veronica Visentin
ACQUISITIONS EDITOR	Darren Lalonde
SENIOR MARKETING MANAGER	Anne-Marie Seymour
EDITORIAL MANAGER	Karen Staudinger
PRODUCTION MANAGER	Tegan Wallace
DEVELOPMENTAL EDITOR	Leanne Rancourt
MEDIA EDITOR	Channade Fenandoe
EDITORIAL ASSISTANT	Laura Hwee
COVER AND INTERIOR DESIGN	Joanna Vieira
TYPESETTING	MPS Limited
COVER PHOTO	© moodboard/Corbis
PRINTING AND BINDING	Friesens

Printed and bound in Canada
1 2 3 4 5 FP 16 15 14 13 12

WILEY

John Wiley & Sons Canada, Ltd.
6045 Freemont Blvd.
Mississauga, Ontario L5R 4J3

Visit our website at: www.wiley.ca

ABOUT THE AUTHORS

JAMES L. NORRIE, DPM, is an Associate Professor at the Ted Rogers School of Management at Ryerson University, where he teaches Introductory IT, Advanced Project Management, Systems and Process Analysis & Design, Intellectual Property Law, and Governance and Professional Ethics. He also undertakes applied research, speaks regularly at industry events, and consults widely in these areas with a particular focus on aligning business and IT strategy to eliminate business risk and improve organization performance. More recently, his focus has expanded to the implications of social media for business strategy and models. Prior to joining the faculty, he was both an entrepreneur and a Fortune 500 executive with a 20+ year track record of creating, growing, and managing technology-related ventures. He is the author or co-author of two other best-selling titles and numerous articles, and is a frequent media commentator on current issues in technology, business, and society, including emerging trends and implications of social media.

MICHELLE NANJAD, BComm, BA, PMP is the principal consultant of Nanjad Project Services, an IT and project management consulting company. In her consulting practice, Michelle personally manages strategic projects, creates and manages PMOs, and customizes and implements best practice project and portfolio management methodologies. Michelle helps her clients realize their strategic goals, whether to achieve cost savings or to successfully introduce new products. Michelle is a skilled coach for IT executives and high level project managers and, on occasion, fills interim executive IT roles. Michelle's clients include companies in the manufacturing, telecommunications, transportation, retail, publishing, software development, and not-for-profit sectors. In the academic world, Michelle has been an instructor and teaching assistant for Project Management, Systems Design, Process Design, Technology Strategy, eCommerce, Introductory IT, and IT Law at Ryerson University.

MARK W. HUBER is Lecturer in Management Information Systems in the Terry College of Business at the University of Georgia (UGA), Director of the Terry College and Franklin College of Arts and Science Leadership Excellence and Development Program (L.E.A.D.), and a member of the UGA Teaching Academy. Over the past six years he has won nine teaching awards, including recognition as Outstanding Faculty at UGA Honors Day, a Terry College Regent's Professor Award Nominee, Outstanding MIS Faculty, a Student Government Outstanding Professor Award, Alpha Kappa Psi (professional business society) Outstanding Management Information Systems Teacher of the Year Award, and three UGA Career Center Student Development Awards. Dr. Huber recently completed a 21-year U.S. Air Force career that included the creation and command of a Combat Communications Squadron and the management and development of strategic information systems projects at the Pentagon. His research interests include group support systems and team and group development. He has written numerous papers for various professional and academic journals, and he co-authored a lab manual published by John Wiley & Sons, Inc. in 2006.

PREFACE

■ WHY WE WROTE THIS BOOK

During our collective teaching careers in both Canada and the United States, we have developed and taught introductory information systems courses to more than 25,000 business students. For most of our students, this was their first exposure to understanding both business and information systems together. From our students, we learned that there was a significant need for an introductory information systems textbook that engages business students across all majors and creates a foundation for their understanding and strategic use of information systems and technology as future business professionals. From our generous colleagues around the world, we learned that providing a textbook that leads with the business context, rather than with a technology focus, helps make introductory IT more interesting and seems a better fit with many courses that are not intended for those pursuing a deep, sustained major in a technology-related discipline.

We hope that as a student or instructor of IT, you will agree that this book represents an innovative and creative way of teaching and learning about an important subject.

■ NEW TO THE THIRD CANADIAN EDITION

The pace of technological innovation is truly staggering, so any IT book needs constant updating. In this new edition you will find new or increased coverage of the following:

- Characteristics of the digital world we live in; Internet crime and cyberterrorism (Chapter 1)
- Internet security; business continuity; cloud computing (Chapter 2)
- Dashboards and visual analytics (Chapter 3)
- Competitive necessity; co-opetition (Chapter 5)
- Technology-based acquisitions; end-user development (Chapter 6)
- Social media usage and trends; search engine optimization (Chapter 8)

New Cases

Each chapter also includes one entirely new case (for a total of two cases in each chapter), plus additional cases that are available through *WileyPLUS*. Some of these cases are based on real-life companies or situations; others are critical thinking exercises that ask students to think of solutions to common business problems.

Study Cards

At the back of the book are detachable Study Cards that students can take with them to study on the go. These cards include a summary of key points for each chapter, including diagrams; a list of the most important key terms (Knowledge Speak); key figures to help students visualize the material; and a Quick Test to test their knowledge of the chapter content.

■ HOW WE WROTE THIS BOOK

Our fundamental philosophy is that within organizations, all business professionals use information systems and technologies to enable and enhance the successful achievement of business goals. We believe that the effective integration of IS with knowledge drives the creation of significant business value, everywhere and every time. As such, most students, regardless of their major, need to understand information systems and technologies and their importance to the success of business organizations. Numerous features of this book are designed to help students and teachers succeed.

Integration of E-Commerce

We approach e-commerce as an important component of commerce and not as an aspect of business that stands alone from an organization's efforts to create business value. So, while we discuss e-commerce business models, strategies, and technologies in significant detail in Chapter 7, we integrate this topic into most other chapters and incorporate relevant examples throughout. The same is true for social media and its implications for marketing, customer service, collaboration, and decision making.

Tech Guides

We wanted to provide a way to extend students' learning experiences, as well as enable instructors to tailor the depth of the material to their course goals, without deviating from our goal of focusing on the business context first. To accomplish this goal, we have included three Tech Guides that provide more extensive coverage of hardware and software, networks, and SQL and XML. Instructors can either cover these as links to appropriate chapters, or use them to motivate students to go beyond what is required for the class and enjoy a deeper look at base technology and systems architecture.

Features to Engage Students

Introduction to Business Information Systems, Third Canadian Edition, is filled with many pedagogical features designed to engage students and enhance the learning process. These features include our chapter-opening student ROI, various within-chapter elements, and relevant end-of-chapter material (including two case studies).

The next few pages will take you on a tour of some of the special features of this edition. We strongly believe that the approach taken in this text will enhance student engagement and help create a foundation for students' understanding and use of information systems and technology. We hope you will agree! I would love to hear from you regarding your experience using this book in the classroom. Please email me with any comments.

Dr. James Norrie, lead author
jlnorrie@ryerson.ca

FEATURES TO ENGAGE STUDENTS

■ GET STARTED ON THE RIGHT FOOT!

Student ROI

The *Student ROI* alerts students to the knowledge and skills they will have after reading the chapter. In other words, this section helps students see the "return" on their "investment" of time to read and understand the chapter material.

STUDENT RETURN ON INVESTMENT ROI

Through your investment of time in reading and thinking about this chapter, your return—or created value—is gaining knowledge. After reading this chapter, you should be able to

1. Define data, information, and knowledge and describe how business professionals engage in knowledge work activities.

The Voice of Experience

Each chapter begins with *The Voice of Experience*, a Q&A session with a business professional that focuses on how the individual uses information systems in his or her job. Some of these interviewees are IT professionals, but most are business professionals who have been able to leverage the power of information systems to create business value. These interview boxes are designed to motivate readers to understand the content covered in the chapter by helping them to see how the chapter material might be useful in their future career.

THE VOICE OF EXPERIENCE

Arti Davda, University of British Columbia

Arti Davda graduated from the University of British Columbia in 2005 with a Bachelor of Commerce. She then enrolled in York University's Schulich School of Business Accelerated MBA program, graduating with honours in 2008. She now works as an Account Manager with Google Canada.

What do you do in your current position? As an Account Manager at Google Canada, my primary focus is client relations. I work with key clients in a strategic role where I help

over the world, and this makes for more timely and cost-efficient meetings. The advertising and sales team members use laptops whether we're in or out of the office, and phones have headsets for ease-of-use. We are also using the latest Google phones so we are always connected. Our new

■ MAKE THE CONNECTION!

Quick Tests

Quick Tests are short quizzes integrated throughout each chapter that provide students with an opportunity to test their understanding of the material in that section.

Quick Test

1. Which one of the following is not an input to the organization as an open system?
   a. labour
   b. productivity
   c. information
   d. technology

2. Fill in the blank. A business carries _____ when it interacts with its environment.

What Do You Think?

What Do You Think? boxes are scattered throughout each chapter and are designed to evoke critical thinking related to the topic just discussed. They pose questions to the students to help them think critically about an aspect of the topic and to help them relate it to their own examples or experience. These boxes are further developed in the Instructor's Manual to provide a basis for leading in-class discussions or debates—techniques that we know are important to instructors who wish to engage students in the classroom.

WHAT DO YOU THINK?

Imagine that you are the CEO of a large global retailer. Recently, your CIO approached you to ask about the requirements for a new business intelligence system to replace an aging MIS application. Answer these questions that you are asked during this meeting:

1: What kinds of information about our business would you like to see on a daily, weekly, or monthly basis?
2: How important is it that this information is accurate and up-to-date for the kinds of decisions that you normally make? Does it have to be accurate by the minute, hour, or day, and why?
3: How would you like to have access to this information? Where and why?

Technology Core

Each chapter includes a *Technology Core* box. These boxes are designed to highlight a technical aspect of the chapter content, showing students how technology facilitates the concept being discussed.

TECHNOLOGY CORE

The details involved in systems projects can be very difficult to keep track of. A lot of information associated with the SDLC flows from one stage to the next. And then there is the issue of changes! When something changes, many, many people need to be informed and many adjustments need to be made. What if you miss one? Keeping track of the details is essential to the success of systems development projects. Integrated development environments (IDEs) are excellent tools to help in this regard. One of the best-

providing an integrated requirements management system that helps to define and manage requirements, especially in the case where requirements change and need to be communicated to team members. Requirements traceability features help determine how requirements are built into the software. Rational, like other IDEs, provides development tools and the ability to develop software collaboratively. Once the software is complete, Rational provides a full quality management system for testing the software prior to

What's in IT for Me?

At the end of each chapter, three boxes—What's in IT for Me? What's in IT for an Organization? and What's in IT for Society?—provide a discussion of applications of the concepts covered within the chapter. *What's in IT for Me?* boxes illustrate personal implications of the concepts, such as how ATMs and online banking have allowed for quick and easy transactions, how databases can make you more efficient, and so on. *What's in IT for an Organization?* boxes highlight how organizations have harnessed the power of IT to be more efficient and more competitive. *What's in IT for Society?* boxes demonstrate the far-reaching implications advances in technology and business decisions have on society as a whole. For example, how did technology speed up relief efforts in Haiti after the devastating earthquake in January 2010? How does the Internet facilitate the tracking of flu cases worldwide? These and other issues are explored in the What's in IT . . . boxes.

What's in IT for me?

What if organizations did not automate, informate, or transform? Can you imagine waiting for the bank to be open to withdraw money or having to use a card file in the library to do the research for your term paper? Successful organizations and businesses are constantly looking for ways to improve. Those that do not are unsuccessful and may even cease to exist. Would you choose a bank that did not offer online banking, for example? IT helps organizations understand their business environment and the needs of their customers by providing vital information.

can then solve problems or capitalize on opportunities that help gain or sustain competitive advantage. When this happens, you, as a customer, benefit. You benefit by dealing with an efficient and innovative organization that knows what you want. IT may also be part of what is offered to you as a customer. Somehow Apple recognized the need for the iPod and invented the required technology to enable it. Because of this one innovative product, the entire music industry has been forced to transform to meet customers' needs. We can only guess what the future will hold as you become business professionals and join in the activity of creating business

■ ASSESS YOUR UNDERSTANDING

Student ROI Summary

The *Student ROI Summary* provides answers to the questions posed in the Student ROI at the beginning of the chapter. As such, it helps students review what they have learned in the chapter.

Knowledge Speak

The *Knowledge Speak* section is a list of keywords found in the chapter, which students should understand as a part of the terminology learned in the chapter.

Review Questions

The *Review Questions* contain various types of questions, all aimed at having students assess their understanding of the chapter material. Types of questions include true/false, multiple choice, fill in the blanks, short answer, and essay.

Team Activity

The *Team Activity* provides an opportunity for students to work as a team to carry out an activity pertinent to the chapter material.

Software Application Exercises

The *Software Application Exercises* ask students to solve a series of related exercises using word processing, spreadsheet, presentation, database, and Internet software.

Case Studies

Two *Case Studies* at the end of each chapter provide short descriptions of an example where information systems have created value, either for an individual or for a business. Case questions or activities are included with each Case Study to allow students and instructors to more deeply discuss the chapter content based on "real world" cases.

INSTRUCTOR AND STUDENT RESOURCES

■ ONLINE INSTRUCTOR SUPPORT MATERIALS

www.wiley.com/canada/norrie

As teachers, we understand the value of support materials for classroom activities. In fact, in creating the supplementary material, we have tried to produce an integrated package that will enhance faculty effectiveness and decrease workload, while simultaneously increasing student interest in the discipline and level of engagement in the classroom. To this end, the textbook is accompanied by a wealth of ancillary materials found on *WileyPLUS*. Materials are class-tested and we are more than happy to help instructors implement them in their own classes. Using this book and its support package should provide a department with confidence that students will receive a rigorous and innovative introduction to IS, and be better prepared to embark upon their future as business professionals creating business value through IS. Go to *www.wiley.com/canada/norrie* to access the extensive support materials for both students and instructors.

Instructor's Manual

The *Instructor's Manual*, written by Michelle Nanjad, is based on the cumulative experience of the authors teaching the course. It is designed to be a useful teaching tool, with an overview of key learning themes for each chapter, suggested answers to the *What Do You Think?* boxes, and suggestions for in-class activities and discussions. It also includes answers to the Review Questions found at the end of each chapter, as well as suggested solutions for the Case Studies.

Test Bank

The *Test Bank*, authored by Dennis Kira of Concordia University, is a comprehensive resource for test questions. Each chapter contains numerous multiple-choice questions to choose from that are labelled based on difficulty—easy, medium, or difficult—and that also include links to the text sections where the concept is discussed. The test bank is available for use in Respondus' easy-to-use software. Respondus is a powerful tool for creating and managing exams that can be printed to paper or published directly to eLearning systems such as Blackboard, WebCT, Desire2Learn, eCollege, ANGEL, and others.

PowerPoint Presentations

The *PowerPoint Presentations* consist of a series of slides for each chapter of the text that are designed to summarize chapter content, incorporating key points from the text. These slides are an excellent starting point for any lecture on the chapter topics. For the Third Canadian Edition, they have been completely revamped into a new format; the new style and a contemporary look and feel should be helpful to instructors and students.

Image Library

All textbook figures are available for download from *WileyPLUS*. These figures can easily be added to PowerPoint presentations.

Clicker Questions

The *Clicker Questions* offer 10–15 questions per chapter that can be used with a variety of personal response (or "clicker") systems.

■ STUDENT RESOURCES

Animations

Selected figures from the text that involve dynamic activity have been animated using Flash technology. These animated figures can be shown as a part of instructor presentations to demonstrate multistep processes.

Practice Quizzes

Students can test their knowledge and better prepare for exams using the *Practice Quizzes*. These quizzes include 15 multiple-choice questions per chapter that give students instant feedback and link to the text so they can review material that they may need to study more.

Flash Cards and Crossword Puzzles

Students can test their comprehension of the Knowledge Speak terms in the chapter using the interactive Flash Cards and fun Crossword Puzzles.

Weekly Update Site

Weekly updates, harvested from around the web by Jim Clark of the University of Lethbridge, provide students and instructors with the latest IT news and issues. These are posted throughout the academic year at *http://wileyisupdates.ca/* and include links to articles and videos, as well as discussion questions to assign or use in class.

Audio Summaries

Students who need to review content on the go can download the podcasts available for each chapter so they can study with their MP3 player!

Microsoft Office Guides

A Microsoft Office 2010 lab manual and projects, prepared by the text authors, and how-to animations for Microsoft Office help answer any Microsoft Office questions students or instructors might have.

Integrative Application Case

Available on *WileyPLUS*, the Integrative Application Case follows two students attempting to start up an Internet company (Campuspad.ca). Each Integrative Application Case builds on the material presented in each chapter, showing students how the content of the text ties together. Case questions, as well as a student task, are included with each Integrative Application Case section.

■ WILEYPLUS

WileyPLUS is an innovative, research-based online environment for effective teaching and learning.

WileyPLUS builds students' confidence because it takes the guesswork out of studying by providing students with a clear roadmap: what to do, how to do it, if they did it right. Students will take more initiative, so instructors will have greater impact on their achievement in the classroom and beyond.

ACKNOWLEDGEMENTS

When we did the first Canadian edition of this book more than five years ago, we had a vision to create a text that would help integrate technology and business in the classroom. The response from the marketplace suggests we succeeded! At that time, Michelle Nanjad was an instructor using the textbook, and she contributed much to its evolution over the second edition—one that proved to be extremely popular with Canadian universities and colleges. Of course, a project such as this is never the work of a single group of authors—rather, it is the combined effort of many people. And this is as true for this new third edition, where we now recognize Michelle's contributions by elevating her to status of co-author, a well-deserved recognition of how much she has contributed to this project over time!

As always, we first wish to thank our many students who have challenged us to develop new and innovative ways of teaching the concepts related to information systems and the value-creating role of IS in organizations. Much of what appears in this new text can be directly attributed to what you have told us about your experiences. This is especially true of our largest school adoptions, where the particular challenges of teaching introductory IT in a large-class format have been a wonderful way of learning more about the pedagogy of IT with newer generations of students in large classes.

Special thanks are due to many people who contributed and worked on this book. To begin with, this project would not exist had it not been for the vision and support of Darren Lalonde, our Acquisitions Editor. He continues to share our vision and this text is of the highest calibre and quality because of his continued support. Similarly, it was Darren who suggested Leanne Rancourt, our Developmental Editor, and it has been great to have her working by our side, day in and day out, bringing all three editions to completion. Our heartfelt thanks go out to the entire Wiley team who have made this book possible: Veronica Visentin, Vice-President and Publisher; Anne-Marie Seymour, Marketing Manager; Karen Staudinger, Editorial Manager; Channade Fenandoe, Media Editor; Laura Hwee, Editorial Assistant; Tegan Wallace and Lynda Jess, Production Manager and Published Services Assistant; and Joanna Vieira, Designer.

And just as there is Leanne and a whole Wiley team behind Darren that makes it easy for him to do great work, we have an entire team behind us that makes us look good. We have to thank Keegan Tremblay, Davis Courneyea, Ashleigh Upton, and Nav Jagdat for their help with research, diagramming, updating Voice of Experience interviews, and working on the new aspects of this book, such as the fantastic study cards. Thanks gang!

Finally, all of the authors would like to thank our families for the gift of time they gave us to pursue this labour of love. Writing is not always an easy task, and it is quite personal, requiring the indulgence of the many to make it possible for the few. To our spouses and children, you know who you are and your love means everything to us!

■ REVIEWERS

We also want to thank the many individuals who took the time to read and evaluate the draft manuscripts prior to production. Our reviewers generously provided their expertise to help us ensure the book's accuracy, clarity, and focus on the needs of today's information systems instruction. Without their many, many helpful comments, the book would not be what it is today. Thank you for your invaluable contributions.

Anne Beaudry, *Concordia University*
Jim Clark, *University of Lethbridge*
Fred Douglas, *Sheridan College*
Bruce Matichuk, *Northern Alberta Institute of Technology*
Shauna Roch, *Fanshawe College*
Alain Ross, *Athabasca University*
Haralambie Stirbet, *Wilfrid Laurier University*
John Trembley, *Fanshawe College*

We would also like to thank the Voice of Experience participants, who took the time to share their expertise and experience with us. They are all examples of what can happen when information technology is used to its fullest potential.

Derek Ball, Entrepreneur, Tynt.com
Ryan Chong, Rogers Communications
Dave Codack, Toronto Dominion Bank
Arti Davda, Google Canada
John Lennie, Investor in e-commerce and social media-related ventures
Chris Moore, City of Edmonton
Joey Peng, Microsoft
Diane Viveiros, Skyline Hotels and Resorts

BRIEF CONTENTS

Logon   2

CHAPTER 1   IT FOR BUSINESS AND BUSINESS PROFESSIONALS   6

CHAPTER 2   TECHNOLOGY ESSENTIALS   46

CHAPTER 3   MANAGING AND USING DATA   90

CHAPTER 4   ENTERPRISE SYSTEMS   130

CHAPTER 5   CREATING BUSINESS VALUE   176

CHAPTER 6   MANAGING IS PROJECTS AND CREATING IS SOLUTIONS   210

CHAPTER 7   E-COMMERCE   252

CHAPTER 8   WEB 2.0, SOCIAL MEDIA, AND ONLINE TRENDS   300

Logoff   334

TECH GUIDE A   THE DETAILS OF IT HARDWARE AND SOFTWARE   338

TECH GUIDE B   THE DETAILS OF NETWORKING   374

TECH GUIDE C   THE DETAILS OF SQL, LOGICAL MODELLING, AND XML   398

Glossary   413

Photo Credits   429

Index   431

CONTENTS

Logon 2

CHAPTER 1 IT FOR BUSINESS AND BUSINESS PROFESSIONALS 6

The Importance of Information Systems 8
Why IS Matters 8
What Is an Information System? 10
IS versus IT 14
The Productivity Zone 14
The Internet 15

What's in IT for Me? 17
IT for Your Personal Productivity and Entertainment 17
IT Is Fundamental for Your Career 18

What's in IT for an Organization? 24
Business Organizations and the Business Environment 24
Types of IS Found in Business 26
Ethics in IT 27

What's in IT for Society? 30
The Global World 30
Characteristics of the Digital World 31
IT and the Economy 33
The Darker Side of IT 34

CHAPTER 2 TECHNOLOGY ESSENTIALS 46

The Components of IT 48
Hardware 49
Software 54
Connecting Over Networks 57

The Internet 60
What Makes the Internet Possible? 60
Accessing the Internet 61
Internet Applications 62
What's Next for the Internet? 65

The World Wide Web 67
    Basic Components of the World Wide Web 67
    Search Technologies 69

Internet Security 71
    Ensuring Security 73
    Disaster Recovery 76

Meaningful Applications of Technology 77
    Collaboration 77

CHAPTER 3 MANAGING AND USING DATA 90

Data, Information, and Knowledge 92
    Lifelong Knowledge Creation 92
    Knowledge Work Activities 93
    Discovery: Finding Data, Information, or Knowledge 93
    Analysis: Investigating and Examining the Available Data, Information, and Knowledge 94
    Transformation: Organizing Discovery Results 95
    Synthesis: The Sum of the Parts 96
    Communication: Sharing Analysis with Others 97
    Summary of Knowledge Work Activities 97

Decision Making and Problem Solving 99
    Classifying Decisions by Type 100
    Using Information in Decision Making 100
    How to Make More-Informed Decisions 101
    The Decision-Making Process and Problem-Solving Tools 102

Databases: The Primary Data Storage for Organizations 106
    The Data Hierarchy 107
    Relational Data Model 108
    Designing a Relational Database 109
    Storing and Accessing Data, Information, and Knowledge 111

Business Intelligence 113
    Using IT to Support Business Intelligence 114
    Business Intelligence Tools 117

CHAPTER 4 ENTERPRISE SYSTEMS 130

Information Systems that Support Business Activities 132
    Building an Understanding of the Value Chain 132
    Functional Information Systems 135
    Workflow Management Systems 137
    Transaction Processing Systems 138
    Supply Chain Management 140

Enterprise Resource Planning   142
Enterprise Systems that Support the Value Chain   143
Strategic Deployment of Enterprise Systems and Technologies   153
The Role of IS Governance and Leadership
in Creating Sustainable Business Value   155

Enterprise Risk Management   157
Applying the Risk Framework   160
Risk-Reduction Methods   161
Control and Controls   163
Conclusion   167

CHAPTER 5   CREATING BUSINESS VALUE   176

Business Organization and Business Processes   178
Businesses as Open Systems   179
How Businesses Organize to Create Value   182
Business Process   183
Innovation and Competitive Necessity   188

Applying IT to Create Business Value   189
Automating to Do Things Faster   190
Informating to Do Things Better   191
Transforming to Gain Competitive Advantage   191

Corporate, IT, and Project Governance   194
IT Governance   196
Project Governance   198
Professional Codes of Conduct and Practice   200

CHAPTER 6   MANAGING IS PROJECTS AND CREATING IS SOLUTIONS   210

Critical Pre-development Questions   213
What Are We Building and Why?   213
Is the Project Feasible?   213
Should We Build or Buy/Lease?   217
Buy or Lease: Which System/Vendor Should We Select?   218
Build: Should We Develop In-House or Outsource?   219

**The Stages and Importance of the System Development
Life Cycle (SDLC)   221**

Managing an IS Project   223
Overview of Project Management Tasks   225
Project Time Management   226
Project Risk Management   228
Program Management   230
Project Management Office   230
Project Management Software   231

IS Development Teams 233
The Importance of Stakeholders 233
A Typical IS Project Team 234

Standard IS Methodology 236
Why Do Organizations Need an IS Methodology? 236
The Traditional IS Methodology: The Waterfall Model 236
Modern IS Methodologies 238
IS Modelling 240

IT Tools for IS Development 241
IS Development Tools 241

CHAPTER 7 E-COMMERCE 252

E-Commerce Defined 254
Beyond the Basic Definition 255
E-Commerce and Products: Physical and Digital 255
E-Commerce Business Models 258

The E-Commerce Advantage 261
Breaking Through the Information Clutter 263
E-Commerce Competitive Difference 266
E-Commerce and Organization Strategy 268
M-Commerce 269

Benefits and Limitations of E-Commerce 271

E-Commerce Between Organizations 275
B2B Transactions and Business Models 275
Using B2B E-Commerce to Improve Supply
Chain Efficiency 277

The Technology of E-Commerce 280
First-Generation E-Commerce Technologies: Establishing
a Web Presence 280
Second-Generation E-Commerce Technologies: Providing Interaction 282
Third-Generation E-Commerce Technologies: Supporting Transactions 285
Fourth-Generation E-Commerce Technologies: Transforming Processes 288

CHAPTER 8 WEB 2.0, SOCIAL MEDIA, AND ONLINE TRENDS 300

Defining Social Technologies and Utility 303
Social Utility 306
Design and Usability 309
Business Utility 309
Legal and Ethical Framework for Social Media 310
Technology Implications and Costs 312
Ignorance Is NOT Bliss! 312

User-Generated Content   314
Finding Content   315
User-Generated Content and Brand Risk   315
Search Engine Optimization (SEO) on Social Sites   316

Creating Business Utility Using Social Media Tools and E-Marketing   317
Harnessing the Power of Social Media   319

The Social and Business Impacts of Web 2.0   320
Social Business Models   322
Conclusion   323

Logoff   334

TECH GUIDE A   THE DETAILS OF IT HARDWARE AND SOFTWARE   338

An Overview of Hardware   339
Evaluating Hardware Devices   339
The Electronics of Hardware   339
Processing Hardware   342
Internal Memory   344

Hardware Devices   345
Input Devices   345
Display Devices   350
Printed Output Devices   352
Storage Hardware   353

Operating Software   355
Comparison of Operating Systems   356
How the Operating System Works   356
What Does the Operating System Do?   357

Application Software   363
Commercially-Developed Application Software   363
Developing Customized Software   368

TECH GUIDE B   THE DETAILS OF NETWORKING   374

Network Architecture   375
Client/Server Architecture   375
Using Client/Server Systems to Increase Knowledge Work Efficiency   376
Peer-to-Peer Networks   377

Network Layer Model   378
Application Software Layer   379
Network Connection Layer   379
Data Component Layer   380

Different Kinds of Networks   383

Local Area Networks   383

The Internet: A Network of Networks   385

Using the Internet to Perform Knowledge Work Activities   387

The World Wide Web   390

Wireless Connectivity to the Web and Internet   394

TECH GUIDE **C** THE DETAILS OF SQL, LOGICAL MODELLING, AND XML   398

Using SQL to Query Relational Databases   399

Relational Database Example   399

Querying a Single-Table Database   399

Using SQL to Display Specific Information   400

Using the LIKE Operator   402

Inserting or Deleting Records   402

Changing Values with SQL   402

Using Aggregate Functions in SQL   403

Using Logical Modelling to Create a Relational Database and Querying Multitable Databases   404

Entity-Relationship Diagramming   404

The Relational Data Model   406

Querying Multitable Databases   407

Using XML for Data Transfer   409

XML vs. HTML   409

Setting Up an XML Document   409

Glossary   413

Photo Credits   429

Index   431

LOGON

Welcome to the start of our journey into the world of the IT-enabled business. As a future professional, entrepreneur, or employee in a business or organization, IT will be an increasingly important part of the work you do. The work world of today is quite different from that of the past. More and more jobs require business professionals who add value to business transactions by transforming data and information into knowledge and wisdom. Making good decisions fast helps maintain competitive advantage and is the priority of global organizations. Organizations use current technology and design information systems to help their workers create this value—and support good decisions. Almost all employees at any level use IT-related systems to perform their assigned tasks. We feel strongly that business strategy should drive these technology and system choices. This is often referred to as "alignment." In turn, this book will help you align your business choices, your career, and your understanding of the technology required to make this happen.

■ SO WHAT DO I REALLY NEED TO KNOW?

Depending on the tasks at hand (which will be different if you are a marketing analyst, sales manager, accountant, operations analyst, project manager, human resources advisor, lawyer, or plant manager, for instance), you will use different kinds of systems to obtain information relevant to your role or function. Regardless of the work you perform, chances are good it will involve a system of some sort. But the degree to which you are interested in the underlying technology of the system, versus the opportunity to improve your results, is the essential question. Most of you will only care about the latter, while the technology underpinnings will be mostly irrelevant to you. But there are some things that you should know at least a little bit about, even if you are intending to be a consumer rather than a designer of technology. Let's try to prove why.

Just as everyone is looking for something different when shopping for a car, each of you will likely be looking for something different from this text. Whether you want to get engrossed in the details of "what's under the hood," or just acquire the IT knowledge you need to succeed as a professional in today's fast-paced business world, this book will help you achieve your goals. But what remains clear is that the knowledge inside has value.

To begin with, think about a car that you might like to buy—your "dream car." Are you thinking about a red convertible with leather seats and speed to spare? Or maybe it's an SUV with a sunroof, DVD player, and 21-inch "spinners"? The way a car looks and how fast it will go are significant and visible differences. But the real purpose of a car, or its value, is to get you from place to place safely and reliably. So while any car you buy will do that, it's the "bells and whistles" that ultimately make the choice. Systems are like that too: they can focus only on utility (getting the job done at the cheapest possible price, easy to operate and maintain, and with no extra features to ease your way). Or, they can be uniquely customized, including the price tag that accompanies that kind of customization. Making decisions about which technology is ultimately best for you requires at least a basic knowledge of what is available to choose from, what your requirements are, and the cost-benefit analysis of features you might like versus need in the technology solution you are choosing. To sort this out, you need at least some knowledge of underlying technology options.

Now take this a step further. You have settled on and purchased your vehicle. There are things that must happen for the vehicle to operate properly. Think about what happens if you forget to fill the car's tank with gasoline or put in the wrong type of fuel. To determine what type of fuel your car's engine requires, for example, you could learn more about "what's under the hood" and investigate the fuel-injection system, combustion chambers, and conduct a similar component-by-component analysis. Or, you could assume the manufacturer has done all that and accept its recommendation, ratings, and warnings. If neither of those options suit you, perhaps a car-rating guide or expert opinion might help. Like a car, a business will stall without its own proper "gasoline"—in this case, clean data—which your technology will eventually process into useful information that helps you make better decisions. And there are many aspects to consider when making technology decisions. Drivers use gasoline to make cars go, and business professionals use data and information to make businesses succeed. So, it may be quite important to understand what will eventually fuel your system and how it will be secured before settling on your option of choice. The quality of the "fuel" you feed a system often determines its long-term health and contribution to your organization.

Those who are majoring in information technology or information systems (IT/IS) will obviously have a different level of commitment to and eventual understanding of the underlying technology being used in the systems—what is actually underneath the hood. They will want to, and need to, grasp much more detail about the systems than a simple technology user will need to know. However, they also need to make sure they understand the business context, since this is where the systems will be used and where the car will be driven as a means of transportation. In other words, they need a client perspective.

We also know that most of you reading this text will not be majoring in IT. You probably care much less about the engine of your car than you do about its features, comfort, and safety. However, you may want to know about fuel efficiency ratings or maintenance costs. The same can be said of your desire to acquire IT knowledge—it's restricted to the minimum you need to know to do your "real job." In fact, this course may be your only required course in the subject and your level of interest will vary, as it should. This is exactly why we wrote this book. We understand your dilemma: you want to understand the practical application of technology, but not necessarily the technology itself. We are going to help by making the book design, writing, and content as business-relevant and interesting as we can.

The authors of this text have all spent many years teaching introductory IT to university and college students around the world. We have come to learn that students vary in their level of interest in and involvement with the subject. Their expectations of the course range from "just get me through it," to "I may want to change my major." Yet there are important learning opportunities available to you, regardless of how much you initially want to study this subject. Information technology is everywhere; it is an essential component of most everything we do. We find it in our homes, in our cars, and at the office. It is in our classrooms from preschool to university. We find it in hospitals and in government offices. We use it to shop, socialize, and find out what's happening in the world. It may be hidden or visible; it may be a help or a hindrance, but it is omnipresent. And to succeed in business today, it must be mastered, not ignored.

Yet mastery is often determined as understanding the definitions and origins of technology. In the Internet age, with its myriad search engines and information-laden sites, this is not the most optimal use of your time as a student. If it is definitions you want, those are easy to get. While we certainly include these in our text (especially in the Tech Guides at the end of the book), we try to provide them in the chapters on a just-in-time basis, to ensure you understand the application of technology in a business context. Only by first ensuring you understand the organizational use of the technology are we safe to assume you may be interested in the origins, operation, and acquisition of such technology. This book emphasizes showing you how technology can be applied to create value, and not justifying the value of the technology itself! In short, our goal is to help you acquire knowledge about how to use IT to accomplish personal, organizational, and business partner goals—the really important stuff of business today.

◼ OUR TEXT'S FEATURES

We designed this third edition with feedback from many colleagues and students in terms of what was and what was not working from the second edition. As a result, we have made some changes that we hope will benefit introductory IT students.

To begin with, there is a balance between acquiring knowledge *about technology itself* versus an understanding of *how to apply technology in business settings*. We attempt to make this distinction by focusing our core content chapters (Chapters 1–8) on the knowledge required to build and manage systems, while deferring the supporting knowledge about the technologies themselves to our Tech Guides (A through C) at the end of the book. This design allows both the student and the instructor to participate in decisions about what level of detailed technology knowledge is required for various kinds of students who may be using this text.

In addition, within each chapter we try to identify the usefulness of systems at three distinct levels: for the individual, for the organization, and for society. You will see these clearly highlighted at the end of each core chapter, in the What's in IT for Me?, What's in IT for an Organization?, and What's in IT for Society? boxes. In addition, we include a standard series of features to help you better master and apply the knowledge gained in each chapter.

Team and individual exercises are included in each chapter, along with hands-on applications of the technology that are relevant to each chapter and one or two mini cases. Again, these are designed to help you and your instructor determine the balance between hands-on and theoretical exercises that will help you learn best.

At the beginning of each chapter, we also include a section called the "Voice of Experience" that highlights people who are putting knowledge about the strategic uses of technology to work in their careers for the benefit of their organizations. These experts' words will help you understand the value of learning to apply information technology in a variety of professions and different situations.

Finally, at the end of the text you will find a series of study cards. These abbreviated, tear-out cards will help you study and prepare for tests, exams, and other assessments in your course. They highlight critical content, important definitions, and major illustrations for each chapter. This feature is a direct suggestion from past course instructors and students and is new to the third edition—we hope you find it helpful.

Online Resources

There is one more essential feature of this text that we would like you to be aware of before we begin our learning journey. *WileyPLUS* includes lots of additional online exercises, relevant content, and even a completely integrative case called Campuspad.ca that spans all eight chapters. This case integrates the knowledge of each chapter with the actual building of an online business and will be of particular interest to those of you considering more entrepreneurial careers involving online businesses. This, along with other additional content, can be found in *WileyPLUS*, which you have access to with your purchase of this text.

So our journey together begins. You now understand our perspective, our goals in writing this text, and how it can help you get engaged in the value and power of IT in business. We hope that you find the text helpful in mastering our digital online world, and that it will help you become the best business professional you can be. Good luck!

1 | IT FOR BUSINESS AND BUSINESS PROFESSIONALS

WHAT WE WILL COVER

- The Importance of Information Systems
- What's in IT for Me?
- What's in IT for an Organization?
- What's in IT for Society?

STUDENT RETURN ON INVESTMENT RO↑

Through your investment of time in reading and thinking about this chapter, your return—or created value—is gaining knowledge. After reading this chapter, you should be able to

1. Describe what an information system is and explain why IS is so important in today's world.

2. Explain why the study of IT is so important to any future business professional.

3. Describe some of the most common types of information systems used in businesses.

4. Describe some of the ways that IT has changed society.

THE VOICE OF EXPERIENCE

Ryan Chong, Ryerson University, Business Commerce

Ryan Chong graduated from Ryerson University in 2008 with a Bachelor of Commerce in Information Technology Management. While in school, he used his entrepreneurial skill-set to co-found SpeechBobble Inc., a cloud-based private social networking platform. Most recently, Ryan has moved into a Product Management role at a major Canadian telecommunications company.

What do you do in your current position? I'm responsible for Product Management (PM) at a large diversified telecommunications and media company. I manage the Product Life Cycle (PLC) for a number of interactive video products delivered to our consumer base through browser, mobile, and cable TV. Working in a life cycle role means that you're focused on maintaining and supporting the products that exist today, and also keeping focused on what products consumers will be using in the future, both short-term and long-term.

What do you consider to be important career skills? Communication and analytical skills are two of the most important skills that an IT worker can have today. I'll explain in the context of PM. For most organizations, PM is an interdisciplinary role; call it the "glue" that binds together engineering and business functions. On any given day, a PM is responsible for a range of tasks that could include explaining business requirements to engineers and software developers, and discussing sales tactics with the marketing team to strategize the best way to take a new product to market. Overarching this, PM is responsible for communicating to executives when and why products are being delivered to customers based on analysis of competitive and market factors.

How do you use IT? IT is an extremely important tool that is used both tactically and strategically to manage the PLC. We use communication systems like email, video, and voice web conferencing, instant messaging, and social networking to connect and collaborate with teams, business stakeholders, and vendors on a daily basis. We use workflow systems like calendaring, software bug trackers, testing/quality assurance systems, project management, and release management tools to drive task completion during new product development. At the macro level, we use traditional IT systems like data warehousing and business intelligence to look

at business trends and financial metrics. We also use these tools to understand customer feedback and monitor how our product lines are performing financially. Finally, we rely on external IT systems like web and media monitoring to stay on top of what our competitors are doing and how the marketplace is evolving.

Can you describe an example of how you have used IT to improve business operations? We rely heavily on IT as a tactical tool to coordinate communication and workflow amongst many people from diverse business functions. Like many product organizations, we have teams from multiple departments collaborate on one common product development and go-to-market activity. This could involve hundreds of people, so we use centralized document management tools to store and share all of our go-to-market information. Regardless of where a team member is located, either geographically or within the company, these documents can be accessed and managed from one central location.

Have you got any "on the job" advice for students seeking a career in IT or business? Become an expert on your "domain," whatever it is! Invest the time and effort to position yourself as the go-to resource for whatever that subject matter may be. This may involve the creation of internal informational tools and/or research libraries that cover your area. Whether they are large or small, companies rely on experts for planning and decision making on a day-to-day basis. Develop a track record of delivering results and your reputation for being the resident expert in your organization will pay dividends for your career advancement opportunities, both inside and out of your company.

Ryan launched an IT start-up while still in school. Using this platform, he worked hard to specialize in product management. Now, Ryan pulls from his broad IT knowledge base to liaise between departments and effectively push products to market. In this chapter you will learn about information systems and why the study of IT is so important to the future business professional.

■ THE IMPORTANCE OF INFORMATION SYSTEMS

Why IS Matters

Before we dive into what an information system (IS) actually is, let's begin by discussing why you should care. It should be obvious to you that information systems are important in your daily life. Without these systems in place, your life would be significantly different. Do you know anyone without a mobile phone, for instance? The rapid adoption of smartphones, particularly in Asia and North America, has created a situation where many people don't even bother with a landline installation in their homes anymore—telecommunications is on-the-go anywhere, anytime. Or consider how strange it is when you meet someone who actually goes into a bank—most of us do our banking online or at automated bank machines (ABMs). Think about what we did before we "googled" information, or how convenient Wikipedia is as a source of ready, if not always perfect, information on a wide range of topics. Finally, think about how quickly new information systems take hold of users, with commonplace social media websites Facebook and Twitter now approaching 700+ million users when they did not even exist before 2004 and 2006, respectively. Can you imagine your everyday life without these types of systems?

Organizations that ignore the impact of technology and information systems when conducting business will likely risk the business itself. The rate of technology change is greater today than ever before. Consumers have completely adopted the Internet in less than a decade, when previous technology shifts, such as from radio to television, took many decades. Organizations and individuals must keep up with these rapid technology changes or risk becoming obsolete. It has been said that you must "run faster to stay in place." To help understand this magnitude of change, we can look to Moore's Law for insight.

In 1965, Gordon E. Moore, a co-founder of Intel, observed a significant trend about the continuing advancement of technology. This observation, now known as **Moore's Law**, states that computing power (as measured by the maximum number of transistors in an integrated circuit) roughly doubles every 18 months (Figure 1.1). This formulation was printed in a volume of *Electronics Magazine*[1] and was based on the founding work not of Moore himself, but of VLSI (very large-scale integration) pioneer Carver Mead. However, it was Moore who connected the notion of underlying changes in the pace of technology with improved consumer access to lower cost and higher performance computing over time. To date, this law has held true, although quite recently other micro-engineering impediments to the ongoing doubling of chip capacity have begun to emerge (e.g., heat and power-consumption related issues), which might affect the durability of Moore's law in future. However, in retrospect and to date, Moore's law effectively explains much of what we have experienced in the last four decades in terms of advances in consumer and business technology speed and cost.

Initially, Moore's Law was an observation on only one component of the technology industry: semiconductors. However, the more widely it was quoted and accepted, the more it began to serve as a standard benchmark for a whole range of consumer technologies within this huge global industry. As technology engineering and marketing strove to keep up with Moore's Law, a technology revolution was born, eventually leading to the rapid introduction of many of the technologies we take for granted today (the original personal computer, the laptop then tablet computer, the cell phone and the more recent smartphone, and so on). Consumers have benefited enormously from this. Since every technology company always presumes that one or more of its competitors would soon introduce a newer, faster, and more feature-rich technology than theirs, the total global technology industry became hyper-competitive and ultimately one of the most productive and innovative industries in the world. The result is cheaper, faster, and better technology all the time!

---

1. Gordon E. Moore, "Cramming More Components into Integrated Circuits," *Electronics Magazine*, 38(8), April 19, 1965.

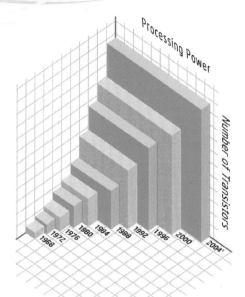

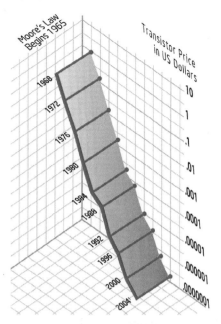

Moore's Law Means More Performance
Processing power, measured in millions of instructions per second (MIPS), has risen because of increased transistor counts.

Moore's Law Means Decreasing Costs
Packing more transistors into less space has dramatically reduced their cost and the cost of the products they populate.

1. Estimate only

FIGURE 1.1 Moore's Law illustrates the rate of change in technology capability over time, and the resulting effect on cost.[2]

While obviously good for consumers, what did this mean for business? Well, consider this: If you wanted to express Moore's Law on a different time scale, you could say that technology improves at an average rate of 1 percent per week. Compounded, this means an increase of 11–15 percent per quarter, depending on the number of days and weeks in any quarter. If you're not in the technology business, but in a business where technology is a part of the business, what must you do to keep up with this ever-present rate of change? Imagine having to either reduce costs or increase sales by that much every single quarter, just to "stay in the game." If you work in a technology industry, you have to. And in this text you will learn that **information technology (IT)**, as a part of any IS, is a key enabler to all organizations (large and small, private or public sector) and impacts all business disciplines (accounting, marketing, etc.). This makes it pervasive and something that you should be interested in knowing a lot more about, regardless of your ultimate career choice.

In fact, as you progress through your career, it will be more important than ever to keep up with changes in technology or risk being left behind. Professionals in any field must continually examine everything that they do to ensure that it is optimally efficient and effective, and makes use of the latest technologies required to do their job well, both now and in the future. This is the essence of **knowledge work**, which involves the discovery, analysis, transformation, synthesis, and communication of data, information, and knowledge. (These knowledge work activities are discussed in detail in Chapter 5.) In today's work environment, it's impossible to do knowledge work without technology.

This brings up another point: How do you predict the future of technology? Well, you can't. Even the easier task of forecasting technology changes in a simple product (for instance, the mobile phone) might have failed to predict the stunning rate at which these devices have become small,

---

2. Intel Corporation.

handheld computers rather than simple phones. So, no matter the product or underlying technology, all you can be sure of is that the only constant is likely to be change itself. You can easily anticipate that technologies will evolve and change in the future, and increasing amounts of base computing power, as predicted by Moore, will bring more and more possibilities to you, to the world of work, and to society itself.

The future often belongs to those whose creativity and innovation are relied on to advance society and change the world. Of course, you could apply this to a technology executive like Bill Gates, or to someone like Helen Keller, whose role in changing the world was less reliant on technology and more reliant on her personal character. And a few of you who are reading this textbook right now will likely change the world of business, of technology, or both. One day, students may be reading your quotes.

One can never consent to creep when one feels an impulse to soar.

—Helen Keller

Success is a lousy teacher. It seduces smart people into thinking they can't lose.

—Bill Gates

So, let's begin your journey to making business history by learning the basics about information systems and how their organization and design impact business.

What Is an Information System?

Like most students, you most certainly surf the Web, shop online, instant-message with your friends on your personal computer, and send text messages on a mobile phone. All of these things demonstrate information systems (IS) in action. So, what is an IS?

> An **information system (IS)** *is an organized collection of people, information, business processes, and information technology (IT), designed to transform inputs into outputs, in order to achieve a goal.*

Are you surprised to learn that an information system is more than a computer? As Figure 1.2 shows, organizations design their information systems to leverage the human ability to achieve business goals through the timely and appropriate application of technology, and the timely delivery of appropriate and useful data, information, and knowledge. That is, information systems enhance work, decision making, problem solving, communicating, and coordinating—all of which are topics we will discuss in detail in this book. Table 1.1 defines the components of an IS model and gives examples for each component.

Data, Information, and Knowledge Of course, at the core of any system is the data that we process that turns it ultimately into information and, perhaps, knowledge. So, we must start our exploration of information systems with a fundamental understanding of those concepts and link them to the nature of knowledge work in a modern context. Table 1.1 very briefly introduces data, information, and knowledge by way of an example.

An information system is much more than just a computer. Sending text messages on your smartphone, shopping online, or even receiving digital copies of X-rays ordered by your doctor are all examples of IS in action.

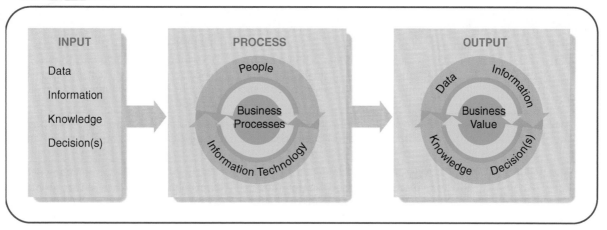

FIGURE 1.2 As this input-process-output (IPO) model shows, a business should design its information system to leverage the human ability to use information technology to its best advantage. By doing this, the output is more than the sum of its parts (data, information, knowledge, decisions)—it is the creation of business value.

Table 1.1	Information System Components	
Concept	**Definition**	**Example**
Input	Items entered into a system to transform them into outputs.	*Input*: Enter your friends' contact information (email address, Twitter ID, web/blog page, phone number, address, etc.) into your contact list.
Process	A series of one or more steps used by a business to transform inputs into outputs.	*Process*: Save to contact database.
Output	The end result of a process. Information is the result of the transformation (processing) of data. From an organizational perspective, the output of a process is a product or a service.	*Output*: Creates an alphabetical list of friends and their contact information that you can access to make phone calls, send email, or check updates. You can use this list to create a group called "spring break trip friends" when planning a trip with your friends for spring break.
Data	Raw, unorganized facts.	*Data*: List of friends who might be interested in a trip on spring break.
Information	Processed/organized/transformed data that are useful.	*Information*: Confirmed list of friends interested in a spring break trip and potential trip locations.
Knowledge	Information plus human experience and judgement.	*Knowledge*: If enough friends can agree on one location, perhaps you can get a group discount on the trip.
Information Technology (IT)	The physical components—typically hardware, software, and connectivity—that make up the IT portion of an IS. Technology is the enabler for processes to perform the steps they were designed to accomplish.	You set up a website for your friends to view the potential spring break location information, with links to tourism boards and travel agencies.
Business Processes	A collection of steps that interact with each other to transform inputs into outputs to achieve a goal.	A function on the website is included for your friends to rank the trip locations in order of preference. Your friends can view which location has the most votes in real-time.

(continued)

Table 1.1	Information System Components (Continued)	
Concept	Definition	Example
People	People or organizations that have both an interest in and an influence on the creation, implementation, or operation of an IS.	Your friends add comments to the website about what locations they like and why to try to influence the selected location.
Decision	A choice made from one or more alternatives to follow or avoid some course of action.	Based on the number of votes received, you select a spring break trip location.
Business Value	A positive return on the investment of resources created through the effective and efficient integration of an organization's people, information, information technology, and business processes.	You have efficiently coordinated your friends to select a location for spring break and negotiated a group discount. You will now have extra money to spend on the trip! You can continue to use the processes in place to keep your friends updated about the trip and count down the days to spring break.

Let's take a closer look at what data, information, and knowledge actually are. Much of what you do as a university or college student, and will do in the future as a business professional, relates to data, information, and knowledge. You collect data about various subjects to transform it into information and knowledge. You learn where to look for quality information and how to store it for future use. Sometimes you share information with others. Information and knowledge are not just words on a page; they have tangible value, and knowledge becomes an important asset.

This is also the case in business. The flow of data and information to create knowledge is what creates value in organizations. You can likely think of occasions when the loss of information had negative results; for instance, a misplaced order from an online supplier, or a phone number that you didn't have a chance to put into your mobile phone and now can't find. Or how about the registration mishaps where you are sure that you registered for a course that's now full? As a student, learning to apply technology to enable this flow helps you and the organizations you will work for improve their results and avoid just these kinds of situations.

Now that you have begun to realize the importance of data, information, and knowledge, let's dig a little deeper into the meanings of each word and their relationship to each other, known as the **data-information-knowledge continuum**. **Data** are raw unorganized facts, numbers, pictures, and so on. **Information** is data that have been organized and are useful to a person. For example, a hair salon owner might include the names of clients, their phone numbers, and their email addresses in an address book program on a smartphone. **Knowledge** is created when a person combines experience and judgement with information. Applying knowledge is how business people create and add value to organizations.

For example, as an international sales manager, you may know the phone numbers and email addresses of your best clients, but you also know your clients' time zones and normal business hours (information). Suppose you decided to email rather than telephone one client. Why did you do this? Most likely, you based your decision on the *information* you have about the client and your personal judgement regarding past experience with this client. Maybe you have found the client doesn't like to be interrupted by the phone or doesn't have voice mail. Therefore, you made your decision based on the *knowledge* you had about that client.

As a student, you use data, information, and knowledge regularly. Remember your first day of classes in your first semester on campus? You had your schedule and the campus map. How did you find your first class? You probably looked on your schedule and found the building name and/or number (data). Once you knew this, you looked at your campus map (information). If your campus was big enough, you might have accessed this using your smartphone, or perhaps you drove there using a mobile GPS device. Were you on time for class? Maybe you were late because, based on the campus map, you decided to take transit instead of driving and parking, but did not realize the stop wasn't close to your classroom because you didn't have the new real-time transit app downloaded onto your phone yet. Or if you did drive, maybe the closest lot was full and the only available parking was far away. You had good information (class time and class and parking lot location or transit route), so what went wrong?

Because you had never driven to this particular class and tried to park in a nearby lot, you had no experience with the process. Assume that the next time you decided to drive, you left earlier and found a space. Now, when faced with the "when-to-leave-for-class decision," you use knowledge, which combines your class time, classroom location, and parking lot location, with your "finding-a-space" experience.

You can extend the data-to-knowledge continuum even further to include wisdom (see Figure 1.3). **Wisdom** adds insight and ethical boundaries to the experience and professional judgement inherent in knowledge. Wisdom enables business leaders to perceive the underlying meaning and nuances of a business situation and ensures that knowledge from all relevant perspectives, disciplines, and sources is considered in the final decision.

Another important thing to note is that the cost and complexity of the system processing tasks to be accomplished increase as you move up the pyramid from simply accessing data to applying wisdom (see Figure 1.3). Information technology and systems assist primarily with collecting, collating, and analyzing data and information. This is their strongest contribution. Some organizations over the years have attempted what are often referred to as **knowledge management systems (KMS)**, which were designed, theoretically, to locate, accumulate, and sort out the vast amounts of unstructured knowledge often used within an organization. Many of these efforts have failed for a variety of reasons, often related to the basic fact that information systems are best when they are dealing with structured, repetitive data and information, and are not quite as good at more sophisticated, nuanced, and layered knowledge sets. While technology is a key enabler, it is still mostly up to humans to take data and information and turn it into knowledge and wisdom.

Think of it this way: in its simplest and lowest form, you have data. These are the raw facts and figures related to any task at hand. By using information technology systems, you can transform this

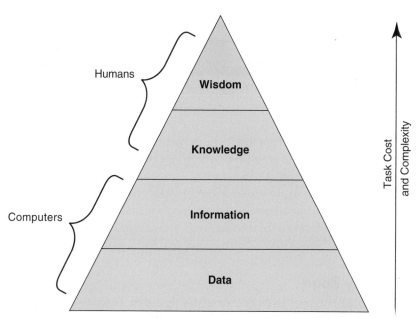

FIGURE 1.3 This knowledge hierarchy shows the relative level of human involvement, cost, and complexity.

data into information by putting it into context, adding it up or sorting it out, summarizing or tabulating, and generally performing various mechanical calculations and permutations that would be both boring and subject to error if performed by humans. The system can then store and retrieve this information quickly and disseminate it throughout the organization as required. At a higher level, you might also expect the system to spot and identify basic patterns in the data or point out anomalies. It might generate warnings about potential problems or about processes or values outside of expected or approved levels. However, after this point, the work of the information system is mostly done. It now falls to the business professional to take this information and interpret it in context; that is, turn it into knowledge. You could also add an ethical or legal interpretation to the knowledge to ensure that the appropriate context has been considered before making a decision. Information that is not used to improve the outcome of a business decision is perhaps interesting, but certainly not useful. So now you can clearly see the boundary of where information systems can and cannot be helpful.

IS versus IT

It is important to stress the difference between information systems (IS) and information technology (IT). In the earlier example in Table 1.1, would the same results have occurred by simply creating a website? Do you achieve good grades in school simply by having the fastest laptop in your class? Obviously not. While a faster processor can help you do more work more quickly, it is still the quality and insight of that work and your ability to present it well and on time that get you good grades.

IT is simply a collection of tools—hardware, software, and connectivity—that enable individuals or businesses to achieve their goals. Without the context of a clear goal (spring break trip), processes (poll for potential locations, vote), and people (friends who are interested in a trip), the information technology itself is irrelevant.

Some of you reading this text may end up with careers in IT, but most of you will not, or may only have an IT position during particular periods of your career. Most of an organization's employees are actually part of the larger goal setting, business process, and people components of an IS, rather than directly involved in the technology components of these systems. However, it is still to your advantage to have a good understanding of what IT can and cannot do to support you in your career since you will most certainly use information systems to do your work.

WHAT DO YOU THINK?

Consider the components of a typical IS outlined in Table 1.1. Reflect on these questions in terms of the systems you use at school to manage your enrolment, course selection, and payments:

1: What are the benefits to the user of an online information system versus a manual alternative?
2: What are the benefits to the institution of an online system? Are these benefits critical for the institution to achieve in its current environment?
3: Errors occur. In the past, you may have experienced an error in your online enrolment, course selection, or payments. Do you think you would have been better off using a manual system to start with? Did you feel you spent more time trying to fix the error than you would have if you had used a manual system?

The Productivity Zone

As mentioned above, IT is simply an enabler to achieving a goal. IT alone does not guarantee success. Consider this another way. Figure 1.4 shows what we call the productivity zone, which is created at the intersection of people, process, and technology. This is where the design of the information system accounts not just for the optimal technology, but also incorporates elements of human design to accommodate how people will use the system. It also carefully considers the optimal design of the process itself, rather than letting the technology guide those decisions. By applying equal weight to all three of the elements and being able to optimally combine each of these elements, businesses can achieve superior productivity and enhance their competitive advantage. For you, this can mean excellent academic results. For businesses, this can mean increased efficiency and greater profits. For government, this could mean better services delivered at a lower cost. For not-for-profits, this could mean enhanced online donor and event management systems.

FIGURE 1.4 The productivity zone occurs at the intersection of people, processes, and technology. A successful IS integrates all three of these components to create business value.

Consider this from a personal productivity point of view. Think of a time when you have been incredibly productive. What elements did you combine to achieve this level of productivity? Can you align these elements with those in Figure 1.4? For example, perhaps you were doing a group project with three other students. To get the project done, you assigned clear roles and responsibilities to one another so that you knew who was going to work on what parts of the project (people). You discussed how and when the work was going to get done. You decided how to research the project material and created a schedule for completion (process). To communicate with one another, you exchanged email addresses and began following one another on Twitter. You agreed to use collaboration software (e.g., Groove, SharePoint, Blackboard) to share your most recent files and information (technology). By addressing each of these elements—people, process, and technology—you achieved a higher level of productivity and achieved excellent results on your group project, perhaps better than other groups in the class who were not as productive.

The Internet

One information technology that you are undoubtedly very familiar with is the Internet. The **Internet** has become an integral part of personal and business lives for the following reasons: communication, information, and commerce. **Communication** generates business value by making it possible for professionals to share information both between themselves and with business partners. The Internet does this by providing newsgroups, chat rooms, bulletin boards, text messaging using mobile phones, as well as email and instant messaging. You may currently use these Internet communication methods, but as you enter the business world, you may find different Internet tools to use.

Another key to generating business value for any organization and to increasing personal productivity is the ability to both make information available, and to find information in a timely manner. Through the **World Wide Web** (www), the Internet has dramatically reduced the effort required to carry out both activities. For example, the Web makes it easy to publish information in a variety of ways. In fact, the Internet and Web have been called the greatest advances in publishing since the invention of the printing press over 500 years ago. After publishing information on the Web, efficient search engines make it possible to locate it quickly.

However, this ease of creating and distributing information also has the potential for **information overload**, and an absence of quality control means not all web sources are created equal. First of all, as of March 2012, WorldWideWebSize.com reported between 7.74 billion confirmed and possibly up to 45 billion indexed pages on the Web. That's an awful lot of information! For your own interest, why not go to that site and see what the number is now? How much has it grown or maybe even shrunk? It might also shock you to know that as of July 2008, Google engineers Jesse Alpert and Nissan Hajaj confirmed over 1 trillion unique URLs in their company's search database.[3] As of May 2009, more than

3. "We Knew the Web Was Big," July 25, 2008 entry into the official Google Blog.

100 million of those URLs were commercial or business-related sites.[4] In fact, there is increasing pressure to open up new base domain names to feed this explosive global growth. There is also a substantial effort afoot within telecommunications engineers to increase the number of digits in IP addresses globally for the same reasons. Our appetite for digitized information seems virtually insatiable. The sheer volume of information on the Web is one of the reasons why you need search engines to even begin to locate a place to start when you are looking for something specific. This is also why some people are abandoning the Web as a reliable and useful information source.

Finally, the Internet generates value by being an avenue for the buying and selling of goods, also known as **commerce**. While still just a small proportion of the total commerce in the world, electronic commerce, or e-commerce, is growing dramatically. **E-commerce** is the use of information systems, technology, and computer networks by individuals and organizations to create business value (see Chapter 5 for more on e-commerce). This occurs especially in the information economy, such as travel, insurance, and banking, where often no physical product changes hands.

WHAT DO YOU THINK?

Besides integrating communication, information, and commerce, there's another reason why the Internet has become such an important part of your daily life—entertainment! Think about your own Web usage in this area and then consider the following questions:

1: What are some of the ways you use the Internet for entertainment?
2: Consider the site you prefer most for music or video downloading. What makes it so useful and interesting?
3: Do you spend too much time using the Web for entertainment? Is it the world's number one procrastination tool, or is this time spent valuable?

Quick Test

1. Which of the following is NOT part of an information system?
   a. Internet
   b. Furniture
   c. Mobile phone
   d. Analyst

2. The productivity zone is _____.
   a. the technology implemented at an organization
   b. a measure of the efficiency of an organization's IT infrastructure
   c. the intersection of people, processes, and technology
   d. the time of day where workers are most productive

3. If you add human experience and judgement to information, you can create _____.
   a. data
   b. knowledge
   c. resources
   d. facts

Answers: 1. b; 2. c; 3. b

4. "Domain Counts," *Name Intelligence*, May 2009.

■ WHAT'S IN IT FOR ME?

You could interpret this question in two ways: either what's in it for you personally, or what's in IT for you. Both interpretations are important. Most obvious is how IT is involved in your everyday life. IT is not only an enabler for you as a student or as someone who is working, but it is also a major source of entertainment and enjoyment. It is safe to say that it would be impossible to be a fully functioning professional today and not use personal productivity tools or have a basic understanding of the Internet, for instance. But more fundamentally, no matter your ultimate career choice, IT knowledge can be a key contributor to your success. You can see examples of this in the Voice of Experience feature at the beginning of each chapter, where both IT and non-IT professionals discuss their engagement with IT systems.

IT for Your Personal Productivity and Entertainment

What does a typical student's day look like? How many times in a given day do you think you encounter technology?

7:00 A.M. – Awake. Check for status messages on Facebook. Check phone for overnight texts and emails. Of course—no missed calls—nobody does that anymore except your Dad! See message from your marketing group that the scheduled meeting will be at the residence food court. Go back to bed and plan to eat breakfast at the meeting.

8:00 A.M. – Your BlackBerry alarm goes off—hit the snooze button for an extra 10 Zs!

9:00 A.M. – Get your breakfast using the money deposited on your student ID card (thanks, Mom!), but can't find your group. SMS a member of your group: "Where r u?"

10:45 A.M. – Get ready to go to your accounting class. Your professor always posts the class notes at the last minute on Blackboard. Use your laptop to access the class website and download the class notes so you can add brief notes to the slides as you listen to the lecture.

11:00 A.M. – Despite getting some extra sleep this morning, you snooze in your accounting class. Luckily the professor will post a podcast of the lecture later in the day so you can listen to the parts you missed. And your friends have already shared their class notes on the FB study group class before you even leave . . .

1:00 P.M. – Eat lunch and take a break. Sign back in to Facebook to see what your friends are up to later. You received a Tweet earlier from your BFF that some photos of you at the party last night are posted on Facebook. No wonder you are so tired today . . .

2:00 P.M. – About to get ready to go to your e-commerce class when you receive an email that class is cancelled! You now have extra time to work on your research project. Find a comfy seat at the nearby Starbucks and use Wi-Fi to sign in to the school library and do your research online. Use Google and Wikipedia to find other sources of information.

4:00 P.M. – Eek! Realize that April will be here before you know it. Better line up a summer job. Post your resumé on several job sites and Craigslist (you never know!). Sign up for RSS feeds on a few job sites to get the latest postings delivered immediately.

6:00 P.M. – What's for dinner? Thai would be good, but not the same old place. Use Google to find a good Thai place close to your school. Make a reservation using OpenTable for the points! Tweet where you are going for dinner in case someone wants to join you.

7:30 P.M. – You get lost on the way to dinner. Use the GPS in your phone to find the way . . . change the reservation time while you're at it!

8:00 P.M. – Use your BlackBerry to catch up on emails while waiting for friends at the Thai restaurant. An RSS feed from SchoolParty blog indicates there is a party at the campus pub tonight. You mention the party at dinner and your friends agree to check it out with you. Post a status update that you are attending and like the event on FB. It's going be another good night! Better set the BlackBerry alarm now for tomorrow . . .

How many times a day do you use technology? Perhaps an easier question to answer is what daily activities do you participate in that *don't* use technology?

Looking at this simple example, you can see there are many times in any given day when people use technology to be more efficient and effective, thereby becoming more productive. For example, this student did not need cash to purchase breakfast, as credit was available on his or her ID card. This may have saved a trip to the ATM. Getting an email about a class cancellation saved a trip to the class. Using Wi-Fi at the coffee shop saved a trip to the library. From an entertainment point of view, this person was able to easily connect with friends and family, find dinner companions, make reservations, and find out about a party. Without enabling technologies, these actions would only have been possible with a lot of effort, or not at all.

IT Is Fundamental for Your Career

You cannot work effectively in any knowledge-intense profession today without superior systems. This means you need to be knowledgeable in the applications of technology in your chosen field, and ensure that you also have well-trained and systems-savvy professionals on board. As an exercise, go to a popular job search site on the Internet, such as *www.workopolis.ca*. Search for jobs in your chosen career, whether accounting, marketing, finance, or another area. Look at some specific jobs. Can you find any postings that do not mention technology skills (e.g., familiarity with MS Office or other more specific systems)?

The following expands on what you learned in the exercise above, and gives you an idea of how IT will fit in to your future career, especially if IT becomes your career.

I Want to Be an Accountant . . . All basic accounting functions today are done using automated systems, and while they respect the ledger system principles, they have actually replaced the ledgers themselves! This also means that all of the audit trail you need access to, either as an external auditor or as an internal accountant performing business analysis, is contained in various information systems. The ability to understand systems, validate the integrity of the systems operation, and assure management that what is being reported is accurate all require IT knowledge. In fact, most professional bodies that certify accounting professionals now require several courses in IT and IT audit skills to even graduate.

Marketing Is What I Want to Do . . . As any good marketer will tell you, information is power. In this field, it is essential to understand how consumers behave, what influences them, and how to reach them to deliver your message. This is increasingly done online, as you will discover in Chapter 8. An understanding of the power of new media and its impact on society is fundamental for a marketer to figure out how to reach audiences, as traditional media are decreasing in both presence and importance. Furthermore, the information on current customers and their purchasing behaviour is likely all collected by the company's customer relationship management (CRM) or enterprise resource planning (ERP) systems and reported through a data warehouse or data mart. We will explore these systems in detail in later chapters because they are essential to the operation of the modern enterprise and to any aspects of e-government. If you choose to be in marketing, part of your job will include structuring these systems to capture the critical information you will need to analyze customer behaviour and adjust product and service offerings accordingly. It is also likely that you will use Web 2.0 technologies and social networking tools to develop and place indirect marketing messages into cyberspace and to monitor developments around your brand. All of this activity requires IT/IS knowledge.

I'm All About Human Resources . . . Perhaps you access online job boards when you look for a job. You may have visited an online career fair in Second Life, or visited the Manpower Island there. Or maybe you investigated an employer rating site to see where the cool places are to work before getting more information about the company from its website. If you work in HR, you better be ready to respond to these new trends because the future generation of workers has moved online. As part of an organization, did you sign up online with an employer for benefits? Or did you report your time into an automated time-tracking system connected to payroll? Or file your taxes online? Modern HR systems are all IT-enabled, and companies increasingly expect professionals in this area to be able to assess the cost-benefit trade-offs of making investments in automation to serve employee and employer needs. IT knowledge is essential to investigating these potential opportunities and making the final business decision about how to proceed. The best HR practitioners understand they need to remain one step ahead of their current and future employees, and therefore need to be linked to developments in the online world.

Finance Is My Game . . . Financial analysis, complicated or simple, is always conducted using systems. Like your colleagues in accounting, the trail of information you need to access is usually only available in company or government databases. You will need to interact with the IT professionals in the company to structure these systems to provide not only the knowledge you need, but also to automatically flag important exceptions so management can deal with them before they become a problem. The only way to model complex systems is to use computing power to resolve multivariate equations that would take months to do manually, if they could even be done. As discussed earlier, information is coming online at a steady rate, and finance professionals need to stay on top of fast-moving economic and market news and events—or risk being left behind and letting their employer fall behind too.

The Front-Line Is Where I Belong . . . Perhaps you are a whiz at working hands-on to get products into the hands of customers in the front-line of business operations. Operations may include roles in manufacturing,

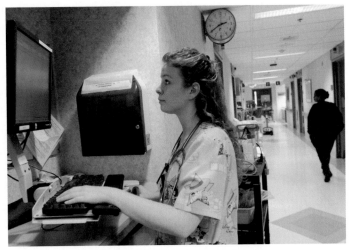

Very few professions today do not require the use of technology in some form. Nurses who enter or check patient information are interacting with a complex health care network that needs to be secure and accessible to other appropriate health care providers.

transportation, distribution, or service areas of the business. Often these are the most expensive areas of the business to operate, and come under intense scrutiny for efficiency and effectiveness. Complex systems, including customer relationship management (CRM) and enterprise resource planning (ERP), support these areas and provide vital information to other business functions. In your operations role you may need to manage staff to ensure that they use systems appropriately. You may need to analyze the efficiency of operations using data from these systems to find ways of increasing efficiency and reducing costs. Let's look at a few front-line positions more in depth:

- In retail, you need to ensure the products that customers want are in the store at the appropriate times. You rely on automatic inventory replenishing systems driven off immediate point-of-sale data from daily transaction summaries at every store location nationwide.
- In hospitality, it is critical that a VIP customer get the appropriate hotel room upgrade. The room was likely booked online, and the customer will be checked in and checked out using front-of-the-house systems linked to electronic card key access systems in each room.
- In health care, you need to ensure that patient records are accurate and distributed to all required parties. Online systems will maintain the privacy and security of these records and ensure that only authorized medical staff can access them.

If you are considering any of these types of roles, IT will be an integral part of your job.

I Am Going to Work for Myself . . . Being an entrepreneur can be a very fulfilling vocation, especially if you have a fantastic business idea and the ability to turn that into marketable products or services. Most of these will rely on some elements of technology to create, market, and fulfill the product or service to customers. You will likely rely on a website as a source of promotion so prospective customers around the world can find you easily. At the beginning of your entrepreneurial career, you will often be a company of one. That is, you will be the accountant, marketer, finance department, and operations expert. Once you have some success and can afford some staff, you will be the HR department too. The previous sections in this chapter described the role that IT will play in your own business. Additionally, you will likely also be the IT department! At the very minimum, you will make technology purchasing decisions like what computer(s) to purchase, who will be your Internet service provider, what mobile and office phone plans you should choose, etc. In the early days, you will likely install all of your computer hardware and software. If there are technical issues, you will likely be your own first level support help desk. Some basic computer skills and IT knowledge will help you to at least understand your requirements and troubleshoot any problems that arise.

The Law Is Where It's at . . . Lawyers today could not cope with the information overload they face without systems. Looking up precedents and codes of law in any jurisdiction around the world in an instant, dealing with colleagues and clients in the firm's offices across the country, or checking on possible conflicts of interest before taking on a new client are all essential IT applications in the legal profession. Collaboration systems have made it easy for multi-team members to create documents and instantly track and approve changes to improve the speed at which final documents are presented to a client. The volumes of information that must be exchanged between the parties in a typical commercial litigation or merger and acquisition can be done online in the blink of an eye, rather than photocopied, indexed, and bundled into boxes and delivered by truck, as was once the case. Furthermore, instead of searching physical documents by reading them, you now search them electronically for the very specific phrase you want, and then the program sorts and presents the results by occurrence including date, time, and document location!

A Career in Consulting Is for Me . . . As a consultant, you will need to quickly understand your clients' businesses and needs. For many businesses, this means IT is the business! You may be asked to evaluate the efficiency and effectiveness of a business and its processes. You may be asked to make business strategy recommendations, or assist in launching a new product. To do any of these activities, you will need to understand the IT the business is using and, perhaps, evaluate new IT that will help your clients reach their goals. If you are an employee of a large consultancy, you will be expected to learn the company's internal systems (including engagement time tracking so your company can bill clients), and knowledge management systems (so that information and tools for engagements can be shared between all members of the firm).

IT Is Going to Be My Career . . . You may, by design or by chance, find yourself with a career in IT, often known as **ICT (information and communication technologies)**. ICT careers pay well. Industry Canada reports that in 2008, ICT employees earned, on average, $61,971, or 47 percent more than the economy-wide average of $42,143. Workers in the software and computer services sector earned the highest average, at $68,126. Industry Canada also reports that ICT employment continues to grow at 2.8 percent per year, with low unemployment.[5] According to IT World Canada, the average IT manager in Canada makes more than $80,000 a year.[6] At the upper end, chief information officers (CIOs) earn well over $100,000. The CIO Association of Canada (CIOCAN) reports that its members have an average base salary of $155,000. At the very high end, Canadian CIOs in mining and financial services tend to have the highest salaries, at $285,000 and $247,000, respectively.[7]

One certainty in ICT is continual change. Moore's Law ensures that ICT affordability and power will continue to increase, and that we will see ongoing innovation of products and services using ICT. The knowledge that you gain in your post-secondary education will need to be replenished multiple times throughout your career, which means that you will need to continually learn as the ICT industry changes.

A significant current shift is the move to a stronger integration of ICT and business, as you saw in the previous sections where no business discipline escapes interaction with IT. Many of the technology components that were once stand-alone, fragmented, and unreliable are being completely integrated with business processes and are highly reliable. Enterprise systems, as you will learn in Chapter 4, have integrated most business processes both within and beyond an organization. David Ticoll, the executive director of the Canadian Coalition for Tomorrow's ICT Skills (CCICT), describes jobs in ICT as focused on innovation and on the application of technology, and less on building or operating the technology. ICT professionals "'package' business knowledge, communications skills, leadership, project management, interpersonal effectiveness—essentially client and general management capabilities with an ICTS (information and communication technologies and services) flavour."[8] He refers to an "Industry-IT Specialist . . . [with] subject-specific business knowledge, combined with applicable ICTS skills, in a domain where a Canada-based IT/business process services centre of excellence,"[9] such as financial services, electrical utilities, and insurance. For Ticoll, ICT skills are most relevant when applied to a business or organizational context.

5. Canadian ICT Sector Profile, Information and Communications Technologies Branch, Industry Canada, August 2009.

6. *www.itworld.com*, retrieved April 22, 2010.

7. CIO Association of Canada, "Women CIOs Out-earn Men," news release, July 14, 2009.

8. David Ticoll, "ICTS Jobs 2.0: How Canada Can Win in the 21st Century Global Marketplace for Information and Communications Technologies and Services (ICTS)," *Developing Tomorrow's Workforce Today*, Information and Communications Technology Council, March 2007.

9. Ibid.

Table 1.2	ICTC Career Clusters and Work Streams[10]
Career Cluster	**Work Stream**
Software products	Analysis Design Analysis Programming Application Software Business Analysis and Service Level Management Programming Software Design and Delivery (Engineering) Technical ICT Architecture Web Design Web Development
Infrastructure	Data Administration Database Administration Capacity and Performance Help Desk Network Planning and Support Operations Problem Management Security Systems Programming User Technical Support
Management	ICT Management Intellectual Property Management Production Management Project Management Supply Chain Management ICT Consultancy
Hardware Products	Design Engineering Hardware Scientist Manufacturing Engineering Product Line Management Technical Marketing
Testing/Quality Control	Audit Validation Quality Assurance Quality Professional
Documentation and Training	Education/Training Management Technical Writing

Table 1.2 presents a list of ICT occupation profiles created by the **Information and Communications Technology Council (ICTC)**, which is funded in part by the Government of Canada's Sector Council Program. On their website, ICTC describes the jobs as they are practised in industry today.

The core competencies that apply to all work streams are analytical thinking, information management, and relationship building. Other competencies that apply to several streams are decision making, leadership, writing skills, and project management. For full details, visit the ICTC website at *www.ictc-ctic.ca*.

---

10. ICT Competency Profiles: A Framework for Developing Tomorrow's ICT Workforce, © 2009 Information and Communications Technology Council Inc.

A long career in ICT can take many paths. Some of you will spend your entire career in one industry, such as banking, retail, or government. Some of you may spend your entire career in one organization, although this has become increasingly rare. Some of you will become entrepreneurs, perhaps starting one or more ICT companies (at one point, Google was just another start-up). If you enjoy project management, consider the Project Management Professional (PMP) designation from the Project Management Institute (PMI). If your skills are more toward business or systems analysis, join the International Institute of Business Analysts and attain the Certified Business Analyst Professional (CBAP) designation. If technology attracts you, consider attaining certification in popular technologies such as Cisco Systems communications, Microsoft operating systems, or SAP enterprise resource planning software.

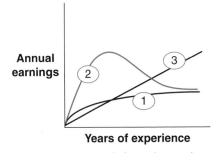

FIGURE 1.5 Begin with the end in mind. As you start your ICT career you can expect interesting, fulfilling, and rewarding work over many decades. Continually invest in your technical and managerial skills and you will be well rewarded.

A key decision that you will face is the need to choose between a technical path or a managerial path. Figure 1.5 depicts three salary paths over a career. The first path plateaus after a few years, so that in the second half of the career, the annual earning increases are small. These people have become specialists in a particular area, and repeat that specialty throughout their career. The second path has an early spike, earning a high annual income, but then decreases to a more reasonable level. This profile is often found in specialty technologies that have a high demand for a short period of time, as was the case with many e-business skills before the dot-com crash. The third path is more balanced, with a steady rise throughout the career. This usually reflects continual growth and development, often with a growing portion of managerial responsibilities. This path leads to senior ICT roles, perhaps as CIO. Remember, top CIOs earn well over $200,000 annually.

In whatever career you choose, in whatever business environment you find yourself, you need to understand your role in the organization (how what you do creates business value) and your organization's goals and information needs. Further, your success depends on understanding the technology solutions that help meet those goals and needs. Why? Ultimately, the need for and the use of information lies at the heart of every business decision and process.

Quick Test

1. A career in the following will involve some knowledge of IS/IT:
   a. finance.
   b. law.
   c. consulting.
   d. all of the above.

2. Fill in the blank. If you've ever worked retail, there is a good chance that you relied on automatic inventory replenishing systems that collected _____ from each and every _____.

3. The core competencies that apply to all work streams are
   a. analytical thinking, information management, and relationship building.
   b. written, oral, and visual communication management.
   c. rapid relationship creation, information dissemination, and computer processing.
   d. information management, multimedia creation, and word processing.

■ WHAT'S IN IT FOR AN ORGANIZATION?

Have you ever purchased something online and noticed that the website suggests other products you may be interested in based on what other customers have purchased, or based on what you purchased in the past? This is a key example of organizations using IT to increase sales. Behind the scenes, systems calculate and compile data to understand customer behaviour. A business might learn that a customer who purchased a Dan Brown novel may also be interested in purchasing a John Grisham novel. As the customer, you may not have considered buying a John Grisham novel, but now that it has been suggested, you may check it out.

This kind of intelligent function is exceptionally important for online stores that need to capture as many dollars per visit as possible. Online stores do not have the benefit of eye-catching impulse displays near the checkouts, so they rely on turning as many visitors to their sites into buying customers as they can. These stores also want each transaction to involve as high a dollar volume as possible to maximize profits. In fact, cross-selling or up-selling has been made very simple using technology that matches your current customer profile to your buying behaviour. Either the system itself will prompt you (if the transaction is self-serve), or the salesperson will be prompted to make a personalized offer to you directly (if the transaction is intermediated personally by a sales or service agent).

In addition to increasing revenue per customer or gaining new customers, organizations use IT to increase efficiency and reduce costs. This helps lower their input costs, which can then either be taken back in the form of higher margins on products and services sold, or by enabling them to reduce their selling price to preserve competitive advantage and retain market share or open new markets. And if you are in government or the not-for-profit sector, reduced costs means the ability to deliver more services for the same amount of money, something any taxpayer or donor truly appreciates!

To help you better understand these concepts, in the following section we examine businesses and their environments and explore the IT that contributes to their information systems.

Business Organizations and the Business Environment

To learn about business organizations and the information systems and technology that support them, we need to start with a brief review of the world of business. When we refer to a **business**, we mean any organization with one or more people who:

1. decide on common goals to pursue
2. work together to locate and organize resources
3. create processes to achieve the desired goals

This definition can include businesses in the corporate, government, or not-for-profit sectors. Typically, a business's primary goal is to generate economic value (make a profit) over a sustained period of time. For example, when you order coffee at Starbucks, this generates value for the company. Or when you sign up for a mobile plan, this service creates business value for the telecommunications company by giving you access to voice and data communication via a national wireless network of networks. In other businesses, such as government and not-for-profit, the goal may be to provide clients with a service, or to gain a donation or participation in an event to help support the work of the organization.

In reality, many different factors drive the selection of business goals. One of the most important factors influencing a business is its environment. As Figure 1.6 shows, a company's **business environment** is a complex collection of political, economic, social, and technological factors that organizational leaders must consider when making decisions regarding goals, organizational forms, and the creation of business value. Businesses are now relying on information systems more than ever before to respond to those factors.

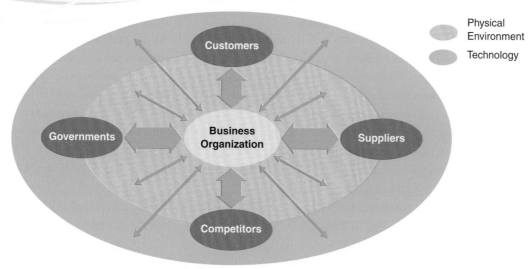

FIGURE 1.6 An organization's business environment is often a complex collection of political, economic, social, and technological factors.

Organizations rely on digital information to gain competitive advantage and to respond quickly to opportunities. As organizations strive to respond quickly, they are changing the way they organize or structure themselves.

Think about an organization from the point of view of a courier carrying documents between the top of the business and the bottom. Perhaps there is a directory to help find the addressee of the package. Or maybe the courier only has the physical address of the big building the company is in, and not the specific floor. The taller the organization, the more "stairs" the courier must descend or climb to find and deliver the package to the appropriate party. At each floor, people stop the courier to read the address on the package, see if it's for them, and comment on the weather or whatever. Or maybe the courier needs to stop to clarify if he is getting closer to his final destination. This additional communication may or may not help the courier to efficiently and effectively deliver the package to its final destination. The process of discovery can take lots of valuable time before the courier finally delivers the package.

Now imagine that the courier could take an express elevator to deliver the package directly to its intended recipient simply by putting the name into an electronic directory at the front desk of the building. The elevator and directory "flattens" the business into two floors: (1) the floor where the courier gets on; and (2) the floor where the courier stops. Often the pathway the information takes, and how many times and who touches it along the way, will have a significant impact on the design and flow of business information systems. It also affects their efficiency and effectiveness.

So, organizations use advanced information systems, such as *decision support systems (DSS)* and *enterprise resource planning (ERP) systems*, like the courier uses the express elevator—to flatten the organization by eliminating unnecessary stops on floors along the way. Imagine the effect of such de-layering in a business. Now a chief executive officer (CEO) can use a decision support system (DSS) to view and understand corporate data. Such a system could very well eliminate the need for layers of middle managers to filter and interpret the data for the CEO. By eliminating the need for these management layers, the DSS helps flatten the organization and may make it more responsive to its business environment. As a student, you do similar things using IS. You no longer need to visit several libraries and access specialized research resources individually to write term papers. You simply use a tool such as Google or your school's online library portal to find what you need.

Types of IS Found in Business

Now that you have an idea of what a generic information system looks like and how it works, let's take a brief look at some types of IS that you will find in a typical business today. From *transaction processing systems (TPS)*, *management information systems (MIS)*, and *decision support systems (DSS)*, to *enterprise resource planning (ERP) systems* and *customer relationship management (CRM) systems*, information systems perform a wide variety of tasks and services. These types of systems use all of the components of IS listed in Table 1.3, and each of these IS is vital to the efficient and effective operation of most modern businesses. As you read about the different types of IS in Table 1.3, you will see that, regardless of the type of IS, businesses connect people, information, hardware, and software to achieve goals and to create value.

If you have ever purchased anything at a retail store, you are probably most familiar with the transaction processing system in Table 1.3. Table 1.4 illustrates each of the IS components within a transaction processing system (TPS).

The next time you purchase something at a store, think about these various components. Are they visible and obvious to you now? Did you purchase more items than were on your list? This may be the result of an IS in action!

Table 1.3	The Business Value of IS Types	
IS Type	**What Does it Do?**	**How Does it Help to Create Business Value?**
TPS (transaction processing system)	Captures and processes transactions to make them available to the organization. A *transaction* is the exchange of something of value the business produces for something in return that the business values (e.g., revenue from product sales).	If a business cannot track its transactions, it will have no way of making decisions about the success or failure of its business processes.
MIS (management information system)	Through processing and reporting features, an MIS provides timely information to decision makers.	Timely reports enable managers to monitor critical processes and avoid costly mistakes.
DSS (decision support system)	Provides analytical and visualization tools to support and enhance decision making and planning.	Enables managers to make data-based decisions and to discover new business opportunities through the use of its tools.
ERP (enterprise resource planning) system	Integrates and standardizes processes, and centralizes and standardizes the storage and management of data.	Reduces costs associated with duplication of processes and effort. Also, can minimize decision-making mistakes due to multiple versions of the same data, information, and knowledge.
CRM (customer relationship management) system	Integrates data collection, transformation, storage, and analysis of customer transaction data, including purchases, service requests, and other forms of customer contact.	Greatly increases the understanding of customers' purchasing and service behaviours and needs. Facilitates the timely and proactive management of customers.

Table 1.4	IS Components of a Transaction Processing System (TPS)
Input	Sales records are gathered at point of sale (POS), when a product's bar code is scanned.
Process	The data are added to a sales database table and removed from an available inventory database table.
Output	The product is sold.
Data	ISBN 978-1-118-29979-1 9 781118 299791
Information	1 medium, white, Concordia University T-shirt, $19.95, Sept. 9, 2010, 4:06 P.M.
Knowledge	Customers who purchased white Concordia University T-shirts were also likely to purchase Concordia University beer mugs.
System	As part of the TPS, the POS bar code reader allows for a sale to take place by managing the sale's inventory. The payment module enables the customer to purchase the T-shirt using a credit card.
People	The clerks in the university bookstore have been trained on the system and are able to serve customers efficiently.
IT	The POS hardware (the bar code reader) uses software to read data that are then input into inventory databases, the accounting system, and banks through network connectivity.
Decision	Move the beer mugs closer to the T-shirts to encourage cross-selling of products during the first weeks of September.
Business Value	More beer mugs and T-shirts were sold in the month of September as students and their parents arrived for the start of the school year.

Ethics in IT

You may remember the famous line from Spiderman, "With great power comes great responsibility." This quote has many applications when it comes to IT in organizations. Organizations, whether they be private companies, government, or not-for-profit agencies, collect a massive amount of data about customers, clients, suppliers, products, and more. With this information, companies like Amazon can determine what types of products you may want to purchase from your past purchasing behaviour. The ethical handling and safeguarding of information is only one area where ethics influence organizations and their handling of IT. This section illustrates common ethical dilemmas in IT that organizations face.

Copyright and Piracy One of the biggest plagues of the software industry is piracy. It should be clear to any professional that copying any protected software, which the licence clearly does not permit, is an unethical practice. It hurts the costs of software in the marketplace (because vendors factor in these costs and pass them along to consumers and businesses alike), does not encourage innovation (why bother if people are simply going to steal your stuff anyway?), and diminishes opportunities for IT professionals (because of less profit to invest in new product development). See the Business Software Alliance website (*bsa.org*) for more detailed studies of this problem.

Similarly, we all sometimes fall into the trap of simply "cutting and pasting" something without referencing it or sourcing it properly. This is another aspect of copyright infringement that is made easier by having access to the Web. It is a significant corporate problem that you have to be aware of, as a CIO or as an employee of an organization.[11]

---

11. See *TYNT.com* for an interesting example of a software solution designed to help address this issue within organizations.

The dispute between Apple and Samsung over patent violations on iOS devices demonstrates how easily disputes can arise in this highly competitive, fast-moving industry.

Patent Violations Although violations rarely happen deliberately, there are still many cases where companies are sued for patent violations. While some of this may be the result of ignorance (in and of itself a potential violation of ethics, since it is easy enough to search for pre-existing patents), much of this is intentional. If you use someone else's work, you should pay for it, and almost every developed nation has its own patent codes, arrangements, and royalty requirements. In the case of patents, that normally means acknowledging the use of and paying royalties on any invention you use as prescribed under various patent regimes in place around the world. To use someone else's invention without paying is not only unethical, it is also theft of intellectual property. An interesting and relevant example of this is the current lawsuit between Apple and Samsung regarding two previously registered U.S. patents, 8,074,172 and 8,086,604, which most prominently involve spelling and auto-correct features from iOS devices. Both companies have been in heated competition in the tablet and touch screen handset markets. While court documentation detailing the financial punishments that Apple wants to lay on Samsung has not been made public, it is clear that trying to keep pace in the quickly evolving tech industry can easily lead to dispute.

Reverse Engineering This topic attracts a lot of attention among academics and practitioners alike, and there is substantial debate about its validity as a professional practice. Essentially, reverse engineering is used most often to find out how another manufacturer created a product (software or hardware), and then attempting to learn from this to either make a better one or find a way to replicate it in a different way to avoid infringing on copyright or paying royalties on a patent. If this process is used as an educational tool (which was its original intention), there are no ethical dilemmas. However, for any other purpose designed to evade respecting other people's originality and intellectual property rights, there is considerable ethical debate about the integrity of this practice.

Spam and Privacy Codes Consumers and businesses hate spam email. However, organizations continue to use it as a marketing tactic, and criminal organizations use it in phishing schemes (e.g., the emails that indicate you are a lottery winner or have been chosen by a foreign national to enter into a business partnership with them). They are all fakes! For up-to-date information on this continuing web scourge, see *www.antiphishing.org*. The ethical dilemma is not the practice of sending promotional email itself; it is seeking permission to do so rather than collecting or buying email addresses where individuals have not provided their consent. This common practice requires IT professionals to implement the systems. However, it is not clear that the profession has taken a stand against unwanted spam email. Similarly, it seems incumbent upon any organization that does happen to have the privilege of obtaining private email addresses to keep them so and not to re-sell them to others without prior permission.

Security Breaches News stories[12] often describe breaches in protocol, usually in IT, or how intrusions or security breaches resulted in the loss or disclosure of valuable personal information. In most countries, including Canada, there are specific requirements to report these privacy

---

12. *www.canada.com/news/Canadian+Tire+cancels+MasterCards+following+breach/1232174/story.html* is a good Canadian example, and *www.pcworld.com/article/158003/massive_theft_of_credit_card_numbers_reported.html* is an excellent American one.

breaches and take immediate action to deal with any negative impact of the disclosure. However, there are exclusions for minor breaches, and the system is also voluntary. Without disclosure, there may be no need to act, and there will likely be no media impact. Would you report it? Of course you should, and ethical practice demands that you do. However, it is clear from the frequency with which consumers are affected by identity theft and not informed about it that not every organization adheres to this regimen. This behaviour is unethical; a privacy breach is a serious matter and must be taken seriously. The law is the law—as inconvenient as it may be—and it should be followed.

Here's an example: In April 2011, the Sony Corporation announced that their PlayStation Network had been hacked. Although this news deeply affected customer trust, Sony was upfront about the fact that information including customers' names, email addresses, birth dates, profile data (including purchase history and billing address), and PlayStation Network/Qriocity password security answers had been stolen. Other possible information stolen included customer credit card data. Despite the negative repercussions they faced, Sony acted appropriately in providing transparent reports about this unfortunate event.[13]

Competitive Intelligence Competitive intelligence is a common practice in business, including in the IT industry. Competitors want insight into what others in the industry are doing so they can respond to the market and maintain market share. Gaining such insights from customers or partners or from observation and deduction are all fine, but beyond that there are a whole host of practices that clearly skirt the boundaries of ethical practice. For instance, having someone pose as a potential customer to get pricing information, hiring away a competitor's employees with the sole purpose of obtaining competitive information, hiring a head hunter to seemingly solicit interest for a non-existing job so employees will disclose confidential plans, or hiring investigators to snoop and obtain private information are all clear examples of unethical practices that have been seen or documented in IT and other industries. Obviously, being a vigorous competitor is one thing; being a crook or a cheat is another.

Hiring Practices, Equity, and Equal Opportunity A vibrant IT sector often helps drive a country's economy through innovation and wealth creation. This often means that demand for talented professionals with the right skills outstrips supply, attracting immigration of qualified professionals to fill that demand. However, there is some evidence that these visa workers are frequently mistreated, not paid fairly, or exploited because they have a limited ability to change employers without affecting their immigration status. They also have to work for a number of years to qualify for citizenship. So, although we need these professionals, we may not always treat them fairly.

The same could be said for those who come to Canada to study in advanced technical programs, often because there are not similar programs in their country of origin. Although they are trained in these programs, they often report having a less than equal access to opportunity. This is a problem within the IT profession; practices that are not completely merit-based are unethical and should be questioned and rectified. All IT professionals should be concerned about this issue.

Green IT The environment is obviously a major global concern of every citizen of every country. And, like any industry, IT is a contributor to environmental damage. IT professionals are becoming aware of what they can do to help protect the environment. Some of the major steps all IT professionals should take are to promote recycling and reduce consumption to create a more sustainable global IT industry.[14]

---

13. For more information, see *www.cbc.ca/news/technology/story/2011/04/26/sony-playstation-network-hacked.html*

14. See *GreenIT.net* as an example of an entire consulting firm dedicated to this emerging trend. Their site has some very interesting and up-to-date information on green IT trends and practices.

Quick Test

1. True or False. Businesses rely on information systems to help them respond to their environment.

2. Of the following types of IS, which type primarily captures and processes data?
   a. DSS (decision support system)
   b. EIS (enterprise information system)
   c. MIS (management information system)
   d. TPS (transaction processing system)

3. Fill in the blank. When a company hires an employee from a competitor with the sole purpose of learning competitive information, it is an example of unethical _____.

■ WHAT'S IN IT FOR SOCIETY?

The Global World

As part of information systems around the globe, IT has had a significant impact on society. Not more than 30 years ago, it would have been inconceivable for you to maintain contact with even one friend in another country on a daily basis without incurring prohibitive phone charges. You might have had an international pen pal with whom you exchanged letters on occasion. Without extreme persistence, this often ended within a short period of time. Now you are in contact with friends and family through email and social networking sites such as Facebook as often as you like, and often 24/7! If you subscribe to Twitter, you can be in contact as much as you like, up to 140 characters at a time, and with many people at one time. You can choose to follow some people, and have others follow you. And with Skype, the cost of calling internationally is either very low, or when done completely online, is free, no matter where your friends or family live. This truly is an example of technology making the world a bit smaller.

Air travel certainly created a revolution in international understanding, allowing individuals to easily leave their country and experience another. But the Internet now provides an even less expensive and far easier way to explore the world. With the ability to enter any search term into a search engine, you can learn about any subject in the world. If you are interested in the Hindu festival Diwali, you simply type it in. In the search results you will find Wikipedia entries describing the festival, pictures of devotees enjoying the festival, YouTube videos of festival events, and perhaps blog entries describing individual experiences of Diwali. If you add a location to your Diwali search term, such as Diwali Calgary, you can learn about Diwali celebrations in Calgary.

As you can see, IT has contributed to globalization on a social level. Globalization has also had an impact on the way business is done around the world. **Globalization** means that modern businesses use information technology to expand their market to customers around the globe, to find the lowest-cost suppliers regardless of location, and even to create 24-hour business days by shuttling work across time zones and nations. Globalization also means paying attention to things like multilingual capability in your customer-facing systems, because geography may no longer be a barrier to having customers around the globe—all speaking to you and wanting to be spoken to in their own language online. On the other hand, it also means the expansion of English as a dominant language of global commerce for this same reason—and big changes in the second languages that students choose to study in secondary school, college, and university.

Globalization also means an increasing focus on universal technology standards and professional mandates. Organizations are adopting the view that one way of doing things around the globe is often better than doing it many different ways according to local custom or practice. This expands the market for truly world-class, standardized IT processes and practices such as we find in ITIL and similar efforts.[15]

Characteristics of the Digital World

Much of the current globalization of business and business's worldwide reach is due to the use of the Internet and Internet-related technologies. Another way to look at this globalization is to consider it as flattening. Just as technology has flattened organizations by requiring fewer organizational layers, the world has become flatter. This idea is explored by Thomas Friedman in his book, *The World Is Flat*.[16] He shows that IT has been a key enabler in making the world flatter and smaller. Of the 10 forces identified by Friedman as responsible for flattening the world, only one is not directly related to technology:

1. Collapse of the Berlin Wall – 1989
2. Netscape – an early search engine allowing the general public to search the Internet
3. Workflow software – using Internet technologies to allow work to be done without human intervention (e.g., the use of PayPal for financial transactions)
4. Open sourcing – allowing online contribution and collaboration
5. Outsourcing – allowing work to be divided between companies or locations, enabling them to be more efficient; the work is then integrated back to the assigning organization; customer contact call centres are often outsourced
6. Offshoring – allowing companies to take their operations to another location, which allows them to produce items better, faster, and cheaper
7. Supply-chaining – using technology to streamline operations and provide products/services to market faster and cheaper
8. Insourcing – allowing companies, small and large, to use outside firms to manage key operations on their behalf, thus allowing them to focus on core business (e.g., a company may insource its warehouse and distribution activities so that it can focus on product design)
9. Informing – the ability to find any type of information online
10. "The steroids" – technology such as mobile phones, iPods, instant messaging, and voice over Internet protocol (VoIP)

As you can see, all of the forces involve technology, with the exception of the fall of the Berlin Wall in 1989. The flattening of the world caused by these forces has brought countries and individuals closer together for interpersonal relationships, as well as for business ventures. With the evolution of technology and especially the Internet, business is done 24 hours a day around the world. It is not uncommon to have project team members located in Canada, the United States, Europe, Japan, and India doing work around the clock. It is also not uncommon to be able to more easily sell or purchase goods and services from other countries. For example, *Elance.com* is a service that connects a variety of professionals

The world is truly becoming flatter. Globalization has impacts on both the business world and individuals, because through a virtual network we can be linked to almost anyone or any organization that has a Web presence.

---

15. ITIL is the most widely adopted approach for IT service management in the world, and it provides a practical framework for identifying, planning, delivering, and supporting IT services to businesses. Go to ITIL's website to learn more: *www.itil-officialsite.com*.

16. Thomas L. Friedman, *The World is Flat*, 2005. Farrar, Straus and Giroux.

looking for contract work with clients that require their services. Using a service like this, a Canadian company can easily hire web designers from Hungary, Turkey, or India for short-term assignments.

The impact of the rapid technological advances of smartphones and their global popularity can also not be discounted as a factor in the new digital world. Everything is going mobile—and there is an app for just about anything you can imagine. Smartphone technology as we know it today originated in 2000, when Ericsson released the first touch-screen mobile phone (the "Smartphone R380," giving us the name for this category). This was the first device to use the Symbian operating system, which opened the possibility for applications to be developed by third parties and added to the phone. In 2002, Ericsson followed the R380 with the Smartphone P800, which was the first phone to include a camera, appealing to the growing trend of user-generated content. Microsoft, Research In Motion, and Nokia followed with their own smartphones and their own various operating systems— each supporting new and cool features consumers and businesses were looking for.

But the market entered a new phase June 2007 with the launch of the Apple iPhone. It became an instant success, prompting a second-generation version just one year later. No one reading this text should be unaware of the hype that precedes any announcement by Apple of a new iPhone version, and the consumer frenzy to acquire one that follows! In 2008, Google launched its own smartphone operating system, Android, as an attempt to define a new standard in mobile operating systems. It could be installed on any manufacturer's device. Products using Android began with the HTC Dream, the first phone on the market to use Android. The appearance of Android and its popularity with consumers globally caused total smartphone sales to nearly double from the third quarter of 2009 to the third quarter of 2010; smartphone sales now represent 19.3 percent of total mobile phone sales, according to a November 2010 Gartner report.[17]

Moreover, in 2011, market research firm IDC reported that the smartphone market grew by over 54.7 percent, while full-year smartphone shipments totalled 491.4 million units, up 61.3 percent from 2010.[18] Software developers continue to focus on new applications that use the still untapped capabilities of smartphones and incorporate a stream of new tools (such as flash photography and GPS location services). Mobile devices fit particularly well with social media applications, creating a very real global trend toward mobile commerce and instant, anywhere access to the World Wide Web.

It may be best at this point to sum up the important fundamentals of this increasingly global digital world. The important issues to address in your business model, often assisted by IS, include:

- Instant access to organization information, reliably and in real-time
- Consolidation and amalgamation of resources to optimize costs through best practices
- Anywhere, anytime mobile access by customers and clients
- Globally savvy marketing and brand reach (often using social media tools)
- Understanding and meeting globally complex privacy and security regulations
- Competing globally, which requires constant innovation to become and remain a leader

None of this should be understood as being easy—in fact, growing global competition has created lots of corporate casualties along the way (for instance, the auto industry), provoking business failures, government bailouts, consolidations, and declining prestige and profits. This is often the result of managers not truly understanding how much and how quickly their markets were "going global," or perhaps due to resistance from employees in understanding that everyone is now measured on a globally competitive basis and jobs will go where wages and productivity enable profits to be made, not where products are sold locally. As transportation costs fall, the means of production will be tied to competition and NOT to geography, truly creating an almost perfect worldwide, singular competitive market in many industries. This is scary for some, enticing for others.

17. *www.gartner.com/it/page.jsp?id=1466313*

18. *www.bgr.com/2012/02/06/idc-smartphone-sales-hit-all-time-high-in-q4-led-by-apple-samsung*

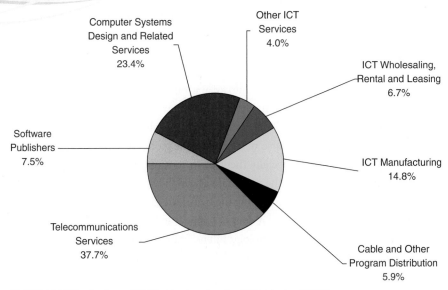

FIGURE 1.7 Distribution of GDP at basic prices by ICT industry, 2008.[19]

IT and the Economy

The information and communications technology (ICT) sector is a major contributor to the economies of the world. In Canada, the ICT sector is divided into several industries, as shown in Figure 1.7. This graph shows the contribution to 2008 GDP (the most recent statistics available) made by each of these ICT industries. As a whole, the ICT sector was a source of 4.8 percent of Canada's GDP, at a total value of $59.2 billion. Surprisingly, the ICT sector outpaced the Canadian economy. The ICT sector grew 2.7 percent from 2007 to 2008, whereas the Canadian economy grew only 0.6 percent. As seen in Figure 1.8, the ICT sector has had a higher rate of growth than the Canadian economy since at least 2002.

In terms of employment, the ICT sector employed 572,712 people in 2008.[20] Fifty percent of these people were employed in the software and computer services industry of the ICT sector. From 2007 to 2008, employment in the ICT sector grew from 3.30 percent of all Canadian employment to 3.34 percent.

What is especially remarkable about ICT GDP and employment growth is that in 2008, all of the economies of the world were slowly sliding into a recession, unlike any other time in history. While the ICT sector is not recession-proof, the sector fared much better than other sectors. And in Canada particularly, our overall economy has fared better than most, including the ICT sector.

It is important to consider not only the ICT sector, but also the impact of the outputs of this sector. Technology is critical to the success of businesses within other sectors of the economy. Without the products and services

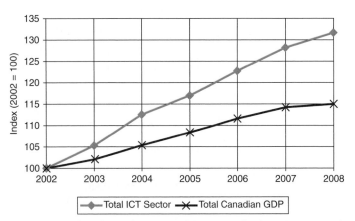

FIGURE 1.8 Indexed growth in GDP at basic prices for the ICT sector and the Canadian economy, 2002–2008.[21]

19. Industry Canada, "ICT Sector Gross Domestic Product (GDP)," November 2010. This reproduction is a copy of the version available at *www.ic.gc.ca/eic/site/ict-tic.nsf/eng/h_it05864.html*.

20. Canadian ICT Sector Profile, Industry Canada, August 2009.

21. Industry Canada, "ICT Sector Gross Domestic Product (GDP)," November 2010. This reproduction is a copy of the version available at *www.ic.gc.ca/eic/site/ict-tic.nsf/eng/h_it05864.html*.

provided by the ICT sector, financial services, resources, energy, manufacturing, health, education, and entertainment industries would be very different. In fact, growth, innovation, and throughput of these industries would be significantly decreased. Imagine the entertainment industry without the Wii, or eBay without PayPal.

To help put the worldwide ICT industry into an appropriate context for Canadian business students, Table 1.5 shows just a few comparative statistics on a worldwide basis for the period 1997 to 2008, as published by the International Telecommunications Union (*ITU.int*).

These statistics provide just a glimpse of how large the global ICT industry is, and how much impact it has had globally. Notice especially the growth in mobile phone devices (confirming the future of mobile commerce), and also the rapid rate at which both personal computers and associated Internet access has occurred. This is driving the size of the global ICT market—adoption of core technologies at unprecedented rates. And it does not appear to be stopping any time soon.

It is also clear that the trend of technology intensification has a social impact, creating both have and have-not nations, and within any nation a group that has easy access and can afford it and a group that cannot. This is referred to in the literature as the "great **digital divide**." It is a very real social concern since access to technology is increasingly associated with access to opportunity, because not everyone can afford equal access to new technologies. Government and social agencies around the world are wrestling with this important issue, as it is clear that investments in technology infrastructure at the national level have an impact on a country's GDP and ability to innovate and prosper in an online world. This is something you need to be aware of and consider as you become a citizen of the world, rather than just a citizen of your own country.

The Darker Side of IT

With all of the good impact that IT has had on society—contributions to the global economy, increasing standards of living, creation of opportunities—there is a darker side to use of IT as an enabler of crime and cyber-terrorism. New types of crime have not only been enabled by IT, but created by IT. That is, these sorts of crimes would not be possible to perpetrate without the use of IT.

Identity Theft Identity theft, which is facilitated by IT, is one of the more common cyber-crimes. Identity theft occurs when a perpetrator uses the personal information of an individual, which may include name, address, birthdate, social insurance number, or a combination of these pieces of information, to fraudulently present themselves as that individual. Identity theft occurs in the non-digital world where a person's identity may be stolen by someone taking mail or soliciting information by phone. Through IT, however, much more information can be gathered about a person's identity and in a much more convenient way. For example, through the use of a virus, spyware, or keylogging program installed on your PC, a criminal can record everything you input into your computer. That includes any online job applications, your online banking information, and online purchases you make.

Internet Fraud Another common Internet crime is fraud, in all shapes and forms. Have you ever been the victim of **phishing**? Phishing occurs when criminals send fraudulent emails posing as legitimate organizations, typically governments or banks, for the purpose of obtaining account numbers, passwords, or other important information that can then be used for a variety of purposes, including identity theft. Phishers even pose as charitable organizations in the wake of disasters by sending out fraudulent emails and setting up websites to collect donations. Internet fraud can also involve things like disrupting data flow between Internet gambling sites and players. One 2001 account saw hackers steal financial information from providers and enact fraudulent transactions using customers' names by obtaining their legal identities.[22]

---

22. *Journal of Gambling Issues*, Issue 24, July 2010. *http://jgi.camh.net/doi/pdf/10.4309/jgi.2010.24.5*

Table 1.5 Key Global Telecom Indicators for the World Telecommunication Service Sector[23]

	1997	1998	1999	2000	2001	2002	2003	2004	2005	2006	2007	2008
Telecom market revenue (current prices and exchange rates), US$ billions												
Services	712	767	854	920	968	1,039	1,126	1,329	1,419	...	...	...
Equipment	234	248	269	290	264	275	300	...	...	...	...	...
Total	**946**	**1,015**	**1,123**	**1,210**	**1,232**	**1,314**	**1,426**					
Other statistics												
Main (fixed) telephone lines (millions)	792	838	904	975	1,034	1,083	1,135	1,204	1,262	1,263	1,278	1,267
Mobile cellular subscribers (millions)	215	318	490	738	961	1,157	1,417	1,763	2,219	2,757	3,305	4,100
International telephone traffic minutes (billions)	81	91	103	114	120	127	141	166	179	183	...	...
Personal computers (millions)	325	375	435	500	555	615	650	775	808	...	...	...
Internet users (millions)	117	183	275	390	489	616	721	867	989	1,168	1,344	1,542

23. International Telecommunication Union, ICT Statistics, *Key Global Telecom Indicators for the World Telecommunication Service Sector, www.itu.int/ITU-D/ict/statistics/at_glance/KeyTelecom99.html.*

All types of Internet fraud are on the rise. In 2010, the Internet Crime Complaint Center (IC3) received 303,809 complaints of Internet crime, the second-highest total in IC3's 10-year history—and these are only ones that are reported![24] Imagine how many victims or near victims there actually are.

Espionage You have certainly heard of hacking, the way in which a malicious computer programmer can gain illegal and unauthorized access to a computer or computer system. But have you heard of spoofing or sniffing? Spoofing and sniffing are ways of gaining access to network traffic to access the information being transferred on these networks. For individuals, spoofing could be used for fraudulent purposes to gain personal information. In case of organizations, spoofing and sniffing can be used to spy on these organizations and gain access to confidential and proprietary information. I am sure you can imagine how valuable information related to Apple's next big product release or the secret recipe for Coke would be!

There are also some who would put Wikileaks into this same category, where individuals deliberately strive to entice those with confidential or secret information to reveal it online for the world to see—often at their own personal peril. Every state has strict national secrecy laws, and it is clear that Wikileaks does not plan to respect them. This brings up a number of interesting ethical and moral issues, as well as the obvious technical one: How do you successfully steal so much encrypted information?

Sabotage and Extortion The same methods as mentioned regarding espionage are used for much more destructive purposes. Once access to a computer or computer network is achieved, anything can happen. In the case of extortion, a perpetrator could copy something confidential and hold it for ransom. Alternatively they could gain access to a network and prevent any other person's access to it until their demands are met. The options are endless! In the case of sabotage, the sole purpose of the Internet crime may be to destroy something of value or add an incredibly destructive virus or worm that could then infect others.

Cyber-terrorism A large-scale form of Internet crime is cyber-terrorism. The FBI has defined **cyber-terrorism** as "The premeditated, politically motivated attack against information, computer systems, computer programs, and data which result in violence against noncombatant targets by sub-national groups or clandestine agents."[25] Cyber-terrorism can take several forms. One form is simply facilitating terror. That is, terrorists use computer systems to organize, gain information, and communicate with one another without physical presence, checkpoints, etc. Their activities over cyberspace are quite difficult to track and infiltrate. Second, IT can be used as the weapon itself.

One method of cyber-terrorism is called a **denial of service (DoS)** attack. This occurs when a network or networks are intentionally overloaded to the extent that they can no longer function. Very famously, Twitter was crippled by a denial of service attack in August 2009 that had the service offline for several hours. Now, think of the impacts of this happening to another, more critical organization, such as air traffic control, sewer operations, or world banks. The results could be catastrophic.

Viruses and worms are also used for cyber-terrorism. In 2009, it was estimated that the Confiker virus/worm had infected between 9 and 15 million computers.[26] The purpose of the virus/worm is still unknown. Likewise, the author of the virus/worm is also still unknown.

Of course, all of the above-mentioned crimes can be committed on a global scale as well, making enforcement and punishment much more difficult. In Chapter 2 we discuss how to protect yourself from these crimes.

---

24. IC3 2010 Annual Report on Internet Crime, Internet Crime Complaint Center, 2011. *www.ic3.gov/media/2011/110224.aspx.*

25. *www.crime-research.org/articles/cyber_terrorism_new_kind_terrorism/*, retrieved September 9, 2011.

26. *http://edition.cnn.com/2009/TECH/ptech/01/16/virus.downadup/?iref=mpstoryview*, retrieved September 9, 2011.

TECHNOLOGY CORE

Throughout this chapter, we have introduced you to the world of information technology and information systems and their role in your daily life, business life, and society at large. At the core of this is what we will generally call *technology*. None of the things discussed in this chapter and subsequent chapters can occur without it. So, how did technology as you know it get started?

For the purpose of this text, we have selected some key events in computing history to highlight.

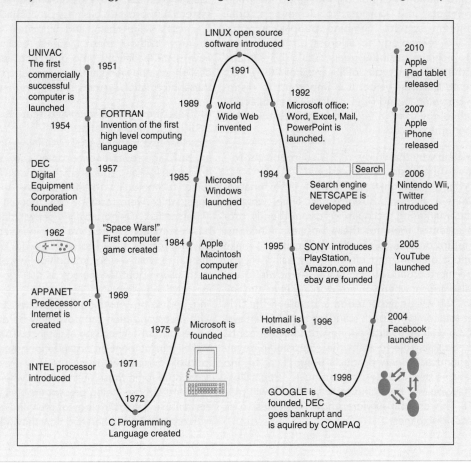

Quick Test

1. Which advancement was NOT one of the 10 forces identified by Friedman as responsible for flattening the world?
   a. Supply chaining
   b. In-sourcing
   c. The fall of the Berlin Wall
   d. Google search

2. True or False. The ICT sector outpaced the growth of the Canadian economy between 2007 and 2008.

3. Fill in the blank. The clear trend of technology creating both have and have-not nations is referred to as the _____.

RO↑ | STUDENT RETURN ON INVESTMENT SUMMARY

1. Describe what an information system is and explain why IS is so important in today's world.

An information system (IS) is an organized collection of people, information, business processes, and information technology, designed to transform inputs into outputs to achieve a goal. Information systems combine people, information, and technology to address business needs and to achieve business goals. Table 1.3 summarizes the different types of IS and how they help to create business value. It is important to distinguish between IS and IT. IT is simply the collection of technology used in an IS that enables the other components of an IS.

2. Explain why the study of IT is so important to any future business professional.

This chapter demonstrates how IT is an enabler in business. In every business discipline, whether finance, marketing, accounting, or another, IT provides essential tools for these business functions. As a future business professional, IT can help make you more efficient and effective. By using IT, you can be more organized and faster. A knowledge of IT is also critical when you are working in an organization. You will be expected to understand the IT in use at the company, both standard and custom systems, as well as evaluate them for improvements. It may be your role to assist the company in developing innovative new products using IT, or to find efficiencies and reduce costs using IT. Regardless of what you will be doing in business, IT will play a part. This chapter explored how IT applies to all business disciplines.

3. Describe some of the most common types of information systems used in businesses.

Table 1.3 summarizes some key information systems used in business: TPS, ERP, CRM, MIS, and DSS. Each system supports key business processes, parts of the business's value chain, and ultimately the business strategy. Without these systems, businesses would have a more difficult time operating and significant challenges innovating and growing. Chapter 4 looks at these information systems and others in more detail.

4. Describe some of the ways that IT has changed society.

It is clear that technology is so omnipresent that, from an early age, everyone becomes comfortable using it to manage all aspects of their lives. This includes using technologies to intermediate social interactions, which were formerly only thought to be done in person (i.e., dating, acquiring new "friends," having business meetings, etc.). We become used to technology not just as an aid to what we do, but as fundamental to what we do. In addition, we become used to thinking about technology as the "go-to" solution for anything—learning, researching, buying, travelling, and so on. Anything that involves an interaction with an organization can now likely be done through some form of technology assistance. This prevalence makes it incumbent on organizations, and particularly for-profit businesses, to ensure they are present and accounted for in those online places where customers are. Furthermore, being present ensures that customers can use the technology of their choice to engage with organizations when and how they want.

KNOWLEDGE SPEAK

business   24

business environment   24

commerce   16

communication   15

cyber-terrorism   36

data   12

data-information-knowledge continuum   12

denial of sevice (DoS)   36

digital divide   34

e-commerce   16

globalization   30

information   12

information and communication technologies (ICT)   21

Information and Communications Technology Council (ICTC)   22

information overload   15

information system (IS)   10

information technology (IT)   9

Internet   15

knowledge   12
knowledge management systems (KMS)   13
knowledge work   9
Moore's Law   8

phishing   34
wisdom   13
World Wide Web   15

REVIEW QUESTIONS

Multiple-choice questions

1. Enterprise resource planning (ERP) systems can reduce:
   I.   costs associated with duplication of processes and effort.
   II. decision-making mistakes due to multiple versions of the same data, information, and knowledge.
   III. reliance on data and information as the basis for decision making.
   a. I
   b. II
   c. I and II
   d. I and III
   e. I, II, and III
2. Data are _____.
   a. letters
   b. numbers
   c. symbols
   d. all of the above
3. To arrange the following terms in order from least complex to most complex, which of the following sequences is correct?
   a. knowledge, information, data
   b. knowledge, data, information
   c. information, data, knowledge
   d. data, knowledge, information
   e. data, information, knowledge
4. Which of the following are included in Friedman's 10 forces that flattened the world *and* involve technology?
   a. inshoring, offshoring, insourcing
   b. the collapse of the Berlin Wall, "the steroids," open sourcing
   c. Netscape, Nintendo, In-forming
   d. workflow software, supply chaining, insourcing

Fill-in-the-blank questions

5. _____ are raw unorganized facts, numbers, and pictures.
6. For a manager, examples of _____ might include the names of clients, their phone numbers, and their email addresses in an address-book program in a personal digital assistant (e.g., a Palm Pilot™).
7. _____ is created when a person combines experience and judgement with information.

True-false questions

8. Moore observed that computing power roughly doubles every 18 months.
9. As an entrepreneur, you will not need to have any knowledge of information technology or information systems.
10. The only factor of importance in a business's environment is competition.

Matching questions

Choose the BEST answer from column B for each item in column A.

Column A	Column B
11. data	a. You listen to the weather report and discover that it predicts a blizzard.
12. information	b. Milk.
13. knowledge	c. You need to buy milk at your grocery store before it starts snowing, or you may find that the stores have sold all their milk.
	d. None of the column B choices are appropriate matches.

Column A	Column B
14. process	a. Raw sales data.
15. input	b. Organize and format the sales data to create a monthly sales report.
16. output	c. A manager's monthly sales report produced by the IS department.
	d. None of the column B choices are appropriate matches.

Short-answer questions

17. Apply the model of an IS to an information system of your choosing. Based on the IS you choose, give an example for each of the following components:
    a. input
    b. process
    c. output
18. Explain how the productivity zone works. Give an example of the productivity zone in action.

Discussion/Essay questions

19. Explain the difference between IS and IT. Expand using examples.
20. Using the input-process-output model of an information system presented in the text, create an example that describes how an information system can create business value for an organization.

TEAM ACTIVITY

As you probably have already discovered, teams can be both fun and frustrating. How can you maximize the fun and minimize the frustration? Here's one way that might help.

If your team is willing to use them, good agendas can facilitate productive meetings. Creating an agenda requires your team to think about why it is meeting and what it wants to accomplish. Agendas help teams to break down meetings and project discussions into manageable chunks. They also provide a way to structure discussions from start to finish. If you have access to Microsoft Word, open Help and use the Answer Wizard to find out how to create an agenda. You can find additional sample agendas by searching the Web.

SOFTWARE APPLICATION EXERCISES

These exercises are designed to complement the material covered in each chapter, as well as to help you as a student and as a future business professional.

1. Internet

The Internet provides a number of resources for internship and job seekers, such as *Workopolis.com*. Use your favourite search engine to locate government (federal, provincial, municipal) sites for information on careers and future job prospects.

2. Presentation

Assume that you have to give a presentation about your background and qualifications to a graduate school admissions committee or a prospective employer. Create a presentation that highlights your strengths and experiences, relates why you chose your major, describes your goals, and then ties it all together to describe why you should be accepted or hired. (This exercise will also help you focus your thinking about possible majors or careers.)

3. Word Processing

Regardless of where you are headed after graduation, you will very likely need two important documents: a cover letter and a resumé. However, many people postpone creating these documents because they don't know where to get started. Further, in the case of the resumé, it is often difficult to highlight and convey the importance of past accomplishments in the space of one page. You can find examples of effective cover letters and resumés by searching the Web. These resources will give you ideas for creating your own resumé. Your school's career centre can also help you create and fine-tune your cover letters and your resumé.

4. Spreadsheet

Are you applying for summer internships? Attending career fairs? Applying for scholarships? Who did you meet? When did you send the thank-you note for that interview? Throw in all your normal school activities, and things can get hectic. However, a well-planned spreadsheet can help you reduce the stress inherent in managing your activities. Visit the course website to view a PowerPoint presentation on creating effective spreadsheets. Then, use this knowledge to create a spreadsheet that will help you track important activities.

5. Database

Here's a chance to see how others create those form letters you receive in the mail. Word processors typically have a MERGE function that will allow you to import or *merge* data from a database (or other source) directly into the document. For this exercise, use database software to create a database of potential employers or graduate schools. Decide what data you need to store (e.g., company name, internship title, school name, graduate program name, and so on). Once you have entered the data into your database, return to your word processor and use its merge function to merge the data into your cover letter (usually called the *merge document*). If you have created your database properly, it's easy to add new companies or schools to your database and print out a cover letter that contains the new data. CAUTION: When using the MERGE function, in a matter of seconds you may create 10 cover letters with the same error. Carefully proofread your cover letter before merging your data into it!

6. Advanced Challenge

Why not create a database that will manage your activities and allow you to provide data for merged documents? If you track activities by date, you can see what has been done in your meetings, as well as what you still need to do. You can use a database to track contacts with companies, the type of contact (phone call, email, thank-you letter, etc.), the employees you contacted, and much more for your internship or job-related activities.

ONLINE RESOURCES

Companion Website

- Take interactive practice quizzes to assess your knowledge and help you study in a dynamic way.
- Review PowerPoint lecture slides.
- Get help and sample solutions to end-of-chapter software application exercises.

Additional Resources Available Only on *WileyPLUS*

- Take the interactive Quick Test to check your understanding of the chapter material and get immediate feedback on your responses.
- Review and study with downloadable Audio Lecture MP3 files.
- Check your understanding of the key vocabulary in the chapter with Knowledge Speak Interactive Flash Cards.

CASE STUDY:
A DAY IN THE LIFE OF A UNIVERSITY STUDENT

Ashley Hyatt attends university, where she is majoring in business administration. The following is a typical day in the life of Ashley.

7:00 A.M. Ashley awakens to new music videos by her favourite artists playing on her computer. These files have been automatically downloaded overnight in compressed format and charged to her credit card. After five minutes, the flat-screen monitor switches from the music videos to a web page displaying news customized to Ashley's interests, including scores from the latest university sporting events.

8:00 A.M.–9:15 A.M. Ashley's first class is Globalization, Regionalism, and Information Technology Systems (commonly known as GRITS), an elective course examining how nations' leaders can use IT to solve global problems. Today the class features speakers from the School of Business Leadership at the University of South Africa, as well as speakers from Botswana and Kenya. The live broadcast is seen by students in Canada, Singapore, Norway, Brazil, and South Africa.

9:15 A.M.–10:30 A.M. After class, Ashley heads off to the combination computer lab–coffee shop where she purchases a bottle of fruit juice and a muffin. As she leaves the food area, she checks the wall-mounted LCD panel to verify that the correct amount was deducted from her account. The mobile device in her backpack communicates automatically with the checkout device. Since her university now uses contact-less smart cards that do not require swiping, all she needs to do is walk through the food area exit. Her mobile device handles all these transactions in addition to other chores. In fact, she can program her mobile device to display selected information on a regular basis; wireless access is continuous throughout the university. For example, for her Finance class, Ashley's team is managing a portfolio of mature Internet stocks, and she has programmed her mobile device to display the portfolio's latest value every 15 minutes. The bottom line of the LCD window shows that the portfolio is down 1.5 percent for the day, based on a number of stock exchanges around the world.

Choosing a seat at a table with an available flat-screen display device, Ashley uses the school's wireless-access capabilities to log on to her network account. Her Web-based to-do list reminds her that she has a quiz to take for her Networked Economy class and a report to finish on *Toronto.com* for the Strategic Management course. The quiz takes about 20 minutes, and she is relieved to immediately find out that she scored 92 on it. Next, to finish her *Toronto.com* assignment, Ashley consults an online collection of databases and checks a few websites. When she finishes the report, she emails it to the professor. Even though the professor is working with an MBA team on a consulting assignment in New Zealand, she knows that he will grade the report within a couple of days and return it with attached audio and text comments. She thinks this mix of classroom lectures and independent learning is good preparation for her business career because she is learning how to learn by herself. She could have done all of this on her mobile device using audio output, but she likes to see the graphics available on the flat-screen display.

10:30 A.M.–11:45 A.M. Ashley attends her Networked Economy class and, via the Web, participates in an interesting class discussion that includes the use of voice over the Internet. Whereas some of her fellow students are in her classroom, others are at home or in offices as many as five time zones away. However, all work from the same web page and wear a special headset–microphone combination that allows them to hear and respond to other class members' comments.

1:00 P.M.–2:30 P.M. After lunch, Ashley's Data Management class team members (Ashley, Eduardo from Brazil, and Tore from Norway) meet to review their design for a data model. They participate in an audio conference with a shared screen, so the team members all see the same high-fidelity model of the timetable for the Sao Paulo subway. They take turns changing it until they agree. The Data Management class is simultaneously taught with partner business schools in Brazil and Norway, and students learn how to design and query databases as they hone their skills in working in cross-cultural teams. After completing the project, Ashley catches a bus to the recreation centre to play racquetball. During the bus ride, Ashley listens to a podcast of her Strategic Management professor's latest lecture to confirm her understanding of the class material.

5:00 P.M.–6:00 P.M. Ashley's Strategic Management class team meets at the video booth in a school lab. Jennifer, an alumna working in Vancouver, has agreed to review the team's presentation. As she watches the presentation on her computer in Vancouver, Jennifer's software tags her comments so that the team knows the portions of the presentation that need more work.

6:30 P.M.–7:30 P.M. During dinner, Ashley's sound system stops playing the latest U2 music downloads stored on her computer and announces the receipt of a priority voice mail. Ashley uses the remote to instruct the system to play it for her; it is from the alumna who viewed her team's presentation that afternoon. Impressed by Ashley's role in the presentation, the alumna asks Ashley to cut and paste her section of the presentation and mail it to the company's recruiter. It takes Ashley about five minutes to locate the video on the university server, edit it, and email it to the recruiter.

11:00 P.M. Before going to bed, Ashley adds comments about her day to the blog she is keeping for the GRITS class.

Case Questions

1. How many of the innovations in Ashley's home or school life are available to you? How many are you actually using?
2. This case mentions many acronyms and technical terms. Research and write a short paragraph about each of the following terms:
   a. blog
   b. wireless access
   c. LCD display panel
   d. podcast
3. Do you believe that any of the information systems involved in Ashley's daily life create only limited value for her?

CASE STUDY:
BUILDING A WEBSITE

You are a member of your local Chamber of Commerce because you decided that you need a place to network for career advancement when you graduate. One of your friends says there is no point in simply joining; to get noticed you need to volunteer to take on some kind of leadership role to build your profile. It turns out they are looking for someone (younger it seems!) to take on a website re-build project. You volunteer and are picked—well actually, you are the only volunteer, but anyway . . .

While they have the vendor and the money to pay to get the site developed, you are asked to present an outline of the basic processes that you feel can be automated that will help secure the most useful design of the new site for club members and executives.

You do some interviews with the president, treasurer, and some key members, and you establish some of the following observations as important priorities that should be addressed in the new website design:

"I want to be able to receive my statement and pay my club dues online . . . but our website doesn't do that today and it should. We are so behind the times."

"There is no good way to track RSVPs for our online events today, which is a problem."

"I would like to know which events are most popular, maybe even have members rate them or tell us what they thought about them so we can improve our services."

"Our mailing list is inaccurate, with more than 10% coming back each month. Members are asked to send in updates on their address information; they never do . . . "

"Some members have said they feel their privacy is not being respected since we only have the option of mailing stuff to them at home right now—what if they don't want that? Or if they only want it electronically or not at all?"

Case Task

1. Before the club's next meeting with the vendor, you decide to create a short PowerPoint (or similar) presentation that will outline the basic processes you feel need to be automated. Your presentation should include simple process diagrams showing the inputs/outputs and results of these new automated processes, and a list of the data and information that will be collected, automated, and stored behind the web pages themselves as a result.

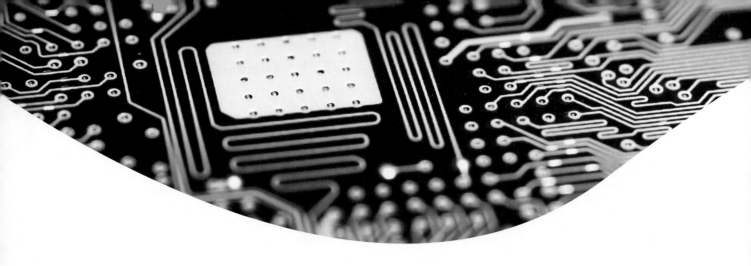

2 | TECHNOLOGY ESSENTIALS

WHAT WE WILL COVER

- The Components of IT
- The Internet
- The World Wide Web
- Internet Security
- Meaningful Applications of Technology

STUDENT RETURN ON INVESTMENT **ROI**

Through your investment of time in reading and thinking about this chapter, your return—or created value—is gaining knowledge. After reading this chapter, you should be able to

1. Describe the fundamentals of information technology and how they come together to help increase your productivity as a business professional.

2. Explain why the Internet is so valuable to businesses, and outline some of the Internet applications available to businesses today.

3. Identify the basic components of the World Wide Web and describe how web pages are located on the Web.

4. Outline important ways individuals and businesses can keep their data and information safe online.

5. Explain how technology has made collaboration in the business world easier and more productive.

THE VOICE OF EXPERIENCE

Derek Ball, University of Calgary

With a Bachelor of Commerce specializing in finance, Derek Ball started out in banking. He recognized the ability of technology to create business value, and soon became involved in the start-up of several technology companies. Derek sold his company, Sonic Mobility, to U.S.-based Avocent in 2004 for over $8 million (U.S.) and has recently sold another technology venture, Tynt.com. As a serial entrepreneur in the technology sector, Derek is already searching for his next venture!

What do you do in your current position? I am now the former CEO and co-founder of Tynt Inc., a company that helps online publishers benefit when their readers copy and paste their content. Tynt was sold to 33Across, a strong sales-oriented company that will combine Tynt with their substantial assets and client base. As the two companies integrate, I am the VP of Publisher Development, where I provide continuity for Tynt customers and help 33Across realize the benefits of Tynt's technology.

What do you consider to be important career skills? Understanding the value technology can deliver and whether it can solve a real-world problem. Just after graduation, I was working in Zurich for a bank, doing financial control. The bank bought computers and dumped them on everybody's desk and didn't tell them how to use them. I was willing to learn and I figured out how to use Lotus 123, a precursor to Excel, to automate financial control functions. Despite the fact that I didn't have any formal IT training, the bank ended up giving me the role of applying technology to streamline operations.

What I am doing currently is probably less about education or skill and more about experience. I have enough technical knowledge to know what is possible. I can be realistic about what problems technology can solve. I learned that technology is a tool. It's a means to an end, but not the end itself. It will always be changing, so it's important to be flexible and adaptable.

How do you use IT? Personally, I don't do voice mail. I try to focus all my communications through email as a way of managing my time. I'm also big believer in mobile devices as productivity tools. I have used the Internet extensively for research and I'm a big fan of software as a service, something that is accessed on a remote server, not installed on an individual hard drive.

Can you describe an example of how you have used IT to improve business operations? At Sonic Mobility, we used IT to provide a secure connection from a hand-held wireless device to a company's backend network. It was an encrypted TCP-IP connection with secure identification. The hand-held would connect with the Sonic Admin server, which would act as a proxy and communicate with the servers that needed to be adjusted through a variety of different protocols, depending on the required action. As an example, our client's IT support staff were about to board a plane to go to a conference when they were contacted about a virus attack. They were able to connect remotely to the network from their BlackBerry devices and use Sonic Admin to stop the virus without returning to the office and missing their trip.

Have you got any on-the-job advice for students seeking a career in IT or business? Your most important resource is the people sitting on your left and right. There's no way that any one person is ever going to understand everything there is to know in any field. Information technology has grown exponentially and will continue to do so. The most important thing you can do is make as many contacts as possible.

Although Derek did not start out in the IT field, he recognized that IT plays a critical role in business success. Early in his career, he had a willingness to learn about new technology and continued to build that learning into successful businesses. This chapter will introduce you to the components and terminology of IT to equip you with a foundation for applying IT in business.

Think about how often you come in contact with information technology (IT) beyond the use of a desktop or laptop computer. For example, a grocery store uses IT to allow you to purchase items more quickly through self check-out. A bank relies on IT to provide you with ATM access. You carry IT with you, such as a mobile phone, PDA, or MP3 player. We could spend all day adding to this list!

Now think about what IT allows you to do. IT allows you to *communicate* with others, such as through mobile phones and instant messaging. IT *enables transactions* between you and the organizations with which you deal, for example, through online purchases. IT helps you to *obtain*, *organize*, *analyze*, and *store data* and *information* that you need through online searches and specific software tools. Finally, IT *provides entertainment* through MP3 players and game consoles. Information technology can help you do all of these things and more, with greater efficiency and value.

Most people are uninterested in opening up IT devices and tinkering with the circuits or boards. They just want to be competent users of technology. However, your use of IT will improve if you know and understand some basic concepts. It's a lot like owning and operating a car: To be a competent driver, you need to know when to get an oil change or that an unusual sound means a trip to the mechanic. And, just like paying for gas at the pump using your credit card, doing many things with your IT devices yourself can save you time.

In this chapter, our goal is to equip you with the IT knowledge that you will need to support your future career. Knowledge of these fundamentals, and using available technical tools, will also help you understand new innovations.

■ THE COMPONENTS OF IT

When you think about it, all IT, including computers, mobile phones, and PDAs, are actually limited to the following capabilities:

- accepting and storing information
- performing mathematical calculations
- applying logic to make decisions
- retrieving, displaying, and sending information
- consistently repeating the above actions many times

The power of IT comes from the fact that it does these things amazingly well. IT devices combine these capabilities in a number of ways to help you work with information more efficiently and effectively. How is this possible?

Information technology consists of three basic categories: hardware, software, and networks. **Hardware** is the electronic and mechanical components that you can see and touch, such as your computer monitor. **Software** is the set of instructions that direct the hardware. While not necessary for all IT devices, **network** technology increases their power by allowing users to share resources, including hardware, software, and information. The three basic categories (hardware, software, and networks) together create a **platform**, as Figure 2.1 shows.

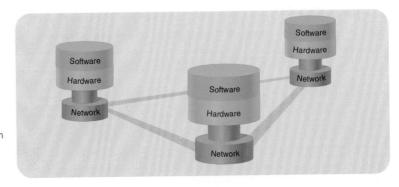

FIGURE 2.1 The IT platform consists of hardware, software, and network technology.

TECHNOLOGY CORE

This chapter discusses the technology that you need to be aware of to be a successful business person. In whatever career you choose, you may need to know more than these basics. When searching for information about technology on the Internet, try these sources:

- *http://mashable.com*: Mashable is a very popular blog that reviews new websites and services, especially in social media.
- *www.cio.com*: This news site for chief information officers provides overview information on technology and related business issues.

- *www.cnet.com*: This technology news site covers all types of technology, including PCs, mobile devices, software, and more.
- *www.gartner.com* and *www.forrester.com*: Gartner and Forrester are technology research firms that often issue press releases on the latest technology and technology usage.

Other sources of information include technology leaders' blogs, such as Bill Gates; leading technology companies' websites, such as Cisco or Microsoft; and idea forums, such as *www.TED.com*.

Hardware

Hardware components represent the physical (hard) parts of a system, as distinguished from the more adjustable (soft) parts, the software. The working parts of IT hardware consist primarily of electronic devices (mostly digital) with some electromechanical parts used with input, output, and storage devices.

When it comes to hardware, IT devices share a common set of system components. In our discussion of these system components, we focus on the personal computer (PC). However, the same architecture and components are common to most modern IT devices.

These general components can be categorized into six basic IT hardware categories (see Figure 2.2), which are discussed in the following subsections.

Processing Hardware Processing hardware directs the execution of instructions and the transformation of data using transistors. A *transistor* is an electronic switch that can be either on (represented by 1) or off (represented by 0). A tiny chip made up of transistors is called a *microprocessor*. This chip contains most of the components that make up the *central processing unit (CPU)*. You notice the speed of the CPU when you are performing a task on your PC. Have you ever done a search or opened a file and had to wait what seemed like an eternity? This speed is called the *clock speed* and

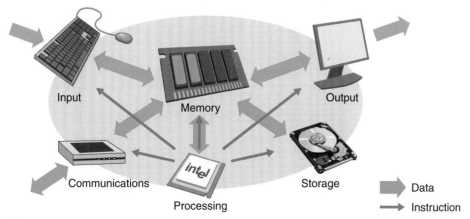

FIGURE 2.2 All IT devices share a common set of six system components.

is measured in *megahertz (MHz)*, millions of cycles per second, and more recently *gigahertz (GHz)*, billions of cycles per second. Higher clock speeds usually translate into faster performance, which is something to consider when you purchase your next computer.

Just as processing hardware is at the heart of any individual IT device, it is also at the heart of business IS. The main difference here is that rather than making decisions about a single processor, organizations typically need to select combinations of processors with varying processing power. A common categorization scheme for processors used in IS is the computer hierarchy.

As Table 2.1 shows, the **computer hierarchy** categorizes processors according to their power. Note that processing power also often corresponds to the computer's physical size. However,

Table 2.1	Computer Hierarchy		
Computer Type	**Relative Processing Power**	**Purpose**	**Example**
Supercomputer	Largest and fastest	Performs processor-intensive computations using parallel processing	Supercomputers are typically used to process large amounts of data. For example, Environment Canada uses supercomputers to analyze data and forecast the weather, military institutions use supercomputers to analyze data concerning national security, and scientists use supercomputers to analyze data to identify trends or make new discoveries.
Mainframe	Large	Carries out many of the organizational processing needs using high-speed processing chips and large amounts of memory	Mainframes are used to process large amounts of data and are often used to process transactions. For example, banks use mainframes for account activity and statement generation, insurance companies use mainframes for managing insurance claims, and your university or college uses mainframes to manage your student records and accounts.
Server farms	Medium/many	Allows multiple servers to handle network processing activities	Google relies on its extensive server farm to operate efficiently.
Personal computer (PC)	Small to medium	Enables users to carry out processing tasks needed to perform their job; usually networked together	All of the major Canadian banks provide Internet banking to their personal and business banking clients. Over their websites, the banks allow clients to manage their accounts, order cheques, apply for loans, and download their account activity in accounting software to manage household finances or create business financial statements.
Personal digital assistant (PDA)/Tablets/Smartphones	Very small	Provides users with portable computing power, often using specially designed applications, and provides the ability to connect to the Internet and email	Smartphones come with many built-in applications, such as cameras and GPS locators. Additionally, there are currently over half a million iPhone applications available, including games and business applications, such as business card readers. Similar applications are available for BlackBerry smartphones and Android phones.
Embedded processors	Extremely small	Provides low-scale processing and/or identification; embedded in appliances and products	Companies like Procter & Gamble incorporate embedded processors into packaging to monitor expiration dates.

comparing computer types on processing power alone can be deceptive. For example, it is possible to combine the processing power of several smaller computers, like personal computers, to exceed that of a small supercomputer. An organization, therefore, has many options to meet its processing needs and will select the most efficient and cost-effective option possible.

In fact, the smallest type, embedded processors, which provide small amounts of processing power, may actually provide the greatest value to businesses. *Embedded processors* are programmable chips built into products to make them "smart." Creative uses for embedded processors include digital signal processors (DSPs). DSPs are special microprocessors that include more math-related functions in their instruction set than the typical processor. DSPs can also process signals in real time.

DSPs process signals in real time, perfect for applications that cannot tolerate any delays, such as mobile phones.

On the other end of the spectrum is **grid computing**. Grid computing involves combining the processing power of several computers by networking them together. Each member in the grid is called a *node*. Each node contributes to the power of the grid and can be as powerful in and of itself as a super computer, or as simple as a desktop computer. The power of the entire grid can be used to solve complex problems or do complicated calculations, or pieces of the grid can be used as back-up for the rest of the grid should any node fail or become overworked.

Memory Memory temporarily locates data and instructions before processing. Long-term memory helps you keep track of facts, like the name of the first Canadian prime minister, or processes, like how to brew coffee when you're only half awake. Short-term memory, on the other hand, is only for items that you need to remember for a relatively short time, such as the start time of a movie. After leaving the theatre, you forget that time, or replace it with other things to remember.

Computers have long-term memory (ROM) and short-term memory (RAM) stored on chips. Memory capacity is measured as the number of *bytes* that the ROM and RAM chips store. Capacities of memory devices range from thousands (kilobytes–KB), to millions (megabytes–MB), and even billions (gigabytes–GB) of bytes. **Read only memory (ROM)** contains instructions and data that only special devices can alter. **Random access memory (RAM)** stores data only until they are no longer needed, or until you shut down the computer. This type of memory is called random access because the CPU can access any item stored in RAM directly (randomly).

Whenever you load software—like Microsoft Word to work on that 10-page term paper that you've been putting off—the CPU retrieves the software instructions and loads them into main memory. As you begin typing the paper, the CPU stores the text that you see on the screen in RAM. As you have no doubt found, if your computer shuts down inadvertently and you have not saved your paper, it will be lost, since the RAM is cleared at shutdown.

Eventually, your computer reaches its RAM capacity. What happens then? It becomes necessary to continuously exchange items stored in RAM with new items from slower storage devices. This can profoundly affect the overall performance of your computer. Consequently, increasing your RAM capacity can be one of the cheapest and most effective ways of extending the life of your computer.

Input Hardware Input hardware provides the interface used for data entry *into* a device. The choice of input device should be tailored to the task to be performed. Have you ever been in a situation when you were using a self check-out counter and the barcode scanner did not read the barcode of an item you were attempting to purchase? Having to enter the 12-digit barcode by hand on a keypad demonstrates that the scanner is a much better way to input barcode data. Input devices you are familiar with include keyboards, pointing devices (such as a mouse, touchpad/screen, or a Wii remote), scanners, and digital cameras. With the creation of the Microsoft Xbox Kinect game console, even humans are input devices! The Kinect registers human movement as the input to the game. No doubt because of this novel input method, Kinect earned a spot in the Guinness World Records as the fastest selling computer device ever, with daily sales of 133,000 units per day between November 4, 2010 and January 3, 2011.[1]

Controlling a computer with a pointing device, such as a touchpad or mouse, allows more natural movements, thereby requiring less user training.

WHAT DO YOU THINK?

You have no doubt used a Wii or Kinect. The Wii gaming remote, invented by Nintendo, connects wirelessly to the gaming console and allows gamers to move the remote to perform activities as if they were in the game itself by sensing motion (e.g., swinging a tennis racket or steering a car). The Kinect does not even require a remote; it simply senses human movement.

1: Are there business applications for this technology?
2: Why would this input method be preferable to others in terms of usability? Are these the same reasons why some gamers prefer this method of input over others?
3: What are the drawbacks? Does this technology make you feel more a part of the machinery than you are comfortable with (e.g., Cyborg)?

Output Hardware Output hardware provides the interface used to retrieve information *from* a device. *Output devices* convert IT-processed information into a usable form. When choosing output devices, business professionals are primarily concerned with the quality and speed of the output. Secondary considerations may include ergonomics, portability, compatibility, and environmental considerations. Display devices make up the most common category of output device, such as computer monitors. However, most users also require printers, and many users now rely on other output devices, such as speakers or MP3 players.

Modern monitors come in all sizes and resolutions. LCD screens are light, thin, and consume less energy than other types of monitors. Printers and plotters output data to paper. Are you familiar

1. *http://mashable.com/2011/03/09/kinect-10-million/,* retrieved October 22, 2011.

with the terms "paperless society" or "paperless office"? In the 1970s, with the adoption of computer technology in business, some predicted that we would no longer require paper output and would simply view documents on screen, and that society would adapt to decrease paper consumption significantly.[2] What happened in reality was quite the opposite. As it became easier to access documents and information, it became easier to print them! The result, for a period of time, was an increase in paper consumption. Today, we do view a lot more information online rather than printing it. The increasing use of e-billing and e-banking are evidence of this. Statistics Canada indicated that up to 67 percent of Internet users paid bills or did their banking online in 2009.[3] In 2011, a labour dispute suspended Canada Post services for two weeks. During this period, even more Canadians signed up for e-billing in order to receive and pay their bills online, causing many people to call into question the relevancy of the postal service itself.[4]

LCD monitors are slim, light, and don't use a lot of power to run.

Think about your personal printing habits. Have you signed up for online billing, for example, as a way to reduce business costs and reduce the use of paper? What types of things do you tend to print rather than view on a screen? Do you think you could go completely paperless? Some of you may be reading this textbook as an eBook. Have you printed it out to read it? Be honest!

Storage Hardware Storage hardware stores data, information, and instructions for the long term. Examples of storage include the computer hard drive, CDs, DVDs, USB flash memory, and external hard drives. How often do you back up your PC? Do you remember to put critical files on an external hard drive or memory key just in case? Have you been in the unfortunate situation of losing your data? To prevent the loss of your data, you can now sign up for an online service that will automatically back up the files that you specify on a scheduled basis. If you have bought a Dell computer recently, they may have provided you with a trial of their Dell DataSafe product, which automatically backs up your data and stores it at a secure storage site. Or perhaps all of your files are stored "in the cloud." Storing your data in the cloud allows you to access your data from anywhere and at any time, and puts the burden of maintenance elsewhere. We discuss the cloud in detail later in this chapter.

Storage is not only a concern for individual business professionals; it is also a major concern for businesses. Later in this chapter we discuss disaster recovery as a way of reducing the risk of data loss. Often businesses keep critical data off-site in case something happens to their internal systems or facilities. This way they can retrieve their data and resume business as quickly as possible.

Communications Hardware Communications hardware connects one IT device to another. Communications hardware, such as the **network interface card (NIC)**, provides the physical connection between a computer and a local network. This ability is vital to many knowledge work activities.

When you are not physically connected to a network, you can use a modem. **Modems**, both wired and wireless, allow you to connect to a remote network over a telecommunications line, such as telephone or cable TV service. A modem converts (*mo*dulates) the digital signals going out from your computer into an analog

A USB flash memory stores large amounts of data and instructions for the long term.

2. "The Office of the Future," *Business Week* (2387), June 30, 1975, pp. 48–70.

3. *http://www40.statcan.gc.ca/l01/cst01/comm29a-eng.htm*

4. *www.techvibes.com/blog/canada-post-union-strike-cost-a-lot-more-than-two-weeks-revenue-as-canadians-take-digital-route-2011-06-28*

signal appropriate for the connection medium used. When receiving a signal, it converts (*demodu-lates*) the analog signal back into a digital signal that your computer can recognize.

Modem speeds, measured in bits per second (bps), significantly affect knowledge work activities. For example, if you frequently research information on the Internet, you will lose valuable time waiting for a telephone modem to download the data. At top transmission speeds of 56 Kbps, telephone modems cannot compete with DSL modems, which offer higher transmission speeds—up to 10 Mbps and higher in many areas. Similarly, cable modems can theoretically reach speeds of 30 mbps, but they are shared with other users.

Finally, recent IT technology has increased knowledge work effectiveness by allowing mobile devices to connect to wireless networks by using wireless NICs.

We have now discussed the main categories of hardware that exist in any IT system. (We discuss each of these components in further detail in Tech Guide A). However, each and every IT device, from your MP3 player to your desktop PC, includes a component that you can't touch but that your device cannot work without. In the next section, we discuss this important component: software.

Software

As discussed, IT devices help you with your knowledge work activities and thereby contribute to creating business value. As such, they always involve working with information in some way. You can think about software as information that specifies how a hardware device should work with other data, information, and knowledge.

To begin to understand the relationship between software and hardware, think about cooking from a recipe. Your mother makes an amazing chicken pot pie, and it has been a while since you had a home-cooked meal. She emails you the recipe and you buy the ingredients. You follow the recipe exactly: 2 cups of chicken, 2 carrots sliced, and so on. You also follow the baking instructions: 1 hour at 350 degrees Fahrenheit. Does the chicken pot pie turn out the same as your mom's? Probably not.

By now you're probably wondering: "What in the world does this have to do with computer software?" Recall that a computer performs functions based on instructions—that is, software. The process by which a computer follows instructions is similar to how you learn and follow instructions for the tasks that you do.

Continuing the example above, even if your mother gives you the exact recipe, she may omit some of the steps that she takes to ensure the perfect chicken pot pie (such as adding a little more salt or pepper to taste). She is able to execute these instructions routinely and without thought. The instructions for this task have become instinctual or built-in, like firmware. Similarly, when you turn on a computer, firmware built into ROM chips allows the computer to start and prepare for use (i.e., boot up). Once the computer is ready, the CPU loads more software into RAM, and the computer can get to work.

After your chicken pot pie is cooked, you begin to do more tasks, such as finding dishes and utensils to eat with. Your *personal application software* for setting the table may instruct your body to select which utensils (fork or spoon) to use. However, it's your *system software* that controls your hands as you place items on the table. Similarly, while you may select the Print command within an application software package, it is the operating system that takes over and carries out the actual print job.

We can divide computer software into three main categories: (1) system software, (2) application software, and (3) middleware.

System Software **System software** includes any software required to control the hardware components and to support the execution of application software. System software includes the operating system and utility software. The **operating system (OS) software** coordinates and handles the details of working with the computer hardware. After the boot program in ROM successfully tests and starts up the hardware, the CPU loads the operating system software into the computer's memory. The OS software performs two main tasks:

1. managing the hardware and software resources of the computer
2. providing a stable and consistent interface between application programs and the hardware

To manage the hardware, the operating system works like a police officer who directs traffic at a busy intersection. Given its role of directing all computer operations, OS software has the most impact on your experience, efficiency, and productivity when using a computer.

An example of the importance of operating systems was illustrated by the controversy over Windows Vista when it was released worldwide in 2007. In its first year of availability, *PC World* rated it as the biggest tech disappointment of 2007[5] and it was rated by *InfoWorld* as number 2 of the 25 all-time technology flops.[6] Although Vista implemented much needed new security features and a different/improved user interface, it was criticized for the hardware requirements needed to run it and its incompatibility with other software. In an effort to encourage adoption, Microsoft decided to no longer support the previous operating system, Windows XP, and to no longer provide XP as an operating system to its channel partners, such as Dell. Soon, this left new PC buyers with no choice but to use Vista. Due to public backlash and criticism of Vista, Microsoft retracted and began to allow the use of XP again. They also increased their efforts on the next operating system release, Windows 7. Who knew that an OS could have such a big impact and create such passion in computer users! The relevance of an operating system is also illustrated by those who use Apple computers versus those who use PCs. It is the difference in the operating systems of these devices that make the user experience so different and that also makes it difficult to switch from one to the other.

Utility software provides additional tools that you can use to maintain and service your system. For example, users often add utilities such as file management software and security programs. A firewall application is an example of utility software that helps guard your computer against unauthorized access when connected to a network.

Application Software **Application software** is a complete, self-contained program or set of programs for performing a specific job. For example, you use a word processing application software, like Microsoft Word, to write a term paper.

An important group of application software for business professionals is known as **productivity software**. Business professionals frequently use productivity software to work more efficiently and effectively with data, information, and knowledge, such as:

- *Document preparation software*, for creating documents composed of text, images, and supporting graphics
- *Electronic spreadsheet software*, for performing general calculations and analyses, such as financial analysis, budgeting, and forecasting
- *Presentation graphics software*, for preparing professional-quality slides and graphics for business presentations; often requires a business professional to be able to access and manipulate large amounts of data
- *Database management system (DBMS)*, for designing, creating, updating, and querying data
- *Personal information management (PIM)*, for managing personal information, such as to-do lists, schedules, and email

5. Dan Tynan, "The 15 Biggest Tech Disappointments of 2007," *PC World* (December 16, 2007), *www.pcworld.com/article/id,140583-page,5-c,techindustrytrends/article.html*, retrieved March 1, 2010.

6. Neil McAllister, "Tech's All-Time Top 25 Flops," *InfoWorld* (January 21, 2008), *www.infoworld.com/article/08/01/21/03FE-25-tech-failures_6.html*, retrieved March 1, 2010.

In addition to these uses of application software for individual business professionals, enterprises also employ application software for business units (e.g., finance, marketing, etc.) or for the enterprise as a whole. This software tends to be specialized for a certain business process and may be further customized for the organization itself. An example of this type of enterprise application software is customer relationship management (CRM) software, which helps organizations manage customer data and interactions. Because these types of application software are so important and prevalent in business today, we discuss them in depth in Chapter 4.

Middleware **Middleware** is software that is more common in enterprises. Its purpose is to link applications that use dissimilar software or hardware platforms and act like a specialized messenger/translator to manage the exchange of information. Figure 2.3 illustrates where a layer of middleware software would fit within an organization's IS to support efficient communication between various business applications and the systems environment.

Middleware is often essential when an organization is implementing new types of software that need to communicate with existing systems. For example, your organization may acquire another company and need to integrate the purchased company's financial systems. Middleware may be written to interface with the source system (the acquired company's financial system) and the target system (your company's financial system).

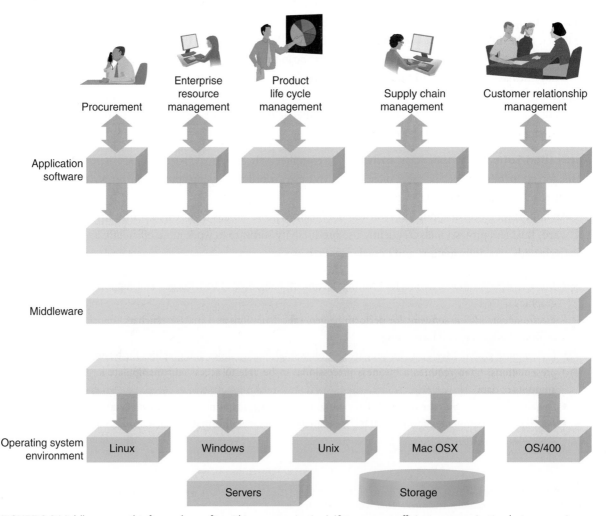

FIGURE 2.3 Middleware, as this figure shows, fits within an organization's IS to support efficient communication between various business applications and the operating system environment.

Open Source Software Open source software is software that can be used, modified, improved, and redistributed. Open source software is usually developed by a community of developers that are interested in the subject matter of the software and want to share their work with others. Open-source programs are often free or have very low cost. The combination of low cost, flexibility of use, and decreasing reliance on a single software vendor has made this software a very popular choice for many e-commerce applications. Commonly used open source software in e-commerce include:

- Linux—used as the operating system for servers (and possibly the clients)
- Apache—a Web server software application
- MySql—a database management system
- Perl, PHP, or Python—a selection of script programming languages
- Ruby on Rails (RoR)—a Web application framework

A report by The Standish Group states that adoption of open-source software models has resulted in a $60 billion loss in annual revenues for software companies,[7] but that also means that it's saving consumers about $60 billion per year.

Now that we have discussed hardware and software (both of which are discussed in more detail in Tech Guide A), we can examine how these connect to other organizational resources and how those resources are accessed and shared.

Connecting Over Networks

Look around. Networks are everywhere! Humans are networking maniacs. Social networks link people through family relationships, friendships, acquaintances, and business contacts. Global transportation networks link cities and towns via roads and highways, as well as by train, bus, and airline routes. There is also a long history of communication networks, such as the Greek message runners, the Pony Express, telegraph systems, and the international telephone system. Today, the fastest-growing network is arguably our global computer network, known as the Internet.

A computer network consists of *network nodes* that represent computer hardware and the network users, with various types of hardware, software, and *communications media* forming the links between nodes. As such, a computer network requires four primary components:

1. data (the resource) that computers share on the network
2. special hardware
3. software that allows computers to communicate and share the data
4. communication media to link the computers together

Networks of connected computers support the core function of data transfer in an organization. But networks serve another critical function: Computer networks are the main technology supporting communication between managers and employees, between employee and employee, and between the organization and its suppliers and customers. They provide a platform for collaboration, allowing users to share data, information, and knowledge.

In the following sections, we briefly review network hardware and software. For a more in-depth discussion of networks, see Tech Guide B: The Details of Networking.

---

7. *www.standishgroup.com/newsroom/open_source.php*, retrieved October 22, 2011.

Table 2.2	Computer Networks		
Network	**Size**	**Purpose**	**Examples**
PAN (private area network) (private)	Covers a very small space that ranges from the size of a human body to a small office	Communication among computer devices in close proximity	A PAN allows your MP3 player to connect to a wireless headset, your PDA to "sync" with your PC, and your car to respond to commands from a Bluetooth-enabled mobile phone.
LAN (local area network) (private)	Within the immediate location or building	Share files, resources, servers, and other hardware among the members of an organization	Common LANs include university computing labs, small office or household networks, and a wireless hotspot (WLAN).
MAN (metropolitan area network) (private/public)	Ranges in size from a few blocks to an entire metropolitan area	Provides data and voice transmission typically at high speeds ($\approx$100 Mbps)	A university may use a MAN to connect LANs across campus; many city libraries use MANs to support centralized cataloguing and searching of resources.
WAN (wide area network) (private/public)	Over a large geographic area	Share data, information, and resources among units of an organization distant from one another	A WAN connects various university MANs/LANs to share research; a corporate network uses a WAN to link national and international locations.
Internet (public)	Worldwide	Share data and information with all stakeholders in the organization, as well as with the general public	The Internet is the largest public WAN; sometimes known as a *global area network (GAN)*.

Network Categories To better understand why so many options exist for network technology, it helps to know the different types of computer networks that exist. The categories we discuss here are important because they represent why different networking components or techniques may be required.

One common method of describing computer networks relies on how much geography the physical size of the network covers. The two extreme sizes are a local area network (LAN) and a wide area network (WAN). Technology requirements are generally more complicated as the physical size of the network gets larger. As Table 2.2 indicates, organizations use all sizes of networks, including PANs, LANs, MANs, WANs, and the Internet, as well as networks based on the Internet protocols.

Network Hardware Forming a network requires a number of devices for making network connections as well as for managing data transmission over the network. There are three basic categories of network hardware:

1. Hardware to connect a device to a network: Hardware that connects computers or other devices to a network includes modems, cable modems, network interface cards (NICs), and wireless cards. Each of these devices connects your computer or device to a specific network. The device

that you use depends mainly on the media that connects to your computer.

A physical link that forms a network connection is referred to as a *carrier* or *communications medium*. There are several different options, including the *plain old telephone system (POTS)* network, which is still the most common for transmitting electrical signals. Alternatively, coaxial and fibre optic cables can transmit information at faster speeds. What type of connectivity do you have? If you connect to the Internet using a regular modem that uses the phone line, you have a POTS connection.

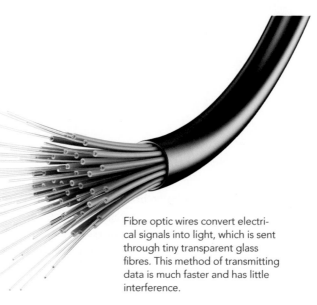

Fibre optic wires convert electrical signals into light, which is sent through tiny transparent glass fibres. This method of transmitting data is much faster and has little interference.

Finally, technologies such as infrared light, radio waves, and microwaves also allow networks to transmit signals through the air. This form of transmission is increasingly important as you seek more mobility with your IT devices. You have likely used Bluetooth technology to speak on your mobile phone using a wireless earpiece, or "beamed" a friend your phone number from your mobile phone to theirs, or used your mobile phone as a modem to connect your computer to the Internet.

2. Specialized hardware for handling network traffic: Devices that help coordinate the data traffic on a network include routers, bridges, repeaters, and hubs. A *bridge* is a device that lets you connect to networks or break a large network into two smaller, more efficient networks. A *router* connects, translates, and then directs data that cross between two networks. A *hub*, also known as a *concentrator*, serves as a central connection point for cables from the devices on the network. A *repeater* is sometimes needed to strengthen or amplify signals that are sent along a long transmission route. Finally, a wireless *access point (AP)* is a special bridge that connects between wireless devices and a wired network. All of these are important because they contribute to the speed of a network.

3. Specialized computers that control the network and the delivery of data on the network: On most networks, specialized computers, called *servers*, manage the various functions of the network. Servers are often assigned a specific task, such as handling email (*email server*), Web traffic (*Web server*), or running programs (*application server*).

A *file server* is a fast computer that requires a large amount of RAM and storage space. Why? Because not only does it store and run the network operating system software, it may also store shared software applications and data files. Further, the file server manages all communication between the devices on the network. (Any computer connected to the file server on a network is called a *client* or a *workstation*.) Because many users may request services from the file server at the same time, you can also see why a computer that can store a lot of data and share it quickly is required. We discuss other types of network servers in Tech Guide B.

Network Software Like PC software, we can divide network software into operating system software and application software. Network operating system software manages network functions and the flow of data traffic over a computer network. Network application software provides the instructions that allow for the creation of data and for this transformation to fit appropriate *protocols* for transmission over a network. A **protocol** is a standard set of rules that allows the communication of data between nodes on a network.

You have no doubt used network application software when you composed an email to a friend and sent it over the Internet. These days, we can include just about every productivity software category as network application software. For example, modern word processing software usually includes features that allow you to email or fax a document directly, or transform and post the document as a web page.

Quick Test

1. All other things being equal, which mix of components allows a computer to simultaneously run multiple programs faster?
   a. 1-GHz processor with 256 MB RAM
   b. 1-GHz processor with 512 MB RAM
   c. 1-MHz processor with 256 MB RAM
   d. 2-MHz processor with 512 MB RAM

2. Imagine that you are in charge of tracking the dues paid by each member of a large student organization. To store these data in an organized form that allows you to easily look up data, which type of application software would you most likely use?
   a. spreadsheet
   b. database management
   c. presentation
   d. word processing

3. Which one of the following is a primary component of a computer network?
   a. communications media
   b. data to share
   c. software
   d. all of the above

Answers: 1. c; 2. b; 3. d

■ THE INTERNET

Strictly speaking, any computer network that connects several networks together is an internet (short for inter-networking). We simply refer to the single largest and most popular internet in the world as the *Internet*. With the Internet, all of the IT components we have discussed so far—hardware, software, and networking technologies—come together to make what is arguably the most useful technological tool of the last few decades. Over three-quarters (80 percent) of Canadians aged 16 and older (some 27.1 million people), went online for personal reasons in 2009.[8] In 2011, it was estimated that over 2 billion people worldwide had access to and were using the Internet.[9]

What Makes the Internet Possible?

The foundation technology that makes the Internet possible is the adoption of standard protocols. The Internet uses the *TCP/IP* suite of *packet switching* protocols. This is a very general, non-proprietary set of communication rules. By adopting these rules and making use of software compatible with the

---

8. *www.statcan.gc.ca/daily-quotidien/100510/dq100510a-eng.htm*, retrieved October 23, 2011.

9. *www.internetworldstats.com/stats.htm*, retrieved October 23, 2011.

TCP/IP standards, any computer, regardless of the platform, processor, and OS, can connect and communicate over the Internet.

Another aspect of the Internet, important to its near global adoption, is that no single organization or governmental entity owns it. Instead, several international organizations provide committees that discuss and propose Internet standards. These committees include the Internet Engineering Task Force (IETF), the Internet Architecture Board (IAB), and the World Wide Web Consortium (W3C). These and other groups have developed standard protocols, sometimes referred to as the Internet protocol suite. This suite offers many useful protocols, such as HTTP, SMTP, and FTP, which we discuss in detail in Tech Guide B.

Accessing the Internet

At home, users access the Internet through dial-up (over traditional phone lines) or broadband (through cable or ISDN). At work, they often connect directly to the organization's LAN or WAN. The organization in turn provides connection to the Internet. All Internet-access methods require specialized hardware—a modem for dial-up access, a cable modem for cable access, and an NIC or wireless NIC for direct connection to a network.

Most users do not connect directly to the Internet. Instead, they contract with an **Internet service provider (ISP)**. ISPs, like Sympatico, Primus, Shaw, and Rogers, purchase the expensive equipment needed to connect to the Internet. ISPs then provide connections for customers to use via dial-up or cable.

Internet access also requires software. Software used to make the connection includes OS utilities and special software that the ISP usually provides. To access and process content, Internet users also need application software, such as an email client and a Web browser.

Wi-Fi (discussed on the next page) has made it possible for business professionals (and anyone else, for that matter) to go mobile. With your smartphone, tablet, or laptop, you can access the Internet from almost anywhere.

You will not only find Internet access at home or the office, but in public locations like libraries, airports, and coffee shops. Access at these places is becoming increasingly simple and universal with the prevalence of *Wi-Fi hotspots*. **Wi-Fi** is the popular name for the 802.11 standards for wireless network access. A hotspot refers to any public space within which a wireless device can connect. With Wi-Fi and other forms of wireless access, business professionals can now go mobile and stay connected to the Internet using laptop computers, PDAs, or a number of other wireless devices. You will find wireless access, free and paid, in all major cities in Canada. For a list of free Wi-Fi hotspots in Canada, the United States, and Europe, visit *www.wififreespot.com*.

Internet Applications

While the creation of and the ability to access the Internet were revolutionary in themselves, it is now what can be done with the Internet that is remarkable. Later in this chapter we discuss the most popular application of the Internet, the Web. But more and more, researchers are finding ways to use the Internet for other purposes. We will first discuss these other notable Internet applications.

Voice Over Internet Protocol (VoIP) One purpose, now commonplace, is the use of **voice over Internet protocol (VoIP)** to make calls anywhere in the world and bypass traditional switched telephone networks. VoIP uses the Internet's foundation technologies of packet switching and TCP/IP to carry voice instead of data. VoIP does this by converting the analog voice signal to digital, creating packets and sending the packets over the same infrastructure as you do your email or Internet searches. Figure 2.4 shows this process at a very high level.

There were challenges when VoIP was first introduced. Packets were sometimes lost or delayed along the network, resulting in conversations sounding choppy. Over the years, however, quality has improved and services such as Skype have become very popular. Skype is especially popular because the calls are free between Skype users. Using the traditional public switched telephone network (PSTN), a call from Toronto to Calgary might cost as much as $3/minute, whereas a Skype VoIP call between those same locations using VoIP-enabled phones or a PC with microphone and speakers is free. Another major advantage of Skype is that it enables video, chat, and screen sharing for free as well! Mind you, with Microsoft's purchase of Skype for $8.5 billion in May 2011, this may change.

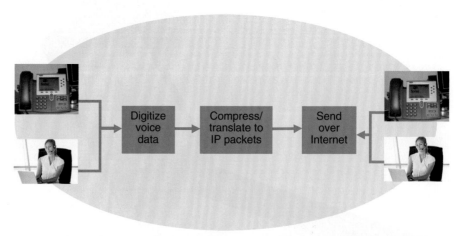

FIGURE 2.4 VoIP takes analog voice calls, digitizes them, and delivers them over the Internet, avoiding the costly PSTN network.

Businesses can also use VoIP to reduce costs, such as reducing the cost of phone calls over the telephone network. More valuable, though, is the ability to use VoIP for unified communication. In this context, you can use VoIP for telephone calls, faxing, voice mail, and more over a single network, which can significantly decrease infrastructure costs. Some business professionals, such as a senior executive at Bell or Telus, might not be so enthusiastic about this cost-cutting measure. How would you respond to this competition if you were one of those senior executives?

Cloud Computing Another advancement in the use of the Internet is **cloud computing**. The term *cloud* has been used as a synonym for the Internet for many years, so cloud computing simply means computing over the Internet. The Internet has made it easy to remotely access computing resources, separating users from the infrastructure they are working on. That is, users can use any Internet connection to access their resources on virtual computers anywhere in the cloud. There is no need to see or even know the location of the server you are using, and there is no need to have a large amount of storage available on a device for all the things you need to do. Cloud computing is used for applications (software as a service), technical infrastructure (i.e., servers for computing power and operating systems, known as *hosting*), security, data storage, and various technical platforms (e.g., email). Without our knowing, cloud computing is enabling many of the services that we rely on daily. For example, in April 2011, Amazon web services experienced an outage that made many popular websites, including redditt and foursquare, unavailable for several hours.[10] This led to the creation of some new dramatic monikers for our everyday vocabulary, including *cloudburst* and *cloudgate*. Despite this type of outage, which rarely happens, there are many advantages to cloud computing:

- Reduced cost because technical infrastructure is not required: Cloud computing is often paid for on a usage, user, or flat fee basis that is significantly cheaper than building and maintaining a technical infrastructure. In addition, many cloud computing applications are available for free, such as Google Docs and gmail, Google's free email application.
- Scalability on demand: The cloud has many available resources, including the ability to increase bandwidth and access common application protocol interfaces (APIs) for extending services.
- Accessibility: Cloud computing is accessible from anywhere there is Internet access.
- Increased collaboration between employees, especially when employees are in several locations: For example, after Virginia-based consulting firm CSC turned to Jive, a maker of cloud-based collaboration software, more than 25,000 people registered, creating 2,100 groups. CSC's president called the results "stunning" and added, "It's the de facto standard for how we collaborate. It's the language of the company."[11]

As you can imagine, cloud computing is especially beneficial for small or medium-sized businesses that do not want to invest in technology and the resources to manage it.

The advantages provide powerful motivation for companies to move to an on-demand service provider, but there is a cost. Clients must be willing to relinquish some control over the applications. Further, they must realize that they will probably not be able to gain a competitive advantage by using these applications. Because your organization finds it efficient to use a certain cloud offering, it is quite likely competitors will do the same. This implies that these types of services would be best

---

10. *www.computerworld.com/s/article/9216064/Amazon_gets_black_eye_from_cloud_outage*, retrieved November 19, 2011.

11. *www.theglobeandmail.com/report-on-business/careers/management/morning-manager/cloud-gazing-what-to-consider-with-online-it/article2234927/*, retrieved November 13, 2011.

suited for business processes that are common to most organizations, like accounting or human resources, which are often provided through software as a service or application service providers.

Software as a service (SaaS) is the most commonly known type of cloud computing. SaaS is a way for organizations to acquire enterprise systems; that is, they essentially rent software. The availability of SaaS for almost every business application has led many to believe that some organizations will eventually stop buying or building their own software. Instead, these organizations will use this model to ensure they always have up-to-date systems in the areas where automation will help them most. As Marc Benioff, the flamboyant CEO of Salesforce.com has put it, "I've said it before, I think it's the end of software."[12] Mr. Benioff's company delivers on-demand customer relationship management (CRM) over the Web. Services at Salesforce.com include sales force automation, customer service and support, document management, and corporate social networking, to name just a few.

Salesforce.com is one of the most successful examples of a company that provides on-demand, or **utility computing services**. Instead of the traditional approach of a firm developing its own IS to support its business applications, utility computing provides services hosted on servers, which can be accessed from anywhere. So software is not really dead, but the concept that a company has to create systems and install the software on premise may be close to extinction. The goal of utility computing is to provide computing resources when and where an organization needs them. Like electricity, clients pay for services only to the extent that they use them.

Does utility computing represent the end of the way we currently think of software? Probably not for all cases, but the $1.7 billion revenue for the fiscal year ended January 2011 and over one million subscribers from about 92,300 companies worldwide that use Salesforce.com seem to provide strong backup for Mr. Benioff's argument.[13] Do an Internet search on SaaS or cloud computing and you will find a number of different offerings in the market. You will also find SaaS that are offered free of charge, like Google Docs, which provides word processing, calendar, and spreadsheet software. It is very likely you have or know someone who has a Gmail account, Google's free email service. All of these are SaaS offered by Google. If you are an Apple user and are using an iPhone, you likely have taken advantage of iCloud, which allows you to share applications and data, up to 5GB for free, from a central source to all of your devices.

Software as an outsourced service is another way software is provided to organizations. An **application service provider (ASP)** is an online technology company that develops and delivers software tools on the Internet. Payment for the service is often based on fees or subscriptions. If you take a quick look on the Web, you will find many examples of ASPs. For instance, ASPNews.com has a directory of more than 1,900 companies that provide ASP services, such as BrightSuite's Web-based groupware, intranet, and team collaboration application. Many of these ASPs are now marketing their wares as SaaS.

ASPs provide several major advantages that are increasing their popularity. When an organization uses an ASP, an external company builds and operates the system. This means that the organization does not need to acquire its own technical resources or hire staff with technical expertise. Since the ASP is the primary service of the provider, it also bears the burden of keeping it up to date to provide a competitive advantage over other ASPs. Further, as ASPs deliver these services over the Internet, the software is available anytime and anywhere. In addition, any device can use it.

ASPs and SaaS are quite similar offerings, and many ASPs are changing their business model to be more like SaaS. Table 2.3 compares SaaS and ASP models.

---

12. Alorie Gilbert, "The End of Software," *http://news.zdnet.com/2100-3513_22-5281034.html*.

13. *www.salesforce.com/company/news-press/press-releases/2011/02/110224.jsp*, retrieved October 31, 2011.

Table 2.3	Comparing SaaS/Cloud Computing and ASP Models	
	SaaS/Cloud Computing	**ASP**
Pricing model	Per use or per user	Monthly, flat fee, or subscription
Ability to customize	Some ability to customize at a cost, but major deviations from the core product are discouraged	More ability to customize at a cost, as each installation is unique to a customer
Control over the system	None	Some; clients are usually provided administrator tools
Data security and privacy	It may be unknown how data are processed and stored, but data are likely contained in common databases with other customers of the SaaS	Negotiable; some ASPs will provide a separate database, keeping it completely secure and separate from their other customers, at a cost
Security	As the applications are generally available over the Internet, the system is subject to the same vulnerabilities as any Internet application	Option is available to connect to the system over a dedicated connection, which increases security, in addition to accessing over the Internet

WHAT DO YOU THINK?

Software as a service is certainly here to stay. Imagine that you are in charge of finding customer relationship management (CRM) software for your small business. Consider the following questions.

1: Are you concerned that your company's customer data are stored outside of your company?
2: What if in the future the software you are renting no longer meets your needs? How will you move from one system to another?
3: Why would a company offer software for free? Should you consider a free CRM system?

What's Next for the Internet?

There is seemingly no limit to what can be done over the Internet. Did you know that the Internet has only been used by the general public for the last 20 years? But look at the advancements made in that short period of time! Below are a couple of projects in the works that will take the Internet to the next level.

- The Next-Generation Internet: This project is working on replacing the basic protocols that make the Internet possible, namely IP (currently version 4), with a next generation protocol called Internet Protocol Version 6 (IPv6). IPv4 is already more than 20 years old and is sorely in need of an update for the Internet to continue to grow. In the early 1990s, experts predicted that by using IPv4, the world would exhaust the available number of IP addresses (4.3 billion addresses!). In fact, the last block of IP addresses was allocated in February 2011.[14] In addition to providing more IP addresses, IPv6 seeks to repair a number of problems with IPv4[15] and add improvements to routing and network configurations.

    Anticipating the need to move to IPv6, the world's largest technology companies, including Google and Facebook, participated in a 24-hour test of IPv6, called World IPv6 Day, on June 8, 2011.[16] The purpose of this test was to determine readiness for the inevitable switch to this new Internet

14. *www.apnic.net/publications/news/2011/delegation*, retrieved October 24, 2011.

15. "What Is IPv6?," *www.ipv6.org, 2010.*

16. *www.worldipv6day.org/*, retrieved October 28, 2011.

protocol. You can test your own IPv6 readiness at *www.worldipv6day.org/*. If your results are not good, don't worry. The Internet for IPv4 will be here for some time. Interoperability between IPv4 and IPv6 is slowly being reconciled, and most of the largest Internet organizations are running "dual stacks," meaning that they can handle both IPv4 and IPv6 traffic. It will be some time before the Internet will be IPv6 only. You can think of the Next-Generation Internet project as a *major* overhaul of the Internet.

- Internet2: A consortium of professionals from more than 200 universities and industry and government agencies is developing advanced network applications and technologies to enable the creation of revolutionary Internet applications and ensure the rapid deployment of new technologies and services to the global community.[17] Internet2 applications are already in use. Check at your school to see if some of the Internet sites that you visit are part of Internet2.

WHAT DO YOU THINK?

There is no doubt that the ability to access the Internet anywhere, at any time, using wireless technology, is changing the way we work and live. Just imagine—there was a time when you could only access the Internet or email by using special terminals in the library! However, some argue that using wireless technology may make us too productive. Consider the following:

1: Have you ever heard the term *Crackberry*? What does this mean to you?
2: Do you think being able to access your email at all times using a wireless device keeps you more or less socially connected?
3: What do you think of the expectation some organizations have that if you are connected wirelessly, you are available 24/7?

For more on this topic, see the article by two professors at Ryerson's School of Information Technology Management, Catherine A. Middleton and Wendy Cukier, "Is Mobile E-mail Functional or Dysfunctional? Two Perspectives on Mobile E-mail Usage," *European Journal of Information Systems*, June 2006, *15*, p. 252.

Quick Test

1. Which one of the following represents the set of primary rules for transmitting and receiving data over the Internet using packet switching?
   a. FTP
   b. HTTP
   c. SMTP
   d. TCP/IP

2. Which of the following is a true statement about the Internet?
   a. Dial-up access generally provides faster access to Internet resources than broadband.
   b. Most home users require an ISP to connect to the Internet.
   c. The Internet is owned by the U.S. government.
   d. It is impossible to use a wireless device to connect to the Internet.

3. True or False. Software as a service essentially allows organizations to rent software.

Answers: 1. b; 2. b; 3. True

---

17. *www.internet2.edu*, 2010.

■ THE WORLD WIDE WEB

For many, the Internet is synonymous with two of its most popular applications, the *World Wide Web (WWW)*, including e-commerce, and *electronic mail (email)*. However, the World Wide Web, often called simply the Web, is not the same as the Internet. Think of the Internet as the technology platform, and the Web as an application that works on that platform.

Some very basic technologies are required to make the Web work:

- client/server networks—the networks over which data travel
- browser—application software that lets users request and view web pages
- HTTP protocol—the standardized rules for exchanging data over the Web
- HTML—the language that guides the display of a requested page

Figure 2.5 shows how these technologies work together. Although there are more complicated technologies on the Web than depicted in this diagram, it provides you with a general overview of the technologies that are still in use today, which are discussed in detail in the following sections. (All of these components of the Web are discussed in more detail in Tech Guide B.)

Basic Components of the World Wide Web

Client/Server Networks When you open a Web browser on your computer, you start a client application. If you type a **uniform resource locator (URL)**—which specifies a unique address for each page that indicates the location of a document—into your browser or click a hyperlink, the browser sends a request out over the Web that makes its way to the corresponding server. The browser formulates the request under the rules of HTTP (discussed below) so that all computers on the Web, especially the destination server, will know how to handle it.

When the request reaches its destination, the server generates a response that includes the requested item and conforms to HTTP (note that a *Web server* is a software application that handles Web requests, not necessarily a separate computer). The server then simply loads the text data from storage, adds the appropriate HTTP information, and sends the item back to the client. This sequence of activities provides a **client/server network**.

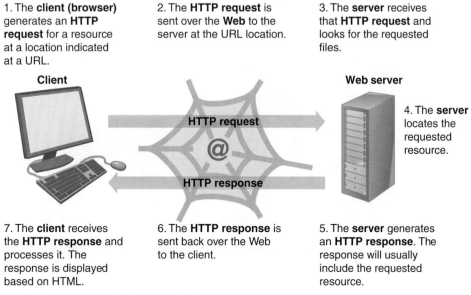

1. The **client (browser)** generates an **HTTP request** for a resource at a location indicated at a URL.

2. The **HTTP request** is sent over the **Web** to the server at the URL location.

3. The **server** receives that **HTTP request** and looks for the requested files.

Client

HTTP request

@

HTTP response

Web server

4. The **server** locates the requested resource.

7. The **client** receives the **HTTP response** and processes it. The response is displayed based on HTML.

6. The **HTTP response** is sent back over the Web to the client.

5. The **server** generates an **HTTP response**. The response will usually include the requested resource.

FIGURE 2.5 The sequence of activities on the Web over a *client/server network*.

A static web page file will typically hold a combination of text content and *hypertext markup language (HTML)* commands. Other requests may include other static file formats such as images, sound, or video. While sound and video might seem interactive, they are nevertheless static because the file contents do not change.

Web Browsers A **Web browser** is a software application that allows you to easily navigate the Web and to view the content that you find there. At its most basic, a browser will let you request, either by typing a URL or clicking a hyperlink, and display a hypertext-based file. Hypertext organizes content into units that are connected using associations called *links*. Figure 2.6 shows an example of a browser displaying a web page and identifies the typical components of a browser.

HTTP–Hypertext Transfer Protocol A client and a server communicate with each other using messages. To do this, they need a standard set of rules for formatting and transmitting these messages. That is where HTTP comes in. The **hypertext transfer protocol (HTTP)** comprises the set of rules for exchanging messages on the World Wide Web. HTTP governs both the request (*HTTP request*) for a file and the transmission (*HTTP response*) of the requested file.

Tim Berners-Lee, the inventor of the World Wide Web, first implemented HTTP while at CERN, the European Centre for High-Energy Physics in Geneva, in 1990 and 1991. He developed HTTP to live at the application layer of networks. That is, once the application composes the HTTP message (request or response), lower-level protocols such as TCP/IP transmit the message. Berners-Lee originally designed HTTP as a lightweight, speedy method of sharing hypermedia information over a client/server network.

HTML–Hypertext Markup Language **Hypertext markup language (HTML)** is the primary language for creating web pages. It is not a true programming language, as the computer does not generally process HTML instructions. Instead, browser software interprets HTML instructions through the use of *tags*, which are interspersed with content. The tags, surrounded by angle brackets (< and >), mark the placement and appearance of the various components of the page. A web page usually consists of several different types of components, such as page layout instructions, formatted text,

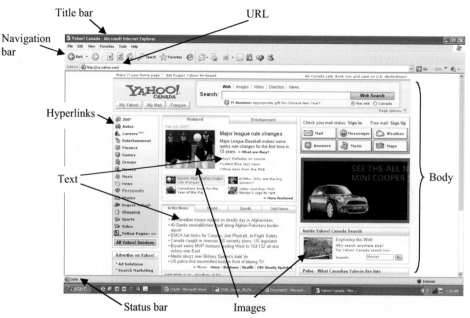

FIGURE 2.6 Most browsers, including Internet Explorer shown here, provide similar components for displaying and viewing a web page.

hyperlinks, tables, graphics, and form objects. Go to any website, right mouse click, and select "view source," and you will be able to see the HTML for that particular web page.

Of course, all of the above happens when users are able to find a website they are looking for. Without search technologies, users would have to know a specific URL to find the website they are looking for. Luckily, sophisticated search technologies are available to help you find what you are looking for, even when you enter the most vague search criteria.

Search Technologies

Have you searched the Web for information lately? If you have, you realize the vast amount of data available. In 2008, Google reported indexing one trillion web pages, and further indicated that more were available.[18] As of 2012, no one is really sure how large the web really is. A group called the World Wide Web Foundation, appropriately founded by Tim Berners-Lee, is on a quest to figure out, with some degree of certainty, how big the Internet really is. Starting with $1 million in funding from Google, the foundation planned on releasing the results of its online forensic search, the World Wide Web Index, early in 2012.[19]

What is absolutely true is that we are at the point of information overload, where huge volumes of useless, old, or unsubstantiated information lives, just because it was once posted on the Web. As a result, how could you locate the best source of specific information on any product, service, or topic without search technology?

Internet **search engines** generally follow the process shown in Figure 2.7. For most sites, users access an HTML form-based web page that allows them to enter their specific search criteria to a

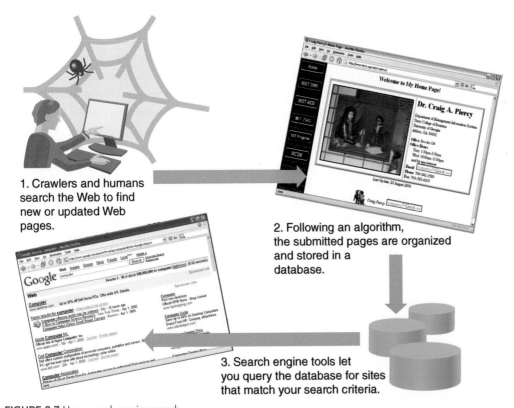

1. Crawlers and humans search the Web to find new or updated Web pages.

2. Following an algorithm, the submitted pages are organized and stored in a database.

3. Search engine tools let you query the database for sites that match your search criteria.

FIGURE 2.7 How search engines work.

---

18. *http://googleblog.blogspot.com/2008/07/we-knew-web-was-big.html*, retrieved March 6, 2010.

19. *http://articles.cnn.com/2011-09-12/tech/web.index_1_internet-neurons-human-brain?_s=PM:TECH*, retrieved October 30, 2011.

greater or lesser extent. Search criteria generally consist of one or more keywords, and possibly other data to limit the search and keep the list of results to a manageable level. The search criteria data are sent to the search engine Web server, which in turn passes it to the application server to search through the sites' databases. In reality, when you search the Web you are actually searching a database that was compiled from previous Web searches.

The main difference between most Internet search engines is how the database of Web locations is created and organized. To search the Web and compile location data in their databases, most Internet search engines use either special software called *Web crawlers*, human submissions, or a combination of the two. Many web pages incorporate special tags, known as *meta tags*, which contain information that describe what a site is about. Crawlers, or spiders, move around from site to site, read these meta tags, and report the data back to their database for storage.

People can also submit sites, which the database also stores. Since people often discriminate between sites better than crawlers, human submissions are often of higher quality or fit a specific profile better than sites found by crawlers. In either case, the actual sites stored in each site's database can vary, depending on what the crawlers and humans find and submit.

Perhaps more important than how the sites are found is the manner in which the database organizes, or *indexes*, the Web data. Each search engine typically uses a different algorithm for indexing the data and applying the search criteria to query the indexed data. For example, a search engine may rank web pages based on the frequency and location of keywords in the page content. Those pages with a higher frequency of relevant keywords may receive a higher ranking. Another method, such as the one made popular by the Google search engine, ranks each page based on the number of other pages that link to the page. A page with a larger number of relevant linked pages is considered to be more important to the Web community, and thus would receive a higher ranking.

In 2011, Google announced it was making significant changes to its search algorithm that would impact up to 35 percent of Google searches. The change was motivated by users' increasing desire for up-to-the-minute information and the competitive forces of social media. The change, code named Caffeine, alters Google's search algorithm to prioritize more recent results when it determines the search query is more relevant to recent events. For example, someone searching *Occupy Wall Street* is likely looking for recent information as opposed to a historical search for a cookie recipe.[20]

When it comes to search engines, there are a lot of questions that can be asked, including:

- What responsibility should search engines have to make sure that the information they are collecting and indexing is accurate and valid?
- What if the information collected is deliberately vague, false, or misleading?
- How can you structure your organization's online presence to ensure that the right information from the right source is displayed to those searching out your business?
- What are the ethical, legal, and related issues that arise if you try to manipulate or otherwise influence search engine "hits" to favour your business?
- To what extent do the business models of search engines influence how, when, and what they display and how they disclose this to you once it is displayed?

Given all of these questions, do you think that using search engines helps you find the information you are looking for? Not necessarily. This is where your experience and skills come into play. If you don't know which search criteria to enter, you may not be able to locate the information you need to succeed. Therefore, learning more about query languages, the construction of Internet search engines, and how that technology works is very useful. You may also consider using a *meta search engine*, a Web-based tool that allows you to review the search results generated by other search

---

20. "Google Changes Search Algorithm, Trying To Make Results More Timely", *The Globe and Mail*, November 4, 2011, p. 20.

engines. A meta search engine sends out a search query (formats the word or words that you enter for use by search engines) to other search engines, and then returns the list to you. The meta search engine uses criteria to select which results it will display. So, if you use a meta search engine like Mamma.ca (*www.mamma.com*) or Copernic.com (*www.copernic.com*), your results will be the top listings from other search engines such as MSN (*www.MSN.com*), Yahoo, and Google.

Quick Test

1. True or False. Text content, hypertext markup language (HTML) commands, and image, sound, or video requests can all be found on a static web page file.

2. To compile location data in their databases, most Internet search engines use software called _____.
   a. data creepers
   b. meta collectors
   c. Web crawlers
   d. site coders

3. _____ is the primary language for defining how web pages are displayed in a browser.
   a. HTTP
   b. HTML
   c. Java
   d. VoIP

Answers: 1. True; 2. c; 3.b

■ INTERNET SECURITY

In this chapter, we have discussed the growth of technology, the Internet, and the World Wide Web. With this growth comes risk. Risk, in the context of the Internet, means security. Internet security is seen as a serious issue around the world. In 2010, the Internet Crime Complaint Center ranked Canada as fifth in the world for the origin of Internet crime perpetrators and second in the world for the number of complaints about Internet crime.[21] It is important to remember that both individuals and enterprises can be the victims of Internet crime. Table 2.4 describes some of the most common Internet security threats. However, there are many more in addition to these. In fact, in 2011, Sophos—a developer of anti-virus software—received around 150,000 new malware samples every day.[22]

The risk of these threats has increased substantially with the advent of social networking. Social networking provides a breeding ground, if you will, for malware. Those worried about the dangers of social networking sites have a right to be concerned, as many malicious attacks, spammers, and data harvesters take advantage of under-cautious users. Most notably, the notorious Koobface worm family became more diverse and sophisticated in 2009. The sophistication of Koobface is such that it is capable of registering a Facebook account, activating the account by confirming an email sent to a Gmail address, befriending random strangers on the site, joining random Facebook groups, and posting messages on the walls of Facebook friends (often claiming to link to sexy videos laced

---

21. *www.ic3.gov/media/annualreport/2009_IC3Report.pdf*, retrieved March 10, 2010.

22. *www.sophos.com/en-us/security-news-trends/security-trends/sophos-security-threat-report-mid-year-2011.aspx*

Table 2.4	Common Internet Security Threats
Security Threat	**Description of Threat**
Malware	The use of malicious code as part of a subversive, organized scheme. Such schemes result in massive intrusions into sensitive financial and intellectual property areas. Viruses, worms, and Trojans are all types of malware.
Scareware	A type of malware designed to trick victims into purchasing and downloading useless and potentially dangerous software. Ironically, scareware is often disguised as virus protection software and shows a window telling you that your PC is not being protected or is currently infected.
Virus	A program that is able to copy itself and infect a computer. Viruses are designed to spread to as many computers as possible. They usually need some human action, like opening an email attachment, to occur in order to spread. There are thousands of known viruses on the Web. Most PC users use anti-virus software to prevent viruses.
Worm	Destructive software that can spread by itself, such as MyDoom and its later version, DoomJuice. The MyDoom worm is particularly nasty. Once started on a computer (by clicking an email attachment), it automatically sends out infected emails to everybody in the user's address book, using one or more of the names on the address book as the sender. In addition to overwhelming email servers around the world (at one point, the virus generated as many as one in three emails in circulation), it creates a "back door" to allow a system to be used to further propagate viruses and malware.
Spam (electronic)	Unsolicited and undesired emails. Aside from being annoying, spam may facilitate the installation of malware or phishing.
Phishing	An attempt to gain personal and confidential information (e.g., passwords, credit card information) for fraudulent purposes such as identity theft.
Denial of Service Attack (DoS)	An attempt to make a website unavailable to its users. An attacker will do this by sending a target so many communication requests that the target server eventually goes down and becomes unavailable. No website is safe from DoS attacks. Both Twitter and Facebook have been the victims of DoS attacks.

with malware). Furthermore, it includes code to avoid drawing attention to itself by restricting how many new Facebook friends it makes each day.[23] Even today, this especially sophisticated virus has active variations. Another favourite method of attack is known as cross-site scripting or Self-XSS. Facebook messages such as, Why are you tagged in this video? and the Facebook Dislike button take you to a web page that tries to trick you into cutting and pasting a malicious JavaScript code into your browser's address bar. Self-XSS attacks can also run hidden, or obfuscated, JavaScript on your computer, allowing for malware installation without your knowledge.[24]

Twitter is just as vulnerable. Imagine that a friend of yours has tweeted a link to a cool song, except that the link to the song contains a virus. It is possible that every one of your friend's followers will click on the link and be infected. Some of those friends might even re-tweet the link to their friends, and so on and so on. In 2011, Twitter accounts were hacked. The hacked accounts were then used to tweet an advertisement, "Get the beach body you always wanted. . . ." with a link to a questionable website. Of course these were not tweets by the account holders, who were very much

23. Sophos Security Threat Report: 2010, *www.sophos.com/sophos/docs/eng/papers/sophos-security-threat-report-jan-2010-wpna.pdf*, retrieved March 10, 2010.

24. *www.sophos.com/en-us/security-news-trends/security-trends/social-networking-security-threats/facebook.aspx*, retrieved October 30, 2011.

surprised to learn of them.[25] In another famous Twitter hack of 2011, the Fox News Twitter account was hacked and a tweet posted announcing the assassination of President Barack Obama.[26]

Social networking sites can also contain a lot of information about individuals. For some reason, people feel it is safe to post information that normally they would keep private. For instance, it is not unusual for people to post pictures or update their status on Facebook when they are on vacation. With some investigative abilities, it would not be hard for someone to take the individual's profile information, the knowledge that the person is on vacation, and other information on the Internet to eventually find the person's address and rob his or her home. There are several stories of robberies occurring as a result of Facebook updates, including one at *http://gizmodo.com/5636025/robbers-used-facebook-to-see-when-people-werent-home.*

Ensuring Security

So what can be done to ensure Internet security for both individuals and organizations? One framework for Internet security is known as the **CIA triad**. CIA is an acronym for Confidentiality, Integrity, and Availability. Security is achieved by adhering to:

- *Confidentiality*—the ability to hide information from unauthorized viewing. Tools such as password policies and encryption support confidentiality.
- *Integrity*—ensuring that data is not changed and represents the original secure data.
- *Availability*—ensuring that data is available to those who need it, when they need it. Tools for data replication and back-up are used to ensure availability

Another framework that addresses Internet security is the McCumber Cube (see Figure 2.8). The McCumber Cube takes the concept of the CIA triad and extends it by considering the state of the information (transmission, storage, processing) and safeguards (human factors, policy and practices, technology). Each individual cube within the larger cube can then be analyzed with respect to security. Think through a bank transaction using the McCumber Cube to illustrate its application.

Can you guess what is the largest security risk? People. This is why the human aspect of McCumber's cube is so important. Of course, there are security threats perpetrated by hackers

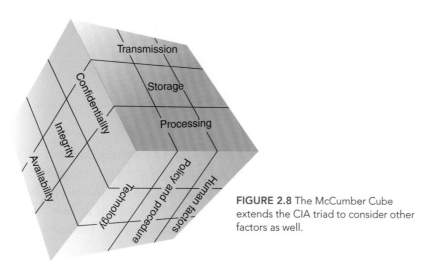

FIGURE 2.8 The McCumber Cube extends the CIA triad to consider other factors as well.

25. *http://nakedsecurity.sophos.com/2011/07/27/twitter-account-hack-beach-body-spam/*, retrieved October 30, 2011.

26. *http://nakedsecurity.sophos.com/2011/07/04/barack-obama-shot-dead-fox-news-twitter-account-hacked/*, retrieved October 30, 2011.

external to an organization, but sometimes the greater risk comes from insiders. Of 500 IT and data security staff attending a conference in 2011, 40 percent boasted that it would be easy to use their knowledge of encryption keys, shared passwords, and loopholes in data security programs to walk off with any information they wanted.[27] Additionally, there are unintentional acts by individuals that put security at risk, such as making errors or not behaving with security in mind.

Both individuals and organizations can take some very simple actions to minimize Internet security threats that are in line with the Internet security frameworks discussed above:

- Install, and keep up to date, both antivirus software and a personal firewall.
- Update your software, such as Windows, to patch security holes or move to less vulnerable systems, such as Linux.
- Do not open email messages or attachments from unknown sources.
- Follow safe computing practices, such as effective password policies.

We often take passwords for granted; however, they play an important part in both online and offline security. Is your password your account name, simply the word *password*, or a common name like that of a friend or relative? Do you use the same password for most or all of your accounts? According to research reported by the Computer Crime Research Center, 21 percent of people use their own or their partner's nicknames for their passwords, 15 percent use their birthdays or anniversaries, and another 15 percent use their pets' names. About 14 percent have a family member's name as their password, 7 percent rely on a memorable date, and 2 percent even more unimaginatively use the word *password*.[28] Splash Data, a company that provides password management software, compiled a list of the 25 worst passwords in 2011:[29]

1. password
2. 123456
3. 12345678
4. qwerty
5. abc123
6. monkey
7. 1234567
8. letmein
9. trustno1
10. dragon
11. baseball
12. 111111
13. iloveyou
14. master
15. sunshine
16. ashley
17. bailey
18. passwOrd
19. shadow
20. 123123
21. 654321
22. superman
23. qazwsx
24. michael
25. football

Why do so many people use weak passwords, especially considering passwords are an important part of authentication for many computer systems? *Authentication* is the process of identifying individuals and ensuring they are who they claim to be. Coupled with a username, a password is perhaps the most common authentication technique used today. Since most of us have important private information stored on various computer systems, using a weak password is like providing easy access to the key to our safety deposit box.

27. "Beware of Vengeful IT Personnel," *The Globe and Mail*, May 27, 2011.

28. *www.crime-research.org/news/17.08.2001/567/*

29. *www.dailyfinance.com/2011/11/15/internet-insecurity-the-25-worst-passwords-of-2011/*, retrieved November 24, 2011.

To ensure that your password is and remains as strong as possible, you should follow these guidelines:

1. Use at least eight characters.
2. Include digits, punctuation, and non-printing characters.
3. Use both upper- and lowercase characters.
4. Use different passwords on different accounts.
5. Change your password regularly and don't reuse passwords or make minor variations such as incrementing a digit.

Of course, these guidelines are hard to follow. The main reason we don't use strong passwords is that they can be hard to remember, and it is more difficult still to remember more than one. So what can you do? Try this: come up with one or more rules that you can use to derive a strong password from something easy to remember—your own password-making algorithm. For example:

1. Start with something easy to remember, such as a favourite song (the *key*), like "*Mary Had a Little Lamb*."
2. Take these initials: MHALL.
3. Make every other initial lowercase: MhAlL.
4. Insert a punctuation mark between each letter: M*h*A*l*L.
5. Append the initials of the account that you want to access; for the office desktop, the password may become M*h*A*l*Lod.

By memorizing just a few items—the song title, the punctuation, and the account initials—you can create a fairly strong and memorable password that is different for each account.

Another area of concern with respect to Internet security is in network systems. As a student, you usually enjoy wireless access on your campus or when you are out at the coffee shop, and are able to connect to your email and browse the Internet. Wireless networks enabled in various hotspots are convenient, but if unsecured, they can pose a security threat. Although we usually think of hackers breaking into computer systems through the Internet, the growing popularity of wireless networks for organizations and homes has created a new type: wireless hackers.

Here is an example of what could happen: a security expert noticed his physician using a notebook to set up appointments and wondered about the level of security in this wireless network. Outside, he noticed a chalk mark on the side of the building put there by a hacker, indicating an open network was available inside—so-called *warchalking*. Sure enough, when the security expert got to his car, he could access the physician's appointment notes, including the one just created for him! While data about appointments are relatively harmless, diagnoses and prescriptions could also have been on this network, leading to a potential loss of privacy or other problems. While warchalking is very unusual today due to the prevalence of free networks available (see any Starbucks!), if you're using an unprotected wireless network, be aware of the potential for so-called *drive-by hackers* to access your files. A hacker may not bother with your files, but instead use your network to assist in propagating malware or creating denial of service attacks that can be traced back to your network. If you are setting up a wireless network at home, be careful to secure it properly to prevent any of these security issues.

Earlier in this chapter we discussed the popularity of cloud computing. One of the major advantages of cloud computing is that data are not resident on one PC or one network, but are available over the Internet from wherever someone has Internet access. From a security point of view, this may make it easier for hackers to access the information, as they no longer need to worry about an individual's authentication, operating system, or firewall. Instead, they can focus their efforts on the system running the cloud computing application (e.g., Gmail) and gain access to many accounts and a lot of information. In January 2010, Google shocked the Internet community by announcing that it (and more than 30 other companies) had been the victim of a targeted hack attack, seemingly focused against the Gmail accounts of Chinese human rights activists.[30] This is just one publicized event. Just type *gmail hacking* into any search engine and you will find more examples, and even instructions!

Disaster Recovery

Let's assume that despite best efforts, the worst happens and security is compromised. This, unfortunately, happens more often than not. To plan for these worst case scenarios, both individuals and organizations need to consider disaster recovery and business continuity plans. A **disaster recovery plan (DRP)** allows an organization to resume operations after a major event that interrupts normal business processes. Such events may include data corruption, software bugs, network failures, network attacks, or natural and man-made physical disasters. Even small amounts of downtime could result in lost transactions, diminished productivity, and reduced customer satisfaction. A disaster recovery plan is IT-focused and is often a subset of a business continuity plan. A **business continuity plan (BCP)** addresses other aspects of resuming business operations, including loss and personnel recovery. Both of these plans are discussed in Chapter 4 in the context of risk reduction strategies as part of enterprise risk management.

When developing either a disaster recovery or business continuity plan, a company needs to determine its critical functions, the level of disaster, and appropriate procedures for recovery. In a disaster recovery situation, IT focuses on having and making available the important data needed to resume business. Reliable data storage and consistent back-up procedures are essential in maintaining data integrity. Imagine if a disaster were to occur and a company lost all of its customer and transaction data. How would it bill customers and receive revenue? Think about your own disaster recovery planning. Would it be acceptable to your professors if you told them you could not turn in your term paper on time because of an unrecoverable hard drive or because your laptop was stolen? Probably not.

Some key components to a disaster recovery plan include:

- Identification of the most critical things to recover and a plan to do so
- Quantifiable success metrics in terms of amount recovered and time to recovery
- Regular tests of recovery
- Regular reviews of the recovery plan to ensure that any changes in the business are accounted for (i.e., changes in priorities, additional priorities)

Quick Test

1. True or False. One framework for Internet security is known as the CSI triad.

2. Which of the following is NOT a guideline to ensuring that your password is and remains as strong as possible?
   a. Use at least seven characters.
   b. Include digits, punctuation, and non-printing characters.
   c. Use both upper- and lowercase characters.
   d. Use different passwords on different accounts.

3. True or False. Cloud computing suffers from security issues.

Answers: 1. False; 2. a; 3. True

---

30. *www.sophos.com/blogs/gc/g/2010/01/14/google-china-censorship-hacking/*.

■ MEANINGFUL APPLICATIONS OF TECHNOLOGY

You have now learned the basics of hardware, software, networks, the Internet and one of its most popular application, the web, and Internet security. This technology is meaningless unless it has a function and creates a benefit. For businesses, this benefit might be the creation of value and competitive advantage. For individuals, it may mean being more efficient and productive. In this section we highlight some applications that might be of interest to you now as a student, or in the future as a business professional.

Collaboration

One of the most important applications of technology is collaboration. Never before have we seen this number of technology tools that allow us to collaborate and communicate with colleagues and friends across the globe. In this section we highlight a few of the technologies that you may be already using, or that you are certain to use as a business professional.

Groupware Software tools known as **groupware** help individuals and teams keep up with their scheduled meetings, monitor projects, share work files, and even conference online. You are likely using some form of groupware now with your professors and classmates. Many universities and colleges use a system called Blackboard that allows professors to post content to all students, send group messages, set up working and discussion groups, and send out and receive assignments.

A commonly-used collaboration software in business is called SharePoint. SharePoint is a very robust system offered by Microsoft that offers many features, including an information repository, a workflow manager, and the ability to manage content, all readily available over a secured Internet connection. Many organizations use SharePoint to store and share all of their files. Files are easily searched for, retrieved, modified (if allowed), and re-saved for the next employee to view. The workflow aspect of SharePoint is valuable from a business process perspective. Imagine a document that requires input from various individuals. SharePoint can manage this interaction through assigning workflow and ensuring that each individual contributes and then makes it available for the next person. This works especially well when approvals are required. And of course, there is an audit trail that shows the progress through the process. Using a system like SharePoint can really improve operational efficiency. In 2010, the International Monetary Fund (IMF), based in Washington, implemented a SharePoint solution for their over 4,000 employees to quickly source economic information about their 187 member countries. This new system boosts collaboration, makes information retrieval fast and easy, and increases user satisfaction.[31]

A key feature of collaboration systems is their ability to store documents that can be worked on and shared with several people. You are likely using free tools, like Google Docs, to collaborate now with your school colleagues. As the documents are created and saved in Google's technical infrastructure, you can share the documents with anyone who has Internet access.

Intranets A less recent method of collaboration for businesses is the use of an intranet. An **intranet** is a set of services for distributing private information throughout the organization using a collection of private computer networks brought together to form an organization-wide, private network (ranging in size from LAN to WAN). At first, most businesses used intranets to reduce publishing and distribution costs for such items as policy and procedure manuals, benefits information, and phone directories. Today, however, the use of intranets has moved beyond the goal of paper reduction to support automated internal transactions, as well as to improve communication, teamwork, and knowledge management.

---

31. *www.microsoft.com/casestudies/Microsoft-FAST-Search-Server-2010-For-Sharepoint/International-Monetary-Fund/ Economists-Quickly-Find-Information-Using-Enterprise-Search/4000011274*, retrieved October 30, 2011.

Using the technologies of the Internet and the World Wide Web, intranets transmit data according to the TCP/IP and HTTP protocols of the Internet, and share the advantages of these protocols. For example, using the Internet as a bridge, an authorized user can access the intranet from any physical location—not necessarily within the organization's physical walls. Further, as with the Internet, employees can also access an intranet using a Macintosh, Windows, or any other PC platform. This is known as *platform independence*, which is usually not the case with traditional LANs and WANs. Finally, intranets can store data using Internet-compatible file formats, such as HTML and XML, thereby allowing users to access the data using a Web browser.

However, an intranet's use of Web technologies, which allow users to access outside resources over the Internet, also make maintaining the privacy of organizational information more crucial. An intranet often incorporates security measures, such as a firewall, and requires users to authenticate themselves with usernames and passwords. As part of their Intranet or a companion technology, organizations are implementing corporate social networking applications. These applications mirror the functionality of widely-used personal social networks such as Facebook and Twitter, but are internal to an organization. The benefits of these corporate social networks are to encourage collaboration and dialogue in a forum that people are accustomed to outside of work, to provide an immediate and interactive forum, and reduce the email burden of staff members. Examples of these corporate social networks include Jive, Yammer, and Salesforce Chatter.

Instant Messaging (IM) Do you think you are collaborating when you use a tool such as Skype? Likely not, but you are. Skype is a popular tool for not only free long distance calls from computer to computer, but also for instant messaging (IM). IM is an online communications service that allows users to communicate in real time over the Internet. In 2008, IM had become so popular it led research firm IDC to predict that it would overtake email as the preferred form of business communication by the second half of 2010.[32] It is unclear whether or not this has become a reality, but what is certain is that IM continues to be extremely popular. With the purchase of Skype in early 2011, Microsoft now commands 68 percent of the instant messaging market. Skype reported 170 million connected users and saw over 207 billion minutes of voice and video conversations in 2010 alone.

Instant messaging serves both important social and business functions in our society. It allows business professionals to communicate in real time for low cost.

There are two main categories of IM applications: public or enterprise (EIM). Examples of public IM include Skype, MSN Messenger, and Yahoo! Messenger. EIM systems, on the other hand, provide features such as restricted access, and security precautions such as encryption. Developed for corporate use, EIM services include Sun ONE Instant Messaging, IBM Lotus Instant Messaging (Sametime), and Web Conferencing.

Users of IM in the workplace cite improved teamwork, time savings derived from faster sharing of information, decrease in email and voice mail, and moments of relief from the daily grind. IM can also be used for communicating with customers. For example, the online clothing retailer Lands' End provides Lands' End Live service, which allows customers to get assistance, in real

---

32. *www.computerworlduk.com/technology/networking/messaging/news/index.cfm?newsid=9887.*

time, with a service representative while they shop online. The representative can even redirect the customer's browser to an appropriate page on the Lands' End site. Lands' End, which has been recognized as a leading e-tailer by various organizations and awards, credits the technology as an integral part of the company's online success.[33]

Risks of using IM include a rise in needless interruptions and distractions, potential security problems, and increased workplace gossip. Have you ever been working on a term paper or studying and just couldn't resist opening your IM tool? Many, however, especially those already accustomed to IM, see that the benefits outweigh the risks, resulting in IM becoming more commonplace in many organizations.

Virtual Meetings As a business professional, you may need to conduct a meeting but may not be able to attend it in person. How will you do this? Some excellent web meeting tools are available to facilitate online meetings. This is especially important if you are working with colleagues in many locations. One of these services is called GoToMeeting. GoToMeeting offers web meetings, voice, and chat for invited participants. To have your meeting, you simply set it up in the meeting scheduler and invite your participants. Participants are given a URL, meeting code, and password so they can attend the meeting. Once in the meeting, you can use your computer screen to run a presentation or a product demo, and all meeting participants will be able to see it. If your meeting participants have questions, they can enter these in the chat function.

Other technologies you may be interested in include:

- RSS feeds: Get updates from your favourite websites and blogs by signing up for an RSS feed. When you sign up, you will receive email alerts to let you know that there is new content you may be interested in.
- Survey Monkey: Survey Monkey is an online survey tool that allows you to set up simple surveys online for free.
- Convergence technologies: You may have heard the word *convergence* before and you may be experiencing it now. Convergence in the context of technology means the merging of technical devices, media, and functions. A current example of convergence is your ability to browse the Internet on your mobile phone. Many more converging technologies are on the horizon.

Quick Test

1. Which of the following is NOT a form of collaborating?
   a. File sharing
   b. Online conferencing
   c. Instant messaging
   d. Word processing

2. True or False. Platform independence is when a user can access the Internet or an intranet from a Mac, Windows, or any other PC platform.

3. True or False. Jive, Yammer, Twitter, and Facebook are all examples of corporate social networks.

Answers: 1. d; 2. True; 3. False.

---

33. *www.landsend.com/newsroom/corp_info/customer_service/index.html*, retrieved March 10, 2010.

What's in IT for me?

Most of you probably own an MP3 player, such as the Apple iPod, to which you can download and listen to your favourite tunes. But, did you know these devices offer more than entertainment value? These personal digital audio/image players and personal computers with digital audio playback capabilities create new opportunities for discovering and learning from experts and others. The primary technology that has allowed for this arguably more productive use of audio devices is known as *podcasting*, a name derived by mingling the words "iPod" and "broadcasting."

Podcasting is a method of publishing audio programs via the Internet that allows users of just about any digital audio device to download broadcasts or to subscribe to a feed of new files (usually MP3s).[34]

Podcasting makes all types of audio content portable and available on demand. Listeners can catch up on audio content—news, entertainment, or learning—while completing other tasks like working out at the gym. Like many Internet technologies, podcasting brings "power to the people" by allowing almost anyone to broadcast audio content. However, podcasting has more recently gained interest in the corporate world. Companies can use podcasts to spread the word about their products and services or to complement other media. For example, CBC Radio offers several podcasts that you can subscribe to at *www.cbc.ca/podcasting*.

One of the more well-known IT-related sites is PodcastAlley.com, which lists over 5,000 podcasts related to technology alone. If you need to increase your knowledge of agile or extreme programming, or IT security, or even what Microsoft is up to next, then the Internet and podcasting can provide you with this knowledge.

Finally, podcasting is one of the ways that professors supplement university and college classes. According to the University of Calgary, it was the first university in the country to introduce podcasting on a large scale when it launched four courses in 2006 featuring portable MP3 technology as a teaching tool.[35]

Podcasts will help you become more knowledgeable in the future. For now, you can become more knowledgeable in your classes by downloading audio files about topics in this book from *WileyPLUS*.

---

34. *http://en.wikipedia.org/wiki/Podcasting.*

35. *www.ucalgary.ca/oncampus/online/march-06/ipod.html*, retrieved March 10, 2010.

What's in IT for an organization?

Technology obviously has many benefits for an organization, one of which is putting together virtual teams. A *virtual team*, sometimes called a geographically dispersed team (GDT), is a group of people who work across geographic distance, time, and boundaries between organizations. They stay connected through telecommunications technology. Like any team, however, the members should have complementary skills, focus on a common goal, and hold themselves mutually accountable.

The number of virtual teams has grown along with improvements in communications, especially with the file-sharing capabilities available over networks like the Internet. Reasons for virtual teams revolve around the differences in the locations and work times of team members. Members may not be physically located at the same place, and it may be impractical or too costly for the team members to travel to meet face-to-face. In addition, the members may work at different times.

Technology to support virtual teams includes hardware, software, and networking.

Hardware may include computers, telephones, and videoconferencing apparatus, either connected over private WANs, or more often using public networks like the Internet. The primary software category in use is groupware. Groupware features can include email, meeting facilitation, group scheduling, and project management tools. In a nutshell, a team, plus groupware, plus a communication network, equals a virtual team.

An organization can derive several benefits by using virtual teams:

- People can work from any place and at any time.
- Organizations can recruit the best people regardless of their physical location.
- Travel and sometimes facilities expenses are reduced.
- There is greater flexibility for workers.

However, virtual teams may need to overcome time zone, culture, and organizational responsibility differences to function effectively as a group.

What's in IT for society?

Technology has the power to mobilize people from around the world. On Tuesday, January 12, 2010, an earthquake with a magnitude of 7.0 on the Richter scale had a devastating impact on Haiti. From the moment the earthquake struck, people turned to technology to find information and organize relief. Below are a few examples of how technology was used in this crisis:

- Almost immediately after the earthquake, tweets and twitpics were posted to Twitter with details of the devastating earthquake. A Twitter group called *#relativesinhaiti* was created and flooded with traffic trying to find out about loved ones. Another Twitter group called *#rescumehaiti* was used to direct rescue efforts to where trapped survivors were located. "Following the earthquake in Haiti, Twitter once again became a platform to disseminate the news and, more important, a way to quickly raise money to support relief efforts," said Mark Evans of social media monitoring and analytics firm Sysomos Inc.[36] Several celebrities posted links to Haiti charities, urging their followers to donate.

- Google responded to the earthquake by working with satellite imagery company GeoEye to quickly make images of the destruction available in Google Earth and Google Maps. The images were taken at approximately 10:27 A.M. Eastern time on Wednesday, January 13, and proved to be a helpful tool for aid organizations.

- A website called *Haitian Earthquake Registry* came online Wednesday, January 13 and allowed people to register and look for missing friends and relatives.

- People were able to donate to various charities for Haiti by sending text messages via SMS and donating flat rate amounts.

- The Facebook group called *Earthquake Haiti* had more than 160,000 members,[37] and celebrities quickly added links to Haiti charities on their Facebook pages to increase awareness.

- Journalists, unable to use conventional media broadcast methods, used the Web and Skype to broadcast the first reports of the devastation caused by the earthquake.

It is hard to measure the impact that technology had on the crisis in Haiti, but what is certain is that without it, the situation would have been much worse. This is one example of the depth and breadth of technology that can be applied when events such as this occur. Given the prevalence and importance of these technologies, you can find similar examples every day.

36. *http://blogs.wsj.com/digits/2010/01/14/twitter-helps-in-haiti-quake-coverage-aid/*, retrieved March 10, 2010.
37. *http://news.bbc.co.uk/2/hi/8461240.stm*, retrieved March 10, 2010.

1. **Describe the fundamentals of information technology and how they come together to help increase your productivity as a business professional.**

An information technology (IT) device can accept and store information; perform mathematical calculations; apply logic (e.g., compare values of numbers to make decisions); and retrieve, display, and send information. As such, IT allows you, a business professional, to communicate your thoughts, ideas, and feelings with others. IT enables transactions between you and the organizations with which you deal. IT helps you obtain data and information that you can use. IT provides tools you can use to analyze data and information to help in your decision making. IT can help you organize and store data and information that is important to you. IT can provide entertainment. Information technology can help you do all of these things more efficiently and with greater value. The meaningful application of this technology will achieve efficiencies, gain competitive advantage, and create business value.

2. **Explain why the Internet is so valuable to businesses, and outline some of the Internet applications available to businesses today.**

The Internet is arguably the most useful technological tool of the last few decades. The Internet uses the TCP/IP suite of packet switching protocols, a very general, non-proprietary set of communication rules. By adopting these rules and making use of software compatible with the TCP/IP standards, any computer, regardless of the platform (processor and OS), can connect and communicate over the Internet. Further, another aspect of the Internet important to its near global adoption is that no single organization or governmental entity owns it.

3. **Identify the basic components of the World Wide Web and describe how web pages are located on the Web.**

If the Internet is the technology platform, the World Wide Web is an application that works on that platform. The Web is the primary Internet application that supports many types of e-commerce, which will be discussed in detail in Chapter 7. The Web basically provides a hypertext system that operates over the Internet. Hypertext allows an easy way to publish information on a network. Hypertext documents can include references (hyperlinks) to other information on the network. Using Web browser software, business professionals can view hypertext documents and use the hyperlinks to browse (or surf) other related documents.

4. **Outline important ways individuals and businesses can keep their data and information safe online.**

Both the CIA triad and the McCumber Cube provide effective outlines to ensuring data and information security for individuals and organizations. Some simple actions that anyone can take to minimize Internet security risks include installing and keeping up to date antivirus software and firewalls, patching security holes with system updates, or moving to less vulnerable systems, such as Linux. Avoiding simple human error is one of the most effective ways to ensure data and information safety. This means users should follow safe computing practices, such as effective password policies and avoid opening email messages or attachments from unknown sources.

5. **Explain how technology has made collaboration in the business world easier and more productive.**

Technological advancements in cloud computing have fostered collaboration over the Internet like never before. Users can now schedule meetings, monitor projects, share work files, and even conference online from any computer platform, regardless of its operating system. By using software such as SharePoint, any user with permissions may access and update a single document for others to see or edit. Through sophisticated new software and secure Internet connections, cloud computing is driving collaboration forward in the business world.

KNOWLEDGE SPEAK

application service provider (ASP)   64

application software   55

business continuity plan (BCP)   76

CIA triad   73

client/server network   67

cloud computing   63

computer hierarchy   50

disaster recovery plan (DRP)   76

grid computing   51

groupware   77

hardware   48

hypertext markup language (HTML)   68

hypertext transfer protocol (HTTP)   68

Internet service provider (ISP)   61

intranet   77

middleware   56

modem   53

network   48

network interface card (NIC)   53

open source software   57

operating system (OS) software   54

platform   48

productivity software   55

protocol   59

random access memory (RAM)   51

read only memory (ROM)   51

search engines   69

software   48

software as a service (SaaS)   64

software as an outsourced service   64

system software   54

uniform resource locator (URL)   67

utility computing services   64

utility software   55

voice over Internet protocol (VoIP)   62

Web browser   68

Wi-Fi   62

REVIEW QUESTIONS

Multiple-choice questions

1. What hardware location temporarily stores data and instructions?
   a. Hard drive
   b. RAM
   c. ROM
   d. USB flash drive

2. _____ software manages and controls the resources of a computer system.
   a. Application
   b. Operating system
   c. Productivity
   d. Utility

3. Which of the following is not a networking technology that allows connection to the Internet?
   a. DSL
   b. HTML
   c. Cable
   d. Plain old telephone system

4. A worm, as it relates to computer technology, is
   a. A virus spread by letting other people use your computer.
   b. A destructive software that can spread by itself and once started, it automatically sends out infected emails to everybody in the user's address book.
   c. The name used for a person who can remotely take over your computer and use it as if you were using it.
   d. An attempt to gain personal and confidential information (e.g., passwords, credit card information) for fraudulent purposes such as identity theft.

Fill-in-the-blank questions

5. The _____ speed of a processor can be measured in megahertz or gigahertz.
6. A major category of productivity software that business professionals primarily use for quantitative analysis is known as a(n) _____.
7. A _____ allows members of an organization to share files, resources, servers, and other hardware with other members of an organization.
8. A _____ merges the technical devices, media, and functions.

True-false questions

9. A pointing device is generally easier to use than a keyboard when entering text data.
10. The Internet is controlled by several independent, international organizations.
11. By right clicking your mouse, you can view the HTML code of most websites.
12. CIA in the CIA Triad for Internet security stands for Component Internet Accessibility.

Matching questions

Choose the BEST answer from column B for each item in column A.

Column A
13. communications
14. input
15. output
16. processing
17. storage

Column B
a. Hardware used to save data, information, and instructions long term.
b. Hardware used to connect one IT device to another.
c. Hardware that provides an interface for retrieving information from an IT device.
d. Hardware that provides an interface for entering data into an IT device.
e. Hardware that directs the execution of instructions.

Short-answer questions

18. Briefly explain why more RAM can speed up your computer.
19. Review the network categories and describe a LAN and a MAN that you are familiar with. How do you know it is a LAN and a MAN?
20. Describe the ways in which you can protect your computer from various types of malware.

Discussion/Essay questions

21. Discuss the impact of open source software on the software industry.
22. Discuss the benefits and drawbacks of cloud computing. Are the risks worth it?

TEAM ACTIVITY

Effective teamwork relies on good communication among team members, as well as between the team and its organization. In this activity, you will explore how information technology can help you with each. First, organize yourself into a team of at least five people. At your first meeting, select a team coordinator and an assignment (e.g., a problem that you've noticed on campus or a team assignment for one of your classes). Then send everyone off with the task of thinking about possible solutions to the problem. Over a period of days, the team coordinator should use information technology to communicate with team members to come up with a set of possible solutions to discuss at the second meeting. The coordinator will also use information technology to schedule the second meeting and inform the team members. At the second meeting, in addition to discussing the problem, discuss how the team used IT to perform these tasks. What worked well and what didn't? How could your team use IT more effectively?

SOFTWARE APPLICATION EXERCISES

1. Internet
Information technology is constantly changing, and many new IT devices can seem exciting and cutting-edge. Search the Web and select five new or future information technologies that interest you. Bookmark these sites for use in the Presentation activity that follows.

2. Presentation
Create a presentation to discuss the technologies that you found for the Internet assignment above. For each technology, use two or three slides to provide a brief description and possible uses. Give your presentation a professional look by incorporating an attractive layout, informative graphics, and appropriate slide transitions.

3. Word Processing
Create a personal disaster recovery plan. Ensure that the key components of a DRP are addressed.

4. Spreadsheet
Acquiring information technology can be expensive! Personal computers and laptops can range from a few hundred to a few thousand dollars, depending on the capabilities and options selected. Assume you are interested in purchasing a new computer. Create a spreadsheet to help you evaluate the relative costs of several options. For each system, include cells to record the possible options and their prices. Be sure to include extras such as shipping or tax, which may apply to some options but not others. Use formulas to calculate the overall cost for each system. For a challenge, try to use special cells and IF statements to reflect various decisions such as Plasma versus LCD flat-screen monitor, or 512M versus 1024M RAM.

5. Database
Expand the data you collected in exercise #4 to include many makes and models of computers, laptops, tablets, and accessories. Create a database so that you can search on one aspect (e.g., GHz) and so the result of the search shows all items with that characteristic in your database.

6. Advanced Challenge
A lot of groupware is available in the market. Search the Web and find the five most popular groupware applications. Create a document to compare their functionality, technical requirements, and pricing. Recommend which groupware application your class should use.

ONLINE RESOURCES

Companion Website
* Take interactive practice quizzes to assess your knowledge and help you study in a dynamic way.
* Review PowerPoint lecture slides.
* Get help and sample solutions to end-of-chapter software application exercises.

Additional Resources Available Only on *WileyPLUS*
* Take the interactive Quick Test to check your understanding of the chapter material and get immediate feedback on your responses.
* Review and study with downloadable Audio Lecture MP3 files.
* Check your understanding of key vocabulary in the chapter with Knowledge Speak Interactive Flash Cards.

CASE STUDY:
SELECTING A COMPUTER

In the end-of-chapter case for Chapter 1, you met Ashley Hyatt, a student in business administration at university. In this case, we continue Ashley's story.

After a successful fourth year, during which she interviewed with a number of companies, Ashley accepted a position with one of the large consulting firms. She starts her new job within a few weeks. Because Ashley will telecommute one to two days per week, her company will fund the purchase of a Windows-based, desktop PC system for her home, worth up to $3,000. However, she is unsure of what system will work best for her job.

Ashley realizes that she should begin by considering her job requirements. Because she'll be carrying out extensive financial analyses, she needs a system with a significant amount of processing and hard disk storage. Because she may be doing some serious number crunching in her new job, Ashley should probably go for the maximum processor speed she can afford. Because she will be storing large data files on her hard disk, she should try to purchase a hard drive with as much capacity as possible, but not less than 500 GB. Further, because Ashley will need to transport large files between work and home, she needs a system that reads and writes DVDs.

Finally, Ashley decides that a large (at least 19-inch) flat-panel monitor, which can also display high-definition television signals, will allow her to check breaking news stories while working on her assigned projects.

Case Questions

1. Using a budget of $3,000 and the requirements mentioned by Ashley, make specific suggestions as to what computer system she should purchase, including a brand name, model, and options.
2. You realize Ashley has overlooked printed output. Considering her budget of $3,000, what options would you recommend?
3. Do you think that Ashley's choice of DVD as a portable secondary storage media is a good one? Why or why not?
4. What upgrades would you recommend that Ashley purchase in the future?

CASE STUDY:
iPADS FOR THE ENTERPRISE

Michael Kennington could not be more excited about his new iPad. He just spent the entire weekend loading all of his favourite music on it and exploring all of its applications. He especially loves Angry Birds! Michael Kennington is also the CEO of a major publishing company, and as such, he has also installed an e-reader on his iPad. He knows this is the future of publishing and he needs to be on board with it.

On Monday morning, Michael runs into the CIO, Roger Mondale, in the elevator. "Roger, have you got an iPad?" Michael asks. Roger replies, "Not yet, but I am really enjoying my iPhone. I heard that with iCloud I can share applications and data between the iPhone and iPad. I am putting an iPad on my Christmas list, but I will wait for the next version." Michael continues, "I can't believe how great this iPad is! Why didn't get one sooner? I feel so efficient! I can listen to music, read my email, read documents, and play games all at the same time! Hey . . . this iPad is way more convenient and easier to use than my laptop. Not to mention how cool I will look in meetings with it," Michael chuckles.

Michael then says, "Roger, send Arnold to me right away. I am replacing my corporate laptop with this iPad. I am truly entering the world of Web 3.0! See you later at the management meeting." "Oh boy," Roger thinks to himself, "Arnold (the head of Corporate Desktop Systems) is going to flip."

Roger calls Arnold to his office. "Hi Arnold. You better sit down," says Roger. Roger describes his encounter with Michael in the elevator and, as predicted, Arnold freaks out. "What happened to the standardized desktop policy ensuring that employees use corporately issued hardware and software? What about security? How am I going to support this? Me and my team are not familiar with iPad and iPad applications. What if something goes wrong? Oh my . . . what if EVERYONE wants one?!!" Arnold says, animatedly. After some time, Roger manages to calm Arnold down. "Arnold, is an iPad any different than my iPhone? I use my iPhone for business. An iPad is just another mobile device, right? Besides, you know Michael, once his mind is set on something—that is it. We are going to have to figure this out."

Case Questions

1. As the above situation illustrates, the corporate use of iPads and other tablets is inevitable. Take the perspective of Michael Kennington and make a detailed list of the benefits of using an iPad or tablet for both business and personal use. Research and provide examples of where there has been a business benefit for their use to support your argument.

2. Then, take the perspective of Arnold, an IT staff member who is responsible for supporting the employees of the organization, ensuring data and organizational security, and managing corporate IT resources. Again, research and use examples of the inappropriate use of iPads/tablets in businesses.

3. Conclude your investigation with a statement of your opinion on the matter. Should iPads/tablets be used in the enterprise?

3 | MANAGING AND USING DATA

WHAT WE WILL COVER

■ What Are Data, Information, and Knowledge?

■ Decision Making and Problem Solving

■ Databases: The Primary Data Storage for Organizations

■ Business Intelligence

STUDENT RETURN ON INVESTMENT **ROI**

Through your investment of time in reading and thinking about this chapter, your return—or created value—is gaining knowledge. After reading this chapter, you should be able to

1. Define data, information, and knowledge and describe how business professionals engage in knowledge work activities.

2. Explain how the structure, quality, and presentation of information influence the nature of the decisions made by business professionals.

3. Describe how databases help businesses store and access their data, information, and knowledge.

4. Explain how business intelligence enhances organizational decision making.

THE VOICE OF EXPERIENCE

Diane Viveiros, Humber College, Business Administration, Marketing and Public Relations

Diane Viveiros is a Digital Marketing Manager at Skyline Hotels and Resorts, a company that offers a collection of urban and country retreats. She manages the brand perception and digital marketing efforts for their multi-faceted offerings by tracking and reviewing the data created by website traffic.

What do you do in your current position? I assist in building and implementing online marketing strategies including social media marketing, banner advertising, and email marketing campaigns for Skyline Hotels and Resorts. Beyond strategy implementation, I also monitor traffic analytics and track changes to optimize our keyword efforts and goal conversion rates. I draw from my public relations knowledge base to update both Twitter and Facebook daily, organizing giveaways and managing the perception of our brand with the help of visitor data collected by analytics programs.

What do you consider to be important career skills? One of the most important career skills you can gain in my field is the ability to perform effective research. You should always read and learn about the newest trends to stay ahead of the game! This not only means keeping up-to-date with current social media trends, but also keeping an eye on the competition.

How do you use IT? Aside from online marketing, I lead the ongoing development of our primary digital property including its design, functionality, and technical maintenance. This means I am always seeking to optimize the visitor experience for our website. The optimal visitor experience is typically achieved when key content sections of our site reflect marketing and organizational priorities.

Can you describe an example of how you have used IT to improve business operations? Our website provides a series of vital functions for patrons looking to stay with us.

Without a successful back-end, clients couldn't book or confirm hotel reservations, send an RFP for an event, or schedule time at the spa. With this in mind, I recently led an Opera hotel systems upgrade to bolster sales and catering. Along with the sales and catering upgrade, I also upgraded our online reservation software to streamline functions that were previously separated. By linking various functions together, we can now increase revenues by maximizing bookings.

Have you got any "on the job" advice for students seeking a career in IT or business? The best advice I can offer to students seeking a career in IT or business is take initiative! Research any upcoming changes in your industry. In my field, it's important to stay current with social media and online trends because they can have a big impact on website traffic!

Aside from research, one of the most valuable resources you can gain is a mentor. To position yourself with a mentor, seek out someone in your field and offer to meet them over lunch or coffee. Tell them what you are trying to achieve and what experiences you would like to gain. Ask if they would be open to a mentor/mentee relationship. I have done this on several occasions and I've found that most professionals in IT do not have a problem spending time each week to help a young professional gain the experience needed to be successful.

In this chapter we discuss data management and how data can be mined and used for business intelligence purposes. Diane is constantly reviewing data to monitor and direct traffic to her company's website. Data created from website visitors is a valuable resource that can be leveraged to help companies gain competitive advantage.

Data and information are as vital to an organization as water is to people. In addition, both individuals and businesses need these resources delivered in a usable form. Using this analogy, we can actually think of IT as the "plumbing" of a business information system (IS). First, we like to get our water when we want it—as soon as we turn on the tap, any time of the day. An organization also likes to get the data and information that it needs when it wants it. Constant access is therefore important. Second, we want a reliable system to provide clean water—the reservoirs, the processing facilities, the pipes that deliver it to our home, and the sewers that drain it away. Similarly, a business counts on its IS to deliver accurate data and information.

However, it is perhaps more enlightening to think of how data and information differ from the water piped to our homes. With water, we basically need only one standard type—clear and clean. With data and information, an organization's needs are much more varied. It wants data in different forms (e.g., number, text, video, audio) and organized in different ways (e.g., tables, reports, graphs). Just think how complex a plumbing system would have to be to deliver water, coffee, or pop with just a twist of the tap!

In this chapter we discuss the equivalent of "organizational plumbing"—the IT systems designed to support different kinds of knowledge work—gathering and storing data, processing information, and making decisions and solving problems.

■ DATA, INFORMATION, AND KNOWLEDGE

Due to the importance of data, information, and knowledge in business and IT, we spent some time in Chapter 1 defining and discussing them. As a review, **data** are raw unorganized facts, numbers, pictures, and so on. **Information** is data that have been organized and made useful. **Knowledge** is created when experience and judgment are combined with information. Applying knowledge is how business people create and add value to organizations. First, we spend a little time understanding knowledge better and learning the activities to gain knowledge.

Lifelong Knowledge Creation

To be a successful business professional, you must always strive to create or acquire new knowledge. Specifically, you need to build on the two types of knowledge that you possess: explicit knowledge and tacit knowledge. **Explicit knowledge** is knowledge that is readily codified, such as the knowledge in this textbook. **Tacit knowledge** is knowledge that you gain through experience, insight, and discovery. These two types of knowledge are complementary halves of a lifelong knowledge creation process.

How does the knowledge-creation process work in the real world? Consider one of your first steps toward becoming a business professional: the business internship or job interview. Interviewers often ask you about their company. They want to assess what explicit knowledge you may have gained about their company by visiting their website or reading the company's annual report. As the interview continues, the interviewer may ask you to describe a situation where you worked as a member of a project team. As you describe your experiences and the lessons you learned from them, you are highlighting your tacit knowledge of working in teams.

Digital audio devices like MP3 players offer opportunities to incorporate the explicit and tacit knowledge of others into your own knowledge through podcasting, thereby enhancing your own knowledge-creation process.

You've learned that data are transformed into information, and information can be transformed into knowledge. Then what? If an organization is willing to hire you because you are capable of creating tacit knowledge that contributes to the organization's success, what does the organization do with the knowledge that you've created? In the next section, we discuss the various knowledge work activities that business professionals engage in to create business value for their organizations.

Knowledge Work Activities

Recall from Chapter 1 that *knowledge work* involves the discovery, analysis, transformation, synthesis, and communication of data, information, and knowledge. Examples in the business world include recommending an investment portfolio to clients or interpreting the monthly sales report to plan for the future. However, even as a preschooler you were already performing knowledge-based activities. How? Say it was your fourth birthday, and you received a bucket of Lego blocks. Inside the bucket you made a *discovery*—plastic blocks in many colours. So, what did you do? You dumped the blocks on the floor and began to *analyze* the blocks and organize the big pile into smaller piles of colours and shapes. Maybe you first decided to build a car, but then realized, "who needs a car when I can build a really big tower and use all the pieces (*transform*)!" So, you started snapping together blocks, until what began as a collection of pieces came together as a magnificent tower (*synthesis*). You were so pleased with your successful creation that you showed everyone around you what you had built. You also probably told them how you built it. In other words, you *communicated* your Lego-building knowledge to others. To apply this analogy to an organization, the steps you went through are referred to as *work flows* and the outcome of your building efforts as the *work product*.

Figure 3.1 depicts these knowledge work activities and shows how they constantly interact around and through you. You did them when you were young (e.g., playing with Lego), you did them recently (e.g., selecting which university or college to attend), you do them now (e.g., preparing for your current classes), and you will continue to do them throughout your life. Because of their importance, we discuss each activity in more detail in the following sections.

Discovery: Finding Data, Information, or Knowledge

Discovery is the finding of data, information, and knowledge relevant to a task, problem, issue, or opportunity (the context). You begin with an idea of what to look for, and then reflect on where information related to the task may exist. You then retrieve relevant data from those various sources

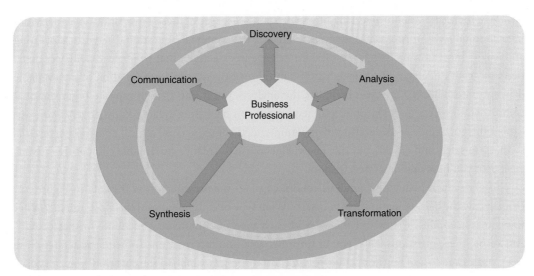

FIGURE 3.1 Knowledge work activities.

Learning from your university or college experiences and course requirements will train you for many knowledge work tasks, especially discovering data and information.

and assess its value to the decision at hand. For example, say you work as a marketing assistant for WildOutfitters.com, a hypothetical retail hiking store. Your manager asks you to find the weekly sales data for the store and its main competitors. This request frames your discovery activities. You now need to answer questions such as, "Where is the sales data for our store located?" and "Who are our competitors?" This type of request is similar to the challenges you face in your search for information to write term papers and create presentations.

You already know how to search the Internet to locate specific data and information. Strong Internet research skills, balanced with an awareness of the limitations of this source of data, can help you create business value for your organization. Reflect on some of the sources you use and trust. What about the sources you reject? Evaluating your search results is an important part of the discovery process. Using sources that you should have rejected will impact the rest of your knowledge work activities, and perhaps lead to incorrect conclusions and poor decision making.

Luckily, discovering information often extends beyond the Internet. In fact, you may have even more powerful job-related information close at hand. The company you work for may have a private version of the Internet known as an intranet. Recall from Chapter 2 that an intranet contains data about the company that only authorized employees can access. If your organization stores information on its intranet about where a similar problem has occurred before and how it was solved, or perhaps tracks the results of decisions made by competitors or partners, it may even help you to discover best practices for solving problems, thereby creating business value for your company.

Analysis: Investigating and Examining the Available Data, Information, and Knowledge

You can think of **analysis** as breaking down the whole into its more discrete parts to better understand how it works. You often perform analysis under other names such as *process mapping* (if you are analyzing a business process), *quality assurance* (if you are analyzing product quality), or *performance testing* (if you are assessing fitness or standards). All of these types of business activities involve some form of root cause analysis to answer the contextual question, "What is happening and why?" Therefore, analysis is a critical knowledge work activity that will help you answer questions and gain understanding through a thoughtful investigation and examination of the available data and information. Once you complete the analysis, put it into the appropriate organizational context, and make a decision or recommendation, you have now created knowledge. If you can extend this to include consideration of any unintended consequences, ethical constraints, or risks so that you safely and quickly put this knowledge to use to create a sustainable competitive advantage, then you have demonstrated wisdom.

To understand better what analysis entails, consider the presentation of the data in Figure 3.2. In analyzing the data, you might ask yourself, "What type of equipment sold the most units?" "What was our total profit?" "How did the sales of each type of equipment contribute to that profit?" Answering these questions helps you to turn this data into information. To better understand the weekly sales and to add business value, you need to continue to analyze the data until you can come to some conclusions. For example, you may come to realize that tents contribute more to profit

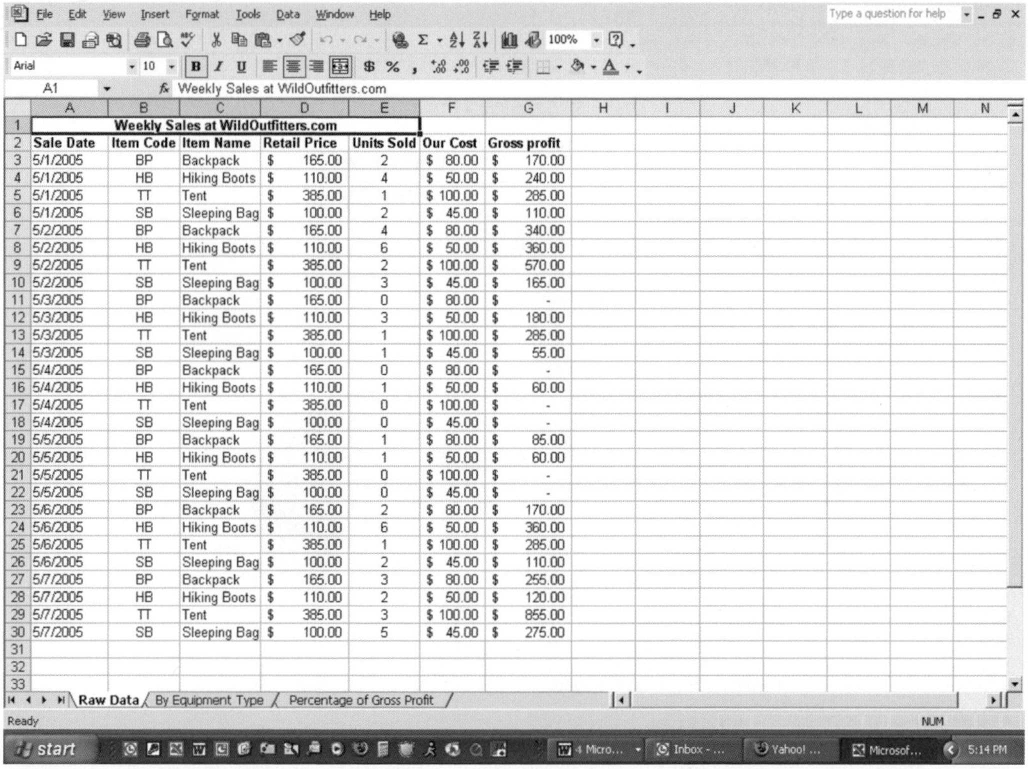

Weekly Sales at WildOutfitters.com

	Sale Date	Item Code	Item Name	Retail Price	Units Sold	Our Cost	Gross profit
3	5/1/2005	BP	Backpack	$ 165.00	2	$ 80.00	$ 170.00
4	5/1/2005	HB	Hiking Boots	$ 110.00	4	$ 50.00	$ 240.00
5	5/1/2005	TT	Tent	$ 385.00	1	$ 100.00	$ 285.00
6	5/1/2005	SB	Sleeping Bag	$ 100.00	2	$ 45.00	$ 110.00
7	5/2/2005	BP	Backpack	$ 165.00	4	$ 80.00	$ 340.00
8	5/2/2005	HB	Hiking Boots	$ 110.00	6	$ 50.00	$ 360.00
9	5/2/2005	TT	Tent	$ 385.00	2	$ 100.00	$ 570.00
10	5/2/2005	SB	Sleeping Bag	$ 100.00	3	$ 45.00	$ 165.00
11	5/3/2005	BP	Backpack	$ 165.00	0	$ 80.00	$ -
12	5/3/2005	HB	Hiking Boots	$ 110.00	3	$ 50.00	$ 180.00
13	5/3/2005	TT	Tent	$ 385.00	1	$ 100.00	$ 285.00
14	5/3/2005	SB	Sleeping Bag	$ 100.00	1	$ 45.00	$ 55.00
15	5/4/2005	BP	Backpack	$ 165.00	0	$ 80.00	$ -
16	5/4/2005	HB	Hiking Boots	$ 110.00	1	$ 50.00	$ 60.00
17	5/4/2005	TT	Tent	$ 385.00	0	$ 100.00	$ -
18	5/4/2005	SB	Sleeping Bag	$ 100.00	0	$ 45.00	$ -
19	5/5/2005	BP	Backpack	$ 165.00	1	$ 80.00	$ 85.00
20	5/5/2005	HB	Hiking Boots	$ 110.00	1	$ 50.00	$ 60.00
21	5/5/2005	TT	Tent	$ 385.00	0	$ 100.00	$ -
22	5/5/2005	SB	Sleeping Bag	$ 100.00	0	$ 45.00	$ -
23	5/6/2005	BP	Backpack	$ 165.00	2	$ 80.00	$ 170.00
24	5/6/2005	HB	Hiking Boots	$ 110.00	6	$ 50.00	$ 360.00
25	5/6/2005	TT	Tent	$ 385.00	1	$ 100.00	$ 285.00
26	5/6/2005	SB	Sleeping Bag	$ 100.00	2	$ 45.00	$ 110.00
27	5/7/2005	BP	Backpack	$ 165.00	3	$ 80.00	$ 255.00
28	5/7/2005	HB	Hiking Boots	$ 110.00	2	$ 50.00	$ 120.00
29	5/7/2005	TT	Tent	$ 385.00	3	$ 100.00	$ 855.00
30	5/7/2005	SB	Sleeping Bag	$ 100.00	5	$ 45.00	$ 275.00

FIGURE 3.2 Sales data for WildOutfitters.com.

due to their low cost. For this deeper analysis, you may need more data and advanced analysis techniques. Two information technologies that can help answer questions about underlying patterns and correlations across large amounts of data are data warehouses and data mining, which are discussed later in this chapter.

Transformation: Organizing Discovery Results

Transformation is knowledge work that requires you to use the results of your analysis to deepen your understanding of the data and information. Why is transformation important? Imagine your university or college course calendar as simply an alphabetic list (e.g., Accounting 350, Acting 102, Art History 210). Each course may contain all the appropriate information, but it is not organized in a useful format. That is, organized this way, you would not know which course is applicable to which degree. When it is organized by course of study (e.g., Business, Fine Arts) or specialty (e.g., Business—Finance) it is *transformed* into information that tells you what courses are required to achieve a particular degree.

Let's revisit your manager's request from the discovery phase, where you need to obtain weekly sales data for WildOutfitters.com and its competitors. Through your intranet and Internet searches, you discover a lot of information. In fact, you find more raw data than you can quickly process. This may be especially true if you work as part of a collaborative project team, where others may discover the data or information and pass it to you to analyze and transform. Fortunately, information technology can help you transform data regardless of who did the discovery and analysis work. For example, spreadsheets and databases are effective tools for organizing and storing information, as Figure 3.3 shows. Note that for this example, you could also use database software. Larger organizations, with many transactions, often use database software for storing and transforming data.

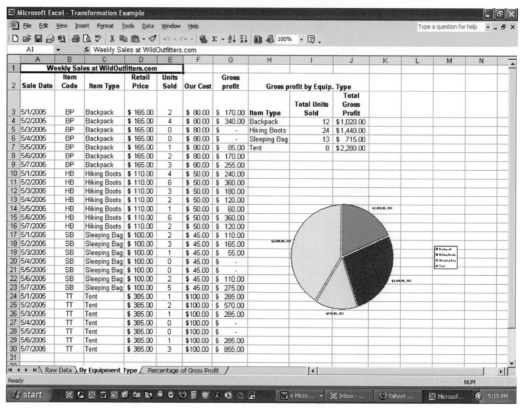

FIGURE 3.3 Further transformation of sales data for WildOutfitters.com.

Figure 3.3 shows additional transformations of the data. Note that you (and your manager) can now easily see that hiking boots sold the most number of units, but tents contributed the greatest percentage to weekly gross profit. By transforming the data into a useful form through the use of a spreadsheet, you begin to make sense of events and issues. You set the stage for the insight and understanding that often result from the next type of knowledge work, synthesis.

Synthesis: The Sum of the Parts

Synthesis allows you to interpret trends or patterns that seem to explain the past and the present, and may suggest courses of action likely to favourably influence the future. Further, while some of these patterns will stand alone—for example, the WildOutfitters.com sales data for each week of the month—isolated information often paints an incomplete picture. As a result, you will probably need to bring together different pieces of data and information to form a complete picture of your current situation. The essential element of synthesis is in knowing which parts, when combined, will create higher total value than the value of the parts themselves. This is particularly true with the synthesis of information. For instance, national security issues are often identified only when one piece of information (otherwise deemed irrelevant or uninteresting) is combined with a similarly unassuming piece of other information to begin to show a pattern of possible terrorist activity. While any one piece of information on its own may seem innocent, when correlated and synthesized into a discernible pattern, there may be a potential terrorist threat to deal with.

Remember, you may need to integrate even more information before gaining a complete understanding or making recommendations. In the WildOutfitters.com example, the weekly sales data may be trending upward, but the last six weeks' data may be trending downward. A synthesis that excludes additional weekly sales data, competitors' sales data, and industry trends may result in an incomplete understanding. For example, if all additional data trend downward except for the weekly sales data shown above, this week may be an anomaly (exceptional case). Or, if other weeks show a downward trend and the overall economy is slowing, you may want to investigate what occurred to generate the increased sales. While systems can provide the summary information, only people have the ability to put this information into the proper context and draw conclusions from it.

Once you have an accurate and complete analysis of your results, you must then communicate them succinctly to others so you can help the organization make better decisions.

WHAT DO YOU THINK?

You have made your way to university or college by doing knowledge work activities. Of course, you may not have known the names of each of these activities or been aware that you were doing them! Consider the activities of discovery, analysis, transformation, and synthesis, and think about the following questions:

1: What activities did you undertake to come to this university or college? This course?
2: Have you purchased a car? Are you thinking of purchasing a car? Which activities will you use to do this?
3: Are you thinking of getting a part-time job? Again, think about what knowledge work activities you will use to find suitable employment.

Communication: Sharing Analysis with Others

As a business professional, you will most likely work for and with others in a business or other type of organization. To help your employer create business value, you must have strong **communication** skills; that is, the ability to share your analyses, ideas, and solutions with others. Even if you work for yourself, you still need to communicate effectively with your customers.

Individuals and organizations can and do use information systems and technologies to help them communicate. Some of the technologies individuals use focus on physically sharing the message, such as email and instant messaging.

Information systems and technology can also allow you to share the meaning behind the message. For example, you can use Microsoft PowerPoint to create a presentation, or other software applications to communicate your knowledge, such as Inspiration (*www.inspiration.com*), Visio (*http://office.microsoft.com/en-us/visio/FX100487861033.aspx*) or Keynote for iPad. Then these can be collaboratively enabled by using tools such as Skype (*www.skype.com*) or GotoMeeting (*www.gotomeeting.com*) to organize and disseminate information throughout a virtual team.

Summary of Knowledge Work Activities

Table 3.1 summarizes and expands on the examples of knowledge work activities we just covered. However, knowledge work activities are only part of the larger picture of a rational decision-making and problem-solving process. To be successful and continue to be successful, businesses must do knowledge work. Once they obtain knowledge, business leaders must make decisions and solve problems based on this knowledge. These decisions and solutions often lead to important changes in the business.

Table 3.1	Examples of Knowledge Work Activities	
Knowledge Work Activity	**Manager's Request**	**Helpful IT Tools and Activities**
Discovery	Find our company's and our competitors' weekly sales data.	Use data from check-out/point-of-sale (POS) terminals, search tools (e.g., Google), and Web searching.
Analysis	Compare the sales data for the first week of May to similar data from our company for the previous two months.	Import the data into a database or spreadsheet application, and use its features and tools to organize the data. Find the previous months' data and import these as well.
Transformation	Identify any trends in the data by week, month, and day of the week. Indicate how our company's results compare with our competition and with the industry as a whole.	Use the data analysis tools in the spreadsheet application to examine the data from different aspects. Consider what your analysis of the data revealed and combine this with your knowledge of your company's goals to add focus to your analysis. Search the Web for other analyses of your company, industry, and competitors. Integrate this with your interpretation of the sales data.
Synthesis	Given your analysis of our company's relative success or failure, suggest ways to capitalize on our strengths and overcome our weaknesses.	With analysis in mind, obtain feedback about specific company products and services. Arrange a brief Web meeting (e.g., with GotoMeeting) of the top sales associates in your company.
Communication	Present your findings and suggestions to management.	Import your spreadsheet data into presentation software. Add the insights gained from your Web meeting.

Quick Test

1. The type of knowledge gained through discovery is
   a. explicit
   b. extraneous
   c. data
   d. tacit

2. Either database or spreadsheet software can be very useful as part of the knowledge work activity known as _____.
   a. discovery
   b. analysis
   c. transformation
   d. synthesis

3. In a business organization, the ultimate purpose of knowledge work activities is the creation of _____.
   a. profits
   b. business value
   c. good employer–employee relations
   d. resources

■ DECISION MAKING AND PROBLEM SOLVING

To truly create business value, a company needs to decide how to best apply the information it has gathered. This section defines a basic decision-making process and provides some problem-solving tools, both critical to everyday business activities.

Before discussing effective decision making, we need to have a common understanding of what a decision is. A **rational decision** is a choice that you make about what actions you will take (or not take) in a given situation after analyzing the consequences of each option. It may involve trade-offs between options, or trying to optimize an outcome given a set of current circumstances and preferences balanced with risk. There may be legal or environmental factors or ethical or moral concerns about certain aspects of the decision.

Often, rational decision making occurs as part of a larger problem-solving process, which we discuss later, within a specific context. This creates natural boundaries and limits around the available options. In other words, you usually make a decision—for example, choosing between University A or College B—in the context of solving the problem of what you want to study and why (the problem-solving process). This involves considerations such as distance from home, climate and language preferences, tuition and living costs, your knowledge of the institution involved, recommendations or rankings by others, quality of program or faculty, accessibility, and perhaps likelihood of being admitted. Once you consider all these factors, the outcome will dictate the first step of choosing where you will go to school (the actual decision). Further, you may also need to consider the ethics of a decision, such as whether or not it is important for you to attend a public or private institution whose selective admission criteria or policies you may not personally agree with, but whose programs may be superior. The good news is, the more practice you have making decisions and learning to anticipate their consequences, the better you become at making them!

Some decisions may be routine, whereas some decisions are more difficult, involving ethical considerations. Think about some of the other decisions that you have made (e.g., what to wear today, what route to take to school, and what career to pursue). These decisions are not equal in consequence or in the need for careful thought and planning.

TECHNOLOGY CORE

Organizations can use IT in several ways to support decision making. For example, businesses use expert systems, a type of knowledge management system. Expert systems originate from the field of artificial intelligence (AI), which attempts to provide computer applications that mimic characteristics of human intelligence. Many other applications use AI technology, from neural networks used for recognizing patterns in stock prices, to genetic algorithms that incorporate theories from genetics into programs that can quickly find an optimal solution to a problem. Expert systems capture and store the knowledge of a human expert so that the organization can permanently store and share it. Special techniques have been developed to capture and codify tacit knowledge (knowledge gained through experience) into an expert system, such as observation and interview techniques. This knowledge includes how an expert performs work and makes decisions. To store the knowledge, special formats capture how the facts relate to the decision rules used by the expert. Expert systems and artificial intelligence will never replace humans, but they can help to advise humans to make better decisions and solve difficult problems.

Putting gas in your car so you can drive it is an example of a routine decision; you don't have to think very hard about whether this is a necessary action!

Classifying Decisions by Type

Your college or university degree program likely requires you to take certain prerequisite courses. When you make your course selections, you know that you must register in these classes. Here, you carry out the required actions associated with a very structured decision. A **structured decision** is one that can be programmed; it is routine or repetitive.[1]

However, not all decisions are so clear cut. Sometimes even simple decisions may have increased uncertainty, or doubt about consequences and outcomes, associated with them. This is the case when you register for optional or elective courses. You may decide to take a course based on your interests or when the course is offered. Some of your classmates may have recommended an elective course that is "easy" or entertaining. Other classmates' opinions may have differed. The choice is not so easy. You are now faced with a **semi-structured decision**.

Let's further complicate this example. You graduate from your course of study and are now faced with doing graduate studies or starting your career in the business world, which is a third kind of decision: the **unstructured decision**. This is a novel, complex situation, with no obvious or single correct decision or decision process. Further, your decision will significantly affect the next few years of your life. What do you do?

To help you decide what to do, you may meet with some graduate students, survey some of the courses you would take, and talk to people working in the business area you are considering. You may also consult your family and friends. Money may also be a consideration. You do some research on the Internet and find that having a graduate degree does not significantly affect initial annual salaries. You make your decision: you will enter the work world and not do graduate studies. But there is still a lot of uncertainty as to the correctness of this decision. If you don't do graduate studies now, when will you? Perhaps you will miss studying with an influential professor. However, given the available information, you have made the best decision you can.

Using Information in Decision Making

This is what rational decision making is all about: using information to reduce uncertainty in the outcomes of your decisions. The above example highlights aspects of the three different types of decisions and their relationship to uncertainty. In general, uncertainty complicates the decision-making process and underscores why information systems are so important to businesses. Information systems help businesses reduce uncertainty by providing information to decision makers. Less uncertainty due to more complete information can lead to better decisions, thereby enhancing the creation of business value.

However, business professionals also have a responsibility to recognize that there is no such thing as perfect information to eliminate uncertainty. Therefore, they also have some responsibility to know when they have enough valuable information to go ahead with a decision, and then to push themselves and their organizations to execute those decisions, even when there is some lingering uncertainty.

---

1. H. A. Simon, *The New Science of Management Decision*, Harper & Row, New York, 1960 and 1977 (re-release); P. G. Keen and M. S. Scott Morton, *Decision Support Systems: An Organizational Perspective*, Addison-Wesley, Mass., 1978.

Another important element of good decision making is what to do when you receive new information. Is it valuable and should it influence your decision? You will be called upon to make these judgments throughout your career as you make important decisions about all kinds of things, both more and less certain, that can affect the organization you work for.

WHAT DO YOU THINK? ❓

People can endlessly analyze information—a never-ending process known as *analysis paralysis*. At some point, analysis should end and lead to some conclusion: a decision or a solution to a problem. To gain competitive advantage, organizations often analyze productivity. **Productivity** is the ability to create business value with the least cost. Examining productivity forces organizations to look at efficiency and effectiveness, defined as follows:

Efficiency: Getting the most output from a given input ("doing the thing right")
Effectiveness: Pursuing the goal or task that is appropriate for the given situation ("doing the right thing")

Therefore, productivity can be thought of as "doing the right thing, right."

Consider the following scenarios to better understand knowledge activities and decision making concerning productivity:

1: Imagine you are a sidewalk vendor of frozen drinks in Saskatoon, Saskatchewan. You get more drinks per amount of ingredients than your competitors; that is, you are highly efficient. But you sell only one frozen drink in January (when the average temperature is −17°C), so your efforts are ineffective.
2: Now imagine you are the owner of a T-shirt-selling business on campus. It is so successful that you always sell out of T-shirts by the end of frosh week. You know you could sell more if you were able to produce more T-shirts by the beginning of September. Not having enough T-shirts to sell is inefficient.

For each of these scenarios, what decisions will you make to improve your productivity? What knowledge work activities will you undertake to assist in making these decisions? What role could IT play in improving productivity?

How to Make More-Informed Decisions

As a business professional, recall that your work will often centre on finding and using quality data, information, and knowledge. As a decision maker, the quality of your decision often depends on the quality of the inputs you use to inform your decision.

In every decision that you make in life, you should always carefully consider the characteristics of the information on which you are basing your decision. Obviously, you must have already considered the source when you either accessed or were provided with the information, and you must assume that the source is a good one. However, beyond that are the nuances of the information itself. Is it complete? How accurate or reliable is it likely to be? If it is not, have efforts been made to address the degree to which it is or is not accurate or reliable? And is the information up-to-date and provided in a timely way?

All of these information characteristics, summarized in Table 3.2, affect the usefulness of data and information for decision making. As someone living in the most intense knowledge era ever, you need to become a good judge of the quality of information.

Table 3.2	Information Evaluation Criteria
Information Characteristic	**Example**
Complete	Your new project team member's mobile phone is 555–1212. Is this enough information? Maybe, but you may also need an area code.
Accurate	You check your printed course schedule and find out that your Intro to IS class meets at 11 p.m. You suspect the schedule is wrong.
Reliable	You receive an unsolicited email offering you a share in millions of dollars if you will help this person transfer money out of his home country. You realize this is a frequent email scam and is, therefore, unreliable information.
Timely	When deciding what to wear, a forecast of yesterday's weather is recent information, but it could be worthless if today's weather is different than yesterday's. Timely information includes recent information, but also requires that the information arrive close enough to the decision to be useful to the decision maker.

The Decision-Making Process and Problem-Solving Tools

Figure 3.4 summarizes a typical rational decision-making process. Initially, decision making requires you to engage in knowledge work activities (discovery, analysis, transformation, synthesis, communication) so that you can make an effective choice about some issue or challenge. You have seen that not all decisions are the same with regard to the structure or uncertainty present in the decision-making environment. Normally, as you progress through the process, you will become more certain and the structure of the decision will become clearer. To make the best decision you can, you need to carefully consider the quality of the data, information, and knowledge and put it into proper context. During the analysis stage, you sort, transform, and organize the data to define options. Of course, in this sense, decisions are just like computer programs: garbage in, garbage out! The quality of the final output of this process (the decision or solution) will likely be based on the quality of the inputs (the information and analysis you create).

Once you have narrowed the options to a final decision, you communicate the conclusion and implement the decision. Obviously, the result will either be a success or a failure. Either of these contributes learning to the process for the next time. You can use this learning to either tackle a new

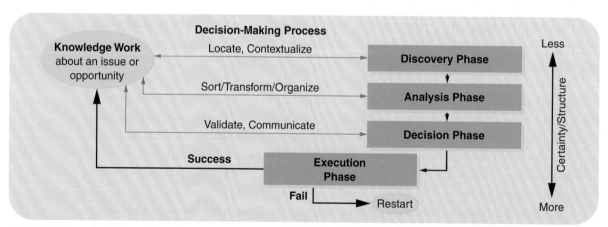

FIGURE 3.4 To make the best decision possible, you should carefully consider the amount of decision certainty and structure, as well as assess the quality of data, information, and knowledge available in the context of the decision to be made.

problem or refine your understanding of the current problem, and repeat the process to make a new decision about a new course of action.

Figure 3.4 illustrates the process of decision making. Let's now discuss the larger context of problem solving, for which decision making is one aspect, and illustrate some tools that assist in the analysis of alternatives. The purpose of decision making is often to solve a problem. In general, a **problem** exists when you find yourself in a situation that fails to meet your goals, needs, or expectations. Further, that current situation often results from a past series of events, or lack of events, that did or did not happen. For example, if you studied and failed to make the desired grade on a test, it's a problem. But it's a different problem if you didn't study at all and failed to make the desired grade on the test. So the first step in problem solving is not only recognizing that a problem exists, but why it exists. You can then take effective and efficient steps to change the situation, to more productively meet your needs and goals. Problems can also be defined as opportunities or challenges. For example, Larry Page and Sergey Brin, frustrated with trying to find information on the Web, thought about how to overcome this problem and help others, too. Who are Page and Brin? They are the co-founders and chief executives of Google.

Fixing some problems is relatively easy, such as using an umbrella to stay dry if it's raining. However, resolving most business problems poses a real challenge. How do business professionals reliably and consistently fix problems? They engage in problem solving. **Problem solving** refers to a series of steps or a process (logical sequence of activities) taken in response to some event or activity.

Let's return to thinking about how you selected a university or college to help you understand the problem-solving process. In choosing a school, you had some ideas about what major to select, but now it is time to get more specific. Assume that you came up with three potential majors: (1) accounting, (2) finance, and (3) management information systems (MIS). In order to solve this problem and make a decision, you must engage in the knowledge activity of analysis. A problem-solving tool known as selection criteria can help. **Selection criteria** are the factors that you think are important and relevant to solving the problem. For example, think about your interests or what you like or don't like to study. You might include your estimate of success in the course work required for the majors as criteria. Or perhaps you view your major as a stepping-stone to your future career. If so, your criteria may include future job opportunities, opportunities for travel and advancement, starting salaries, or lifelong earnings potential, for example. Table 3.3 illustrates this method. For your problem, you might enter the possible solutions in the rows of a spreadsheet, and the criteria for choosing in the columns. You can then score each possible solution by evaluating it against each criterion according to some scale [e.g., 1 (low) to 5 (high)]. You may also want to add some kind of emphasis or weighting on one or more of the criteria. For example, ask yourself if it is more important to study what you are interested in or to earn the highest possible starting salary upon graduation. In a sense, before you can rank your solutions, you may have to rank your criteria.

Table 3.3 Scoring Alternatives Based on Criteria					
Criteria Scale: 1 (low) to 5 (high)	Personal Interest	Estimated Starting Salaries	Forecasted Job Demand	Friends in Major	Total Score
Accounting	4	4 [$41,000.00]	5	3	16
Finance	5	3 [$40,000.00]	4	5	17
Management Information Systems	4	5 [$44,000.00]	5	5	19

Another approach might help you develop useful and relevant criteria. Of the proposed solutions, think about the positive benefits or characteristics of each. As you list these characteristics, consider which ones you view as more important than the others and weight them accordingly. This method may help you develop criteria for choosing which solution to develop further.

Which criteria you apply to your decision greatly affects the data that you gathered. For example, if you select future job opportunities as a criterion, but you didn't gather the data, it will be difficult to use this as a meaningful criterion. You will then need to find more data about your proposed solutions to complete your analysis.

At the end of this analysis, you will have several alternative solutions to choose from. Take the time to think creatively to generate as many viable solutions as possible. Much of the data you have gathered will probably pertain to one or two majors in which you were already interested. However, there may be some surprises as well. Maybe you visited your university or college's career or student centre and took an aptitude test. You can use the results as data to generate alternative majors. Remember, as you generate alternative solutions or choices, you may need to gather more data. You will choose the best solution from those available to solve the problem, meet the challenge, or capitalize on the opportunity.

Is it just that easy? No, not usually. Decision making is often more complex and uncertain. One choice may not be clearly better than the others, or you may need to combine elements from one or more solutions to create a more comprehensive one. Or, if none of the proposed solutions seems workable, you may need to go back and generate more alternatives.

As a business professional, you will often repeat the problem-solving process. Furthermore, each stage of this process may require individual decisions that use the decision-making process. To assist you further in making decisions and solving problems, you could use a framework or model, such as IADD (Investigate, Analyze, Do, Decide) or others available on the Web. These models are quite helpful in structuring data and information to assist in decision making and problem solving.

The best organizations use their most precious resource (people) to focus on their most strategic and urgent priorities (their goals). These resources gather data and information, analyze it, and identify problems or opportunities. Problems may include inefficient processes in need of reengineering or faulty outputs that are reducing profits. Opportunities may be innovative product improvements or new market opportunities. Whether problem or opportunity, business leaders must engage in problem solving and decision making to take action. In the organizational context there are three levels of decisions. At its most fundamental level, organizations make **tactical decisions** every single hour of every single work day. They are usually made by the person doing the actual work, based on appropriate guidelines or policies. Systems may or may not be useful or required at this level. For instance, if you are a shipping clerk, you might make choices about which form of shipping to use, which carriers or companies to call, and so on. While these decisions may be informed by information such as what rate was charged for shipping on the invoice, the promised delivery date, or other information contained in a system somewhere, the decisions are not complex or multi-faceted.

At the next level we have **operational decisions**. Continuing with the same example, an organization might do some overall analysis of shipping patterns, perhaps informed by systems that report on these trends by vendor, product type, date ranges, or similar analysis. The organization might determine that it could save money by implementing a preferred vendor program that focuses on volume in return for discounts on rates or improved service commitments to customers. Since this involves a more global perspective, perhaps across the entire supply chain and using data from all parts of the shipping department, it is more likely that a manager would look at this issue and make decisions about it rather than an individual shipper. Again, as decision making takes on more impact at a higher organizational level, you see the value of having data and information on overall shipping patterns and trends available to that manager as these decisions are considered.

At the highest level of the organization, executives likely face **strategic decisions** such as whether or not to continue even offering the product in a shippable form. Instead, the organization could move to a self-serve model where the customer interacts directly with the organization's systems, makes product choices and payments, determines how they are to be shipped, and so on. This might involve significant investment in new systems, new ways of marketing the product, changes in internal business processes, and/or adjustments to staffing levels and functions. This is clearly a decision involving much more than just the shipping department. Here again, systems could be used to model various scenarios, calculate and examine possible impacts on the company's P&L, perform competitive analysis, do detailed customer analysis to pick candidates to invite to a focus group, and so on. At this level, data and information are not only critical, they may also come from both internal and external sources, and might include actual data along with modelling, forecasting, or other intelligent extensions of data to improve decision making. Building and using these systems is more complex than tactical or operational systems, and requires a significant understanding not only of IT, but perhaps of statistical analysis, data modelling, and other complex skill sets, in addition to an obvious understanding of database and related kinds of technologies.

In an organization, IT plays a key role in problem solving and decision making by providing critical information and organizing it to increase the quality of the information. IT may also be part of the solution. For example, IT can automate the less useful and more routine tasks to free up resources to concentrate on the priorities. These activities make organizations successful, and also make them great places to work. If your problem or opportunity is complex, you will have an abundance of data to organize, classify, store, and so on. Fortunately, databases and database management systems (DBMS) software are excellent tools for organizing and storing data. Further, certain types of DBMS can even harness the power of the relationships that exist in the data (we discuss how in Tech Guide C). Once you have organized and stored the data and relationships, you can use other tools to manipulate the data. For example, you can ask questions of your database through structured query language (SQL) queries, or use special software programs to explore the data to discover previously undiscovered relationships and patterns. We cover the detailed aspects of databases and data management in the following sections, as well as organizational tools that facilitate business intelligence.

Quick Test

1. Fill in the blank. The level of uncertainty faced by a decision maker can be reduced through the discovery and use of _____.

2. True or False. The more you make decisions, the better you will be at anticipating the consequences of making them.

3. The need for data that are from a trusted source determines if the data are _____.
   a. accurate
   b. complete
   c. timely
   d. reliable

Answers: 1. information; 2. True; 3. d

■ DATABASES: THE PRIMARY DATA STORAGE FOR ORGANIZATIONS

From our previous discussion on data, information, and knowledge, it is clear that data are important—and often abundant! How do businesses keep track of all these data so that they are readily available and can be found when needed? All business information systems rely on the use and storage of data. The primary technology used to store, manage, and allow efficient access to data is the database.

A **database** consists of interrelated data that are stored in files and organized so that computer programs can quickly and easily access specific pieces of data. For example, a bank stores information about its customers in a database. The bank can then access and update the database as customers make deposits and withdrawals at an ATM. A **database management system (DBMS)** is a collection of software that allows users to create and work with a database. That same bank uses a DBMS to obtain and print a customer's monthly bank statement. Together, a database and a DBMS make up a *database system.* As Figure 3.5 shows, the DBMS controls access to the data stored in the database.

The people who create and manage the database, sometimes known as *database administrators (DBA),* use the tools in the DBMS to do their work. Other business professionals who need to access the database typically do so through other application software that can connect to the DBMS and query the databases that it manages.

In this section, we briefly introduce databases. As a business professional, you will use business applications that depend on databases. Some of the more prevalent databases used today are provided by Oracle, Microsoft, and IBM. You may work closely with other business professionals who are certified as database administrators for Oracle databases and/or Microsoft SQL servers. For more in-depth coverage, including a more thorough discussion of how to design and model a database, see Tech Guide C.

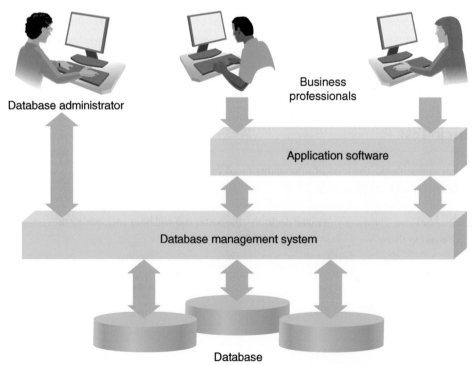

FIGURE 3.5 The DBMS controls access to the data stored in the database.

The Data Hierarchy

To organize data in a database, most users rely on the **data hierarchy.** As Figure 3.6 shows, the data hierarchy organizes stored data in increasing levels of complexity. At the lowest level, the data hierarchy stores all data using electronic bits that can be 1 (on) or 0 (off). A specific combination of bits represents each data *character.* The exact number of bits needed for a character depends on the type of data and the encoding scheme. For example, the ASCII encoding scheme uses eight bits (one byte) to store a letter of the alphabet. Unicode stores the same letter using 16 bits (two bytes). A combination of characters representing a data item, such as a name or a price, is known as a *field.*

The next higher level of the data hierarchy stores collections of fields known as *records.* By using a record that includes fields holding values for FirstName, LastName, Gender, and Age, you find that Bob Smith is a customer who is a 21-year-old male (Figure 3.6). At the next level up, the data hierarchy assembles records into a collection called a *table* or *file.* For instance, at this level you would find a set of records listing the age and gender of all customers, not just Bob Smith. Finally, the top level compiles the organized collection of files into a database.

Using a database system to organize data provides several advantages:

- The organization of the data is independent of any one software application. This allows all applications to access the data in a standard manner.
- The organization of the data reduces data redundancy; a DBMS may need to store only one record of data for a particular product.
- The DBMS can include features for maintaining the quality of the data, handling security, and synchronizing access by simultaneous users.
- The database system allows for capabilities such as improved data access, allowing different views of the data for different users, and report generation.

These advantages improve the accuracy of the data stored (*data integrity*), as well as increase its use.

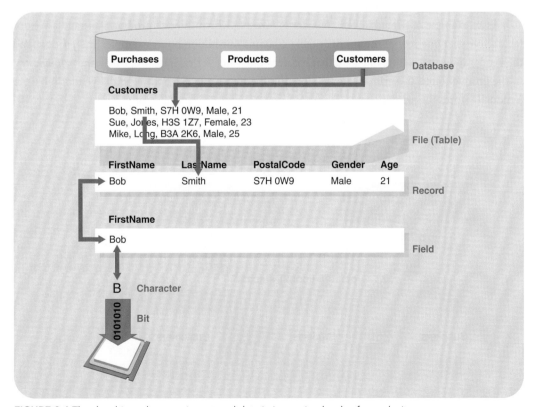

FIGURE 3.6 The data hierarchy organizes stored data in increasing levels of complexity.

Relational Data Model

In the early 1970s, Dr. E. F. Codd developed a method for logically organizing data in a database that was independent of the method used to physically store the data. In this method, known as the **relational data model**, databases store information about entities, such as suppliers and products for a retailer, and the relationships between those entities. Databases then use these defined relationships to store the connections between the entities, such as which suppliers provide which products.

The relational data model has since become the standard way of storing large amounts of data. Researchers at various universities and business organizations (notably University of California at Berkeley and IBM) developed systems based on Codd's relational model. These systems are now known as **relational database management systems (RDBMS).** Figure 3.7 shows a typical relational database management system.

The relational data model stores data in one or more tables, corresponding to entities. Tables consist of records, represented by the rows of the table. The records generally hold data about a single instance of an entity. For example, a single record might store contact information for a single supplier. A record, in turn, consists of one or more fields that hold data about an *instance* of an entity. Because the data values in the fields often describe an instance of an entity, the fields are sometimes called *attributes*. The columns of the table represent the fields of all the records.

For example, suppose that a company decides to create a relational database to store data about its products. It begins by identifying the generic category "Product" as an entity. The company then determines that an *instance* of the product category is a set of data about a specific product, such as "hiking boots." The attributes of the hiking boots product include ItemCode (HB), ItemName (hiking boots), RetailPrice ($110.00), and ItemCost ($50.00). Because the company wants to store data about the same attributes for all of the products that it sells, its product table will include fields for ItemCode, ItemName, RetailPrice, and ItemCost. (You can imagine that the field names are the column headings for a table.) When the company fills in a row in the table with values for the attributes—HB, hiking boots, etc.—then it has a data record for a product.

As an example of related tables, consider Figure 3.8, which shows a product table and a vendor table. Note that one row of the product table contains our hiking boots example. The product and the vendor tables each store one field that has a unique value for each record, called the *primary key*. In the product table, the primary key is stored in the ItemCode field, while in the vendor table the VendorID stores the primary key.

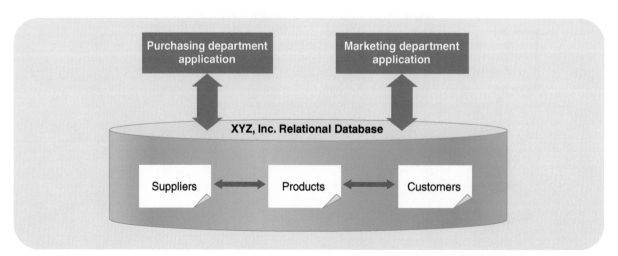

FIGURE 3.7 The relational data model has become the most popular method for organizing and storing large amounts of data.

ItemCode	ItemName	RetailPrice	ItemCost	VendorID
AM	Air Mattress	$100.00	$60.00	SFJ
BP	Backpack	$165.00	$80.00	BRU
CC	Child Carrier	$175.00	$85.00	SFJ
CK	Cookset	$50.00	$32.50	DOL
DP	Day Pack	$105.00	$60.00	WED
GC	Ground Cover	$20.00	$12.50	FEU
HB	Hiking Boots	$110.00	$50.00	DOL
HH	Heater	$75.00	$44.00	BRU
PL	Propane Lantern	$35.00	$20.00	FEU
SB	Sleeping Bag	$100.00	$45.00	DOL
TT	Tent	$385.00	$110.00	WED

Product Table

VendorID	VendorName	Contact	PhoneNumber	Discount
BRU	Backpacks R' U	Nick Estelle	415-555-8328	5.00%
DOL	Doleman Manuf	George Burdell	770-555-4505	6.00%
FEU	Feuters Campin	Chris Patrick	406-555-2103	4.00%
SFJ	SFJ Enterprises	Ashley Hyatt	239-555-0308	5.00%
WED	Waters End	Todd Keegan	715-555-1212	7.00%

Vendor Table

FIGURE 3.8 In this example of related tables, note that the VendorID field (stored as the primary key for the vendor table and the foreign key for the product table) provides the link between the two tables.

Backpack Profit SQL Statement:

```
SELECT Product.ItemName, Vendor.VendorName, Vendor.Discount, [RetailPrice]-[OurCost] AS Profit
FROM Product, Vendor
WHERE Product.VendorID = Vendor.VendorID
AND (((Vendor.VendorID)="BRU"));
```

Backpack Profit Query Result:

ItemName	VendorName	Discount	Profit
DayTripper	BackPacks R' Us	5.00%	$85.00
Mountaineer	BackPacks R' Us	5.00%	$31.00

FIGURE 3.9 Organizations often use SQL queries, similar to the one shown here, to obtain specific information from their databases, such as profit calculations. This example shows that of the two items BackPacks R' Us supply, the DayTripper provides more profit per item. Another query can be done to combine this profit information with sales information.

Note that the product table also contains a VendorID field. To relate the data in one table to data in the other table, the company can simply use the VendorID as a reference. By matching a VendorID stored in the product table with the unique record that it references in the vendor table, the company can pull data about the product and vendor from both tables. In our hiking boots example, you can see that VendorID DOL provides hiking boots, cooksets, and sleeping bags. This code relates to the vendor table that provides all of the details about vendor DOL. When a second table uses the primary key of one table as a reference field in its table, the field is called a *foreign key*.

Of course, designing and storing data in a database is just the beginning. The power of a database comes from how organizations use it. The relational database model provides powerful, standardized methods for maintaining and working with the data. The primary method for accessing and using data in an RDBMS is a query. A *query* is a method for asking a question of a database. For the relational database model, a standard and popular language called Structured Query Language (SQL) (often pronounced "sequel" for short) provides general rules for formulating the queries on relational databases.

For example, Figure 3.9 shows standard SQL queries, which use keywords in capital letters (e.g., "WHERE") and refer to the data by field names and the tables in which they reside (e.g., Product. VendorID). This example also shows that a query can produce values (Profit) that it calculates based on data stored in the database. With one or more SQL queries as a basis, organizations can create forms and reports to simplify data entry and reporting for their employees. A more detailed discussion of SQL is contained in Tech Guide C.

Designing a Relational Database

The following sections discuss the most common methods of designing a relational database.

Data Modelling Data modelling is the process of analyzing the data required by the processes of an organization to support it both operationally and strategically. As an example, a business cannot determine what sales tax it needs to remit to the government if it has not gathered this information at the point of sale of its products or services. Therefore, that piece of data must be collected, stored, and able to be reported on when required.

Data models are often the first, high-level step in designing a relational database; in this process the required data is defined and any integration with other systems is determined. Typical products of data modelling include a data dictionary, which documents the origin, format, and meaning of the data, and other more detailed models such as an entity relationship diagram and a data flow diagram.

Entity-Relationship Diagram and Logical Data Model The **entity-relationship diagram (ERD)** and the **logical data model (LDM)** are the two most commonly used models for designing the organization of a relational database. The LDM is a representation of an organization's data, which focuses on documenting the business requirements aspect of data.

The ERD is the first step in logical data modelling and provides a high-level view of the logical data model. The ERD indicates the entities and relationships for the data that the IS will store (see Tech Guide C for a more detailed discussion of ERDs). The logical data model then translates the ERD into a diagram of the tables in the database. Figure 3.10 shows a partial ERD and logical data model for an electronic voting system.

In practice, the ERD and LDM are not separate, defined steps, but are done at the same time with the result being the detailed logical data model. Once a logical model is approved, a physical model of the database can be constructed that will describe all of the technical aspects of the database.

Data Flow Diagram As the name implies, a **data flow diagram (DFD)** is a traditional IS model that depicts how data move or flow through a system (see Figure 3.11): (1) external entities (boxes) that send input or receive output from the system; (2) processes (boxes with rounded corners) that show activities that move or transform data; (3) data stores (open-ended boxes) that usually correspond to tables in the data model; and (4) data flows (arrows) that connect the components.

Figure 3.11 shows a partial DFD for an electronic voting system. In this figure, one external entity, the voter, interacts with the system. Three data stores (tables from the logical data model in Figure 3.10) indicate the need to store various data items. The boxes with rounded corners represent four processes, each of which transforms the inputs into outputs. The DFD uniquely identifies all of the components with a number. At this point the model does not specify how to implement the components. For example, to authenticate a voter, the system may rely on an automated process developed by programmers during the construction phase of the System Development Lifecycle (SDLC), which we discuss in Chapter 6, or a manual process (e.g., an election volunteer).

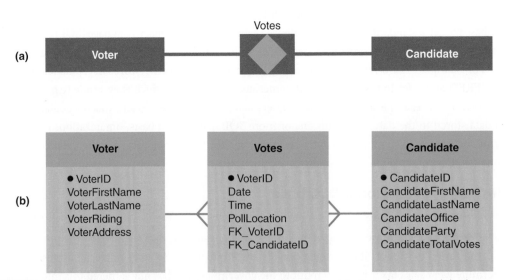

FIGURE 3.10 The two most commonly used models for designing the organization of a relational database are the (a) ERD, which here depicts a one-to-one relationship between a voter and a candidate, and (b) logical data model, used here to represent an e-voting system.

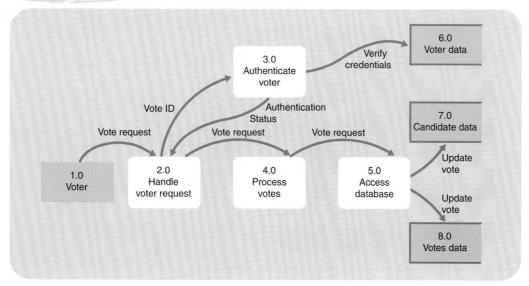

FIGURE 3.11 A DFD depicts how data move through a system; the partial DFD shown here provides more details building on the ERD and logical data model shown in Figure 3.10.

Storing and Accessing Data, Information, and Knowledge

As it turns out, databases are not the only, nor necessarily the best, form of storage for all business needs. For example, to analyze how a product change might affect sales, a marketing manager may need to access several databases. Or, the manager who needs to examine historical sales data may discover that the database does not include this information. In this section, we look at other ways that IT can support the organization, storage, and sharing of data.

Data Warehouses A **data warehouse** is a means of storing and managing data for information access, typically composed of data from one or more transaction databases. It thus consists of *transaction* data, cleaned and restructured to fit the data warehouse model and to support queries, summary reports, and analysis. For example, an organization like the Royal Bank of Canada (RBC) or the Bank of America would rely on a data warehouse to incorporate data from its many locations and business units, such as retail banking, investments, and mortgages. RBC or Bank of America would use the data warehouse to provide insight into customer behaviour, manage risks in its lending portfolios, and prevent fraud, among other things. Table 3.4 lists several differences between database and data warehouse technology.

Table 3.4	A Comparison of Database and Data Warehouse Technology	
	Database	**Data Warehouse**
Supported Activity	Operational (transactions)	Analytical (knowledge work)
Response Time	Fast response time (seconds)	Can be slower (minutes, sometimes hours)
Age of Data	Mostly data for current transactions	A lot of historical data
Scope	May support a limited area within the organization	Should provide view of entire organization
Data Variability	Mostly dynamic, changes often	Mostly static, infrequent changes
Source	Transactions from operational domain; business rules	Combined from multiple sources (including operational databases)
Data Model	Based on business rules of operational application	Aligns with overall business structure

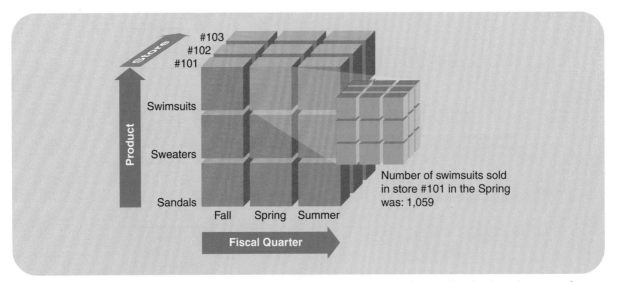

FIGURE 3.12 Data warehouses often provide support for organizing multidimensional data, such as the three dimensions for retail sales shown here, which allows businesses to more easily identify trends.

Because data warehouses are very large (in terms of the amount of data stored) compared with the typical database, they work with tools that allow users to more easily deal with these vast amounts of data. For example, a data warehouse may provide information to an area-specific data mart such as a marketing data mart. A **data mart** extracts and reorganizes subject-area-specific data to allow business professionals to focus on a specific subject area.

Data warehouses often provide support for organizing multidimensional data, which are based on two or more characteristics (dimensions), such as time and place. Organizing data in this way allows businesses to more easily identify trends. For example, Figure 3.12 shows data with three dimensions for retail sales. The company can then organize each data item according to three dimensions: store, product, and fiscal quarter. Retrieving data organized in this way is sometimes referred to as *slicing-and-dicing*; that is, the process of cutting off portions of the data until the needed information is obtained.

As Figure 3.13 shows, businesses access and use a data warehouse for four main reasons:

1. *Automatic production of standard reports and queries:* When users need a particular report, they simply view the report that the data warehouse already generated rather than creating one.
2. *Queries against summary or detailed data:* Data warehouse tools include simple query tools like those used with databases. Queries can involve summarized data or can be drawn against stores of detailed data.
3. *Data mining in detailed data:* **Data mining** includes a set of techniques for finding trends and patterns in large sets of data. Data mining tools can incorporate advanced technologies such as artificial intelligence. Some provide aids for *data visualization*—organizing and presenting data in ways that allow humans to better spot and analyze the patterns.
4. *Interfacing with other applications and data stores:* A company will often connect a data warehouse to applications that use it as the source of data. A data warehouse may feed data to other data warehouses, data marts, or application programs.

Regardless of how a business uses it, maintaining a data warehouse (or DBMS) can be vital to a company's success. This is why the focus of disaster recovery and business continuity planning is on the data. What might happen to a business if it loses all of its data about products, vendors, or customers?

Once captured and stored, businesses process data to create information, which they in turn use for decision making and problem solving. Although a business can always develop information

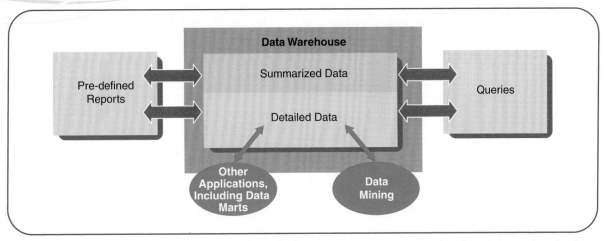

FIGURE 3.13 Businesses access and use a data warehouse for four main reasons: reports, queries, data mining, and applications.

"on the fly" with queries to a database, this is not always practical. In addition, an organization may periodically need the same information. Therefore, rather than re-creating information from a database and storing that information as-is, using a management information system, which we discuss below, is often more efficient.

Quick Test

1. A _____ is a collection of interrelated data that are stored in files and organized so that computer programs can quickly and easily access specific pieces of data.
   a. database
   b. DBMS
   c. program
   d. none of the above

2. A _____ key is a field that has unique values for each record in a relational table.
   a. primary
   b. foreign
   c. data
   d. relational

3. A _____ combines large amounts of data from many sources, including databases, to provide support for analysis.
   a. data mart
   b. data warehouse
   c. relational database
   d. file system

Answers: 1. a; 2. a; 3. b

■ BUSINESS INTELLIGENCE

Business intelligence (BI) is a process for gaining competitive advantage through the intelligent use of data and information in decision making. BI is, therefore, a key part of a corporate information strategy. It enables business leaders to make better decisions, which often translate into increased profitability. BI also plays a role in identifying and solving problems that may not have been uncovered otherwise.

Table 3.5	The Stages of Business Intelligence
Stage	**Description**
1. Data sourcing (Acquisition)	Mining data and information from text documents, databases, images, media files, and web pages
2. Data analysis (Organization)	Producing useful knowledge from the collected data and information, using tools such as data mining and text/image analysis techniques
3. Situation awareness (Analysis)	Culling and relating the useful facts and knowledge, while filtering out irrelevant data
4. Risk assessment (Analysis)	Identifying decision options and evaluating them based on expectations of risk and reward
5. Decision support (Decision)	Using interactive software tools to identify and select intelligent decisions and strategies

Using IT to Support Business Intelligence

To enable businesses to reach intelligent decisions, data and information must go through several stages. Table 3.5 lists the stages of business intelligence and how IT assists at every step. In the first stage, organizations get data, often from multiple sources. These myriad data from various sources are then analyzed. Analysis may include looking for trends, combining and summarizing data from different sources, or filling in gaps by predicting missing information. Next, to ensure relevant analysis, business professionals must match key items to information needs and filter out irrelevant items. With relevant data in hand, an organization can then evaluate plausible decision or action options. To do this, it may assess risks, compare costs and benefits, and weigh one option against another. Do you notice how similar these stages are to the knowledge work activities we discussed earlier?

Figure 3.14 presents a hierarchical model of how IT supports these business intelligence stages, with each stage building on and being dependent on the other.

For example, it is quite unlikely that an organization would have a data warehouse without operational data, such as transactions, being collected and stored. The transaction processing systems (TPS)—which we discuss in detail in Chapter 4—at the base of the pyramid represent the primary source of data from business operations. This is data that is created, for example, when a sale occurs in a retail outlet. Businesses then store and organize the data in databases and, at times, data warehouses, which constitutes the next level in the hierarchy. Once the data is stored, specialized BI and online analytic processing (OLAP) systems can help analyze, synthesize, and create knowledge. And finally, at the top of the pyramid, management uses the created knowledge to guide its actions, decision making, and problem solving.

The BI systems in the third level of the pyramid may include specific systems that are important to organizational decision making and problem solving. These systems include decision support systems (DSS), which allow rapid and creative knowledge creation by decision makers, knowledge management (KM) systems, which facilitate access and distribution of

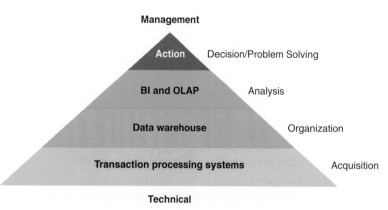

FIGURE 3.14 The business intelligence pyramid.

Table 3.6	Types of DSS	
Type of DSS	**Description**	**Examples**
Communications-driven DSS	Focuses on communications, collaboration, and shared decision making	Conferencing tools; online bulletin boards and chat facilities; email; meeting support applications
Data-driven DSS	Emphasizes access to and manipulation of internal company data, and sometimes external data	Executive information systems (EIS); geographic information systems (GIS); OLAP-enabled data warehouses
Document-driven DSS	Focuses on retrieval and management of unstructured documents	Document management systems (DMS); search services; tools for working with oral, written, and video documents
Knowledge-driven DSS	Provides special problem-solving tools that help decision making by suggesting or recommending actions to users	Expert systems (ES); artificial intelligence applications; data mining tools
Model-driven DSS	Emphasizes access to and manipulation of a model	Financial, statistical, optimization, and simulation models

knowledge throughout an organization, and/or management information systems (MIS), which store management reports.

Decision Support Systems Decision support systems (DSS) help businesses use communications technologies, knowledge, and models to organize and access data to perform decision-making activities. There are five types of DSS, shown in Table 3.6, each of which has a specific decision-making focus. Although businesses rely on all these types of DSS, model-driven DSS continue to make the most significant contribution to decision making.

Model-driven DSS provide tools that enable analysts to create and work with models, including the following:

- *Financial models:* use financial mathematical models and financial data to support financial decision making
- *Statistical models:* use statistics and probability to describe or forecast possible scenarios
- *Optimization models:* incorporate relatively certain data into a mathematical model of a situation; solving the model helps to find the "best" solution
- *Simulation modelling:* a technique for conducting experiments that test possible outcomes resulting from a quantitative model of a system

Model-driven DSS use data and parameters to help decision makers analyze a situation, but they are not usually data-intensive. Instead, these systems often include smaller databases, with data that may be culled from the larger data stores of the organization. They often incorporate innovative user interfaces that provide analysts with graphic views of their models. Organizations often combine model-driven DSS with other types of DSS to form hybrid systems.

Knowledge Management Systems Of the three informational resources—data, information, and knowledge—knowledge is the most difficult to store and share. Why? Recall that earlier in this chapter, we discussed two types of knowledge: explicit and tacit. *Explicit knowledge* includes anything that

Table 3.7	Collaborative Software Categories
Communication tools	• Facilitate the sharing of information and data with tools that enable people to send messages, documents, files, and data between each other (e.g., email, text messaging, voice mail, and Web publishing)
Conferencing tools	• Provide a more interactive facility for the sharing of information • At a minimum, can provide real-time text discussions and a common "whiteboard" that each participant can edit • Can also enable voice and/or video using special equipment or computer networks • Some organizations build special facilities for conferencing supported by these tools
Collaborative management tools	• Can help to manage and facilitate the activities of a team (e.g., electronic calendars or scheduling events and automatically notifying participants) • Can provide shared workspaces to store and share work products that group members may modify • May overlap with project management systems to keep the group aware of a project's status

can be written down, stored, and codified (e.g., business plans, patents and trademarks, and market research). *Tacit knowledge* includes the know-how that people have through learning and experience, which is difficult to write down and share. Tacit knowledge, while important to an organization, represents a major challenge to an organization's **knowledge management (KM)**; that is, how the company recognizes, generates, manages, and shares knowledge.

To support tacit knowledge, knowledge management systems often rely on collaborative software, which supports teamwork with technologies that enable communication and sharing of data and information. This software category, also known as **groupware**, can be a simple communication tool like email, or it can be more complex, providing shared workspaces to store common files and tools for conferencing and meeting support. Table 3.7 summarizes how groupware is divided into three levels of support.

The benefits of knowledge management are often difficult to calculate. Some benefits directly increase revenue or reduce costs, while others do not. To derive the most benefits from knowledge management, clear business goals must drive the process for sharing relevant knowledge throughout the organization. For example, an effective KM program can allow business professionals to streamline the value chain. This in turn will improve customer service and boost revenues as the organization gets products and services out to the market faster. Further, an effective KM program can increase employee morale. Employees often feel greater appreciation when organizations recognize the value and use of their knowledge. They are then often more eager to share their information and ideas, which can foster innovation throughout the organizations.

Management Information and Document Management Systems In the early days of information systems, businesses typically developed systems known as **management information systems (MIS)** specifically to meet the need of storing processed transaction data as reports for managers. These early systems were often rudimentary and produced large volumes of information because of their limited ability to sort and process data to specific user needs. MIS typically generate three types of reports:

1. *Periodic reports,* such as a company's annual financial statements or monthly sales reports, which are updated and generated after a specific time period has passed.
2. *Exception reports,* which monitor when, and perhaps why, exceptions occur of key values, defined as critical to the operation.
3. *Demand reports,* which are generated based on user requests. Many systems also include a library of such reports from which a user could choose.

As organizations and systems capability both progressed, many businesses began to create specific systems to serve specific needs. One example is **executive information systems (EIS)**, designed to provide summary information about business performance to those making higher-level strategic decisions. This often involved creating "views" of data about business trends that gave rise to graphic displays of information.

Similarly, organizations began to recognize data management needs that revolved around business documents (as distinct from business information). These systems are known as **document management systems (DMS)**. A DMS enters, tracks, routes, and processes the many documents used in an organization, including but not limited to the three types of reports just discussed. A DMS can create the documents electronically or convert them to electronic form using *imaging technology.* Imaging technology includes scanners like those discussed in Chapter 2, as well as special software that can recognize printed characters and convert them to specific data formats to work with application software.

Businesses can use DMS to support workflow systems by managing the storage and routing of documents. They can also use DMS to maintain large archives of forms and documents in a much more efficient and flexible manner than with traditional paper documents.

Business Intelligence Tools

There are a number of business intelligence tools in the marketplace. Some are independent, stand-alone applications that work with any organizational data mart or warehouse. Others come as part of an enterprise resource planning (ERP) system, which we discuss in Chapter 4. A company called SAS has been a leading provider of business intelligence tools since 1976 and offers several products that contribute to business intelligence. Their core BI offerings allow companies to integrate and visualize organizational data. They also offer analytics products that help organizations further analyze the data and enable forecasting. SAS and other business intelligence tools provide users with a very simple interface to build their own queries, models, and dashboards. Essentially, users drag and drop data elements or make drop-down list selections to build their data sets. Once finished this set-up step, they may end up with an information dashboard that looks something like the example in Figure 3.15.

On SAS's website, *www.sas.com*, you will find several success stories, including one for Passport Canada. Passport Canada used SAS tools to analyze and predict demand for passport applications. This project came about in 2007 when Passport Canada was taken by surprise with the increase in passport applications as a result of the United States requiring Canadians to use passports to enter their country. By using predictive models based on combined historical data and external data, Passport Canada can now predict, plan, and act before it experiences increases in passport demand. This has now enabled it to consistently provide passports within 10 business days.[2]

A more recent success story is that of Expedia. Expedia is an online travel provider that allows customers to book flights, hotels, cars, or entire vacation packages. Expedia used SAS tools to

---

2. *www.sas.com/success/Passport-Canada.html*, retrieved December 19, 2011.

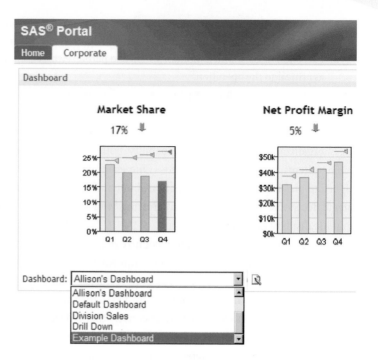

FIGURE 3.15 Example SAS®
dashboard.[3]

analyze vast amounts of data to discover innovative ways of increasing customer satisfaction and loyalty, while increasing annual gross bookings and revenue. Expedia can now identify what marketing channels influence and drive revenue conversions on the site; optimize its marketing spend by channel; increase customer lifetime value; improve the overall experience for customers while on the site; and discover usability glitches that can lead to lost revenues. Joe Megibow, Vice President and General Manager of Expedia US, said "SAS inspires creative analysis. We may know what the problems are or know where we've done something wrong, but SAS helps us figure out how to do things better. We actually have a backlog of opportunities from research that we've done. We've been able to capitalize on SAS's experience in solving so many different problems in so many industries. This is an unsung asset of SAS that helps creative thinkers apply solutions in new ways to solve challenging problems."[4]

Figure 3.15 shows one example of a dashboard. A dashboard is a common way of organizing and presenting BI or related information sources that we discuss below. The purpose of a **dashboard** is to provide critical information to business users at a glance. Often these mechanisms link an organization's strategy to a series of clear measures or indicators that they monitor to determine if they are on-track or not in executing this strategy. For example, Figure 3.16 shows an example of a sales dashboard. This dashboard is very likely the result of combining and storing several data sources, applying calculations, and then feeding the results into this easy-to-view interface that, at a glance, indicates if sales and market share targets are being achieved.

Dashboards can be used for many purposes, including tracking personal finances. In fact, Dashboard Insight (*www.dashboardinsight.com*) awarded Dashboard of the Year in 2011 to a personal finance dashboard that allows users to track spending versus saving targets.[5]

3. Copyright 2009, SAS Institute Inc., Cary, NC, USA. All Rights Reserved. Reproduced with permission of SAS Institute Inc., Cary, NC. *http://support.sas.com/documentation/cdl/en/bidbrdug/61856/PDF/default/bidbrdug.pdf*, retrieved December 20, 2011.

4. *www.sas.com/success/expedia_travel.html*, retrieved December 19, 2011.

5. You can view the winning dashboard by going to *www.dashboardinsight.com/dashboards/screenshots/dashboard-design-contest-personal-finance-dashboard.aspx*.

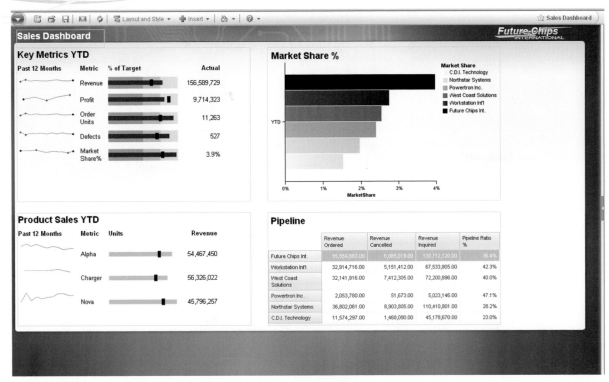

FIGURE 3.16 Example of a sales dashboard.[6]

A balanced scorecard is a very popular type of dashboard used by many businesses. The **balanced scorecard** was originally developed by Drs. Robert Kaplan (Harvard Business School) and David Norton as a performance measurement framework that added strategic non-financial performance measures to traditional financial metrics to give managers and executives a more "balanced" view of organizational performance.[7] The balanced scorecard examines vision and strategy in the context of financial, customer, internal business process, and learning and growth perspectives, each equally weighted (see Figure 3.17). Each perspective has objectives, measures, targets, and initiatives. Most important from a dashboard perspective are the measures and targets. If you go to *http://ppsblog.members.winisp.net/Img/StrategyMapsinPerformancePointServer_C0B0/image_thumb.png* you can view a sample of how a simple dashboard based on an organization's balanced score card might look. The actual column shows the measures recorded numerically, while the colour target indicators show green if on target, yellow if borderline on target, or red if not on target. Upon viewing this dashboard, management can take immediate action on those measures that are red or yellow.

The technology behind dashboards has recently been enhanced to provide business users with visual analytics. **Visual analytics** extends a dashboard by enabling a user to examine data in-depth, reorganize it dynamically, and change information parameters to do "what-if analysis." Figure 3.18 extends a personal finance dashboard to show related visual analysis of expenses. You can see how

6. *http://www.performance-ideas.com/2011/10/02/cognos10-dashboarding*.

7. *www.balancedscorecard.org/BSCResources/AbouttheBalancedScorecard/tabid/55/Default.aspx*, retrieved December 24, 2011.

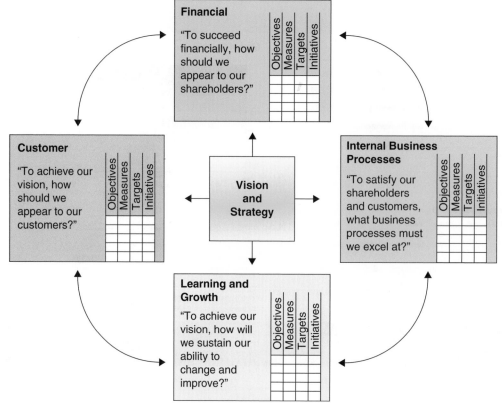

FIGURE 3.17 The balanced scorecard framework.[8]

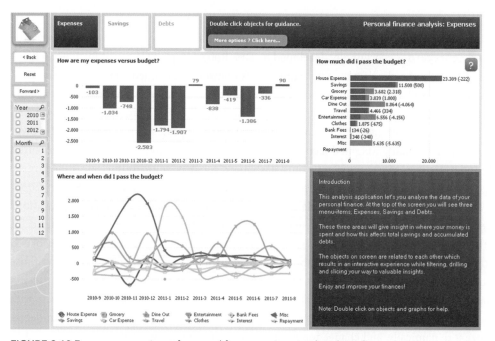

FIGURE 3.18 Expense comparison of personal finances using visual analytics.[9]

---

8. Adapted from Robert S. Kaplan and David P. Norton, "Using the Balanced Scorecard as a Strategic Management System," *Harvard Business Review* (January–February 1996): 76. Courtesy of Balanced Scorecard Institute, *www.balancedscorecard.org/BSCResources/AbouttheBalancedScorecard/tabid/55/Default.aspx*, retrieved December 24, 2011.

9. Patrick Tehubijuluw of Credis. *www.dashboardinsight.com/dashboards/screenshots/personal-finance-visual-analysis-interface.aspx*, retrieved December 24, 2011.

this presentation might help individuals better understand their finances; the same is true of business professionals' understanding of their business functions.

Regardless of what systems and tools an organization uses, what is clear is that decisions made in organizations should be based on data and information. Decision support and knowledge management systems are designed to turn basic information into knowledge that can create organizational wisdom. Regardless of whether the role you play is in IT or within another business function, you must have more than a passing level of knowledge about how to build and use these kinds of systems. They are important for IT to create, but even more important for users in the business to access for a reliable source of data to inform decision making. Properly designed systems can improve the quality of decisions made and therefore improve business outcomes—all important goals for IT to contribute to and a major reason why DSS, BI, and related systems and data structures are often a significant focus area for most modern IT functions.

WHAT DO YOU THINK?

Imagine that you are the CEO of a large global retailer. Recently, your CIO approached you to ask about the requirements for a new business intelligence system to replace an aging MIS application. Answer these questions that you are asked during this meeting:

> 1: What kinds of information about our business would you like to see on a daily, weekly, or monthly basis?
> 2: How important is it that this information is accurate and up-to-date for the kinds of decisions that you normally make? Does it have to be accurate by the minute, hour, or day, and why?
> 3: How would you like to have access to this information? Where and why?

Quick Test

1. The process of gaining competitive advantage through the intelligent use of data and information in decision making is called _____.
   a. automating
   b. business intelligence
   c. value chaining
   d. modelling

2. _____ are interactive computer systems that enable the decision and analysis stages of business intelligence.
   a. Decision support systems
   b. Groupware
   c. Transaction processing systems
   d. Workflow management systems

3. True or False. Business intelligence is only used for strategic decision making.

What's in IT for me?

You may have heard the quote "knowledge is power," by Sir Francis Bacon. Do you think this is true? Certainly accurate and timely data is critical for business success. But it is also true for you as a student and as a business professional in the future. Here is a list of ways to obtain up-to-the-minute information that might make you more efficient than your colleagues:

- Bookmarks—researching and bookmarking websites provides you with easy access to important information

- Contact databases—maintaining an in-depth contact database on your mobile phone and PC provides you with email and phone numbers at your fingertips
- Organized files in a directory structure—organizing your documents in folders on your PC ensures fast and easy retrieval and makes you more efficient
- RSS feeds—identifying and signing up for RSS feeds keeps you informed about important events and developments

The above are just a few examples of how obtaining and organizing data can help you be more efficient and knowledgeable.

What's in IT for an organization?

It should be obvious to you by now that data are critical to an organization. One organizational database that you will likely soon come into contact with is the human resources recruiting database. Have you ever applied for a job online? Wonder what happens to your application and resumé when you hit "submit"? Do you think that an HR analyst reads every submission? HR recruiting databases store submitted applications and resumés and provide search capabilities for HR staff to quickly sort, categorize, and filter candidates. Just imagine how many candidates apply to a company for a position; it would be impossible to manually review each one. One major benefit of these systems is that candidate data can be saved for the long term. Then, when a position opens up again, the HR analyst can simply search the recruiting database for suitable candidates rather than re-posting the position. For this reason, HR databases keep candidate resumés on file for future consideration. Because of these systems, it is important for you to ensure that your applications and resumés are in a suitable format (HTML, plain text) and have keywords that relate to the position you are applying for. This will help HR analysts find you in their large candidate database.

What's in IT for society?

In 2009, the world faced a flu pandemic predicted to be unlike anything experienced in the modern age. The flu strain, H1N1, threatened to become a widespread plague affecting millions of people. Because, by definition, a pandemic is an epidemic over a wide geographic area, it was critical to track and monitor cases from mild to severe, along with the number of H1N1-related deaths worldwide. Health organizations and hospitals around the world were equipped with data entry tools to upload their data on the pandemic to various health agencies, including the U.S. Centers for Disease Control (CDC) and Prevention. This data was then aggregated to the city, region/province/state, and finally country level. With this data, health officials could track the movement of the flu, do statistics to determine if the flu was increasing or declining and in what areas, and measure the impact of vaccination programs. Similar statistics continue to be kept by the CDC for the United States. Go to *www.cdc.gov/flu/weekly/* to see the latest week's seasonal flu activity.

More recently, health officials are now using data collected from social networks such as Twitter to track the flu. The Social Network-Enabled Flu Trends system, or SNEFT, uses a continuous data-collection framework that monitors all flu-related tweets.[10] This network can provide even faster indications of flu outbreak than that provided by the CDC, meaning that preventative measures can be taken earlier.

With this type of data, medical professionals, governments, and individuals could make decisions about how to prevent all types of flu on a global scale.

10. *www.uml.edu/News/stories/2011-12/Flu-Twitter.aspx*, retrieved December 21, 2011.

ROI | STUDENT RETURN ON INVESTMENT SUMMARY

1. Define data, information, and knowledge and describe how business professionals engage in knowledge work activities.

Data are the lifeblood of an organization. Organizations collect this raw information to begin to understand their operations and determine whether or not they are achieving their business objectives. Information takes data one step further by organizing it in a way that is useful, meaningful, and more easily accessible. Organizations attain knowledge through the knowledge work of the business professionals they employ. Knowledge work involves the discovery of data and information, its analysis, transformation, and synthesis, and finally the communication of conclusions, which may be solutions to problems or decisions. Throughout this process, individual and organizational experience is applied and value is added. It is with this knowledge that organizations can create competitive advantage.

2. Explain how the structure, quality, and presentation of information influence the nature of the decisions made by business professionals.

A decision is a choice you make about what actions you will take (or not take) in a given situation. Decisions can vary in the amount of structure and uncertainty, from structured and certain decisions (e.g., selecting prerequisite courses) to unstructured decisions that give little guidance about what to do, how to do it, and what the likely outcome will be. The amount of structure and the level of uncertainty can influence how much time business professionals will spend in different knowledge work activities, and how certain they might be about the outcomes of their decisions. Further, because the gathered data and information form the foundation for the analysis, the quality of data and information directly affects the quality of the decision.

3. Describe how databases help businesses store and access their data, information, and knowledge.

Through the use of databases, businesses can quickly and easily access interrelated data that are stored and organized in files. The ability to access and combine data enables businesses to understand and learn about the operations of the business. For example, this data helps businesses answer questions such as, How many sales were made in the last hour, day, week, month, quarter, year, decade, and for all time? What is our market share compared to our competitors? These data also support more advanced systems, such as decision support systems (DSS) and knowledge management (KM) systems, which are able to transform data to organization knowledge to inform strategic decision making, preserve knowledge beyond individuals, and improve efficiency.

4. Explain how business intelligence enhances organizational decision making.

Business intelligence (BI) is a process for gaining competitive advantage through the intelligent use of data and information in decision making. The goal of BI is to increase profitability by enabling business leaders to make better decisions. Decision support systems (DSS) provide computer-based tools designed to support business intelligence.

KNOWLEDGE SPEAK

analysis   94

balanced scorecard   119

business intelligence (BI)   113

communication   97

dashboard   118

data   92

database   106

database management system (DBMS)   106

data flow diagram (DFD)   110

data hierarchy   107

data mart   112

data mining   112

data modelling   109

data warehouse   111

decision support systems (DSS)   115

discovery   93

document management systems (DMS)   117

effectiveness   101

efficiency   101

entity-relationship diagram (ERD)   110

executive information systems (EIS)   117

explicit knowledge   92

groupware   116

information   92

knowledge   92

knowledge management (KM)   116

logical data model (LDM)   110

management information systems (MIS)   116

operational decisions   104

problem   103

problem solving   103

productivity   101

rational decision   99

relational database management systems (RDBMS)   108

relational data model   108

selection criteria   103

semi-structured decision   100

strategic decisions   105

structured decision   100

synthesis   96

tacit knowledge   92

tactical decisions   104

transformation   95

unstructured decision   100

visual analytics   119

REVIEW QUESTIONS

Multiple-choice questions

1. Which of the following is not an example of data?
   a. 25 degrees Celsius, 77 degrees Fahrenheit
   b. address book
   c. book, backpack, computer
   d. $345,200, $40, $2,000

2. The knowledge activity where a business professional uses the results of analysis to gain a greater understanding of the data and information is called_____.
   a. analysis
   b. transformation
   c. communication
   d. discovery

3. Which of the following is NOT a characteristic of a data warehouse?
   a. historical data
   b. contains a lot of data
   c. slower than online systems
   d. includes only transactions for the operational domain

4. At what level of decision making would data modelling technologies normally be applied?
   a. strategic
   b. operational
   c. tactical
   d. all of the above

Fill-in-the-blank questions

5. A(n) _____ is a collection of interrelated data that are stored in files and organized in a way so that computer programs can quickly and easily access specific pieces of data.

6. A(n) _____ key is a field in a relational database table that is used to reference a record in another table and thus represents a relationship between the two tables.

7. Organizational _____ is created when you take base data and information and perform analysis and modelling to turn it into knowledge that can be applied to improve decision-outcomes.

8. A(n) _____ is designed to provide summary information about business performance to those making higher-level strategic decisions.

True-false questions

9. An unstructured decision includes little or no inherent uncertainty.

10. The purpose of a dashboard, with respect to business intelligence, is to indicate the direction the strategic plan should take.

Matching questions

Choose the BEST answer from column B for each item in column A.

Column A	Column B
11. synthesis	a. Find addresses for bars and clubs near campus.
12. transformation	b. Combine all of the data about the bars and clubs, including cover charge, hours of operation, location, and ratings.
13. discovery	c. Develop a recommendation of where to go on Saturday night.
14. analysis	d. Review the ratings other students have given the bars and clubs.

Short-answer questions

15. Discuss the advantages of relational database systems.

16. Explain the business intelligence pyramid and why it is a hierarchy.

Discussion/Essay questions

17. Explain the knowledge work activities of discovery, analysis, transformation, synthesis, and communication, using the creation of a term paper as an example.

18. Explain the possible applications of a data warehouse for a manufacturing company and a services company. How would the data differ between these organizations?

TEAM ACTIVITY

As a team, draw the entity relationship and data flow diagrams that you think represent the data contained in your student records. What do you think the major tables are? What primary and foreign keys relate the tables?

SOFTWARE APPLICATION EXERCISES

1. Internet

Do an Internet search and find the website for Cognos, a popular business intelligence tool. Watch one of the demos on the site to get an idea of how business intelligence tools work.

2. Presentation

Create a presentation to explain the importance of data to an organization. Be sure to present all of the uses of business intelligence in an organization.

3. Word Processing

Recommend the purchase of a business intelligence system to your boss. Provide an evaluation of two popular business intelligence tools and recommend which you think is the best one.

4. Spreadsheet

A spreadsheet is basically a rudimentary database. Create a spreadsheet that catalogues the clothes in your closet. Include columns for the major attributes of the clothes (e.g., size, colour, type, short sleeve, brand, etc.). Assign an ID to each article of clothing. Sort and total some of the attributes of the spreadsheet to gain knowledge about your wardrobe.

5. Database

Imagine that you are a business owner and create a database to track your organization's assets. For each asset, include the following: asset ID, description, category, and status; employee to whom the asset is assigned; department to which the asset is assigned; vendor that provided the asset; make and model of the asset; date acquired; purchase price; and date of the next scheduled maintenance. For each employee, store the following data: employee ID; first and last name; title; work phone number; and email address. Store the following for each department: department ID and name. For each vendor, store the following data: name of company; first and last name of company contact; contact's title; and contact's phone number.

6. Advanced Challenge

Think about a relational database that you could create to support your efforts as a student. What would the tables be? How would they relate? What intelligence would this provide you with? Would using a database like this give you a competitive advantage?

ONLINE RESOURCES

Companion Website

- Take interactive practice quizzes to assess your knowledge and help you study in a dynamic way.
- Review PowerPoint lecture slides.
- Get help and sample solutions to end-of-chapter software application exercises.

Additional Resources Available Only on *WileyPLUS*

- Take the interactive Quick Test to check your understanding of the chapter material and get immediate feedback on your responses.
- Review and study with downloadable Audio Lecture MP3 files.
- Check your understanding of the key vocabulary in the chapter with Knowledge Speak Interactive Flash Cards.

CASE STUDY:
DELL INC.

When it comes to purchasing new computers, Dell has been the top choice for many individuals and corporations. What makes this somewhat surprising, considering the salesperson assistance generally required for these purchases, is that Dell sells only directly to its customers, without any retail stores. Dell initially did this by using telephone sales, but has aggressively moved into e-commerce as a way of connecting with its customers. Total 2003 online sales were over $50 million *per day*, resulting from more than 7,000 visits to its website each *minute* of the day.

The Dell website (*www.dell.com*) originally made the direct sales model the heart of its business model, and it was 100 percent reliant on e-commerce as its primary sales method. By providing greater convenience and efficiency to its customers, the site simplifies the process of selecting and purchasing a computer. Dell custom-builds every computer so that customers get exactly what they want and the latest in technology. Dell also improved its support services by making its website work as a front end to its internal databases so that its customers and suppliers can see the same support information it uses internally.

Dell had always sought efficiency in its operations, as evidenced by the fact that its expenses dropped to an almost unheard of 9.9 percent of net revenue in 2003. With this level of efficiency, each Dell employee is generating over $1 million in revenue each year—three times the level of their competitors. This search for efficiency is also demonstrated by its move to the use of radio-frequency identification (RFID) chips that it attaches to parts. Using RFID allows Dell to convert online orders into radio signals that instruct automatic parts-picking machines to find the parts needed for each PC. These same radio signals transmit assembly blueprints to workers and track the shipping of the finished product, enabling Dell managers to watch the entire process online. These are examples of using systems at the operational and tactical levels to automate business processes and improve decisions and business outcomes.

Recently, Dell has moved beyond personal computers by offering printers, personal digital assistants (PDAs), and plasma screen televisions. While it does not manufacture all of these products itself, Dell uses its e-commerce engine to sell these products in an innovative way. For example, if you have a Dell printer and it is close to running out of ink, a message will appear on your computer screen. If you agree to order a new ink cartridge, the e-commerce engine will automatically contact the Dell website and arrange to ship an ink cartridge overnight to your home or office. Compare this with the problems of determining which type of ink cartridge you need, finding a retail outlet that carries it, and then scheduling a trip to the store to purchase the cartridge.[11]

Of course, you can now also walk into a computer retailer any place in the world and buy a Dell PC or laptop. This was big news a few years ago when Dell made the decision to participate in the traditional retail channel in addition to continuing to sell its product direct to the consumer. These two business models had not previously co-existed that well. Some of that has to do with the very different systems, processes, and skills required to manage a retail channel versus a distribution business. Given what you have studied in this chapter and the preceding ones, you should be able to discuss what must have been involved in Dell's IT department to make all of this happen in preparation for participating in this new business model.

Case Questions

1. How does Dell use IT to differentiate itself from its primary competitor in terms of its direct sales and distribution of its products? How would this discipline relate to being in the retail channel, or does it?
2. Discuss ways in which Dell is using its online capabilities, business intelligence, and decision-support systems to improve both sales and service.
3. Why do you think that Dell made the strategic decision to begin to sell through traditional retail channels, even while remaining the dominant online supplier of laptops and PCs? What kinds of changes in Dell's systems do you think this would necessitate?

---

11. "e.biz 25," *Newsweek*, September 25, 2003, pp. 116–126; Todd Weiss, "Dell Posts Record Revenue of $11.5B for Q4 2004," *Computerworld*, February 12, 2004.

CASE STUDY:
DATA, DATA, EVERYWHERE....

Are you aware of every time data is collected about you? Think about it for a moment. From the minute you are born, data is collected about you—your name, the time you were born, your weight, your parents' names, etc. As you go through school, more data is collected about you. And as an adult, even more data is collected, and you add to this already extensive pool of data by your actions online. Have you ever thought about this? What conclusions could be drawn about you from this data?

Here are some examples of new types of data collection.

A recent article in the *Globe and Mail* newspaper entitled "Data Scrubbing: Hospital's Surveillance Tools Help Track Infections," detailed a new system being implemented at a Toronto hospital to monitor staff's hand-washing practices.[12] In this pilot project, doctors, nurses, and other hospital staff who interact with patients wear a wristband that transmits to over 1,000 ultrasound receivers installed at the hospital, recording hand-washing data. This data is then fed into an interactive database where it can be viewed and reported on. The article indicates that the purpose of this system is to collect data to help prevent infection, especially in high-risk patients such as organ transplant recipients.

Another health-related data collection story is taking place in Ontario, where a government agency called eHealth has been working for years to create an electronic health record for all Ontarians. The purpose of this record is to allow all health practitioners—doctors, clinics, labs, hospitals, and even pharmacies—to access a patient's complete health history to provide them with a better level of service. So, when a patient is admitted to a clinic or hospital, even if the patient has never been there before, the person's full medical record would be accessible to the staff.

In another example of data collection, for Valentine's Day 2012, Facebook reported the number 1 love song to be Jason DeRulo's "Don't Wanna Go Home."[13] Facebook chose this song by tracking songs played on Spotify, a service that plays music online, just after members updated their relationship status. Facebook also reported the top five break-up songs.

Case Questions

1. Read the full article "Data Scrubbing: Hospital's Surveillance Tools Help Track Infections," which you can find on *WileyPLUS*. This article focuses on the benefits of this type of system in preventing infections. What about the negative aspects? List the potential negative aspects of this data collection from the perspective of doctors, nurses, and the hospital.

2. Imagine that your eHealth record could be combined with other data sources. What if it was combined with your credit card purchasing history? What if it was combined with your student record and marks? What conclusions could be drawn from this combined data? List three ways in which this data combination could be used.

3. What could be the commercial uses of the song data collected by Facebook? Why would it bother to collect this data?

---

12. *www.theglobeandmail.com/life/health/new-health/health-news/data-scrubbing-hospitals-surveillance-tools-help-track-infections/article2337289/*, retrieved February 13, 2012.

13. *www.theglobeandmail.com/life/the-hot-button/whats-the-no-1-love-song-according-to-facebook/article2337214/*, retrieved February 15, 2012.

4 | ENTERPRISE SYSTEMS

WHAT WE WILL COVER

- Information Systems that Support Business Activities
- Enterprise Resource Planning
- Enterprise Risk Management

STUDENT RETURN ON INVESTMENT ROI

Through your investment of time in reading and thinking about this chapter, your return—or created value—is gaining knowledge. After reading this chapter, you should be able to

1. Describe ways in which organizations can apply IT to build business value.

2. Explain how businesses can use enterprise resource planning to strategically fit IT to the organization.

3. Describe IT's role in managing enterprise risk.

THE VOICE OF EXPERIENCE

Dave Codack, University of Toronto, summa cum laude

Dave's career has spanned over 20 years and more than nine industries. He has worked in many organizations as both an entrepreneur and as an "entrepriseneur" (one who is entrepreneurial within an organization). Dave's current position is VP of Employee Technology and Network Services at the Toronto Dominion Bank. Dave is the winner of the 2010 IT World Leadership Award for Mentoring.

What do you do in your current position? In my current position as VP Employee Technology and Network Services, I oversee all aspects of employee-related technologies and networks. This includes network connectivity, desktop, printing, assistive technologies, and branch and contact centres.

What do you consider to be important career skills? During my career I have had the good fortune to be involved with two start-up companies—one involved software in the construction industry, and the other was an online consumer magazine. Two very different industries! Being a part of these start-ups, running a publicly-traded company, and working with large multi-national publicly-traded companies has shown me how important basic business skills are to augment one's technology acumen. While I have been involved in many disciplines (architecture, system design, product development, maintenance, and infrastructure), it is the business development, finance, and operations competencies that I rely on constantly in whatever role I find myself. My advice: ensure you round out your technical skills with business-related expertise and run your area of responsibility as a business.

Can you describe an example of how you have used IT to improve business operations? Over the course of my career, the most value-adding applications of IT I have seen involve improving the consolidation, application, and use of data. By making data accessible and understandable, it can be used to inform process improvements, generate revenue opportunities, or help organizations better engage their customers. In the consumer magazine start-up I was involved

with, data was an integral part of delivering value to customers as it was aligning relevant material (articles, value-added information) to each customer's preferences—data was the product. The bank, as with many industries, mines data to develop and deliver innovative banking products to our customers.

How do you use IT? There is more and more technology available today—it is changing every day and in every field. With this modality, technology becomes the conduit for collaboration and unified communication—the lifeblood of healthy organizations. It used to be that we thought unified communication meant one device. Today, we realize it is multiple devices such as desktop/laptop, smartphones, tablets, etc., but where there is a blending of enterprise and personal personas.

Have you got any on-the-job advice for students seeking a career in IT or business? There are two pieces of advice that I give to people early in their career (and I mentor a lot of people!). The one piece of advice I give them all is to establish and maintain personal networks—nurture them, as they are your most important asset. The second piece of advice I give is to stay current and upgrade your skills regardless of what area your discipline is in. Change is constant, and these changes are reflected in new and different roles that may not have existed before. Technology is filled with examples of roles that didn't exist 10 years ago. Just think of the new roles that the advent of social media has created.

Dave has had experience in many industries and roles. The time he spent in start-ups gave him first-hand experience with the value chain and how IT supports it. In his role now, he provides value through supporting the bank's over 80,000 employees in their varied roles and in supporting the many enterprise systems the bank has implemented.

Recall that a business or organization is made up of one or more people and creates products or provides services to earn a profit or satisfy a societal or client need. It does so through core processes it designs and manages that add value. Sounds easy enough, right? Not necessarily. To become successful, businesses must manage many activities. Consider any large airline international airline, like KLM, for instance. It provides revenue-producing services by flying people and cargo to and from various destinations, resulting in it needing to operate globally 7/24. To do this productively, KLM must purchase or lease aircraft; hire pilots, mechanics, flight attendants, and other employees; create an optimized schedule of flights covering authorized routes that will maximize revenue; procure, store, and dispense fuel and other supplies for its aircraft; cater, clean, and maintain its fleet of aircraft; and locate and secure capital for current and future operations. And these are just some of the many different resources and processes that KLM must manage to create business value that customers ultimately pay for by flying KLM.

Putting all of these various business processes together comprises something called the *value chain*. Simply put, this is a serial map of each activity that must happen from initial customer interest and eventual purchase through to ultimate delivery of the product or service to the customer or end-user. For most businesses that sell more than once to the same customer, the value chain does not even stop there, as it often necessitates functions to deliver post-sale services and support, ongoing product communications or upgrade opportunities, and tracking and nurturing existing customer relationships to support additional future sales. So value chains can be quite complex and involve many steps, functions, and outcomes.

Regardless of the business model the organization uses or what steps it undertakes to create its business value, in this chapter we will discuss the concepts of the value chain and how IT is used to create and support it.

■ INFORMATION SYSTEMS THAT SUPPORT BUSINESS ACTIVITIES

There are many ways to understand what businesses do to create value. Michael Porter provides one useful way by providing a strategic framework for businesses to plan how they can become and remain competitive within their chosen industry (see Figure 4.1). For the purposes of this chapter, we are less concerned with delving into strategic questions about what industries and activities a business decides to participate in (although that is an important exercise in its own right); rather, we are more concerned with reviewing the typical components of a fairly generic value chain, and then discussing how businesses can use IT, and particularly enterprise systems, to improve results through efficiently and effectively deploying an optimized value chain.

Building an Understanding of the Value Chain

The **value chain** is a connected series of activities, each of which adds value or supports the addition of value to the firm's goods or services.[1]

We begin our exploration of the value chain with the five core components of a typical value chain, as shown in Figure 4.2. To make this chapter easier to understand, we will use generic terms that clump similar activities together. For instance, *inbound logistics* includes receiving, warehousing, and inventory control of raw materials required to create a product or service. *Operations* are the value-creating and often proprietary activities that transform the raw inputs into the final product and can include R&D, manufacturing, and product design elements, for instance. *Outbound logistics* are the activities required to get the finished product to the customer, including packaging,

---

1. Michael E. Porter, "How Competitive Forces Shape Strategy," *Harvard Business Review,* 1979, pp. 137–145.

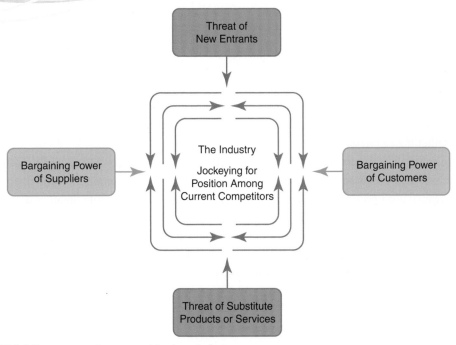

FIGURE 4.1 Forces governing competition in an industry.

FIGURE 4.2 An organizational value chain is a connected series of processes and activities, each of which adds value, or supports the addition of value, to the firm's goods or services.

warehousing, and order fulfillment, or perhaps exclusively the online provisioning of goods and services in today's digital world. Again, this depends very much on the particular business model of the organization and the type of goods and services that it produces and provides to customers. *Marketing and sales* are all activities associated with defining and securing target market interest, getting buyers to purchase the product, including working with distributors, retailers, or online channels, and activities like competitive analysis, advertising, and pricing decisions. *Service activities* are those that maintain and enhance the product's value, including customer support, repair services, warranty, and recall. As you move through these processes in Figure 4.2, you should be **adding value** at each step such that the customer ultimately pays for all these steps as part of the product or service purchase.

Obviously, while these five components are more often identified with traditional manufacturing businesses (as shown in Figure 4.2), they can also be associated with newer IT-enabled businesses that really form part of a digital value chain instead—this is, where the majority of the enterprise is focused around online sales and service or product delivery. These firms use the same five components to hire programmers and other technical specialists, manage the project to create the software product, package and deliver the software to the customer, create sales documentation, and provide after-sales technical support. However, the steps are simply conducted mostly online and relate to a digital rather than a physical product.

The value chain components can be further classified into primary and secondary activities. We normally think of *primary activities* as those directly related to the production and distribution of the organization's products and services. These are the activities that create the most direct business value for the organization and its customers. But most organizations will also require additional *support activities* that surround the primary ones. Support activities are value chain activities that an organization conducts in support of or expansion of the business value created by the primary activities. Experts like Porter and others typically identify four critical support activities that almost always exist in some form or other for most firms:

1. firm infrastructure (often called administration)
2. technology development and R&D
3. human resource (HR) management
4. procurement

Briefly, most organizations need some kind of infrastructure to exist. This can include various forms of incorporation and registration with governments and agencies for the purposes of taxation, licensing, protecting legal rights, banking, and so on. This might also include the need for office space or production facilities. Technology development and R&D are the obvious inclusion of whatever technology resources and systems the organization needs to support its value chain—the very purpose of this chapter is to discuss that in detail. Often embedded in these activities are project management and similar kinds of activities designed to help the organization constantly improve and deploy new and better technologies to support improvements in the value chain.

Moving down the list, HR management and policy directly affect the people who perform the work that creates business value. HR manages the compensation and benefits that reward employees for their work (e.g., pay, bonuses, and retirement plans). As an organization grows its revenues and volumes, if must often add employees, and this function gets more complex as an organization scales globally. More motivated employees often create more business value, and so the emphasis of a modern HR function in an organization often focuses on how to hire and retain the best talent available to enable the organization to outperform its competition. Regardless of how different types of employees might be engaged in various kinds of operational activities (e.g., programming software or calling on possible customers to buy the software), HR management efforts must support them to focus on their value-creating activities.

When you put this all together, you can see that an organization's value chain is the sum of its primary and secondary support activities, working together to create business value for the organization and its customers. As such, the value chain model is yet another way to view the organization from a systems perspective as discussed in Chapter 1 (inputs → processes → outputs). It is important not to get overwhelmed in this analysis; although value chains might seem complex, their operations are always similar in any organization.

The value chain is also a useful tool for defining an organization's core processes and the activities and competencies that it can use to gain a sustained competitive advantage over its competitors.

Often this is measured in terms of reducing process cycle costs or improving the efficiency or effectiveness of steps in the value chain. And through the intelligent use of IT, a business can increase its competitive advantage by incrementally changing the value-adding activities themselves, or by making it possible to configure the value chain in a new way, sometimes because of technology advances that enable new functionality previously not available or possible with older IT systems. Therefore, the value chain in most organizations is always changing, adapting, and improving.

So now that you have a good idea of what a typical generic value chain is at a high level, we will now discuss how information systems can support the entire enterprise across all of these business activities. Later in this chapter we will also look at specific systems that support each individual component of the value chain. For now, let's explore some general information systems that support the value chain. Within these general types there are often hundreds of core systems and subsystems, often specific to an organization. The common information systems classifications include:

- functional information systems
- workflow management systems
- transaction processing systems
- management information and document management systems
- supply chain management
- enterprise resource planning (ERP)

Keep in mind that this list does not *begin* to cover all of the various information systems that organizations use to support knowledge work and business processes; however, it is a way of classifying some of the most common types of systems that organizations use. Also important to note is that there are entire textbooks written on each of these types of systems. Here we provide simply an overview to raise your awareness of them. If you choose to either major in IT or focus on an area of study that heavily relies on IT, then you may go deeper into the details of each of these types of systems and the alternatives available to an organization to accomplish its strategic and competitive objectives in deploying these various systems.

Functional Information Systems

Traditionally, organizations divided their IS along lines that corresponded to their functional departments, such as operations, accounting, and marketing. Referred to as **functional information systems (FIS)**, they focus on the activities of the functional department to improve its efficiency and effectiveness. For example, an accounting information system focuses not only on automating basic accounting activity, but more importantly, providing instant access to reliable and up-to-date information about an organization's ongoing accounting activities. This can include activity such as reporting taxes and revenues to authorities, determining product costs and margin amounts that determine break-even points for sales, tracking payroll and employee productivity date, and so on. These systems are what help managers both inside the accounting function and elsewhere in the company use accounting data to improve results. Without such systems, the work would be tedious, too manually intense, and take too much time to remain up-to-date and would be far less efficient for most firms.

Similarly, there are normally a series of functionally-oriented systems in each major area of an organization, as shown in Table 4.1. Often, these functions get acronyms such as HRIS or CRM, which we have also included. We have also provided some examples of commercially available systems, which you may recognize or which you may wish to explore in more detail online to further educate yourself about the range of IT systems available to help an organization manage these functions effectively. See how many of these systems you recognize.

Table 4.1	Some Common Functional IS
System	**Description**
Accounting (AIS) **Example systems:** QuickBooks; AccPac/ Peachtree; Sage Simply Accounting; Great Plains; and so on.	• Typically dedicated to the reporting of a firm's financial health and up-to-date information on business results • Relies on input from transaction processing system (TPS) since it must record and process all transaction data according to normal accounting practices and standards • Provides both internal and external reports of a company's financial status, which may include regulatory reporting
Marketing IS (CRM) **Example systems:** InfusionSoft; Zoho CRM; ClaritySoft; Salesforce.com; and so on.	• Supports marketing research and decision making in developing and distributing products and services • Includes input from TPS, strategic plans, and corporate policies, and sometimes external sources and databases • For charities and not-for-profits, this function might involve donor management systems, for example • Includes marketing research outputs to support the four Ps of marketing: product development, pricing decisions, promotion, and product placement
Human Resources IS (HRIS) **Example systems:** SimpleHR; Epicor; Triton; Ceridian; Avanti; and so on.	• Supports activities related to managing the organization's employees, including HR planning, recruiting, hiring, payroll, training, talent management, succession planning, etc. • Includes input from TPS, strategic plans and corporate policies, and external sources such as tax tables and other compliance and regulatory information particularly for payroll • Supports interface with job boards and other online services • Enables administration of government-required records
Financial (FIS) **Example systems:** SAP; Sage Solutions; Treasury Sciences; Advent; and so on.	• Provides financial information to the organization's financial managers, including management of cash balances, treasury functions, and corporate investments • Includes both internal input items—TPS, financial objectives, and project needs—and external input items—competitor and environmental data or information on market trading and share prices, for instance • Generates both internal and external audit reports, supports management of funds and cash balance management
Manufacturing IS and Enterprise Resource Planning (ERP) **Example systems:** SAP; Sage Solutions; Oracle; Netsuite; OpenERP; and so on.	• Comprehensive information system that supports manufacturing and production processes and activities, including both primary and secondary functions • Includes input from TPS, AIS, CRM, strategic plans and corporate policies, and external sources • May be structured as an "end-to-end" standardized system or suite of software, or built as a "best of breed," function-by-function set of software integrated across the enterprise • Uses outputs primarily for controlling processes: design and engineering, control of inventory, resource planning, and computer-aided manufacturing, for instance

In all of the examples in Table 4.1, you have an important choice to make regarding a best-in-class functional system with its rich features and options, but which might lack easy integration with other systems (many companies now find that they need to integrate these systems with the rest of their organization's systems by using middleware—software that links separate systems; see Chapter 2). Alternatively, you can turn to large enterprise systems, such as enterprise resource planning suites like Oracle or SAP, that are already integrated and provide multiple function capability, but perhaps with some compromising of customizability or more limited but fully integrated functionality.

Regardless of the choice, some parts of any enterprise will require specific functional information systems for specialized areas like medicine (e.g., a patient information system or diagnostic systems) or for a specific functional purpose (e.g., CAD/CAM for design-intense applications). Depending on the function that the IS is related to and the industry an organization is in, your enterprise may need to or choose to build its own systems. This will normally only occur if a business is so specific that there may not be enterprise software available to fulfill its needs. However, this is a very costly and complex undertaking and most organizations are better served by using existing software and application suites whenever possible. These types of considerations are covered in more detail in Chapter 6, when we discuss IS projects and the considerations when determining to buy or build software.

Workflow Management Systems

A **workflow** represents the steps, organizational resources, input and output data, and tools needed to complete a business process. By focusing on a business process from beginning to end, a **workflow management system (WMS)** (also referred to as *business process management* or *BPM*) supports activities that several departments of the organization may carry out. For instance, perhaps marketing requires specific reports organized around specific regions or customer segments to perform analysis about your firm's competitive position. Obviously, there is a workflow associated with determining the information required; locating that information and verifying the underlying reliability of the data sources being used; preparing the report itself, likely including some mathematical tabulations and manipulations of the base data to turn it into useful information; and drawing conclusions from the report and determining the next appropriate actions. Any of this *could be done manually*. However, if this process recurs frequently (as it is likely to for a marketing report, for instance), then it may be prudent to consider ways that IT systems might assist with this workflow to reduce the human intervention and labour costs associated with these manual tasks. This way, the emphasis can be on *interpreting the report and making decisions*, rather than on collecting data and producing the report itself. This improves the costs and efficiency of the business and contributes to competitiveness.

A WMS typically provides tools for modelling the steps of the process. The model shows the flow of work, along with the state of components. For example, Figure 4.3 shows an example of workflow for a typical online product order. Information and documentation are needed and generated at each step in the workflow. However, workflow management is not just about how the documents and information flow through the process. A computer program manages the process itself, such as assigning the work, monitoring work progress, and getting the required approvals.

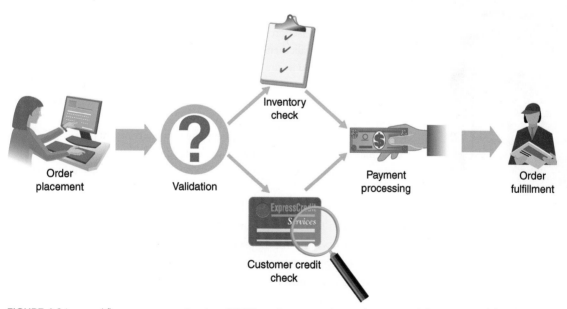

Order
placement

Inventory
check

Validation

Customer credit
check

Payment
processing

Order
fulfillment

FIGURE 4.3 In a workflow management system (WMS), each step requires and generates information and documentation.

A WMS often leads to several benefits. First, misplaced or stalled work is often reduced, which improves efficiency and quality. Second, managers can focus more time on business decisions rather than on tracking work. Third, because developing a WMS requires formal documentation of all procedures, more analysis and tighter control of the processes often result. This, in turn, leads to better work assignments—the best person for the job—and produces more efficient scheduling.

Workflow systems include tools and features that allow users to work with and manage the processes and the system itself. Administration and modelling tools provide a means for users to create and work with workflow models and definitions. Finally, particular workflow systems will generally not have all of the capabilities needed to support the business rules of the organization. A **business rule** is a statement that defines or constrains some aspect of the business. It is intended to assert business structure or to control or influence the behaviour of the business.[2] For example, a business may decide that it will only accept cash payment. To support enterprise-specific business rules, the system can directly activate plug-in or custom-tailored tools to add capabilities to the system, and the workflow client application manages the interactions between the system and added applications.

Transaction Processing Systems

Business transactions are often one of the most critical of the core activities an organization performs, and the enterprise-wide process used to activate and record them is a critical system to pay attention to. Without transactions there are no sales, and without sales there is no business! They also provide the foundation of information on which a number of other systems (CRM, ERP, and so on) must rely. For this reason, we will look at transactions and transaction processing systems in depth.

A **transaction** is an exchange of goods or services (value) between two or more parties (businesses, individuals, or a combination of the two) that creates a relationship between the parties. For example, a customer using a bank's ATM to withdraw money is a transaction between the customer and the bank. When you download software you have purchased online, you have completed a transaction.

Businesses must record, act on, complete, and report transactions in an accurate and timely manner. This is where transaction processing systems play a critical role. **Transaction processing systems (TPS)** enable transaction activities and capture the key data created by the transaction.

From a technical standpoint, a transaction is a unit of work that has the following characteristics:

A customer using an ATM is a transaction between an individual (the customer) and an organization (the bank providing ATM service).

- *Atomicity*—A transaction must be unequivocally completed. If an error causes the transaction to fail, then the entire transaction to that point should be undone and the data reset to its previous state (e.g., when a sale is voided or reversed).
- *Consistency*—All unchanging properties of data must be preserved. This means that the data captured by the transaction must fit within the rules of data storage.
- *Isolation*—Each transaction should execute independently of other transactions that may occur at the same time on the system.
- *Durability*—The characteristics of a completed transaction should be permanent.

These characteristics, together known as ACID, allow organizations to create systems that can handle large numbers of simultaneous transactions. Defining transactions that have the ACID properties also helps organizations ensure that the activities of any one transaction all succeed or fail as a group. Why is this important? Think about how a bank relies on its ATM transactions. Say a customer

2. *http://en.wikipedia.org/wiki/Business_rule*

decides to transfer $100 from his savings to his chequing account. This account-transfer transaction has two simple activities: (1) subtract $100 from the savings account, and (2) add $100 to the chequing account. Imagine the problems that would occur if the first activity succeeds but the second one fails. Now think about this problem multiplied by the bank's daily ATM transactions. You can see why a TPS must handle both of these activities together as a single transaction.

Figure 4.4 shows how a TPS brings together the common components of IT—data storage, data processing, data capture, and software—when a customer makes a purchase at a store. First the store's product is scanned, requiring the TPS to capture the bar code, collect product information from the database, display results, and update the transaction totals (1). This process happens instantaneously for each item! Once all products are scanned, the TPS calculates and displays the taxes and totals, which prompts the customer to pay the required monies (2). The customer must then input her payment (3), and once her payment is received, the TPS must generate a receipt and update the store's inventory and the transaction record's database (4). Processing in a TPS must control the flow of both the activities and data involved in the transaction. Depending on the configuration of the system and the network connections, the processing power that handles the transaction can include PCs, servers, and/or mainframes. TPS software applications must incorporate the logic for controlling and enabling the transaction, the business rules of the organization that apply to the transaction, and necessary error-handling logic. Regardless of the business model of your organization, chances are quite good that you will need to have some kind of transaction processing system in place to track sales and customer orders.

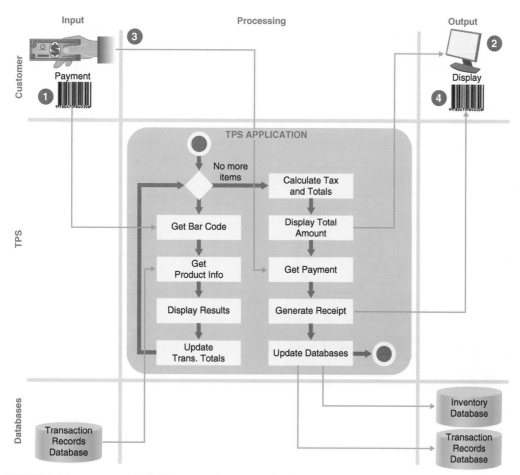

FIGURE 4.4 An automated POS-TPS process brings together the common components of IT—data storage, data processing, data capture, and software—as it creates value for the organization.

Data storage, most often in the form of one or more databases, is important as a source of input data and as storage for the captured data of a TPS. For example, most retail stores use a point-of-sale (POS) system to capture and store much of the data about their products. A bar code value, assigned as an ID for each product, serves as the primary key for accessing this data, such as the product name and price. Finally, a TPS uses network technologies to connect both its components as well as its system to the organization. The databases that the TPS accesses are usually stored on special database network servers. An important aspect of networks in a TPS is how the company uses the networks to update the central data stores of the organization with the new transaction data. As discussed in Chapter 3, this data can then be used to make important business decisions.

Supply Chain Management

Every business has a supply chain. A **supply chain** is a system of organizations, people, technology, activities, information, and resources involved in moving a product or service from supplier to customer. Supply chain activities transform natural resources, raw materials, and components into a finished product that is delivered to the end customer. In sophisticated supply chain systems, used products may re-enter the supply chain at any point where residual value is recyclable.[3]

Historically, especially in established economies throughout North America and Europe, there has been a traditional three-tier distribution system: the manufacturer sells its products to various national or regional wholesalers who, in turn, re-sell the product downstream to their established retail network for sale to the end customer. This system evolved for a variety of reasons related to the costs of product transport, support, and the desire of manufacturers to have a limited number of centralized wholesalers as customers rather than "selling direct" to individual customers. However, the primary disadvantage of this system is that it adds a layer of cost that increasingly does not add value—that is, the "value chain" of this model is eroding. This is especially true because modern transportation infrastructure makes it feasible to manufacture just about any place in the world and deliver to any other place in the world quite quickly and efficiently, thus making local warehousing and distribution increasingly less relevant in the value chain of many firms.

Similarly, as the Internet grew in scope and popularity, it became easier to "disintermediate" those in the middle; the famous phrase about "eliminating the middle man" was inspired by this notion. Early online success stories like Amazon.com are classic examples, as they disintermediated both regional book wholesalers and local retailers as well. Consumers could find an unlimited variety of books online at prices that a three-tier distribution system could not match. And the rest is history! In fact, one of the most common economic impacts of the Internet has been forcing huge efficiencies into the supply chain of most industries as consumers demand lower prices, better selection, and quick delivery of goods. Whether or not

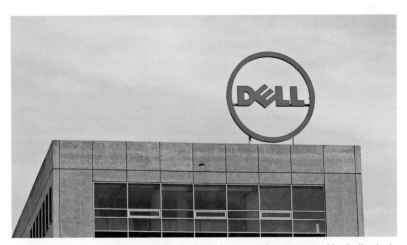

The eroding value of traditional supply chains began with companies like Dell, which moved to a "just-in-time" manufacturing model, creating products that were made based on an order placed directly by the consumer. This offered the advantages of lower cost and more product selection.

3. Anna Nagurney, *Supply Chain Network Economics: Dynamics of Prices, Flows, and Profits.* Edward Elgar Publishing, 2006.

production occurs overseas or in North America, disintermediation will continue to thrive because of these benefits.

An organization's supply chain includes several components of its value chain, as well as links into the value chain of other organizations. Consider the beverage you may drink at the end of exam week. The beverage producer's supply chain includes getting the materials to manufacture the drink. The production of those materials is the end of another organization's supply chain, but the beginning of the beverage producer's. Similarly, the end of the beverage producer's supply chain is the start of the restaurant or bar's supply chain, and so on.

To manage the supply chain, businesses engage in **supply chain management (SCM)**. SCM manages materials and inventory levels, supply information, and finances as they move from supplier to manufacturer to wholesaler to retailer to consumer. A more robust definition is provided by the Council of Supply Chain Management Professionals (CSCMP):

> *Supply chain management encompasses the planning and management of all activities involved in sourcing and procurement, conversion, and all logistics management activities. Importantly, it also includes coordination and collaboration with channel partners, which can be suppliers, intermediaries, third party service providers, and customers. In essence, supply chain management integrates supply and demand management within and across companies.*[4]

Supply chain management systems seek to optimize the supply chain to create business value and competitive advantage. If one organization can produce and distribute its products faster and better than another, it will certainly have the best business results (increased profit and reduced cost).

Typical modules in any supply chain management software system include:

- *Materials management*—the procurement, storage, and use of raw materials to be used in the end product; may connect externally to supplier supply chain systems
- *Inventory management*—finished goods inventory
- *Order management*—orders by customers, distributors, retail outlets
- *Logistics management*—plans for shipping the product and tracking it from origin to destination and related shipping documentation

In addition to the above, supply chain management systems often include various levels of reporting, forecasting tools, and asset management. Because supply chain management encompasses so much of the value chain, it is often the cornerstone and starting point of enterprise resource planning (ERP) system implementations, which are discussed next.

WHAT DO YOU THINK?

It is easy to see how a supply chain works in a manufacturing or retailing business, but what about a services business such as an accounting firm, a financial planning business, or an IT consultancy? Consider the following questions when thinking about the supply chain for a services business:

1: What would the supply chain look like for an accounting firm? Would it have the same primary and support activities as a manufacturing business? How might they differ?
2: What would the "materials" or other inputs be for an accounting firm?
3: How do you think services firms manage knowledge and knowledge-based products to create business value for their clients?

---

4. *http://cscmp.org/aboutcscmp/definitions.asp*, retrieved February 10, 2010.

Quick Test

1. True or False. More value is created by keeping each component of the value chain separate, focusing only on its contribution to business value.

2. A _____ allows the data from a transaction to be processed and passed on immediately to organizational data storage.
   a. human resources information system (HRIS)
   b. functional information system (FIS)
   c. workflow management system (WMS)
   d. transaction processing system (TPS)

3. For more efficient production and distribution, supply chain management modules typically include which types of process management?
   a. materials, inventory, ordering, and logistics
   b. materials, ordering, sales, and reordering
   c. materials, logistics, sales, and inventory
   d. inventory, ordering, logistics, and sales

Answers: 1. False; 2. d; 3. a

■ ENTERPRISE RESOURCE PLANNING

One way to integrate the departments and functions across an entire organization is to use **enterprise resource planning (ERP)** software. With ERP, a company runs all of its applications from a single database, often known as a "data warehouse." Each functional unit of a company, such as finance, marketing, and sales, still uses its own supporting enterprise software applications (either provided by a single suite of applications from a single vendor or by linking together best-in-breed solutions from several vendors); ERP sets out to link these various applications and ensure their compatibility via common data processing and storage. This creates a situation where data is only captured or entered *once* but used multiple times as required across multiple applications. This tends to reduce data errors and improve both the availability and reliability of an organization's data about its ongoing operations.

For example, imagine that a customer contacts a company's salesperson to place an order. Accessing the ERP sales module, the salesperson obtains all the necessary information, such as the customer's contact and billing data, product data, and the product's forecasted availability. The salesperson enters the order data in the ERP sales module, which stores the data in a central database that everyone in the company using other ERP modules can access. This update creates an automatic trigger for all of the other required processes in the value chain related to filling this order. As the sales data are updated and the product is taken out of inventory, the financial data are updated to reflect an accounts receivable entry and a customer invoice is generated. Elsewhere, the paperwork required for product logistics is created (e.g., picking and packing slips) and if the salesperson is working on commission, her commissions due are updated with the value of the sale she just processed to be included on the company's next payroll run. More importantly, any of the company's employees working in any capacity can quickly obtain the status of the order at any time by accessing the ERP system—especially critical to the customer service function that might field a call from the customer enquiring about the order status, for instance. All of these actions undertaken in the ERP system are coordinated and shared without any additional human intervention from that very first source of data entry—the sales order.

Have you ever tracked a letter or package sent via Canada Post, anxious for its delivery? The reason you can is that a few years ago Canada Post improved its organizational efficiency and effectiveness by deploying an ERP system. This system created value by providing visibility throughout its delivery network (inbound logistics, operations, outbound logistics), enabling new business (sales), and reducing costs through process standardization (administration). Canada Post's ERP demonstrates that the application of IS to its value chain's primary and support activities can support multiple important business processes and can create value for a business.[5]

As this example illustrates, a benefit of an ERP system is to streamline business processes. Companies want to get orders to customers faster and at less cost, and also receive sales revenue quicker. In this case, Canada Post provided a key benefit to customers and was able to respond to competitive pressure from shipping companies. ERP can support all areas of the value chain, both primary and supporting processes, helping to achieve efficiencies not possible with independent systems.

However, the primary disadvantage of the ERP system is that, like the organizations they support, the system can become incredibly complex and difficult to manage as it grows. ERP systems need to be customized for the specific business processes and rules that it is supporting. Sometimes this customization is

Canada Post's ERP system allowed the organization to streamline its business processes while simultaneously creating value for customers by providing visibility throughout its network.

extensive, and businesses come to rely on ERP vendors and service providers, such as SAP, Oracle, and IBM, to develop and maintain their ERP installation. These arrangements require close relationships between the client and the service provider. It is important that businesses not become over-dependent on service providers and end up paying expensive fees for support. In these situations, businesses can find themselves losing the cost savings they have achieved through efficiency. And examples of failed ERP implementations abound, including Waste Management suing SAP for $500 million for a failed ERP implementation, Hershey Foods' 19 percent drop in profits from a failed SAP implementation at Halloween time a few years ago, the complete bankruptcy of FoxMeyer Drug, a $5-billion pharmaceutical distributor, over a failed $100-million ERP implementation, and, perhaps most troubling of all, the over $1 billion spent by the U.S. Navy on four different ERP systems, all of which have failed.[6]

In the next section we will discuss the individual components of the value chain and provide examples of the enterprise systems that support each component.

Enterprise Systems that Support the Value Chain

Some IT systems are specific to particular parts of the value chain or specific organizational functions. For example, logistics management systems may be specifically designed to support inbound logistics, accounting systems might only serve the needs of that department, and software development tools are generally only used by IT for in-house technology development. On the other hand, some systems, such as ERP, are used across all parts of the value chain.

5. Adapted from *www.sap.com/solutions/business-suite/scm/pdf/CS_canada_post.pdf*, retrieved February 10, 2010.

6. *www.generalatlantic.com/en/news/article/1223*

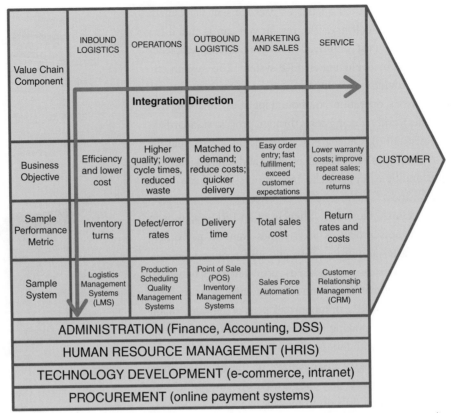

Value Chain Component	INBOUND LOGISTICS	OPERATIONS	OUTBOUND LOGISTICS	MARKETING AND SALES	SERVICE	
	Integration Direction					
Business Objective	Efficiency and lower cost	Higher quality; lower cycle times, reduced waste	Matched to demand; reduce costs; quicker delivery	Easy order entry; fast fulfillment; exceed customer expectations	Lower warranty costs; improve repeat sales; decrease returns	CUSTOMER
Sample Performance Metric	Inventory turns	Defect/error rates	Delivery time	Total sales cost	Return rates and costs	
Sample System	Logistics Management Systems (LMS)	Production Scheduling Quality Management Systems	Point of Sale (POS) Inventory Management Systems	Sales Force Automation	Customer Relationship Management (CRM)	

ADMINISTRATION (Finance, Accounting, DSS)

HUMAN RESOURCE MANAGEMENT (HRIS)

TECHNOLOGY DEVELOPMENT (e-commerce, intranet)

PROCUREMENT (online payment systems)

FIGURE 4.5 IT supports the value chain both horizontally and vertically, including some common applications in each component. Performance metrics are associated with the value chain component, business objective, and the sample systems that support the value chain components.

The sample systems shown in Figure 4.5 are often referred to as enterprise systems. **Enterprise systems** are large-scale applications deployed across the organization that support specific business units or functions; they are another way that an organization might apply IT to its value chain. The specific systems listed in this figure are discussed in detail later in this section. And by no means does Figure 4.5 provide an exhaustive list of enterprise systems. Further, note that some of the systems listed in the figure may support more than one activity (in which case the systems are integrated across multiple functions or units).

To understand the possible impact of enterprise systems on the value chain, let's consider the types of activities within each component of the value chain, some possible ways to measure the business impact of deploying these systems, and the types of business goals they support.

Inbound Logistics While we discussed earlier in the chapter the notion of the value chain and its outbound touch points (i.e., getting products and services to the customer), for many organizations there is much to be gained in terms of business efficiency by paying attention to the inbound logistics component of the value chain. This includes such primary activities as:

- raw material procurement
- warehousing
- materials management
- production coordination

Raw material procurement involves sourcing and ordering materials from suppliers, keeping track of expected arrival dates of materials, receiving and checking the materials upon arrival,

An RFID tag (left) can be invaluable for organizations to keep track of inventory, and QR codes (right) allow consumers to connect directly to an organization simply through scanning.

approving the packing slip/bill and authorizing payment, distributing the materials to the correct location, storing the materials, and monitoring supply levels. When the operation is ready for the materials, they must be located and transported to the correct location for use in the operations process. Many manufacturing organizations today apply "just-in-time" methods for the inbound logistics function to keep warehousing costs to a minimum; this way, the raw goods literally go from supplier directly onto the production floor for immediate use. This increases efficiencies and reduces costs—imperatives if you want to be globally competitive.

For many years, most consumer products have had a universal product code (UPC), which is also called a *bar code* because of how it looks. You commonly see these on products as you scan them at a retailer on checkout; but that is far from the only technology that is helping support advances in *logistics management systems (LMS)*. LMS are typically highly customized as they need to match the specific organization's business rules and requirements, and any organization with any form of significant manufacturing or product delivery in their value chain will pay significant attention to this area of their enterprise because of its value and profitability impact. More general aspects of LMS include transportation management and warehousing systems, which often form a sub-set of LMS technologies.

One example of a specific technology that is becoming more critical to inbound logistics is *radio frequency identification (RFID)*. RFID uses radio waves to automatically identify objects and transmit this information to an IT system. The most common type of RFID stores a serial number on a microchip that is attached to an antenna. The antenna enables the chip to transmit the identification number to a reader. The reader converts the analog radio waves from the RFID tag into digital information. The ID number can then be matched against data stored in a database to obtain information, such as a product's name and price. This kind of technology can greatly assist with tracking inventory, picking orders, and performing inventory counts for audits—which are just a few examples of its value. Today, these tags can also be accessed using mobile device readers (such as handheld devices), smartphones, iPads, and similar types of devices. As the computing interface itself has become more portable and mobile, business processes can be designed to incorporate these technology enhancements in an effort to increase efficiency and lower costs.

Because RFID tags are small and cheap, they may soon replace bar code technology for many applications. One advantage of RFID over bar codes is that it does not require "line-of-sight" scanning. For a bar code, the scanner uses a laser to read a printed label. To do this, the scanner must have an unobstructed view of the label. Have you ever used a self check-out counter at the grocery store? Did you ever try to scan an item and the bar code just would not be read? Frustrating! Since radio waves can pass through and around objects, a reader can read an RFID tag as long as it is in range. Another benefit is that an RFID tag can be read as soon as a tag is within range. This eliminates the need for a user to present the tag to the reader. RFID identification is quickly taking over because it is faster and more accurate than other forms of product ID.

QR codes are another form of printed or embedded technology that provide a similar function to RFID, but which are somewhat more passive since they do not emit but rather must be scanned. They are seen most often in promotions to consumers and are featured in off-line advertising campaigns directed at consumers who are "on the move" and who want point-and-click convenience in obtaining product or service information. QR codes can be created with ease by using sites such as *http://qrcode.kaywa.com*, meaning almost anyone can use this new technology. Many business cards are beginning to feature QR codes that link to content most relevant to potential customers. If you are a new graduate looking for work, consider including a QR code on your business card that links to your industry-relevant blog. The ability to brand and customize these codes is also possible, as seen in the Corkbin example shown on the previous page. When QR codes are combined with facial recognition or eye-tracking technologies (all of which exist and are now commercially available through a variety of vendors worldwide), a wealth of new information about consumers becomes viable to collect and analyze at any point in time.

But, as with almost any new technology, there are always concerns about potential uses and abuses that can occur. New technology enables new capabilities, the full extent of which might not initially be recognized. In the case of RFID, Walmart was a known leader in the use of IS for competitive advantage and began pushing the adoption of universal RFID tagging by its suppliers. By requiring that products from its suppliers possess an RFID tag, Walmart was able to increase the efficiency of the warehouse and logistics processes in its own supply chain. For suppliers, however, especially smaller ones, RFID can be costly to implement and requires them to transform many of their business processes. But since Walmart had mandated the change, these suppliers have no choice but to follow or lose a lucrative customer. Of course, smart suppliers and manufacturers will think of this and build emerging technologies that their customer might demand into their future product strategy. All organizations should constantly consider how technological innovations could improve their performance.

Technologies like this inevitably have privacy and data protection implications. Advocates of individual privacy rights worry that RFID could allow for the real-time tracking of customers. In addition, there is a concern that additional private information might become available to a mobile phone carrier, for instance, when a consumer clicks on a QR code that might include information about where that customer was located when he or she clicked on it. In some mobile phones, GPS information transmitted to geo-sensitive applications, combined with QR and other coded data, might generate enormous insight into consumer buying behaviour. For example, grocery stores could use the information to identify where consumers are and what they are buying at any given moment. But should they be able to tag and track your movements and your intentions within their store simply because they can? Would you be OK with your grocery store using facial recognition technology to determine the gender, and potentially the race, of purchasers in its stores, and how various store layouts, displays, inducements, coupons, and similar techniques support sales of different kinds of products? Privacy advocates caution that this could lead to abuses of those who seek to collect data without consumers' knowledge and permission.

Here's another example: What if a clothing manufacturer embedded a micro RFID tag into its clothing? Perhaps it is trying to figure out if its brand appeals to wealthy patrons who regularly go out to public events. It could then contract with theatres, performance halls, museums, and similar venues to track and measure the number of people in the audience wearing its particular brand—or where they sit and what they watch. The data may then be used to make decisions about product promotions, positioning, or advertising. While this may be innocent enough, the potential for abuse is clearly there.[7] As far as we know, there are no reported examples of abuse of this technology to date, but it is possible and likely that this is mostly because the technologies we are discussing here remain in their infancy in terms of adoption rates.

Operations All of the activities required to actually create the product or service and make it available for sale to the marketplace are contained in the operations component of the value chain. If you are a manufacturing company, this is where

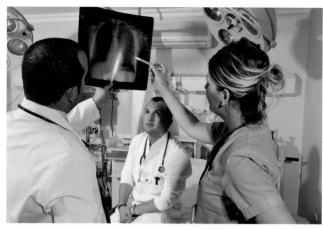

Clearly, the operations of an emergency department in a hospital are much more complex than the operations of a family doctor's office.

you manufacture the product; if you are a services company, you create and deliver the service. Of course, the scale of operations can vary considerably; a local doctor's office is a great example of a small enterprise delivering mostly services. While the scale of a medical clinic might increase with the number of doctors in it, or the extent of its operation if it includes an after-hours clinic, for instance, the basic activities of operations in a doctor's office will be well understood, fairly common, and consistent. As a result, a large number of IT vendors will flock to this space to provide innovative IT-based solutions for the operations value chain of a traditional medical clinic.

However, the scale of operations in a hospital, while seemingly related in nature as they are also medical, increase significantly in terms of scope and complexity. In fact, while there may be doctors in the hospital who are practising the exact kind of procedures and work that they do in their own clinics, their application inside an acute-care hospital setting change the nature of the operations of that treatment considerably in terms of something even as simple as tracking and monitoring who is doing what inside the hospital.

Now imagine that you are responsible for a set of regional hospitals, all working together. Or perhaps you are a large HMO in the United States with hundreds of sites and millions of patients on your rolls across the country. Any of these would again significantly change the nature of the operations in your enterprise and demand different types of IT solutions to properly manage their complexity. Yet again, extend this to perhaps a global pharmaceutical manufacturer or a global medical billing agent, and the requirements grow in scope again. All of these examples would be classified as part of the larger "pharma" or "medical" industries that exist anywhere, but they certainly are all unique in scale and their specific IT needs, aren't they?

So this example speaks to why the execution of "operations" tends to be unique to each organization and will often feature proprietary practices that contribute to competitive advantage. Both supply chain management and enterprise resource planning systems are deployed in the operations of a company to monitor work in progress and the efficiency of the operations processes, regardless of the scale or geography involved. For instance, if your operations include the design and manufacture of buildings, you do that by creating engineering documents and 3D architectural and design images and plans. And it is possible you might be even called upon to design a hospital or large clinic. This is another important industry (building and design) that is linked to but quite different from

7. David H. Williams, "The Strategic Implications of Wal-Mart's RFID Mandate," *Directions Magazine,* July 29, 2004. *www.directionsmag.com/article.php?article_id=629&trv=1*, retrieved January 6, 2007.

the operation of the hospital itself. However, how well the hospital is designed, which flows from an understanding of how hospitals operate, is ultimately what will determine how well it functions post-construction. And, it is quite likely that the uniforms worn by those in the hospital (doctors, surgeons, nurses, security staff, etc.) were all designed, produced, and ultimately delivered using various other forms of enterprise systems appropriate to that industry. So we see in this example how various supply chains are interconnected and co-dependent on each other.

Another common enterprise system used in the operations component of the value chain is production scheduling tools. These automated tools optimize the production machinery and availability of staff to run the machinery. Imagine the operations of Campbell's Soup, for example. It likely uses the same machinery to produce both tomato and mushroom soups. In between making each of these soups, the machinery would need to be cleaned (you don't want mushrooms in your tomato soup!) and new raw materials and ingredients delivered to the production area. This takes a specified length of downtime that must be taken into account in production schedules, or else the recipe will not be successful and the soup production will fail. There might also be scheduled maintenance required on the equipment from time to time that must be factored into production schedules. Perhaps there is seasonality where a particular soup might be at unusual levels of demand, which has to be recognized and planned for well in advance (consider Turkey at Thanksgiving for instance). Or maybe it has particular staff or required experts who may only work on tomato soup or mushroom soup, and they need to be scheduled accordingly for when those soups are being made. All of this must be managed so that production meets demand and sales are optimized.

Another critical function in a manufacturing setting is quality management. Quality control/management systems monitor and control the quality of the products being produced. In our soup example, the quality control system might monitor the temperature at which the soup is cooked, cooking time, and so on. These processes may specify when and how many taste tests are required and what particularly is being controlled for in those taste tests (for instance, saltiness). The quality system may also govern any time and temperature constraints around canning the soup that might impact things like avoiding contamination or damaging the quality of the end-product. If the quality control rules are not followed, defects may occur that result in a substandard product.

Of course, in the case of a food or drug manufacturer, the consequences of not following a strict regime of quality control could result in the product causing illness or death. In that situation, a company is legally liable and may face financial losses, either from reduced sales or settling law suits. Even if the situation is not life or death, a company's reputation can be significantly damaged if quality issues are reported in the media. To reflect on that, all we have to do is go back in time to the Tylenol product tampering scare in the United States, the Maple Leaf Foods Listeria-infected packaged meats example in Canada, or other similar situations to see what can happen when a company gets caught by the public with product quality or integrity issues. In the case of Maple Leaf Foods, what began as a curious uptick in listeriosis cases quickly unfolded into a massive public health problem in the summer of 2008, as hundreds of people fell ill after eating tainted meat.[8] Maple Leaf Foods cited two identical slicing machines as being at fault, with the bacteria lingering "deep inside" their mechanical components.[9] The negative effects on the company included broken public trust, lost lives, and plummeting sales.[10]

And what about a service business? Do you remember the last time you stayed in a hotel or motel? Chances are it used a reservations system to manage your booking and to assign you a room. Perhaps that system included items like special requests that needed to be booked in advance or

---

8. *www.cbc.ca/news/health/story/2008/08/26/f-meat-recall-timeline.html*

9. *www.citytv.com/toronto/citynews/news/local/article/4715--maple-leaf-foods-update-ceo-points-at-cause-for-listeria-outbreak*

10. *www.thestar.com/Business/article/527152*

specific room requests. Maybe you used a self-service system through the television in the room to settle your bill or to enter a room service order. These are all examples of operational systems that use IT to improve product and service delivery.

Outbound Logistics Outbound logistics involves the warehousing of finished goods and the distribution of those physical goods to their proper destination. While that obviously includes end-customers, it may also include distributors, wholesalers, and retailers (see Figure 4.6). Of course, in today's digital world, it may also be the case that a product is delivered completely electronically and only online. Most consumer software sales are now done this way. Music downloads and e-books are other examples of electronic products that are quickly displacing traditional physical products. While these products require a slightly different business model, much of what we discuss in terms of outbound logistics for physical products can still apply to digital products delivered online. So while we acknowledge the different construction of the digital supply chain in advance of our discussion, the concepts we will discuss can equally apply to both types of products.

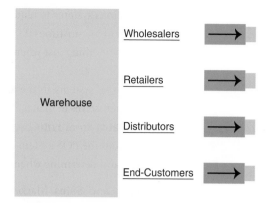

FIGURE 4.6 Outbound logistics include both the warehousing and delivery of finished goods.

As with inbound logistics, logistics management systems and RFID are used in outbound logistics also. *Transportation management systems (TMS)* can be exceptionally important: a lot of time, effort, and cost have been invested in the finished product, and it is important that it ends up in market how and when it is intended to. Imagine Valentine's Day chocolates arriving in store on February 15! That kind of a disaster can be career-ending if you are in the logistics business, so it is vital to understand how long it takes to ship a product to its endpoint and the optimal way to achieve that in terms of timing and price of delivery.

Enterprise systems supporting the outbound logistics component of an organization's value chain include systems that get products into the hands of consumers, on time, and at the right cost. These include transaction processing systems (TPS), which we discussed in detail earlier in this chapter. One extremely popular type of TPS is the point of sale (POS) system (refer to Figure 4.4). The POS system conducts the transaction between the organization and the customer at the location of the sale. This is often at a check-out counter in the case of a grocery or clothing store, and sometimes even at your table in a restaurant. The shopping cart function of an e-commerce website can also be considered a type of POS. In recent years, a lot of effort has been made to put POS in the hands of customers themselves. Self check-outs, chip technology in credit and debit cards, and mobile commerce are all moves in this direction.

Fulfillment systems are also an important part of outbound logistics systems. These come into play when you order something online or at a retail store, such as furniture. Stock must be checked and released to the order, and the order must picked, packaged, and processed to be delivered to the customer. It is imperative that proper information on the availability of current inventory be made available to the system to help manage customer expectations. If a product is temporarily or permanently out-of-stock, this fact must be known and transmitted to the customer. Perhaps the product is going on sale shortly—again, to avoid complaints and disappointment, it may be wise for systems to know and flag this order in advance based on the date range of when the order was placed and when the sale will start so that automatic, and unexpected, positive price adjustments are made when the final product is delivered and paid for.

As transactions take place and goods transfer to the hands of customers, inventory must be updated. *Inventory management systems (IMS)* constantly monitor the supply of finished goods to ensure that enough supply is on hand to meet demand. Of course, this may involve communicating with operations systems to request that more of certain products be made available. IMS help enable the concept of just-in-time (JIT) inventory, which optimizes the manufacturing process (making just enough of something just when it is needed), and ensures that excess inventory does not need to be managed and stored.

Enterprise systems in the area of inventory management have enabled organizations to allow suppliers themselves to manage the inventory on store shelves. Have you ever been in a store and seen a representative from Frito-Lay or Pepsi re-stocking the shelves rather than a store employee? Sales of goods from the POS system are transmitted directly to these suppliers, who then monitor inventory levels and determine when the shelves need re-stocking.

Marketing and Sales Marketing and sales is always a critical component in any organization's value chain. This can even apply to not-for-profits or charities, which rely on the promotion of their cause to attract donor support. Without marketing, there is nothing that helps the end-customer or target client know what it is you are all about! The marketing and sales area investigates what customers, partners, donors, or others imperative to your operation might need to engage with you. These efforts help determine the products and services that will best meet those needs. Marketing and sales are information-intense activities that rely on enterprise systems to help provide and organize this data. It is essential that companies closely monitor existing sales for trend identification and for input into sales forecasts. Do products need adjusting, or do products need to be discontinued entirely? Much of the data and sales analysis done by marketing and sales is fed back into the other primary activities of the value chain.

You may have heard the term "sales force automation" (or SFA). If not, you might want to proceed online to *Salesforce.com* and have a peek at their site as a starting point to better understand this element of the value chain. This term is used for popular enterprise systems that support sales forecasting, contact management, order management, and lead tracking. All of these are critical activities of the sales team. Of late, sales force automation activities have been encompassed in customer relationship management (CRM) systems, which we discuss in the next section.

Service Once a product or service is in the hands of a customer, the post-sales service component of the value chain begins. Sometimes firms do not invest as heavily in this as they do the efforts to get buyers to purchase their product or service in the first place. However, that is a mistake because much research demonstrates that a bigger impression is often made on the consumer or client by virtue of the value of post-sales service and support than by initial sales efforts. By far the most popular enterprise system supporting this aspect of the value chain is the **customer relationship management (CRM)** system. According to a report by Consona CRM,[11] service and support make customers successful, which in turn help to make the company's offerings more valuable to customers, increasing product usage and adoption. This ultimately drives loyalty, referenceability, retention, and repurchase.

CRM systems provide organizations with the tools to service customers better through knowing their past purchases, their purchasing patterns, and even what their future needs may be. Have you ever been shopping online and noticed an area that said something like "Other customers who bought a blue shirt also bought a blue skirt"? This is a CRM system at work, and this action is called *up-selling*. While the CRM system enables servicing a need a customer has about a past purchase, it may also provide information to encourage the customer to make a new purchase. And this doesn't only occur on the Web. A very common installation of CRM systems is in call centres. CRM systems help route customer calls to the most appropriate agent to help them. When the call is answered the agent has all of the customer's information, including past purchase history, and the system may even

---

11. *http://crm.consona.com/content/whitepapers/consonarevenueenginewhitepaper.pdf*

suggest potential purchases for the agent to offer the customer. CRM systems not only enable companies to be more efficient in servicing customers, they can also increase revenue through up-selling and increased customer satisfaction.

Administration and Finance Systems Administration is an important supporting activity in the value chain, but it is usually seen as being too expensive to perform manually and too costly without directly contributing to the primary activities that generate value in an organization. Because of this, several enterprise systems are aimed at automating and optimizing administrative processes in the hope of reducing costs and ensuring these processes are efficient.

Administrative activities include functions related to finance, accounting, payroll, and legal, as well as activities like knowledge management and decision making, as we have already discussed elsewhere. In many businesses, administration may primarily be known as billing or accounting, but it is just as important as actually providing the product or service; without these activities, customers would not be properly invoiced or pay their bills. Think about your mobile phone bill. As you make calls, send texts, and use the Internet on your mobile device, your telecommunications provider is tracking your billable actions. It would be tedious to have to do this manually, so they automate this task and link it directly to your individual mobile phone number and billing account. As a result, they are able to bill you properly at the end of the month—a good thing! This bill is then sent to you and a record of this receivable is added to the company's accounts receivable ledger where it will stay until you make payment. And if you don't make a payment, the collections department will be informed to seek payment and perhaps contact technical services to suspend your service until you do. Most of these kinds of tasks are performed automatically by an enterprise system based on pre-determined business rules. This keeps human intervention to the level of exceptions and follow-up only.

If your provider has good IT systems linked to its value chain, it will also know when you have stepped out of your standard billing package and therefore add a billable event to your bill. Or it may be able to see changes in usage patterns and call you to see if everything is all right or to suggest another kind of plan. If you are not on a pay-as-you-go plan, the provider can also control the volume of calls it allows on credit before calling for additional security or payment terms. Or, if you miss a monthly payment for whatever reason, it may route your account to a collections agent to call you while temporarily blocking your service. These are all examples of business rules, and a clear understanding of these is required before building enterprise systems. For instance, how long will a credit situation be allowed to continue before a call is made? How big does the credit default have to be before it justified a personal call—which is, by definition, quite expensive to make? At what levels do we distinguish between simply flagging the need for a call to sort things out versus temporarily freezing an account—a delicate balance between respect for our customers and protecting our own financial risk. While seemingly simple, often the role of IT, and particularly IT project managers, is to determine just exactly this level of specificity to ensure that the business rules we live by can be automated successfully.

Every text you send or call you make on your mobile phone is being tracked by your service provider to ensure proper billing. Could you imagine a company doing this task manually? While administrative functions like this might seem routine, they are extremely important to the success of any business.

Other administration systems inside an organization handle accounts receivable and payments from customers, generate cheques for accounts payable to others, calculate taxes collected and payable to the government (HST, GST, and PST for instance), and handle the general ledger and account balancing to ensure reliable financial statements are available to management. Other systems (often referred to as treasury management or cash management systems) track cash assets, execute investment and asset management functions, and perform many other similar tasks required to legally operate a company in most places. Often these systems are linked to online banking systems to help a large company reconcile its accounts to its cash balances and to manage its cash flow.

Human Resources Information Systems (HRIS) If you have ever been an employee of an organization, you have been involved in the human resources component of the value chain. Typically, human resources is responsible for recruiting and hiring staff, and managing staff compensation and training. Even the smallest of companies must manage basic human resources processes like hiring and interact with payroll to ensure that staff members are paid. *Human resource information systems (HRIS)* are enterprise systems that enable this component of the value chain. HRIS systems house information about employees, including contact information, years of service, experience, and training received. All of this kind of employee-related information is critical in terms of understanding the costs associated with staffing an organization. HRIS systems should be able to answer critical questions like, What is the monthly expenditure on salaries across the organization? What is the average number of hours per week worked by non-salary staff? What is the company's portion of benefits paid for each employee? Data contained in an HRIS are very important to organizational decision making. Having accurate information that can be accessed quickly is a major benefit of HRIS.

Technology Development The technology development component of the value chain is quite specific to individual organizations. The sole purpose of technology development is to support the value-creating activities of the organization. If the organization is a retail operation, certainly the creation and maintenance of an e-commerce website would be an example of an enterprise system supporting this area of the value chain.

Most companies now have intranets as a way of supporting value-creating activities. Intranets provide employees with important information about their employer, employee benefits, and administration information such as telephone numbers and locations. Intranets may also act as a knowledge management system, providing information to employees critical to performing their jobs. In addition, organizations may use specific systems or programs to create custom developed enterprise systems to support the business. Development systems, such as integrated development environments (IDE), are discussed in Chapter 6.

Procurement All companies must purchase materials of some kind. As a student you procure books, a laptop, software, pens, paper, and so on to enable you in the business of studying. Procurement supports all primary components in the value chain, especially inbound logistics, as the raw materials necessary for the product or service to be produced are acquired in the procurement process. Enterprise systems for procurement are often part of the financial systems of the company. These systems help to manage preferred vendor lists, indicating which vendors supply what items. If suppliers are required to issue bids when a company is purchasing something, procurement systems can assist by tracking and ranking bids. Most often, procurement systems issue purchase orders when it is determined that something needs to be purchased. Depending on the size of the purchase, a procurement system may manage the approval process required for the purchase. Procurement can be a time-consuming and document-intense activity. Because of this, organizations seek to automate many procurement functions using integrated e-commerce and online payment systems (which we will discuss in more detail in Chapter 7).

Of course, any system that a business chooses to install should be linked to its value chain and to a measureable performance metric that helps it manage the impact of that system on its overall success. An appropriate measure (always linked to business strategy) can help determine how effective these systems are and, in effect, how effective or efficient the value chain activities become when using them. Some sample performance metrics listed in Figure 4.5 are associated with the value chain component and the sample systems.

As an example, let's say a company invests $2 million in a new quality management system. Once implemented, the company monitors product defect rates and compares them to the rates prior to the quality system implementation. What would you expect to happen? Surprisingly, at first rates may increase. Sometimes the act of monitoring brings previously unknown issues to light. As the underlying issues are resolved, however, defect rates should decrease.

Enterprise systems support every area of the value chain so an organization may have several of them. Some of these systems can be bought off-the-shelf; others require a high degree of customization to work with the specific business rules of an organization. Enterprise systems, either bought or built internally, can be very expensive to implement and maintain. Because of this, companies look for more economic ways of fulfilling the need for these systems. Software as a service (SaaS) application providers and "the cloud" are in some cases possible alternatives.

TECHNOLOGY CORE

What makes enterprise software like SCM, ERP, or software as a service (see Chapter 2) possible? In Chapter 2 we discussed network technologies, and in Chapter 7 we will discuss e-commerce technologies. These are the foundation of enterprise software; without these technologies we could not operate most organizations the way we do today. By using a combination of server-side programming to create the software, payment, and security systems that process and authenticate clients, and Web services for quick delivery of data, enterprise systems are used throughout organizations, with external partners, and over the World Wide Web. It is not uncommon for a manager in the U.K. to be monitoring U.S. sales using their integrated ERP system. Again, this is only possible because of both global networks and the associated IT-related technologies that enable e-commerce and web-based systems. Without these advancements in technology, enterprise systems as we know them today would not be possible.

Strategic Deployment of Enterprise Systems and Technologies

IT can be used to support just about anything inside an organization. With such a wide range of possible scope, how do you decide what the priorities are? Investing in IT takes money, and most organizations do not have unlimited amounts of that available to invest. In this section we are going to examine the ways in which IT can fit strategically within an organization and how the best organizations approach these important decisions.

There are primarily four ways in which a business can derive benefit by applying IT to support the organization and its processes:

1. *Supporting the value chain* – as we have discussed in previous sections, systems, such as an ERP, can be applied directly to the value chain to make it more efficient and effective
2. *Automating* – business processes and functions can be automated, enabling cost reductions, normally through the consumption of less labour and increased efficiency and reliability

3. *Informating* – IT systems create, store, and make available data that can be used to improve the quality of business decisions, as discussed in Chapter 3

4. *Gaining a competitive advantage* – implementing a new system that creates new capabilities may give an organization a temporary competitive advantage over their competitors

These views, summarized in Table 4.2, demonstrate that a business can use IT not only to support current operations, but also to gain strategic benefits. To help clarify what we mean, in addition to listing the scope and benefit of each tactic noted above, in Table 4.2 we also apply IT to an example, handling newspaper subscriptions, so that you can understand the applications of these four tactics in a real business setting.

As you can see from the newspaper subscription example, the four different tactics are not mutually exclusive. By using IT to allow new customers to subscribe online, the newspaper company can gain benefits that coincide with all four tactics simultaneously. By focusing on the subscription process itself, it gains greater efficiencies through automation. Through informating, it collects data that may help it further improve the process. The company may use the data it collects when users subscribe to gain a competitive advantage, by using it to support publications targeted at key customers or through some other means. While the process itself may fall within the marketing and sales activity of the value chain model, the company can use the collected data to make decisions about all of its primary activities. This is what the strategic application of IT is really all about.

Some would go so far as to believe that companies can gain a unique advantage through an exclusive use or application of IT. This was a widely-held view during the so-called dot-com years of the late 1990s and early 2000s. However, in recent years, some have challenged this view. In his provocative article, "IT Doesn't Matter,"[12] Dr. Nicholas Carr argues that since the core functions

Table 4.2	Comparing IT Strategic Tactics		
Tactic	**Scope**	**Benefits**	**Newspaper Subscription Application**
Support of value chain	Organization-wide	• Views organization as a system with need for integration of components and activities • Allows a focus on enabling value-adding activities • Helps to fit IT applications and infrastructure to organization	• Use subscription data to forecast demand and to better schedule inbound logistics, production, and outbound activities • Use demographic data for targeted marketing promotions and improved customer service
Automating	Process/transaction	• Allows for cost reduction, efficiency, quality, and consistency	• Use online subscription for newspaper to reduce printing and handling costs of paper-based, mailed subscription forms
Informating	Process/transaction	• Allows for knowledge and learning of core competencies	• Use transaction data to understand subscription process • Collect demographic data during online subscription application and use it to better understand customers
Competitive advantage	Organization-wide	• Connects automating and informating of processes to organizational strategy	• Develop a unique competency for delivering targeted content to various customer segments as identified by demographic and subscription data

---

12. Nicholas Carr, "IT Doesn't Matter," *Harvard Business Review*, 81(5), May 2003.

of IT—data processing, data storage, and data communications—are available and affordable for anybody, it isn't possible to develop sustained distinctive competencies on IT alone. In other words, if a company can put together an IT system that helps it automate a particular process, then so can its competitors. This is especially true when competitors can use SaaS providers to simply and easily access the same application suite at the same cost. This drives a significant question of **competitive necessity,** the need to keep up with competitors to stay in business rather than simply having competitive advantage. A company can only gain a sustained edge over its competitors by doing things that they can't do; yet the direction of the IT industry in providing massive and complete, but incredibly similar, application suites across the full realm of enterprise systems might drive a firm to believe in some ways that IT has simply become a commodity. The issue becomes getting access to systems we need at the lowest possible price in order to operate the business efficiently, while relying *solely* on product and service differentiation to establish and maintain a competitive advantage. In the alternate, only the largest and most successful global firms in any market will be able to sustain the level of investment necessary to even contemplate building their own systems, and that would create for the firm a competitive advantage born only of necessity in their marketplace.

The IS community continues to debate Dr. Carr's ideas. Dr. Carr maintains that IT is an essential part of the infrastructure of a competitive company, but ultimately inconsequential to strategy. Much of the business world agrees with Dr. Carr's view because many believe that competitive advantage built on systems is too ephemeral—that is, any advantage you gain cannot be sustained long enough to be worthy of the time and money invested in IT (because it's so easily copied by competitors, in most instances). However, this suggests that either there is a better place to invest those funds, which may be doubtful because improvements in efficiency and effectiveness deliver higher overall organization returns for long periods of time, even if competitors copy the IT capabilities themselves and the advantage ceases to be unique. It also suggests that there is absolutely no opportunity to gain competitive advantage with IT; and this is a statement with which we do not agree. There are some instances, albeit perhaps not as many or as often as some CIOs believe, where creatively and uniquely deployed IT systems can truly create a disruptive, innovative, or sustainable competitive advantage.

However, one cannot rely on technology vendors that create and sell IT naturally to help you figure out these strategic applications; most vendors take a position that sustained competitive advantage never comes from a particular technology itself, but from the intelligent application of IT to support business strategies and leverage distinctive competencies and the value chain of an organization.[13] They argue that the components they build and provide can be combined and altered in ways that make their application unique to a particular enterprise. This may or may not be true—and we will not attempt to settle that debate here. Rather, we encourage you to join the debate and continue thinking about the value and potential for competitive advantage offered by the strategic deployment of IT, and continue to acquire knowledge about how IT can make you a more successful business professional as you embark on your future career.

The Role of IS Governance and Leadership in Creating Sustainable Business Value

Recall our earlier discussion of Porter's value chain model, which showed the activities that create business value. Effective IT governance and leadership combine Porter's competitive strategies

---

13. E. K. Clemons and M. Row, "Sustaining IT Advantage: The Role of Structural Differences," *Management Information Systems Quarterly*, 15(3), 1991, pp. 275–292; L. M. Hitt and F. Brynjolfsson, "Productivity, Business Profitability, and Consumer Surplus: Three Different Measures of Information Technology Value," *Management Information Systems Quarterly*, 20(2), 1996, pp. 121–112; J. B. Barney, "Firm Resources and Sustained Competitive Advantage," *Journal of Management*, 17(1), 1991, pp. 99–120; and B. Wernerfelt, "A Resource-based View of the Firm," *Strategic Management Journal*, (5), 1984, pp. 171–180.

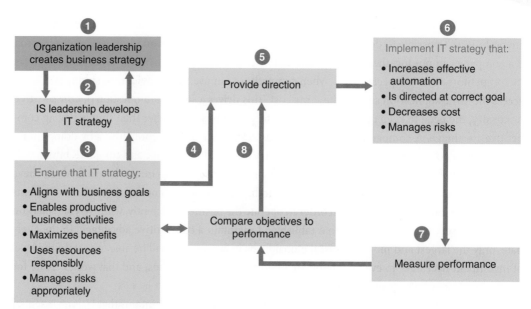

FIGURE 4.7 As this figure shows, effective IT governance and leadership, when combined with Porter's value chain model, can help create business value.[14]

with the value chain model to help create business value. To see how IT governance and leadership can do this, consider Figure 4.7. The figure includes numbered boxes that correspond to our discussion here.

For example, IT leadership can suggest how a business can integrate technology to reduce or eliminate costs throughout its value chain, until it becomes the lowest-cost producer or retailer (1). From this overall business strategy, IS leadership can develop a specific IT strategy, which enables the business to implement its lowest-cost strategy (2–5). Two possible ways for IT to help reduce costs are to automate a process or to support the **outsourcing** of a process to another location or vendor that can perform the process more efficiently and effectively. This is often referred to as business process outsourcing (BPO). This could include processes in IT, such as desktop support, help desks, hosting (often called IT outsourcing), or non-core processes in other parts of the business, such as accounting, human resources, or sales. The reduced process cost helps the business offer a lower price for its products or services, thus improving global competitiveness (6). If outsourcing a business process to another country, IT leadership will need to develop a strategy that includes how to support global operations (back to 1). Another way to support the low-cost strategy is to find efficiencies within the value chain. Some businesses do this by closely integrating business processes and systems with their suppliers to reduce time spent executing value chain activities. This may mean implementing SCM or ERP.

Regardless of whether implementing automation, outsourcing, or optimizing the value chain, the business must measure the performance and total costs of the effort against the unit cost savings for the production and delivery of the product or service. Remember there is also a need for many global organizations to have multi-lingual and multi-jurisdictional systems in place because their supply and value chains are global in nature. This might suggest a governance model for IT that is world-wide in outlook. Or it might drive a regional IT strategy in some instances, where this chart might be applied regionally to different types of operations globally. For instance, if you distribute software on the Internet, you will need to have a sales interface in multiple languages;

deploy tax tables appropriate to the jurisdictions you sell in; and have contracts and service agreements in place for different parts of the world. Or instead you might have a European division that operates distinctly from its U.S. and Canadian counterpart, and they might have different system needs and requirements than we have in North America. Either way, whether you are deploying a regional or global strategy model, these considerations for the global context of most IT strategies is another factor not specifically identified in this chart, but which will often add complexity to IT decision-making.

When all of this is taken into account, it determines if the IT strategy aligns with and meets the needs of the "lowest-cost" global business strategy (7–8). If not, the IT leadership must act to bring performance in line with expectations (5). Especially while pursuing a low-cost strategy, a business may not only be trying to create enhanced business value, but simply be trying to stay in business against global competitors. This suggests some companies may have to constantly improve their use of IT out of sheer competitive necessity, driving down unit costs quarterly or annually to remain cost-competitive.

You will notice in box 6 of Figure 4.7 that IT also manages risk. Risk is an essential element of business and no organization, even those in the public or not-for-profit sectors, can eliminate it entirely from their operations. This means that IT has a role to play to both tracking and managing risk, not only for its own operations, but also for the whole company in some instances. In the next section we discuss enterprise risk management (ERM) and the role of IT in this important task.

Quick Test

1. True or False. Metrics are not necessary when implementing an enterprise system because enterprise systems always improve the efficiency of the value chain.

2. Which of the following is NOT a source of enterprise systems?
   a. ASP
   b. IDE
   c. custom development
   d. SaaS

3. Fill in the blank. Because operations are the value-creating and often proprietary activities that transform raw inputs into a company's final product, operations are almost always _____.

Answers: 1. False; 2. b; 3. unique

■ ENTERPRISE RISK MANAGEMENT

All businesses face threats and risks. They cannot be eliminated completely, only anticipated and minimized. These can occur in real-time and impact current operations, or be forecast as possible threats or risks against future operations; regardless, there is a role for IT to play in monitoring and mitigating potential business risks.

Value is maximized when management sets strategy and objectives to strike an optimal balance between growth and profit goals and the inherent risks associated with these activities. For instance, if you work in mining and have operations only in Canada, but you can only grow revenues and profits if you expand abroad, there is obviously more risk in doing so than in operating only within the borders of Canada.

Let's reflect on this specific example for a minute. By going abroad you might have to deal with issues such as currency exchange risk; the risk of political instability in countries where you might want to build and operate mines over many years; the risk of changes in local tax and capital investment strategies that could affect returns; and so on. If you were the CIO of a mining company, you might be concerned with the security and integrity of systems and data in such remote locations; the stability and reliability of telecommunications and network services; or not being able to find local technically qualified staff who are skilled enough to avoid the additional costs of having to bring in expatriates from Canada to staff your local IT function. What other risks can you think of that might occur for a Canadian company operating in the mining industry abroad? We are certain you will easily think of others, confirming that business risks are real—but then, so are the potential rewards. Otherwise, organizations would not bother to expand and take on additional risk without return.

Obviously, businesses cannot anticipate or plan for all risks and threats. However, when creating and implementing a business strategy, a business must attempt to identify, address, and eliminate elements of risk before they threaten its success. To do this, businesses apply **enterprise risk management (ERM)**. One common definition of ERM is provided by the Committee of Sponsoring Organizations of the Treadway Commission (COSO) as:

A process effected by an entity's board of directors, management, and other personnel, applied in strategy setting and across the enterprise, designed to identify potential events that may affect the entity, and manage risk to be within its risk appetite, to provide reasonable assurance regarding the achievement of entity objectives.[15]

What this means is that everyone involved with planning for and enabling the success of the organization, including any external directors, is responsible for figuring out what can go wrong and how to manage it. This also consists of deciding how much risk they can stand (*risk appetite*) and still achieve their business goals.[16]

To help businesses identify risks and threats, the COSO developed an integrated ERM framework. This framework, shown in Figure 4.8, identifies four overlapping categories of business objectives for focusing on risk assessment and management:

- strategic—high-level goals, aligned with and supporting its mission
- operations—effective and efficient use of its resources
- reporting—reliability of reporting
- compliance—compliance with applicable laws and regulations

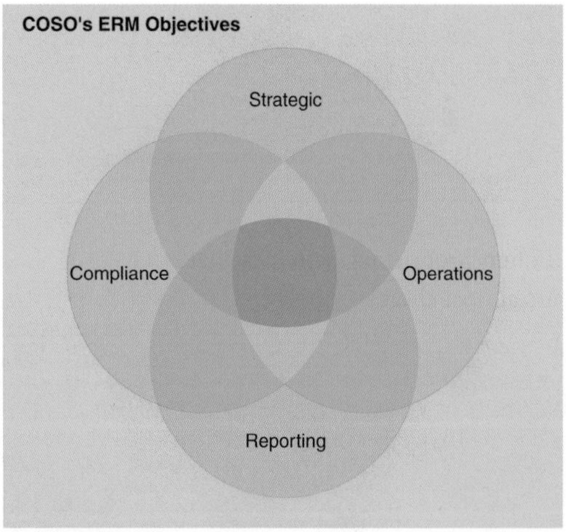

FIGURE 4.8 The COSO ERM framework identifies four overlapping categories of business objectives for focusing on risk assessment and management.[17]

IT has a role in supporting each of these categories. With respect to *strategy*, IT can provide important data for executive

15. Committee of Sponsoring Organizations of the Treadway Commission (COSO) ERM Integrated Framework Executive Summary, September 2004, p. 2. COSO (*www.coso.org*) is a "voluntary private sector organization dedicated to improving the quality of financial reporting through business ethics, effective inter-control, and corporate governance." ITGI, "IT Control Objectives for Sarbanes-Oxley," April 2004, p. 27.

16. *www.coso.org/Publications/ERM/COSO_ERM_ExecutiveSummary.pdf*

17. Adapted from the Committee of Sponsoring Organizations of the Treadway Commission (COSO) ERM Integrated Framework Executive Summary, September 2004, p. 3.

decision-making in setting goals and strategies that align with an organization's mission and that mitigate business risk. So far in this text we have seen many ways in which IT supports *operations* by automating, informing, and transforming, and through the implementation of enterprise systems. Through these activities, IT enables the organization to be more effective and efficient. Accurate, timely, and reliable *reporting* is simply not possible without the support of IT. With the appropriate IT systems in place, on-demand reporting provides organizations with critical information that they need to manage their business.

Lastly, IT supports compliance. **Compliance** reduces risk through policies and processes that, for example, ensure proper financial and accounting procedures or protect employee and customer data. Compliance practices and audit trails must be built into IT processes that store, process, and transmit data, for instance. Compliance efforts increase stakeholders' abilities to trust the integrity and accuracy of information reported by internal information systems, and ultimately to the public in the case of a public entity. Compliance with laws and regulations ensures that stakeholders and the general public can trust that organizations are performing as stated and are prudently managing risks as they try to achieve their business goals. IT helps organizations with compliance by ensuring that appropriate checks and balances are in place in the systems used by the organization on a daily basis, and that information required for any external audits, accounting or system, is provided.

Why is non-compliance such a risk? Trust is an important cornerstone of global economic and financial systems. Trust is supported through effective continuous compliance practices; non-compliance destroys trust and opens the door to fraud, waste, and mismanagement. For example, after the publication of details involving the financial scandals of Enron and WorldCom, people generally began losing trust in the entire financial industry. This was most recently followed by the bankruptcy of Lehman Brothers and Bear Sterns, which caused equal skepticism about banks. In fact, one might argue these bankruptcies started the most recent global recession. Now consider what happened in the European Union with Greece and the developing debacles around other European countries like Italy, Spain, and Ireland in 2011. When you can no longer trust even the government to pay its debt, then who really is a good credit risk? What does that mean for the cost of capital, interest rates, and the general legitimacy of our banking systems?

As mistrust caused market chaos, resulting in global repercussions for governments, corporations, and individuals, the U.S. Congress intervened in the form of legislation, most notably the Sarbanes-Oxley Act of 2002. Individual organizations involved in financial regulation have also stepped in, such as the Canadian Public Accountability Board (CPAB) and the Auditing and Assurance Standards Oversight Council (AASOC), which were formed primarily to encourage compliant practices. And because Canadian and U.S. capital markets are co-dependent, the Canadian Securities Administrators (CSA) have adopted multilateral instrument (MI) 52-109, which essentially demands the same level of certification of financial statements for Canadian public firms that the United States does. International organizations, such as the International Monetary Fund (IMF) and the Financial Stability Board (FSB), are working on international financial issues and compliance matters, particularly as they relate to limiting the deficits of national governments to a lower and more sustainable standard, thus using a compliance mechanism to protect global liquidity and debt markets. And, as always, these actions affect IT.

Why has a piece of legislation that focuses on corporate financial reporting and accounting practices become so important? And why is it relevant to understanding and using information systems in business? Consider technology author Ben Worthen's suggestion: "Imagine, if you will, that Sarbanes-Oxley is a water purity test. What ultimately matters is the quality of the water coming out of the faucet. But no responsible organization would let its water be tested before thoroughly examining

Legislation that focuses on corporate financial reporting has been compared to a water purity test. If the source and all of the plumbing used to deliver the water is clean, then the water itself will be clean. Likewise, if the IT supporting an organization is secure and meets all compliance regulations, then the data from that organization will also be "clean."

and repairing its plumbing, especially when failure means multimillion-dollar fines, a ruined reputation, and possibly jail time for top executives."[18]

If the plumbing (IT) is clean and intact from source to spigot, then as long as the source is clean (IT governance and auditing), so will be the water (data). Because information systems store the majority of a modern business's financial data, these systems must have proper controls in place if the data and the financial reports are to be accurate, reliable, and trustworthy. This is why any accounting firm conducting an audit of a public company today will spend as much time auditing their IT systems and practices as they do the actual "books." Without determining the integrity of the underlying IT systems, the audit of only the financial results would be an inadequate job that would not be able to draw a reliable conclusion otherwise.

Applying the Risk Framework

How do businesses apply the ERM framework to address enterprise risk? They first identify and categorize potential risks. For example, if you are the CEO of a specialty e-tailer (strategy), your customers will buy your goods using the Internet (operations). Accordingly, you need to have secure Web servers (compliance and control) to provide shopping and account management services to your customers (operations), as well as to collect, analyze, and communicate financial, transactional, and other data (reporting and compliance).

Once a risk is identified, the next step is to assess risks and threats using two primary criteria: impact and likelihood. Continuing on with our example, you realize you risk loss of business due to a denial of service (DoS) attack launched against your servers (denial of service is discussed in detail in Chapter 2). How would you assess this risk? You might begin by estimating the dollar-value impact (cost) of your servers' inability to respond to customers' requests. Say your business averages daily sales of $1 million. What if the server problem persists for several days? What if the servers are outsourced to an offshore vendor in a different time zone? You can see that an extended denial of service would severely affect your current operations and the execution of your business strategy.

You next need to determine the likelihood of a DoS attack. How do you estimate this? You can collect data from a reliable source, such as the 2007 e-Crime Watch Survey.[19] Using the data from the survey, you determine that there is a 49 percent chance your organization could experience a DoS attack.

18. Ben Worthen, "Sarbanes-Oxley: The IT Manager's New Risks and Responsibilities," *www.cio.com/article/31900/ Sarbanes_Oxley_The_IT_Manager_s_New_Risks_and_Responsibilities?page=2*

19. "2004 e-Crime Watch Survey," CSO magazine, U.S. Secret Service, CERT® Program, Microsoft Corp, *www.cert.org/ archive/pdf/ecrimesummary07.pdf*, retrieved February 11, 2010.

Now you have to decide whether or not this risk is acceptable. Recall that you previously estimated $1 million in lost sales per day if your business experiences a DoS attack. As a result, you decide to implement improved security procedures and invest in IT security infrastructure improvements as necessary.

As in our example, once an organization has addressed its ERM objectives, it needs to focus its greatest effort on managing risk, especially where high-probability risks will have the greatest impact. Figure 4.9 shows the enterprise risk matrix that helps organizations classify risks. The upper-right corner of the ERM matrix shows the area where there are high probability and high impact risks that must be addressed. Businesses should also manage applicable risk (the orange area in Figure 4.9) *before* it evolves into high-impact/high-probability risk. Finally, businesses should note the *immediacy* of a risk. Due to the diminished amount of time available to discover and implement mitigation policies or processes for immediate risks, businesses need to proactively manage these risks rather than react to them.

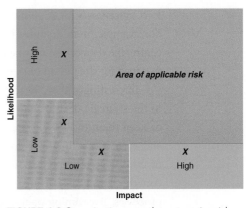

FIGURE 4.9 Organizations use the enterprise risk matrix, where X indicates a potential risk, to ensure that they focus their efforts on addressing high-probability risks that will have the greatest impact (upper-right corner of the ERM matrix).[20]

Risk-Reduction Methods

Once an organization identifies risk, it must find ways of responding to those risks. IT is a critical enabler in responding to risk. In fact, many risk responses would not be possible without IT. Table 4.3 lists some examples of organizational responses to enterprise risk; let's examine how IT plays a supporting role in the risk responses listed in Table 4.3.

Risk Transfer Through the use of IT, organizations can use outsourcing to transfer risk. Earlier in this chapter we discussed outsourcing as a way to make business processes more efficient. Outsourcing can also shift risk outside of an organization to another business that may be better equipped to mitigate risk. For example, several organizations outsource the management of their data centres (facilities housing servers that contain applications and data). Data centre management companies are up to date on the latest technologies and developments in the area of data storage and data facility design. These data centre facilities provide the ideal environment for an organization's hard-working servers and provide staff knowledgeable in monitoring and maintaining this equipment. Because the care of this equipment is the sole focus of these centres, it is likely that the risk of adverse events is reduced. Also, organizations used for outsourcing are often held to strict *service*

Table 4.3	Types and Examples of Organizational Responses to Risk
Risk Response	**Action**
Risk transfer	Move the risk to someone who is more able to deal with it
Risk deferral	Postpone exposure to the risk until circumstances are more favourable or resources are available to address the risk
Risk reduction	Either reduce the probability of the risk occurring or lessen the impact
Risk acceptance	Realize that some risks are unavoidable and make sure that contingency plans are in place
Risk avoidance	Eliminate the possibility of the risk occurring; however, that may close the doors on some business opportunities as well

20. Applicable risk as defined by the Institute of Chartered Accountants of England and Wales, cited in "How 7799 Works," *Gamma, www.gammassl.co.uk/bs7799/works.html*

level agreements (SLA), which penalize the organization monetarily should the SLA not be met. For example, if an organization's data or applications are not available due to an issue at the data centre, the data centre may be required to reimburse its client for lost revenue, or at least refund any fees paid for the period of the outage.

Interestingly, there is also the opposite of outsourcing, called in-sourcing. **In-sourcing** refers to the strategic decision made by a business to bring various services or functions back in-house, or keep them in-house, rather than globally source them. Firms concerned with security, quality, and even cost reduction may decide to bring a formerly outsourced IS development, call centre, or other business application back in-house. For example, in 2003, Farmers Insurance Group, an American insurance group with revenues of $11.5 billion and 19,000 employees, in-sourced its IT processes, reassuming operation and control of mainframe IT support, application, and development. According to former Farmers' CIO Cecilia Claudio, Farmers realized an annual savings of $6 million within one year.[21] Of course, in-sourcing reverses risk transfer and the organization must account for the increased risk.

More recently, starting in 2007, Ford planned to in-source more than 2,100 jobs by 2012, exceeding by roughly 35 percent the original contractual commitment to bring 1,559 jobs back to UAW-Ford employees through 2011.[22] They noted the ability to hedge currency fluctuations and rising commodity prices, mitigating unforeseen supply chain issues, and the ability to achieve just-in-time production as the reasons for this change.

Risk Deferral Sometimes IT is used to defer risks. One example of this strategy in action was during the Y2K crisis. As the year 2000 approached, companies became aware that their existing systems would not be able to handle the year format ending in "00." This created frantic activity to investigate new systems to install to avoid any adverse effects. As many of the systems available at the time were too complicated and difficult to install prior to the year 2000, many companies hired programmers to alter existing programs—sometimes coding line by line—to defer the risk of adverse activities at the turn of the century. Once the year 2000 arrived, many companies then pursued new systems to ensure long-term stability. ERP systems were among those selected, boasting sales of this new type of system and launching ERP vendors.

Risk Reduction One of the most common ways that IT reduces risk is by enabling disaster recovery. Many organizations have developed disaster recovery, business continuity plans, or both. These plans address what to do should the organization be faced with an event causing significant business risk. Important considerations for a disaster recovery plan were discussed in detail in Chapter 2. A disaster recovery plan is a subset of a business continuity plan that concerns primary IT resources, such as data. A business continuity plan addresses problem prevention, response to crises, resumption of business, recovery of losses, and restoration of systems and processes. The business continuity plan is exactly that—a plan to ensure the survival of the business in all aspects.

Risk Acceptance Not all risks can be transferred, deferred, proactively reduced, or avoided. Organizations must accept some risk; for example, when they go into new ventures or introduce new products. Without risk there is no chance of a greater return. If you have financial investments, you know this to be true. Businesses make changes all the time. We have discussed how businesses pursue competitive advantage through automating, informating, and transforming, as well as implementing strategic enterprise systems. With each of these actions, organizations accept a certain level of risk. Even though the level of risk is acceptable, it is prudent to have a contingency plan in place should something unexpected occur.

---

21. Stephanie Overby, "Bringing I.T. Back Home," *CIO Magazine*, March 1, 2003.

22. *www.fordahead.com/home/u-s-investment/in-sourcing/*

In the case of system changes, one contingency plan is to have a roll-back strategy. A **roll-back strategy** essentially involves being able to reverse every action that took place to make the change happen such that everything is returned to its original state with no damage done. Another common contingency plan is to plan a budget contingency should an unexpected expenditure occur on a risky venture.

Here is a very simple example you may have experienced with respect to risk acceptance. You have invited your girlfriend/boyfriend over for dinner and really want to impress him or her. You select a delicious sounding French recipe that you have never made before. You are accepting the risk that it may not turn out exactly like it is pictured on *www.allrecipes.com*, but if it does, your girlfriend/boyfriend will think you're a kitchen superstar! You accept the risk, but buy double the amount of ingredients in case it doesn't turn out the first time and you have to try to make it again (roll-back strategy). You also buy a frozen lasagna, just in case (contingency).

Risk Avoidance Probably the most popular risk response is avoidance. Isn't it human nature to avoid risk at all costs? No one likes to be put in a compromised situation. One way organizations avoid risk is to implement controls, which we discuss in detail in the next section.

Control and Controls

Implementing controls is not only a way of avoiding risk, but it may end up providing a control advantage through IT. We define **control advantage** as the strengthening of internal controls and compliance through the application of IT-based controls to business processes, policies, and procedures. Table 4.4 lists some frameworks that organizations rely on to attain this control advantage.

To help you understand how IT can enhance corporate control efforts, we first discuss control and controls in general. We then review the overall process of internal controls, using an example to highlight how IT can enhance the effectiveness and efficiency of controls.

Defining Control and Controls Businesses generally base control around three key concepts:

1. Control is a process that runs throughout the organization.
2. Control influences how people behave at work.
3. Control can only provide reasonable, not absolute, assurance of achieving objectives.[23]

Controls are specific actions, including policies and procedures, designed to ensure the achievement of business objectives. *Effective controls* prevent, detect, and correct actions that increase the enterprise's risk of failing to meet business objectives, such as inappropriate financial and accounting practices, fraud, misuse of resources, and ineffective physical and electronic security practices.

COSO defines **internal control** as

a process effected by an entity's board of directors, management, and other personnel, designed to provide reasonable assurance regarding the achievement of objectives in the following categories:

- *effectiveness and efficiency of operations*
- *reliability of financial reporting*
- *compliance with applicable laws and regulations*[24]

All these categories should incorporate three broad types of controls: preventive, detective, and corrective. *Preventive controls* are designed to prevent increased exposure to risk by stopping some

---

23. K. H. Spencer Pickett, *Internal Control: A Manager's Journey*, New York: John Wiley & Sons, 2001.
24. *www.coso.org/resources.htm*

Table 4.4	Selected Compliance and Control Frameworks and Standards[25]
Frameworks and Standards	**Description and URL**
COSO (Committee of Sponsoring Organizations of the Treadway Commission)	A framework for internal controls, in addition to an Integrated Enterprise Risk Management framework (See *www.coso.org*)
COBIT (Control Objectives for Information and Related Technology)	A framework for effective governance and control of enterprise IT and information (See *www.isaca.org and www.ITgovernance.org*)
ISO 17799 and BS7799	A framework from the International Organization for Standardization that focuses on information security controls ISMS is the means by which senior management monitor and control their security, minimizing the residual business risk and ensuring that security continues to fulfill corporate, customer, and legal requirements; it forms part of an organization's internal control system[26]
Information Technology Infrastructure Library (ITIL)	A set of best-practices standards for IT and service management; the U.K. Central Computer and Telecommunications Agency (CCTA) created the ITIL in response to the growing dependence on information technology to meet business needs and goals (See *www.itil-officialsite.com*)
Capability Maturity Model Integration (CMMI)	Guides process improvements across organizations, especially those associated with software development (See *www.sei.cmu.edu/cmmi/index.cfm*)
UCCnet, a subsidiary of GS1 U.S.	A standards organization that provides an Internet-based supply chain management (SCM) data registry service for e-commerce companies and companies that have an e-commerce component (See *www.gs1us.org*)
RosettaNet	An organization set up by leading information technology companies to define and implement a common set of standards for e-business (See *www.rosettanet.org*)
Institute on Governance (IOG)	A non-profit organization that promotes effective governance, including technology governance (See *www.iog.ca*)
Standards Council of Canada (SCC)	Facilitates the development and use of national and international standards and accreditation services; offers IT security evaluations and accreditation (See *www.scc.ca/en/programs/lab/it_secureval.shtml*)

25. Adapted from D. Cougias, "Moving into Compliance Mode: Realizing the Benefits, Cutting the Costs," *Hotel OnlineSpecial Report*, March 2005, *www.hotel-online.com/News/PR2005_1st/Mar05_MovingIntoCompliance.html*

26. *www.computersecuritynow.com/* and *www.gammassl.co.uk/bs7799/works.html*

action or process before it occurs. An example of preventive control is requiring employees to change their corporate network password every 30 days. *Detective controls* reduce risk by discovering when preventive controls have failed and providing notification that action must be taken. For example, if an employee has not changed his or her password in 25 days, then the employee may get a warning email message asking him or her to do so immediately. Lastly, *corrective controls* aim to remedy the situation and try to keep it from recurring. If the employee has not changed his or her password by the 30th day, then he or she could be locked out of the system until such time as they become compliant with the password change standards.

Specific Internal Control Processes Now that you have an understanding of controls, we next discuss seven generic categories of controls, highlighted by K. H. Spencer Pickett in his book *Internal Control: A Manager's Journey.*[27] The seven categories are:

1. segregation of duties
2. authorization
3. security
4. ID codes
5. verification
6. control totals
7. supervisory review

Segregation of duties (Figure 4.10) means that jobs do not span lines of control that would allow mistakes or fraud to go undetected. For example, say you only have one programmer who creates your critical e-commerce applications. A problem can arise if she is also the only person responsible for testing, debugging, and certifying the system. Further, if she leaves the company, who would know if she had created a back door in the e-commerce software, allowing her to hack the system

FIGURE 4.10 Segregation of duties helps to prevent any mistakes or fraud from going undetected.

---

27. K. H. Spencer Pickett, *Internal Control: A Manager's Journey,* New York: John Wiley & Sons, 2001.

and steal sensitive data? Another programmer should review the code and the changes and possibly test, debug, and certify the system.

Authorization controls prevent scope creep and cost overruns in various situations, such as major projects or operations management. Allowing an individual programmer to make minor system changes is efficient. But some changes to the system can be very costly and may commit resources that are already assigned. As a result, another person, such as the project team leader, should sign off (authorize) any significant changes.

If the team leader and programmers are working on an e-commerce application, they will need access to a development database to develop their application. However, for the majority of their application development process, they do not need to access the organization's actual transaction database (production database). Executing untested new code against a production database is a recipe for disaster. To provide *security* for the production database, application developers should therefore log in separately to the development and production databases.

It is also a good idea to track the login IDs and activities of all users, as login IDs are a useful type of *ID code* (as is your student ID number). Tracking login IDs and other ID codes creates an audit trail that organizations can follow to ensure proper controls are in place and working. Organizations can also use them to detect and document attempts at unauthorized use.

Depending on how the application is implemented ("goes live"), *verification* controls can confirm that the application is accomplishing e-commerce functions (e.g., order placement, payment) without error. For example, verification controls can monitor return of merchandise counts to ensure that the new system is sending customers what they ordered.

Control totals can help detect fraudulent actions. Imagine that you return a product. Now say a dishonest employee credits a fictitious account that he created rather than your account. If the organization lacks control totals, which compare a customer's paid orders with credits received, it cannot detect this fraud. The item would have been returned and a proper credit in the correct amount given to a customer, just not the right customer.

Finally, supervisors should periodically audit and review processes and transactions. In the case of your e-commerce system, *supervisory review* could consist of ordering an item, calling customer service, returning the item, receiving credit for the item, and documenting the process. The supervisor would share any discrepancies with the responsible person(s), and then make improvements or take corrective actions.

Quick Test

1. Which one of the following is NOT an organizational response to risk?
   a. risk acceptance
   b. risk avoidance
   c. risk behaviour
   d. risk reduction

2. Fill in the blank. _____ reduces risk through policies and processes that ensure proper financial and accounting procedures, as well as protects employee and customer data that corporate IS stores, processes, and transmits.

3. True or False. Corrective controls reduce risk by discovering when preventive controls have failed and providing notification that action must be taken.

Conclusion

Enterprise systems is a very complex topic to cover; for those of you pursuing more in-depth careers in IT, you will certainly spend more time in the future learning much more about their selection and deployment to support the enterprise's mission. For those who are going to be spending their careers outside of IT, you have learned enough by now to realize that these systems will be central to the work that you do providing information, automating tasks, and delivering competitive advantage. You have learned about the value chain (both inbound and outbound logistics and their impact on efficiency and effectiveness) and you have learned that organizations must make critical decisions about how to strategically choose their approach to automating their enterprise. We delved into the thought-provoking idea, advanced by Nicolas Carr, that there is no sustainable strategic advantage that comes from IT alone, and that it should be treated in a utilitarian way that minimizes IT spend. Alternatively, we considered the various ways in which organizations can choose to make these types of decisions, and particularly how to do so with an eye toward minimizing risk while maximizing return—something to which all organizations ultimately aspire.

Now, with all this enterprise systems knowledge firmly in our minds, we move forward to explore specific elements of specific technologies that dominate much of IT today—the Internet, e-commerce, and social business are some examples of areas of focus, along with the important role that data and data management methods play in supporting these systems.

What's in IT for me?

When you are a business professional, you will likely use enterprise systems in your role. This is a good thing. As you have learned in this chapter, enterprise systems make organizations more efficient. They also make individuals more efficient. Imagine a time, not long ago, when accountants had to manually add up revenue numbers receipt by receipt and manually enter them into the appropriate general ledger. Now, with the touch of a button, they can see sales in total, or segmented in any possible way for any possible period, and all transactions are posted electronically directly from the source. The same is true in the marketing field. Marketers had to manually keep track of their product sales to specific accounts. Now it is possible for sales to be made through e-commerce or SCM systems and tracked automatically without any intervention by the salesperson. They simply collect their enterprise system-calculated commissions!

These two examples illustrate how enterprise systems take care of the more mundane or rote functions of a position. These functions are sometimes known as *non-value-added*, meaning that, while necessary, they do not add value to the activity or organization. Using enterprise systems frees up time for individuals within an organization to focus on more knowledge work or *value-added* activities. In the case of the accountant, this might mean having the time to investigate money-saving tax strategies, or in the case of the marketer, being able to focus on new ways to fulfill customers' needs. These activities improve the operations of the organization or increase revenue and are, therefore, value-added. Certainly, from an individual's point of view, these activities are more interesting and ones where business professionals can use their skills to the fullest. Thanks to enterprise systems, when you graduate, you will be able to use your knowledge in your role instead of doing the boring tasks you won't want to do!

What's in IT for an organization?

We have spent this chapter discussing the benefits of enterprise systems for organizations. One aspect not yet covered is how enterprise systems can benefit not-for-profit organizations. With tight funding and the reliance on donations and grants, not-for-profit organizations can find it challenging to acquire or build systems. With software as a service (SaaS), where organizations can pay on a per use basis, not-for-profit organizations are better able to manage software expenditure.

One popular SaaS in the not-for-profit area is called eTapestry. eTapestry offers not-for-profits online fundraising and donor management software. The software tracks donors, prospects, and alumni, while managing gifts, pledges, and payments. It is available on the Web and can be accessed by anyone in the organization with login permission. The system is hosted by eTapestry, so in-house technical resources are not required to manage the system. Without a service such as

eTapestry, individual not-for-profits may try to manage donor data using spreadsheets or ad-hoc database systems, never being able to analyze or understand their donor data to make the most of donation opportunities. Or worse, by not recognizing the need for a system for this purpose, not-for-profits might invest their hard-earned donor dollars in expensive systems to the detriment of the community or clients they are trying to serve. SaaS is often the perfect solution for the needs of the not-for-profit sector.

What's in IT for society?

Software is big business around the world. In 2011, Gartner Research predicted worldwide enterprise software revenue to be $267 billion, a 9.5 percent increase, despite the global recession.[28] Every country in the world has an information and communications technology sector. What does this mean for society? In a word: employment. Of course the research, programming, and marketing of the software create employment, but the sale and purchase of software is just the beginning. Often associated with the sale are consulting and training services. These actions impact employment and maybe even future employment as people acquire new skills by using the purchased software. The software purchased may improve business processes or operations or increase the revenue of the purchasing organization, all potentially leading to more employment. Sometimes the purchased software can lead an organization to obtain a global presence. Perhaps it has purchased web development software that allows it to sell online internationally or work with remote workers around the world. Despite the pressures felt by the software industry from open source software, SaaS, and cloud computing, the software industry is here to stay and the benefits to employment will continue.

---

28. *www.gartner.com/it/page.jsp?id=1728615*

RO↑ | STUDENT RETURN ON INVESTMENT SUMMARY

1. Describe ways in which organizations can apply IT to build business value.

Businesses can use IT to create a value chain, mapping each activity that must happen from initial customer interest and eventual purchase through to ultimate delivery of the product or service. By organizing departments into functional information systems, companies are able to archive and obtain past and current information about operations, accounting, or marketing to measure successes and optimize weaknesses. In order to carry out business processes within these departments, management teams must use workflow management systems. These systems outline the steps, organizational resources, input and output data, as well as the tools that are required to complete tasks. On front lines, transaction processing systems can add significant business value by tracking items that are sold, updating stock levels, and prompting the suppliers when replenishment is required. If a transaction processing system does prompt suppliers to replenish stock, it ties into that company's supply chain management, which takes into account all of the materials, inventory, orders, and logistics of product delivery. By using these information systems, businesses are able to optimize internal management, production, and front-line sales.

2. Explain how businesses can use enterprise resource planning to strategically fit IT to the organization.

Information systems, like the organizations they support, consist of more than IT. When applying IT, a business must consider the interaction of technology with the people who create and use it, the organizational structure and culture, the business processes, and the environment within which the organization resides. In other words, a business must consider the strategic fit of IT within the context of the organization as a system and what it is trying to accomplish. Table 4.2 and Figure 4.7 provide additional insights into IT and its strategic fit with organizations. One specific way that IT supports business strategy is through the implementation of enterprise systems that support individual components of the value chain, like logistics management systems in the inbound logistics component, or across all value chain components in the case of ERP. These systems support business objectives (as set out in the strategy) and are measured by performance measures to ensure that they are creating the expected value.

3. Describe IT's role in managing enterprise risk.

IT plays an integral role in both identifying and managing risk. IT helps to identify risk by providing data to management that may help them to recognize a threat. In managing risk, businesses turn to IT to: implement technology and controls supported by technology to minimize or avoid risks; assist with outsourcing to transfer risk; undertake activities to defer risk; and assist with contingency plans to minimize the impact of unavoidable risks. In the case of a disaster, IT is called upon to recover important data and ensure that the business can return to an operational state as soon as possible.

KNOWLEDGE SPEAK

adding value   133

business rule   138

competitive necessity   155

compliance   159

control advantage   163

controls   163

customer relationship management (CRM)   150

enterprise resource planning (ERP)   142

enterprise risk management (ERM)   158

enterprise systems   144

functional information systems (FIS)   135

in-sourcing   162

internal control   163

outsourcing   156

roll-back strategy   163

supply chain   140

supply chain management (SCM)   141

transaction   138

transaction processing systems (TPS)   138

value chain   132

workflow   137

workflow management system (WMS)   137

REVIEW QUESTIONS

Multiple-choice questions

1. The following is NOT a system that supports the marketing and sales component of the value chain.
   a. CRM
   b. production scheduling
   c. salesforce automation
   d. ERP

2. A system that enables transactions and captures key data created by transactions is
   a. a WMS.
   b. an ACID.
   c. a DSS.
   d. a TPS.

3. Organizations generally consider control as _____.
   a. a process that runs through the organization
   b. based around people and how they behave at work
   c. providing reasonable, not absolute, assurance that objectives will be achieved
   d. all of the above

Fill-in-the-blank questions

4. The area of _____ includes a set of risks that are predominately high likelihood and high impact.
5. _____ are large-scale applications deployed across the organization that support specific business units or functions.
6. The risk response where an organization tries to reduce the probability of a risk or minimize its impact is called _____.
7. The value chain model is a useful tool for defining an organization's goals and the activities that it can pursue to gain a sustained _____.

True-false questions

8. The application of IT to an organization can be seen from four different views: (1) automating, (2) informating, (3) competitive advantage, and (4) value chain support.
9. A workflow represents the steps, organizational resources, input and output data, and tools needed to complete a business process.
10. IT is solely responsible in an organization for enterprise risk management.

Matching questions

Choose the BEST answer from column B for each item in column A.

Column A	Column B
11. automating	a. Amazon.ca's use of patented "one-click" technology
12. informating	b. Gathering data about search patterns of online purchasers
13. competitive advantage	c. Having customers fill out their own online loan applications
14. support of value chain	d. Scanning bar codes on incoming materials to determine if they meet purchase orders

Short-answer questions

15. Describe the characteristics of a transaction. What happens if any one of these is not achieved?
16. Think of a business organization with which you are familiar, and list operations that would fall under each primary activity within Porter's value chain model.

Discussion/Essay questions

17. Some businesses create business value by extending the value chain outside of their organization to suppliers and others. From a value chain perspective, argue for or against external company involvement in managing support activities.

18. Considering your answer to the preceding question, how can information technology help transform organizational value chains?

19. Use the ERM framework and enterprise risk matrix to identify and assess risks that you may be facing as a student (e.g., no summer job). Determine a response to each of the risks in your area of applicable risk.

TEAM ACTIVITY

As a team, discuss a business you are familiar with, such as a food outlet in a nearby food court. Discuss the value chain of this business and the potential systems that support it. Create a diagram like the one in Figure 4.5, filling in the specific business objectives, systems, and performance metrics.

SOFTWARE APPLICATION EXERCISES

1. Internet

When you begin searching for a full-time job, you may find several positions require experience with SAP. SAP is the predominant supplier of ERP systems in the world. Go to *www.sap.ca* and learn more about its products. Find some customer testimonials and see how it is used in specific companies.

2. Presentation

Assume that your boss asks you to present one of the information systems in this chapter that support business to the CEO. Your presentation should provide an overview of the system; that is, describe what it is and how the organization could use it. Include both the benefits and risks of using the technology, potential vendors, and one or two examples of how others have used the system. Incorporate graphics as needed. Your presentation should be visually appealing as well as professional.

3. Word Processing

Prepare a disaster recovery and business continuity plan for yourself. Outline each of the critical things that you would need to recover or do to continue to function as a student should you find yourself without your possessions, including your computer.

4. Spreadsheet

Many companies have a lot of money tied up in physical assets such as machinery and IT hardware. To keep up with these physical assets and their value, companies typically maintain an equipment inventory. Often this information is contained in an inventory management system (IMS). Create a spreadsheet to track an equipment inventory for yourself. For each item, record or calculate values related to the physical condition and the financial status of the item as follows:

- *Physical condition*: Provide columns to record an asset or serial number, an item description, a location, a physical condition, the name of the vendor, and the years of service left.
- *Financial status*: Provide columns to record the initial value, a down payment, a date purchased or leased, a loan term in years, a loan rate, a monthly payment, monthly operating costs, total monthly cost, expected value at end of loan term, annual straight-line depreciation, monthly straight-line depreciation, and a current value. Calculate these values as follows:

     Monthly payment—if an initial payment is entered and it is not equal to the down payment, use an appropriate function to calculate this value

     Total monthly cost—monthly payment + monthly operating cost

Annual straight-line depreciation—use an appropriate function and parameters to calculate this value; if you are unfamiliar with depreciation, search the Web for more information about it

Monthly straight-line depreciation—annual straight-line depreciation ÷ 12

Current value—use an appropriate formula to subtract the current depreciation amount from the initial value of the item (*hint*: use the now() function in your formula; this one is challenging)

5. Database

Create a database of at least 10 suppliers that you use on a regular basis, such as the pizza delivery place. Include the suppliers' names, addresses, phone numbers, email addresses, and other relevant data such as hours of operation. If possible, export this database to your mobile device for easy access. You have now created a database that supports your procurement process.

6. Advanced Challenge

Imagine that you are a sales rep for a consumer goods company. Write a detailed job description for this position including a "day in the life" description. Imagine the types of systems that you need as support in the field as you visit customers. How will you know if inventory is in stock? How will you place orders for your customers? How will you track your sales commission? Develop a set of requirements for the systems you need. With these in hand, search the Internet to find available open source software that could support you.

ONLINE RESOURCES

Companion Website

- Take interactive practice quizzes to assess your knowledge and help you study in a dynamic way.
- Review PowerPoint lecture slides.
- Get help and sample solutions to end-of-chapter software application exercises.

Additional Resources Available Only on *WileyPLUS*

- Take the interactive Quick Test to check your understanding of the chapter material and get immediate feedback on your responses.
- Review and study with downloadable Audio Lecture MP3 files.
- Check your understanding of the key vocabulary in the chapter with Knowledge Speak Interactive Flash Cards.

CASE STUDY:
WALMART

From its humble beginnings in Bentonville, Arkansas, Walmart has grown to be the world's largest corporation in terms of revenue. As measured by the Fortune 500 before the 2006 oil price rise, it surpassed such corporate giants as General Motors and Exxon Mobil, the only two other companies to hold this position. On top of that, *Fortune* named Walmart as the "most admired" company in 2003, the first time the top Fortune 500 company has also had that honour. Reasons for this admiration? Walmart's constant efforts to lower prices for consumers actually influences the U.S. economy by keeping inflation at low levels and forcing productivity up. Famed investor Warren Buffett calculated that Walmart contributes $10 billion a year to the U.S. economy.

Founded in 1962 by Sam Walton, a large part of Walmart's move to the top of the Fortune 500 ranking resulted from its aggressive use of information systems and technology. Unlike many of its competitors, Walmart always considered information technology as a competitive advantage rather than an expense. Walmart was one of the first companies to use POS terminals and bar codes at check-outs.

Other retailers also eventually used this same technology, but Walmart applied it innovatively. For example, rather than hoarding or selling the data that bar codes and POS systems generated, Walmart shared it freely with its suppliers, such as Procter & Gamble, as a way of improving its incoming logistics. The suppliers thus obtained the data necessary to replenish Walmart's products without waiting for the retailer to order them. This process resulted in an average savings of 20 cents per shipping case for both Walmart and the supplier.

In 1991, Walmart took this sharing process one step further. It formalized sharing with an information system named Retail Link, which enables suppliers to look up sales and prices of their products in any Walmart store. This information helps the supplier plan its production and distribution to Walmart, leading to better and cheaper products. Over 40,000 suppliers now use Retail Link. Walmart is also pushing a web-based version of EDI as a way to provide suppliers with even more information and data.

Another important part of Walmart's philosophy of sharing information was the introduction in 1995 of collaborative forecasting and replenishment (CFAR). With CFAR, vendors can access Walmart data from their home offices and adjust for causal factors themselves. Walmart does not collaborate with vendors over public exchanges, but instead works with them through Internet connections to its retail link system.

This commitment to the use of IT is most obvious in Walmart's supply chain; that is, the flow of products from its suppliers to its shelves. As one observer put it, "Grocers always invest in new stores. Walmart invests in the supply chain, then in new stores." By using the latest in technology to squeeze inefficiencies out of the supply chain, Walmart keeps its costs down, which enables it to offer lower costs than its competitors. For example, recently Walmart has been a leader in pushing the adoption of radio frequency identification tags (RFIDs) in products coming into its distribution centres. These RFIDs are tiny tags that replace bar codes as a way of identifying products. They have the advantage that they do not require direct contact or line-of-sight scanning to identify the product, and make it possible for retailers to know exactly what is in a pallet coming into the loading dock without having to be near it.

Walmart also uses information technology for competitive advantage in product distribution. For example, Walmart uses its POS data to minimize warehouse inventory. By using the warehouse as a "pass-through" point, where goods come in from the supplier at one side and go out to the store on the other side the same day over miles of conveyor belts, Walmart saves time and money. To improve this process further, Walmart was also an early member of UCCnet, the data synchronization and registry service of the Uniform Code Council that sets the codes used in bar code systems. This avoids problems with pallets with bar codes that fail to match the purchase order listing, which delays processing at the loading dock. If a pallet has a high-demand product on it, the result of the delay could mean lost revenue and unhappy customers.

Case Questions

1. In what ways does IT contribute to the growth of Walmart?
2. How is Walmart using IT to share data and information with suppliers? Why does this lead to lower prices for consumers?
3. What are Walmart's recent IT innovations, and how will they lead to lower costs?

CASE STUDY:
JEM ENTERPRISES

You have just been hired as the new marketing analyst at JEM Enterprises. They are a manufacturer of small consumer electric devices for the Latin American market, which your company does well with because your President is Venezuelan. You have some manufacturing capacity based locally in several South American countries to avoid tariff rules, but also do some design and engineering in the United States. Your head office and most of your accounting, marketing, operations, and finance activities are in Canada because that is where the company started many years ago and where the owner prefers to live.

The company is getting ready to purchase and install a complete ERP system, company-wide, that will integrate its operations globally. Of particular interest are the improvements in supply chain management this will bring to the enterprise. However, while the project is full of folks from operations and manufacturing, they did not (until recently) have a marketing representative; you were just assigned to join this team. To bring you up to speed, they provided you with several large documents that lay out the project background, provide justifications for decisions, and outline the business case and project approach. They all seem pretty good to you. The team is just at the point of deciding between SAP and Oracle as the preferred vendor for their ERP system.

Two weeks ago, each vendor was invited in and presented basic system information,
including estimated pricing (although this will not be a deciding factor, since both are affordable for the company). So, it will come down to a more difficult fit and function decision. As a result, the President has called a project team meeting for next Tuesday to gather perspective on this important decision. The project team asks you to develop "marketing's position" on this choice by then.

To do this, you develop a list of key questions you think you need to find answers to:

1. What are the differences and similarities between the two systems?
2. Is one or the other better for customers or customer data tracking?
3. What have other manufacturing companies experienced with the vendors?
4. If marketing wants a CRM in future, which is easier to integrate with?
5. What else can you find online that might be helpful sources of insight?

You do not want to be completely uninformed when participating in this discussion, so you decide to go online and do some research on these points before going into the meeting. You will also need to secure the support of the VP of Marketing for your position before presenting it, and you know he likes short and precise, not long and exhausting, analysis.

Case Activities and Questions

1. Summarize what you find out from your research in a single page "position paper" that outlines what you think the marketing department's initial position should be on this critical company decision.
2. Is there anything else that should be considered or that marketing should raise with the other departments that they might not think about in this decision?
3. If it was you, how else would you go about ensuring this IT system decision remains optimal from a marketing perspective?

5 | CREATING BUSINESS VALUE

WHAT WE WILL COVER

- Business Organization and Business Processes
- Applying IT to Create Business Value
- Corporate, IT, and Project Governance

STUDENT RETURN ON INVESTMENT **ROI**

Through your investment of time in reading and thinking about this chapter, your return—or created value—is gaining knowledge. After reading this chapter, you should be able to

1. Explain how businesses organize and use business processes to achieve competitive advantage.

2. Describe how IT helps create business value.

3. Explain the various types of organizational governance and state why governance is important in today's business world.

THE VOICE OF EXPERIENCE

Chris Moore, Computer Programming, Centennial College

Chris Moore is the Chief Information Officer for the City of Edmonton. Graduating from Centennial College with a Computer Science Diploma in 1983, Chris believes in continued learning and encourages everyone in IT to stay relevant with industry trends. Chris has worked with small, medium, and large organizations to create business value by actively pursuing collaboration and co-creation.

What do you do in your current position? I provide leadership and vision for the City of Edmonton's information and technology direction. I advocate open ecosystems, open data, and information sharing, encouraging everyone to be paper-free and use information in its digital form. I'm often experimenting with new social media to understand and articulate its value to others.

What do you consider to be important career skills? In IT, people often move up in an organization because of their technical skills, but it's important to hone your people skills as well. Knowing how to effectively communicate and coach others is crucial. To be an efficient people leader in IT, you must know how to effectively compromise and negotiate. You have to be able to listen and quickly analyze a situation to root out the cause then take action.

How do you use IT? I use IT solutions to conduct meetings, generate reports, and monitor the newest developments in my industry. I'm a big advocate of cloud computing where everyone can access one source of truth, collaborating together. At the City, we hold paperless meetings and, prior to these meetings, my team collaborates to build a meeting agenda. During meetings we project the agenda on a large screen so that everyone can work on it in real-time. Throughout the meeting, everyone makes notes in the document to minimize the chance of someone misinterpreting what someone else has said. In this way, technology is a tool to collaborate.

Can you describe an example of how you have used IT to improve business operations? In 2009 we launched an open data catalogue with 12 data sets. As of 2012 we've

grown that catalogue to 129 data sets. Before we launched this catalogue, I had to produce a report for council that explained open data and answered the questions that council posed. I had 12 weeks to produce the report, so I set up a Google document, logged onto Twitter, and asked my network if anyone wanted to be a part of my open data report. I ended up with 38 report authors from around the world with experience and expertise on open data. My challenge was taking the 10 pages that the collaborative group produced and translating it into a succinct two-page council report. I didn't want to compromise the contributions, so I placed a link to the Google doc within the council report so that people could still see the original source and every author's work could still be accurately attributed.

Have you got any "on the job" advice for students seeking a career in IT or business? Make sure IT is your passion. Keep asking "why?" and don't relent. IT is going through a huge transformation. In 60 years, two generations of people have gone through the industry. Some traditional IT workers struggle with change. They believe that if the systems work and they are robust, they should be left as-is. Don't get sidetracked by these traditional thinkers. Keep challenging the system because you're bringing in the next generation of IT. The way we've been developing IT is not sustainable. Large multi-million dollar budgets are a thing of the past. The information world is becoming more open and accessible. This means you have to be current, agile, and flexible to keep growing.

In this chapter we will discuss how business value is created by reviewing business strategy, business organization, and the business process. In the IT sphere, Chris creates value by centralizing documents to foster collaboration. Chris advocates transparency and data sharing to make value creation accessible for all businesses.

Building on the knowledge you have now gained about enterprise systems, you may realize that technology is not an end in and of itself, but rather it is a means to an end. Put simply, technology is a collection of tools that enable desired results. The design of great technology is outcome-based; it is built with the end in mind! An example of this might be the serial success of many new Apple consumer products where new technology so easily meets innovative forms and functions that people clearly and quickly embrace. Similarly, from a business perspective, technology enables strategy, competitive processes, and innovation, which ultimately define competitive advantage for an organization. In this chapter we will focus on these issues and help you deepen your understanding of applying IT to create business value.

■ BUSINESS ORGANIZATION AND BUSINESS PROCESSES

Because of the sheer number of different tasks that need to be coordinated to deliver the end product or service, organizations need a **business strategy**. As we discussed in Chapter 4, the organization's strategy devolves from its core purpose and analysis of its value chain. Properly constructed, the strategy becomes a road map for what needs to be done to create high business value and lower costs, leading to competitive advantage. Some organizations seem to over-think when planning their strategy, perhaps by not focusing on its simplest form: a clear statement about what they have to do well. If an organization cannot create this basic premise, then it is hard to align IT systems to optimize organizational performance. Having a clear strategy is what creates the focus for IT in an organization, so we need to study this further.

Often when you seek out an organization's strategy, it will be linked to a series of other important statements about the organization. You might imagine it like a series of concentric circles, like in Figure 5.1. The organization's mission is *why it exists*. The vision is *what it does*. And the values represent statements about *how it achieves its mission*. The purpose of an organization can then be defined as where mission, vision, and values meet to create opportunities for strategic action. Of course, surrounding and influencing this are an organization's various stakeholders, as shown in the outer circle of Figure 5.1. We will discuss this in more detail in sections to follow.

Sometimes strategic conversations in an organization involve fundamental questions like: Why do we exist? What can we be the best in the world at? What are we most passionate about? And how do we want to behave as an organization? Seeking even temporary answers to these types of profound questions is an important exercise that helps an organization understand itself and its evolving role in the world over time. It also enables the organization to attract and retain committed investors and employees who actively support the mission and vision. However, while these loftier conversations are important, they may lack specifics or may not completely define the complete strategy.

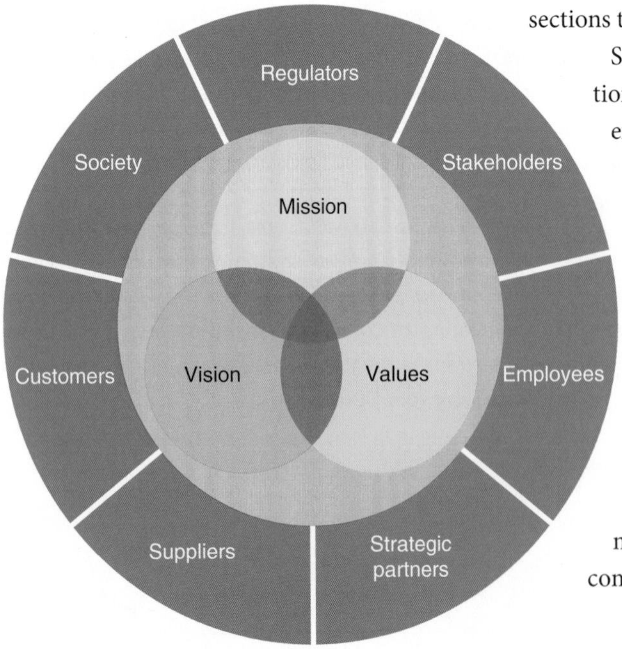

FIGURE 5.1 Business strategy influences.

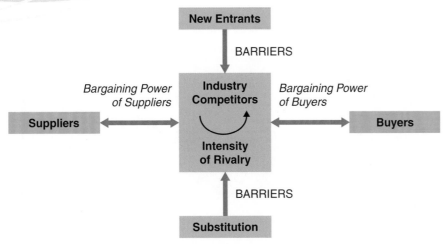

FIGURE 5.2 Porter's five forces model.

One of the better-known thinkers on strategy, Michael Porter, states that a *strategy* is:

a broad-based formula for how a business is going to compete, what its goals should be, and what plans and policies will be needed to carry out those goals.[1]

This simple and elegant definition complements our earlier understanding of an organization's core purpose. He suggests that the intensity of competitive rivalry in any industry or service sector can be attributed to forces that define that industry. If the industry is attractive and there are fewer barriers to entry, then more competitors will enter the industry, thereby increasing competition. If there are barriers to entry (such as requirements for large amounts of capital or government regulations), then it will be harder for new competitors to gain entry. Similarly, the industry has to consider the threat of consumers substituting a new product or service for existing ones, and the bargaining power of both suppliers and buyers to determine strategies to create and sustain competitive advantage. These are referred to as five strategic forces. Porter's "five forces" model, as shown in Figure 5.2, illustrates how these forces determine the competitiveness of an industry.

In today's world, of course, IT is an essential element of any organization's strategy. The major strategic contribution of IT professionals is to ensure that their efforts are aligned to help the business deliver its intended end result. However, before we discuss how businesses use IT productively, you need a good understanding of business fundamentals. Let's begin by considering the analogy of business organizations as open systems.

Businesses as Open Systems

Looking at an organization as a system helps you see how organizations use various resources, processes, and structures to create business value. In Chapter 1 we used an input-process-output model to define an information system. In this chapter, we expand the model into a general model of an organization.

As Figure 5.3 shows, the **open systems model** indicates that a business operates by transforming inputs into outputs and by constantly interacting with its environment. To understand this model better, we will begin by discussing two significant components of the business environment: stakeholders and boundaries.

Stakeholders and Boundaries in the Business Environment

Different businesses face different business environments. How businesses adapt to their environment contributes greatly to how their

---

1. Michael Porter, "What Is Strategy," *Harvard Business Review*, November 1996, pp. 69–84.

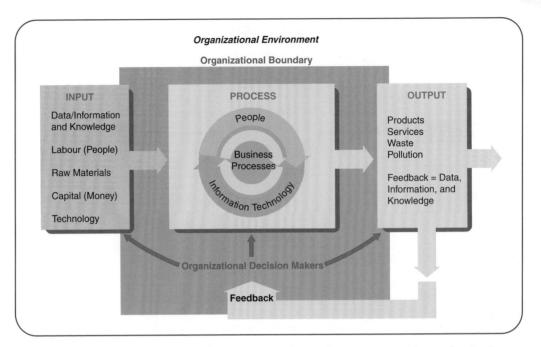

FIGURE 5.3 As this open systems model of an organization shows, a business operates by transforming inputs into outputs and by constantly interacting with its environment.

structure develops, and helps determine whether they succeed or fail as a business. What is in this environment that has such a profound effect on organizations? Stakeholders.

A **stakeholder** is a person or entity, for example a government agency or a shareholder, that has an interest in and an influence on how a business will function in order to succeed (or in order to not fail). A stakeholder may be external (in the environment) or internal (within the organizational boundary) relative to the system. Note that *influence* is an important part of the definition of a stakeholder. That influence may be actual or potential, great or small. It all depends on how the organization's decision makers perceive it in relation to a stakeholder's interests.

For example, you may be interested in how a certain company handles online shopping transactions. But if you don't shop at the company's website, you probably have no influence over how the company conducts its e-commerce operations. However, if you are a frequent customer and you email the company describing problems with its website, your suggestions may influence future e-commerce operations. Because you have both interest and influence as a customer of this organization, you are now a stakeholder in the organization's environment. Figure 5.4 shows other examples of external and internal stakeholders for a business.

Another important aspect of an open system is the **organizational boundary** (the perimeter of the green rectangle in Figures 5.3 and 5.4). Businesses must remain open to their environment. Why? An open boundary primarily allows a business to receive inputs and to produce outputs. Further, a business must be aware of what is going on in its environment so it can take steps to remain competitive by responding to opportunities or threats. In addition, a business needs external information to run its operations or processes on a daily basis. For example, before making business decisions, soft drink manufacturers like Coke or Pepsi need information about purchases of their competitors' products in various regions of the country, the expected cost of high fructose corn syrup (sweetening ingredient), and even the government's recent changes to tax laws. These are environmental factors that impact the organization and its performance.

As it interacts with its environment, a system will normally expand its boundaries to capture as much opportunity as it can. This is particularly true of private sector enterprises that have a profit-maximizing motive. So where competitive performance and opportunity both permit, the

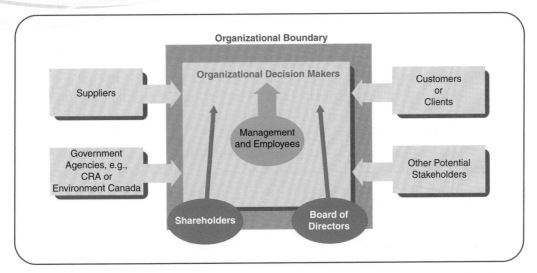

FIGURE 5.4 Organizational stakeholders, whether external or internal, have both an interest in and an influence on how a business will function in order to succeed.

organization can expand its boundary and increase its scope, seeking instinctually to maximize. But if competition intensifies or the business environment turns hostile, the same organization may also be forced to reduce its scope and focus on a lesser number of activities at which it can truly excel at a world-class level. Often organizations do not wish to face this reality and may wait too long before acting—to their own detriment. All of this has to do with the extent of opportunity present in the environment and how an organization exploits it. Obviously organizations must constantly make these critical strategic decisions, and they do so by constantly conducting **environmental scans**.

But interaction with the environment also carries risk, especially when an environment changes constantly. There is even the threat of extinction in some cases (think typewriter companies, for instance!). New technologies drive innovation and can become a serious threat to an organization if they are not managed proactively. For example, organizations that use the Internet face new threats by online criminals that include the use of stolen or fraudulent credit cards and attacks against their online infrastructure. Yet, for all of its security challenges, most businesses and organizations must use the Internet because so many customers and clients do business this way. So the organization seeks to balance opportunity and risk. It is really a double-edged sword: you have to be in the game and play to win to stay competitive, but playing the game is risky and you can still lose!

WHAT DO YOU THINK?

In today's networked economy, organizational boundaries are not always clearly defined. Many organizations are blurring the boundary between their suppliers and their organization to gain greater efficiencies in their supply chain and create more business value. A recent evolution by some large retailers requires that suppliers manage the inventory bound for store shelves using sales data provided by the retailer. If supplies of a product are low, it is up to the supplier to recognize this and immediately ship whatever is needed to that store. With this in mind, consider the following questions:

1: How might retail businesses gain or lose from having suppliers directly manage their in-store inventory levels?

2: Are suppliers who don't provide this level of service to retailers at a disadvantage? Do they ultimately have a choice about complying?

3: Are there any risks associated with expanding an organization's boundary in the way these retailers have?

How Businesses Organize to Create Value

If you want to get something done in an organization, you need to know where to go for the information and how to get to the authority required to accomplish your task. To some degree, all business organizations possess structures that organize information, responsibility, and authority. When used appropriately, organizational structure helps get the job done. When misused, organizational structure can grow to an unmanageable size and density and can create a bureaucracy that seems to inhibit rather than facilitate productive work.

Figure 5.5 shows four representative types of organization structures. Companies often adapt these structures to their unique business situation or combine them in novel ways that suit their competitive environment, strategy, and preferences.

Consider Figure 5.5 from the viewpoint of a CEO. What do you notice? In **functional** and **decentralized structures**, the lines of authority (who has the right to tell whom to do what) and communication are vertically oriented. The **matrix structure** blends the functional and decentralized organizational structures; however, it has a risk of a more diffuse sense of authority. From top to bottom, the matrix is organized as a functional structure; from left to right, the matrix follows a product-focused (or project- or customer-focused) structure that creates teams across business units. Teams are an important part of business, and you would be hard-pressed to find a business that does not rely on the work of teams. In fact, this team orientation is one of the most oft-cited benefits of a matrix organization, most particularly in global multinationals where coordination across multiple geographies and product or service lines of business is required.

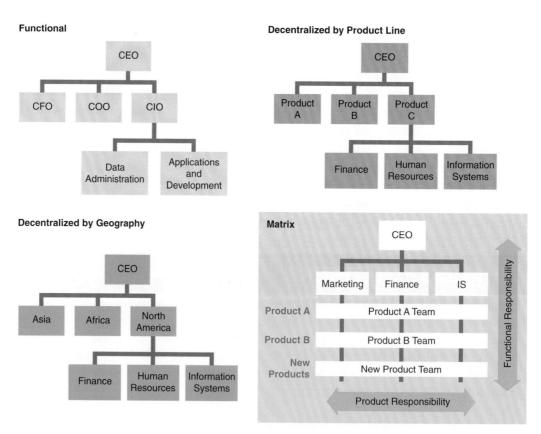

FIGURE 5.5 Functional, decentralized, and matrix organizational structures: modern organizations blend and extend these forms to adapt to a complex and changing global business environment.[2]

---

2. Adapted from Weinshall, 1971, from *Understanding Organizations*, Charles Handy, Oxford University Press, 1993, p. 257. Matrix organization diagram added by authors.

Table 5.1	Advantages and Disadvantages of Functional, Decentralized, and Matrix Organizational Forms[3]	
Organizational Form	**Advantages**	**Disadvantages**
Functional	• Economies of scale through efficient use of resources • Significant technical expertise found in the functional areas • Clear chain of authority and communications within a function	• Poor communication and coordination between functional areas • Relatively inflexible or slow to respond to change in the business environment • Employees may focus on functional area goals rather than organizational goals
Decentralized	• Faster response and greater flexibility • Greater communication and coordination between organizational units • Greater development of breadth of managerial skills	• Duplication of resources and efforts across organizational units • Technical knowledge not as in-depth relative to functional organizational form • Less direct control by upper management
Matrix	• Increased flexibility and responsiveness to business needs and environmental changes • Enhanced problem solving, cooperation, communication, and resource sharing • Decision making occurs lower in organization and closer to customer	• Frustration due to dual lines of authority and responsibility • Increased need for coordination between functional areas consumes time and resources • Potential for goal conflict between functional and decentralized components of matrix (e.g., marketing manager vs. product A manager)

In addition to the benefits of teams, a business might use a matrix structure to take advantage of the strengths, as well as make up for the weaknesses, of functional and decentralized forms. And organizations often combine organization types by, for instance, having a matrix structure within a "head office" to promote collaboration across the corporation globally, while defaulting to a geographic or functional structure within each major region of the world.

Table 5.1 lists some advantages and disadvantages of matrix, functional, and decentralized organizational structures. Finally, although functional, decentralized, and matrix structures represent more typical forms, modern organizations blend and extend these forms to adapt to a complex and changing global business environment.

Business Process

The preceding sections introduced you to the strategy and the concepts of businesses as open systems. This led naturally into a discussion of how businesses organize themselves to create business value. This suggests there is a goal in mind (strategy), the environment has been scanned and understood (boundaries set), and people are organized in a way to make it happen (organizational structure). What comes next? The business processes to execute the strategy. In fact, many CEOs that we have dealt with in our careers will admit that setting strategy is often the easier of the two tasks—bringing it to a successful conclusion is a major focus of business operations, with a constant emphasis on ensuring the entire organization understands the strategy and aligns behind it to make it happen.

---

3. Based on Richard L. Daft, *Management*, 3rd ed., pp. 300–312; and John R. Schermerhorn, *Management*, 7th ed., pp. 259–264.

To transform inputs to their main outputs (the products and services the organization provides or sells), organizations need to perform a series of steps known as a **business process**. A business process, as defined by Michael Hammer and James Champy in their influential book *Reengineering the Corporation*, is:

a collection of activities that takes one or more kinds of input and creates an output that is of value to the customer.[4]

Modern businesses are full of various processes and sub-processes. Some, like manufacturing processes, directly create output—a product like a car or a Blu-ray player—while others may offer a supporting service—like a help desk for internal IT systems. Before examining business processes, consider what a process is and how we go about studying them.

A process is often shown as input → process → output (refer to Figure 1.2). A process receives input(s), undertakes some action(s), and then produces output(s). Processes are all around us. As you read this book you are in the process of studying, for example. In this case, the input is this book, the process is studying, and the output, hopefully, is knowledge about information systems in business. This is a simple example of a process at a very high level.

Typically there are hundreds of processes involved in running a business. These processes link together and interact with one another to achieve the various goals of the business. Business processes can be incredibly complex and layered. The study of business processes is often compared to peeling the layers of an onion. You begin by looking at a high level view of the processes of an organization and continually delve deeper, uncovering more and more detailed processes and sub-processes. A sub-process is one or more tasks that accomplish a significant portion or stage of a process. Figure 5.6 illustrates a simple example of a process that you are likely quite familiar with—ordering coffee at a coffee shop.

This string of actions (or sub-processes) constitutes the process of buying a coffee. Does this process look complete and detailed? It might be surprising to learn that you can break this process down further into detailed sub-processes. Figure 5.7 shows the sub-process, *Order Coffee*, in more detail.

As you can see, even the most deceptively simple process can involve several sub-processes and steps, some of which seem so automatic or obvious that you hardly think of them as a process step!

One method used to analyze and better understand processes is called **IGOE**. Shown in Figure 5.8 in simple graphic form, this method used in process mapping illustrates the inputs (I), guides (G), outputs (O), and enablers (E) of a process.

Inputs to a process are those resources needed to start a process. In addition, in a series of processes, the output of a previous process may be the input of the next. To help illustrate this point, Table 5.2 lists representative types of inputs that are, at a high level, essential to any organization. *Guides* are rules, specifications, or policies within which a process must successfully operate. These

FIGURE 5.6 The process of buying a cup of coffee.

4. Michael Hammer and James Champy, *Reengineering the Corporation: A Manifesto for Business Revolution*, Harper Business, 1993.

FIGURE 5.7 The sub-process of the process *Order Coffee*.

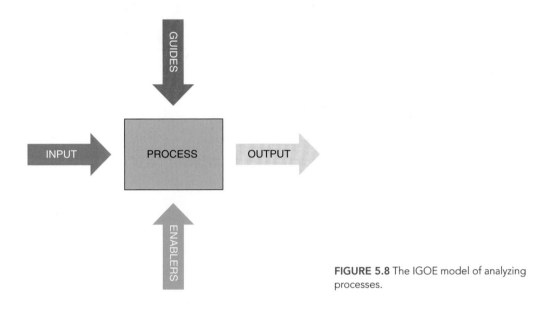

FIGURE 5.8 The IGOE model of analyzing processes.

Table 5.2	Examples of Inputs
Input Type	**Description**
Data, information, and knowledge	Raw facts, summarized data, information derived from research, and expert knowledge relevant to a business's goals (e.g., census data, consumer purchasing data, industry analysis, and a consultant's assessment of a business's IS security capabilities)
Labour	People hired to carry out all or part of the essential business processes or supporting functions (e.g., a production employee hired to make a product or a human resource analyst who manages an employee benefits program)
Raw materials	The "ingredients" from which the company makes its products (e.g., for an automobile manufacturer, a partial listing of raw materials includes steel, plastics, glass, and rubber)
Capital	The money that businesses need to operate (different forms of capital include cash, debt instruments like bonds, and stock—shares of company ownership)
Technology	Available in many forms, and greatly extending beyond PCs and software applications (e.g., robotic welders, computer-controlled assembly lines, mobile phones, and database and Web servers)

may also specify the performance, speed, cost, and other parameters and measures associated with operating the business process to a specified quality level that are essential to ensuring the business is competitive. In fact, fundamentally, the smooth and consistent operation of world-class business processes will almost always create sustainable competitive advantage in most industries and sectors. *Outputs* are the results of the process. *Enablers* are a special kind of input or resource that facilitates a process. These can include special tools, facilities, or perhaps

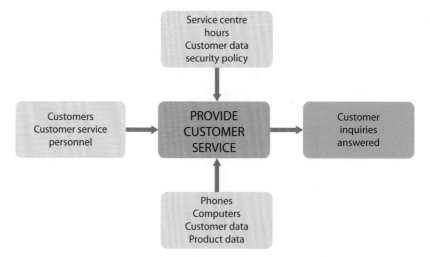

FIGURE 5.9 The business process of providing customer service analyzed using the IGOE model.

IT systems that support the business process design. So in its simplest form, *every* business process can be made to fit into this simple over-arching design, even though the complexity of the processes that you design and develop in an organization will vary considerably.

If you consider the process of studying, you would find the following:

1. Inputs – you, your textbook
2. Guides – you want to re-sell your textbook, so you do not use a highlighter
3. Output – your knowledge about information systems in business
4. Enablers – you download the lecture notes to follow along when reading the textbook

Now consider a high-level business process, *Provide Customer Service*, using an IGOE diagram (Figure 5.9). It seems quite simple when viewed this way, but let's consider how this unfolds from the perspective of a customer service agent and customer.

In this case, either a customer or customer service representative initiates the process. The process can only occur during service hours and only when the customer in the interaction proves his or her identity. Normally, the customer service agent verifies this using some type of internal CRM (customer relationship management) software, as we learned about in the last chapter. The customer, of course, will be searched by some kind of criteria such as name, address, phone number, or perhaps customer or transaction number. Often there may be validating questions that need to be asked to confirm the customer's identity, which are established by a guide to security. This same guide likely also provides restrictions on what can be done with a customer whose identity cannot be validated.

The CRM system tracks customer interaction with a company at all contact points, from the time of first purchase through to providing customer service. Technology might also provide the agent with some type of database for common queries to product-related problems; or perhaps a wiki that has FAQs from customers in past calls. It is probably technology that routes this particular customer call to this agent in this centre, and that manages the wait time and messaging to the customer while on hold. It's also likely this system is linked to a payroll and HR system that tracks working hours, on and off the phone times, and performance statistics such as average wait time, call length, and perhaps call resolution and escalation rates—things that call centre managers are quite interested in.

All of these process elements, and the technology that support them, contribute to the output of the customer's inquiry being answered. And the centre and agent would be far less efficient without the technology enablers designed to support the customer service process.

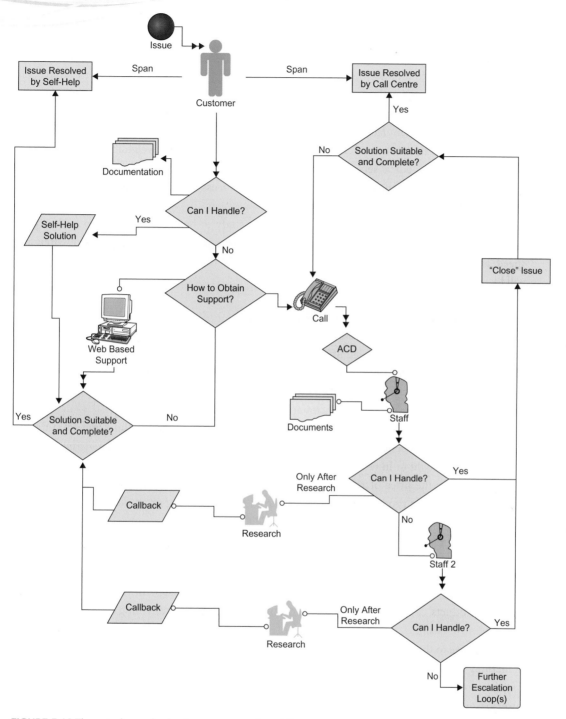

FIGURE 5.10 The actual complex business process of providing customer service.

Most business processes are not quite this simple, however. Complex businesses require complex processes, and you should not expect them all to be as neat and tidy as this simple example is. To this point, Figure 5.10 shows a far more complex customer service process that introduces branching for things like online customer self-serve versus call-centre provided resolution, and significantly more detail on how service issues are tracked and resolved. This is more likely the type of example process map you may encounter in business today.

Let's consider the role that feedback plays in the business process design. **Feedback** is a special kind of measurement created by a business process that is then returned to the system ("fed back") to control the system's future inputs, processes, and outputs. Normally, this feedback will include information such as error or failure rates, processing speeds, process costs, and information on approvals and controls required in the process, and if they are being respected. Businesses often use this performance feedback to monitor the efficiency and effectiveness of a given process. For example, if a company assembles personal computer systems and has a lot of small parts left over, it should realize it needs to adjust its assembly and/or inventory management process to reduce unused or wasted parts and thus lower manufacturing costs. In fact, the perfect process would theoretically have no waste at all! However, the costs of creating a perfect business process outweigh the benefits in all but a few cases (such as medical services). In the case of extra computer parts, the physical presence of "too many leftovers" is feedback to the system that the process is not working as it should, and the company must decide what to do about this.

Business process reengineering (BPR) is the study of business processes to find ways of making them more efficient. The goals of BPR are usually to reduce costs, increase throughput and speed, and increase quality and service. By undertaking BPR and achieving these goals, a business will likely increase its competitive advantage.

Innovation and Competitive Necessity

In today's hypercompetitive business environment, all organizations must focus on improving results all the time. However, there are significant differences between **continuous improvement** of what exists and **continuous learning**, which strives to innovate and redefine the future instead. Both of these traits are hallmarks of successful enterprises—those that are never satisfied with good enough, but strive to set new standards and benchmarks all the time.

To achieve this, all employees in an organization must be empowered to think and act at the top of their game. They must be encouraged to creatively seek ways to make things better. The notion of *better* is often thought of in terms of reducing the costs of a business process, decreasing the costs of goods sold or the price of raw materials, or improving revenue by increasing prices through branding or improved product quality. And while all of these are important and valid, we think of **competitive advantage** as an equation that looks like this:

Competitive advantage = Quality of insight + Speed of execution + Cost competitiveness[5]

Simply put, unless your efforts at work improve the quality of insight of your organization (into markets, products, consumer needs, pricing, competitor behaviour, or anything else you can think of that matters in business) or improve the speed of execution or cost competitiveness of your organization's response to that insight, then your effort is futile and will not add value. This equation also has something to say about innovation. Often we think of innovation and creativity as the same thing, but they are not. Creativity, while good, may take one outside the boundary of what is possible or probable as a business solution or product. And while this type of thinking is necessary in society, innovation is more often thought of as bounded creativity—that is, thinking not outside the box, but inside the box! Innovations must be doable if they are to have value to the organization, and this equation can help guide a company's efforts to be innovative.

Similarly, good IT systems are deployed to improve the quality of insight of those making decisions, to improve the speed of execution, to reduce costs, and/or to increase the efficiency of processes. Otherwise, there is no other good reason to spend money on the system in the first place. It is not that IT professionals cannot creatively design systems that would be interesting to build, but

---

5. Adapted from Carol-Ann Hamilton and James Norrie, *The A to Z Guide to Soul-Inspiring Leadership*, Epic Press, 2003, p. 129.

rather that what the organization needs from them is innovative systems that actually help install and sustain competitive advantage. While perhaps less interesting as a focus than being purely creative, this type of focus generates stellar business results, which is what our next section is about.

TECHNOLOGY CORE

Although most technological solutions are introduced to improve processes and increase business value, there are many technologies that hinder productivity. Some companies and managers perceive social media as one of these hindrances, and over the past five years some businesses have begun to block social media websites in the workplace because of their perceived negative effects. However, some businesses are actually harnessing the power of social media to create business value. By implementing internal private social networks (PSNs) , businesses are able to increase real-time communications and replace email with a user friendly, media-rich network. Networks such as Yammer, SharePoint, and Igloo allow employees to collaborate and share ideas in a professional and open forum.

Community managers are an important part of a PSN's success. Although these custom social networks are placed behind company firewalls, it is up to the community manager to track and curb comments or behaviour that might damage the company. Community managers are also expected to mediate conversations and coach good usage practices. Ideally, as employees become more and more accustomed to their PSN, the community manager's actions become less needed.

Quick Test

1. Which one of the following is not an input to the organization as an open system?
   a. labour
   b. productivity
   c. information
   d. technology

2. Fill in the blank. A business carries _____ when it interacts with its environment.

3. Which one of the following is not an organizational form?
   a. matrix
   b. functional
   c. CEO-based
   d. decentralized by geography

4. True or False. Teams are a key part of the matrix organizational structure.

Answers: 1. b; 2. risk; 3. c; 4. True

■ APPLYING IT TO CREATE BUSINESS VALUE

This section expands on the general focus of the value of enterprise systems described in Chapter 4. In this section we define three aspects of strategically applying IT to create business value and competitive advantage: automating, informating, and transforming business processes.

Bar code scanners are one of the more obvious ways automating can help companies do things faster. The bar code contains all of the information the store needs to keep track of its inventory and sales.

Automating to Do Things Faster

One of the first ways that a business seeks to apply IT is through **automating** tasks (using automation to execute repetitive, routine tasks without human intervention). This frees up employees to concentrate on tasks that have the potential to add high value, or tasks that require judgement or insight to complete. By automating, a business can also complete tasks with more speed, economy, consistency, and possibly accuracy. Automation may provide additional benefits by allowing a business to perform work in different ways than before.

When automating a process, a business first tends to apply technology to do the same things as before, but with greater efficiency and accuracy. Later, as the organization learns from the new technology, it looks to use technology to do new things. Table 5.3 presents several examples of how companies have used IT automation to increase business value.

When applying automation within an organization, management usually thinks in terms of improving a single process (or a small group of interrelated processes). It starts by considering answers to such questions as these:

1. What is the main goal, and what are the steps of the process to be improved?
2. What are the current costs, quality level, and other parameters of the process?
3. Is the process performed occasionally, frequently, or 24/7? Where is it done?
4. What data and information are required to carry out the steps in the process?
5. What data are generated in each step? How do data flow between steps?
6. How should the data be protected and stored appropriately?
7. What types of human intervention (if any) are required for the process to work?
8. How is the process interrelated with other processes of the organization? What systems does it use in common with those other processes?
9. When should/does it occur? What triggers the process to start? How does the output affect or feed into other processes?

These questions do not address the specific IT hardware or software used to enable the process. Instead, the most critical issues when applying IT automation are related to how the process fits within the competitive imperative, and the business organization, strategy, and goals.

Table 5.3	Using IT Automation to Create Business Value	
Industry	**Automation**	**Benefits Derived from Automation**
Banking	ATM machines, online banking	• Reduces costs associated with the processing of deposits, withdrawals, and money transfers • Increases flexibility and improves access of services to customers
Grocery/Retail	Bar code inventory systems	• Increases speed and accuracy of product transactions • Improves accuracy (assuming correct entry of products' prices into the system) • Reduces costs and transfers control to customers (e.g., self-service kiosks and check-outs)
Travel	Reservation and scheduling systems	• Allows airline reps and travel agents to process reservations more efficiently and with less cost • Allows transfer of processes to customers (self-serve model) through online services

For example, consider automated teller machines (ATMs), which operate 24/7/365. Prior to ATMs, the bank had to be open and a teller had to be available for a customer to withdraw cash. The bank customer filled out a withdrawal slip to present to the teller to receive cash. The teller accessed the customer's account, determined if there were enough funds for the withdrawal, and, if so, updated the account and gave the cash and a receipt to the customer. The use of 24-hour ATMs, however, eliminated this requirement for serving customers. Relative to the old way of serving customers who needed cash, ATMs met a bank's goals of increasing customer service (e.g., cash is "always" available) and saving money (e.g., no teller or branch visit is involved in the transaction, so the bank doesn't need to be open).

ATMs are not only convenient for customers (an example of how automating makes businesses more responsive to customer needs), they are also an application of informating. When you use the ATM, you are providing your bank with information about the services you use most often, which might tell the bank what other services you might be interested in.

Informating to Do Things Better

Another way companies view the application of IT is known as informating.[6] **Informating** is recognizing that executing processes (e.g., customers accessing their bank accounts to make deposits or withdraw funds) also creates new data and information. An organization may then process the new data to improve its decision making and to change or improve the process itself.

In most cases, companies derive informating and automating benefits from some of the same applications of IT. For example, building on the examples in Table 5.3, installing ATM machines not only reduces costs and increases flexibility, it also tracks the use of services to provide the most popular and profitable services to customers. Likewise, a barcode inventory system improves the ability to track inventory and predict demand for various items. With an informating view, IT can deliver more long-term benefits than from automation alone. In addition, an automation-only view may result in simply speeding up a "bad" process. Informating, however, allows a business to identify flaws in the process and then use its new-found knowledge to do things in entirely new ways.

To gain the benefits of informating when applying IT to a process, a business needs to step back from the details of executing the process and ask three crucial questions:

1. Does the IT store data so that it can also be used for learning and decision making?
2. Is the business process being IT-enabled already optimized for high performance?
3. How could IT enable a better (more efficient or more effective) business process or capability that delivers higher value or additional competitive advantage?

Transforming to Gain Competitive Advantage[7]

The primary goal of most for-profit companies is to achieve a sustainable competitive advantage that results in high profits. For their public sector or not-for-profit equivalents, it is usually to provide services efficiently, effectively, and at the lowest possible cost. In some cases, companies are concerned

---

6. The concept of informating was first described by Dr. Shoshana Zuboff in 1988 in her book, *In the Age of the Smart Machine*.

7. The two types of competitive advantage were first identified by Michael Porter in his book, *Competitive Advantage: Creating and Sustaining Superior Performance*, 1985, which is now considered a classic text on organizational strategy. "Transforming" is a term suggested by Professor Richard T. Watson to complement and extend the concepts of automating and informating.

with competitive necessity: the need to stay in step with competitors and continue to stay in business. In other situations, it is important to outperform or outdo the competition. This is often referred to as **transforming** the business.

The transformative view of IT is one where companies use IT to help them acquire or maintain a competitive advantage. This can be to overcome their competition or to be in line with competitors, but either way it involves changing the way an organization goes to market or performs its business functions. Transformative changes are usually not incremental improvements; rather, they are extraordinary leaps of competitive prowess that involve taking advantage of new technologies to invent new ways of doing business—to truly innovate. The benefit of this approach is that a company then possesses a competitive advantage that sustains higher-than-average profits within its industry, often paying back the investments made in IT at the outset. Even organizations in the not-for-profit or government sector, which have efficiency as their objective, see IT in a similar transformative light.

There are two basic ways of obtaining competitive advantage: cost and differentiation. A company gains a *cost advantage* when it delivers the same benefits to customers as its competitors, but at a lower cost. A company gains a *differentiation advantage* over its competitors when it delivers superior benefits to customers. By trying to achieve a cost or differentiation advantage, a company can provide better value for its customers and increased profits for itself. It is often difficult to obtain both a cost and differentiation advantage, however, because attempts to achieve greater differentiation usually result in greater costs. This strategy will only work if the differentiation delivers higher market share and results in more revenue.

In a simple resource-based model of competitive advantage, a company gains competitive advantage through the development of distinctive competencies. A company forms its distinctive competencies from a combination of its capabilities and resources. Distinctive competencies enable innovation, product quality, process efficiency, and customer responsiveness. Applying IT strategically can assist in all these areas. Through automation with IT, a business can use its resources and capabilities more efficiently to achieve a lower cost structure. Through informating with IT, the business can learn new ways to increase or transform its capabilities, and better ways to manage its resources to differentiate its products and services.

Collaboration and Co-opetition How often have we heard students complain about group work in class? No matter how professors assign the work or create the groups, it never seems satisfactory. If groups are self-selected, they are often exclusionary or tinged with commitments of friendship rather than productivity. And if they are assigned or randomly picked, then the adhesiveness and productivity of the group seem to vary dramatically, causing student distress. So why do professors continue to insist on group work?

The simple answer is that collaboration is required in the workplace for an organization to be successful. And it should be noted that in the world of work, you will not likely have much control over or choice about your work teams. You will simply be placed on teams, normally by virtue of either the role you have in the company or your availability or implied suitability for the project team's assigned tasks. In fact, it is likely that no matter what career you choose, working in collaboration with others will be among the most important job-related skills that you will have to develop and demonstrate to get ahead.[8]

Furthermore, an organization's ability to build competence internally around collaboration practices can often become a competitive advantage in and of itself. Why? Well, the ability of

---

8. Still don't believe us? See the Society for Human Resource Management's (SHRM) report, *Critical Skills Needs and Resources for the Changing Workforce, www.shrm.org/Research/SurveyFindings/Articles/Documents/08-0798CriticalSkillsFigs. pdf.* Figure 1 shows that 35 percent of experienced workers believed teamwork was much more important in 2008 than it was in 2006, compared to only 26 percent of new workers.

an organization to optimize its use of resources suggests that effective collaboration can result in faster decision making, more certain project execution, and a more engaged and committed workforce. All of these, perhaps argued by some as less tangible business outcomes, can provide a competitive edge for an organization. In Chapter 3 we talked about collaboration technologies and the support systems that can assist those collaborating across geographies or functions. However, the competitive advantage is not about the systems elements so much as it is about the internal organizational culture that promotes collaboration. This very important skill starts with individual employees who recognize the importance of collaboration and are willing to do so when it is called for.

Similarly, there is a new term emerging in the business literature and practice of global commerce: **co-opetition**.[9] This term implies that organizations can collaborate in one endeavour (for instance, a joint venture), while they compete in other areas. This may vary by geography, line of business, or some other particularly unique feature that drives an organization to awareness that collaborating, even with competitors in some instances, is a better alternative than going it alone and being less effective.

In a Canadian context, this is best illustrated by a fairly recent development in the world of sports, where two distinctly competitive companies—Bell Canada Enterprises and Rogers Communications Inc.—came together to purchase the assets of Maple Leaf Sports and Entertainment. These two companies are fierce competitors in the mobile and home phone business, as well as in cable and satellite TV operations. Yet, rather than face negotiations with a third party buyer, the two competitors came together to put in a winning bid to acquire this sports franchise and its associated broadcast rights and assets. Given broadcasting is a major part of each of their business models, cooperating on this content is a win-win situation. It means that instead of competing to purchase Maple Leaf Sports, they purchased it together, divided their use by geography, and will share the profits that result, which will be higher since Maple Leaf Sports cannot play each of Bell and Rogers against each other in a competitive bidding process. The deal is an excellent example of co-opetition in action.[10]

Co-opetition should not be confused with collusion (which is an illegal practice in most parts of the world), price-fixing, or other kinds of practices that are not truly collaborative or transparent. While it is true that true collaboration or co-opetition often attract questions about competitive practices, monopolies, or restraint of trade (all questions that need answers before a commercial deal can proceed), co-opetition is a simple admission by many corporations and organizations, and especially those that operate globally, that they cannot be good at all things for all customers all the time. Collaboration and co-opetition are options to creatively address these competitive gaps by letting each party focus on what they are good at and then cooperating where necessary to create sustainable competitive advantage.

The CEOs of Bell, George Cope (left), Maple Leaf Sports and Entertainment, Larry Tanenbaum (centre), and Rogers Communications, Nadir Mohamed (right), announce the purchase of MLSE by the two competing companies.

---

9. Barry J. Nalebuff and Adam M. Brandenburger, (1997) "Co-opetition: Competitive and cooperative business strategies for the digital economy," *Strategy & Leadership*, 25(6), pp. 28–35.

10. If you want to learn more about this deal, do a simple Internet search. Articles were written by most major Canadian news agencies, including the CBC, *Financial Post*, *Toronto Star*, and even *Marketing Magazine*.

Using IT or collaboration to create business value is obviously important, but an organization's strategy and purpose cannot be truly realized without some level of governance. Keeping an eye on operations to make sure the organization is fulfilling its strategic goals is the topic of our next section.

Quick Test

1. Fill in the blank. A business can improve a process or the decision making behind that process by _____ to capture and review valuable data.

2. True or False. Using IT to transform is a practice undertaken by both for-profit and not-for-profit organizations.

3. When companies collaborate in one area of business but compete in another it is called _____ .
   a. neutral business value
   b. co-opetition
   c. cooperative competitive investment
   d. collaborative negative value

Answers: 1. informating; 2. True; 3. b

■ CORPORATE, IT, AND PROJECT GOVERNANCE

Corporate governance can be simply defined as the highest level of decision making, involving basic questions of status, financial viability, strategy, and compliance within an organization. Clearly, IT would be of use in making decisions about any of these organizational outcomes and should therefore be included in any governance process. Effective governance is a critical enabler for success in the global economy, for securing the enterprise's information resources, and for creating competitive advantage. Often the responsibility for corporate governance in the private sector lies with a board of directors; in the public sector it may be a board of governors or advisory board, while it may be a ministry or cabinet arrangement in government. Regardless of the jurisdiction or type of organization, it will certainly have some form of governance providing strategic rather than managerial oversight at the highest level.

One of the primary responsibilities of board members/governors is to appoint the chief executive of the organization who reports to them. At this next level, normally a chief executive officer (CEO) is ultimately responsible for running the organization; all the other officers and senior managers within the organization report to the CEO. While many public sector companies use the CEO title, the top executive, particularly in the public or not-for-profit sector, may also carry titles such as president, country executive, director general, managing director, minister, and the like. A series of vice-presidents, senior directors, deputies, and so on report to this position.

While the CEO and the management team are responsible for formulating and proposing the strategy of the organization, it is ultimately the governance processes of the organization that approve it, including the possible financial implications that accompany any strategy. The governance function also seeks regular updates on strategy execution and expects that any deviation from the annual plan will be discussed and approved along the way. For functional implications, the executive responsible for the area is expected to understand and contribute to formulating both the organization's overall strategy, and then also translating this into a series of actions to be executed by the function he or she is responsible for.

In IT, for instance, this is likely to be a chief information officer (CIO), or a vice-president or director of IT or IS. To be effective, they must translate the overall strategy into a functional strategy in support of the organization's mission. This will often involve establishing metrics to monitor the strategic performance of IT and creating decision filters to help sort out internal priorities (see Figure 5.11). This improves collective action by aligning each part of IT to the overall strategy. Many companies still have senior IT directors reporting to the finance or administration departments rather than the CEO, but this is beginning to change. As IT becomes more and more important to strategy execution, other executives want the head of IT sitting with them when they make important decisions. We will talk in more detail about the functional responsibilities of the CIO shortly.

There is a great deal of literature on the relationship between good governance and solid management. Much of the literature contends that good governance is often linked to improved financial performance and higher executive accountability. Noted MIT business scholar Peter Weill estimates that businesses with strong governance create 20 percent more business value than similar firms with less-robust governance.[11] Others note there are companies that follow all the rules of good governance but still face challenges and suffer poor performance, suggesting more factors contribute to performance than simply good governance. Yet one thing is certain: all companies are re-evaluating their governance in light of relatively high-profile corporate scandals (notable examples include Enron, WorldCom, and the recent U.S. investment bank failures) to bring it in line with emerging global standards and legislated requirements. As a rule, this is currently and generally improving the overall state of corporate governance globally.[12]

Corporate governance can only be considered effective when the leadership (including both governors and managers) of a business are directly accountable to its owners (i.e., shareholders) for *proper operation and financial control* of the organization. This is what shareholders expect, given they have invested funds and trust that management knows what it is doing. This further

FIGURE 5.11 To be effective, the management team must develop a clear strategy that includes measures, new projects, plans, and budgets that all align to ensure the organization achieves its desired results. Many CEOs require an IT member on the executive team to ensure measurements and metrics are set appropriately.

Corporate governance took a front-row seat in everyone's consciousness in 2001 when the Enron scandal broke. Several top-level executives, including founder Kenneth Lay (pictured here) and president Jeffrey Skilling, were indicted and later convicted of several fraud-related charges all connected to the collapse of Enron. Skilling is currently serving a 24-year prison sentence, and Lay died of an apparent heart attack in July 2006, although some speculate it was suicide.

includes deliberate and complete disclosure and reporting of results, including mandated reports and certificates for public companies (i.e., if shares are traded on a stock exchange somewhere in the world). Given the global expansion of businesses and public demand to control what many see as massive corporate excess and global fraud, it is no surprise that stakeholders such as national governments have increased their involvement in ensuring effective governance and reporting.

---

11. Peter Weill and J. W. Ross, "IT Governance: How Top Performers Manage IT Decision Rights for Superior Performance," Harvard Business School Publishing, Boston, 2004, p. 2.

12. Janet McFarland and Elizabeth Church, "Do Better Boards Make Better Companies?," *The Globe and Mail*, October 24, 2006, B1.

Government and business leaders around the world are enacting laws (such as Sarbanes-Oxley in the United States), writing regulations (such as IFRS financial statements[13]), and establishing policies and guidelines for the control of financial systems (such as new compensation restrictions on banking executives[14]). As well, they are using existing laws and regulations regarding the security and confidentiality of sensitive data and personal information.

IT Governance

Most businesses still need to take corporate governance one step further than they have in the past. Since managers and employees are the business professionals who implement and follow governance policies and processes, they need to understand technology and its impacts on both corporate and IT governance. Most modern businesses are heavily invested in and dependent on information systems, technologies, and data. Any requirements, especially around reporting and disclosure, clearly rely on fundamental assurances that what is in an organization's IT system is reliable, safe, and secure. This is particularly true as accounting records in most organizations now exist only online. It certainly would not be prudent to simply assume that because something is "in the system," it must be right! Therefore, for an organization to understand and manage its operations, it must provide for effective governance of all of its information-related assets, just as it would for its financial assets.

IT governance is the "distribution of IT decision-making rights and responsibilities among enterprise stakeholders, and the procedures and mechanisms for making and monitoring strategic decisions regarding IT."[15] This means that IT governance begins as a very high-level process that specifies: (1) how the organization will set goals, objectives, priorities, and policies for IT; (2) how it will integrate IT with business strategies and goals; and (3) which organizational members will make decisions regarding, and be responsible for, the successful completion of these tasks (the "who" of IT governance).[16] This leads to a discussion of the role of IT in an organization and how it must help support proper governance. One of the largest associations of IT professionals in Canada, Canada's Association of Information Technology Professionals (CIPS), has published a very relevant code of ethics that helps address this responsibility in the context of an IT professional (see *www.cips.ca/ethics*). Of course, if we strive to be better professionals, one of our obligations is to continually enhance the role of our profession as it relates to contributing to society and not just remain self-interested. CIPS, among some other like-minded professional associations globally, has been leading this discussion since the 1980s. CIPS is a good starting point for you to start exploring these issues, even before you begin practising in the field. This brings us to our next discussion: the role of the CIO in promoting good governance practices.

The CIO: Managing IT Governance The CIO must ensure proper and secure use of all the organization's information resources, and particularly the organization's compliance with privacy laws and regulations in *every jurisdiction* in which it operates. For most organizations today, this has become a monumental task involving a complex web of overlapping laws and different standards that requires a significant amount of specialized knowledge to sort out. In fact, IT relies heavily on legal professionals to help sort out these complexities even before systems are designed and implemented. As a result, the connection between IT, finance, and legal in most organizations is an important triumvirate where those colleagues must work together if the organization is to function well. To give you some insight into these complexities, Table 5.4 summarizes just a few of the applicable types of legislation around the world that might apply to various IT operations of a typical organization.

---

13. See *www.ifrs.org* for more details on this global regulatory regime.

14. See *http://online.wsj.com/article/SB125324292666522101.html* as an example of this issue.

15. Ryan Peterson, "Crafting Information Technology Governance," *Information Systems Management*, *www.ism-journal.com*, Fall 2004.

16. Adapted from IT Governance Institute® website, *www.itgi.org*, retrieved June 15, 2005.

Table 5.4	Selected Governance- and Compliance-Related Laws and Regulations
Laws and Regulations	**Description**
Personal Information Protection and Electronic Documents Act (PIPEDA)	The Canadian government act sets out ground rules for how private sector organizations may collect, use, or disclose personal information in the course of commercial activities. The law gives individuals the right to access and request correction of the personal information these organizations may have collected about them.[17]
Bill 198	This Ontario legislature bill amends the Securities Act and Commodity Futures Act. Among the amendments are those giving the Ontario Securities Commission (OSC) rule-making authority to require reporting issuers to appoint audit committees and to prescribe requirements relating to the functions and responsibilities of audit committees, including independence requirements. The OSC also has rule-making authority to require reporting issuers to establish and maintain internal controls, disclosure controls, and procedures, and require CEOs and CFOs to provide certifications related to internal controls and disclosure controls and procedures.[18]
EU Data Protection Directive	Each EU member nation is required to pass legislation requiring confidentiality and integrity controls for networks, systems, and data containing personal information for both employees and customers.[19]
Basel II Accord: International Convergence on Capital Measurement and Capital Standards	The regulations from the Bank for International Settlements are designed to encourage banks to adopt and follow rigorous risk assessment, management, and controls practices.[20]
Sarbanes-Oxley Act	The U.S. act holds a company's officers personally responsible for providing accurate public financial information to investors. Emphasis is on internal controls.[21]
Multilateral Instrument 52-109	Since March 2005, CEOs and CFOs (or persons performing similar functions) of reporting issuers are required to personally certify in each interim and annual filing that: 1. He or she has reviewed the filing; 2. Based on his or her knowledge, the filings do not contain any untrue statement of a material fact or omit to state a material fact required to be stated or that is necessary to make a statement not misleading in light of the circumstances under which it was made; 3. Based on his or her knowledge, the financial statements together with the other financial information included in the filings fairly present in all material respects the financial condition, results of operations, and cash flows of the issuer; 4. He or she and the other certifying officers are responsible for establishing and maintaining disclosure controls and procedures and internal control over financial reporting, and they have designed disclosure controls and procedures and internal control over financial reporting (or caused them to be designed under their supervision); and 5. He or she has caused the issuer to disclose changes in internal control over financial reporting with material affect or reasonably likely material effect on internal control. In each annual certification, the certifying officers must also disclose under item 4 that they have evaluated the effectiveness of disclosure controls and procedures and caused their issuers to disclose their conclusions regarding their evaluation.[22]

(continued)

17. Ibid.

18. Ontario Securities Commission Notice of Proposed Amendments to the Securities Act and Commodities Futures Act, *www.osc.gov.on.ca/en/SecuritiesLaw_ar_20021115_bill-198.jsp*, retrieved January 15, 2010.

19. *www.cdt.org/privacy/guide/protect*

20. *www.bis.org/publ/bcbsca.htm*

21. *www.aicpa.org/_catalogs/masterpage/Search.aspx?S=Sarbanes-Oxley+Act*; *www.law.uc.edu/CCL/SOact/soact.pdf*

22. *www.kpmg.ca/unitymail/accountability/en/issues/elert2006-007.html*

Table 5.4	Selected Governance- and Compliance-Related Laws and Regulations
Laws and Regulations	**Description**
Privacy Act	This Canadian government act imposes obligations on some 150 federal government departments and agencies to respect privacy rights by limiting the collection, use, and disclosure of personal information. The Privacy Act gives individuals the right to access and request correction of personal information about themselves held by these federal government organizations.[23]
Provincial Privacy Legislation	Every province and territory in Canada has privacy legislation governing the collection, use, and disclosure of personal information held by government agencies. British Columbia, Alberta, and Quebec are the only provinces with laws recognized as substantially similar to PIPEDA. Others, such as Ontario, have their own legislative framework (FIPPA). These laws regulate the collection, use, and disclosure of personal information by businesses and other organizations, and provide individuals with a general right of access to, and correction of, their personal information. In addition, Alberta, Saskatchewan, Manitoba, and Ontario have passed legislation to deal specifically with the collection, use, and disclosure of personal health information by health care providers and other health care organizations (HIPPA in Ontario, for example).[24]

This part of governance is known as *compliance* for its obvious outcome of ensuring the organization's practices remain compliant with the law. In some instances, compliance might also involve reporting things systematically to authorities (for instance, in the banking sector, where certain types of transactions must be disclosed to authorities to investigate for criminal or terrorist links). However, while that part of compliance is obvious to most of us, there are also significant internal compliance issues that dominate much of IT governance efforts in most organizations. These involve maintaining global practices that might include architectural standards, using only preferred vendors, and privacy or security regimes that go beyond the minimums required by law. These are developed by the organization for its own purposes and in compliance with what it has determined its internal needs are, or perhaps as a brand or service commitment to customers. Whatever the reason, global standards need to apply. So when we discuss *compliance*, we are talking about governance that ensures the organization remains *internally compliant* with its own IT standards and practices in addition to those imposed upon it by the law or local regulations.

However, since not all organizations have a formally designated CIO, the role of ensuring that IT governance is properly in place is actually the responsibility of the senior executive team and the board of directors. Ultimately, it is up to them to decide who will be responsible for IT governance within their organization. The most basic point here is simply to ensure that overall IT governance and the resulting alignment to strategy that it produces is not an afterthought, but rather a forethought.

Project Governance

IT as a function is heavily project-oriented, so another important element of internal IT governance are efforts to align the selection and management of projects to the organization's strategy. These two aspects of project governance (selection and management) are quite separate and need to be properly understood. **Project management**—which encompasses single, multiple, and even enterprise program

---

23. Office of the Privacy Commissioner of Canada, Privacy Legislation in Canada Fact Sheet, *www.priv.gc.ca/fs-fi/02_05_d_15_e.cfm*, retrieved January 15, 2010.
24. Ibid.

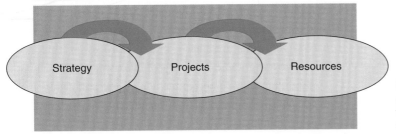

FIGURE 5.12 Organizations have to select projects that will create competitive advantage by aligning with the organization's strategy and available resources.[25]

management efforts—focuses on a singular objective: delivering projects on-time, on-budget, and on-quality. It is a virtual certainty today that any IT organization likely has adopted, created, or purchased a methodology to help it properly manage its projects once they have been selected. We will address this in more detail in the next chapter when we talk more about developing IS solutions.

However, a separate process that involves **project portfolio management (PPM)** can be more strictly defined as the internal process used to *govern strategic project selection*. This process directly addresses the question of strategy execution and involves how an organization chooses to create, estimate, and select the batch of projects that it has underway at any point in time to *maximize its strategic alignment*. The process adopted by the organization must establish the connection between its strategy and the project proposals so that scarce resources (a fact in any organization) focus only on key projects that will ultimately create competitive advantage (see Figure 5.12). It is then up to IT to manage the required resources and budgets to create sufficient capacity to execute the portfolio quickly and efficiently. This also suggests *not* letting the IT budget become a determinant for how many projects are selected; rather, the business must decide how many projects IT must perform for the organization to remain competitive, and then assign the supporting resources to ensure projects can be accomplished. This often involves trade-offs with other budgets and competing interests and is why PPM is appropriately treated as a governance issue rather than a managerial process—it is not solely up to IT to determine for itself what the budgets or project portfolio should be for the organization.

Project selection enables the organization's strategy, so careful selection of the projects, even before we turn our minds to managing them, is actually the more strategic of the two activities. Sadly, however, research shows that many IT professionals spend more time on project management practices than on getting the project selection right in the first place, thus becoming part of the problem instead of the solution![26] Making a wrong choice, even if a project is brilliantly conceived and properly delivered, will produce a less than strategic outcome unless it is carefully crafted to align with required competitive advantages.

Because of these constraints, many IT organizations put a fairly strict emphasis on involving senior executives and lines of business heads in making project selections, which helps drive engagement and alignment for the sponsorship of those projects. Since IT will ultimately be expected to deliver on these projects, this is a critical subset of IT governance practices in most organizations.

A significant issue that CIOs and other senior IT leaders must deal with when thinking about portfolio and project management methodologies and processes are the trade-off decisions they

25. James Norrie, *Breaking Through the Project Fog: How Smart Organizations Achieve Success by Creating, Selecting and Executing On-Strategy Projects*. Toronto, ON: John Wiley & Sons Canada, 2008. P. 23.

26. Ibid.

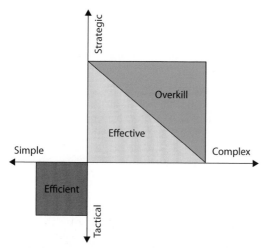

FIGURE 5.13 PPM methodologies and trade-offs. There are two dangers when implementing a project—oversimplification and overkill. Either will lead to a project that doesn't deliver the competitive advantage results an organization hoped for.[27]

represent. As noted in Figure 5.13, an organization must seek a balance to make sure that the methodologies do not *oversimplify* what are clearly strategic processes. This means acknowledging some level of complexity and ensuring the methodology chosen and implemented will sufficiently incorporate methods that help staff handle complex tasks without adding complexity. This is not always easy to do and is a key feature of good managers—they simplify without sacrificing effectiveness.

Similarly, another dimension noted in Figure 5.13 is the trade-off between a process that is overly tactical but that ignores longer-term strategic implications. This may occur, for instance, when those involved in a project argue to skip architectural reviews or compliance steps in favour of speedy execution. No matter how urgent the project, ignoring internal standards in favour of quick action ultimately sacrifices potentially critical benefits, such as lower-cost IT infrastructure that is highly efficient over time and across many competing project platforms.

Again, these kinds of operational trade-offs involve a balance between short-term, tactical deliveries and longer-term, often more diffuse, strategic objectives. The objective is to maintain a balance between efficiency and effectiveness without moving into overkill—this is where a smart and experienced CIO can make a difference!

Professional Codes of Conduct and Practice

A major part of good governance is understanding what the ethical and appropriate governance practices are to apply. So industry associations, professional bodies, and industry think-tanks for many professions—IT included—often develop, publish, and promote **codes of conduct**. These codes are relevant to any profession and help guide the professionals within the field in terms of what is and is not acceptable and ethical behaviour. This clearly has a direct impact on governance practices since the individual employee's conduct can be informed by an external, referenced standard of behaviour.

Many professions have very strict codes of conduct (medicine, law, accounting, and engineering, for example), where the consequence of not following them normally results in expulsion from the profession and the payment of compensation for malpractice. In many of these professions, a clear duty of care is in place between the patient or client and the professional, and often the relationship is fee-based. In addition to the CIPS example cited earlier in this chapter, most other IT-related professions have looser guidelines or lesser means of imposing sanctions and are considered as voluntary rather than punitive codes of conduct. Specific examples of these in IT include the following:

- Project Management Institute (PMI): *http://www.pmi.org/About-Us/Ethics/~/media/PDF/Ethics/ap_pmicodeofethics.ashx*
- Association for Computing Machinery (ACM): *www.acm.org/about/code-of-ethics*
- Association of Information Technology Professionals (AITP): *www.aitp.org/resource/resmgr/forms/code_of_ethics.pdf*
- Computer Society of the IEEE (IEEE-CS): *www.ieee.org/portal/pages/iportals/aboutus/ethics/code.html*

---

27. Ibid., p. 14.

WHAT DO YOU THINK?

There is a school of thought that argues that IT is not a profession in the strict sense of the word. There is no mandatory licensing, no commonly agreed upon body of knowledge and standards of practice, and no self-regulating peer review process for complaints and lapses in standards as there are in many other professions.

However, others argue that many in IT are certainly engaged in *professional practice*. This means that they purport to have expert knowledge in a specific field, on which others must rely, and for which they are paid.

What do you think? Is IT a profession or simply a job? On what basis would you compare and contrast IT to other professions to make this assessment? What could be done to improve IT professionalism in your opinion?

Many large private companies in Canada also have internal codes of conduct that relate to employee conduct and maintaining high ethical standards. The Royal Bank of Canada (RBC) is a good example. RBC's Code of Conduct includes the following principles:

- upholding the law
- confidentiality
- fairness
- corporate responsibility
- honouring our trust in you
- objectivity
- integrity
- individual responsibility[28]

These kinds of codes are often in place in organizations with high risk profiles (such as financial services, natural resources, hospitals, community services, etc.), where the risk of unethical behaviour has high financial or human costs.

If the organization or business you belong to has one of these codes, it may be important to review it before you accept employment. If the organization does not have one, perhaps that too should be a question you address during the interviewing and hiring process. Regardless, arm yourself with knowledge about these kinds of issues, the various kinds of codes of conduct that exist, and how different organizations approach and respond to ethical dilemmas. Knowledge is power, and the ability to think about these issues before you face your first real test in business will help you respond better when you do.

Quick Test

1. True or False. All business professionals who use organizational technologies should understand how technology can affect corporate and IT governance.

2. True or False. IT governance includes the distribution of IT decision-making rights and responsibilities among enterprise stakeholders.

3. The_____usually leads the organization's information and technology efforts, especially as it relates to the creation of business value.
   a. CEO
   b. CFO
   c. CIO
   d. COO

Answers: 1. True; 2. False; 3. c

---

28. The full Royal Bank Code of Conduct can be found at *www.rbc.com/governance/pdf/RBCCodeOfConduct.pdf.*

What's in IT for me?

What if organizations did not automate, informate, or transform? Can you imagine waiting for the bank to be open to withdraw money or having to use a card file in the library to do the research for your term paper? Successful organizations and businesses are constantly looking for ways to improve. Those that do not are unsuccessful and may even cease to exist. Would you choose a bank that did not offer online banking, for example? IT helps organizations understand their business environment and the needs of their customers by providing vital information. With this information, organizations can then solve problems or capitalize on opportunities that help gain or sustain competitive advantage. When this happens, you, as a customer, benefit. You benefit by dealing with an efficient and innovative organization that knows what you want. IT may also be part of what is offered to you as a customer. Somehow Apple recognized the need for the iPod and invented the required technology to enable it. Because of this one innovative product, the entire music industry has been forced to transform to meet customers' needs. We can only guess what the future will hold as you become business professionals and join in the activity of creating business value and competitive advantage.

What's in IT for an organization?

This chapter covered a lot of ground, from strategy to process to governance and ethical conduct. A key member of the executive team who contributes to all of this is the chief information officer (CIO). This person normally reports to the CEO/chair, COO/president, or sometimes the CFO. The CIO leads the organization's information and technology efforts, especially as they relate to the creation of business value and competitive advantage. What does it take to become a CIO? Several studies concluded that critical skills for CIOs include strong communication skills, the ability to think strategically, and a thorough understanding of the business processes and operations of the company. With these skills, a CIO champions the use of IT in identifying efficiencies and information that will help sustain or gain competitive advantage. The CIO is also responsible for understanding how new technologies might enable existing business processes and potentially automate, informate, and/or transform.

As you continue through this text, keep in mind that you are gaining the basic foundation for becoming a CIO. Through experience and increased business and technical knowledge, you may one day aspire to fill the CIO position.

What's in IT for society?

When companies transform to gain competitive advantage, they benefit from increased profit while society benefits from a cheaper, more valuable, more efficient, or more convenient product or service. What do you think would happen if businesses in North America didn't transform? For starters, entrepreneurs wouldn't be given a creative outlet, and consumers wouldn't be given new products or services. Both entrepreneurs and consumers would then begin to look elsewhere to satisfy their needs, sending more money and intelligence to competing markets. Markets must always encourage transformation to stay competitive.

In Web 2.0, websites informate to collect relevant data from their visitors so that they can observe the demographics and tendencies of their target market. One of the most common byproducts of this type of informating is implementing relevant cross-promotions on e-commerce sites. Amazon.com is a pioneer in this practice, where shoppers looking at product A are automatically shown products B, C, and D, which are products that other people purchased alongside product A. These relevant cross-promotions are a result of Amazon collecting large amounts of transaction data over a long period of time. By practising this type of cross-promotion, Amazon is able to gain competitive advantage by creating precise suggestions for their customers, while their customers are able to benefit from finding more of what they like faster.

RO↑ | STUDENT RETURN ON INVESTMENT SUMMARY

1. Explain how businesses organize and use business processes to achieve competitive advantage.

Business organization dictates business growth. If you want to get something done in an organization, you need to know where to go for the information and how to get to the authority required to accomplish your task. Too much business structure could create bureaucratic barriers that stunt the growth of a company, and too little structure can create chaos where employees are not held accountable for their actions. Team structures like the matrix structure play an important part in business because they facilitate the free flow of information between employees while holding members of the group accountable to one another. Competitive advantage is the result of creating more business value than competitors, and good business organization can be a key factor in maintaining or increasing advantage.

2. Describe how IT helps create business value.

Businesses continually analyze their competitive position to, at minimum, maintain competitive advantage and hopefully increase advantage. In these endeavours, IT helps businesses to both identify and implement ways to increase business value and competitive advantage. First, IT enables businesses to more efficiently gather, process, and analyze data and information. Through these actions, business professionals can identify areas for improvement or opportunities that will lead to competitive advantage. Second, IT may be a crucial part of the business product or service that is offered to market. It certainly may be part of the way the product or service is produced. IT may assist by automating or informating processes to be more efficient and informative, or may transform products to be highly successful in the marketplace.

3. Explain the various types of organizational governance and state why governance is important in today's business world.

Corporate governance involves basic questions of status, financial viability, strategy, and compliance within an organization. It ensures that the organization's efforts are all geared toward the organization's goals, mission, or purpose. IT governance is managed by a company's Chief Information Officer. The CIO must ensure proper and secure use of all the organization's information resources, and particularly the organization's compliance with privacy laws and regulations wherever it operates. By managing IT governance, CIOs are able to protect individuals that digitally communicate with the organization externally and internally, while protecting the company from unknowingly committing illegal actions in the global IT realm. Effective governance is a critical enabler for success in the global economy, for securing the enterprise's information resources, and for creating competitive advantage.

KNOWLEDGE SPEAK

automating 190

Bill 198 197

business process 184

business process reengineering (BPR) 188

business strategy 178

codes of conduct 200

competitive advantage 188

continuous improvement 188

continuous learning 188

co-opetition 193

corporate governance 194

decentralized structure 182

environmental scans 181

feedback 187

functional structure 182

IGOE model 184

informating 191

IT governance 196

matrix structure 182

open systems model 179

organizational boundary 180

Personal Information Protection and Electronic Documents Act (PIPEDA) 197

project management 198

project portfolio management (PPM) 199

stakeholder 180

transforming 192

REVIEW QUESTIONS

Multiple-choice questions

1. For a business to begin, it must start with
   a. strategy
   b. processes
   c. organizational structure
   d. all of the above

2. Which is not a stakeholder in creating business strategy?
   a. society
   b. employees
   c. suppliers
   d. technology

3. Which of the following is NOT a type of organizational structure?
   a. autocratic
   b. matrix
   c. decentralized
   d. functional

4. A process is often shown as:
   a. Input -> output -> process
   b. Process -> output -> input
   c. Process -> input -> output
   d. Input -> process -> output

Fill-in-the-blank questions

5. _____is the study of business processes to find ways of making them more efficient.
6. When _____ a process, a business might apply technology to do the same things as before, but more efficiently.
7. Complex businesses require _____ processes.

True-false questions

8. The G in IGOE, the process analysis method, stands for *gather*.
9. IT governance specifies how an organization will set goals, objectives, priorities, and policies for IT.
10. The CIO of an organization must ensure the organization is compliant with privacy laws and regulations in *every jurisdiction* in which it operates.

Matching questions

Choose the BEST answer from column B for each item in column A.

Column A	Column B
11. input	a. fermentation tank
12. guide	b. raw materials, including barley
13. output	c. beer
14. enable	d. heat measurements

Column A	Column B
15. data	e. money that businesses need to operate
16. labour	f. raw facts
17. capital	g. "ingredients" used to make products
18. raw materials	h. people hired to carry out business processes or supporting functions

Short-answer questions

19. How can automation increase business value?
20. What is the difference between creativity and innovation?

Discussion/Essay questions

21. What are some of the advantages and disadvantages of decentralized structures of business?
22. Give one example of co-opetition and explain why competing companies collaborate.

TEAM ACTIVITY

Work with two or three other classmates and map the process for a task that someone in the group has completed today. Pick a task that interests the group and brainstorm all of the technology enablers involved in the process. Approximately how much time did these enablers save you? How could technology further expedite the process? Is there a financial gain in speeding up this process? Plan your technological improvement on paper first, and then use the activities below to implement it.

SOFTWARE APPLICATION EXERCISES

1. Internet

Research how to incorporate your technological improvement into the process. Does this technology already exist or is it the combination of a few different technologies? Research potential competitors and see what sort of technology exists in their processes.

2. Presentation

Create a presentation outlining exactly how your technological improvement would benefit the process. Present your ideas to your class and/or a professor. Give your audience insight into the look and functionality of your proposed improvement, providing examples of how one real-world company could implement it.

3. Word Processing

Use a word processor to write five different pitches for your technological improvement. Each pitch must be 140 characters or less. Imagine you are writing these pitches to attract stakeholders via the micro-blogging site, *Twitter*.

4. Spreadsheet

Technological improvements cost money. Prepare a budget with projected costs, including an assessment of labour costs (e.g., your hourly rate—research these rates for a realistic cost). Include charts from your financial estimates for the presentation assignment above. Calculate how much it would cost to implement your technology into the process of the existing real-world company you listed above. How would the costs increase if you were to launch an independent company selling this tech improvement B2B or B2C? Would there be any economies of scale?

5. Database

How many people would benefit from the process improvement? Compile data about your target demographic and use these figures for your presentation. These figures could also be incorporated into your presentation when calculating the projected profitability of your technological improvement.

6. Advanced Challenge

Create an account for this exercise on *Twitter*. Use this social media platform to engage with potential stakeholders and broadcast the pitches you created above. Gather feedback about how stakeholders perceive your tech improvement and use this information to support or improve upon your automation.

ONLINE RESOURCES

Companion Website

- Take interactive practice quizzes to assess your knowledge and help you study in a dynamic way.
- Review PowerPoint lecture slides.
- Get help and sample solutions to end-of-chapter software application exercises.

Additional Resources Available Only on *WileyPLUS*

- Take the interactive Quick Test to check your understanding of the chapter material and get immediate feedback on your responses.
- Review and study with downloadable Audio Lecture MP3 files.
- Check your understanding of the key vocabulary in the chapter with Knowledge Speak Interactive Flash Cards.

CASE STUDY:
BLUEFIN LABS

A product of the MIT Media Lab, Bluefin Labs is a tech start-up that has catapulted into the spotlight since its academic founding in 2008. The Massachusetts-based firm is at the forefront of social TV analytics, where massive amounts of TV-related data are collected and analyzed from social media platforms like Twitter and Facebook.

Prior to this technology, broadcast companies could only measure how many people were watching a show at a given time. Now, using social media measurement techniques, Bluefin is able to reveal how many social comments a television event or show generates and how much of the social share it holds during a specific time. Furthermore, using a combination of machine learning and cognitive science, Bluefin captures tweet and status data related to a television show or event and measures the response as positive, neutral, or negative. This gives broadcasters and marketers a much clearer vision of how many viewers a show is engaging, and what emotions viewers are feeling toward the show.

In 2012, Super Bowl XLVI garnered 12.2 million social media comments. This represents an increase of almost 600 percent from the previous Super Bowl, where 1.8 million social comments were tracked. Data compiled from the event lead to a detailed breakdown of the most socially commented on moments of the game—and more importantly for advertisers, the most talked about Super Bowl commercials. Table 5.5 shows a breakdown of the top 10 socially commented on commercials.

While H&M's "Bodywear for H&M" ranked first in total social comments, Doritos "Man's Best Friend" ranked first in sentiment, with 61% of comments being positive, 29% neutral, and 10% negative, according to Bluefin's measurement tools.[29]

By specializing in this type of niche informating, Bluefin gives broadcast companies, marketers, and advertisers the data required to improve upon specific television marketing avenues. In this way, Bluefin creates measurable business value in the social media sphere.

Table 5.5		Top 10 Super Bowl Commercials Ranked by Social Commentary.[30]	
Rank	Brand	Title	# Social Media Comments
1	H&M	"Body Wear for H&M," featuring David Beckham	109,000
2	Chrysler	"It's Halftime in America," featuring Clint Eastwood	96,000
3	NBC	*The Voice*: "Vocal Kombat," featuring Betty White	90,000
4	Doritos	"Man's Best Friend"	74,000
5	Pepsi	"King's Court," featuring Elton John and Melanie Amaro	45,000
6	Chevrolet	Chevy Silverado "2012"	41,000
7	Doritos	"Sling Baby"	41,000
8	Skechers	"Go Run Mr. Quiggly "	35,000
9	Bud Light	"Rescue Dog"	29,000
10	Samsung	"The Next Big Thing"	26,000

Case Questions

1. In what way has Bluefin improved upon traditional broadcast metrics? Why are these improvements important to broadcasters? Why are they important to advertisers?
2. Explain how consumers might benefit from Bluefin's services. Can you think of an example where social analytics could improve product offerings?
3. Draw upon the data provided to explain why it is important for Bluefin to measure the sentiment of social comments. Why would measuring sentiment be important in evaluating the success of political ads? How do you think not-for-profit industries might use Bluefin's services?

29. Simon Dumenco, "The 10 Super Bowl Commercials That Blew Up the Biggest in Social Media," *Advertising Age*, http://adage.com/article/special-report-super-bowl/10-super-bowl-commercials-won-social-media/232548/
30. Ibid.

CASE STUDY:
THE TRANSIT NETWORK

You are a business analyst and have been hired by a local municipality. It is pretty cool to be working for the city in which you live. Until now, you had no idea just how complex the business process and workflows were in a municipality. And the number of regulations and laws that they are subject to is overwhelming! But you are learning fast.

Your latest project involves city transit. Riders are demanding more and more instant access to information and just-in-time system updates on their next train, bus, or important service announcements. Recently the transit authority began to dream of a my.transit portal project. Transit Network is an important initiative for the mayor, and everyone assigned to transit projects is in the limelight. In their budding plans, regular riders of city transit would sign up and be able to create a profile that includes mapping their daily commute and registering their system "likes"; get instant access to schedule and route information; connect to live, online help if required; buy tickets or renew transit passes online; and so on. They would link to Facebook and Twitter, and tweet comments from satisfied riders and new portal subscribers—transit planners are sure it will be a viral hit! Commuters would even be able to subscribe to a free mobile app for their smartphone that would link them to a mini version of the portal all day long, including updates of where their connected family and friends are currently on the system. Everyone in the transit department thought this would be very cool, and they convinced management to assign you to help prepare initial specifications for the project.

Fortunately, well before any discussions about the massive technology implications of all this, your undergraduate business degree taught you that municipalities are subject to intense legal frameworks around privacy. You also know that security and data integrity will be core issues that need to be addressed well ahead of any functional planning. To date in your conversations with your transit client, you have heard none of this being talked about and you are a bit surprised. Their portal plans involve significant amounts of personal information, and you aren't even sure if you know what exactly is private or public about a transit rider's journey!

So, you decide that a good starting point would be to:

- Establish what privacy regulations apply specifically to municipalities in your area
- Establish what privacy or related legislation applies to any business in that same jurisdiction that would have to also be respected in the portal design
- Frame what kinds of information needed to make a transit portal work might be considered private versus public, and how that will impact on your final design

You are then going to lead an initial conversation with your client that will highlight some of these concerns so they can be incorporated into your portal specifications.

Case Question

Create a very brief presentation (perhaps 8–12 slides long) that will outline your concerns and establish a joint understanding of how the project will govern itself to remain compliant with privacy legislation from the outset.

6 | MANAGING IS PROJECTS AND CREATING IS SOLUTIONS

WHAT WE WILL COVER

- Critical Pre-development Questions
- The Stages and Importance of the System Development Life Cycle (SDLC)
- Managing an IS Project
- IS Development Teams
- Standard IS Methodology
- IT Tools for IS Development

STUDENT RETURN ON INVESTMENT **ROI**

Through your investment of time in reading and thinking about this chapter, your return—or created value—is gaining knowledge. After reading this chapter, you should be able to

1. Describe the major decisions organizations must address before developing an IS system.
2. Explain the activities organizations must consider within each of the seven stages of the system development life cycle.
3. Describe the key tasks in managing an IS project.
4. Outline the importance of an IS development team and name some of the people who might be included on such a team.
5. Outline the methods organizations use to ensure that they obtain the best IS to help meet their strategic goals.
6. Describe some of the IS development tools available to businesses today.

THE VOICE OF EXPERIENCE

Joey Peng, Bachelor of Science, University of Toronto

Joey Peng is a Program Manager at Microsoft. He graduated from the University of Toronto in 2011 with a Bachelor of Science degree, majoring in Computer Science and Economics. Joey worked as a developer while in school. Now he manages program features and works with other developers and testers to deliver them.

What do you do in your current position? I currently manage and lead feature design in my capacity as Program Manager at Microsoft. While this position isn't solely focused on project management, it does play an important part in the success of feature design. I often work across different product and feature groups at various horizontal integration points within the company. Aside from project management, I also conduct research to ensure my feature meets client needs and undertake requirements writing to outline deliverables.

What do you consider to be important career skills? Leadership skills are among the most important skills in my current position. Incorporated in this is the ability to work in teams and communicate effectively. As a Program Manager I have to be able to bring people together in a room and drive them to consensus. To stay on top of my particular feature, I have to organize work for others and communicate with senior leadership.

How do you use IT? I use a variety of Microsoft products including Outlook, Exchange, Lync, and SharePoint. These are used to organize tasks and collaborate with others on a daily basis. The entire office communicates using email, chat, or VoIP technologies. Through this suite, we're also able to hold online meetings where users can dial in from their computer or phone and share screens to follow along with presentations. From the initial digital meeting invite and onward, e-meetings like this enable everyone to stay on the same page despite busy schedules and different geographic locations.

Can you describe an example of how you used IT to improve business operations? Earlier in my career I had the opportunity to work on a significant website redesign. In my position, I had the responsibility of architecting and building

a new infrastructure for the user interface. The initial version of the website was slow and unstable. I had to make it easier for us to create new content and new types of pages, and allow customization for our users. Much of the site was hardcoded so I needed to rewrite things in a modular way. With the new infrastructure we were able to simplify processes to decrease dependency across different features. This meant that features on the website became independent, so if there was ever a problem with one feature, that problem wouldn't completely disrupt other features. Simplifications like this are very important for a growing site because as features grow, the complexity of a site grows exponentially. By simplifying the UI infrastructure, I was able to increase efficiency for business expansion in the future.

Have you got any "on the job" advice for students seeking a career in IT or business? Don't pursue pure business. If your end goal is to become a CEO or business executive, I think you may be going about your schooling incorrectly. Finding a job becomes the major concern for a lot of students after graduation and often new graduates will do anything to get a job they perceive as good. However, I think once you start working you begin to miss what it is you truly love doing. That's why I think you need to find an industry you have passion for; one that you want to see grow. If you want a career in IT, there are a lot of certifications you can gain to give you a competitive advantage. IT allows for a variety of specializations, so focus on building a strong background in whatever IT technology interests you most.

Joey's features are implemented into Microsoft Dynamics CRM (Customer Relationship Management) software. This information system helps drive customer retention and increase sales. Joey uses various technologies to help collaborate, make decisions, and advance the design of each feature he works on. In this chapter you will learn about project management, including project feasibility, information system methodologies, and the system development life cycle.

Toward the end of the last chapter we introduced project portfolio management (PPM) and the importance of IS projects to an organization's strategy and competitiveness. Despite what you have already learned in this text, you may think that creating information systems is easy. However, information systems are the result of hard work put in by project teams including project managers, developers, and business experts. We often take these systems—which we may use every day—for granted, rarely giving a second thought to how they were created. Yet all systems start with someone's idea or a group's belief that a particular IS could help an organization achieve a goal, solve a problem, or create an opportunity. Consider the following examples of successful information systems created in real companies:

- A collection of three Toronto, Ontario, hospitals—the University Health Network (UHN)—created an information system to streamline the delivery of medication to patients. Prior to the implementation of the Medication Order Entry and Administration Record System (MOE/MAR), patients did not receive their medication until forms were manually filled in, entered into a records system, and signed off by doctors, nurses, and pharmacists. With the improved ability to deliver medication to patients, UHN has enhanced patient care and increased the efficiency of caregivers. As an additional benefit, physicians, nurses, and pharmacists were brought together to discuss processes and policies, which resulted in needed organizational change.[1]

- The Ontario Ministry of Government Services had a collection of websites that were not meeting the needs of Ontarians. With the implementation of ServiceOntario, a new interactive website, the government reaches the public through the Internet, public kiosks, and access terminals, and provides a variety of services including drivers' licence renewal and business licence application. This implementation substantially improved service by allowing many transactions to occur online at any time, and helped to streamline operations.[2]

- In 2002 John Deere embarked on an ambitious supply chain project. Their goal was to reduce the inventory-to-sales ratio by half, and as sales increased, keep inventory levels stable with 2,500 dealer/owners and 100 product families, each with 10 to 15 configurations. John Deere products include everything from ride-on lawn mowers to golf course maintenance equipment, aerators, and utility tractors. Plus, 65 percent of all retail sales occur between March and June. Since the project began in 2002, Deere has reduced inventory to the tune of $1 billion. It went from the traditional push model of inventory to a pull model. It took an investment of between $1 million and $3 million, but the ROI has been dramatic.[3]

By embarking on an ambitious supply chain project, John Deere was able to reduce their inventory-to-sales ratio by half, resulting in a $1 billion reduction in inventory for the company. That number makes the $1 to $3 million spent on the project seem pretty low.

What do these examples all have in common? These information systems all created business value and helped to create

1. A recent Canadian Information Productivity Awards (CIPA) winner.

2. A recent Canadian Information Productivity Awards (CIPA) winner.

3. An Irresistible Supply-Chain Story, *Infoworld*, April 18, 2005. *www.infoworld.com/d/developer-world/irresistible-supply-chain-story-705*, retrieved January 12, 2012.

competitive advantage. So, what steps did they take to ensure that these systems matched their needs and were successfully implemented?

In this chapter, we answer this and other important questions that business professionals (that will be you soon!) in any organization should be asking about their IT systems. Let's first turn our attention to a few critical questions that must be addressed before considering embarking on designing and building a new information system.

■ CRITICAL PRE-DEVELOPMENT QUESTIONS

To support a complex organization, employees often need complex information systems, like the enterprise systems we discussed in Chapter 4, for example. The more complex a system, the more difficult it can be to build, buy, and manage. In addition, not every organizational problem can be solved by building a new system. Often, as we discovered earlier in the text, problems may be related to strategic choices or forces, flawed or inefficient business processes, or an unsuccessful business model. In these kinds of situations, it is unlikely that an information system solution will do anything except hasten failure or speed up the chaos! Before implementing a new system, an organization needs to address four critical questions. We call these "pre-development" questions because they happen *before* an organization decides to start an IS project—referred to as the *concept and inception* stages of the systems development life cycle, which we discuss later. The questions to consider, in order, are:

1. What are we planning and why?
2. Is the project feasible?
3. Should we build or buy/lease?
4. If we build, should we do it in-house or outsource it?

Let's look at each of these questions in detail.

What Are We Building and Why?

As already discussed in the previous chapter, an organization can plan to improve the performance of its business processes by automating, informating, and transforming (either to seek competitive advantage or out of competitive necessity). It should also look for ways an IS could add value to its new or existing products and services. When an organization recognizes that an IS can help it exploit an opportunity or solve a problem, the process of determining the best IS design for its needs begins. The process starts with the all-important question of what are we building and why. By answering this question early on and in some detail, an organization begins to understand its *high level system requirements* and also the *business case* for why it makes sense to build the system. Once it has an understanding of what the IS is going to accomplish and how (the *concept*), it moves to the next important question.

Is the Project Feasible?

A **feasibility study**, sometimes known as the *business case*, is a detailed investigation and analysis of a proposed development project that is undertaken to determine whether it is technically and economically possible to successfully build or acquire a proposed system. A project is technically feasible if the required technology is available (or can be created—although this is a riskier proposition, as we will discuss below). The study must conclude that the company is technically capable of both acquiring and deploying the required technology for the IS solution it envisions. An organization can determine *technical feasibility* by examining potential solutions and evaluating these solutions based on its capabilities and the capabilities of any technology partners it may choose to work with.

A project is *financially feasible* if the organization can pay for the project and the project presents a sound investment of the organization's limited resources. To determine financial feasibility, an organization must show that it can afford to build or buy an information system, and that the IS will financially benefit the organization. Organizations often use several common financial measures to assess this, such as return on investment (ROI), net present value (NPV), internal rate of return (IRR), and payback period. Other business texts discuss these in detail and you may already be familiar with these measures from other courses. Keep in mind that IS projects can be very costly to implement, so understanding these financial measures is important to justify their expense. For example, when a company is proposing to implement an ERP system (which can cost hundreds of thousands or even millions of dollars), it will want to use these measures to estimate when it will see the benefits of implementing the system (payback period) or how much benefit it can expect (ROI, NPV, IRR).

Figure 6.1 shows sample calculations for an IS project. You can see that the company is not expecting payback on its investment for three years. Now imagine a parallel assessment of a comparative project, perhaps using a different software vendor. In this analysis, ROI, IRR, and NPV (the returns on investment) are *greater than* the project shown in Figure 6.1. In the project in Figure 6.1, the software has a higher initial cost than the comparative project, but a lower ongoing maintenance cost. If all other assumptions are the same, will the organization select the comparative project simply because it has a higher return on investment? Not necessarily; financial feasibility and justification are just one piece of the IS development puzzle. Perhaps there is a technical, strategic, or other reason to prefer the project shown in Figure 6.1. Perhaps the organization is more confident in the

Assumptions	
Software Price	$1,800,000
Maintenance Costs (per year)	$75,000
Increase in Customer Revenues (per year)	10%
Decrease in Overall Marketing Costs (per year)	2%
Number of Customers (in Year 1)	80,000
Increase of Customer (per year)	5%
Average Revenue per Customer (no software)	
Year 1	$75
Year 2	$100
Year 3	$125
Overall Marketing Costs (no software)	$2,000,000
Discount Rate	10%

Cash-Flows (in Dollars)	Software Project					
Year	0	1	2	3	Sum	Metrics
Costs						
Purchase of Software	($1,800,000)					
Software Maintenance		($75,000)	($75,000)	($75,000)		
Revenues						
Decrease in Marketing Expenditures		$40,000	$40,000	$40,000		
Additional Revenues by using Software		$600,000	$840,000	$1,050,000		
Number of Customers		$80,000	84,000	84,000		
Additional Revenue per Customer		$7.50	$10.00	$12.50		
Total Yearly Expenditures	($1,800,000)	($75,000)	($75,000)	($75,000)		IRR
Total Yearly Revenues	$0	$640,000	$880,000	$1,090,000		14.00%
Net Cash Flow	($1,800,000)	$565,000	$805,000	$1,015,000		
Discount Factor	1.00	0.91	0.83	0.75		
Discounted Costs	($1,800,000)	($68,182)	($61,983)	($56,349)	($1,986,514)	NPV
Discounted Benefits	$0	$581,818	$727,273	$818,933	$2,128,024	
Present Value for Period	($1,800,000)	$513,636	$665,289	$762,585	$141,510	$141,510
Cumulative Discounted Values	($1,800,000)	($1,286,364)	($621,074)	$141,510		ROI
				Payback Period		7.12%

FIGURE 6.1 Decision makers often use a spreadsheet, such as the one shown here, to calculate financial feasibility metrics as part of the cost-benefit analysis for the feasibility study or business case.

maintenance cost estimates provided for that project, or is more comfortable working with the provider of that software. Like any major decision, the financial context is only one element of the final business decision.

The difficulty in calculating the financial measures is in obtaining the exhaustive list of all costs and benefits, and then placing a monetary value on each of them. Some costs and benefits are *tangible*, which means that a value can easily be applied, such as the salary of software developers. Other costs and benefits are *intangible*, meaning they are difficult to measure in monetary terms. Sometimes a company will undertake an IS project for either offensive or defensive strategic purposes that are hard to justify on a purely economic basis.

For example, an intangible benefit of a cosmetics company's website might be the goodwill obtained after customers read about a no-animal testing policy for its products. How would the company measure this goodwill amount? What about the cost of not having a website at all? Have you ever searched for a company and were not able to find a website for it? What did you think? The absence of technology and the "do nothing" approach may also come at a cost. As a result, due to the many intangibles that an organization must often consider in a major IS development project, the financial measures are, at best, good proxies for the project's final costs and benefits. Some of the decision making around IS investments will be based on the judgement and intuition of executives and managers.

To analyze all of the costs and benefits, both tangible and intangible, a more structured and comprehensive cost-benefit analysis is often undertaken. This type of analysis typically uses all of the financial measures listed in Figure 6.1 and others:

- Internal labour cost—It is important to recognize and calculate the effort required by the organization's project team to implement a new system, as well as the cost to maintain the system over time. This cost is usually calculated based on a standard hourly rate set by an organization's finance department.
- Capital costs—The costs of any capital expenditures, such as for equipment or patents, need to be accounted for in the cost-benefit analysis.
- Expected life span of the system—As we will cover later in this chapter, an IS does not last forever! It needs to be upgraded and replaced over time. The expected number of years that a system will be used will impact the amortization period for the system and impact the financial measures shown in Figure 6.1.
- Productivity savings—The implementation of a new system may result in time savings for various types of organization personnel. While this is not considered an intangible, it can be difficult to estimate. It is best to estimate this conservatively. Again, the hourly labour rate for types of personnel (e.g., customer service agents) is often provided by an organization's finance department.
- Customer satisfaction—This intangible benefit is often included in business cases. Of course, customer satisfaction can be measured using surveys, focus groups, and the like, but when proposing it as a benefit of a new IS, it has to be conservatively estimated.
- Brand image—The implementation of an IS can enhance the image of an organization's brand, similar to goodwill.

What is included in a cost-benefit analysis for the feasibility study or business case will vary based on the type of IS proposed and the organization. As you can imagine, a business case for a not-for-profit IS will look quite different from that of a major corporation or a government agency, especially in terms of revenue or the types of intangible benefits (e.g., societal good).

You may recognize the concept of the cost-benefit analysis from our previous examination of decision making and problem solving in Chapter 3. The goal of the feasibility study or business case is to make a decision on the viability of an IS system and make a recommendation (decision) on

Table 6.1	Major Costs and Benefits of a Proposed IS	
Criteria Scale: 1 (low) to 5 (high)	**Proposed IS Project**	**Alternative Project**
NPV	3 ($141,510)	4 ($175,000)
IRR	4 (14%)	4 (16%)
ROI	3 (7.12%)	4 (10%)
Customer satisfaction increase	4 (25%)	4 (25%)
Brand image	4 (25%)	4 (25%)
Goodwill	4	4
Vendor relationship	3	−1
TOTAL SCORE	**25**	**23**

how to proceed. To make this recommendation, the above financial measures and intangibles can be structured in the form of a cost-benefit analysis, and this cost-benefit analysis can be used to compare alternative solutions as we discussed earlier. Then, whether looking at a single alternative or several, another level of analysis can be applied: criteria analysis. Criteria analysis looks at costs and benefits using selection criteria. In Chapter 3, we applied selection criteria to the decision of selecting a major. Here we apply selection criteria to the costs and benefits of a proposed IS. In Table 6.1 we list the major costs and benefits, both tangible and intangible, of a proposed IS and apply some selection criteria.

Criteria analysis can be used in many ways. As shown in Table 6.1, the analysis is used to compare alternatives. The alternative with the largest total score should be the recommended course of action in the feasibility study or business case. The criteria analysis can also be used for a single alternative. Often criteria weighting is a reflection of an organization's goals. For example, in any given year, an organization may be focused on sales or market share. In another year, it may be focused on cost reduction. If the organization values sales or market share more than cost reduction, the criteria for IRR or customer satisfaction may be weighted higher than for ROI, for example. This method helps ensure that costs and benefits are assessed relative to organizational goals. A second way of using criteria analysis for a single project is to determine the overall desirability of the proposed IS. A corporate directive may be that any proposed IS must have a total score of at least 20 in order to proceed to further evaluation. A score of anything less indicates that the IS is not desirable. This ensures that projects with the highest scores, as weighted by organizational goals, proceed.

Criteria analysis is also used in project portfolio management (PPM). As discussed in Chapter 5, PPM is emerging as a critical consideration for companies that are focused on competitive advantage and that want to select only those IS projects that align to their strategic goals. These companies believe that project management should not only be about doing the projects right, but also about doing the right projects!

PPM is ultimately about selecting and approving projects that will accomplish the organization's strategic objectives. While often considered part of project management, it is actually a planning process that precedes the project management process by defining which projects will get activated and assigned to a project manager and project team. The selection of projects aligned to an organization's overall strategy that provide the company with a benefit is of utmost importance. In this selection process, projects are examined to determine which are the most critical and of the highest priority. This is often done using some form of criteria analysis, as we did above. Once this is determined, resources are allocated across the projects in the portfolio. Of course, new projects begin and projects end or are cancelled all the time. Therefore, the portfolio is always changing. The project portfolio is constantly being analyzed and monitored. It is even possible for projects to change priority over time,

Assigned Priority	Budget	Expected ROI	Projects	Dept.	Project Sponsor	Supported Strategic Goal	Project Type	Status	Projected End	PM	Other Allocated Resources (IT and SMEs)
1	$5M	$15M	CRM System implementation	Customer Service	Barb Thomas	Excellence in Execution	Cost Reduction	Execution	Aug 2013	Sam Elliot	Mary Jones, Bob Levy, Sutesh Singh
2	$150K	$3M	VoIP	IT Infrastructure	Ivana Romonov	Stability	Cost Reduction	Initiating	Jan 2014	Linda Chow	Robert Simon, Ted Martin
3	$3M	$10	New product development	Sales and Marketing	Indira Keshavji	Growth	Revenue Generating	Planning	May 2014	Michael Alphonso	Hitesh Bala, Angela Marie

FIGURE 6.2 A simple example of a project portfolio.

and resources may be shifted between projects. Figure 6.2 shows a sample of a very simple project portfolio. In this example you can see some of the critical measures determined during the feasibility study or business case, the assigned priority, which is likely based on the results of the cost-benefit analysis, and the strategic goal that the project supports.

After the feasibility of an IS is determined and the business case accepted, it is time to do some further analysis and determine, in detail, how the project will proceed—will the IS be built or bought/leased or other? It is possible that these alternatives may have been examined as part of the feasibility study or business case. Because these are important decisions in creating an IS, we discuss these at length below.

Should We Build or Buy/Lease?

An organization usually chooses one of three primary options for obtaining an IS: (1) buying, (2) leasing, or (3) building. To select which option is best in any given set of circumstances, the organization needs to examine its requirements and the advantages and disadvantages of each option. Building a new system from scratch often ensures the best matching of an IS with an organization's requirements. It is also the best option for obtaining a sustainable competitive advantage, because the system's capabilities are not easily copied by competitors if they are custom built. However, building a complete IS can be a long and costly process. When time and cost have greater importance than competitive advantage or customization, a firm often pursues buying or leasing.

Obviously, if there is a time-to-market factor in the decision (that is, unless we get to market fast, we are going to lose the opportunity), this may be the most important factor in any decision about buying or building the new system. CIOs today must deliver better systems faster than ever before to support their organization's competitive position.

When buying an existing system, an organization may still need to make adjustments, particularly by compromising its ultimate list of preferred requirements with the actual capabilities of the existing system. However, this option saves time and cost over building a new system. For some systems, like a customer relationship management (CRM) system, it may be possible to lease a system. Leasing refers to using software as a service (SaaS), as available in the cloud, or using an application service provider (ASP), discussed at length in Chapter 2. This often involves a pay-as-you-go approach based on transaction volumes or usage, or it can involve renting access to an application on a renewable monthly or yearly basis. In addition to lower development costs and time savings, the major advantage with leasing a system is that the vendor is responsible for maintaining and updating it. Table 6.2 provides a more complete listing of the advantages and disadvantages of the three options.

Table 6.2	Advantages and Disadvantages of Buying, Leasing, or Building	
Development Choice	**Advantages**	**Disadvantages**
Buying	• Generally faster and less costly than building an entire system from scratch	• Little or no competitive advantage; may need to compromise on some features • Dependent on vendor for product updates
Leasing SaaS (cloud or ASP model)	• Lowest cost and fastest to put in place • Vendors are in charge of maintenance and updates • Does not require an in-house IS staff	• No competitive advantage • Little to no control over system features • Dependence on vendor for entire system • Can get locked into an undesirable contract
Building	• Most likely to provide a competitive advantage • Retain complete control over system • Customization of the system to specific requirements	• Longest time and highest cost to put in place • Requires IS staff with time and development knowledge

Buy or Lease: Which System/Vendor Should We Select?

If an organization decides it is going to buy or lease a system, it will likely follow the organization's approved procurement process. In the case of acquiring an IS, most organizations will issue a **request for information (RFI)** to companies. Often the purpose of the RFI is to gather information about a product and/or vendor capabilities. An RFI is usually sent to as broad a range of vendors as possible. It attempts to gather quite general information, such as basic facts about a vendor and high level product specifications. An RFI is usually followed by a **request for proposal (RFP)**, a more detailed request, only to those vendors of interest, after evaluating the RFI responses. An RFP is a document that initiates a bidding process for potential vendors. This is why it is also known as a *request for quote* or *request for tender* (required for government and many not-for-profits).

The purpose of an RFP is twofold:

- to determine the suitability of the vendor's offered products or services in relation to the proposed IS requirements
- to gather bids from qualified vendors for price comparison

The size and complexity of an RFP depends on the IS being considered. The requirements for building a simple informational website will be few and more simple than the requirements for an ERP system (RFPs for this large a system can be 100+ pages!). It is important that the RFP list as many specific requirements as possible so that vendor responses can be properly evaluated.

A key part of the RFP process is evaluation and selection. The selection of a vendor using the RFP process is to be completely unambiguous and non-prejudicial. That is, all vendor responses are evaluated and treated equally in every way. Communications with responding vendors, including responses to vendor questions, are logged and shared with all vendors. The RFP itself often lists the selection criteria and requirements weighting to make the process completely transparent to all vendors. RFPs must be submitted by the deadline specified in the RFP. Late RFPs are never accepted. A typical RFP includes the following sections:

- introduction and purpose of the RFP
- submission process and rules, which may include the required submission format

- statement of need or scope of work including the detailed requirements; often respondents will be asked to rate their compliance to the requirements on a scale and provide a description of how their product of service meets the requirement
- schedule and cost information
- vendor information, including biographies and resumés of employees who may be involved with the project/company
- appendices, which may include vendor financial information and references

Upon receipt of the RFP responses, an organization begins the evaluation and selection process. Responses are evaluated based on the prescribed criteria and, at times, are done using an automated program. Often vendors are short-listed and asked to present their solution to the IS selection committee. Sounds a lot like a job interview, doesn't it? It is, but is one that can be worth hundreds of thousands of dollars and multi-year contracts.

Finally, the end of the process is the selection of the vendor. Like the cost-benefit analysis described previously, the price of the IS solution may not be the main factor in selecting a vendor. A more expensive vendor may be selected if it is deemed to better meet the requirements or if the vendor is considered to be preferable to others (e.g., good references, solid management team). The RFP process can take a significant amount of time and effort and it is often a relief to finally select a vendor and get the project started. However, before the project can begin, contracts and purchase agreements must be created and signed. These documents are critical to setting expectations and ensuring that the selected vendor delivers what is required. Ensuring that requirements are met is one part of vendor management. **Vendor management** is the management, control, and monitoring of third party providers or suppliers to the organization. It is the role of the *vendor manager* to keep vendors apprised to what is happening in the organization, including any new requirements for vendors. It is also the job of the vendor manager to ensure that vendors are doing and providing what is expected. This is sometimes known as **contract compliance**—adhering to the terms of the agreements.

A critical error that organizations make is to hire a vendor without appointing someone as the vendor manager. This often results in a vendor that is not well managed and that does not meet requirements. Organizations often underestimate the time, effort, and necessity of vendor management. Without it, costs can end up being substantially more than the cost of vendor management due to miscommunication, mismanagement, and vendors going rogue! Of course, some companies avoid the issue of vendor management entirely if they decide to build an IS themselves, using their own staff. Mind you, if they decide to outsource the build, the issue of vendor management is raised again.

Build: Should We Develop In-House or Outsource?

If an organization chooses to build an entirely new system, the next big question is whether to use its own staff (**in-house development**) or hire another company (**outsource**), such as IBM or CGI, to build all or part of it. When the outsourcing company is located primarily in a foreign country, the practice is known as *offshoring*.

An organization needs to carefully consider the advantages and disadvantages of outsourcing versus in-house development. As with the build-or-buy question, an organization must examine its present situation and capabilities and choose the option that most closely matches its current needs. Table 6.3 compares these two options. Dimensions to be considered in this decision include any time-to-market imperative (which puts the priority on speed), current financial performance (businesses in crisis or that are underperforming must pay closer attention to costs), and an organization's risk tolerance (which must be greater to take on building a system from scratch versus buying a system that is not perfect or customized, but that meets its most important requirements).

Table 6.3	Advantages and Disadvantages of In-House Development vs. Outsourcing	
IS Development Source	**Advantages**	**Disadvantages**
In-house development	• Firm retains complete control of the project • Process builds internal knowledge through learning and experience	• Generally higher development time and costs • Distraction of in-house IS staff from other duties
Outsourcing	• High level of skill and expertise • Internal staff provides project oversight, which is less time-intensive than full development • Generally lower time and costs	• Firm loses some control of project since it is necessary to give outsourcer some decision-making authority • Internal staff has less opportunity to build experience • Requires good contracts, oversight, and vendor management

SOURCE: Adapted from Patrick G. McKeown, *Information Technology and the Networked Economy*, 2nd ed., 2003, Boston: Course Technology, 328.

A final and more unusual way of acquiring an IS, that we have not mentioned so far, is by technical acquisition. A **technical acquisition** occurs when a company possessing a desired technology is purchased by another organization so that the acquiring company can own and use the technology of the acquired company. In the case of a technical acquisition, an organization does not need to build or buy an IS—it simply buys the company with the IS! A well-known technical acquisition is eBay's purchase of Paypal in 2002. At the time, eBay had another online payment processing system called BillPoint. BillPoint was not as popular as Paypal and did not have all of the functionality that PayPal did. PayPal was the market leader in online transactions, including those done on eBay itself. Rather than continuing to develop and work with BillPoint or outsourcing online payment processing to PayPal, which would have been very costly considering the volume of eBay transactions, eBay decided to purchase PayPal for $1.5 billion.[4] In doing this, eBay also gained a significant additional source of revenue.

Regardless of how an IS is acquired, it has the same life cycle as any IS project—the systems development life cycle, which we discuss next.

Quick Test

1. Which of the following is one way of acquiring an information system?
   a. buy
   b. build
   c. lease
   d. all of the above

2. True or False. Companies always send an RFI before an RFP.

3. Criteria analysis is used to
   a. determine the value of a proposed IS
   b. analyze costs and benefits using selection criteria
   c. help eliminate intangibles from cost-benefit analysis
   d. ensure a buy decision

Answers: 1. d; 2. False; 3. b

---

4. "eBay Picks up Paypal for $1.5 Billion," CNET. *http://news.cnet.com/2100-1017-941964.html*, retrieved January 12, 2011.

■ THE STAGES AND IMPORTANCE OF THE SYSTEM DEVELOPMENT LIFE CYCLE (SDLC)

The **system development life cycle (SDLC)** is the common term used for the stages and activities of system development. The SDLC is composed of processes that occur from the beginning stages of a system to the end of its useful life when the system is retired and likely replaced with something new. Or, perhaps the organization may exit a line of business or sell a division, thus eliminating the need for the system altogether. Regardless, you must understand that a system created today, no matter how good, cannot last forever. Organizations are therefore perpetually designing and implementing systems.

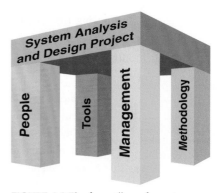

FIGURE 6.3 The four pillars of a system analysis and design project; failures in any one of these areas can cause the whole project to come crashing down.

You must also keep in mind what was said at the very outset of this text: an information system is far more than just technology. Similarly, an information systems project involves more than just technology. Those involved in the systems analysis and design process need to remember that four distinct pillars impact an IS project, and all four must be addressed to succeed (Figure 6.3): (1) you need the right people with the right skills (your IS development team); (2) they must have the right tools and (3) methods to build the system; and (4) you need to manage the process carefully to ensure success. The failure to pay attention to any one of these pillars can cause your project to collapse!

This also suggests that each stage of the SDLC is associated with a set of activities within both the project team (which we will discuss) and the development team (usually housed in an IT department or outsourced). Therefore, throughout the life cycle, various departments or functions will be doing different things to support the IS as it progresses through the stages of the SDLC.

Diagrams typically show the phases or steps of the traditional SDLC as flowing from one to the next from top to bottom, similar to a waterfall, as shown in Figure 6.4. In fact, many systems professionals refer to this as the *waterfall method* for that reason, although we distinguish between the steps of the SDLC and the specific steps the IT development team goes through to build the actual system and the tools and methods they use while doing that (a methodology). At a high level, the SDLC simply starts with an idea. We call this the *concept*, yet early on, the person

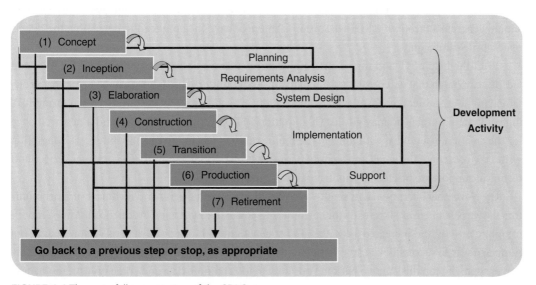

FIGURE 6.4 The waterfall presentation of the SDLC steps.

proposing the idea is unlikely to have details of what the final solution will be. But the SDLC begins when there is an opportunity that likely involves technology or information systems and flows as follows:

1. *Concept* (also known as pre-inception or idea phase)—An organization must foster an environment that promotes ideas that can improve its bottom line. Ideas to gain competitive advantage or reduce costs must be collected, documented, and initially evaluated. The ideas with the most potential and merit advance to the next stage, inception, for further analysis and planning.
2. *Inception* (also known as the feasibility or planning phase)—This phase begins when an organization has the idea to build an information system. The focus is on understanding the problem to be solved or the opportunity to be addressed and planning the project. Early interactions with stakeholders of the system take place at this time to complete the feasibility study or business case (discussed in detail earlier) required to be approved to proceed to the next phase of the SDLC, elaboration.
3. *Elaboration*—In this phase, the project team finalizes the requirements for the system and the project plan, and designs the system architecture. The team also creates conceptual models of the systems and subsystems.
4. *Construction*—During this phase, the team builds the initial running system. The team usually implements core functionalities first, and then incorporates additional features.
5. *Transition*—At this time, the team finalizes the system, tests it, and puts it in place. In addition, the team completes the final training of users and management of users during the transition.
6. *Production*—Once the system is up and running, the organization must continuously monitor, maintain, and evaluate it. The organization must also keep users of the system up to date with the latest modifications and procedures.
7. *Retirement*—At some point, the system may lose its value to the company. This phase often marks the concept of a new system to replace the obsolete one. The old system may retain some usefulness as it is phased out over time by the replacement system.

Let's illustrate the SDLC using an example. As the marketing assistant at WildOutfitters.com, a hypothetical retail hiking-goods store, you suspect that sales are not as high during December as they could be. You come up with an idea to increase website sales for the holiday season (Concept). You analyze sales data for the month of December for the past five years and prove that they are significantly less than sales during the summer. You call a meeting with your manager and your IT department to discuss this information and your idea. They agree that your idea is feasible and should generate a favourable ROI (Inception). You now have the go-ahead to determine the details of a website campaign.

With the help of IT and the advertising department, you design the content and the look and feel of a campaign that will be sent via email to all WildOutfitters customers (using contact data contained in the customer database), with a link to a gift-list generator that encourages them to add hiking equipment to their holiday gift list (Elaboration). IT builds the mailing list and a new web page for the creation of a gift list with links to the online product catalogue and shopping cart. Marketing writes the content of the email and website (Construction). You make sure that customer service and technical support are briefed on this campaign (Transition).

On November 30, the email is sent to all WildOutfitters.com customers. Technical support monitors the website to ensure it is ready for customers to create their gift lists (Production). After a month of frantic activity and increased sales, the gift list generator web page is turned off (Retirement). The campaign was so successful you are promoted to website marketing manager and you are not sure how you are going to top this! You go back to your desk to look at more data and come up with more ideas (Concept again).

WHAT DO YOU THINK? ?

As you can imagine, answering the pre-development questions and developing an IS involves a significant amount of decision making and problem solving. Review the sections on decision making and problem solving in Chapter 3 to consider the following questions:

1: What types of information will you gather to determine if the IS under consideration aligns with the strategic goals of the business?

2: How would you decide between building or buying a system? What types of information will you gather and how will you evaluate these data to come to a solution?

3: During the elaboration phase of the SDLC, many decisions are made about what the system must do. Many times there are a lot of requirements to consider. How would you determine which requirements are more essential than others?

Quick Test

1. Which of the following are required for a successful IS development project?
   a. tools
   b. methodology
   c. management
   d. people
   e. all of the above

2. True or False. The system development life cycle of an IS begins when the system is ready to be used by the organization and ends when the organization retires the system.

3. At which phase does an organization finalize an IS and put it in place?
   a. construction
   b. inception
   c. production
   d. transition

Answers: 1. e; 2. False; 3. d

■ MANAGING AN IS PROJECT

Project management is "the application of knowledge skills, tools, and techniques to project activities to meet project requirements."[5] For IS development, a project manager simultaneously oversees three main project elements: the scope of the project, the resources needed, and the time to complete it, all balanced with a view toward accomplishing the organization's strategy through successful project delivery. The project scope defines what the project should accomplish. Resources can include people, equipment, material, and money. Time estimates consider project activity times and how they depend on each other.

---

5. Project Management Institute, *A Guide to the Project Management Body of Knowledge* (PMBOK® Guide) Fourth Edition, 2008, p. 6.

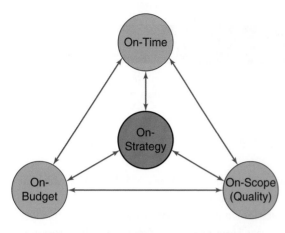

Good People + Good Process + Good Strategy = Extraordinary Results

FIGURE 6.5 The project management triple constraint with the strategy dimension added.

Management of these elements is always a balancing act. A manager often makes decisions to actively set the levels of two elements and then calculates the third accordingly, while always realizing that all three are important and must be accomplished. For example, if the client requires specific software features, these features define the scope and, of course, the ultimate quality of the project. Or the client may prefer to focus on a set time deadline for receiving the final software, often at the expense of incorporating every single last requirement—known as *de-scoping*. By containing enthusiasm for an endless set of features, the project can often be delivered sooner and additional functionality put into a future release or upgrade. The project manager then calculates the resources, which then result in cost estimates needed to meet the scope and time constraints as demanded by the project sponsor.

As Figure 6.5 illustrates, you can think of the three project management elements as the three sides of a triangle; in some project management circles this is referred to as the *triple constraint*, or *iron triangle*, because of its immutable nature and because it is perceived as nearly impossible to deliver on all three components successfully (on time, on budget, and on scope). And, as you might recall from geometry, once you know the length of two sides, you can calculate the length of the third. However, while Figure 6.5 shows all points on the triangle as equal, it should be clear to you that project scope/quality is often the starting point for arriving at the other two points of the triangle. That's because, among these three elements, project scope is often the most important to manage: increases in scope will drive increases in time and/or resources needed. Subsequently, changes or limitations in time and cost can affect the quality delivered by the project.

All that being said, competitive pressures often require the delivery of all three. In fact, we suggest that there is actually a quadruple constraint in most organizations today, where linking project outcomes to strategy is crucial to success. Therefore, the project management triangle, like any other part of the development methodology, must work inside the organization's strategy and mission, as shown by the centre circle in Figure 6.5. By selecting systems projects that enable faster and more certain execution of business strategy, and by executing those projects more successfully, an organization can lock in competitive advantages that make it a force in its industry.

To effectively execute a systems project, each step in the project management process should be linked to a part of the SDLC and have the associated required approvals to proceed to the next step, as shown in Figure 6.6. This requires that project managers of an IS project have at least a comparable

Milestone Approval	Project Selection and Approval	Release to Prototype and Design	Release to Development	Release to Testing	Release to Production	Maintenance Releases
System Development Life Cycle Step	Concept Definition	Concept Development	System Design	System Development	System Development	System Operational
PMI Project Management Life Cycle Step	**Initiating** Planning Executing Controlling Closing	Initiating **Planning** Executing Controlling Closing	Initiating Planning **Executing** Controlling Closing	Initiating Planning **Executing** **Controlling** Closing	Initiating Planning **Executing** **Controlling** Closing	Initiating Planning Executing Controlling **Closing**

FIGURE 6.6 The link between project management steps and the SDLC.

knowledge of the steps of the SDLC and the ability to coordinate activity between the project team/project sponsor and the development team and assigned IT resources.

Overview of Project Management Tasks

Project management activities may occur as early as the concept phase. However, they normally begin at the point at which the organization has approved a project proposal and selected it to be executed as part of their project portfolio. It is important to note one important difference between the system development life cycle (SDLC) and the project management activities to support a particular project: A project has a beginning and an end, whereas the SDLC is a continuous stream of activities over time. Even though a project finishes when the system is complete and released to production, the SDLC activities continue until the system is retired. While many of the activities in project management occur before the system is constructed, most of the SDLC will not begin for that system until the project is started. The project ends when the system is in production and transitioned to day-to-day operational staff; however, the operational staff monitors and maintains the system until it is retired.

Figure 6.7 shows the nine key components of a project management methodology that support the life cycle of the project. Although the project manager should develop knowledge and skills in all of these areas, the following four core functions lead to specific project objectives:

1. *scope management*—identifying and managing all the tasks required to complete a project
2. *time management*—estimating the duration of the project, developing an acceptable schedule, and managing the project to ensure timely completion
3. *cost management*—preparing a budget and managing the costs of the project to stay within budget
4. *quality management*—ensuring that the finished project satisfies its defined goals

The facilitating functions support the project activities. Human resources management focuses on making productive use of the team members. Communications management involves the supervision of shared project information. With risk management, the project manager seeks to identify

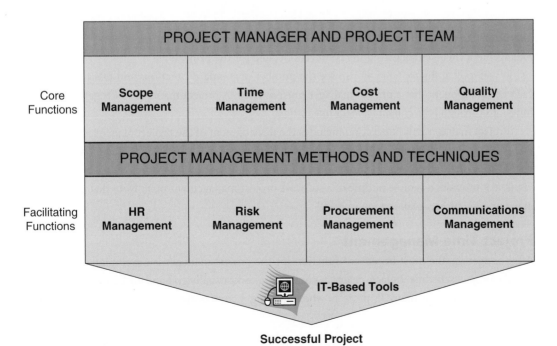

FIGURE 6.7 The nine key components of a project management methodology that create a successful project.

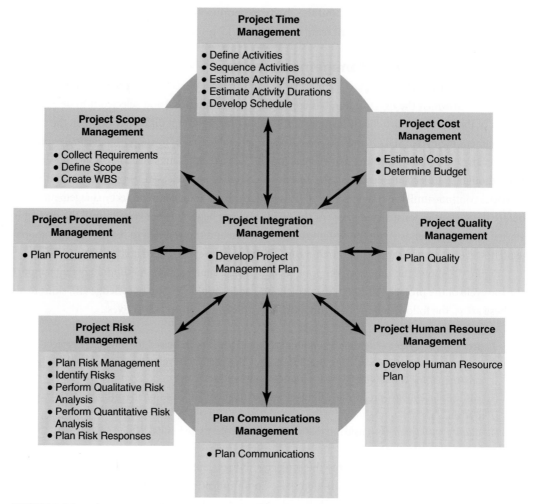

FIGURE 6.8 A project manager must oversee any number of tasks within each of the nine key components of a project management methodology.[6]

and prioritize potential risks and develop contingency plans in case a risk occurs. Procurement management involves acquiring the resources needed for the project.

If you look at Figure 6.8, you can see the number of standard functions and tasks listed under each key component that a project manager must oversee. A project manager ties together all these functions through *project management integration*.

Project management integration includes the development of the project plan, execution of the plan, and the coordination of changes to the plan as they occur. The project manager uses a project plan to coordinate all project documentation and help guide the execution and control of the project. Figure 6.9 provides a sample outline of a software project management plan. Note that creating and managing the project plan is a job in itself!

Project Time Management

After budgeting, the most important function for the project manager is developing and controlling the project schedule. In fact, delays in completing tasks usually go hand-in-hand with increases in costs. However, for many IS projects where gaining a competitive advantage is a goal, creating

---

6. Adapted from Project Management Institute, *A Guide to the Project Management Body of Knowledge* (PMBOK® Guide) Fourth Edition, 2008, p. 47.

Title Page

Change History

1. Introduction

2. Project Management Approach

    2.1. Project Organization

    2.2. Roles and Responsibilities

    2.3. Project Stakeholders

    2.4. Schedule Summary

    2.5. Budget Summary

3. Project Scope

    3.1. Assumptions and constraints

    3.2. Project Deliverables

4. Milestone List

5. Work Breakdown Structure

6. Schedule

7. Project Change Control Process

8. Communications Management Plan

9. Cost Management Plan

    9.1. Budget

10. Procurement Management Plan

11. Project Scope Management Plan

12. Schedule Management Plan

13. Quality Management Plan

14. Risk Management Plan

15. Resource Management Plan

    15.1. Staff Management Plan

    15.2. Contractor/consultant Management Plan

    15.3. Vendor Management Plan

16. Sponsor Acceptance

Appendices

FIGURE 6.9 Sample project management plan.

and maintaining a schedule that produces a quality product as quickly as possible can be more important than costs. For example, think about what might have happened if another company developed its website before *eBay.com*. Could a delay in eBay's development schedule have allowed a competitor to become the first big Internet auction site instead? The main activities of project time management include:[7]

- *define activities*—identify the activities required to produce project deliverables
- *sequence activities*—identify and document relationships between project activities
- *estimate activity resources*—estimate the type and quantity of material, people, equipment, or supplies required by each activity

7. Project Management Institute. *A Guide to The Project Management Body of Knowledge* (PMBOK® Guide) Fourth Edition, 2008, p. 129.

- *estimate activity durations*—approximate the number of work periods needed to complete individual work activities with estimated resources
- *develop schedule*—analyze activity sequences, durations, resource requirements, and schedule constraints to create the project schedule
- *control schedule*—monitor the status of the project to update project progress and manage changes to the schedule baseline

To manage all these activities, project managers often use a **Gantt chart**. Gantt charts (see Figure 6.10) provide a standard format for displaying the results of the first four time-management activities. This chart lists the project activities, along with the start and finish dates, in a calendar format. On the calendar, horizontal bars that correspond to start and end dates represent activity durations. Patterns or colours on the bars represent various categories of activities. Arrows show when the start time of one or more activities depends on the completion of an earlier activity. While the project is ongoing, the project manager updates the chart to show actual project durations, serving as a project evaluation and schedule control tool.

Project Risk Management

Every IS project contains an element of risk. Uncertainties or unexpected events can and do occur. For example, a key project team member might leave unexpectedly, or management might suddenly decide to reduce funding. But most project risks reflect the fact that much of an IS plan relies on estimates. Since these risks are inherent in the project plan, they can be manageable.

The job of **risk management** is, therefore, to recognize, address, and eliminate sources of risk before they threaten the successful completion of the project. This is the responsibility of all project team members. In general, project risk management tasks fall into one of two main categories: (1) risk assessment and (2) risk control.

The first step in risk assessment is to identify potential project risks. A project manager often obtains an initial list of risks by asking several questions: What could possibly go wrong? How likely is this to happen? How will it affect the project? What can I do about it? Since the greatest risks often occur where

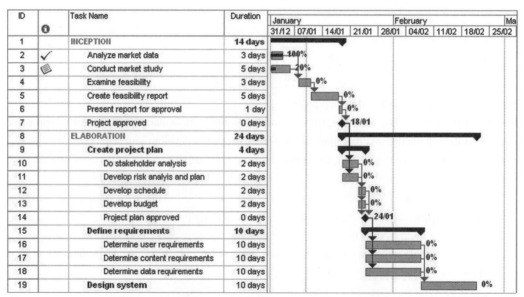

FIGURE 6.10 A Gantt chart provides a standard format for displaying the results of activity definition, sequence and duration estimating, and schedule development; this chart lists the project activities, along with the start and finish dates, in a calendar format.

Table 6.4	Common Areas of Project Risk[8]
Project Risk	**Description**
Feature creep	As the project progresses, user requirements may increase beyond the team's ability to handle them within the original project scope.
Requirements gold-plating	A project has more and perhaps unnecessary requirements than are really needed and that are additional to those envisioned during inception.
Short-changed quality	If a project is rushed, corners are often cut in areas such as testing, documentation, and design tasks.
Overly optimistic schedule	Setting an overly optimistic schedule can cause abbreviations in critical planning and design tasks, as well as put undue pressure on team members.
Inadequate design	When not enough time is allocated to design, the quality of the design can suffer.
Silver bullet syndrome	This occcurs when a project team latches on to a new practice or technology and expects it to answer all of their problems.
Research-oriented development	This occurs when a design attempts to push the boundaries of what is technically feasible in too many areas.
Weak personnel	This occurs when the skills and knowledge of the team members are not up to the project tasks.
Friction with customers	This can be caused by perceived lack of cooperation on one side or the other or personality conflicts.

there is an interface, such as between systems, departments, processes, or organizations, particular attention is paid to these areas. This is where the input of subject matter experts (SMEs), who we discuss later, becomes critical: What do you see as being a risky aspect of the project? What can be done to mitigate these risks? Table 6.4 lists some of the most common areas where risks can occur in an IS project.

After obtaining a list of potential risks, the next step is to actually assess these risks; that is, to analyze each of them for likelihood and potential impact to the project. This assessment will come primarily from the experience and knowledge of project stakeholders and others consulted during the risk analysis process. As Figure 6.11 shows, the greatest effort to manage risk will focus on addressing the risks that are most likely to occur (high probability) and those that will have the biggest impact (high impact) if they do occur. In other words, project managers usually concentrate on those risks that fall in the upper right corner of the matrix.

To manage risk effectively, a project manager directs a team member to allocate each risk to an identified owner. This should be someone within the project team who is responsible for monitoring the situation and ensuring the initiation of any necessary mitigating actions. Table 6.5 lists responses to risks.

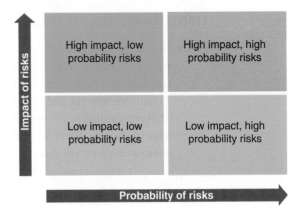

FIGURE 6.11 A project risk matrix helps managers focus on those risks that will have the biggest impact if they occur.

8. Steve McConnell, *Rapid Development*, Microsoft Press, 1996, p. 85.

Table 6.5	Risk Response Action[9]
Risk Response	**Action**
Risk transfer	Move the risk to someone who is more able to deal with it (e.g., a contractor).
Risk deferral	Adjust the plan schedule to move some activities to a later date when the risk might be lessened.
Risk reduction	Either reduce the probability of the risk occurring or lessen the impact; for example, increase staffing resources on the project.
Risk acceptance	Accept the risk and then ensure that contingency plans are in place.
Risk avoidance	Eliminate the possibility of the risk occurring; for instance, use alternative resources or technologies.

Managing risk is an ongoing task throughout the project life cycle. The nature of the risks faced by the project team will change as the project progresses. For example, staff recruitment may be a big issue at the inception of a project, while staff retention becomes more of an issue as the project draws near to an end.

Program Management

Sometimes it may be useful to either break down a very large project into a series of smaller, interrelated projects, or to group a series of related projects into a single work effort. When this happens, the result is often called a **program** and the activity of managing several projects together is known as **program management**—essentially the same tasks as those involved in managing a single project, but across multiple teams. Programs are often created because there are dependencies between projects. Think of a program as similar to graduating with your degree. Inside this program are the individual courses you must take in order to graduate. Think of each of these courses as a project, and some of these courses are prerequisites (dependent). Within each course, specific deliverables and deadlines must be met. Taken together, each course must be accomplished for you to graduate and for the program to end. In systems projects, a program may be created because a project is too large to be organized as one project and the dependencies between large tasks are critical. For example, a project to create a new line of business for an organization would be run as projects within the program, such as creating the technical infrastructure, developing the product for sale, determining customer service practices, and so on.

Project Management Office

When organizations are very project focused, they may have one or more project management offices (PMO). The role of the PMO in an organization or department is often twofold:

- To provide standards and best practices for all projects such that they follow the same process and methodology—With standard documents and methods in place, project execution becomes repeatable and the organization becomes more efficient at project delivery.
- To facilitate, monitor, and report on the project portfolio—Members of the PMO may assist with developing project selection criteria and apply it to projects to determine their priority in the portfolio. In this role, the PMO tracks the status of projects and facilitates any necessary changes to projects within the portfolio.

Depending on the size of the organization and the projects that have been approved, one or more PMOs may exist. For example, there may be an enterprise PMO (ePMO) that monitors all projects in the organization, and there may be an IT PMO that tracks IT internal projects as well as IT participation in enterprise projects.

---

9. Steve McConnell, *Rapid Development*, Microsoft Press, 1996, p. 87.

As the above discussion illustrates, the scope and complexity of an IS development project is often difficult to manage. To assist project managers and ensure that there are standards in the project management profession, the Project Management Institute (PMI) has developed a guide, the Project Management Body of Knowledge (PMBOK®). Much of the information in this section of the text can also be found in the PMBOK® guide. If project management interests you, we encourage you to visit *www.pmi.org* to learn more about the profession and project management standards. Following standard practices helps project teams do the right things (be effective). Using technology helps project teams be more productive and do things right (be efficient).

Project Management Software

Project management (PM) software is designed to support and automate project management and decision-making tasks. PM software is usually classified into three levels:

- *low-level packages*—for entry-level users; include tools for basic scheduling, project control, reporting, filtering, and sorting
- *mid-level software*—adds to these functions by providing resource-levelling, resource-allocation, cost-control, and flexible-charting capabilities; allows for effective management of large projects, with up to about 2,000 tasks
- *high-level software*—provides advanced functions including scheduling by user-defined rules, programming languages, resource management for multiple projects, and risk management; can identify conflicting demands for the same resources, as well as allow the manager to set priorities among projects that require the same resource

Table 6.6 lists the common capabilities/features of project management software.

Most PM software includes graphic tools for scheduling and tracking tasks, such as the Gantt chart shown in Figure 6.10. Another possible tool is the **program evaluation review technique (PERT) chart**. Like the Gantt chart, a project team uses a PERT chart to schedule and manage the tasks within a project. In Figure 6.12, the PERT shows the project as a network of tasks (represented

Table 6.6	Project Management Software Features
Feature	**Description**
Task scheduling	Allows the project manager to assign start and end times to a set of tasks that are subject to certain constraints, such as time or resources
Resource planning	Helps determine and control what resources (people, equipment, materials), and in what quantities, are needed to perform the activities of the project
Time tracking	Helps the project manager ensure that the project is meeting the schedule, budget, and quality targets
Estimating	Estimates task-completion times and amount of resources needed for each task
Risk assessment	Helps identify project risks and then develop strategies that either significantly reduce or avoid the risks altogether
Reporting/charts	Includes capabilities for reporting on the project status (e.g., the use of charts)
Collaboration	May include a shared database as well as email, chat, and virtual meeting capabilities
Process/methodology	Provides tools geared toward supporting a particular development method
Hosted or local install	May be locally installed or hosted on the Web by an application service provider (ASP)

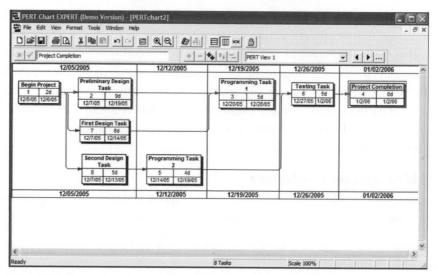

FIGURE 6.12 A PERT chart, such as the one shown here created from PERT Chart EXPERT software, clearly shows the sequence and dependencies between tasks. The project manager uses it to organize and track project deliverables.

by rectangles) that are linked by arrows. An advantage of the PERT chart is that it clearly shows the sequence and dependencies between tasks. (A dependent task cannot be started until another task is completed.) Each task in the diagram is labelled with a task number, the duration of the task, an estimated start date, and an estimated end date.

An important use of the PERT chart is to identify the critical path. The *critical path* is the sequence of tasks that determines the overall completion time of the project. If any of the tasks on the critical path are delayed, then the entire project will be delayed. Tasks not on the critical path may have the luxury of extra time, called *slack*, for completing the work. Note that as the project goes on, the critical path of tasks may change. This can occur if tasks on the critical path are completed early or tasks not on the critical path are delayed beyond their allowable slack time.

Quick Test

1. A _____ chart is used to show sequences of project activities and to identify the critical path.
   a. data-flow
   b. Gantt
   c. PERT
   d. sequence

2. True or False. After setting the project scope and time frame, an organization can then calculate the amount of resources needed to complete a project.

3. The risk that the desired scope of a project will continue to increase as the project progresses is known as _____.
   a. feature (scope) creep
   b. requirements gold-plating
   c. short-changed quality
   d. silver bullet syndrome

■ IS DEVELOPMENT TEAMS

The people associated with an IS project usually belong to one or both of the following groups: those on the actual project team, and those who are stakeholders in the IS. While ultimately the stakeholders must both design and use the system, without a correspondingly excellent IS development team, the system cannot actually be built.

The Importance of Stakeholders

For most IS development projects, identifying the key stakeholders is a very important task that should be thought about right from the beginning. Why? Because the attitude of a powerful stakeholder toward a project can dramatically affect the project's eventual success or failure. In addition, the various stakeholders who are the SMEs can best inform you about various aspects of the system in which you are not an expert. As a result, a **stakeholder analysis** should begin as part of the project feasibility study. The project manager should then continue to use this analysis during the course of the project to reduce the risk of negative stakeholder attitudes.

A stakeholder analysis begins with a list of the stakeholders, including what each has at stake, as well as the degree of impact each stakeholder has on the project. The analysis must also consider whether the team can expect resources from the stakeholders. Further, the analysis should also attempt to identify each stakeholder's attitude toward the project and any risks. Finally, a project manager should assign team members the responsibility of managing different stakeholders, with an anticipated strategy for each one.

Figure 6.13 shows an example of a stakeholder analysis for a generic IS. Note that this analysis lists potential stakeholders, along with how they will affect and be affected by the project. The analysis also estimates the potential impact that each stakeholder can have on the project's success, along with a strategy for dealing with the stakeholders to ensure they have input into the project and are fully engaged in its eventual success. Finally, the analysis includes the assignment of a team member to oversee and carry out the strategy.

Stakeholder	Stake in the project	Potential impact on project	What does the project expect the stakeholder to provide?	Perceived attitudes and/or risks	Stakeholder management strategy	Responsibility
CEO	Policy and process owner who determines organizational policy and procedures	High	Experienced staff to be involved in user group and user acceptance testing. Commitment to implementing change.	Lack of clarity about preferred approach. Views project team as too technically oriented.	Involvement in Project Steering Board, Regular update meeting with project leader.	Project Manager
Department Head	Manages admin staff who will operate the new system at local level and secretarial staff who will indirectly input and directly extract data	Medium	Commitment to implementing change.	Lack of interest in project.	Involvement in briefing sessions at quarterly meetings.	Project Sponsor
Admin Staff	Will operate new system	High	Contribute to system and process design and testing.	Concern about increased workload. Worried about what training they wil receive.	Involvement in user groups.	Admin SME

FIGURE 6.13 A stakeholder analysis lists potential stakeholders, along with how they will affect and be affected by the project.[10]

---

10. Adapted from Stakeholder Analysis Template, JISC InfoNet, *www.jiscinfonet.ac.uk/InfoKits/project-management*.

A Typical IS Project Team

The size of both the project team and the associated IS development team will vary with the specific characteristics of the project. These factors can include the scope of the project, the budget, and the available resources. The project team's skill requirements also vary along these lines. However, most IS development projects require teams with the following roles:

- *Project sponsor*—This individual ensures that the project goals correspond to the organization's business objectives and is often a senior executive or someone in a position of authority. The project sponsor needs to consider the strengths and weaknesses of both the business and the teams, identify opportunities and threats both internal and external to the organization, understand the financial aspects of the project such as budget and the project's return on investment, and manage risks and planning needs. Any major project decisions, including changes to scope, need to be approved by the project sponsor.
- *Project manager (PM)*—This role demands knowledge of methods and techniques to ensure delivery of the project on time and on budget, and the ability to communicate project goals and requirements to the project team and coordinate the workflows of everyone on the project team. The PM is the primary liaison with the project sponsor and the project steering committee and project management office (PMO), if these are in place.
- *Account management*—Typically, this group is part of the development team when the project team works as an outsourcer. This team is responsible for the sales and service of the project team. They provide the initial point of contact to the client (the people who need the IS), as well as daily communication with the client.
- *Architecture and design*—The project members who work in this group ensure that any proposed system is architecturally sound, fits in with the existing or desired technical infrastructure, and meets technical goals and standards. Depending on the type of project, members of this group may be responsible for providing a well-designed user interface. Many user interfaces include multimedia components that require special skills in art and design.
- *Analysts*—Members of this group may have many titles, but they all provide the methods and processes to translate high level requirements in their particular area into lower levels of detail that can be turned into code by programmers. For instance, a *systems analyst* often deals with technical requirements; a *business analyst* more often deals with process and system design; and a *database analyst* handles the data mapping, data dictionary, data structures, etc.
- *Developers*—This group actually creates the system itself by coding and deploying the technical infrastructure of the system and programming it to perform required tasks. This function requires knowledge of both the hardware and software needed by the system to function.
- *Specialists*—This group handles unique aspects of the project; members are often called **SMEs (subject matter experts)**. For instance, a client-facing system may need an artificial intelligence (AI) specialist on the project team to handle specialized interfaces that learn as they go. Likewise, a website for a news organization requires a resource with journalistic or editorial skills on the team to ensure systems meet specific professional requirements of those in the field.
- *Client interface*—A client may be an internal or external customer of the team's organization. In either case, the client has responsibilities that ensure the successful completion of the project. The client must define system requirements, negotiate contract terms, and maintain oversight of the teams as the project progresses. The client may also need to supply resources to the project team.

The exact mix of jobs required will depend on the nature and scope of the project. The project manager is responsible for assembling a team of talented people who can each fill one or more of these jobs. On large and complicated projects, the project manager may decide or an organization may require that there be a **project steering committee (PSC)**. The PSC includes members of senior management who may not be involved directly in a project but who have an interest or stake in the project. Most certainly the project steering committee includes the project sponsor, who may be required to make presentations or answer questions from the committee, and the CFO or controller who may be carefully monitoring the budget of the project. The PSC has regular meetings, typically scheduled and facilitated by the project manager, to discuss the progress of the project. This steering committee provides a level of project governance, which we discussed in Chapter 5, in that the committee's role is to ensure project and organizational goals are met, required resources are provided, contingencies are managed, and expected benefits are realized.

The typical IS project team incorporates many different business professionals with many different skills. Each one needs to contribute his or her expertise to the project for it to succeed.

Team composition is perhaps the most important aspect of project management. The lack of a good team can increase the risks to a project's successful completion. Most successful project teams consist of technical IT people, as well as those with non-technical skills. Non-IT skills range from business skills, such as accounting or business strategy, to creative skills like artistic design and journalism. Thus, no matter what your major, you may have skills that an IS development team needs.

Quick Test

1. A _____ is used to list and analyze those that have an interest in a project.
   a. client interface
   b. project plan
   c. project steering committee
   d. stakeholder analysis

2. True or False. The most important role of a project sponsor is to support the project by clearing obstacles to success.

3. Imagine you are the project manager for a new marketing website. Members of your project will include _____.
   a. you and a website developer
   b. you, project sponsor, PSC, marketing SME, website developer, finance SME, products SME, database analyst, and hardware technician
   c. you, project sponsor, marketing SME, and website developer

■ STANDARD IS METHODOLOGY

A **methodology** provides a framework for executing both the project management and technical processes of an IS project throughout the SDLC. Selecting a methodology that matches a project's needs helps to ensure the successful completion of the development project.

There was a time within the IT profession when there was essentially only one accepted methodology, which initially evolved from the SLDC. In fact, it was even called the *waterfall methodology* as a result. However, while this methodology works well and is still extensively used in practice, it is very structured, and as a result, is sometimes seen as too slow to respond to the fast-changing business environments of today. Because of this, other methodologies have emerged. In this section we briefly discuss and describe the more common approaches to structure IS development and the methods and tools used to implement these methodologies.

Why Do Organizations Need an IS Methodology?

Initially, system developers tended to work in a very ad hoc way, called the **build-and-fix model**. In short, those who knew simply did! In this model, developers sat down briefly with the boss or a customer to find out the requirements, then they wrote programs, created databases, and knit together hardware to create a rudimentary system. After building the system, developers tested and debugged it. As you might imagine, this approach often led to problems. Because developers spent little time analyzing requirements or developing a design, systems developed using the build-and-fix model often did not fully satisfy customer requirements, nor did they easily allow new developers to join the project and understand what had already been done. Because of this lack of a common approach or a shared understanding and documentation of the system itself, organizations often depended on the individual developers' knowledge of a system for any future modifications or upgrades that needed to be made. The loss or resignation of a developer often impaired the future evolution of the system.

As a result, IT managers and developers began to think about improving this early process and improving the methods of the development life cycle so that a project team could rely on structure to ensure that everyone, including the developers, was working toward the same project goals. The methodology defines most of the development activities that are part of the plan developed by the project manager, and form a subset of the overall activities within the SDLC.

Of course, developers do their work using systems and tools designed to produce software. These development tools are often designed to support a particular methodology. A formal methodology brings several benefits to an IS development project, as Table 6.7 shows. In the sections to follow, we discuss both traditional and modern development methodologies, but many of them offer similar advantages and disadvantages.

The Traditional IS Methodology: The Waterfall Model

The first development model to gain wide acceptance among system developers was based on the **waterfall model**. As discussed earlier, the waterfall model defines a set of phases, and a new phase begins only after acceptable completion of the preceding phase. The same is true with the development activities that occur to support the phases of the SDLC, as shown in Figure 6.4. If developers discover mistakes or other problems, they then return, if possible, to a prior phase. As a result, development activities tend to move downstream through the phases in a formal, detailed manner. The idea is that if things are done right in each phase, there will be little or no need to move back upstream to an already completed phase, thereby achieving one of the primary benefits of a structured methodology.

The waterfall model is a document-driven and highly structured process. Work during each phase generally produces a document or another type of deliverable. For example, in the inception

Table 6.7	Importance of Methodology to IS Development[11]	
Advantages	**Disadvantages**
• Improvement in fundamentals—methodologies can help team members understand and apply best practices • Avoidance of rework—the process can be oriented toward avoiding repeating tasks in the event of changing requirements • Risk management—because of its structured approach, a methodology systematically helps identify and manage risks • Quality assurance—helps detect errors earlier, when they are easier to correct • Customer orientation—focuses the development team on customers' needs and requirements rather than on building technology for technology's sake • Planning improvement—makes it easy to identify and organize the activities required by the project and helps target resources toward the activities that need them the most at the right time	• Increased bureaucracy—can be overly rigid and bureaucratic • Increased cost—commercial products and services have a substantial cost and often involve training or require hiring in-house experts to support it • Increased structure—because by definition methodologies are designed to avoid ad-hoc development processes, sometimes customers who are developing system requirements may find the process too structured and get frustrated about why IT cannot "simply get it done"; however, without structure the methodology cannot deliver on its benefits

phase, developers undertake planning activities that result in an initial project plan. During the inception phase, and often at the beginning of the elaboration phase, developers assist users with defining and analyzing the requirements. That is, they develop the business requirements document for the system to be constructed. At the end of elaboration, a system design document, which often includes logical models (diagrams) that show how the system will satisfy business requirements, is produced. In the construction phase, developers implement the system; they code its components and modules, integrate them, and create user interfaces. As these are completed, the system moves

It's easy to see how the waterfall model got its name—activities flow downstream, just like water on a downward slope. The problem with the waterfall model is that it is difficult to go back upstream if the need arises (which it often does); just imagine trying to climb up a waterfall, against the force of the water.

into the transition phase, where the system is tested and implemented into the live production environment. The deliverables of the transition stage include program code, test documents, user documentation, and a completed system. Finally, during the production phases, the developers support the system by keeping detailed records of changes and upgrades. As a result, one of the criticisms of this approach is that it is too focused on output (documents) and not sufficiently on outcomes (the results of the work itself). Sometimes those working with developers on the IS find it too structured and oriented toward an IT perspective rather than the business requirements.

11. Adapted from Steve McConnell, *Rapid Development*, Microsoft Press, 1996, 14.

While successfully used for many years and still applied in some organizations, the waterfall model does have other weaknesses. First, the model is usually only effective when users can express their exact needs. Precisely defining the business requirements is crucial for this approach to work. Developers must understand the problem in detail so they can respond with an effective system design. Otherwise, developers may not detect errors or omissions until late in the transition phase when the system becomes available for testing. A closely related problem is that users often cannot adequately express their requirements until they have something to work with and see. This is called a *prototype*. With the waterfall model, there is nothing to show the user until the entire process, through transition, is complete.

In addition, the sequential nature of the waterfall process can delay progress. For example, construction must wait until approval of the system design. In truth, developers can often start some design work while still finalizing user requirements, and similarly for some elements of generating the actual code. However, a strict reading of the waterfall model prevents earlier starts for tasks or for completing activities in parallel. As a result of all these constraints, developers today rarely use a rigid waterfall model.

Regardless of its limitations, it is still important for you to know about and understand the waterfall model and its associated development activities. It is the most frequently referenced model for describing the development process, allowing developers to share a common language when discussing the development of an IS. This approach also proved the need for consistent documentation and carefully defined system requirements. As such, the waterfall model provided the basis for more modern methodologies, and fundamentally can be credited with adding structure to a formerly ad-hoc approach to development.

Modern IS Methodologies

With more modern methodologies, developers produce a partial running system that they evaluate and then revise and enhance. An **evolutionary model** fits this approach to development. With an evolutionary model, developers first investigate, specify, and implement an important core part of the system with minimal functionality. The team then tests and evaluates this version of the system to plan for the next version. With each iteration of the cycle, the team adds new functionality and features to the system. Figure 6.14 broadly depicts an evolutionary development method.

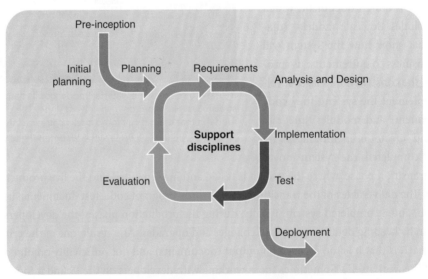

FIGURE 6.14 Using an evolutionary model of IS development, developers produce a partial running system that they evaluate and then revise and enhance.[12]

12. Adapted from Philippe Krutchen, "What Is the Rational Unified Process," *The Rational Edge*, Rational Software, January 2001.

A common approach in the evolutionary model is to use **prototyping**. With prototyping, the project team works with customers to progressively build the system from an initial outline specification using visual mock-ups of screens, diagrams of data relationships, and similar tools that help users see what is going to be built. The final system essentially evolves from that initial prototype. This process can help team members and users better understand the requirements.

However, one problem with an evolutionary model is that developers often neglect to create a well-defined set of documents. This makes it difficult to monitor and control the project, which in turn can cause other problems such as adhering to schedule or estimating the true final costs of development.

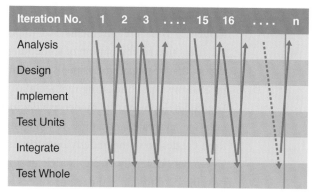

FIGURE 6.15 Because an agile process is designed to satisfy continuously changing requirements, the team develops software in short development cycles or increments.

This shifts responsibility onto project managers, who are often experts in their own field and NOT in development, so they become reliant on the developers' self-reporting progress that may or may not be accurate. If decisions the developers made were not correct or were inadequate, this will only be obvious significantly later in the development life cycle than would have otherwise occurred with a more rigid or structured approach.

A current trend is to develop systems using an **agile development** methodology. Because an agile process is designed to satisfy continuously changing requirements, the team develops software in short development cycles or increments. Each cycle may include all of the primary phases of the process, as Figure 6.15 shows. Many of these development methodologies also rely on creating mock-ups or templates that show how the system will look once developed. These templates are then shown to users and compared to the requirements in real-time, often shortening the cycle of getting to a final system design in a similar way as prototyping does.

Evolutionary and agile development methodologies are an attempt to reduce the somewhat constricting formality of the pure waterfall approach. A well-known agile development method is the rational unified process (RUP). This is not only a development method and process, but also comes with software tools of its own to enable the method. RUP is built on six best practices that occur in each development phase: (1) develop iteratively, (2) manage requirements, (3) use component architecture, (4) model visually, (5) verify quality, and (6) control changes.

The choice between any of these development methods can depend on the importance and complexity of the project itself. In general, the greater the complexity and importance of the project to the strategic mission of the company, the more formality is needed in the development process.

WHAT DO YOU THINK? ?

There is much debate in the IT community about the use of waterfall and evolutionary methodologies for system development. Given what you now know about these methodologies, consider the following:

1: Imagine if you were to do a term paper using *agile* writing. How would this work? What would be the benefits and drawbacks of completing your term paper this way?
2: Do you think that the type of system being developed (e.g., website vs. ERP) should determine the development methodology to be used, or should user preference determine the method?
3: Is it possible to use both methodologies in the development of the same system? How would this work?

IS Modelling

Modelling system requirements is an important part of any IS development methodology. A **model** is a simplified representation of something real, such as a building, weather pattern, or information system that business professionals can manipulate to study the real item in more detail. Models can be of many types, including mathematical equations, computer simulations, and graphs or charts. For IS development, the model usually includes one or more diagrams that developers can use to examine, evaluate, and adjust to understand the system and performance requirements derived from the design of the underlying business process that the system is trying to automate or support. Developers generally create models during the elaboration phase of the SDLC to help them align possible IS solutions to the requirements of each step in the business process.

UML Diagrams Unified Modelling Language (UML) has become a very popular modelling tool, as it works particularly well for developing object-oriented systems. The UML consists of several graphic elements that, when combined, form a set of diagrams.

The purpose of UML diagrams is to show multiple views of a system. Together, the set of UML diagrams is known as the *system model*. Like other models, such as ERDs, logical data models, and DFDs that were discussed in Chapter 3, a UML model describes the purpose of the system, but not how to implement it. The most commonly used UML diagrams include class, object, use case, state, sequence, activity (Figure 6.16 is an example), communication, component, and deployment diagrams. We focus on use cases and sequence diagrams here so that you can see how they help the IS development process.

The UML *use case* diagram notation captures all the possible ways to use a system. It shows which users employ which use cases, as well as the relationships both between the users and between the use cases. A use case describes a system's behaviour from a user's standpoint. Business professionals often create use cases as a tool for determining user requirements. For example, Figure 6.16 shows a use case diagram for an electronic voting system. You will recall that we used this example in Chapter 3 when we discussed diagrams that illustrate databases. Here, the use case diagram identifies the possible users of the system and their primary interactions with the system (the ovals). The ovals represent activities that the system needs to support. Business professionals, such as business analysts, can further investigate these activities by using other UML diagrams, such as activity or sequence diagrams. Use case diagrams are usually drawn while gathering user requirements during the inception and elaboration phases of the system development life cycle. These are sometimes

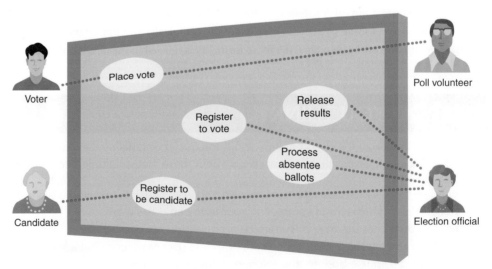

FIGURE 6.16 The UML use case diagram notation captures all the possible ways to use a system, in this case, an e-voting system.

accompanied by a *sequence diagram*, which shows the order of various activities and by who, and how they interact with the various system components as they occur in order.

Regardless of the method you use to model requirements, the important point is that they are understood, documented, and shared among the team. This enables the developers to ensure that when the system is programmed, it will actually function as it was intended to, and the data required are available to users.

Quick Test

1. Which of the following is *not* an advantage of the waterfall development method?
   a. less rework
   b. increased structure
   c. ability to manage risk
   d. increased quality through early error detection

2. True or False. Evolutionary development methodologies are considered to be less formal and more agile than the traditional waterfall development method.

3. Through _____, which usually includes one or more diagrams, developers can better understand the system and performance requirements that are derived from the design of the underlying business process that the system is trying to automate or support.
   a. programming
   b. prototyping
   c. modelling
   d. waterfall development

Answers: 1. b; 2. True; 3. c

■ IT TOOLS FOR IS DEVELOPMENT

What types of IT tools can project teams use in IS development? Project teams routinely use personal productivity tools, such as spreadsheet software, to explore financial feasibility or create a budget. They also use word processing software to write reports and documentation, such as the project plan. In fact, most of you have probably used many of these same tools for your group work during your studies, and you know how collaboration software helps group decision making and communications between team members. Since you should be familiar with these types of tools, we focus next on specific software categories that are geared primarily toward the development of information systems.

IS Development Tools

Ironically, software—often the end result of IS development—also supports the execution of IS development tasks! The project team needs software to model the system, write the software, and develop the database. Developers need tools to create and document code, and test and deploy systems.

Integrated Development Environments (IDEs) Most software programs currently rely on **integrated development environments (IDEs)**. Instead of using separate software packages, an IDE allows developers to complete several programming tasks within the same software application. The typical IDE includes a text editor to allow the user to write program code, a file system to store programs, a compiler to translate the program into machine language, and debugging tools to find and correct errors. Many IDEs feature visual editors that allow the programmer to develop graphic user interfaces by dragging and dropping components onto a palette. Popular IDEs include Microsoft Visual Studio and Eclipse, an open source IDE.

TECHNOLOGY CORE

The details involved in systems projects can be very difficult to keep track of. A lot of information associated with the SDLC flows from one stage to the next. And then there is the issue of changes! When something changes, many, many people need to be informed and many adjustments need to be made. What if you miss one? Keeping track of the details is essential to the success of systems development projects. Integrated development environments (IDEs) are excellent tools to help in this regard. One of the best-known tools in the market is simply known as Rational.

Rational is a very comprehensive suite of tools that helps IS project managers and team members keep track of the enormous amount of information required for an IS project. Rational starts out by providing an integrated requirements management system that helps to define and manage requirements, especially in the case where requirements change and need to be communicated to team members. Requirements traceability features help determine how requirements are built into the software. Rational, like other IDEs, provides development tools and the ability to develop software collaboratively. Once the software is complete, Rational provides a full quality management system for testing the software prior to implementation. Encompassing all of these activities, Rational offers project management tools to tie it all together. It is funny when you think of it—a project team, including programmers, worked on a project to create software to develop and manage projects!

Modelling Tools and Code Generators Using graphic diagrams in modelling systems is an important activity in information system development. A number of software packages offer a toolbox with common diagramming elements to make building diagrams easier. Perhaps the most significant trend in this category is the move toward code generation.

With **code generation**, a developer can use graphic diagrams to define a system's components and how they are related. Then, with a simple click of a button or by selecting from a menu, a developer generates code that corresponds to the diagram in a language like C++ or Java. Table 6.8 lists a number of specialized tools that focus on the development of specific IS components.

CASE Tools Computer-aided software engineering (CASE) is the use of computer-based support in the software development process. CASE tools support the creation and maintenance of the many documents, diagrams, and data that the project team creates over the course of the IS development life cycle and integrates them in a CASE environment accessible to all users. A current trend

Table 6.8	Authoring Software Categories	
Category	**Description**	**Representative Software**
Database (DBMS)	Allows developers to build and manage the databases that are a key part of most IS	Oracle Database, InterSystems Caché, MySql, MS Access
Web development	Provides tools for developing web pages and applications Ranges from simple HTML editors to full-blown IDEs	Macromedia Dreamweaver, IBM Websphere, WordPress
Animation/video	Provides tools for developing animation and video components	Macromedia Flash, Shockwave, QuickTime
Graphics	Allows users to format and edit visual content	Adobe Photoshop
Audio content	Allows users to format and edit audio content	Adobe Audition, Wavepad

in CASE environments is to support the analysis and design of business processes, along with the technology to support business processes.

Although project management, development, and CASE tools have dramatically improved the IS development process, there are some risks in using these tools. One common error is to focus on managing the software tools rather than the content of the project itself—which can lead to a quantity over quality outcome where the final product is not going to accomplish the system's objectives, even if it's on time. Another common problem is known as the *silver bullet* syndrome. This occurs when there is an overreliance on the tools for the success of the project, while neglecting the other pillars of a development project. For a successful project, it is important to keep the tools in perspective and view them as support for the primary activities of the project.

Because IS development tools have become so advanced, it is now easier for non-IT personnel to develop systems on their own. This is known as **end-user development**. Do you have your own web page, for example? A blog? If so, you could very loosely be called an end user developer. With tools such as Microsoft Access, WordPress, and the advanced functions of Excel, anyone can be considered end user developers. In organizations, end users may purchase software with development tools that give them control over that software on behalf of the organization. This is the case for content management systems (CMS) to manage corporate websites, for example. It is said that the major benefit of end-user computing is that it puts control in the hands of the ultimate creator. That is, the person with the idea is also the developer and is intimately involved in every step of creating the IS. Along with this benefit, there may savings in terms of cost and time. On the other hand, end-user development disadvantages might include poor design and architecture, missed requirements due to lack of methodology, and poor security. End users are not always well versed in the latest IT methodologies and security protocols. There is also a risk, similar to the build-and-fix model that was used in the early days of IS development, that should the end-user developer leave the organization or become disinterested in the system they developed, it will cease to function.

This chapter has introduced you to how information systems are acquired, developed, and implemented in organizations. You now know how the systems we discussed early in this text come into existence. In the next chapter we look at the result of many IS projects and systems that many of us use every day—e-commerce.

Quick Test

1. Fill in the blank: A(n) _____ allows developers to complete several programming tasks within the same software application, and provides a text editor to allow the user to write program code, a file system to store programs, a compiler to translate the program into machine language, and debugging tools to find and correct errors.

2. True or False. IS development tools are so advanced now that most projects do not require developers.

3. You can be considered an end user developer if you _____.
   a. collaborate with an IS project team
   b. are a project sponsor
   c. are a C++ programmer
   d. design and build an automated spreadsheet in Visual Basic

What's in IT for me?

Project management is a desirable career path for many. It is possible for a project manager to work on projects in many areas of an organization, including operations, finance, and human resources. A project manager can also manage projects that involve each of these groups in a cross-functional project team. Project management is an important part of an organization's efforts to transform problems into solutions that create business value.

For over 40 years, the Project Management Institute (PMI) has been working to increase the profile and professionalism of project management. Since the 1980s, PMI has been certifying project managers and bestowing the following professional designations:

PMP—Project Management Professional: certifies that an individual has in-depth experience in leading projects

CAPM—Certified Associate in Project Management: certifies that an individual has been a contributor to projects

PgMP—Program Management Professional: certifies that an individual has the requisite experience in managing multiple projects as part of a program

PMI also offers certification in risk management (PMI-RMP), scheduling (PMI-SP), and Agile (PMI-ACP). All PMI certifications are earned by proving experience and writing an exam. If you are interested in project management or becoming a project manager, find out more information at *www.pmi.org*.

What's in IT for an organization?

Project management adds value to organizations. Several studies indicate that project management is beneficial to entire organizations, especially within IT. One study, conducted by Canadians Mark Mullaly, PMP, and Dr. Janice Thomas of Athabasca University, sought to identify the value that organizations receive by managing projects. They studied 65 organizations from around the world and discovered the following key findings:

- Tangible benefits of project management were realized in 47% of the organizations studied. They ranged from cost savings (17%), increased revenues (27%), and decreased write-offs (15%), to customer retention (22%) and increased customer (17%) and market share (7%).

- Intangible benefits of project management included attainment of strategic objectives (63%), more effective use of human resources (63%), improved overall management (61%), improved corporate culture (56%), improved reputation (53%), improved regulatory compliance (24%), improved competitiveness (22%), greater social good (15%), new product/service streams (8%),

improved staff retention (8%), and improved quality of life (3%).

- It was found that the fit between the organization's strategy, culture, industry, economic environment, and resources (human and other) and what is implemented to help manage projects seems to determine the level and kind of benefits realized.[13]

For more on this study, see *www.valueofpm.com*.

What's in IT for society?

Project management and systems development have benefited society, as we have addressed many times throughout this text. Two things we commonly access and enjoy that are the result of projects being initiated and executed—systems projects in particular—that followed the systems development life cycle include:

- Text messaging—Text messaging (SMS) was first conceived as a project in the early 1980s. Several collaborators came together to develop the technology that allows SMS messages to be sent on GSM cellular networks by simply upgrading the software at each mobile station.
- Microsoft Windows—In the early 1980s, Microsoft began a project in response to growing interest in the marketplace for graphical user interfaces (GUI). At first the product was called Interface Manager, but by the time it went to market it was called Microsoft Windows. Over the years, Microsoft has come to call its strategic projects by a code name with only project team members knowing the details of the "secret" project.

We could list many more pieces of technology in place today that started as a project, following the systems development life cycle. Give some thought to technology that provides some benefit to society, and remember that a project team created it.

13. *www.financialpost.com/executive/story.html?id=930145&p=2*. Retrieved March 30, 2010.

ROI | STUDENT RETURN ON INVESTMENT SUMMARY

1. Describe the major decisions organizations must address before developing an IS system.

Organizations need to ask four major questions when considering obtaining an IS: (1) Do we need an IS? Business professionals in an organization are constantly looking for ways to improve their operations; (2) Is the project feasible? During project inception, an organization needs to determine whether or not the project has a reasonable chance of success; (3) Should we build, buy, or lease the IS?; and (4) Do we build the IS ourselves (in-house), or do we contract with an outside firm (outsource) to build it? Answering each of these questions requires that decisions be made. Sometimes it is difficult to make those choices, and there may not be a "right" answer. See Chapter 3 for a discussion on decision making and problem solving.

2. Explain the activities organizations must consider within each of the seven stages of the system development life cycle.

The system development life cycle is a series of events viewed over time from the initial concept through to the retirement of an information system. In other words, the system is born, develops, has a useful work life, and then retires. We can divide the life cycle into seven main phases: concept, inception, elaboration, construction, transition, production, and retirement. The retirement of one system often means that an organization is about to transition to another system. Figure 6.4 depicts the SDLC and development activities as a waterfall. As you can see by our very simple example at WildOutfitters.com, there are a lot of activities going on. Every project is unique in terms of the specific types of activities required to bring a system to life, but the SDLC provides a general guideline to the actions required in each of the seven stages.

3. Describe the key tasks in managing an IS project.

IS projects are among the most complex projects to manage. Many IS project managers use a methodology such as the one outlined in the Project Management Book of Knowledge (PMBOK®) published by the Project Management Institute. It is important to consider all of the project management knowledge areas, including time management, scope management, procurement management, risk management, HR management, quality management, cost management, and communications management. The key tasks in managing IS projects are related to time management, scope management, cost management, and quality management. It is these tasks that will have the biggest impact on the success of the project. As an IS project manager you want to be able to say that your project delivered on time, on budget, and at the expected scope and level of quality.

4. Outline the importance of an IS development team and name some of the people who might be included on such a team.

Without IS development teams, new systems would not be developed and many of the things that we take for granted today, such as Microsoft Word or email, would not exist. Each IS development team may be composed of different members and will vary in size depending on the IS being developed. Most commonly, though, an IS development team involves a project manager, a business subject matter expert (SME), and at least one technical staff member. If the IS is being developed by an end user, it could be the SME doing the project alone as an end-user developer. If it is a multi-year, multi-functional ERP system being implemented, then the IS development team may number up to 50 members with various roles and responsibilities.

5. Outline the methods organizations use to ensure that they obtain the best IS to help meet their strategic goals.

The ultimate goal of any IS methodology is to provide a thoughtful and thorough approach to the process of obtaining information systems. Without a methodology, developers and users usually attempt a make-and-fix or buy-and-fix approach. The waterfall model is a well-known methodology that proceeds from concept through inception, elaboration, and construction, to transition and production. More modern methods involve a more evolutionary approach and use prototyping and agile development to complete IS projects.

6. Describe some of the IS development tools available to businesses today.

There are a number of IS development tools available today, many of which are open source and can be used at no cost. A popular tool is the integrated development environment (IDE). IDEs provide developers with everything they need to design, develop, de-bug, and document their programming code. Other development tools include modelling and CASE tools, which first provide a visual representation of the system to be developed and then can actually automatically generate code for developers.

KNOWLEDGE SPEAK

agile development   239

build-and-fix model   236

code generation   242

computer-aided software engineering (CASE)   242

contract compliance   219

end-user development   243

evolutionary model   238

feasibility study   213

Gantt chart   228

in-house development   219

integrated development environments (IDEs)   241

methodology   236

model   240

outsource   219

program   230

program evaluation review technique (PERT) chart   231

program management   230

project management   223

project management (PM) software   231

project steering committee (PSC)   235

prototyping   239

request for information (RFI)   218

request for proposal (RFP)   218

risk management   228

stakeholder analysis   233

subject matter experts (SMEs)   234

system development life cycle (SDLC)   221

technical acquisition   220

Unified Modelling Language (UML)   240

vendor management   219

waterfall model   236

REVIEW QUESTIONS

Multiple-choice questions

1. In the _____ phase of the IS life cycle, the project team finalizes the requirements for the system and designs the system architecture.
   a. inception
   b. elaboration
   c. construction
   d. transition

2. In the _____ phase of the IS life cycle, the organization recognizes a need for an IS and defines the project.
   a. inception
   b. elaboration
   c. construction
   d. transition

3. Which of the following is NOT a project management task?
   a. activity sequencing
   b. use case creation
   c. resource planning
   d. scope verification

4. Which of the following risk-mitigating tactics means that the project manager will act to eliminate the possibility of a risk occurring?
   a. risk reduction
   b. risk deferral
   c. risk acceptance
   d. risk avoidance

Fill-in-the-blank questions

5. _____ is perhaps the most important aspect of project management.
6. A(n) _____ consists of several graphic elements that, when combined, form a set of diagrams that provide multiple views of a system that highlight the system's purpose.
7. A(n) _____ is a software package that combines several tools used to write software into one package.

True-false questions

8. The IS life cycle enterprise disciplines include configuration and change management, project management, environmental scanning, and operations and support.
9. An RFP is a Request for Proposal, the beginning of a bidding process for vendors.
10. A stakeholder analysis is useful for understanding how well the team members will work together.
11. An important part of a CASE tool is the central repository of project items.

Matching questions

Choose the BEST answer from column B for each item in column A.

Column A	Column B
12. buying	a. Developing an IS by purchasing an already designed system, customizing it, and then installing and maintaining it in-house.
13. in-house development	b. Hiring another company to design and build all or part of an IS.
14. leasing	c. Subscribing to IS services from another company, which also maintains and controls the IS.
15. outsourcing	d. Building an IS using internal staff members to analyze, design, implement, and maintain it.
	e. Using computer-based tools to support IS development.

Short-answer questions

16. List and define the stages of an information system life cycle.
17. Modelling is an important part of many business applications in addition to IS development. List some examples of models that you have seen lately.
18. Discuss why an evolutionary development approach is an improvement over the waterfall model.

Discussion/Essay questions

19. What is the ideal system development life cycle? Is this ideal possible to achieve? Why or why not?
20. Should managers rely on purely financial techniques when determining an information system's feasibility? Why or why not?

TEAM ACTIVITY

Form a discussion/study team to discuss the remaining weeks of your classes for the term. Think of the successful completion of the term as a project. Identify the goals and the tasks that you will need to complete, and create a simple project plan that defines and assigns steps required to meet these goals. In your group, brainstorm the risks you might face that can keep you from meeting the goals, and then develop a risk checklist for the remainder of your class term. Consider how using this plan might help you achieve the outcome you want for the term versus not having undertaken any advance planning at all.

SOFTWARE APPLICATION EXERCISES

1. Internet
As you've learned, many methodologies are used to develop information systems. Use a search engine to locate and read about rapid application methodologies. Read the Database assignment below and decide which methodology you would use to develop the database if you were the project manager.

2. Presentation
Assume that you are an IS analyst working for the IS department in a large retail organization. The Database assignment below will be built for use by project managers (not just IS project managers) in your company. Create a stakeholder analysis that shows the interest and influence of organizational stakeholders for the Database project.

3. Word Processing
Based on your stakeholder analysis in the above Presentation assignment, your company should consider the benefits and costs of outsourcing the database development to a third party. Prepare a request for proposal (RFP) that lists the requirements for the projects and any other relevant items.

4. Spreadsheet
Create a spreadsheet that supports your financial analysis of the Database project. Use the financial feasibility metrics discussed in this chapter: return on investment (ROI), net present value (NPV), internal rate of return (IRR), and payback period. You will find built-in functions for some of these metrics in Excel. Use Excel Help and your own research to determine how to calculate these values. Create two sets of data for each metric: (1) in-house development cost and (2) outsourced cost.

5. Database
Create a database that a manager can use to track projects. The database will need to track information about projects, the employees who work on them, and the activities that they perform.

6. Advanced Challenge
Pull together all parts of your analysis and project management database project work. Create a seamless presentation for management that includes development options, stakeholder analysis, feasibility studies, responses to your RFP, and a prototype of the database. Make the presentation to your professor or to your class.

ONLINE RESOURCES

Companion Website
- Take interactive practice quizzes to assess your knowledge and help you study in a dynamic way.
- Review PowerPoint lecture slides.
- Get help and sample solutions to end-of-chapter software application exercises.

Additional Resources Available Only on *WileyPLUS*
- Take the interactive Quick Test to check your understanding of the chapter material and get immediate feedback on your responses.
- Review and study with downloadable Audio Lecture MP3 files.
- Check your understanding of the key vocabulary in the chapter with Knowledge Speak Interactive Flash Cards.

CASE STUDY:
GOOGLE INC.

"Do you google?" The search engine known simply as Google has become so well-known that some people now use the word *google* as a verb. *Google.com* is the most popular search engine in use today, with over 5 billion web pages indexed and available in less than one-half second. At last count, 53 percent of all searches originated on Google. What spurs this popularity? Basically, Google found a better way to determine which pages match the user's term using an approach called PageRank. This approach ranks a page in the returned search results based on how many other web pages point to it that share similar relevant content. In addition, they refined the natural language search process and its interface to make the search experience for the user easier and (hopefully!) more accurate. This approach usually avoids links to pages that have nothing to do with the user's query. This has made the work of business professionals much easier, including those in IT.

What makes Google different from so many search engine start-ups that failed and vanished or merged out of existence? First and foremost, Google adds business value by making information much easier to find and much more relevant to the needs of the person doing the searching. Because of this, industry giant Yahoo! picked Google as its search engine, thus giving the company an early source of steady income. Second, Google made

money from the very beginning by using innovative advertising on its website. Through a product called AdWords, Google allows anyone to create a simple advertisement for products or services that it displays on related Google search pages.

Third, Google remains open to accepting improvements to its system from its users. Google's open-system approach has resulted in innovative and profitable products being built on top of the Google search engine. Finally, Google constantly looks for new ways to leverage its search engine prowess into other areas, such as indexing images, groups, and products. The company has also added a web log system called Blogger, as well as a free email system called Gmail to compete with existing email systems like Hotmail, and which is now integrated with a simple-to-use calendar system. It is now moving into offering applications software in the form of Google Apps.

Learning how to use Google well for business-related searches is an important skill for any student to acquire; that is primarily what this case is about. Using Google to find information about best practices, state-of-the-art tools or resources, and free information on topics you need to know about to be successful is important to your career success. Therefore, you will use Google to help you find relevant and up-to-date information on enterprise systems development and project management related to this chapter.

Case Questions

1. Using Google, develop five different queries related to the same topic (for instance, project management tools or integrated development environments, etc.). State them in different word orders or using different terms. Working backward from analyzing the results you get on the front page, what do you notice?
2. Zero in on three specific sites that offer you free information that you might find useful as a systems development professional. How might you use this information to improve your organization's systems development results?
3. Choose a specific commercially available automated tool that is used either for project management or systems development. Investigate it online and write a simple one-page recommendation to your manager justifying your choice. Include why the organization you work for should purchase and use this tool by defining how it will help improve your work results.

CASE STUDY:
THE S2S STUFF EXCHANGE

Sienna and Chelsea met toward the end of their first year of university and have been friends ever since. Sienna is an aspiring investment banker and Chelsea is taking computer science. They have decided that for their third year of schooling they are going to move out of residence. They have never lived on their own before and are very excited. They recently found a two-bedroom apartment near campus—the perfect location! But it is not furnished. In planning for their big move, they realize that they are going to need a lot of stuff!

Sienna and Chelsea start to think that other students must have the same problem: They have doubles of some things and nothing of others. Chelsea does have a toaster, at least, and Sienna has a printer. But they don't need two coffee makers! They have seen loads of stuff at the curb at the end of the school year and have seen students going "dumpster diving." There has to be a better way to get rid of and acquire the household goods that students need when they move out on their own. They are very familiar with eBay and Kijiji, but students at their school don't seem to use it much.

Chelsea says, "Sienna, why don't we start our own student stuff exchange website? It will be awesome! You can take care of the money and I can do all of the Web stuff. What do you say?" "Like B2B (business to business), but S2S (student to student)!" replies Sienna. Sienna definitely sees the potential but is a bit concerned. She has an idea of how they could make money (a transaction fee) and how it could work in an eBay/Kijiji kind of way. On the other hand, she is not sure how they are going to market this service, how will it look, who will do the creative work—and will Chelsea have the time to do all of the development work required? Chelsea does not do much database work as part of her studies and she does not know anything about payment processing. She is more of the visionary for the website. And this does seem like a lot of work. Sienna doesn't want to put a damper on Chelsea's enthusiasm, but she knows that she will be the one to work out all of the details.

After some thought, Sienna says, "Ok, Chelsea. I'm with you! I think this is a great idea. Let's work through some of the details. Maybe our parents will help us by investing in our company. If we are going to ask them, we better get our 'stuff' together."

Case Questions

1. Sienna is an aspiring banker; she is all about the money and she wants a decent return on her investment. Create a business case for this venture. Is it a good idea?
2. Assuming that the business case is favourable, the next step is to determine how to make this website a reality. Sienna and Chelsea are facing a classic build, buy, or lease decision. Examine their options and make a recommendation.
3. Create the project team for this website implementation. Who are the SMEs, the project sponsor, the technical staff? What are their roles and responsibilities?

7 | E-COMMERCE

WHAT WE WILL COVER

- E-commerce Defined
- The E-commerce Advantage
- Benefits and Limitations of E-commerce
- E-commerce Between Organizations
- The Technology of E-commerce

STUDENT RETURN ON INVESTMENT ROI

Through your investment of time in reading and thinking about this chapter, your return—or created value—is gaining knowledge. After reading this chapter, you should be able to

1. Define e-commerce and describe how it is a part of today's economy.

2. Explain how e-commerce creates value and helps organizations stay competitive.

3. Describe the benefits and limitations of e-commerce to both consumers and businesses.

4. Explain how organizations can use e-commerce to enhance the delivery of products and services, manage trade with business partners, and improve their supply chain efficiency.

5. Describe the evolution of e-commerce technologies and explain how these technologies have benefited both consumers and businesses.

THE VOICE OF EXPERIENCE

Arti Davda, University of British Columbia

Arti Davda graduated from the University of British Columbia in 2005 with a Bachelor of Commerce. She then enrolled in York University's Schulich School of Business Accelerated MBA program, graduating with honours in 2008. She now works as an Account Manager with Google Canada.

What do you do in your current position? As an Account Manager at Google Canada, my primary focus is client relations. I work with key clients in a strategic role where I help them to set up digital campaigns that will be effective and maximize ROI. I help clients use all of the tools that Google offers—Search, Display, YouTube, Mobile, website metrics, and advertising to help them be successful and reach their goals. More and more, clients are taking advantage of YouTube as a way of getting their message out and educating customers and prospective customers with "how to" videos about their products.

What do you consider to be important career skills? I think it's important to be flexible and to easily adapt to change. Working at Google you see that things change quickly—industry and businesses change quickly, and technology is always evolving. Recognize that change is constant, and embrace it; change keeps things exciting! Also, try to take the initiative whenever opportunities present themselves. Volunteer for things outside of your regular role. My role is not a technical one, but it is important that I understand the technology and be able to communicate how it can benefit my clients.

How do you use IT? At Google, technology is ingrained in the company and corporate culture. We use Google Docs, which makes it easier to collaborate, access materials anytime from anywhere, and not have to worry about version control. I use Gmail and its chat feature so I can quickly and easily communicate with people in the office or team members who are on the road. Our conference rooms are set up for audio and video conferencing; we have staff and clients all over the world, and this makes for more timely and cost-efficient meetings. The advertising and sales team members use laptops whether we're in or out of the office, and phones have headsets for ease-of-use. We are also using the latest Google phones so we are always connected. Our new social media platform, Google+, is

becoming an important IT tool in the way we work. I really like the "Google hang-out" feature, where you can connect with up to 10 people for a live video chat.

Can you describe an example of how you have used IT to improve business operations? We encourage clients to track activity on their website using Google Analytics. It provides them with details about who visits their site, how much time users spend on the site per visit, which pages users access, and user activities such as purchases. This gives our clients a lot of information about how their website is used. I find it rewarding to see clients use this information to make decisions that benefit their business.

Have you got any "on the job" advice for students seeking a career in IT or business? I found that having a mentor is very important. Either before you start your career or when you start your job, find a mentor. This person can help in so many ways. My mentor helped me get where I am today and continues to advise me. Someday you'll be able to return the favour by mentoring someone else.

Arti works for Google in a non-technical sales and marketing role. While in school, she probably never imagined she would work for a technology company—let alone the world's most well-known and innovative technology company! In this chapter, we discuss e-commerce and the technology, such as the metrics that Arti works with, behind it.

Earlier, we defined organizations as creating competitive advantage through a chain of value-producing activities. We also noted that each organization operates in an environment of stakeholders and clients or consumers: those individuals, partners, or suppliers with an interest in and an influence on that particular organization and who ultimately consume the value the organization creates. This implies that *all organizations must have a business model*, regardless of their status—profit-centric or not. Even governments must decide how to efficiently and effectively deliver services, and not-for-profits have to wrestle with how to reach donors and spend those funds wisely. Of course, enterprise systems (discussed in Chapter 4), including ERP and CRM, are some fundamental elements of the technology designed to help create this value.

However, through the evolution of the World Wide Web and various related Internet technologies, including more recently social media, how organizations establish and manage these same relationships among customers, partners, and suppliers is rapidly changing. Organizations can now create business relationships and carry out transactions either completely or partially online through *electronic commerce*, or *e-commerce*. In this chapter, we discuss the many ways that e-commerce is creating business value for organizations. By the end of this chapter, you will see that for an organization to efficiently and effectively engage in e-commerce, it must tie together business processes, enabling technologies, and its human resources and integrate them into its own unique electronic and digital value chain to enable it to execute its business strategy.

■ E-COMMERCE DEFINED

For as long as there have been merchants and markets, there has been the desire to improve the efficiency of the retail channel. Advances in technology, product variety, and consumer demand have brought an accompanying change in retailing strategy (as seen in Figure 7.1). For instance, the arrival of the telegraph enabled orders to be placed rapidly and shipped by mail. Ubiquitous rail and cheaper and more available airline transportation brought new and rapid possibilities for order fulfillment, expanding the possible markets available for manufacturers. This same transportation infrastructure enabled cheaper, centralized off-shore production of goods instead of a series of small, local plants dotted across the world. As a result, the industrial landscape changed forever. In addition, the telephone call centre has changed our definition of customer service, as we no longer assume that we are speaking with someone local, even though our problem may be localized.

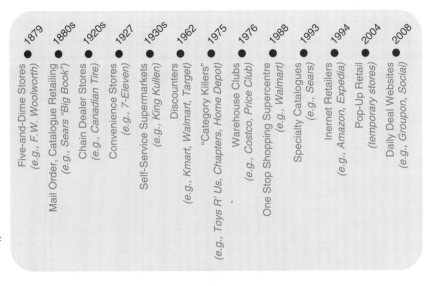

FIGURE 7.1 A brief history of retail innovations.

It seems inevitable that the invention of the Internet would create another revolution in commerce. Specifically, the arrival of e-commerce created a way of doing business around the world in an instant without the need for a physical business presence. The Internet also introduced the forces of *build to order* as a way for manufacturers, such as Dell and others, to directly solicit orders from consumers and deliver products directly, rather than relying on a global network of wholesalers and distributors/dealers. This is known as **disintermediation**—the elimination of the so-called "middle man"—and is a step closer toward creating perfectly competitive, direct global markets for many types of goods that go directly from manufacturer to consumer without any steps in-between.

But what exactly is e-commerce? Quite simply, **e-commerce** is all of the technologies that allow organizations to conduct business online, including the application of these technologies internally and externally. Some have tried to distinguish between *e-commerce* (transactions that involve buying and selling goods and services through the Internet) and *e-business* (the broader use of Internet technologies to reduce operating costs, such as extending the electronic supply chain to partners and suppliers). We have chosen not to make this distinction. Why? We believe that Internet technologies are now sufficiently involved in continuous development cycles that their rapid evolution as a vital part of business operations continues even as you read this. Regardless of how an organization chooses to use Internet technologies to support their business model, what is clear is that every organization can and should use this technology for many aspects of the organization. It is also clear that these technologies are no longer new, but rather are becoming mainstream for organizations.

Because there is still further potential for these technologies relating to everything we do as a society, we feel that artificial distinctions will not help you to better understand this basket of technologies. In this text, we have grouped these technologies together and simply call it *e-commerce* for the convenience of a fulsome discussion of Internet technologies in an organizational context.

Beyond the Basic Definition

When you hear the term e-commerce, you may initially think of an online retail company like *Amazon.ca*. However, the wholesale or business-to-business level is far larger and more important to the global economy than the retail level. In fact, while online retailers measure sales in the billions of dollars, online wholesalers and industrial suppliers measure them in the *trillions* of dollars. But e-commerce is more than just sales. Consider this more formal definition of e-commerce:

> *E-commerce is the use of information systems, technologies, and computer networks by individuals and organizations to carry out transactions to create or support the creation of business value.*

This general definition of e-commerce therefore includes all types of computer networks, all types of transactions, and all types of business relationships and models.

To help you better understand the full potential of e-commerce in various settings, we first describe the parties involved on each side of the transaction to identify the type of e-commerce that is occurring. For instance, we refer to a transaction where a consumer buys a product or service from a business as *B2C*. Table 7.1 summarizes the transaction types.

E-Commerce and Products: Physical and Digital

Think about the wide range and types of products that consumers can buy. We can divide such products into two primary categories: *physical* and *digital*. Physical products include anything that requires an actual shipment of the item from a central distribution point to the buyer (whether an end-consumer, wholesaler, or to another company). This also requires an off-line supply chain to handle the sales, order processing, and delivery of these goods, even if they are discovered and purchased online. On the other hand, consumers can receive digital products directly over the Internet

Table 7.1	Types of E-Commerce Transactions and Example Websites	
Transaction	**Description**	**Example Websites**
Business-to-consumer (B2C)	Online equivalent of the retail store as well as other services	*www.chapters.indigo.ca* *www.barnesandnoble.com* *www.telus.ca*
Business-to-business (B2B)	Electronic exchanges between companies	*http://wwre.globalsources. com/* for the Worldwide Retail Exchange
Business-to-government (B2G)	Online sales to government agencies, as well as electronic payment of taxes	*www.doingbusiness.mgs.gov. on.ca/mbs/psb/psb.nsf/index/ english?openDocument* for businesses wishing to provide goods or services to the Government of Ontario
Consumer-to-government (C2G)	Electronic payment of taxes as well as purchase of various types of licences	*www.netfile.gc.ca/* to electronically file and pay taxes to the federal government
Consumer-to-consumer (C2C)	Use of online auctions like eBay and similar other sites	*www.ebay.com* *www.craigslist.com* *www.kijiji.com*

Most of you are probably quite familiar with purchasing and downloading digital products. What types of digital products have you bought in the past?

or other computer networks (such as downloading music on iTunes versus going to a store to buy a CD). This usually requires the use of a completely IT-enabled supply chain. These differences should be very easy for you understand, given most of you have certainly purchased both types of products before!

The main difference between physical and digital products is in the delivery process, as shown in Figure 7.2. Even though a computer network can transmit information about the order, it obviously cannot ship the actual physical goods. So even though a Web presence and online ordering processes and systems may be essential to many e-commerce transactions, the business must still have these *back-office elements* in place to handle order fulfillment. This often requires substantial technology interfaces between the Web and the enterprise's existing computerized business systems (known as *web integration*). Further, any company in the business of accepting orders and shipping goods to customers must also handle returns, the reverse operation of the diagram shown at right for a traditional business. This physical process is often as complicated as, if not more complicated than, the actual order fulfillment. Yet, by definition, a returns process may not even be applicable to a pure online business (which may not offer the ability to "return" something once it is successfully downloaded—say iTunes songs or e-books, for instance). This often has to do with the fact that, once downloaded, electronic products or services have immediate value and often cannot be *off-loaded* (deleted or otherwise disabled) with any certainty by the vendor, thus defeating the analogous concept of a "return" as it was typically applied to physical goods in the pre-digital era.

Regardless, companies already experienced in physical order fulfillment and returns tend to more successfully implement e-commerce. New companies, especially those only planning to sell

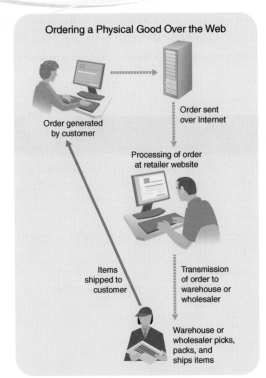

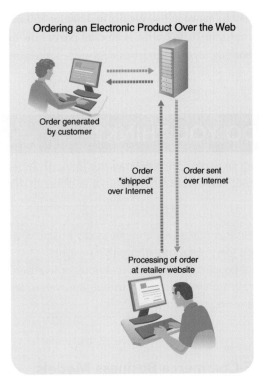

FIGURE 7.2 When buying a physical good over the Web (shown on the left), the company must still pick it from a shelf in a warehouse, pack it for shipment, and physically move it from the warehouse to the customer. The dotted lines indicate electronic communications, and the solid lines refer to physical shipments of products. When purchasing an electronic product (shown on the right), the delivery process is simplified and speeded up as it avoids the need to physically pick, pack, and ship the product. This is why pure online business models are often more profitable to operate.

their goods online, often underestimate the costs and complex process and support issues that often arise in an electronic sales channel. Telephone and mail-order companies also have vast experience in handling returns, so returns from Web orders pose no special problems for them. In this situation, e-commerce often simply means extending an organization's existing business model. Or in some cases, it may only mean adding another direct channel for interacting with customers—that is, the Web simply becomes another channel (place) for customers to buy the physical goods.

Now consider pure digital products. Say that instead of receiving an actual DVD, the company electronically sends you the movie file that you can play back on your computer. In this case, as the right side of Figure 7.2 shows, the company sends you the electronic product directly over the Internet, thereby avoiding any picking, packing, and shipping issues. There are also no return problems. If a problem occurs with the electronic product, the company simply sends a new one for you to download as a replacement, or restores your right to re-download the same content if it is accidentally erased or otherwise compromised. Of course, with the transfer of a physical copy of a software file comes the issue of piracy and illegal duplication—something else for a new online company to consider. Many products come with some kind of associated security feature, such as a digital lock, to address this concern.

Another e-commerce business model has emerged that addresses copyright and piracy concerns. A new technology, known as **streaming**, allows you to purchase the right to *view* the product, but not to physically download it. A number of business models are now using streaming, such as Netflix. Netflix has over 25 million members in the United States, Canada, and Latin America, and was a main contributor to the downfall of physical video rental stores like Blockbuster. Blockbuster had a chance to buy Netflix in 2000 for $50 million, but declined; Blockbuster later declared bankruptcy in 2010. Netflix is an example of how Internet technologies continue to evolve and push the boundaries of existing business models, creating new opportunities for both retailers and consumers.

WHAT DO YOU THINK?

There has been an explosion in online sales in North America in the past few years. Almost everybody has purchased something online at one time or another. In thinking about e-commerce sites you use, consider the following:

1: What features make you choose to do business with an online vendor? What features or aspects make you leery about dealing with a vendor?
2: Are there products or services you would never purchase online? Why?
3: What makes online shopping useful, enjoyable, and fun for you? What types of offers or features encourage you to shop online?

E-Commerce Business Models

The whole story of e-commerce does not only involve questions of how a digital product or service is supplied. In fact, that is often the easiest part of the equation for most e-commerce sites. The harder question is how to develop a business model to ensure the company is profitable for the product it produces or offers in an age where consumers often expect everything on the Internet to be free. An **e-commerce (or virtual or social) business model** combines a specific type of website (transactional, virtual reality, or social presence) with a successful revenue model that produces profits for the owners. These assets can include websites; virtual worlds and goods; videos, audio files, and podcasts; e-books, blogs, and similar digital assets that may be paid for, subscribed to, or promoted to audiences to obtain advertising revenues, and so on. Regardless of what combination of digital assets we consider, for them to turn into a business model there still has to be value created that someone will ultimately pay for!

The question of Internet business models is one of the most important strategic questions for most Internet-related businesses, and is often tied to more than simply the type of site that the business plans to operate. This is also an issue you need to address if you are involved in planning for a not-for-profit or government service, and you seek to be profitable or cover your costs as a result of operating online. Of course, for an online retailer, the answer is quite simple: sell good products at good prices, delivered on time, that leave the business with enough margin (the difference between the selling price and the cost of goods sold) to make a reasonable profit to pay for the website's operation. However, what if you do not actually sell online goods? What if the site you operate is more of a community model based on common interests and shared commitment? How do you monetize that? Or perhaps you are an infomediary, expert site, or news-related site. Some of the most profitable sites are virtual worlds where the purchase of virtual goods (with no real cost of production attached to them) are bought and sold online with real money simply to entertain users.

Some of these business models didn't exist until just a couple of years ago. Who would have thought that anyone would pay for non-existent goods that disappear when they either stop playing or cancel their account? What other business and revenue models will exist in the future that can help you make money online? Regardless of how far they push the current boundaries of consumer behaviour, a series of existing generic business models deal with how Internet companies, and traditional companies using the Internet wisely, can make money online. While future innovations are bound to change this list quite regularly, here are the top ways in which most companies currently make money on the Web today:

1. displaying advertising and being paid for click-throughs from the online community to those advertising products or services (the traffic monetizing or advertising model)
2. selling either physical or virtual goods and services online (typically a transactional, wholesale, or retail merchant model)
3. earning royalties, access fees, or revenue sharing from selling access to their platform to third party developers (known as the API or applet model)
4. selling aggregate data about online user behaviour or selling controlled access to users with their permission through targeted offers; sometimes called *infomediaries* (the information or data aggregation model)
5. getting users to subscribe to a service, usually on a monthly or annual basis (the subscription model)
6. selling upgrades to a premium subscription service by first offering a free service with more limited capacity or capability (the *freemium* model)
7. imposing a very slight fee for specific transactions that add value beyond some kind of initial free access, which are added up and billed or deducted from a user account (the micro-payments model)
8. charging a portion of any transaction facilitated for others either as a brokerage or as a re-seller, as a traditional middle man (the revenue share or royalty model)
9. using an auction or co-operative model that is a derivative of a transactional or retail site, but with pricing controlled by the marketplace and the variations in supply and demand (the auction or co-operative model)
10. selling a company to a strategic buyer (the build to sell model)
11. charging users to post/automatically aggregate feeds (e.g., contests, deals) from their site into one central location (the online aggregators model) (e.g., *www.dailydealzone.com*)

Another way to understand e-commerce is to look at the purpose of the website used to implement the various business models. That is, having a great e-commerce business model will not generate a profit if it is not associated with a website that brings in customers or visitors. As with business models, there are a number of ways to classify websites by purpose, as listed in Table 7.2.

Looking at Table 7.2, note that the same website (Yahoo) is an example of two classifications because most B2C websites try to serve as large an audience as possible. This makes their sites more valuable to advertisers and serves as a source of information about their Web visitors for other companies. For example, Yahoo started out as a type of search engine, and then became a portal by using its popularity to charge for adding links to other websites. But as we also know—and this should act as a cautionary tale—there is a danger in trying to be too many things to too many people online. We are entering an age of both online specialization and consolidation where in many online markets, only the largest dominant competitor and a raft of small, precise specialists will survive, with not much in between.

Yahoo currently seems to have quite a challenge on its hands in this regard—what does it want to do strategically when its core market (search) is dominated by a competitor that is constantly innovating, while also driving down the average ad cost for its site? Yahoo turned down an early acquisition offer to remain independent, only to find that this has not done well for shareholders as business results continue to decline. As economics begin to suffer, the brand takes on a "has-been" or "passé" flavour, and competitors outmanoeuvre and outpace the company. So what does the company do? Sell? Persevere? Or re-position the brand and company to do something completely different and new? Just as we see with off-line competitors, being an online innovator is no certain recipe

Table 7.2	Websites Classified by Purpose		
Website Type	**Purpose**	**Example**	**Business Model**
Portal	Provides a gateway to many other websites	Yahoo, MSN	advertising, affiliate
Search engine	Finds websites that contain a word or phrase	Google, Yahoo, MSN, Dogpile, Bing	advertising, affiliate, infomediary
Browse or search and buy	Sells goods and services	Dell, Chapters.indigo.ca, iTunes, VRBO	merchant, infomediary, manufacturer direct, co-operative
Sales support	Provides information on a product before or after the sale	Microsoft, Dell, McAfee, Telus	community, infomediary
Information service	Provides news, information, and commentary	National Post, TSN, Economist	subscription, community, affiliate
Auction	Facilitates sales between third parties	eBay, Priceline, PayPal	brokerage
Travel	Sells travel tickets and tours	Expedia, Travelocity, Orbitz, itravel2000	merchant, brokerage, co-operative
Special interest or services	Provides information, product sales and support, and contacts between visitors	Microsoft support groups, Google Groups, Match.com, Craigslist	community, merchant, affiliate, infomediary, advertising
Group buying	Aggregators of discounted offers from merchants, often run as a "daily deal" or similar	Daily Deal Zone, Living Social, Groupon	merchant/brokerage, affiliate, advertising

for sustained future success. Internet competition is fierce and growing daily, even for incumbents with long histories of past success. Who knows—at some point after the printing of this book, maybe Yahoo as a separate company may not even exist. (That is, assuming they can find a strategic partner that actually wants to buy them now . . . timing truly is often everything in business.)

On the opposite end of this spectrum we have the phenomenon of group buying—and the recently announced IPO of Groupon—as an example of business model innovation. There is not much that is unique about Groupon's approach; group buying has been around for a long time in the form of buying clubs, travel groups, and so on. However, Groupon enabled it to happen on the Internet and scaled quickly to become the dominant player globally. Now they are poised to reap the reward of this insight and quick action. Of course, as noted above, there are already multiple copycat competitors to Groupon (including LivingSocial, WagJag, Redflagdeals, DealFind, etc.). Specialization is beginning to occur (for instance with *GroupDudes.com* targeting guys and *Spaphile.com* targeting only spa deals), which is a sign the market may be maturing quickly. This opportunity seems to mostly have passed (unless a company is highly specialized), and this business model, although only a variation of a traditional buy/sell model, is now well-established as a permanent part of the e-commerce digital landscape.

While none of the e-commerce business models is particularly complicated, they do not always interact easily with each other. And too much complexity in a business model may defeat business success. Most online companies choose to focus on only one or two of the models to maximize their focus and their profits. In fact, some of these business models are mutually exclusive and could not even co-exist. Yet there is still room for innovation. For instance, e-commerce and social computing are intersecting with business in new ways, and "social business" models (based on social media technologies) are currently a hot area for technology and business innovation. Perhaps you will become an online pioneer after you graduate by building a company with a new e-commerce business model!

Quick Test

1. Fill in the blank. Selling your vintage Star Wars action figures on eBay.ca is a form of _____ e-commerce.

2. Which of the following is NOT a known e-commerce business model?
   a. infomediary
   b. auction
   c. subscription
   d. pay-as–you-go

3. True or False. As long as you have visitors to your e-commerce site, you will have a successful e-commerce business model.

Answers: 1. C2C; 2. d; 3. False

■ THE E-COMMERCE ADVANTAGE

The use of private computer networks to carry out transactions between buyers and sellers started well before the Internet arrived. These networks created significant early e-commerce advantages in the worldwide economy. The Internet has only expanded this movement and globalized it further through standardized technologies and lower costs. As a result, this advantage is often referred to as the *frictionless economy*—the transactional ability of the consumer to move from thought to action (i.e., buying to instantly receiving the product) creates new opportunities for businesses to operate at lower costs by easing the burden of the supply chain electronically.

To cite just one interesting example of these frictionless transactions, think of Craigslist. How did consumers sell an item in decades past? Likely, if the item had sufficient value, they would advertise it in the newspaper classifieds (now a dying business in many markets). However, that cost money and took significant time: to write the ad, to call the newspaper and book it, to review the proof copy, and then to authorize it to run. And, of course, this also implied waiting another day or so before it actually ran in the printed copy of the newspaper. In turn, the buyer had to respond to the ad itself, normally through a phone call (if the seller dared include a telephone number), or by writing to an assigned post-office box. Such lapsed time and cost meant that this method really only made sense for items of real value—in fact, versus the cost, many consumers would have opted for other kinds of methods to sell the unwanted stuff. For instance, there were flea markets (now almost extinct in their previous form), or perhaps a garage sale or yard sale that would only attract local buyers. Regardless of the method, to actually mount the effort to sell the merchandise took some planning, effort, and cost.

Now think about the Web equivalents—eBay or Craigslist, for instance. In a nanosecond, anyone connected to the Web can post an ad, often without cost, depending on the site. Consumers in turn can immediately access an ad from any place in the world and transact business—no more relying on the local neighbours or drive-by types looking for a bargain. Other interesting business models (auctions, commission-based sites, etc.) also help drive new value into the process of classified advertising, and have re-invented it. As the cost of posting an ad approaches zero and becomes increasingly easy to do, sellers do it more often for even lower-cost items.

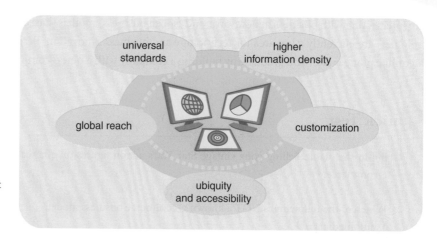

FIGURE 7.3 Impact of e-commerce technologies on business.

This is a great example of the impact of frictionless transactions and the reason why so many newspapers are suffering drops in profit as a result of consumers abandoning an antiquated model for a new, more robust online equivalent.

To understand this better, consider the technology, competitive issues, and strategy associated with e-commerce around the world. When you examine the business use of computer network technologies, especially those associated with the Internet, you find that they offer a number of unique benefits, as Figure 7.3 shows.

People around the world now have Internet access to varying degrees. Some have it only in local Internet cafes; some have a connection directly in their homes or on mobile phones, laptops, smartphones, iPads, or other PDAs. This has resulted in the *marketplace* becoming a ubiquitous *marketspace*, with more than 2 billion potential customers (people with Internet access) as of March 2011 (see Figure 7.4).[1] In Canada, national Internet usage penetration rates are high, with over 82 percent of the population having some form of regular access to the Internet—one of the highest rates in the world.

While still a minority of the world's total population, Internet users are a fast-growing group with significant buying power; yet that power is often concentrated, because those with Internet access often represent a more economically-advantaged class. Businesses cannot ignore this group

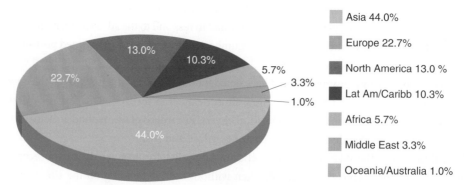

FIGURE 7.4 Internet users around the world number approximately 2 billion. This chart shows the distribution of where those potential consumers are located (as of March 31, 2011).
SOURCE: www.internetworldstats.com/stats.htm

---

1. *www.Internetworldstats.com/stats.htm*, reported as of September 2011.

when making marketing plans, especially not organizations in North America and Europe, where the Internet is a powerful and growing force for commerce.

The Internet relies on the use of universal technical standards to make it available in the same way, no matter what corner of the world you access it from (see Chapter 2 for more information on underlying Internet technologies; later in this chapter we discuss e-commerce technologies). When combined with open source software applications and development tools, universal standards increase accessibility to the marketplace while also lowering entry costs and encouraging innovation. The innovative uses of the Internet in business have produced truly global competition. Sellers can reach virtually any potential buyer in the world and can easily create a global electronic presence. This moves us ever closer to the *perfect market*, described for decades by economists as an ideal situation that theoretically produces the highest consumption at the lowest price for the most goods.

While this global marketplace is great for large retailers like Walmart, it also allows the almost instant creation of niche businesses targeting small markets that would not be dense enough in any single area to support a small, local retailer. When aggregated online, however, these businesses produce a viable volume of sales to support a global Internet retailer. Smaller businesses like this can compete successfully by targeting specific customers for one-to-one attention. One example of this is *Etsy.com*. Etsy is essentially an online craft fair. Sellers post their handmade items such as knitted slippers, original artwork, or handmade jewellery, and buyers purchase the items through the site's online store. Some products on Etsy are highly customizable and include specific requests from the buyer that might include adding the buyer's name to artwork or selecting custom colours. Without e-commerce, access to these products would be limited to connecting with the artisans directly, likely by word of mouth or seeing them at a local or travelling craft show. With e-commerce, both buyers and sellers have access to the world's marketplace. And instantly, formerly small, local artisans can expect to sell their goods around the world!

You may not have heard of Etsy and, if some of the sellers on Etsy had websites of their own, you may not have heard of those either. Beyond the need to have a business model that makes you sufficient money that you can afford to offer your service for free, there are the issues of attracting people to your site and marketing to an often overwhelmed consumer. In the following section we discuss information clutter, a growing issue on the Web that may ultimately start to interfere with the effectiveness of the Web as a commercial vehicle.

Breaking Through the Information Clutter

The expansion of global e-commerce has also increased buyers' level of **information density**; that is, the quality and quantity of information about products and services of interest to them. For example, websites like *PCMag.com* or *CNet.com* offer product guides, reviews, and prices on many different kinds of technology, from PCs to printers to digital cameras. Websites such as *PriceGrabber.ca* and *Shopbot.ca* provide a wide range of price and quality information on electronics and computers, making you more knowledgeable when you visit an electronics store. There are also a wide range of product rating sites that enable consumers to help other consumers, along with online versions of formerly printed buyers' guides like Wine Spectator, Consumers Report, and many others. However, the ability of buyers to obtain almost endless amounts of business information also creates new business challenges: How do I get noticed among all this clutter? Some businesses have responded by choosing to create business value based on a customization-oriented approach (mass customization or personalization) linked to e-commerce, rather than solely on a low-cost producer strategy.

It is clear that simply having a great website is not enough; you have to make it possible for potential customers to find it, and that is not easy, particularly in categories where the business is not unique and may have many online competitors or lookalikes. Online merchants use a number of important strategies to accomplish this goal. The following sections outline a few common marketing strategies for online businesses that you will likely recognize, having experienced them yourself.

Online Advertising The challenge of attracting attention to your site can be partially solved online using the same method as is often used off-line—advertising. Google AdWords (see *https:// adwords.google.com*) is a way of linking paid advertising to key word searches by consumers. For instance, if you have villas for rent in Hawaii, then you might choose to associate your online ad with searches having to do with vacations, Hawaii, villas, rentals, and so on. If you want to be less specific but have a target budget in mind, you can also buy coverage in the form of *cost per click* (CPC) maximums, which work almost like an auction of those competing for placement against popular words and phrases. Costs to advertise online have fallen dramatically in recent years as the possible inventory of ad placements has increased. Ironically, this same trend is due to the very same information clutter that makes it hard to find a site in the first place. With the abundance of sites on which to advertise, proper targeting and ad placement become essential parts of getting online advertising campaigns to work.

Yahoo and almost all other search engines offer similar options and alternatives for online advertising linked to searches, as do certain types of specialized aggregators and placement agencies. Similarly, banner ad placements (either in bulk or targeted to specific sites) may help you reach your target market online. These can often be purchased with the assistance of either a digital agency (that specializes in the creative aspects of your ad and its effective placement) or, if you make your own ads, from one of the larger media placement firms that can manage directing your ad to the right inventory at the right cost and monitor click-through rates and ad effectiveness for you.

Search Engine Optimization All search engines use a technology called *spiders* to crawl the Web and catalogue its content—including your organization's or businesses' new website. How it then gets labelled and ranked becomes important to its visibility to others online. A variety of techniques are related to making your website both more visible to search engines and more relevant to the way these search engines rank sites to increase the likelihood of appearing higher in the list of any relevant search by consumers. A big part of this is ensuring that your site uses technologies that are easy to search (for example, by avoiding too much use of Flash or embedded video), creating lots of links between your site and others (which in many cases increases your rank), and making good use of meta-tags and content density to appear like a site that offers lots of information and value (a tactic that also creates higher website rankings on search engines).

However, like everything on the Web, this space is fast-changing and practices that work today may not continue to work tomorrow, or search engine practices may change as companies develop newer and better ways of providing search results. Again, specialist firms can help you to optimize your search engine ranking, and consulting them on the latest practices and trends in this constantly-changing domain is often worthwhile.

Partnering and Traffic Trading You can almost always think of complementary business partners in the off-line world that target a similar (or even the same) market as you, but with different products and services, or perhaps different price points and features. An example of this in the off-line world is the common dinner and movie pairing. A restaurant near a movie theatre may offer a dinner and movie package for less than the regular cost of one dinner and one movie, thereby encouraging customers to eat dinner at their restaurant prior to the movie. Similarly, in the online world you can partner with other sites and each of you can cross-list the others' website and trade potential traffic that comes to one site. Customers may or may not buy, but they could be interested in something else on your site. In most cases, it's easy to track the origin of traffic and reward the partner site with a commission or fee related to sales it generates for you and vice-versa. This is also a low-cost method of online promotion since it only requires that you identify and contact potential partner sites. Often the parties only pay for results (click throughs, actual sales, etc.) and not any type of set-up or maintenance fee.

Once you have managed to get a potential customer, or *prospect*, to your site, you must find a way to capture his or her interest and, hopefully, encourage a purchase. **Mass customization**, or the ability to create custom products or services on-demand, is one way that Dell has succeeded in the consumer PC business. Through its website, customers can choose from a wide variety of ways to customize a standard Dell PC to match their needs and desires. Other manufacturers have tried this approach as well. For example, you can visit *www.bmw.ca* or *www.mercedes-benz.ca* and customize a vehicle that the company will deliver to a dealer in your area.

Some businesses use e-commerce to customize their products, such as this website that allows consumers to build their own Mini Cooper.

Netflix recommends shows or movies you might like based on your past selections or ratings of past selections.

Businesses also use personalization as another way in which e-commerce sites can better reach their customers. **Personalization** is a marketing message that a business customizes for each potential customer's interests, based on his or her searching, browsing, and buying habits. By using personalization, businesses can make marketing messages more effective and efficient. For example, if you register with *Amazon.ca*, you can view a list of book recommendations and why Amazon recommends the books to you. Personalization of this nature is often only possible because you previously shared information with the website through a registration or sign-up form, or through the data you provided to purchase items from the site. Netflix is another example of a business that uses this functionality with their TV and DVD streaming. You rate the shows you have watched and it recommends other similar shows you may enjoy. iTunes has also incorporated this functionality with their Genius selections, pairing songs in your library that go well together, automatically generating playlists you might like, and providing a sidebar that recommends songs from iTunes to help you discover new music that fits your tastes.

Web Usage and Statistics Once you have your website up and running, besides using some of the methods above to generate new traffic, make sure to pay attention to how visitors who find your site use your site. What pages do they visit and how long do they stay? Do they come back? To what kinds of marketing messages and offers do they respond? Do they join or otherwise indicate some kind of commitment, and how do you measure this in stages and encourage consumers to take the

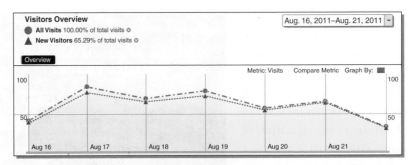

FIGURE 7.5 A simple but important Web statistic is the number of unique visitors to a website. This metric helps to measure if your website is attracting traffic. The sample above shows the number of unique visitors and page views by day. Some analytics providers, like Google Analytics, allows you to hover over any specific point to get information about the total visits that day as well as new visits.

next step? Both IT and non-IT related business people need to be asking these kinds of questions all the time.

Many Web statistics reporting software programs are available, many for free. Some require that you install software on your Web server; others operate as SaaS (software as a service). All of these software programs contain the basic required Web metrics for various time frames, including number of unique visitors, number of page views, where users are coming from (a way to measure the effectiveness of partnerships), which page users exit from on your website, which search engines visitors use to find your website, and more. Figure 7.5 shows the output of one of these programs, indicating the number of unique visitors and page views for several days. Some Web statistics programs offer advanced logging functions, graphing, trend analysis, and integration with other Web programs. For a comprehensive Web analytics tool, view the Google analytics product tour at *www.google.com/analytics*.

E-Commerce Competitive Difference

E-commerce dramatically affects competition between organizations in a number of interesting ways, such as:

- reducing barriers to market entry
- preventing any company from "owning" the market
- enhancing collaboration/alliances
- multiplying market niches
- changing marketplace drivers

To consider each of these impacts, let's use the example of a vacation home rental.

A vacation home is often a sound investment. As the owner, you can use it as well as rent it to others to help cover the costs of the property. Further, because you will probably purchase the vacation home in an area subject to significant increases in property value over time, you can later sell the investment for a large gain.

While investing in a vacation home can be a good idea, it does have problems, especially with traditional commerce. First, you might need to hire a rental agency located in the same area as your property, or advertise in newspapers in those areas where you believe your potential renters might live. However, a rental agency usually charges a significant commission (as much as 50 percent in some cases) and might neglect your property in favour of other rentals that it handles. Advertising in newspapers is expensive and is a hit or miss situation, depending on where potential renters live.

An e-commerce solution to this problem is the use of a **co-operative website**, like *VRBO.com*, *CanadaVacationRentals.ca*, and *HomeAway.com*, where owners of vacation properties co-operate by advertising on the same site. Such websites serve as a meeting place between property owners and renters. For example, the *VRBO.com* (Vacation Rentals By Owner) site claims to list over 160,000 properties from around the world, with 42 million visits to the site each year by renters.[2]

Rental websites also provide an e-commerce solution. Potential renters find these sites through search engines, advertisements on other websites, or even in traditional travel magazines. These types of websites have quickly become popular with both property owners and renters, for whom the website is basically a meeting place. The actual discussions of availability, price, and rental conditions are handled on a one-to-one basis between the potential renter and the owner. But potential renters can see layouts, complete a virtual tour in some cases, learn about the property location or community services, and so on.

Co-operative websites, such as the one shown here, reflect one significant e-commerce difference in competition by reducing the barrier to entry.

In looking at e-commerce co-operative websites, it should be easy to see how they have dramatically changed the face of the vacation rental market. They have reduced *barriers to entry* by not requiring that a rental agent have an expensive building in a well-travelled location near the vacation area, a list of rental properties to offer potential renters, or a well-known name among past and potential renters. Instead, owners can rely on a much less expensive rental website that will act as a gateway to their individual vacation property website. Even another dominant website does not create any barriers to entry, given the wide open nature of the Internet.

In addition, e-commerce keeps any one rental agency or website from owning the market. The Internet, with the proliferation of search engines, is now the first way that many travellers look for a place to stay on their trips. This bypasses the traditional rental agencies, which often restrict themselves to travellers who happen by their building.

Further, many of the rental websites on the Internet today are co-operative sites that thrive on collaboration—even if the collaborators don't know each other! By co-operating on a popular rental website, property owners virtually ensure that search engines find the site so potential renters can visit it. Finally, a co-operative rental website also enables contacts between property owners in different parts of the world, which can result in alliances between them.

Traditional rental agencies also typically lack the resources to compete in a niche market, such as renting to travellers interested in visiting a specific beach known for its high-quality shells. Such agencies must rent to the broader market to cover the high fixed costs associated with having a physical location. On the other hand, vacation property owners can easily set up and advertise on a niche

2. *www.vrbo.com*, as of September 2011.

rental website. **Niche markets** are one area where e-commerce has shown itself to be superior to almost any existing form of marketing.

Finally, time, distance, and price all drive the traditional marketplaces, but e-commerce can easily overcome these limitations (as we described earlier in the Craigslist versus classified newspaper advertising example). Now websites allow a business to stay open on a 24/7/365 basis, and the owner and potential renter can communicate almost instantaneously from virtually anywhere in the world, at any time. This means that a property owner in Canmore, Alberta, can just as easily rent to somebody from Germany as to somebody from Edmonton. This was not really feasible prior to the Web because of time and cost. In terms of price, because the Internet generates so much data, a seller or renter can determine demand patterns based on prior experience or on data from other users. This means that negotiations on price between owner and potential renter can rely on availability and demand, rather than on a one-size-fits-all pricing scheme. And since pricing is a very strategic issue for any business regardless of size, this brings us to our next important topic: the integration of e-commerce into business strategy.

E-Commerce and Organization Strategy

Technology advances normally require adaptation, and often changes in organization strategy. To better understand this statement, consider *business strategy* in general terms. Henry Mintzberg, a professor at McGill University and a leading thinker on strategy and leadership, suggests that strategy is a plan, pattern, position, and perspective. This is very sound and, when broken down, becomes quite comprehensive in terms of guiding the action of an organization. He argues that strategy emerges and evolves over time in natural response to a constantly emerging competitive landscape and the individual performance level of any competitor in that marketspace. A change in either a company's performance in relation to the competition or a major change in competition (for instance, the emergence of a disruptive industry force, the emergence of a new competitor, innovations in business models, or the introduction of new government regulations) could necessitate revisiting business strategy. A strategy may start as a perspective (vision, direction) that calls for a certain position, such as being a low-cost provider, and then evolves into a plan that is implemented, and emerges as a pattern that is evident in actions and decisions.[3] Of course, in today's highly tech-dependent world, where the Internet is certainly a major force for innovation and change, no business strategy would be complete without addressing the question of how to integrate the Web and e-commerce into the overall business strategy.

E-commerce strategy is a general term for how a business intends to use computer Web-based networks and information systems to compete in its global marketplace. For example, Manheim Auctions is the largest automobile remarketing service (automobile auction) in the world. In 2002, when the Internet was starting to become a force, Manheim was the first automobile auction to explore ways to use the Internet to protect its market share from potential encroachment by competitors. This is a good example of what Mintzberg calls ever-green strategy. Manheim chose to strategically apply e-commerce to the wholesale used car market by creating an online purchase system, an online bidding system, and a co-operative system that enables individuals to sell their automobiles. They did this, even at the expense of revenue in their legacy business model, rather than wait for a competitor to do it and change their leadership position. The Internet cannot be ignored. Manheim changed its perspective and looked for ways to use the Internet to further its competitive goals of serving its customers better, demonstrating this co-dependence between strategy formulation and the impact of new technologies as a way of maintaining business performance and competitive

---

3. Henry Mintzberg, *The Rise and Fall of Strategic Planning*, (1994), Basic Books.

position. And their strategy has paid off—in 2010, Manheim handled nearly 10 million used vehicles, facilitating transactions representing more than $50 billion in value.[4] Today, Manheim offers Android and iPhone apps to enable vehicle search, bidding, and buying.

Building a meaningful e-commerce strategy requires two different views of an organization's strategy: what it wants to do (conceptual strategy), and how it will do it (technology strategy). Often there will be a gap between the two that must be addressed if you are to successfully execute your strategy. Obviously, the two views are interlinked (see Figure 7.6). For example, having the technological capability to carry out an activity will result in business failure if no market exists. Similarly, relying on a new technology to create competitive advantage has both costs and risks associated that will have to be recovered in new sources of profit (see online references to *Pets.com* or the story of Friendster losing its initially leading market position to Myspace and Facebook as great examples of this strategic risk). Just ask the people who lost money in one or more of the dot-com companies in the late 1990s about the business complications of balancing these two challenges!

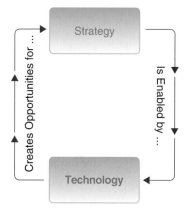

FIGURE 7.6 The interaction of strategy and technology.

An important strategy that many companies are using is to connect their online Web strategy to their existing *customer relationship management (CRM)* systems to create an integrated one-to-one marketing experience for their customers. The Web generates a huge amount of data on customer buying habits and preferences that can be stored and instantly recalled and applied with each new visit (using cookies or other technologies discussed later in this chapter, for instance). With these data, companies can use CRM to tailor the products on their website to the individual buyer, or perhaps create customer-specific offers and campaigns or keep track of specific discount levels or specific inducements or entitlements offered to repeat buyers. For example, your organization could create automatic shipping notifications when orders leave the warehouse so customers know their order is on the way. You can then follow up with automatic online surveys to ensure a highly satisfied customer. This creates a closer match to the customers' real needs, which, in turn, increases the probability they will return to the website for another purchase. However, this can also give rise to privacy concerns, and many of these strategies require customers to give their consent to storing critical information about them (Chapter 1 addresses privacy and other ethical concerns).

The value of overcoming privacy concerns is that the use of CRM can also create switching costs for customers. Going to another seller means that they will have to retrain a new website to understand their preferences. Good service from an existing supplier is a known factor in repeat-purchase decisions, and online vendors should take this seriously.

Other e-commerce strategies that companies use to increase business value to consumers include use of virtual showrooms, increased channel choices, wider component choice, and use of mobile technology. Of course, just as the Web itself was a disruptive technology, the rapid expansion of mobile data networks, tablets, and smartphones are other current examples of technology innovations that demand a strategic business response.

M-Commerce

Possibly the largest new channel for many businesses (both online and traditional business models) is the use of mobile devices on wireless data networks to access the Internet. This technology enables mobile commerce (m-commerce) applications to become a reality, and ensures that consumers can

---

4. *www.manheim.com/about/*, October 2011.

immediately react in the moment to any marketing message (rather than waiting to get home to their computers to access the Internet). **Mobile commerce** is the use of laptops, tablets, mobile telephones, and PDAs to connect to the Internet and Web to conduct many of the activities normally associated with e-commerce, but in real time and without regard to where the user may actually be at the moment. Firms now have two-way interaction with customers through these mobile devices and in new ways that can enable entire new applications. For instance, one company is currently exploring the issues of providing consumers with instant-use coupons in grocery stores. Using a combination of a pre-registered customer ID, a smartphone number, and the phone's geolocating ability, as the buyer navigates the stores aisles, the smartphone becomes a coupon and information dispensing device that reacts to where the buyer is and what the buyer's preferences and buying habits are. What is the strategic business objective for the merchant? To influence cherished loyal buyers' behaviour at the point of sale while they are actually in the store, helping them sell more through inducements and tailored offers.

Of course, it is not just the retailers who have caught on to this, but also those who design and provision stores and store displays. If, for example, you are shopping in Loblaws and you have enabled a mobile coupon application like GeoQpon, it will detect small electronic sensors in the aisles of the supermarket to "ping" you with an instant coupon. The sensors can also detect things like you passing rapidly by products (indicating you are likely not interested or possibly only interested if you get pinged) or when you are stationary (perhaps suggesting that you are browsing the shelves of competitive products and that an electronic offer in the moment might cause you to buy one product over another on that shelf). On the other hand, if you like the group buying phenomenon, you can sign up for a limited amount of time for a group buy, redeem your coupon (sent to your mobile device), and take home your new treasure—and save money too. Similarly, experimental technologies are now underway that use facial recognition technology to follow your eyes in a store and, if you look at a display, change what it is offering to match your gender, approximate age, race, and so on.

Mobile commerce is continually changing the way people shop. Shopping apps allow consumers and companies to interact in exciting new ways.

Sometimes these technologies pose interesting ethical issues and certainly touch a nerve with regard to privacy and consent—but nonetheless, they are soon coming to a store near you! If you are responsible for creating an organization's strategy in this area, mobile commerce cannot be ignored.

To offer the service to consumers for free, the application charges both the product manufacturers and the grocery stores for the technology and application, as well as occasionally charging a commission or fee (this varies) to the product or service seller. The hopes of the companies involved are obviously to gain the ability to influence sales to consumers by learning more about what offers, purchasing patterns, and available choices interact to cause consumers to buy more or different products through different devices at various times of day.

Now that you have a better understanding of e-commerce and the difference it makes, let's look at the business-to-consumer (B2C) and business-to-business (B2B) sectors.

Quick Test

Choose the BEST answer from column B for each item in column A.

Column A	Column B
1. customization	a. competing sellers partnering on a common website
2. frictionless transaction	b. creating products on demand
3. co-operative website	c. providing products/services efficiently and reducing cost and involvement of the provider

Answers: 1. b; 2. c; 3. a

■ BENEFITS AND LIMITATIONS OF E-COMMERCE

Recall our discussion of *business strategy* in Chapter 5, and specifically Michael Porter's five forces model. In general, because having information about and access to larger markets increases the buyer's knowledge of a good deal, Porter's model suggests that e-commerce increases competition. This often results in lower prices and better services for all consumers, online or not. However, there may be disadvantages or limitations for consumers in the form of shipping time and costs, download speeds, security, and payment sizes that create some barriers to the use of this technology for some kinds of transactions or industries. On the flip side, the increased competition, lower prices, and better services that consumers now expect can create problems for inefficient businesses as newer, more tech-savvy competitors enter the industry. Table 7.3 lists some advantages and disadvantages of B2C e-commerce for both consumers and businesses. You are probably familiar with most of these advantages and disadvantages for the consumer.

In looking at Table 7.3, note the number of advantages of B2C e-commerce for businesses. Expansion of the marketplace enables businesses to reach customers far beyond their local area with

Table 7.3	Benefits and Limitations of B2C E-Commerce	
	Benefits	**Limitations**
Consumer	• Lower prices • Shopping 24/7 • Greater searchability of products worldwide • Shorter delivery times for digital products • More sharing of information with other consumers • Improved customer service	• Delay in receiving physical products, plus shipping charges • Slow download speeds in areas without high-speed Internet • Security and privacy concerns, especially with the rise of phishing (a scam intended to gain private information for fraudulent use) • Inability to touch, feel, smell, try out, or try on products prior to purchasing • Unavailability of micropayments for purchases of small-cost products
Business	• Expansion of marketplace to global proportions • Cheaper electronic transactions • Greater customer loyalty through customized web pages and one-to-one marketing • Expansion of niche marketing opportunities • Direct communications with customers through website, often resulting in better customer service	• Increased competition due to global marketplace • Ease of comparison between competing products drives prices down • Customers want specific choices and will not accept substitutes • Customers control flow of information instead of companies

SOURCE: Some, but not all, of these are from Efraim Turban et al., *Electronic Commerce: A Managerial Perspective* (2002), Prentice-Hall: Upper Saddle River, NJ, pp. 26–28.

a minimal capital outlay. Businesses also reduce their cost of dealing with paper-based transactions by carrying out transactions digitally over a computer network.

Customizing individual web pages to the interests of customers also creates greater customer loyalty. *Amazon.ca* has turned this into a key advantage that keeps customers coming back, since they don't have to train a new website to know their interests. The use of niche marketing helps companies react to changing competition. For instance, many travel agencies use specialized travel niches (for example, those specializing in a specific area, such as *www.findcroatia.com*). Finally, more direct communication with customers, even when an intermediary sells the product, results in better customer service. For example, a large company like Moen (*www.moen.com*), which markets kitchen and bath products, can provide customers with detailed drawings of its products directly over the Internet, as well as design information prior to the sale. It also gives customers the ability to use their online tool to see what faucets would look like in a simulated bathroom or kitchen.

However, e-commerce has definite disadvantages for inefficient companies that often mirror the potential advantages. A global marketplace means that companies from around the world can compete for a business's local customers, creating a very intense industry rivalry. More competition driving down prices is like having a Walmart next to every business. If a business is not ready to compete on a price basis, then it must offer some service that its competitor cannot, like more customized products or more individual attention. Finally, with a wide variety of advertising media, companies must know how to attract customers to their websites.

One way to attract customers to websites is to ensure protection of sensitive data, such as credit card information. As a result of consumer concern, many online vendors resort to third-party endorsements of their security practices to help build consumer confidence. An example of this would be overlay brands, such as *www.truste.org*, that an organization qualifies for and then advertises on its site. It is important that online businesses are secure and that they safeguard consumer information.

WHAT DO YOU THINK?

What stalled e-commerce in its early days was consumer distrust of online payment systems, especially if they involved giving out credit card information. Over time, this has become less of an issue as secure computing has gained consumer trust and as various new types of "digital cash" systems have emerged on the Web, such as PayPal. Consider these questions as an Internet user:

1: Have you ever used an online payment system like PayPal? If so, for what? Did you trust that it would work the first time? Why or why not?
2: What are the signs of legitimacy that you look for in a website before providing your credit card information for payment?
3: Have you ever had a payment problem on the Internet? What were the consequences or solutions to the problem?

Another way companies are attempting to increase consumer comfort levels with e-commerce is through the use of technology provided by credit card companies. Have you ever been on an e-commerce website and been asked to provide your credit card security code as part of the transaction? Figure 7.7 shows the location of the security code on the flip side of a Visa or MasterCard. It is assumed that if consumers are able to provide the security code, they have the physical card in their possession, and that the card number is not being used by anyone other than the card holder.

If you make a large purchase online (e.g., airline tickets, computer) you will see a higher level of security offered by credit card companies. During the e-commerce transaction process, an additional

FIGURE 7.7 E-commerce sites often ask for credit card security codes (circled in red in this figure) during a transaction to provide a higher level of security.

screen is presented asking you to enter a special code. This screen is provided by the credit card company, "Verified by Visa" and "MasterCard SecureCode," respectively, and collects a code that is required to authorize purchases. Again, this assumes that only the card holder is doing the purchase online, and that this security code has not been shared with anyone.

TECHNOLOGY CORE

Having an e-commerce business idea would be irrelevant without the technology to enable it. Later in this chapter we discuss the technology of e-commerce and briefly discuss order and payment systems, including the protocols (SSL) and standards (SET) used for transactions. Here we focus on encryption, the most common method of providing security to e-commerce transactions. Encryption is the process of scrambling a message so that it is meaningful only to the person holding the key to deciphering it. To everyone else, the message is gobbledygook. The reverse process, decryption, converts a seemingly senseless character string into the original message.

There are two primary forms of encryption systems: (1) private key and (2) public key encryption. *Private key* encryption uses the same private key to encrypt and decrypt a message. A key is an algorithm used to encode and decode messages. While private key encryption may sound like the simplest method, there are significant problems with it. For example, how do you securely distribute the key? You can't send the private key with the message, because if the message is intercepted, the key can be used to decipher it. You must find another secure medium for transmitting the key. Do you fax or telephone the key instead? Neither method is completely secure, and each is time-consuming to use whenever the key is changed. In addition, how do you know that the key's receiver will protect its secrecy? Another problem with private key encryption is that you have

to create a separate private key for each person or organization with which you will exchange encrypted messages.

In contrast, a *public key* encryption system has two keys: one private and the other public. The public key is freely distributed and used to encrypt messages coming to you. In contrast, the private key remains secret and is only used to decrypt the messages encrypted with your public key. For example, you would distribute your public key to anybody who might need to send you encrypted messages. They would encrypt a message with your public key. Upon receiving the message, you would apply the private key, as shown in Figure 7.8. Your private key, the only key that can decrypt the message, must be kept secret to permit secure message exchange. Public key encryption is widely used in e-commerce to ensure the safety and privacy of transactions.

Did you know that this encryption/decryption process is done each time you provide information on the Web, and especially when transactions are involved? Feeling a bit more secure now?

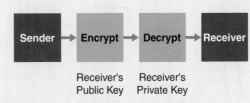

FIGURE 7.8 The process of public key encryption.

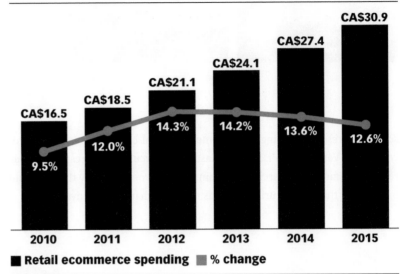

Retail Ecommerce Spending in Canada, 2010-2015
billions of CA$ and % change

FIGURE 7.9 This chart shows the anticipated growth in online retail in Canada.[5]

Note: includes travel, digital downloads, event tickets and spending on foreign sites
Source: eMarketer, Feb 2011

124239   www.eMarketer.com

All in all, however, the advantages of e-commerce continue to outweigh any limitations. As a result, businesses are turning to e-commerce business models to find more ways to compete in the global marketplace. In 2010, consumers in Canada spent $16.5 billion on domestic and foreign sites for products and services (including travel). By 2015, online spending is projected to nearly double, reaching $30.9 billion (see Figure 7.9). Shoppers are increasingly comfortable buying high-consideration goods online, such as home electronics and apparel. The allure of group buying is also introducing more consumers to e-commerce.[6]

Although these B2C numbers are impressive, e-commerce is an essential aspect of B2B companies as well. B2B organizations that choose to adopt an e-commerce platform will benefit as the economy continues to improve over time, and those that fail to adopt such strategies are likely to fall significantly behind their competitors.[7] The ability of businesses to reach new customers/markets is made possible through e-commerce by decreasing the costs of maintaining and supporting a direct sales force.

Quick Test

1. Which of the following is NOT an e-commerce benefit for businesses?
   a. Expansion of marketplace to global proportions
   b. More expensive electronic transactions
   c. Greater customer loyalty through customized web pages and one-to-one marketing
   d. Expansion of niche marketing opportunities

---

5. According to e-marketer, Inc.

6. *www.emarketer.com/Report.aspx?code=emarketer_2000767*

7. *www.oracle.com/us/products/applications/atg/b2b-ecommerce-reinventing-333314.pdf*

2. In order to read an encrypted message, what process must occur?
   a. subscription
   b. decryption
   c. recryption
   d. post-encryption

3. True or False. E-commerce platforms should only be used for B2C transactions.

■ E-COMMERCE BETWEEN ORGANIZATIONS

Even though most of the emphasis in the popular press has been on the B2C form of e-commerce, B2B is by far the larger market in terms of volume of transactions and dollar amounts. One business or organization doing business with another markedly differs from the B2C process. For example, if you decide you need a new computer, you think about what you need in a new PC and then search for computer merchants that sell the product that meets your needs. You most likely make the purchase with a credit card and set it up yourself when it arrives. You then pay the bill from your personal bank account.

On the other hand, if an organization decides it needs new PCs, it's not just ordering one computer at a time, but potentially thousands of PCs. This larger-scale purchase results in a more complex decision-making process, like that discussed in Chapter 3, requiring a great deal of thought and preparation. One or more authorized individuals must consider a number of factors, including the existing organizational technology infrastructure.

B2B Transactions and Business Models

We can broadly divide B2B transactions into two types: (1) spot buying and (2) strategic sourcing. **Spot buying** is much like what you do when you make a stock market transaction—you buy at market prices determined by supply and demand from someone you do not know. Companies often engage in spot buying to purchase goods and services that are commodities; that is, they are usually uniform in quality and differ only somewhat in price. Examples include gasoline, paper, and cleaning supplies. Whenever a company engages in spot buying, it needs to find a public marketplace or *exchange* that sells these desired products and services. Although it can be a physical marketplace, most B2B e-commerce exchange transactions occur through an online intermediary.

On the other hand, **strategic sourcing** involves forming a long-term relationship with another company. The companies set prices through negotiation. Both the buyer and seller are usually well known to each other and wish to continue a trading relationship into the future. A company's large-scale computer purchases probably result from strategic sourcing.

Strategic sourcing often relies on a one-to-one business model, although company-centric and exchange models are also used.[8] In the **one-to-one marketing model**, two companies collaborate to create a trading relationship that is good for both of them. In this form of B2B, both trading partners win from the relationship, as with strategic sourcing transactions. While they are not always of the same relative size, neither company dominates the trading relationship. From an e-commerce point of view, the two companies often seek to use computer networks to facilitate the supply chain from one to the other. (We discuss this model in more detail in a later section.)

---

8. Efraim Turban et al., *Electronic Commerce: A Managerial Perspective* (2002), Prentice-Hall: Upper Saddle River, NJ, pp. 220–221.

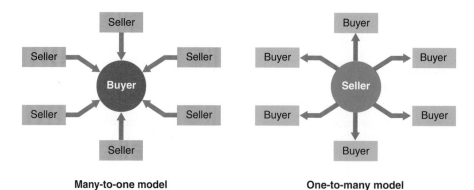

Many-to-one model **One-to-many model**

FIGURE 7.10 With the company-centric business model, a company is either a buyer from many companies (many-to-one) or a seller to many other companies (one-to-many).

With the **company-centric business model**, a company is either a seller to many other companies (one-to-many) or a buyer from many companies (many-to-one), as Figure 7.10 shows. In either case, the single company tends to dominate the market. It often completely controls the information systems that support the transactions, including the supply chains between it and its smaller trading partners. In this model, the large buyer or seller wants to use e-commerce to improve its profitability by increasing prices and/or reducing costs of doing business with the many smaller trading partners.

With the one-to-many model, the seller often provides a Web-based private sales channel through a private network, called *electronic data interchange (EDI)*, or through a protected form of the Internet, called an *extranet*, to link trading partners while keeping others out (we discuss both EDI and extranets in more detail later). Such sales can be at a set price or via an auction. For example, *Carbid.ca* uses an extranet to enable car dealers to purchase used cars online, thereby avoiding a costly trip to the physical auction. It has specified prices for cars, as well as online auctions at which dealers can bid on automobiles.

Because the many-to-one model provides a single buyer with products that it needs to carry on business, this is a part of the *procurement process*. When using e-commerce, it is commonly referred to as **e-procurement**. A buyer can conduct this process in a number of ways, including reverse auctions, aggregating catalogues, or group purchasing.

With an e-procurement reverse auction, the buyer posts projects to a secure website to which sellers respond with bids for providing goods and services for that project. In this case, the bidder with the *lowest* bid wins, hence the name *reverse auction*. The aggregating catalogues model assembles together the catalogues from all suppliers on the buyer's server. The buyer then uses them to make all purchases. This tends to centralize the procurement process. Finally, with group purchasing, two or more buyers work together to achieve lower prices from their suppliers. Smaller buyers can do this through websites that aggregate demand and then negotiate prices with suppliers.

In the **exchange model**, many companies use an exchange to buy and sell from each other through spot-buying transactions. The exchange can be a co-operative venture among a number of the companies, owned by an independent organization like that run by the National Retail Federation for the benefit of its members. It can also be run by a larger company that has found a way to profit from the transactions. The airplane parts exchange created by Boeing is an example of the last type of exchange (see the Case Study at the end of this chapter).

We can categorize exchanges into two groups: (1) verticals and (2) horizontals. *Vertical exchanges* meet the needs of a single industry, such as retailing. On the other hand, *horizontal exchanges* deal with products and services that all companies need, regardless of the industry (like office supplies). Figure 7.11 shows how buyers and sellers come together in an exchange. From an e-commerce point of view, an exchange is typically a website where buyers and sellers post their needs and offerings. For example, for a fee, the *Workpolis. com* website posts both resumés and job openings.

Using B2B E-Commerce to Improve Supply Chain Efficiency

Recall from our discussion of the *value chain* in Chapter 4 that the inbound and outbound logistics (movement of goods or services from supplier to organization and from organization to customer, respectively) of a company are linked to the logistics of other companies via its supply chain. Also recall from Chapter 4 that a *supply chain* is a system of organizations, people, technology, activities, information,

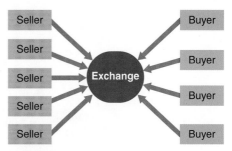

FIGURE 7.11 From an e-commerce point of view, an exchange is typically a website where buyers and sellers post their needs and offerings.

and resources involved in moving a product or service from supplier to customer. More specifically, it is a network of facilities and distribution options that performs the functions of procurement of materials, transformation of these materials into intermediate and finished products, and the distribution of these finished products to customers.[9] Procurement plays a large part in any supply chain, and the use of e-commerce for procurement is an important way for organizations to save money. To understand why, we need to first review the traditional procurement process.

Traditional Procurement Process For procurement to occur between businesses, there must be an information flow between the entities in addition to the flow of goods. Traditionally, this paper flow has involved three key elements: (1) the purchase order, (2) the invoice, and (3) the receipt of goods. Figure 7.12 shows the typical steps in the process.

1. The buyer sends a purchase order to a vendor. A *purchase order (PO)* is a document from an organization requesting another organization to supply something in return for payment. It typically provides product specifications and quantities, with this information often coming from the supplier's catalogue.
2. The vendor responds to the PO by sending the goods to the buyer along with a *bill of lading (BOL)*, which describes the contents of the shipment.
3. After receiving the goods and BOL, the buyer sends back a signed copy of the BOL to the vendor and internally files a *receipt of goods*.
4. The vendor sends an invoice to the buyer. An *invoice* is a detailed list of goods shipped from the supplier, along with a list of all costs and discounts. In essence, it is a detailed bill and request for payment.
5. The buyer's accounting department compares the original PO with the receipt of goods and the invoice to ensure they match. After confirming a match, the buyer pays the vendor.

As you can see, the traditional procurement process relies on paper-based documents. The employees in the accounting department have to pull all of them together and make an item-by-item comparison. Not only is this very tedious and time-consuming, it is also subject to errors and fraud.

Using E-commerce to Improve the Procurement Process E-commerce, with its digital information, replaces the paper documents in traditional procurement systems. Employees can quickly compare the digital files with far fewer errors and less opportunity for fraud. While companies still compare all three key documents—PO, receipt of goods, and invoice—prior to payment, automating

9. Ram Ganeshan and Terry P. Harrison, "An Introduction to Supply Chain Management," *http://lcm.csa.iisc.ernet.in/scm/ supply_chain_intro.html*.

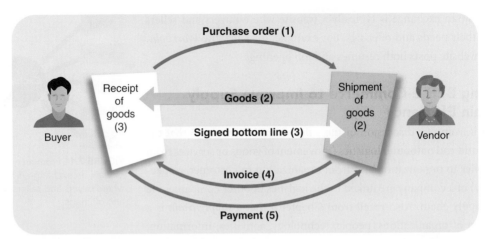

FIGURE 7.12 The traditional procurement method, which requires documents at every step, is often an inefficient process.

the process is a giant step in the right direction. In fact, some companies have moved ahead by authorizing payment on receipt, thereby eliminating the need for invoicing (Steps 4 and 5 in Figure 7.12).

E-procurement is also evolving into a tighter integration and coordination of the activities of a supplier–buyer relationship through the creation and use of interorganizational systems. An **interorganizational system (IOS)** is "a networked information system used by two or more separate organizations to perform a joint business function."[10] IOS can help to create 24/7 communications between organizations and their suppliers and customers, as well as enable paperless transactions throughout the supply chain. An IOS often involves electronically linking a production company to its suppliers or to its customers in such a way that raw materials are ordered, production takes place, and finished goods are sent to the customer with little or no paper changing hands. IOS can therefore enable supplier and customer organizations to carry out transactions almost as if they were parts of the same organization.

The two most common forms of IOS in use today are based on **electronic data interchange (EDI)**, which uses value-added networks (VANs) or private networks instead of the regular telephone system, and **extranets**, which are collaborative networks that use Internet technology to link businesses with their suppliers, customers, or other businesses that share common goals.

EDI allows the exchange of structured information between two computer applications, using a minimum of human involvement. EDI works because of a set of agreed-upon message standards that allow both applications to understand and process the exchanged data. In EDI terminology, the organizations that send or receive documents from each other are called *trading partners*. These partners agree on which specific information to exchange and how to use it.

Although the initial purpose of EDI was to replace the exchange of paper-based documents with more efficient and flexible electronic documents, trading partners have since realized several additional benefits from its use. An EDI system can save unnecessary recapture of data, which leads to faster data transfer, fewer errors, and a more streamlined business process. Firms can also use EDI as a platform for automating existing processes. This can help to reduce costs further, as well as improve the quality and speed of services. Finally, since EDI requires co-operation between trading partners, it can also serve as a catalyst for improving interorganizational processes and overall supply chain efficiency.

---

10. James I. Cash, Jr., Franklin Warren McFarlan, James L. McKenney, and Lynda M. Applegate, *Corporate Information Systems Management: Text and Cases*, 1994, 4th ed. Homewood, IL: Irwin, p. 339.

EDI is older technology that is often overshadowed by the newer cutting-edge technologies such as the World Wide Web and XML. Nevertheless, EDI remains an important part of business. It is still the engine behind a majority of all e-commerce transactions in the world.

An extranet uses Internet technologies to interconnect the intranet of an organization with the intranets of its business partners. Through the extranet, customers, suppliers, consultants, and other trading partners can access selected sites and data available on the internal intranet. Keep in mind that while an extranet extends access to the network outside the boundaries of the organization, usually over the Internet, it is still a private network. Security measures, such as usernames and passwords, usually control access to the extranet. Companies may also use the additional security measures of encryption and firewalls.

As companies realized the advantages of sharing data and information with trading partners, they began to develop extranets as a way to allow these trading partners to access limited areas available on the intranet. An extranet is somewhere in-between a private intranet and the public Internet. There is still a firewall between the intranet and public access, but it is now set to open for selected outsiders. Because EDI requires the use of expensive VANs or private networks, most businesses find it too expensive. However, through the use of an extranet, the Internet enables smaller companies to take advantage of IOS. Another way of connecting with customers or partners is by using a customer portal. A customer portal is available over the Internet and is secured through the use of HTTPS protocol and customer/partner authentication. Table 7.4 highlights some differences between EDI, extranet-enabled, and customer portal B2B e-commerce.

Table 7.4	Comparing EDI and Extranet-Enabled B2B E-Commerce		
	EDI	**Extranet**	**Customer Portal**
Security	More secure due to use of private network	Less secure than EDI due to use of Internet, but can be made safer through use of security measures (e.g., strong passwords, encryption)	About the same level of security as using an extranet; limits public access by using HTTPS protocol, but is public facing and is available wherever the Internet is available
Cost	More costly due to proprietary software and use of VANS	Less costly because with enhanced features, an organization's extranet can evolve as an extension of its intranet, allowing for the use of existing networks and possible reuse of Internet-enabled applications	Even less costly than the others as it simply uses a Web front end to access internally available applications
Flexibility	Less flexible because proprietary software limits use primarily to standard business documents	More flexible because it is based on the Internet, which permits greater customization and wider access to development tools	Similar to extranets in that anything that is possible on the Web can be done on a customer portal; further customization by customer may be possible by changing the look of the Web interface to be specific to each customer when it enters the portal
Trend	Gradually being replaced by extranet-based applications	Gaining wider acceptance due to lower costs and increased use of the Internet	Becoming widely used as it tends to be simple to set up and maintain

Does e-procurement work in the real world? Absolutely. For example, Scotland exploited technology to facilitate collaboration and change through use of a common platform, *eProcurement Scotland (ePS)*. The results so far have been very positive. Since its creation in 2002, governmental entities have placed more than 260,000 orders for goods and services from thousands of suppliers, spending in excess of 271 million Scottish pounds. In fact, this effort has been so successful that ePS was a finalist for Scotland's National e-Government Excellence Award.[11] The government of British Columbia has also introduced procurement technology, called BC Bid®. This software gives businesses that would like to sell to the provincial government the ability to access, create, browse, and compete on public sector opportunities at any time.[12] The Canadian federal government and other provincial governments have, at minimum, posted rules and procedures for selling to their governments on their websites to facilitate procurement.

Throughout this chapter, so far we have touched on the strategic importance of the technology that enables e-commerce. The next section discusses aspects of the technologies themselves in more detail to provide in-depth knowledge of what makes e-commerce work in practice.

Quick Test

1. Which of the following outlines the traditional procurement process between businesses?
   a. purchase order, goods, signed bottom line, invoice, payment
   b. invoice, goods, signed bottom line, payment, purchase order
   c. invoice, signed bottom line, goods, payment, purchase order
   d. signed bottom line, payment, purchase order, invoice, goods

2. True or False. An extranet is a semi-private network that enables organizations to electronically handle the trading process.

3. Fill in the blank. A(n) _____ is a networked information system used by two or more separate organizations to perform a joint business function.

Answers: 1. a; 2. True; 3. interorganizational system

■ THE TECHNOLOGY OF E-COMMERCE

In its relatively brief history, e-commerce has been through several distinct generations of growth. These generations, shown in Figure 7.13, represent important shifts in the evolution of e-commerce and its enabling technologies. Note that the increasing heights of the bars in Figure 7.13 represent both the growing number of users and increased technology capability. Also, notice how the time frames listed on the bottom of the figure overlap somewhat. That's because we can only approximate the dates when each stage began. Similarly, we can also only estimate the end of each stage; that is, the point at which most Web users adopted the technologies of that generation and began to move on to the next stage.

First-Generation E-Commerce Technologies: Establishing a Web Presence

In the first generation of e-commerce, the available technologies delivered static content through a Web presence. **Static content** refers to fixed information, such as company information, online marketing, and electronic versions of company brochures. A *Web presence* means the business has

---

11. *www.eprocurementscotland.com/default.asp?page=1*
12. *www.bcbid.gov.bc.ca/open.dll/welcome*

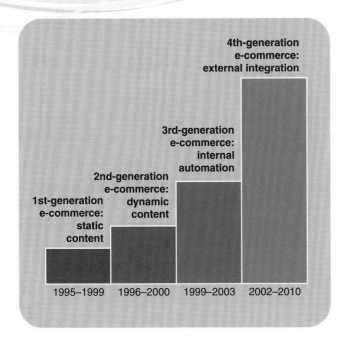

FIGURE 7.13 Generations of e-commerce.

established its existence on the World Wide Web by creating a set of pages that users can access. Very simple technologies are required to create a website with static content only. These standard web technologies include client server networks, web browsers, HTTP protocol, and HTML. These are basic technologies and were discussed in detail in Chapter 2, Technology Essentials. Businesses that use only these technologies for their websites are limited to providing static content, but these technologies also represent a low-cost and relatively easy way for new businesses to begin e-commerce transactions.

A term often used to refer to sites with only static content is *brochureware*—a direct reflection of how today's consumers negatively view this low level of sophistication in any organization's website. However, as companies race to improve their respective website capabilities, it is interesting to note that some companies have recently downgraded from more sophisticated e-commerce sites and are reverting to more information-intensive applications. For instance, in early 2009, Canadian Tire stopped selling merchandise on its website, indicating that the website did not make enough money to justify its expense. They felt that the site was being used primarily for research purposes prior to a consumer visiting a retail location.[13] Canadian Tire didn't downgrade quite as far as a first-generation e-commerce site, since their site contains many interesting features including "do-it-yourself" tutorials and additional product suggestions when a product is selected. Yet in late 2011, they revised this position somewhat with the announcement that they were re-launching their website to sell only tires online, an industry that is worth between $2.5–3 billion of annual sales. This move is both on-strategy due to the company's shift back to its automotive roots, as well as a response to competitive pressure from European e-tailers and start-up His Tires and Co.[14]

Similarly, we have the example of HMV—a global music retailer in the United States, United Kingdom, and Canada. It has had difficulty competing with online music downloading as the retail music industry suffered disintermediation. The obvious strategic reaction seemed to be a change in their website to provide music downloading capability, to sell digital music players and gear, and so on. Not quite so easy. The dominance of online music seller iTunes makes for fierce competition, and

13. *www.financialpost.com/story.html?id=1195152*
14. "Canadian Tire Rolls out Online Tire Business," *The Globe and Mail*, September 20, 2011.

recently, HMV has reverted to a more socially oriented "music lovers" website designed to entice frequent shoppers, hobbyists, and music lovers and supporters to patronize HMV stores. Again, an interesting set of changes that may or may not work but which speak to the difficulty of a one-size-fits-all rule in today's rapidly changing online world.

While the first generation of e-commerce technology represented a significant advance in sharing information, it was the ability to exchange dynamic information that allowed e-commerce to really take off. Let's turn next to the second-generation e-commerce technologies that made new capabilities possible.

Second-Generation E-Commerce Technologies: Providing Interaction

At some point in the mid-1990s, newer technologies allowed for the delivery of dynamic content, moving us into the second generation of e-commerce. With **dynamic content**, information on a web page can change depending on a number of factors. For example, the time or date, user profile, or browser location might trigger web page changes. In addition, other capabilities became available, such as delivery tracking and personalization of content to match user preferences.

Dynamics and interaction occur based on input data and programming instructions. To create dynamic content, the following needs to occur: obtain input data, pass data to the server, hold data in memory, and execute programming instructions to process the data. Input data can come from several sources:

- the header in the HTTP request contains data about the client requesting the page
- the server system clock
- client data from a *cookie* along with the request. A **cookie** is a small bit of data, usually created by programs running on the server, stored on the client machine, and passed back and forth in the HTTP request and response. With a cookie, the server can store one or more data items on the client that it may need for subsequent requests.
- user input in an HTML form. You have probably come across a web page that asked you to enter data. The components of a page that allow you to enter input are called HTML *form controls*. Figure 7.14 shows some common form controls. HTML forms are the primary means by which a business can get the data it needs for online transactions. For example, think about the type of information you may have input when ordering items online, such as your name, address, and credit card information. Because this information is critical to successful e-commerce transactions, a business will carefully select the form controls with two major goals in mind. First, the form components must fit the data needs of the transaction. Second, a business selects the form components for ease of use and to minimize the chance of incorrect data entry.

Storing Data on the Client Side With second-generation e-commerce, once data are received, they can be stored. This overcomes the issue of first-generation HTTP protocol being stateless and connectionless, meaning that every request is independent of any other so that a server could not recognize that a previous client was making another request. Now that a cookie can be stored on the client side, data can be retrieved that identify the client and the application can then respond specifically to that client. Of course, you are used to "signing up" for this type of function already. This action is exactly what happens when you click on a "remember me" box or, if you are using Internet Explorer, you might see a box asking if you'd like Internet Explorer to remember your password. When you agree or click the box, this creates a cookie that is stored on your PC.

By allowing a cookie to store data on the client side, the cookie data can remain until the user returns to the website. When data remain available for a period of time, it is known as *persistent data*. Persistent data allow Web applications to benefit both users and the businesses that run the sites. Because the main use of the cookie is to identify the user, this allows websites to provide *personalization*, an advantage of e-commerce that we discussed earlier in this chapter. Businesses also often use cookies to keep up with

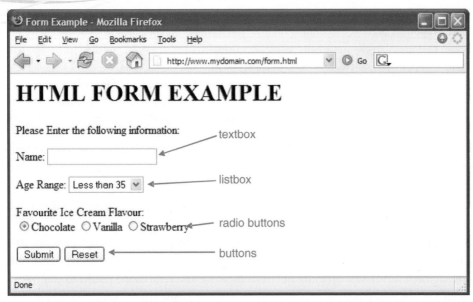

FIGURE 7.14 HTML forms, such as the one shown here, are the primary means by which a business can get the data it needs for online transactions.

data, such as a shopping cart of products that customers want to buy or a customer's wish list. A database is an essential component for any interactive e-commerce site. Databases provide another means of maintaining the state of client interaction with the server and storing persistent data on the server side.

The advent of this capability also began to give rise to the first substantial tests of privacy on the Internet. In most jurisdictions, there are specific privacy measures in place to restrict the collection of personal information and storing or using it for anything other than a single purpose and single transaction. However, with cookies and other data tracking technologies, websites could now make it easier and more convenient for users by storing ("remembering") who they were and maintaining data about them for future use. Government and privacy advocates continue to insist on scrutinizing these types of practices, and publicly promote the dangers of having too much personal information stored outside of your knowledge and control. However, consumers have clearly embraced a "post-private" world in which they seem to prefer convenience over their statutory privacy rights. They often give permission for the site to retain the data and merrily continue browsing, not quite sure of where that data might end up, but sharing it nonetheless.

So where is all this data stored and how is it manipulated? For interaction, a computer needs to execute programming instructions. The server, the client, or both may execute instructions. Let's take a look at the primary technologies used for executing program instructions with Web applications.

Making the Client Side Dynamic and Interactive On the client side of a Web application, the browser generally executes instructions by using a scripting language, downloadable code components, or a plug-in. A **scripting language** is a high-level computer language that another program—in this case the browser—interprets when executed. Businesses often use client-side scripting for data validation to ensure that user information is in the correct form before sending it to the server. The most common client-side scripting language is JavaScript. Scripts are primarily used for simple processing tasks such as enabling those annoying popup windows you likely block. For more complex tasks, a browser relies on specialized components designed to interact with the user and perform advanced instructions, such as ActiveX, Java applets, and plug-ins:

- *ActiveX* is a set of technologies that Microsoft designed to support the sharing of information among different applications. The ActiveX technology allows you to link data from one document to another. For example, a marketing report created using a word processor might link to a chart in a spreadsheet. Businesses generally use ActiveX controls in their e-commerce applications for more complex actions. Depending on how you have set up your browser, you may have blocked sites that use ActiveX. Some believe that sites using ActiveX are vulnerable to viruses and malware and that any users who access those sites may be infected.

- A *java applet* is a small independent Java program that is typically used for online games.
- You undoubtedly have several *plug-ins* installed on your PC right now. Do you use Adobe to view documents? That is a plug-in. What about the Google toolbar or a media player? All plug-ins.

Most businesses use server-side programming to deliver truly dynamic content. **Server-side programming** is just what it sounds like—programs that run on the server in response to browser requests. Server-side programming is more powerful and can therefore do much more than client-side scripting. It also allows the owners to retain control over their programs so that they can better manage their websites.

Almost every major e-commerce site uses server-side programming. When a site requires you to log in, a program on the server checks that you are a registered user. When you type keywords into a search engine, a server-side program queries a database and returns the results to you. When you shop at an e-tailer, server-side programs display the products and handle your transactions.

A short listing of some things that server-side programming can do should convince you why it is important for e-commerce applications. With server-side programming, a business can:

- deliver content that it customizes for the individual user
- dynamically modify content for any page
- access data stored in a server-side database and send it to the client's browser
- take action on queries and data sent from HTML forms
- provide access control and security for a website
- optimally manage the traffic to the site

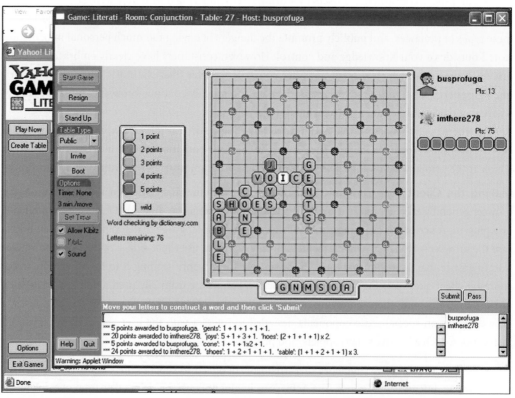

Due to their small size, applets are ideal for applications like online interactive games.

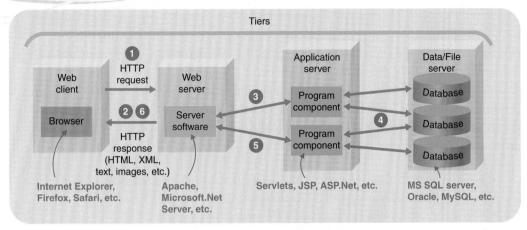

FIGURE 7.15 A four-tier e-commerce infrastructure; depending on its capabilities, any e-commerce application that you build or use might consist of one or more of the Web, application, and data tiers.

When we discuss second-generation e-commerce technologies, we often refer to it being implemented in a tier system. Figure 7.15 and the explanations below it illustrate how a typical transaction would travel through a four-tier e-commerce system.

1. By entering a URL, clicking a button, or any of several other ways, you send an HTTP request to a *Web server*.
2. The Web server receives the requests and determines how to generate a response. If the request is for a static HTML file, the server simply retrieves the file and sends it back as part of the response to the client's browser.
3. If the request requires a dynamic response, the Web server acts as a controller that routes messages and data between the client and the *application server*.
4. When needed, applications contact the *data server* to perform queries on the databases that it controls. The application uses the data to perform its tasks.
5. The results of an executed application are formulated into a browser-compatible web page that combines the output of the application with the appropriate HTML tags.
6. The Web server includes the dynamically-generated page in an HTTP response and then sends the result to the browser.

Third-Generation E-Commerce Technologies: Supporting Transactions

As the power of the World Wide Web became clear to businesses, demand for new technologies grew. Consumers liked using the Web, and organizations moved to respond. The third generation of e-commerce saw demand for technologies that would extend to support real-time, online transactions. Companies began to automate both internal and external business processes. Automated transactions enabled advanced capabilities on the Web, such as data mining and the delivery of instant status information through portals (FedEx and Canada Post now do this with full-cycle individual-item tracking systems). Companies sprung up around the globe with new business models that took advantage of enhanced technology and network capabilities, often challenging well-known incumbent firms to catch up and move more quickly into the e-commerce age.

Early in the evolution of e-commerce, businesses recognized that they must contend with several important aspects of commercial transactions for e-commerce to work. An essential element of commerce is paying for goods and services received. That meant prospective online customers must have a way to order and pay online and feel secure in doing so.

Order and Payment Systems and E-commerce System Security An e-commerce site needs to include components for processing orders and accepting payments. The four primary components of a typical e-commerce site are: (1) the shopping and ordering system, (2) the merchant account, (3) the payment gateway, and (4) the security system.

Many e-commerce firms manage the shopping and ordering processes on their own servers or privately leased servers. The main tasks are to track the products that the user selects to purchase during browsing of the site, and then to record the order for those products so that the firm can gather and ship them to the user. A site may use several methods to do this, such as:

- a non-secure HTML order form, with the results sent to the firm's email address
- a secure HTML order form, with the results sent to the firm's email address
- a "shopping cart" system that tracks customer orders using a database
- a shopping cart service provided by a third party

Possibly the best and most popular choices are to use a secure HTML order form or an in-house shopping cart system. The secure HTML order form is simpler to use and is a viable choice if users typically order a small number of items. Firms use shopping carts for more complex sites with lots of shopping options. This makes the users' shopping experience easier by allowing them to continue their browsing after selecting each product and then checking out only once.

Concerning the payment process, firms again have several options. In fact, many sites offer more than one of these options. Businesses can allow payment in more traditional ways, such as billing for payment by cheque or by manually processing credit card information. This is known as *deferred payment*. Smaller sites with limited infrastructure can also use third-party merchant accounts, like those provided by PayPal, CCBill, or Click Bank. These sites process payments between the customer and merchant for a transaction fee. While this can be a good solution for those with limited site capabilities, the fee can eat into profits. However, consumers love services like PayPal. Originally designed by a group of entrepreneurs who worked together at eBay, and later purchased by them, PayPal essentially created a form of online currency that made a series of smaller consumer transactions possible and convenient by aggregating them through one account that is settled automatically. Especially popular with eBay and other trading site users, PayPal has now become an essential part of online commerce.

For large sites, the preferred method for processing payments is to use real-time credit or debit card authorization that they process themselves. This eliminates a "middle man" and improves margins on sales. However, it also makes the sites responsible for all of the issues (security, privacy, etc.) that come with accepting payment information directly into their own systems. With real-time processing of credit cards, the merchant handles the payment almost immediately. The merchant then simply needs to ship the goods. This type of payment system, however, requires the merchant to set up a merchant account and to establish a connection to a payment gateway. The same or a similar system is used for debit card payments.

A *merchant account* is basically a bank account that allows merchants to receive the proceeds of credit card purchases. After establishing a merchant account, the acquiring bank agrees to pay the merchant for all valid credit card purchases in exchange for the right to collect the debt owed by the consumer. A **secure gateway provider** is a company that provides a network to process encrypted transactions from a merchant's website. It then passes the transactions on to the issuing banks of the customers' credit cards for approval. Some of the most popular gateway providers include Verisign, Symantec, and *Authorize.net*.

A secure gateway provider will generally offer a payment gateway and a processor. A *payment gateway* links an e-commerce site with the banking network. The processor handles the financial data submitted by the shopping cart application by accepting the data from the shopping cart, properly

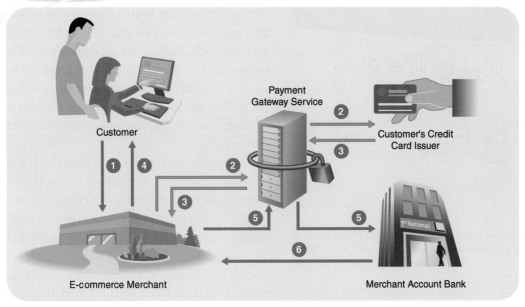

FIGURE 7.16 A payment gateway links an e-commerce site with the banking network.

formatting it, and entering it into the banking network. It is then handled just like any other credit card transaction. Figure 7.16 shows the steps involved in this payment system.

1. The customer places an order with the merchant through the e-commerce site.
2. The payment gateway provider detects the placement of an order. The provider securely encrypts the transaction data (discussed below) and passes an authorization request to the bank to verify the customer's credit card account and available funds.
3. The gateway provider returns a response, indicating whether or not the transaction is authorized, to the e-commerce merchant. This process typically takes less than three seconds.
4. Upon approval, the e-commerce merchant notifies the user and fulfills the customer's order.
5. The gateway provider sends a settlement request to the merchant account's bank.
6. The merchant account's bank deposits the transaction funds into the e-commerce merchant's account.

The order and payment systems must be secure to protect both the customer and the merchant. In 2009, half of all Canadians reported that they were very concerned about online credit card use.[15] While this trends down with the more Internet experience a user has, it is still a concern that must be addressed. Have you ever been on an e-commerce site that did not make you feel comfortable about making a purchase? What made you uncomfortable or suspicious?

Most e-commerce security technologies relate to the **secure socket layer (SSL)** protocol. SSL, developed by Netscape and RSA Data Security Inc., allows a client and a server to communicate in a way that prevents eavesdropping, message forgery, or tampering. A server that encrypts data using the SSL protocol is known as a *secure server*. How do you know if you are connected to a secure server? You just need to look at the URL. The URL of a secure server starts with HTTPS in place of the usual HTTP. You may also see a closed lock icon in the lower corner of your browser. A website can signal that it uses SSL to encrypt data by purchasing an *SSL site certificate*. The site can own the SSL certificate itself, or a hosting service can provide it. When you connect to a secure server, the server will first identify itself to your browser using the SSL certificate. The SSL certificate works to verify the identity of the secure server, much like your driver's licence can be used to identify you (except the SSL certificate is much

15. *www.statcan.gc.ca/daily-quotidien/100927/dq100927a-eng.htm*, September 2010.

Secure servers often have a small lock either in the address bar or in the lower corner of your browser, and they always start with HTTPS.

more difficult to fake). When a customer connects to a secure server, the server and the browser use SSL to provide each other with the information needed to encrypt the data. SSL is currently being replaced by a newer protocol called the *transport layer security (TLS)*. TLS and SSL cannot work together, but a message sent with TLS can be handled by a client that uses SSL.

Microsoft, Netscape, Visa, MasterCard, and others also endorse another security standard called the *secure electronic transaction (SET)* protocol. SET combines several security standards to provide a system that can ensure private and secure transactions.

Finally, we should also mention the importance of cookies to payment and security technologies. Previously, we discussed how businesses use cookies to track activities on the Web. However, the payment and security systems that we have reviewed in this section may not work without cookies. For instance, these systems often use cookies to authenticate users or to hold data to match users with their shopping cart. In this case, businesses and consumers must consider the trade-off between convenience and security.

Fourth-Generation E-Commerce Technologies: Transforming Processes

We are currently in the midst of the fourth generation of e-commerce, characterized by increasing integration of all enterprise systems with external customers, partners, and suppliers all linked over the World Wide Web. The Web itself is undergoing a transformation, from enabling transactions between humans and Web applications to allowing transactions between two Web applications. In fact, fourth-generation e-commerce technologies are moving to the realm where computers at one business automatically interact with computers at another business. These newer technologies are improving the ability to exchange small amounts of data via the Web and to standardize the support of transactions. We will look at the primary fourth-generation e-commerce technologies of XML and Web services here, which are quickly becoming web standards.

The **eXtensible markup language (XML)** organizes data based on meaning rather than how the data should appear. HTML's goal is to describe how to display data. As such, XML complements HTML, and the two are often used together. XML has become a major component in a set of technologies that are helping to make the Web even more interactive. By combining XML with JavaScript and dynamic HTML and HTTP protocols, a technology called *AJAX* allows web pages to respond more quickly to user actions. With AJAX, much of the processing related to user actions happens on the client side rather than sending a request to the server and having the user wait for the server's response. Instead, requests for only a small amount of XML formatted data are made when needed and then used to adjust the web page interface. This speeds up overall interaction for the user because an AJAX engine on the client side can handle any action that doesn't require a request from the server, like simple data validation. These cutting-edge uses of JavaScript and XML provide a much richer user experience.

A **Web service** is a standardized way for one computer program to request and run another computer program over the Internet. The two applications may reside on different computers that are connected in some way, for instance by a LAN, or more commonly by the Internet. The most popular and most discussed Web services are self-contained business functions that operate over the Internet.

A Web service is a platform-independent software component that can be:

- described using a standard description language
- published to a public registry of services
- discovered using a standard method
- requested through an application program interface (API)
- combined with other services and procedures to compose an application

Web services are important because they enable different systems to interact more easily than before, meaning that partners can more efficiently and quickly link and share data. Web services give companies the ability to do more e-commerce business, with more potential business partners, and in different ways than before, at a reasonable cost. There's no doubt that Web services are valuable for e-commerce. First, a Web service is like a spare part that can be incorporated into any program that has access. Once written and made available, developers can simply request a Web service as needed. This saves time. Second, Web services provide a way for two computers to automatically pass data between each other. This saves more time. These two advantages are so important that many organizations are setting up an infrastructure known as **service-oriented architecture (SOA)** to support full-scale use of Web services.

Web services continue to gain in use and popularity as they create value for companies. For example, *Amazon.ca* and Google both provide Web services that others can use to access their huge databases. One recent trend is to cobble together Web services from various sources to make an application known as a mashup. A *mashup* is a Web application that seamlessly combines information from more than one source into an integrated experience. Mashups are not only creating new services for existing companies, but also entirely new companies. For example, *www.orderit.ca* is a current online offering that allows users to browse the menus of local restaurants, based on their current location, and order through the site for delivery—even if the restaurant doesn't offer delivery itself. It makes additional money through the delivery of this food at a premium for the convenience.

Quick Test

1. Which of the following is a small data file that can be used to store data on the client's computer?
   a. ActiveX
   b. cookie
   c. crumpet
   d. plug-in

2. Which of the following is a company that provides a network to process encrypted transactions from a merchant's website?
   a. merchant account gateway
   b. payment processor server
   c. secure gateway provider
   d. shopping cart system

3. Which of the following is true regarding XML?
   a. XML tags define the look and feel of a web page as it is displayed in a browser.
   b. XML is platform-independent and can be used by many different applications.
   c. All devices using XML must use primary XML with no new tags defined.
   d. XML is only used for database query data.

What's in IT for me?

Have you ever thought of opening your own e-business? Perhaps an e-commerce site? Today, more than ever, opening your own e-business is easy to do as long as you have basic knowledge of how to register a retail business in the province in which you live. Once you have your company name and retail sales tax registrations in hand, you can simply visit *www.ebay.com/stores*, pick your options and—voilà—you're literally in business overnight. Much easier than opening a retail store location and, better still, online you can sell to the world!

If eBay stores is not for you, there are several services available online that will help you create an e-business. Check out *www.estore.com* or *www.zen-cart.com*. Both services have a simple, build-it-yourself interface, along with all of the order and payment processing components you need to run your business.

What's in IT for an organization?

Just as you can save yourself money through group buying with *TeamSave.com* or *Groupon.com*, businesses are also starting to participate in consortiums to buy things that all organizations might need. For instance, many industries are similar vertically, with common suppliers, and are therefore setting up *group purchasing organizations (GPOs)*. These entities are created to leverage the buying power of their member businesses. A good U.S. example of this model can be found at *www.supplychainassociation.org* (Healthcare Supply Chain Association), or the very similar Canadian organization, the St. Joseph's Health System Group Purchasing Organization (*www.sjhcs-gpo.com*). By joining together and integrating their individual supply chains (process and technology) and using B2B e-commerce, they achieve economies of scale and discounts that they could not achieve individually.

What's in **IT** for society

Economists have always talked about the creation of a perfect labour market being a panacea for workers—one where workers and employers could find each other and simply interact directly to let market supply and demand set up their employment arrangements. The theory is that this would enable workers to get the best possible price for their skills and abilities, and align labour rates to value-added activities created in the business. Today, it's much more common for jobs to be sourced through headhunters, agencies, or others with a vested interest in the outcome of the search, and often with an economic incentive to artificially raise or lower the labour rates being negotiated (depending on their business model).

The Internet gets us one step closer to that perfect market concept by making it possible to create online labour markets. One example of this would be *Elance.com*, a site designed specifically to connect professionals with available projects. This site, for example, enables Turkish programmers to bid for Canadian Web development projects, and Canadian programmers to bid for Turkish Web development projects. Elance's website provides running totals of the number of professionals registered on the site and the earnings these professionals have collected. See *www.elance.com/skills_central* for today's total. As of June 2011, this page listed 453,461 professional with earnings of $431,965,359. Clearly they are doing something right!

RO↑ | STUDENT RETURN ON INVESTMENT SUMMARY

1. Define e-commerce and describe how it is a part of today's economy.

E-commerce is the use of information systems, technologies, and computer networks by individuals and organizations to carry out transactions to create or support the creation of business value. With each evolution of the technology behind e-commerce, more and more functionality is created, increasing the capabilities of businesses, customers, and individual users. Almost all sectors of today's economy rely on it: business (B), consumer (C), and government (G). The primary relationships between these sectors result in C2C, C2G, B2C, B2B, and B2G e-commerce.

2. Explain how e-commerce creates value and helps organizations stay competitive.

E-commerce creates value for businesses in a number of ways, including technology, competition, and strategy. For example, the use of technology in e-commerce has resulted in information density, which businesses have responded to through mass customization and personalization. In terms of competition, e-commerce (1) reduces barriers to entry for consumers and new businesses; (2) helps keep any one company from owning the market; (3) provides more opportunities for collaboration and alliances among various stakeholders; (4) increases the number of market niches; and (5) affects the traditional marketplace drivers of time, distance, and price. Finally, e-commerce demands specific strategy, such as CRM, which allows businesses to create a one-to-one marketing experience.

3. Describe the benefits and limitations of e-commerce to both consumers and businesses.

E-commerce provides both advantages and limitations to consumers and businesses; see Table 7.3. To emphasize the advantages, most organizations rely on e-commerce models. However, having a great e-commerce business model will not generate a profit if it is not associated with a website that brings in customers, or at least visitors.

4. Explain how organizations can use e-commerce to enhance the delivery of products and services, manage trade with business partners, and improve their supply chain efficiency.

B2B transactions are usually of two types: (1) spot buying or (2) strategic sourcing. Companies often engage in spot buying to purchase goods and services that are commodities; that is, they are usually uniform in quality and differ only somewhat in price. On the other hand, strategic sourcing involves forming a long-term relationship with another company. Strategic sourcing often relies on a one-to-one business model, although company-centric and exchange models are also used.

In addition, e-commerce can benefit a company's supply chain. A supply chain is a network of facilities and distribution options that performs the functions of procurement of materials, transformation of these materials into intermediate and finished products, and the distribution of these finished products to customers. Traditional supply chains involve a number of paper-based transactions, but e-commerce-based supply chains involve an interorganizational system (IOS). An IOS can help create 24/7 communications between organizations and their suppliers and customers, as well as enable paperless transactions throughout the supply chain. The two most common forms of IOS in use today are based on electronic data interchange (EDI), which uses value-added networks (VANs) or private networks instead of the regular telephone system, and extranets, which are collaborative networks that use Internet technology to link businesses with their suppliers, customers, or other businesses that share common goals.

5. Describe the evolution of e-commerce technologies and explain how these technologies have benefited both consumers and businesses.

As e-commerce technologies have moved from being static ("brochureware") to integrated and interactive, businesses have benefited from being able to bring more dynamic online services to consumers, and consumers have benefited from being able to directly replicate more of the offline shopping experience online: virtual store fronts with incredible moving and changing displays; the ability to "try on" items remotely with an avatar that resembles you; and data-rich forms for processing your checkout quickly and flawlessly are all part of the new world of online e-commerce.

KNOWLEDGE SPEAK

business-to-business (B2B)   256
business-to-consumer (B2C)   256
business-to-government (B2G)   256
company-centric business model   276
consumer-to-consumer (C2C)   256
consumer-to-government (C2G)   256
cookie   282
co-operative website   267
disintermediation   255
dynamic content   282
e-commerce   255
e-commerce (or virtual or social) business model   258
e-commerce strategy   268
electronic data interchange (EDI)   278
e-procurement   276
exchange model   276
eXtensible markup language (XML)   288
extranets   278

information density   263
interorganizational system (IOS)   278
mass customization   265
mobile commerce   270
niche markets   268
one-to-one marketing model   275
personalization   265
scripting language   283
secure gateway provider   286
secure socket layer (SSL)   287
server-side programming   284
service-oriented architecture (SOA)   289
spot buying   275
static content   280
strategic sourcing   275
streaming   257
Web service   288

REVIEW QUESTIONS

Multiple-choice questions

1. Which of the following is considered a benefit of B2C e-commerce?
   a. Consumers are uncomfortable about the security of their personal data.
   b. Delivery of the product is delayed and may incur an extra cost.
   c. Distance to markets is shortened.
   d. Micropayment systems are not yet standardized.

2. With _____, many companies use an online market to exchange products or services.
   a. an exchange
   b. a reverse auction
   c. spot buying
   d. strategic sourcing

3. Which of the following technologies can be used to make a website dynamic?
   a. a Java applet
   b. an ActiveX control
   c. server-side programming
   d. all of the above
   e. none of the above

4. Which of the following components of a four-tier client/server e-commerce system will display results of a request in a browser?
   a. application server
   b. data/file server
   c. Web client
   d. Web server

Fill-in-the-blank questions

5. _____ is the use of information systems, technologies, and computer networks by individuals and organizations to carry out transactions to create or support the creation of business value.

6. A _____ is a network of facilities and distribution options that performs the functions of procurement of materials, transformation of these materials into intermediate and finished products, and the distribution of these finished products to customers.

7. The message that contains the web page sent to a client from a server is part of an HTTP _____.

8. A _____ is a small Java program that can be downloaded and executed within a browser window.

True-false questions

9. Using a variety of techniques to make a website both more visible to search engines and more relevant to the way they rank sites to increase the likelihood of appearing higher in the list of any relevant search by consumers is called search engine optimization.

10. Due to the popularity of e-commerce, it is more difficult than ever to create business alliances.

11. Websites collect statistics about what pages visitors access and where visitors exit the website.

12. The majority of websites today provide only static content.

Matching questions

Choose the BEST answer from column B for each item in column A.

Column A	Column B
13. traffic monetizing	a. An e-commerce business model where products are shipped directly from the manufacturer to the consumer.
14. revenue share	b. An e-commerce business model where websites are paid a fee when purchases come through them.
15. infomediary	c. An e-commerce business model where data on consumers and consumption habits are provided.
16. transactional	d. An e-commerce business model that brings together buyers and sellers for a fee.

Short-answer questions

17. Why is it important for an e-commerce company to have a business model?

18. List the tiers that make up the typical four-tier e-commerce infrastructure. What is the purpose of each tier?

Discussion/Essay questions

19. Discuss how e-commerce is changing many aspects of business today for both customers and businesses.

20. Describe the four generations of e-commerce. Provide current examples of sites in each generation.

TEAM ACTIVITY

Find two or three other students in your class who are in, or are interested in, the same major that you are. Think about creating an e-commerce portal/site for your major or your intended major. What information needs to go on the web pages that make up the site? What links are necessary? What about collecting membership dues? Could you also use the site to raise money for the student organization associated with your major? Plan the site on paper first, and then use the activities below to implement it.

SOFTWARE APPLICATION EXERCISES

1. Internet

Research how to build an e-commerce site for your major (see Team Activity assignment above). Look for open source tools that introductory IS students can use (for free) to create and maintain a website. Visit hosting sites to check on hosting plans, and ask your academic department if it is willing to host student sites.

2. Presentation

Create a presentation on how to build and host a major-related e-commerce site (see Internet assignment above). Present your ideas and solutions to your class and/or a professor in your major. Use presentation software to create prototypes of screens that give your audience insight into the look and functionality of your proposed website.

3. Word Processing

A very important aspect of an e-commerce site is the user interface. The designers must make sure that they design the site to convey the right message (e.g., that supports the business strategy). Several design factors are important to consider for any website. For example, the content must be appropriate to communicate your message to the users and to hold their attention. In addition, the overall site must be organized so that the users can easily understand how to use it (as well as navigate it). You can use most word processors to create quick web pages. Use a word processor to create mock-ups of how your pages will look on your website (see Internet assignment above).

4. Spreadsheet

E-commerce sites cost money, whether you host them at school or offsite. Prepare a budget with projected costs, including an assessment of labour costs (e.g., your hourly rate—research these rates for a realistic cost). Include charts from your financial estimates for the Presentation assignment above. If you decided to deploy this type of website across your entire school (organization), how would the costs increase? Would there be any economies of scale?

5. Database

Research open-source databases, and design and create a database that will support the membership and e-commerce components of your website (see Internet assignment above). You may also use a commercial DBMS like MS Access if this fits better with your school's IT architecture.

6. Advanced Challenge

Think about some of the stakeholders mentioned in the preceding Internet assignment (e.g., fellow students and faculty in your major). Once you have their support, consider what other stakeholders might influence your ability to effectively implement your website. Assume that all stakeholders have approved your e-commerce site. Use an iterative development approach to create the site and test its functionality. Find a suitable hosting site (verify faculty approval to implement) and "go live."

ONLINE RESOURCES

Companion Website

- Take interactive practice quizzes to assess your knowledge and help you study in a dynamic way.
- Review PowerPoint lecture slides.
- Get help and sample solutions to end-of-chapter software application exercises.

Additional Resources Available Only on *WileyPLUS*

- Take the interactive Quick Test to check your understanding of the chapter material and get immediate feedback on your responses.
- Review and study with downloadable Audio Lecture MP3 files.
- Check your understanding of the key vocabulary in the chapter with Knowledge Speak Interactive Flash Cards.

CASE STUDY:
USING B2B E-COMMERCE AT BOEING

Assume that you are the spare parts manager for an airline operating a fleet of Boeing 737s in Asia, and you need to order spare parts in a hurry. At one time, this process would have involved digging through the Boeing parts manual, finding the correct part numbers, and then calling, faxing, or telexing your order to the company parts warehouse in Seattle. Upon receipt of your order, Boeing would then send you a number of automatic faxes or telexes to acknowledge the order and let you know its status. And this assumes that you have updated your maintenance manual with the continual revisions sent by Boeing—a process that usually took 60 to 90 days.

Sound like a big job? It was! However, today, with Boeing's *MyBoeingFleet.com*, customers and suppliers have a portal to Boeing's Web-enabled, B2B extranet. This site, and the functions it offers, makes the parts-ordering process much less painful for companies operating Boeing aircraft. The password-protected website is open to airplane owners and operators, as well as maintenance, repair, and overhaul shops—basically anybody who needs products or information for their Boeing airplanes. While it is not open to the general public, you can read a product overview brochure at *www.boeing.com/commercial/aviationservices/myboeingfleet/* for more details about the site's functionality.

In mid-2005, 30,000 industry professionals from 550 companies had access to the extranet site, with more than 4,000 logins per day and 4 million hits per month. In addition to ordering parts from *MyBoeingFleet.com*, customers can access engineering diagrams, up-to-date maintenance and flight manuals, service bulletins, and other pertinent information.

The PART Page

A key part of Boeing's global B2B e-commerce effort is the sale of spare parts for the more than 7,000 Boeing aircraft in operation. These parts are handled out of spare-parts centres in eight cities, with the largest such centre being located near the Seattle-Tacoma airport. This centre contains over $1 billion (U.S.) in spare parts stored in a building covering over 6 hectares! In 2004, the centre shipped an average of 3,000 orders each day. These orders contained almost 300,000 different parts and weighed 3 million kg. The centre handled all of these orders using an automated conveyor delivery system more than 3 kilometres long.

To handle this huge spare-parts e-commerce operation, Boeing created a special element for the overall *MyBoeingFleet.com* website. Termed the PART page, this site allows customers to order spare parts on a 24/7 basis and provides tracking information on the orders. Customers can work with the latest information without having to deal with reams of paper updates. This site currently lists more than 6.5 million types of spare parts and handles an average of 130,000 transactions per week. This online supply chain management process is a win–win process for both Boeing and its customers: Boeing dramatically reduces staff required to handle telephone calls, faxes, and telexes, while customers save hundreds of thousands of dollars each year in paper and distribution costs. For example, a customer can now access information equivalent to 80,000 pages of text—a stack of paper 7.5 m high, weighing 360 kg!

Spare Parts Economics

Why does Boeing concentrate on the spare-parts business as the keystone of its e-commerce system? There are actually several answers to this question. First, it simply is not possible to sell multimillion dollar airliners over the Web. Second, Boeing makes a great deal of money from its maintenance program. In fact, aircraft maintenance is a much higher-margin business than selling the original aircraft. While Boeing has a 9 percent margin building planes, it has a 20 percent margin servicing them. Finally, even if Boeing stopped building aircraft tomorrow, it would still have a very profitable aircraft maintenance business for many years into the future. Finding ways to more efficiently handle this business, through e-commerce, is just smart.

Case Questions

1. What aspects of the website *MyBoeingFleet.com* qualify it as an extranet?
2. How does this website help enable the Boeing supply chain to assist operators of aircraft built by Boeing?
3. Why is the PART page referred to as the key e-commerce element of the *MyBoeingFleet.com* website? Do you agree with the economic analysis for concentrating on spare parts? Why or why not?

SOURCES: James Wallace, "Aerospace Notebook: Boeing's Got Parts—15 Whole Acres of Them," *Seattle Post-Intelligencer*, March 2, 2005. Elizabeth Davis, "Portal Power: E-business at Boeing Gaining Velocity," *www.boeing.com/commercial/news/feature/ebiz.html*. Fred Vogelstein, "Flying on the Web in a Turbulent Economy," *Fortune*, April 30, 2001.

CASE STUDY:
KNITTING FOR DUMMIES

Your mother is aware that you are studying business and heard you were taking an IT class. Suddenly, she thinks you are an expert and has been calling you for advice about her small business—Knitting for Dummies—which sells knitting patterns and detailed instructions, including pictures of what each step should look like, to those trying to learn how to knit. Despite your DNA, you have absolutely no interest in knitting and can't imagine anyone wanting to buy any of this stuff; but you also realize the profits from this are helping to pay for your university education . . . so, you try to help her as much as you can.

Today's call was about enabling her existing website to take online orders. She lives in Montreal and sells her products by mail across Canada and occasionally to other mostly-English-speaking countries, like the United States, the United Kingdom, and Australia. The mail order business is declining and your mother recently went to her bank to enquire about taking credit cards online. They were not very encouraging and she is frustrated. Surely there must be a way for her to take online payments that is simple, fast, and easy to integrate onto her website?

You decide to start by verifying the challenges of taking credit cards directly. You research the online offerings of the major Canadian chartered banks and discover that almost all of them make it easy to process credit cards if you have a physical location (like an office, store, or restaurant, for instance), but are not very welcoming of online transaction processing. In fact, their silence is deafening. You conclude, as your mother already has, that this will be a difficult thing for a small business to accomplish and would probably take too much time and effort to make it worthwhile.

Instead, you suggest PayPal as an option—something with which you are already personally familiar. Your mother disclaims any knowledge of this type of payment system and asks you many questions that you can't answer: What's involved? Where are these payments accepted? Are there any other companies like this in business elsewhere? How should she start? What is required to make sure she gets her money? You realize that this is not going to be as simple as you thought. You hang up, her telling her that you will get back to her shortly with more information. What do you do now? You know your mother can't do this alone and you want to help, but it will require that you guide her through this process in its entirety . . . so you get to work. You decide to start at *www.paypal.com*. There must be something there that will help you get started!

Case Task

1. Make notes as you research how PayPal works. Describe what you plan to share with your mother in your next phone call about online payment processing options and how you will help make this happen for her.

8 | WEB 2.0, SOCIAL MEDIA, AND ONLINE TRENDS

WHAT WE WILL COVER

- Defining Social Technologies and Utility
- User-Generated Content
- Creating Business Utility Using Social Media Tools and E-marketing
- The Social and Business Impacts of Web 2.0

STUDENT RETURN ON INVESTMENT RO↑

Through your investment of time in reading and thinking about this chapter, your return—or created value—is gaining knowledge. After reading this chapter, you should be able to

1. Define Web 2.0 and describe what features can make a social website more successful.

2. Explain social utility and how it is leveraged to encourage user-generated content.

3. Explain the benefits businesses can obtain by harnessing the power of social media.

4. Describe how social media has changed the way people consume media and how this has affected social business models.

THE VOICE OF EXPERIENCE

John Lennie, Ryerson University

John Lennie graduated from Ryerson University in 1987 with a Bachelor of Business Management. John previously worked in banking and product management in non-technology roles, but now works with technology companies to help develop technological products. He is a strategic and active investor in a variety of e-commerce and social media-related ventures.

What do you do in your current position? I invest in new technology product development as a strategic—not passive—investor. I work with company management and provide advice on the operations of technology-focused companies. I also help develop and manage sales and service channels for technology-based products. I directly contribute to a company's success by accessing new and expanded markets for its products.

What do you consider to be important career skills? You need to be a realist in business. For example, when planning development time or sales cycles, people with less experience underestimate the time it takes to bring a product to market and the time it takes to close deals in the sales funnel. Being realistic helps to build trust and build a reputation for being trustworthy, which in turn results in market loyalty. When it comes to product development, it is always best to under-promise and over-deliver whenever that's possible.

How do you use IT? IT permeates every aspect of business and I use it to get a full, 360-degree view of customers and prospects. IT is the cornerstone of all of our products, which I use on a daily basis. I've developed our own software platforms for sales, service, etc. There are some technologies that drive engagement, and we've pulled those out and developed products around them. One example of this is the creation of a social media-based group buying site for guys—a place where they engage, create, and comment on content and also engage in e-commerce. These

kinds of models didn't even exist a year ago, and now they're booming!

Can you describe an example of how you have used IT to improve business operations? These days I don't really get involved in projects at that level. But early in my career I worked on the marketing team that launched Lottario, an Ontario lottery product. We were the first to use computers to create and sell lottery tickets. I understood the IT capability even though I'm not a programmer. Now I'm trying to help businesses understand the value of social networking tools. Although it might make sense to dissuade staff from using social networking tools while at work, they can actually help businesses and their use should be encouraged, I think. And if you can engage employees at work, you'll reduce staff turnover and absenteeism. Social networking tools can improve productivity when used properly. The problem with these tools, though, is that not many people know how to use them effectively. Many companies just try to use all of them in the hope that something will stick. Others ban their use entirely. Neither of these methods is the answer. Skills in social media utility are skills that businesses need to develop.

Have you got any on-the-job advice for students seeking a career in IT or business? Get to know as much as you possibly can, including business processes. That knowledge will enable you to provide more value to the business and inform strategic work. Try to "get into the weeds" of an organization. Find out about sales, operations, finance, etc. The more you learn, the more you know, and the better you'll do.

In this chapter we discuss Web 2.0, social media, and online trends. The companies that John works with are all involved in these areas, creating, implementing, and selling new technologies that are becoming more commonplace every day.

How often have you heard the term "Web 2.0" and wondered what exactly it meant? Or even how someone decided we had suddenly left the world of Web 1.0 and why we are already talking about the "semantic web," now known as Web 3.0? These are critical terms and concepts with which you will need to become very familiar in your future business pursuits.

And you would not be the only one to feel a bit confused when imagining how to apply these rapidly-evolving social tools to organizational settings. Some talk about these trends in technology terms, particularly about multi-media capabilities; for others, it is more about the user experience and higher levels of engagement with web content that comes with the social web model. Some see this as revolutionary, but most simply regard it as an evolution and extension of our existing global reliance on web-based technologies generally. We believe that the technologies simply mirror underlying social and psychological behaviours that human beings generally embrace and demonstrate. It is important to keep this in mind as we explore social media in an organizational setting.

Going back into recent history, the term Web 2.0 was first coined by Tim O'Reilly (founder of O'Reilly Media[1]) and used publicly at a trade conference in 2004. Through common usage more than anything else, **Web 2.0** has come to represent what most people refer to as the interactive web—that is, moving from a passive site that basically displays information to a site that permits interaction with visitors or users and encourages them to become involved in content creation and sharing (see Figure 8.1). Socially-enabled sites often look and feel more interactive and are supported by significant multimedia capability. They are often enhanced by audio and video tools focused on various forms of **user-generated content (UGC)**, such as blogs and conversation threads. The ability for an Internet site to become a two-way communication tool also significantly enhances its ability to promote a sense of online community, an important part of social media's advantage over the traditional static web. Therefore, the term is often associated with websites that expect higher levels of user engagement and involvement, designed to evoke and promote self-expression. The **semantic web** is a next-generation—but not entirely separate—web that makes information sharing and exchange easier by focusing on content, searchability, and interpretability at a technical level. You might even hear this called Web 3.0. These technology evolutions will continue to drive new possibilities in the future for even more amazing content-rich, information-sharing applications.

FIGURE 8.1 The term Web 2.0 can mean many different things to different people. What different site types can you find above?

---

1. *http://oreilly.com/*

Obviously this trend has significant implications for businesses because it changes the way consumers use the Web. More particularly, any trend that has a significant social impact will also have a collateral business impact and, in this case, it will generally increase expectations among users that your organization's website will offer these social features and functions. In this chapter we will explore the intersection of the changing social trends on the Web, and their implications for society and businesses alike.

TECHNOLOGY CORE

Without the advances in technology that took us from Web 1.0 to 2.0, many of the social media websites we are so accustomed to today would not exist. The following list highlights a few of these important technologies.

- **Adobe Flash** – Nearly every browser comes with Adobe Flash. It allows interactivity, animation, and streaming of audio and video. Without Adobe Flash, you would not be able to view your favourite YouTube video or play online games. To avoid the time delays of downloading, many sites embed a Flash video player and you simply click the play button and the content streams directly and quickly to your desktop—instant video-enabling! During the summer of 2011, however, Apple announced that it will not support Adobe Flash in iOS mobile devices anymore. This move will greatly decrease Flash usage, leading some to believe that Flash will soon be replaced in desktop browsers as well. In the fall of 2011, Adobe announced that they will be using HTML5 programming language for mobile.
- **HTML5** – Hypertext mark-up language is the industry standard for developing websites. Version 1 was released in 1990, and there have been a steady stream of improvements since. The current version, HTML4, is now under revision and slated for release in early 2012. HTML5 will focus on incorporating more multimedia and real-time graphics capability (particularly scalable vector graphics, SVG), adding new standard elements and attributes, and improving the existing capabilities of HTML to keep pace with the data and graphic-rich environments in which websites and mobile sites are developed today.
- **Javascript** – Simply put, Javascript is the communicator between your computer and the Internet. This program runs locally on your computer and allows you to quickly open windows, menus, and toolbars. It also draws the user's attention to graphical interfaces on mouse-overs, for example. Without Javascript, you would be pressing enter to view a friend's photos on Facebook, and be waiting and waiting and waiting for it to load.
- **API** – In the Web 2.0 world, there is an Application Protocol Interface (API) for everything. Through the use of APIs, developers are able to access established programs and use their functionality. For example, several sites use the Google map API to automatically show locations of stores, bars, restaurants, and much more. As a further example, the Intel Museum of Me uses the Facebook API to aggregate users' data and compile it into a personal museum showcasing their life. Don't forget that the cool iPhone applications we all seem to love would be impossible without iPhone APIs.

These are just a few of the technologies that make social media happen.

■ DEFINING SOCIAL TECHNOLOGIES AND UTILITY

Technologies that find their centre in the psycho-social fundamentals of human interaction truly constitute social media technologies. For instance, if you think about blogging, the technology is quite simple: a platform gives users the ability to post a story and gives readers the ability to respond with comments in time-stamped threads. Nothing about this is purely "technology-driven" in the traditional sense. Our need to self-express—and perhaps to be opinionated—is a fundamental characteristic of most individuals and our society. We love to talk about how we think and feel about things! So, blogging really only involves a re-deployment of existing technological capability (threaded conversation) into a more usable and specific form that supports our desire to self-express. In other words, social technologies are simply *purpose-built collections of existing capabilities and tools*, in most cases bundling together a combination of existing and occasionally some new online concepts to create a novel technology-enabled online experience paralleling off-line socializing.

Given all of that, it may be helpful to have a taxonomy about what types of sites actually constitute "social media" and where we see the social web trending to in terms of popularity of applications. Table 8.1 briefly outlines some common categories.

Table 8.1	Common Categories of Social Media
Site Type	**Current Examples**
Blogs: • allow people to author stories and share opinions • frequently implemented by companies looking to increase transparency by sharing relevant insight into company or industry trends and operations	Blogger; Wordpress; Blogspot; Tumblr
Wikis: • foster knowledge sharing • large organizations often implement Wikis to create a fluid set of principles or practices for everyone to see	Wikipedia; Wikileaks
Social Bookmarking: • allows users to save and share web pages, images, or rich media to a globally accessible website • helps users discover relevant and interesting media pertaining to various subjects	Delicious; Digg; StumbleUpon; Reddit
Social Networking Sites: • enable users to connect with friends, entertainers, brands, and business professionals • some platforms, like Tagged, focus on specific niches, such as friend discovery	Facebook; MySpace; Tagged; LinkedIn
Social Updating Services: • offer short and pointed social updates • allow viral sharing through succinct information, media, and link sharing	Twitter; Yammer
Virtual Worlds: • allow users to create and nurture virtual avatars • enable users to interact and develop relationships within these platforms	Second Life; HABBO; The Sims Online
Social Endorsement/Rating Sites: • allow for patron-to-patron promotion and information sharing of real-world restaurant and business experiences • allow for patron-to-business reviews of service and product offerings	Yelp; TripAdvisor; DineHere.ca; Urbanspoon
Media Sharing Sites: • generate viral proliferation by sharing rich media across a global public audience	Flikr; YouTube
Geo-Location: • allows users to earn status and badges while businesses collect real-time social data by sharing geo-location information	Foursquare; Gowalla
Forums: • encourage knowledge and experience sharing focused on specific topics	IGN boards; babycenter.com

It is this last point that is so vital to understanding what is occurring online today: the development and deploying of technology enables fundamental human social instincts. These include the need to connect with others and to feel connected; to express; to lead and follow; to join and belong; and to meet and exploit many of our basic human psychological and social traits. This is what happens when a new technology (the web itself is only some 20 or so years old) begins to catch up with what users expect from the experience of using the technology—the technology begins to improve and align itself to users' needs. This begins the trend of the technology interface adapting to humans rather than humans conforming to the technology.

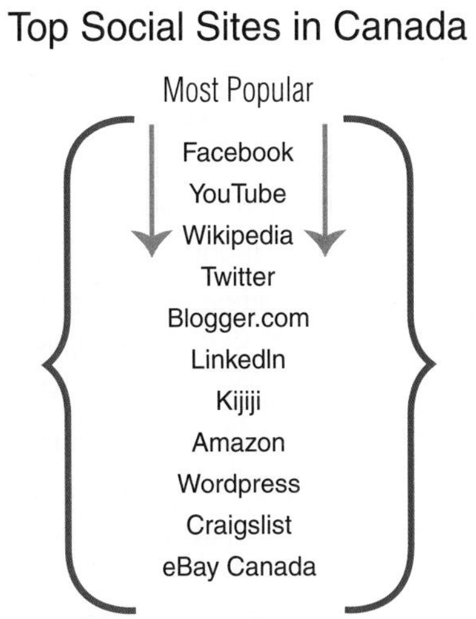

This linking of *form* to *function* is an important point regarding the social web. Once the core technology functions are working, developers can turn their attention to replicating and refining the paradigms of human social interactions to enable them to occur more smoothly online and with fewer unnatural impediments. To do this, developers study how the original technology was absorbed and used to improve the interface by making it more seamless and effortless. For instance, in terms of blogging, it is only a short leap to move from the notion of a speech (blog post) to a conversation (a set of multi-party posts happening in real time). Think also about living in a community, joining a club, or belonging to a particular group, or perhaps even online dating. These notions are originally social in nature, and define how people think about and describe themselves. These activities existed long before technology came along. When you think about the social web, you are really only thinking about doing something that human beings have done forever (converse, connect, gather, join, belong) and translating that into an online context.

Examples of websites that belong to this category include Facebook, YouTube, Twitter, LinkedIn, Wordpress, Wikipedia, and many others that you may be all too familiar with (see Figure 8.2). Their primary purpose is to connect you with friends, family, partners, or colleagues. They may help you discover new friends or people of interest, or share your life in the form of pictures, videos, blogs, and updates on your daily activities. They might be oriented mostly toward a specific demographic (e.g., business networks and colleagues in the case of LinkedIn) or aimed more generally at the world (in the case of Facebook). In some cases, different demographics or geographies will adopt one site over another, giving it a social flavour that is different than a similar site elsewhere.

Research suggests that the trend crosses all demographic ranges. For instance, a recent study by Nielsen showed that the popularity of social networking and blogging is not limited to younger teens and adults:

> Females make up the majority of visitors to social networks and blogs, and people aged 18–34 have the highest concentration of visitors among all age groups. Americans aged 35–49 are also avid visitors: 4 percent more likely than average to visit social networks and blogs than they do any other site and 27 percent of these sites' audience.[3]

In addition, the Nielsen Online survey reported that "Social Networks and Blog sites rule Americans' Internet time, accounting for 23 percent of time spent online, more than twice the amount of time spent on the #2 category, Online Games. To further put this into context, time spent on the 75 'Other' online categories combined only accounts for 35 percent of Americans' total Internet time."[4]

Top Social Sites in Canada

Most Popular

Facebook
YouTube
Wikipedia
Twitter
Blogger.com
LinkedIn
Kijiji
Amazon
Wordpress
Craigslist
eBay Canada

FIGURE 8.2 Can you find a classmate who has never been to one of these sites? Likely not; social networking is very popular among young teens and adults, but it is also growing among older generations too.[2]

2. Alexa, The Web Information Company, "Top Sites in Canada," *www.alexa.com/topsites/countries/CA*, retrieved September 2011.

3. *www.nielsen.com/content/dam/corporate/us/en/reports-downloads/2011-Reports/nielsen-social-media-report.pdf*

4. Ibid.

A website does not have to be a general purpose application to include a social component. A social site may aim to help you share your world through videos and photos (YouTube or Flickr), or to help you find a date in the city in which you live (*MeetmeinTO.com*, for example). If you are interested in starting your own blog, consider visiting *Blogger.com* or *Thoughts.com*. In addition, social media trends follow basic social trends. For example, it is often said that people avoid talking about sex, politics, or religion except in private, safe gatherings. Not surprisingly, you can find blogging sites for politics (*Bloggingcanadians.ca* or *Bloggingtories.ca*) parenting (*Themommyblog.net*), religion (*Religionnewsblog.com*), sports (*Cagepotato.com*), and, of course, sex (*Sexblogs.org* or *Erogs.com*, which stands for erotic blogs). Again, many of these sites do not specifically deploy any new technology as such, but they do provide a new technology context for users to do online what they do offline. Form follows function to help create sites enabled by cool technology where people want to participate socially.

Social Utility

In our research at Ryerson University, we have borrowed from other fields (primarily economics) to gain a better understanding of why people are willing to spend so much time online—and what they get out of it. We have coined the term **social utility** to address this. This term suggests that you only spend time on sites that are *useful* to you, and that the time invested on socially-oriented websites must somehow contribute to your happiness or social satisfaction, or create social opportunities for you, or we hypothesize that you wouldn't or shouldn't bother. In fact, the *only* reason that most people spend any time on Facebook or such similar sites is that they provide something of social value in return for spending valuable time creating profiles, updating entries, and so on. Therefore, to invest time on a site, you need to feel like you get a return or you will go elsewhere.

One way to better understand the concept of social utility is to visualize it using our **Three Pillars of Sociability**, shown in Figure 8.3. The concepts attached to each pillar are rooted in social psychology, the study of how people congregate and why—which explains why so often cultures and groups demonstrate almost tribe-like behaviour in their operations. Let's consider each of these important concepts in turn to see what they can teach us about online social behaviour. As a result of their general applicability, organizations can use these same basic concepts to explore why and how they too can use social media technology to improve their business models and operations.

Affiliation The first step, beyond simply being aware of the opportunity to join something, is to ensure that users want to be *affiliated* with your group. The underlying psychological driver of this is the need to belong. This may include wanting to belong to something because it is popular or will make a person popular, or it may be just the opposite and rooted in exclusivity and the fact that only the chosen or a few belong. Regardless of the specific reason why someone wants to belong, you must trigger in your target user the desire to be affiliated with your site. Of course, to create the desire to affiliate, they must know you exist and be able to discover you—this is why you must first figure out where your target user congregates and go to them. Similarly, if your organization wants to attract new customers or members, it must first learn to stand out online and offer an attractive reason for targeted groups to want to affiliate with it.

This same pillar also explains the massive fragmentation and specialization that is now occurring in social media sites. While in the early stages you have only a few large platforms that initially grow exponentially as they become popular, critical mass often renders them too big and too general to meet specific affiliative needs. That is, people become bored being in a general community and want to join a specific community of like-minded people with shared interests, which is often smaller, or perhaps unique, or even has

FIGURE 8.3 The Three Pillars of Sociability.

The Three Pillars of Sociability apply to both real life and the online world. The desire to affiliate, participate, and be validated by others is a key factor of the human existence; social networking sites allow users to do this online.

some particular caché in being affiliated with it. A good example of that is *Tagged.com*, which seems focused on the younger demographic of club-goers and online music lovers. Even if someone on *Tagged.com* has a more general profile on Facebook or Myspace, they may feel more connected to others who share their love of urban music on *Tagged.com*.

Participation Once new users have made the leap to wanting to join your site (that is, to publicly declare their desire to affiliate with you), you must help them easily understand the rules of *participation*. Every group of humans, no matter how large or small, has both spoken and unspoken rules regarding conduct in the group. Some things might be obvious (for instance, if you join a photo sharing site, you likely want to indulge in photo sharing and understand that others will in turn view your photos), but there might also be other rules (for instance, regarding limitations on the types of photos that can and cannot be shared or how many are allowed, etc). These kinds of rules are often printed or implied and are easily mastered by users.

However, there are often other, more subtle codes in groups. For instance, making sure that tags attached to photos are authentic and not deceptive simply to help your photos get viewed or become popular. Or NOT using personal names in tags unless that is socially permitted or approved by others in the photos. These are often much more subtle rules, perhaps even more like guidelines—and what if those norms are not obvious to a new user? These rules may be internal to the group or relate to when, where, and how it's okay to move outside the fixed social boundary of the existing private group into the outside world of the all-encompassing cloud. Continuing with our photo-sharing example, this might mean it is fine to post photos and invite others to view them, but perhaps it is not all right to follow up with emails or pokes asking them to comment on them (a common complaint of many sites with an emphasis on sharing) unless they are already also members of the group.

Since it is important for the growth of your online community that users understand rules of behaviour and conduct (both formal and informal), effective community managers must find ways to help make participation *socially safe*. Recall your experiences in high school, when every little social gaffe or blunder might have had significant reputational consequences and you worried about doing, saying, and being the right thing. This was not necessarily a socially safe context for many, and it often prevented people from participating fully. And where was the printed rule book that helped you with this? Right, there wasn't one. You learned by doing, as risky as that may have seemed. Similarly, the most successful social networking sites focus on ensuring an **invitational design**, borrowing a psychological term for finding ways to welcome new people into an online group and making it safe for them to learn and master the norms. The best sites encourage play and discovery and make the site design intuitive. This is an essential consideration in the design and marketing of any social networking site. Elements of this may have helped explain why *Friendster.com* was first to market, but ultimately Facebook and MySpace ended up the category winners. Comments at the time suggested that Friendster may not have had the community elements of its design right, and users clearly abandoned it in droves for other sites.

Validation The third pillar of sociability to consider is how to *validate* the user's ongoing social experience, thereby constantly reinforcing the social utility of your website. This may not be the same for every user, since each user will have a different level of social comfort, involvement, and confidence. But it does mean finding tangible ways of demonstrating social value—perhaps even involving elements of competition, an age-old concept that human beings have willingly engaged in for centuries. For example, a simple but powerful reason why Facebook ultimately beat Friendster in the race to dominate social computing in its early days may have had to do with two critical points:

1. Facebook initially appeared to be a focused and targeted site that had exclusivity (you had to be a registered student in a university or college with an active institutional email ID to join). Friendster was a general purpose site that allowed anyone to join and touted this fact in its marketing. This may have driven down the desire for some to affiliate with it because it was perceived as too easy and too common versus its competition.
2. The *friend* feature in Facebook enabled an instant form of social validation for its participants. In fact, others can easily see how many friends you have and you can find validation by inviting friends to connect with you.

These two facts may have helped create the social desire for people to get in and stay in, contributing to Facebook eventually being forced to broaden its membership base after its initial success. Had it not increased the opportunity for full and continued participation, its growth would have stopped and it would not be the success story we speak of in glowing terms today.

It is not possible to definitively prove this particular hypothesis about these two sites so late in their respective evolutions and with their now fixed competitive order in the marketplace. However, recent studies of online social behaviour suggest that when a social media platform combines constant social validation of its users (through a variety of techniques that are relevant to its purpose and design), with a slight dose of competition as a way of encouraging users to compete for external forms of validation from other members, it drives up social utility and interest in the site among both users and non-users. This is an interesting and useful finding for those wanting to learn more about what makes a particular social computing website more or less popular with consumers and users, and helps explain why some sites succeed and others fizzle and fail.

Facebook's homepage encourages new users to sign up by creating the image of an exclusive community.

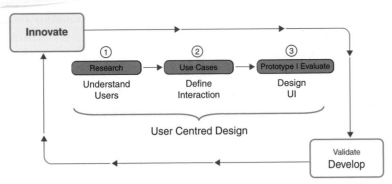

FIGURE 8.4 Intuitive user interface design is constantly developing new and innovative UI changes to give users a fresh experience while still abiding by principles of interaction that define user tendencies.

Design and Usability

It is becoming clear that design esthetic and usability are critical components to building a successful interactive media site, and that the most powerful of these become almost addictive to users (see Figure 8.4). In fact, as with any social phenomenon, there are going to be users who cannot stay away or keep their desires in proper perspective. This has always been true offline, so it is inevitable that inappropriate uses of social computing will take place as well.

A site has to look good and be attractive to users, while also functioning well and being intuitively obvious to users. We refer to this as **social transparency**. This means that the social elements of your technology design must intuitively map to the same ways that the social interactions take place off-line. Simply put: if you make it easy to navigate, people will use it; if you don't, they won't. But it is not always easy to create this seamless combination. Close working relationships between developers and designers need to be established to help each discipline maximize its contribution during the site development phase. Companies can no longer afford to code first and then visually integrate good design. The best sites do both concurrently and rapidly, constantly changing and refining the site's technology, flow, and architecture based on users' feedback about what they do and do not like about the site. Successful sites also normally employ a minimalist design perspective that simply says that everything must matter and be just a short click away. This means eliminating the layers, barriers, and complexities of navigating the site by making sure that users can easily find and use a specific function.

Of course, if companies expect users to interact on their sites, they must also design sites that both encourage interaction and make it easy for users to do so. Keep in mind that users are often not very sophisticated in their use of technology. As a consultant in the field once said to a client, "It's not about the technology, stupid!" Rather, it's about what the technology can do for users.

Companies should also be aware of just how possessive users can be about their chosen platforms and interfaces. Recall the number of times that Facebook has encountered controversy when trying to make unpopular changes to its site and how users reacted.[5]

Business Utility

This discussion brings us to a critical question—as students of IT, what can you do to learn how to translate online social utility into business utility that helps drive value for the companies and organizations you serve or intend to create? Essentially, this means exploring how to deploy social media platforms and technologies to create business outcomes (e.g., increased sales, higher customer

---

5. For example, see *http://latimesblogs.latimes.com/technology/2011/09/facebook-users-protest-changes-to-news-feed.html*.

loyalty, lower transaction costs, etc.) that have real value for an enterprise, but are also acceptable to users. This can be harder to accomplish than you might think. Many business models associated with social computing and media are emerging, and the jury is still out on what is and is not working well. We will discuss a few examples of how social media and Web 2.0 technologies can help businesses later in this chapter. However, simply assuming that consumers or clients will share information with you because you want them to is naive—they will only do so when there is utility, when they get something back in return that they want (e.g., products and services, information, access to other buyers, etc.).

Legal and Ethical Framework for Social Media

While social media is perceived by many to be "new" (and some elements, as we have discussed already, are quite innovative or novel), it is important to remember that in a business context, existing legal frameworks still apply to any organizationally-mandated social media efforts. For instance, the same legislation that applies to off-line advertising and competitions will apply to online competitions in whichever jurisdiction you operate in. For Canada, this includes provisions of the Criminal Code (around false and misleading advertising, fraud, and so on), the Competition Act (around a whole host of issues including price fixing, competitive practices, advertising and promotion claims, etc.), and various provincial consumer protection acts. In addition, in almost every leading jurisdiction around the world there will be some form of privacy legislation that applies—which we discuss later—and sometimes uniform commercial codes or legislation related to online commerce and transactions.

In most jurisdictions, unique laws and regulations apply when your social media (or other online promotional efforts) involve children specifically, or those who meet a jurisdictional test of being a "minor." (Age of a minor varies greatly around the world, by the way—another complication of the Internet being such a global phenomenon.) And, beyond the law itself, most jurisdictions also have some form of industry self-regulation around advertising in particular. In Canada that is the Advertising Standards Council of Canada (ASCC), *www.adstandards.com*, whose primary role is to create and enforce ethical codes for advertisers, promoters, agencies, media companies, and the like. In the United States, the Federal Trade Commission is the highest authority on the subject. These bodies often produce extensive resource information for both their members and the public about various kinds of advertising, promotions, and contests. They can be an excellent and informed starting point for information about local standards if you plan to engage social media as part of your organization's marketing efforts.

For the most part, online social media efforts normally involve as their primary purpose the acquisition and engagement of new and existing customers, clients, donors, or supporters. In some form or other, this will eventually touch on all of the normal legal and ethical issues that intrude into regulating how organizations go to market and what they can and cannot do. Just because something is novel does not mean it operates in a lawless environment. Professionals engaged in the creation and deployment of social media campaigns or efforts need to be mindful and seek good professional advice on what codes apply to what issues and when. What is clear from many examples we have seen is that the law of unintended consequences can certainly apply in any instance where you do not consider the legal, ethical, and moral implications of the promotion, campaign, or contests you run in a social media setting, running the risk of a negative backlash against your brand that goes viral!

Privacy and Security There are also implications for *privacy* and *security* for any social website, both of which are topics covered in Chapter 1 in some detail. These issues have a direct implication for sites where users post and share both public and private information of various types, formats, and levels of risk if they are shared by accident. If you lose your users' trust because of a security breach or because you cannot help them keep their private information protected, you will not succeed at retaining them. Your site will fail to attract new users because of concerns that will likely be widely disseminated on the Web (much to your embarrassment) and, of late, we have seen numerous examples of this exact event smear some significant global brands. A recent example of this is Sony's failure to secure the private information of 77 million PlayStation users, ranking as the worst security breach in 2011.[6] Not only was this breach embarrassing, it also resulted in a major fall in Sony's stock price.[7] This is also an area of great *legal risk* since various privacy codes around the world (such as the Freedom of Information and Privacy Protection Act, or FIPPA, or Personal Information Protection and Electronic Documents Act, PIPEDA, in Canada and similar types of legislation in both the United States and European Union) create obligations that companies and organizations must adhere to by law to operate locally.

What is completely clear is that the answer is not as simple as suggesting that because your site is based in a particular jurisdiction (for instance, Canada), you must only meet the codes of that host country. It would appear from recent precedents that the instant you gain a registered user in another jurisdiction, you may be subject to the privacy and security laws of that country. This was proven recently when the privacy commissioner of Canada engaged in very significant discussions and negotiations with Facebook to ensure its site met Canadian privacy laws. If Facebook does not comply, the commission has the ability to prevent it from operating in Canada or accepting Canadian registrations—a significant business and technical risk for a global firm.

Of course, as with many things legal in origin, there is not a standardization of the codes and their requirements. As a result, those wishing to operate in multi-jurisdictions are stuck trying to figure out compromises in site design and operation, which mostly comply with the common denominators of security and privacy legislation in most jurisdictions. Alternatively, they can voluntarily opt out of doing business in some jurisdictions instead of attempting to comply with local regulations and laws.

When we specifically address not just the online security of your website, but the added layer of highly personal information normally involved in social computing applications (think of the treasure trove of personal insights contained in the average profile!), which legal codes do you have to understand and honour? And how would you have to change the design of your social technology to accomplish this when the codes are different everywhere and no single solution will likely leave you globally compliant with all aspects of local law?

One principle of privacy law that is almost universally found in various jurisdictions is the notion of "informed consent"—for greater certainty, this principle is worth generally adhering to in your social website. This suggests the following:

- Collect information only when it's required and for a specific purpose.
- Use the information *only* for the purpose it was collected for initially.
- Inform the user of the privacy policies and codes that apply in advance of collection.
- Ensure there is a clear and unambiguous agreement from the user for the collection.

These four basic rules will ensure a high degree of compliance between your data collection strategy and most privacy codes and help reduce complaints or privacy breach risk for your organization.

---

6. *www.theglobeandmail.com/news/technology/tech-news/massive-data-theft-77-million-users-exposed-in-sonys-playstation-security-breach/article2000201/*

7. *www.infosecisland.com/blogview/14224-Sony-Stock-Hammered-in-Wake-of-Security-Breaches.html*

Technology Implications and Costs

When you think about social computing websites from a technology perspective, several obvious issues arise. The first (and likely least obvious) one is the sheer cost of *accumulating and storing* all of this often multimedia-intense content. Of course, storage of information also comes at a cost to any organization, and should be a factor in your long-term strategy of information retention, particularly as it relates to social media applications you host yourself. While costs of storage are generally falling, volumes of storage are increasing, often offsetting these rate reductions. While software-as-a-service (SaaS) applications are the norm for many social media platforms, they often exclude commercial uses without permission and/or the payment of fees related to the use of their site for commercial purposes, mostly to offset these costs for themselves that your users will generate through usage of the SaaS application.

Additionally, running a site oriented toward interactive media requires significant bandwidth (to simply serve up all the content on demand) and massive amounts of storage to keep it all instantly available and properly tagged and indexed. This has a direct operating cost for social media sites, since both bandwidth and storage become more expensive the more volume a site receives. This means that Web 2.0 sites are more expensive to create and run than traditional websites. It also means increasing demand for **compression technologies**, which help reduce the costs of storage and transmission (particularly of image and video-based formats) and improve download speeds for users. In addition, developers who know how to code and implement systems that efficiently handle large amounts of information are in demand.

Ignorance Is NOT Bliss!

The same costs associated with hosting a social website are involved in its use. In 2012, Robert Half Technology interviewed 1,400 CIOs in Canada as an update to their 2009 Robert Half organization survey. The findings show the following:

Many businesses don't like the idea of their workers using social networking sites at work, but others accept that most business professionals today are multitaskers who might be able to harness the power of social sites for business value.

- Approximately 31 percent of companies prohibit all access to social media sites, down 23 percentage points from 2009.
- 51 percent of companies permit access for business purposes only (up from 19 percent in 2009).
- 14 percent of companies permit access for limited personal use (down from 16 percent in 2009).
- 4 percent of companies permit any access for personal use (down from 10 percent in 2009).[8]

Limiting social media usage within an organization is seen by many experts as an unfortunate stance that has several potentially negative consequences. The first is what this tells potential employees about a company's corporate culture (that it lacks trust in its employees), and this may damage an organization's "employee brand." Employees today expect access to social media, both for themselves in their personal lives but also in their professional lives.

Second, it fails to recognize the way in which work is viewed as an ongoing activity to be woven into a complete 24-hour period, and that multi-tasking is now the norm for most employees.

8. *www.prnewswire.com/news-releases/social-work-more-companies-permit-social-networking-on-the-job-robert-half-technology-survey-reveals-122650448.html*

Many of us may not even "go" to work; instead, we work at home, from client or customer sites, using a mobile phone, on Bluetooth devices in a car moving between calls. Even if we go to an office, work is something that we integrate into other aspects of our social world. Work and play, so long as they remain in balance, now occur spontaneously in the moment. Soon organizations will catch on that granting freedom to employees to perform well, including control over how they spend their time to accomplish their assigned work, will enhance productivity in the long run and improve employee satisfaction and engagement, not diminish it. A part of this is accepting the integration of social media into our world of work.

WHAT DO YOU THINK?

You are graduating and looking for a job. You recently heard in the news that a company you are considering applying for a job with has banned Facebook and Twitter for its employees at work. Would this affect your opinion of the organization? Would you still apply for a position with the company? Is it fair for employers to restrict access to social sites when they have no problem with you checking your corporate email at home in the evening (and indeed often expect you to)? If you were a business owner, would you allow your employees to access social networking sites at work?

Third, it is just plain ignorant. Trying to restrict access to social media in the workplace ignores an important fact about social media trends—there is no undoing this revolution outside the walls of the organization. This is a permanent social shift. Like any other social change, we must learn to embrace and adapt it, not ignore it.

Fourth, limiting employees' exposure to new technologies doesn't make business sense. Many CIO's argue that social computing does not belong in the business realm. Yet businesses or organizations will not survive unless they begin to understand the social web and, in turn, begin to integrate it into their organizations to engage in social business models. The very employees who "get it" the most and who could help an organization do the same will no longer feel attracted to working for organizations that ban social networking sites. They will not bring their talents and insights to the organization to help it master these new technologies. An organization cannot deploy technology that employees do not understand. Who is going to help an organization discover what it should be doing about this trend if no one at the company is allowed to participate in it?

And finally, a technological concern arises from banning social networking sites: many employees will find a way to get around the ban and access the sites anyway. After all, employees can be pretty creative. CIOs around the world are realizing that many employees are becoming tech-savvy, and they can easily deploy proxy servers and other techniques to get around site-specific bans (for instance, check out *Hidemyass.com* as just one example of a site targeted at exactly this kind of workplace ban). However, using sites like this can compromise corporate security protocols and open up access to outside intruders. Employees may not be aware of this access, and the average CIO would likely want to discourage it. Yet another reason to embrace technology that employees want access to instead of hiding from it.

These are the kinds of important issues you must explore about this brave new world of social computing as either an IT professional, someone in a business or other organization deploying social media, or even a user! Fortunately, clearer answers are now starting to emerge as the social web emerges with breathtaking speed as a worldwide force of great social change, providing more guidance than was initially available at the outset of this new wave of technology innovation. This is making it less risky to move to the forefront of this trend for organizations.

Quick Test

1. True or False. Web 2.0 is clearly a revolution in the web world.

2. Which of the following contribute to the success of a social networking site?
   a. usability
   b. attractiveness
   c. intuitive navigation
   d. all of the above

3. Fill in the blank. People participate on social networking sites only if the site provides _____.

■ USER-GENERATED CONTENT

An essential ingredient that most experts agree is fundamental to most social media applications is the concept of *user-generated content*. This suggests that in most instances, true social sites focus on providing the *context* in which users generate content themselves, rather than providing the actual content. Participants in social media sites must register, identify themselves, and decide how to present themselves. This may be done by creating and posting a profile (as in the case for LinkedIn and Facebook-type sites) or perhaps by adopting an avatar or fictitious online personality (as in the case of many interactive gaming sites and sites such as *Secondlife.com*). Regardless, the primary purpose of a social site is to have participants interact, which means they must actively join and self-identify in some form before they can participate.

Good psychology suggests that before you affiliate with a group, you must *discover* and *trust* its social motives and intentions. For this reason, most successful social media sites permit some form of restricted observation or discovery before requiring registration or identification. If you move to restrict access solely to registered members, you are limiting your growth to those who trust before having reason to do so. Studies suggest these people make fickle members at best, since they move around to the latest, newest sites. Instead, successful sites restrict visitors to watching, observing, or learning about the site, its intentions, and user behaviour by limiting what non-registered users can do. Using this method, before new users can participate fully they must demonstrate a willingness to disclose or create a **participating identity**. They will use this identity to create and post additional content or take the actions required to begin to fully participate in the online community.

Again, this mirrors the offline world: before joining a club, you are often invited by a current member to attend a meeting or learn more about it. If you then decide to join, you become a member, which infers certain privileges but also certain obligations or responsibilities. Similarly, when you join various social sites, you may also face restrictions such as user or member agreements, codes of conduct, or requirements to participate only in certain ways. The community might also be **self-regulating**, where members report conduct they feel is outside the group norms to a moderator who is responsible for drawing the inappropriate behaviour to the attention of the member or removing or restricting the member's privileges. Again, when you consider these functions as technology, you miss the point—these technologies are not actually innovations for technology's sake, but rather are simply *technological interpretations* of normal social conduct. The online and off-line worlds mirror each other more in this space than in just about any other found on the World Wide Web.

Finding Content

To make your own content useful to other users, you must label or tag it. **Tagging** involves associating keywords with your content to make it searchable so that other users can locate it and interact with it. In turn, by using collaborative tagging and comparing and coalescing how other users tag the same or similar content, you derive a **folksonomy**, or collective cloud tag, that helps users access information quickly and efficiently.

Again, while the content and how it is tagged and searched will depend on the purpose of the site, the technology of tagging and searching is actually not new and was certainly available in the days of Web 1.0. What is different is how the technology is deployed to permit **viral social interactions**, where something that is funny, unusual, shocking, interesting, or newsworthy almost instantly spreads online from its origins to nearly every corner of the world. If you speak with your classmates or friends, you will likely be able to recall a recent example of something that went viral. What do you think made it go viral? How many people who you know saw it? How did they see it? These are the kinds of questions that marketers are now asking themselves as they try to address how consumer behaviour on the social web is changing, and how it impacts information consumed online.

WHAT DO YOU THINK? ?

Choose a specific theme like "hockey." Go to *www.youtube.com* and search for a video that falls within this theme. When your search results appear, click on a video that you want to watch and then click on a related video that YouTube suggests. After watching the related video, click on another related video; repeat this action seven times. Do you think the seventh video still falls under the specific theme you originally searched? Is there a tag that relates the seventh video to the first video you watched? Retrace your steps. Can you think of tags that might link the first video you watched to the second video? How about the second video to the third video? Create a chain to illustrate which tags linked your videos together.

User-Generated Content and Brand Risk

If you think about business for a second, having something good about your business (perhaps a story of outstanding products or services, for instance) go viral would be wonderful. This might often be a company's stated objective. However, in keeping with the psychological concept of **schadenfreude** (drawing happiness from others' misery or misfortune), negative stories go viral more often than positive ones. For instance, recall the viral video of the bride with her hair on fire as an example that later turned out to be part of a stealth advertising campaign. This kind of example should act as a warning to organizations that might misunderstand the power of the social web and try and harness its benefits without realizing its risks. This also suggests that one essential element of any company's **online social strategy** should be an awareness of the risks of undertaking any kind of online social campaign that might backfire.

Companies need to make sure that they monitor the online messages being posted about their enterprise or organization. Probably one of the best examples of an online campaign gone wrong can be found by searching Google for "Dove Mashup" or "Unilever Disrobed," or going to *Shapingyouth. org* and searching the same terms. Unilever is a massive, global consumer products company that owns both the Dove and Axe brands—products aimed at separate and distinct demographics (older women and younger men, respectively). The world of social media permitted anyone to compare and combine the messages that Unilever was using in two separate campaigns. For Dove, Unilever employed the "talk to your daughters before the beauty industry does" campaign, which stressed the "natural products that bring out the natural beauty in you." For the Axe line, the "spray more get more" campaign had an overtly sexual overtone and was seen by many as being demeaning to women.

Within days of the campaigns being activated in traditional media, there was a user-generated **mashup** of the two campaigns that juxtaposed them side-by-side in a way that Unilever obviously never intended nor thought would happen. This is called a **brandstorm**—a situation where a traditional brand faces an online storm that can quite literally damage the value of its brand overnight. While the intention was not to directly attack Unilever, the online world was imposing *media transparency* by forcing Unilever into the awkward position of justifying its seemingly unauthentic positions. The result, of course, is that the online world was instantly abuzz with negative messages about the two campaigns and the company's intent to deceive its customers, regardless of the company's actual intent. This is what is so damaging about a brandstorm; in many cases, the storm is created not on the basis of fact, but perhaps only by implication, or in some cases from outright fiction. An example of this is the online video showing a Kryptonite bike lock being sprung by a Bic pen cap. It was later proven to be false using time-lapse photography, but it was too late and the damage to the brand was done.

Ironically, the mashups in these instances are often many hundreds of times more popular online and viewed by more surfers than the original product campaign videos or statements by the company defending itself. Even if Unilever had wanted to respond with its side of the story, it would never have been able to purchase the same amount of media coverage that occurred when the original message went viral. This gets to the heart of the matter: indirect messages, whether based on fact or fiction, are increasingly more potent than any equivalent direct message from the company itself, and this can put brands at risk. In fact, there was very little official response from Unilever to the Dove mashup (likely a strategic move to have the tizzy go away over time rather than risk adding to it), yet it remains a nearly perfect example of the importance of social media strategies to companies today.

Search Engine Optimization (SEO) on Social Sites

Search engine optimization is the practice by which websites streamline their code and emphasize keywords and concepts that are relevant to their industry or internal goals. By enacting SEO techniques on a regular basis, websites are able to guarantee that search engines like Google, Bing, and Yahoo will position their content higher in search results. No one doubts the importance of the search for both users of the web and those trying to ensure their websites can be easily located; in fact, there is an entire industry dedicated to search engine optimization and search-based marketing. Much has been written about how to optimize your website's static content and particular strategies around tagging and linking, as ways of ensuring that your website rises to the top of search engine rankings for your key words. Of course, for a site that is only static in nature and that does not encourage UGC or user interaction and self-tagging, there is a high degree of control over what actions you might take to ensure your site is optimized for search engines.

However, as you socially enable your site, users become a more dominant force in the creation of and tagging of content on your site. They might also pick media (for instance, video) that renders great content less searchable and, perhaps, less valuable to you as a way of improving your site's search engine rankings. In addition, the same creativity that makes their contributions so interesting and valuable will also extend into tagging and titling where their creativity may not match your site's search engine strategy. What is a web manager to do?

Linkings and click-throughs matter to crawlers—the software tools that various search engines use to review and rank individual website content in their databases. These operate all the time, roaming everywhere over your site and picking up what's new and how that should affect your ranking when a user presents a key word search to their search engine. So, among other things, your refresh rate will attract more frequent crawls and often can be a factor in improving your rankings.

There are other types of emerging strategies that can work to address some of these problems. One element of this emanates from your site design and architecture—for instance, can you create interfaces that encourage users to make contributions to the site, but use a structure for tagging, titling, and so on that optimizes your content density around your selected key words. This strategy alone will almost instantly increase rankings of content on your site and improve search engine performance. You can do this by, for instance, allowing tagging from a drop-down box or check box list of tags that are common and consistent. As you will have already learned elsewhere, having common and consistent standards in anything improves the adaptability of your system to a rules-based system which, by definition, any IT system is and which any search engine ultimately is as well. So, think in rules-based terms but in a way that remains user-centric and your site's rankings will improve. You can also find experts in this field who can conduct a **site audit**, which might help detect areas where the re-positioning of pages or content, changes in tagging consistency or weighting, and other types of changes can help escalate your appearance higher up in search engine rankings.

The technology architecture of your site also matters. Some technologies and tools are more "search friendly" than others—and the content contained in them is more visible to the bots and crawlers trolling your sites. When making a decision to use a specific tool or technology on your site, first investigate if it will help or hinder your most important search engine rankings. This kind of information changes frequently, but there are numerous online resources that can help you make these kinds of decisions.

Rather than trying to list and enumerate those here, we refer you instead to these types of online resources, many of which you can find in the *WileyPlus* site for this text.

Quick Test

1. True or False. Tagging your content helps users locate and interact with your content.

2. To join a social media website, you must create:
   a. a mashup
   b. an identity
   c. your own website
   d. a folksonomy of your content

3. Fill in the blank. A situation where a traditional brand is facing an online storm that can damage the value of the brand is known as a _____.

Answers: 1. True; 2. b; 3. brandstorm

■ CREATING BUSINESS UTILITY USING SOCIAL MEDIA TOOLS AND E-MARKETING

The early advent of desktop computers did not have much initial impact on marketing. Instead, it had an impact on other elements of business, such as accounting, finance, customer service, and fulfillment, for instance. In fact, if you were working in product or service marketing during the 1980s, you were likely dealing only with the need to get aggregate information through electronic data files and databases (e-info). Otherwise, the two disciplines remained fairly separate (see Figure 8.5).

When the World Wide Web started to become more prominent and adoption was rising, mostly through the early and mid-1990s, marketers began to see it as a tool that would enhance their *direct*

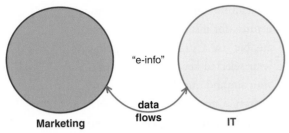

FIGURE 8.5 Phase 1: Early on, marketing's use of IT technology rested solely on gathering and using e-info data.

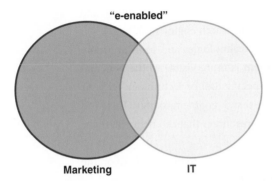

FIGURE 8.6 Phase 2: As the Web began to grow, most companies began to use IT as a way to communicate directly with their customers. However, the communication was still only one way—from company to consumer.

brand marketing efforts. Most companies and organizations began to create an online presence (see Figure 8.6). **Direct marketing** means just that: messages, offers, or promotions that come directly from the company to the consumer in some form (e.g., advertising, mail, targeted events, or samples). This moved companies into a new phase of computer-enabled marketing where the two disciplines began to work more closely in tandem. This phase is associated with the creation of mostly passive websites and the slow beginning of basic online marketing techniques such as email lists (and the associated plague of spam). Eventually, companies began to refine their efforts to understand online customer behaviour and to track statistics about online buying behaviour to customize offers presented to customers and to refine marketing campaigns. Around this time, most companies began to offer some method of buying products and services online, or at a minimum, introduced store or dealer locator features to make buying easier (see Chapter 7 for more on e-commerce). However, customers were not yet interacting with the company; companies were still only putting traditional marketing materials and information online, and were changing very little about the practice of marketing.

However, the arrival of the social web changed all of that. Consumers began to realize the power of interacting online, and began to demand that companies operate with a view to how *they* wanted to access product and service information and buy online when and how they wanted. As a result, the balance of power between marketers and consumers shifted. What *others* were saying or doing with products became more important, and consumers began to seek out **indirect sources of information** (e.g., product and ranking review sites, relying on word of mouth to find new products, etc.). This meant an emerging distrust in some instances for the direct marketing messages coming from companies, and more emphasis being placed on validating what companies were saying about their brands and products.

While not quite creating the notion of "perfect markets through perfect information," as economists suggest is ultimately what happens when buyers have access to complete information, the World Wide Web quickly became an important global source of influence on customers. Consumers were able to share information at such a rapid rate, it was hard for traditional marketing to catch up. To see just one simple example of this, check out *www.tweetedbrands.com*. This site provides information on the most tweeted brands on Twitter in the last 24 hours. It is fascinating to see how this changes over a period of time. Similarly, if you go to Google news, a simple news search engine, and type in any well-known brand name, you will be instantly rewarded with a list of every possible citation of that brand on the Web in the recent past. These kinds of tests will help you see how real the indirect messaging around brands really is online.

Not just marketers have this information—consumers do too. This puts traditional practices such as differential pricing (i.e., the same product sold around the world at different prices that are not purely exchange-rate driven) at risk because consumers became savvy and could shop around globally. Right around mid-2000, just as Tim O'Reilly was introducing the term Web 2.0, the world of marketing was changing so rapidly that marketing and IT became interdependent.

E-dominated marketing emerged as a new paradigm as every company, organization, or entity was affected by these trends and had to effectively navigate the risks and rewards of this new online social world to succeed (see Figure 8.7).

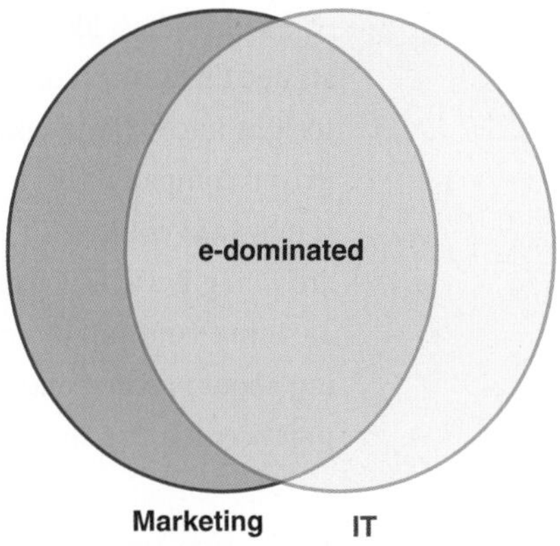

Harnessing the Power of Social Media

How should companies strategically use social media technologies in their business? Here are a few examples to explore online to answer that question:

FIGURE 8.7 Phase 3: As the social web began to take over, marketing became e-dominated, where use of the Web is an integral part to marketing's communications with consumers.

- To facilitate employer/employee engagement (*www.speechbobble.com*)
- To create brand-related clubs/forums (*www.redtag.ca/forum/*)
- To manage online communities (*www.hootsuite.com* or *www.tweetdeck.com*)
- To facilitate online review sites (*www.traveladvisor.com* or *www.yelp.com*)
- To promote geo-purposed sites (*www.aroundme.com* or *www.sysomos.com*)
- For application creation (see application creation for Facebook, *www.involver.com*)

Each of these sites has the features that appear to make social-media sense for a business. They have a purpose attached to community, common membership, or interests, and they support a specific brand or product and/or a geographical overlay that helps draw local traffic. Of course, this is not to suggest that there is not room for more general-purpose social media sites (often referred to as **platform plays**) that rely on the widespread adoption of their system as a result of a first-mover or technology advantage, making them a superior context for most common social applications. Rather, as a market matures, it tends to fracture into **micro-markets.** These are purpose-built sites (or forums or groups) designed to meet a specific need. It behooves all businesses to consider this trend and to ensure their own social media strategy takes into account how their target market is consuming social media and where. It is almost always better to *go to where they are* rather than trying to *bring them to where you are*, both in terms of the cost and likelihood of success. As a result, one of the more important elements of an online strategy is to find out where your target market is currently "hanging out" online. This is perhaps similar to finding out what they like to do offline, and then advertising or promoting your product or service to them there.

Media transparency—making sure your brand and advertising messages are coherent and consistent—has also become increasingly important in this context. Any deviation from this practice will absolutely enrage Internet users and likely backfire. Avoid trying to be all things to all people; instead, be who you intend to be for people likely to buy your product or service, and do it well. This often results in organizations moving away from brazen brand marketing (promoting the message endlessly, widely, and without regard to any risk of how it is perceived by other consumers) to a more benign form of marketing involving more emphasis on product placements, targeted sampling, and promoting word-of-mouth awareness through loyal buyers or users.

But if you are going to design, operate, or participate in a loyalty or review site, remember our earlier instructions about self-regulated communities. For instance, early in its online career, Ford North America launched a customer feedback and loyalty site for truck owners. Unfortunately, it seemed as if initially they were conducting themselves like a brand-driven company by filtering out negative messages and only leaving positive posts online. They quickly got caught, demonstrating the value of transparency. While it might have scared the company to post negative comments, it would have been better to trust that their loyal, Ford truck-loving customers could take care of themselves online and judge all feedback, good or bad, accordingly.

Other sites, like *Tripadvisor.ca*, which operate with clear policies of transparency, have demonstrated that unfair comments are quickly corrected within the community; those that are not provide insight into what a company needs to improve or correct, insights that matter to any customer-driven company. This is emerging as a whole new realm of market intelligence for companies. While it may take courage to enable customers to say anything about your product or service online, they are doing it anyway. Why not encourage it to happen where you are aware of it and can count on an active community to participate and correct any unfair comments? This is a new way of thinking about product and service marketing, and it will take some time before online social marketing practices mature and best practices emerge.

Quick Test

1. True or False. When advertising online, it is more effective to create a place for consumers to come to you rather than finding where consumers already are.

2. Fill in the blank. A more general purpose social media site is known as a _____ because it relies on widespread adoption.

3. Social media is benefiting businesses by
   a. making it easier to respond to negative publicity.
   b. using viral campaigns that are more innovative and cheaper for launching new products.
   c. increasing favourable mentions on the Web through the creation of brandstorms.
   d. allowing for the fracturing of large markets into micro-markets that are easier to manage.

Answers: 1. False; 2. platform play; 3. b

■ THE SOCIAL AND BUSINESS IMPACTS OF WEB 2.0

Another important development for business has been the generational impact of the Web on entertainment choices. For instance, there has been a rapid decline in the consumption of network TV as more and more choices have become available and cable broadcast systems have increased their global penetration, thus ushering in the age of specialty networks.[9] Yet, this alone is not the most fundamental trend. More disturbing to many advertisers is the similar decline in the consumption of newspapers, magazines, radio, and most other forms of mass media. Where are all these listeners, viewers, and readers going? Online, of course. In fact, the amount of time spent online by the average citizen has steadily increased every single year for 15 years as more and more people spend more and more time online. While many thought this trend was mostly related to young computer-savvy people hanging out online, the rates of online usage are rapidly rising across all demographics. Most startling for many advertisers is the recent fact that one of the fastest rising online demographics is retired seniors who seem to have time on their hands and a willingness to spend it learning about new online resources! This has driven a corresponding explosion in online advertising spending (see Figure 8.8).

As social patterns change and people spend more time online either consuming entertainment (e.g., by watching Internet TV, gaming, or possibly gambling, which now occurs more often online than in licensed casinos) or creating and posting content on sites like YouTube and Flickr, they are not seeing or responding to advertising the way they used to. In fact, the kinds of advertising that

---

9. See *www.reuters.com/article/technologyNews/idUSTRE5817CE20090902* for a good discussion of the implications for the use of TV and the Internet at the same time by the same user.

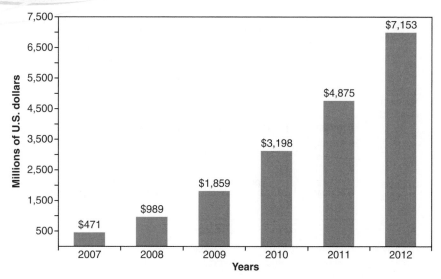

FIGURE 8.8 U.S. online video advertising spending, 2007–2012.[10]

will work in a broadcast medium (think the "killer commercial" you used to see during the Super Bowl) are now being replaced by very different efforts that take advantage of the unique technology properties of the Web. For instance, the ability to podcast very specific ads to very specific groups is simply not feasible on conventional TV, but it is on Internet TV.

To understand what this means, look back to the 1950s and the unbelievably quick adoption of the television. Television displaced the earlier and dominant technology of radio, particularly as related to having a source of news and current events. While radio was superior in terms of currency over printed newspapers, what is interesting is that newspapers, radio, and TV all co-existed quite nicely until the invention of the Internet. Citizens often consumed all three in a day, reading newspapers in the morning, listening to the radio in the car on the way to work, and then watching television in the evening. As a marketer, this was the heyday of advertising, with lots of ability to bombard the consumer with brand and product-related advertising of all kinds.

However, the Internet changed all that. People have virtually stopped buying and reading newspapers. Why bother when all the news you want is no longer cost effective to print and is only a click away? People are listening to Internet and satellite radio, which are commercial free and subscription based (or even free in some cases!), are watching a decreasing amount of TV, and are more likely to be found online in the evening. In fact, a recent study noted that even when the TV is on in a household, it is likely that a laptop or computer is also running and is being used during the program itself, and most certainly, during commercials. So, as Figure 8.9 shows, there has been a dramatic and continuing decrease in the dominance of broadcast media worldwide and an associated rise in personalized "mycasting" online that seems destined to continue.

WHAT DO YOU THINK?

If you were marketing a product or service to students today, where and how would you market it? What role would the Internet or social media technologies likely play in your strategy?

This presents a significant challenge for companies wanting to advertise, and likely explains the almost 10-fold rise in annual spending in online social advertising that is expected to occur

---

10. Based on data from eMarketer.com.

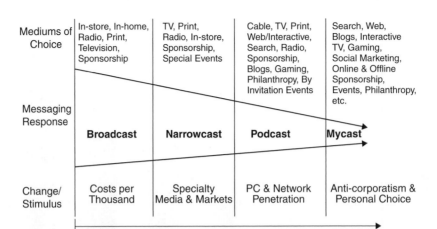

Mediums of Choice	In-store, In-home, Radio, Print, Television, Sponsorship	TV, Print, Radio, In-store, Sponsorship, Special Events	Cable, TV, Print, Web/Interactive, Search, Radio, Sponsorship, Blogs, Gaming, Philanthropy, By Invitation Events	Search, Web, Blogs, Interactive TV, Gaming, Social Marketing, Online & Offline Sponsorship, Events, Philanthropy, etc.
Messaging Response	**Broadcast**	**Narrowcast**	**Podcast**	**Mycast**
Change/ Stimulus	Costs per Thousand	Specialty Media & Markets	PC & Network Penetration	Anti-corporatism & Personal Choice
	1950's	1970's	1990's	2010's

FIGURE 8.9 The way advertisers reach consumers has changed significantly since the advent of the Internet. We have moved from an age of broadcasting to mycasting, and the ability of advertisers to target their audience has narrowed in the process.

worldwide between 2007 and 2012. The focus of online advertising is shifting from search and banner ads to social media sites.

Social Business Models

With all this change in marketing and advertising, what are the social business models of the future? How will this trend impact how businesses deal with their customers and build their brands? The answers are still emerging, but there are some early signs that you should pay attention to. The first one is that best practices for social marketing are different. Look for up-to-date sources of what leaders in this space are doing and follow them. Good sources for this information might include sites like *www.mashable.com* or *www.econsultancy.com*. For those of you interested in the not-for-profit space, it too is adopting the social web in interesting ways (see *www.frogloop.com* for the latest and greatest social networking ideas in that space, including a social network return on investment calculator!). If you look carefully at any of these sites, you may find that they really do practise what they preach, and they will make it easy for you to find out about them. For instance, on the front page of *Mashable.com* you will see four distinct ways to access information about their latest findings, including Twitter, RSS, daily email subscriptions, or their Facebook group. Of course, as they discover new ways, this list will likely change, as it should for all organizations using social media. To use the social web, you have to be part of the social web!

Companies might also seek the help of a local interactive media marketing agency. This is an emerging field, often linked to traditional marketing agencies. Its sole purpose is to help you maximize your online social presence and brand. But all of this is useless unless there is a way to monetize or assetize your traffic and brand, as discussed earlier in Chapter 7.

What if a company is not an online company, but rather is a traditional bricks and mortar company that simply wants to use social networking to its full advantage? What should it be doing in the social web? Here again there is continual innovation and new applications for ways to save money, ways to do things more efficiently or effectively, or ways to improve business outcomes with consumers. Here is a short list of some recent things being done

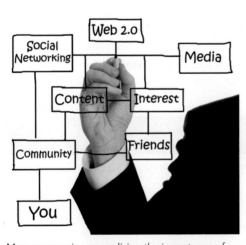

Many companies are realizing the importance of social media in their marketing efforts and are putting more advertising dollars into these sites than more traditional online advertising, such as search and banner ads.

in the social web to great advantage, and which begin to help define the business benefits of social computing in new ways:

1. Conduct online focus groups for new product development (faster, easier).
2. Run viral campaigns to launch new products (innovative, cheaper).
3. Hold virtual recruiting and job fairs in Second Life (more targeted; attracts a different demographic; cheaper than head hunters).
4. Replace annual online employee engagement or satisfaction surveys with new virtual equivalents that run 7/24 (more cost effective, up-to-date, and interactive).
5. Use social media tools to move from a broadcast to podcast model for training and development and internal communication with employees (on-demand, more flexible, just-in-time).

As shown in the list above, the opportunities to apply social media tools, both internally and externally, are vast for any business regardless of its size, geography, or industry. We are presently in the early stages of adoption. Yet even by the time you read this textbook, more and more organizations will be using these tools online to create, build, and promote their organizations to engaged and involved online consumers. What is clear is that no one can ignore this trend—it is real and it is now.

Conclusion

What does all this mean? It means that all businesses and organizations are ultimately affected by any underlying social trend of any magnitude, and that the example of Web 2.0 is no different. As the usage of online social computing in all age groups continues to increase, businesses will have to adapt and figure out what this means for their target markets. It also means that you cannot afford to ignore the technology trends and contents outlined in this chapter, regardless of what role you plan to have in any enterprise, anywhere in the world!

WHAT DO YOU THINK? ?

Social media has moved from affecting consumer relations to affecting the entire decision-making process. We already know that social media has greatly impacted marketing agencies and internal marketing strategies for companies. Consider how social media has impacted human resources, sales, and IT departments. Where do you see the future of social media going?

Quick Test

1. Free time and a willingness to learn have allowed this demographic to become one of the fastest-growing online demographics today.
   a. Computer-savvy youth
   b. 18–25-year-old students
   c. Retired elderly
   d. Middle-aged parents

2. Fill in the blank. Since the 1950s we have witnessed media consumption shift from broadcasting to the personalized form known as _____.

3. True or False. Offering employees the option of podcast training sessions creates a more flexible learning environment because employees can learn the newest information on demand, when it fits their schedule.

What's in IT for me?

Have you Googled yourself lately? What have you found? More and more information can be found about individuals online. Perhaps you were quoted in the school newspaper, had your triathlon results published, or made a charitable contribution noted on a charity's website. Your activity on Facebook, LinkedIn, and Twitter may also come up when searching about you. On one hand, this is good; on another, not so good. With a profile on LinkedIn, for instance, you give employers the ability to find and contact you. This good impression of you may be obliterated, however, by the pictures your friend posted on Facebook of you at Oktoberfest.

It is becoming very important to be aware of your online image and take steps to manage it. Below are some selected tips from Robert Half Technology, a firm specializing in recruiting technical employees, for protecting your professional reputation when using social networking sites:[11]

- Know what's allowed. Make sure you understand and adhere to your company's social networking policy. If you are not permitted to blog or tweet about what you are doing at work, don't. Confidentiality is key.
- Use caution. Be familiar with each site's privacy settings to ensure personal details or photos you post can be viewed only by people you choose.
- Keep it professional. When using social networking sites at work to make connections with others in your field or follow industry news, be professional in the use of your language.
- Stay positive. Avoid complaining about your manager and co-workers. Once you've hit submit or send, you can't always take back your words—there is a chance they could be read by the very people you're criticizing.
- Polish your image. Tweet or blog about a topic related to your profession. You will build a reputation as a subject matter expert, which could help you advance in your career.

Above all, use common sense. When using social networking, realize that you are broadcasting. The results are much the same as being on TV or radio, but with a more permanent effect.

What's in IT for an organization?

Recently, while conducting research on trends in social computing as related to organizations, we became aware that many innovative organizations respond to new trends by adopting them as a way to promote the organization online. While this is one interesting application of new technology, as researchers we wondered how to apply these kinds of technologies internally within organizations. As a result,

---
11. Robert Half Technology Canada, *http://rht.mediaroom.com/index.php?s=131&item=790.*

a new idea was born. As essentially a collection of social networks (departments, functions, reporting relationships, groups with assigned leaders, a social and power hierarchy, etc.), most medium- to large-sized companies could benefit enormously from deploying Web 2.0 technologies internally; yet the focus of most organizations has been purely on their use externally. The most innovative CIOs will never forget their internal users, for they are the core of productivity and innovation, something every company should care deeply about. To see more about how this approach might work and what is being done about it, check out *Speechbobble.com*.

What's in IT for society?

As a social trend, Web 2.0 technologies are game-changing in the world of politics. As just one example, the Obama presidential campaign in the United States was able to raise more money than any other campaign in history, and from a larger number of donors, through the use of social media. Rather than relying on targeting large corporate donors or the obviously wealthy, the Obama campaign was a grassroots response to a rising social phenomenon.[12] And, of course, social computing was the enabler of this. Without the ability to reach millions of people, seemingly able to connect with them on their issues, and then offering them the chance to donate online, this campaign would never have succeeded. Now that's a social trend in politics worth noting!

12. *http://webtrends.about.com/od/web20/a/obama-web.htm*

RO↑ | STUDENT RETURN ON INVESTMENT SUMMARY

1. Define Web 2.0 and describe what features can make a social website more successful.

The term Web 2.0 represents the interactive web as distinguished from the static, for-information-only web of Web 1.0. Web 2.0 has functionality that allows the creation of communities, input of user-generated content (UGC), and two-way communication. All organizations, businesses, not-for-profits, and governments need to be concerned about Web 2.0 because it is the standard that consumers and stakeholders expect. When you contact organizations, you expect responsiveness and interactivity. In fact, you expect fun! This is why more people are using the Web for information and entertainment than radio, TV, and print.

For a social website to be successful, it must have social utility. That is, it must be useful and contribute to your happiness or social satisfaction, or create social opportunities for you. The most successful social websites provide an opportunity for their communities to participate and add content of interest to the whole community. This then attracts more like-minded participants, who add more content. In addition to this, for a social website to be successful, it must be attractive and easy to navigate.

2. Explain social utility and how it is leveraged to encourage user-generated content.

Social utility suggests that users receive social value by spending time creating content on social media networks like Facebook. The theory explains that users must desire to be affiliated with a site in order to join. Once they join, users must then feel compelled to continually participate on the site to validate their initial desire to affiliate. In other words, if a user joins a social network because they desire to be "cool," continually participating on the network must make them feel cool. By satisfying this basic desire, social networks are able to encourage users to generate multimedia and textual content that keeps the social network in a continual cycle of renewal. This process then attracts more like-minded participants, who add more content and contribute to the growth of the network.

3. Explain the benefits businesses can obtain by harnessing the power of social media.

By harnessing the power of social media, businesses are able to facilitate employer/employee engagement, create brand-related clubs/forums, manage online communities, facilitate online review sites for their products or services, or promote geo-purposed sites or application creation. Each of these types of benefits have a purpose attached to community, common membership, or interests, and each supports a specific brand, product, or geographical overlay that helps draw relevant traffic to businesses.

4. Describe how social media has changed the way people consume media and how this has affected social business models.

Media consumption has shifted from a broadcast to mycast model, where each consumer is choosing which media they consume and when. In the 1950s generic media was projected to the masses through radio, television, and print. During this time, if consumers wanted to consume a certain media program, they had to schedule their day around that program. Today, the Internet enables people to consume media when it is most convenient for them. Through social media sharing, consumers pass relevant content from one person to the next, eliminating their dependency on the mass dissemination of media from broadcast stations. As a result, marketing and advertising through social media channels has skyrocketed. In turn, social business models are constantly adapting by applying new tools internally and externally to help complete business tasks such as training, recruitment, research, and new product launch.

KNOWLEDGE SPEAK

brandstorm   316

compression technologies   312

direct marketing   318

folksonomy   315

indirect sources of information   318

invitational design   308

mashup   316

media transparency   319

micro-markets   319

online social strategy   315

participating identity   314

platform plays   319

schadenfreude   315

self-regulating community   314

semantic web   302

site audit   317

social transparency   309

social utility   306

tagging   315

Three Pillars of Sociability   306

user-generated content (UGC)   302

viral social interactions   315

Web 2.0   302

REVIEW QUESTIONS

Multiple-choice questions

1. Running a social media site requires a lot of _____ to deliver multimedia intense content.
   a. marketing
   b. legal advice
   c. pixels
   d. bandwidth

2. The type of marketing that occurs when marketing and IT are interdependent is known as:
   a. e-info
   b. e-dominated
   c. e-commerce
   d. e-enabled

3. The first step in the Three Pillars of Sociability is _____, which is the step where a user would want to belong to a site.
   a. affiliate
   b. placate
   c. validate
   d. participate

4. Mycasting mediums of choice include:
   a. print, TV, radio
   b. Web, TV, radio
   c. Web, search, social marketing
   d. print, TV, special events

Fill-in-the-blank questions

5. For a user to want to continue to use a social networking site, the site must constantly reinforce its social utility and _____ the user's social experience.

6. Because social media sites must store massive amounts of multimedia content, there is a high demand for _____ and _____ who know how to handle large amounts of information.

7. Due to the amount of user-generated content on social media sites, both the providers and users of these sites need to be concerned about _____ and _____.

8. Some businesses might use _____ as a way to cheaply recruit more targeted and hipper job candidates.

True-false questions

9. In March 2009, it was reported that social networking sites were more popular than email.

10. For a social media site to be successful, it must create and produce a lot of content.

11. If a company experiences a brandstorm, the best course of action is to counter-attack online with competing blogs and videos.

12. It is likely that when a TV is on in a household, so too is a laptop or computer.

Matching questions

Choose the BEST answer from Column B for each item in Column A.

Column A

13. Web 1.0
14. Web 2.0
15. semantic web

Column B

a. You post a cool photo of the sunset on Twitter for your followers to see and re-tweet

b. You need to sell your mountain bike so you post a classified ad on your school's student association website.

c. After booking a trip online, an automated agent searches for hotels and rental cars that will complement your trip.

Short-answer questions

16. What is media transparency? How is this facilitated in social media?
17. What is a blog? How are blogs used in business?

Discussion/Essay questions

18. Select a social networking site. Map this site to the Three Pillars of Sociability. Explain how the site exhibits the three pillars.
19. Imagine you are a marketer. Which social networking sites would you monitor to stay on top of potential brandstorms? Why these sites? What would give you the indication that something is going viral?

TEAM ACTIVITY

Select a brand as a team. Go to *www.youtube.com* and search for videos about this brand. Review the titles of all of the videos that you found. Watch a few of the videos whose titles appear positive to the brand, and a few that appear to be negative to the brand. Discuss your findings as a group. What do you think is the overall impression of the brand on YouTube?

SOFTWARE APPLICATION EXERCISES

1. Internet

Go to *www.ning.com*. Search through the available networks and see if one is appealing to you. Create a social network based on your course work, a hobby, or as a fan of something if it does not already exist. Invite some friends and/or classmates to participate in your social network.

2. Presentation

Blogging may be a good way for you to earn a little money toward your tuition. Do some research to understand what it takes to set up and maintain a blog. Then do some research to determine how you can make money with your blog. Create a presentation to share this information with the class. Ensure that you cover why your blog will be successful.

3. Word Processing

Choose a local company, perhaps a bar/restaurant that you frequent. Develop an online strategy for it that includes the use of existing social media sites such as Facebook, Twitter, and LinkedIn. Document this strategy using your word processing software in the form of a consulting recommendation report.

4. Spreadsheet

Go to *www.tweetedbrands.com*. Select one of the brands that appears in the listing and note the number of associated tweets. Using a spreadsheet, list this brand and the number of tweets it receives for one week. Graph the data. Did the number of tweets remain constant, increase, or decrease for your selected brand? What may have contributed to this trend?

5. Database

The website *Alexa.com* is an excellent example of an incredibly valuable database application if you are in business. For any website in the world, it will give you an instant ranking of relative traffic. You can also find out if the traffic to a website is increasing or decreasing, as well as other information. Go to this site and pick your top five websites, including at least one or more social media sites, and compare them on a number of dimensions using the Alexa data. Compare your favourite online news site with CBC, for instance, and see which one has more popular influence.

6. Advanced Challenge

How are you managing your online image? Do you have profiles on LinkedIn, Facebook, MySpace, Flickr, or other social media sites? If so, review all of the content you have put in these sites. Does the content reflect the image that you want to portray? If you are not using any of these sites, research professional social networking sites such as LinkedIn and Plaxo. Determine which one might be best to join as a job-seeking graduate. If you think it is a good idea, set up a profile and start networking.

ONLINE RESOURCES

Companion Website

- Take interactive practice quizzes to assess your knowledge and help you study in a dynamic way.
- Review PowerPoint lecture slides.
- Get help and sample solutions to end-of-chapter software application exercises.

Additional Resources Available Only on *WileyPLUS*

- Take the interactive Quick Test to check your understanding of the chapter material and get immediate feedback on your responses.
- Review and study with downloadable Audio Lecture MP3 files.
- Check your understanding of the key vocabulary in the chapter with Knowledge Speak Interactive Flash Cards.

CASE STUDY:
WEB 2.0 APPLICATIONS AT EASTERN MOUNTAIN SPORTS

Eastern Mountain Sports (EMS; *Ems.com*) is a medium-sized specialty retailer (annual sales $200 million U.S.) with over 80 physical stores, a mail order catalogue, and online sales. Operating in a very competitive environment, the company uses leading-edge IT technologies and lately has introduced a complementary set of Web 2.0 tools to increase collaboration, information sharing, and communication among stores and their employees, suppliers, and customers. Let's see how this works.

The Business Intelligence Strategy and System

During the last few years, the company implemented a business intelligence (BI) system that includes business performance management and dashboards. A BI system collects raw data from multiple sources, processes them into a data mart, and conducts analyses that include comparing performance to operational metrics to assess the health of the business.

Figure 8.10 illustrates how the system works. Point-of-sale (POS) information and other relevant data, which are available on an IBM computer, are loaded into Microsoft's SQL Server and then into a data mart. The data are then analyzed with Information Builders' business and analytics tool (BI analytics). The results are presented via a series of dashboards that users can view via their Web browsers; they are invited to make comments via blogs. In this way, users can access a

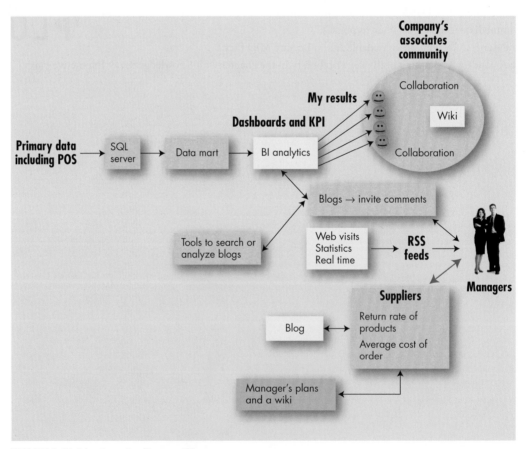

FIGURE 8.10 A business intelligence (BI) system.

unified, high-level view of key performance indicators (KPI) such as sales, inventory, and margin levels, and drill down to granular details that analyze specific transactions. Communication and collaboration is conducted mainly using blogs, wikis, and other Web 2.0 tools that are described next with the process.

The Web 2.0 Collaboration, Sharing, and Communication System

The company created a multifunction employee workbench called E-Basecamp. It contains all of the information relevant to corporate goals, integrated with productivity tools (e.g., Excel) and role-based content, customized to each individual user. Then, it added a set of Web 2.0 tools (see Figure 8.10). The system facilitates collaboration among internal and external stakeholders. EMS uses 20 operation metrics (e.g., inventory levels and turns). These also include e-tailing where e-commerce managers monitor hour-by-hour Web traffic and conversion rates. The dashboard shows deviations from targets with a colour code. It uses the following Web 2.0 tools:

- *RSS feeds*. These are embedded into the dashboards to drive more focused inquiries. These feeds are the basis for information sharing and online conversations. For example, by showing which items are selling better than others, users can collectively analyze the transaction characteristics and selling behaviours that produce the high sales. The knowledge acquired then cascades throughout the organization. For instance, one manager observed an upward spike in footwear sales at store X. Investigation revealed that store X employees had perfected a multistep sales technique that included recommending special socks (both online and in stores) designed for specific uses, along with an inner sole. The information was disseminated using the RSS feed. As a result, sales of footwear increased 57 percent in a year.
- *Wikis*. Wikis are used to encourage collaborative interaction throughout the company. Dashboard users are encouraged to post a hypothesis or requests for help, and invite commentary and suggestions, almost like a notepad alongside the dashboard.
- *Blogs*. Blogs were created around specific data or a key metric. They are used to post information and invite comments. Then tools are used to archive, search, and categorize blogs for easy reference. For example, store managers post an inquiry or explanation regarding sale deviations. Keeping comments on blogs lets readers observe patterns they might have overlooked using data analysis alone.

Going to External Business Partners

In the next phase, suppliers are added. For example, suppliers can monitor the return rate of their product on the dashboard and invite store managers to provide explanations and suggestions using wikis or blogs. Assuming proper security of data is installed, suppliers can get almost real-time data about how well their products sell so they can prepare a better production plan.

The objectives are to build a tighter bond with the business partners. For example, by having store managers attach blogs to the suppliers' dashboards, the suppliers view current sale information and post comments to the blogs. Product managers use a wiki to post challenges for the next season, such as a proposed percentage increase in sales, and then ask vendors to suggest innovative ways to achieve these goals. Several of the customers and other business partners subscribe to RSS feeds.

Called *extreme deals* (big discounts for a limited time), blogs are also embedded into the EMS product management lifecycle (PLM) tool. This allows vendors to have virtual conversations with the product development managers.

The major impact of the Web 2.0 collaboration tools is that instead of having conversations occur in the hallway (where you need to be in the right place at the right time), conversations take place on blogs and wikis where all interested parties can participate.

Case Questions

1. Why not just have regular meetings and send emails rather than use blogs, wikis, and RSS feeds?
2. What are the benefits to EMS of combining its BI system and Web 2.0 tools?
3. In what ways is corporate performance bolstered?
4. What kind of community is this? Who are the members?
5. Can the company use any other Web 2.0 technologies? If so, what and how?
6. What information on *Ems.com* is typical for what you find in social network sites?

Efraim Turban and Linda Volonino, *Information Technology for Management: Improving Performance in the Digital Economy*, 7th edition. Hoboken, NJ: John Wiley & Sons Inc., pp. 321–322.

CASE STUDY:
MARKETING THROUGH SOCIAL MEDIA

Your company is launching a new product. While its final form has to remain secret for competitive reasons until launch day, what is known is that it is a new technology that is anticipated to appeal to on-the-move, urban new professionals in the 22–30-year-old range. While past buyers of your product have mostly been guys (about 70+ percent), the company believes that the design and interface of this new product may allow it to crack the female-buying segment. That is a significant marketing objective and the company has invested quite a bit of time investigating how it can promote this new product to women.

You recently joined the IT team as a business analyst and your client is in marketing. You were approached by the brand manager for this new product with a challenge. Your client is a very experienced product marketer who has been with the company for about 14 years. While very smart, she admits to not being very technically savvy. You have previously had lunch with her to indicate your eventual interest in marketing as part of your career plan, and you are really hoping the work you are doing with her on this will impress her and open up career advancement opportunities. You really want to be quite independent and do great work that impresses her.

She wants to use social media as part of an integrated marketing campaign for the new product, but she doesn't really know a lot about what's available that she could use. She mumbles something about needing to look at Facebook and Twitter and "all those kinds of things." She has now turned to you for a recommendation for either buying, sourcing, or using 3–5 social media tools for the new campaign. She explains her requirements:

1. The tools should be selected to appeal to women and where and how women obtain information about new products they may be interested in buying.
2. The use of the tools must comply with the company's privacy policy, including the fact that the data stored in the system must either be private or permission to use it must be secured from the user, and all customer data should be stored in Canada to the extent possible or practical.
3. Given the tools will be used in a marketing campaign, the marketing team needs access to data and information about the use of the tools by women and how many of them eventually either request information about or actually buy the product, again to the extent possible.

Case Activity

1. Using only the information above, the knowledge gained from this chapter, and your own experience or data sources, prepare a written recommendation for the product marketer. This should be in the form of either a detailed memo or small business case that outlines the social media choices you are recommending, their cost range, operation, potential benefits, recommended uses, and how they comply with your client's requirements. Questions she will be looking for answers to include:
   a. Why is this platform a good choice for young, urban, women consumers?
   b. What do you hope women will do on this platform that encourages them to buy?
   c. How will you measure the contribution of social media to the product launch?

LOGOFF

We hope that you have enjoyed this journey, learning to combine your business and technology knowledge in ways that create value for the organizations that you will one day join. We also hope that the practical approach we took helped make the subject matter accessible and useful to you—we feel it is vital to everyone's future business success to understand IT/IS.

Good system design must focus on seamless, connected systems that enable your organization's processes to do their work and become more efficient and effective. These systems are best designed with the input of those closest to the work: business professionals like you. You will ultimately use these systems to increase your own productivity and create business impact. And creating impact is what will make your career successful, regardless of what it is!

Even though we are at the end of our learning journey, we could not resist incorporating a couple of final examples showing how business and technology intersect in unusual and interesting ways—proof positive of our hypothesis about its use affecting every single function in an organization.

Several years ago, United Airlines experienced an operational mishap, leading to a passenger's luggage being damaged. (The specific details of the incident don't particularly matter, but for more information on this incident, check out the links in *WileyPLUS*.) The luggage that was temporarily lost and damaged was a guitar—quite an expensive professional guitar—belonging to a musician. Needless to say, the musician was upset about this and complained . . . and complained . . . and complained, all to no avail. No one listened to him or helped him!

So how does an incident like this involve technology? As you will see, and as you have hopefully learned throughout this book, technology is pervasive and persuasive, and its use in business can create an undeniable competitive advantage. But that advantage can also be used to hold organizations accountable and to promote their failures online, creating instant attention that was never before possible.

In the past, organizations were structured largely by business functions and, while they may have cooperated across departments, there was limited opportunity for customers to learn how to effectively navigate these various functions to resolve their problems. Frustrations with customer service remained pretty much within customer service, and even if they were escalated, often they would simply move upward within the same function. How could an individual customer really have any impact on a global brand?

In our example, the musician decided to write a song about United Airlines. And, through YouTube and other social media, he was able to instantly produce and publish his work, which went viral very quickly. By the time United became aware of the "United Guitar Song," the video was already trending as the most downloaded video of the day! So, while United apparently could not use technology and process design to avoid damaging their customer's guitar, their customer was certainly able to use technology to make his point about the lack of attention to his concerns and what he felt was a complete lack of customer focus inside the organization.

Global organizations are large, complex affairs and mistakes will happen. Especially in something like the airline business, one cannot expect everything to go as planned all the time. But it is critical that organizations understand the requirement to rapidly and successfully recover from customer service mistakes. To do this, especially in a global context, organizations must deploy technology systems to support that objective, and then empower people to use these systems to make an immediate difference for customers. As you will see in much of the press coverage of this story (links are available on *WileyPLUS*), it was the endless loop of nobody being willing to do anything to help this customer (either because they were not empowered to or because they lacked the proper information about his situation to help effectively) that sparked his rage.

And an angry consumer in today's world is a brand destroyer. More than ever before in the history of commerce, the phrase "businesses are built one customer at a time" applies! And technology is a major part of that. We all know that happy customers are generally silent customers, and for that we are often grateful. But the brand storm that engulfed United Airlines in this case was the result of a consumer being willing to deploy technology rapidly to express a complaint about a brand. As a result, businesses must be willing to deploy that same technology to resolve problems at web speed to avoid this happening.

To prove our point, let's explore another example. This one involves a large global hotel chain with an established luxury brand that truly goes above and beyond. Fairmont Hotels and Resorts

Most organizations have outlets or telephone/online services available, like United Airlines' baggage services office, where customers can complain or get help to resolve their problems. However, they only work if employees are actually able to do something about the problem.

has a reputation for outstanding service. In speaking with the director of marketing recently about this reputation, one of the authors of this text wanted to explore what made this possible. While learning all about their progressive knowledge of their internal systems, all focused on the customer and particularly those who are part of the elite President's Club, the author heard one important thing: the director talked about how grateful she was for Twitter. Why? In addition to tweeting for marketing purposes (and they also blog!), the director of marketing indicated that the in-house customer service team monitors 24/7 every major function held on one of their properties that has a Twitter handle attached to it. They have learned that solving a customer service problem immediately, no matter what it is, is far more powerful than efforts to avoid every single problem in the first place. Just as with an airline, sometimes things do not go according to plan, and since the organization can only fix what is reported to it, Twitter is one of the quickest ways of learning about a problem. Consumers love to tweet, and they tweet the good, the bad, and the ugly. Who would have imagined that a major hotel would be spending time monitoring a Twitter feed to improve their customer service? That is a changed world—and it is the one in which we all now live. Technology is pervasive and powerful.

■ FINAL THOUGHTS

One of the most powerful concepts that we keep returning to in our professional and academic lives is the power of properly combining and balancing people, processes, and technology to achieve productivity in organizations. It might help you to recall this concept by making final reference to one of the first diagrams we used in Chapter 1.

Whether we are talking about the United Airlines example, or the outstanding customer service that is technology-enabled at Fairmont Hotels and Resorts, or maybe even your own local business or branch of a charity that you work for, technology is essential to their operations. But it is even more essential to the development of relationships, both inside and outside the organization; to the delivery of outstanding customer service; and to the smooth operation of the organization's processes and workflows. In fact, you can no longer separate the people, processes, and technologies found in most organizations because of how intertwined they are. The most productive organizations understand this, exploit this, and empower it to happen; they enter their "productivity zone" not with fear, but with the anticipation of a great future that is more powerful and productive than anything we have previously experienced as a society.

We hope this book has helped you realize the power of this simple concept. Many of those profiled in our Voice of Experience sections spoke about the need to remain on top of technology to master its use in business. We hope they have convinced you of its importance as you progress in your career. If your knowledge of technology now includes how to make yourself and others more productive, and how to ensure business processes run more smoothly in your organizations, then we have accomplished what we set out to do. Good luck!

TECH GUIDE

A | THE DETAILS OF IT HARDWARE AND SOFTWARE

WHAT WE WILL COVER

- An Overview of Hardware
- Hardware Devices
- Operating Software
- Application Software

STUDENT RETURN ON INVESTMENT ROI

Through your investment of time in reading and thinking about this Tech Guide, your return—or created value—is gaining knowledge. After reading this Tech Guide, you should be able to

1. Describe the elements that affect the processing capability of hardware.

2. Describe the various types of input, output, and storage hardware that business professionals should keep current with.

3. Explain why the operating system is so important to the use of all types of computers.

4. Explain how business professionals obtain and use application software.

Hardware is the physical component of information technology (IT). The working parts of IT hardware consist primarily of electronic devices (mostly digital), with some electro-mechanical parts used with input, output, and storage devices. *Software* provides the instructions that IT hardware needs. The two major categories of software are operating system software and application software. Except in special situations, both software types run at the same time, each serving a different purpose.

In this Tech Guide, we provide a more detailed look into commonly available hardware, operating systems, and application software. Much of our discussion will focus on the personal computer (PC), as its architecture includes components common to all information devices and it is the system you are most familiar with. Our objective is to provide you with enough knowledge of the technology to allow you to make savvy decisions.

■ AN OVERVIEW OF HARDWARE

Entire books are written about certain types of hardware. Here we introduce key concepts concerning hardware and discuss commonly used hardware to give you a basic knowledge of this area of IT.

Evaluating Hardware Devices

If you have ever been to an office supply store such as Staples or Office Depot, or an electronics store like Future Shop or Best Buy, you will know that selecting the right IT devices can be an overwhelming decision. How do you know which ones will serve you best now and in the future? These decisions often include evaluating the following factors:

- *Cost*—You want the device to be within your budget and to provide the most value for each dollar you spend.
- *Compatibility*—Hardware devices work together to form a system. Each device needs to work correctly with the other devices.
- *Data and Information Needs*—You choose devices based on a desired task. You need your IT devices to work with data and/or information in a specific way.
- *Accuracy*—You rely on your devices to handle data and instructions without errors.
- *Speed*—You would like to work with your data and instructions as quickly and efficiently as possible.
- *Portability*—Because you may want to work with information as you travel, you need to be able to easily move the devices.
- *Form Factor*—The size, shape, and physical arrangement of IT hardware can affect how and where you use a device.

Some, or all, of these factors influence your selection and use of hardware devices, whether the device concerns processing, memory, input, output, communication, or storage. In this Tech Guide, we will look at various types of hardware devices. However, before considering the many types of hardware devices on the market, we first examine the electronics behind them.

The Electronics of Hardware

The primary electronic component of IT hardware is the transistor. A **transistor** is a very small device made out of semiconductor material that acts as a switch to control electronic signals. Millions of transistors, each too small to be seen by the unaided eye, are combined to make the computer's microprocessor and memory chips. Both types of chips are quite small themselves.

Microprocessor chips carry out many different processing operations within a computer, including handling input and output, as well as the actual conversion of data into information. Over time, the number of transistors on a microprocessor chip has expanded, resulting in increasingly powerful computers. For example, Intel's popular Core i5 microprocessor chip contains 774 million transistors. Intel chips power the vast majority of all PCs in the world today, including those built by Apple Computer. Microprocessor chips are also built into virtually all electronic devices.

Memory chips also use transistors to store data within the computer. As with microprocessor chips, the amount of internal memory stored on chips has also risen dramatically as more transistors are built into the memory chips.

How Transistors Work Think of a transistor as an electronic switch that can be in one of two states: off or on. You can represent the two states of a transistor using **binary** mathematics, which uses ones (on) and zeros (off). Thus, transistors store and transmit all data in a computer as combinations of 1s and 0s. Data that transistors store as a sequence of discrete symbols from a finite set, like the set {0,1}, are referred to as **digital data**. When you consider technologies like digital cameras or MP3 players, you can bet that the data processed in these devices are represented as binary numbers. Let's take a closer look at binary data.

Binary Data In binary, the basic unit, a **bit**, corresponds to a power of two, or as they say in mathematics, binary is *base 2*. For example, you can use binary to describe the *base 10* decimal number 234 as follows:

$$11101010_2 = 1_{10} * 2^7 + 1_{10} * 2^6 + 1_{10} * 2^5 + 0_{10} * 2^4 + 1_{10} * 2^3 + 0_{10} * 2^2 + 1_{10} * 2^1 + 0_{10} * 2^0$$
$$= 128_{10} + 64_{10} + 32_{10} + 8_{10} + 2_{10} = 234_{10}$$

Similarly, you can convert other binary values to decimal values; vice versa, you can convert decimal numbers to equivalent binary values simply by taking the decimal number and repeatedly dividing it by two. In each case, the remainder of the division will be 0 or 1. The composite of all such remainders is then the binary equivalent of the decimal number. Let's use the number 234_{10} again. If you take all of the remainders and put them in reverse order from the divisions, you have the corresponding binary number:[1] 11101010_2. See Table A.1.

You may be questioning the usefulness of binary data if they only concern data such as decimal numbers. But many other types of data can also be stored as binary, like the letters and punctuation characters on your keyboard, as well as graphics, music, and videos. How do hardware devices use binary codes to store different types of information? Through character encoding.

Character Encoding Binary codes represent letters and numbers through **character encoding**. Character encoding permits a specific combination of bits to represent each character. Can anyone design a character-encoding scheme? Yes, but that would make it virtually impossible for all types of hardware and software to work together. When software works with a hardware device or when two hardware devices work together, they are said to be compatible. Therefore, independent national or international committees write most schemes, including ASCII, Unicode, and EBCDIC, to ensure IT compatibility.

Standard ASCII The oldest encoding system used on mainframe computers is the *Extended Binary Coded Decimal Interchange Code (EBCDIC)*, which is an eight-bit coding system. For personal

Table A.1	Finding the Binary Equivalent to Decimal Numbers	
Beginning Number	**After Division**	**Remainder**
234	117	0
117	58	1
58	29	0
29	14	1
14	7	0
7	3	1
3	1	1
1	0	1

---

1. For an explanation of why this works, see *http://en.wikipedia.org/wiki/Binary_numeral_system*.

Table A.2	Comparison of Coding Schemes—Binary Representations		
Character	EBCDIC	ASCII	Unicode
A	1100 0001	0100 0001	0000 0000 0100 0001
Esc	0010 0111	0001 1011	0000 0000 0001 1011
%	0110 1100	0010 0101	0000 0000 0010 0101
2	1111 0010	0011 0010	0000 0000 0011 0010
π	Not available	Not available	0000 0011 1100 0000
⅔	Not available	Not available	0010 0001 0101 0011

computers, the first encoding system was the **Standard ASCII (American Standard Code for Information Interchange)**. Standard ASCII uses seven bits to represent the following: the unaccented letters of the English language, a–z and A–Z; basic punctuation; numbers; space; and some control codes, such as the Enter key. Using binary-to-decimal conversion, the maximum number of characters that standard ASCII can code is $01111111_{binary} + 1_{decimal}$ (for 00000000_{binary}) $= 127_{decimal} + 1_{decimal} = 128_{decimal}$ characters. This limits standard ASCII mostly to English characters and punctuation. However, virtually all computers recognize an extended form of ASCII that uses eight bits to provide 256 characters, thereby adding accented characters from common foreign languages. However, this limit of 256 characters has become a problem with the increasing global use of computers.

Unicode To deal with the increased globalization of business and use of PCs, most IT devices now rely on a more recent standard called **Unicode**, which extends ASCII by providing a 16-bit character set. Unicode adds eight characters to the extended ASCII eight-bit character assignments to include the characters of the major modern written languages. As with standard and extended ASCII, Unicode is available on virtually all recently manufactured PCs.

Today, virtually all computers can work with all three types of encoding systems. Table A.2 lists some examples of character codes under each of these standards.

Machine Instructions We've seen how a computer can represent numeric and character data, but what about instructions? Hardware devices, such as a computer or PDA, execute instructions as a sequence of binary strings known as **machine instructions**. The sequence used to represent a specific instruction is assigned in a similar manner as that used to assign binary sequences to character data (e.g., the ASCII code). For example, Figure A.1 shows the machine language instructions for a Pentium chip, seen as a series of instructions to sum the digits 1 to 100.

However, there is one significant difference for machine instructions: no default standard exists for how to encode instructions. Instead, this is left up to the manufacturers of microprocessors, which can therefore result in incompatibility between software and hardware. For example, a machine language instruction for an Intel chip will differ from the same instruction on the chips used in larger computers.

The importance of binary mathematics goes beyond the coding of data. You can express most important measures of performance and capacity in computers based on powers of 2. Table A.3 lists

Instruction	Explanation
10111000 00000000 00000000	Set Total Value to 0
10111001 00000000 01100100	Set Current Value to 100
00000001 11001000	Add Current Value to Total Value
01001001	Subtract 1 from Current Value
01110101 11111011	If Current value is not 0, repeat

FIGURE A.1 The machine language instructions for a Pentium chip.

Table A.3	Important Powers of 2	
Power of 2	Decimal Value	Description
2^3	8	Number of bits in a byte
2^8	256	Number of characters that a byte can code
2^{10}	1024	1 kilobyte (KB)
2^{20}	1,048,576	1 megabyte (MB)
2^{30}	1,073,741,824	1 gigabyte (GB)
2^{40}	1,099,511,627,776	1 terabyte (TB)

A computer motherboard is the main circuit board in an electronic device.

some important binary values that you will often encounter when determining hardware capabilities. For example, a **byte** is typically used to represent a character in ASCII, *megabytes* are used to measure the amount of memory in a computer, and *gigabytes* are used to measure the storage on a hard disk. Now with the advent of huge media files, memory and storage are being expressed in *terabytes*.

Now that you have a basic understanding of the electronics involved in hardware devices, let's look at how they affect processing hardware capabilities.

Processing Hardware

At the core of all computing operations is the microprocessor. It contains the majority of the components that make up the **CPU** or **central processing unit**. The CPU works together with memory to control the execution of all instructions and the processing of all data. The CPU is located on the system's **motherboard**, the main circuit board in an electronic device. The motherboard contains the microprocessor as well as other chips and circuits. The motherboard and CPU chip are found in the **system unit**, the box that we often think of as the computer when we look at it.

Often, the speed and performance of the CPU are the key considerations in determining the processing capability of IT devices. Because it's so vital to IT hardware, let's look at the CPU in more detail.

The CPU The CPU consists of several components, shown in Figure A.2:

- *Control Unit (CU)*—Performs the following four basic functions: fetch, decode, execute, and store. One time through each of these tasks in a sequence is called a *cycle*.
- *Arithmetic Logic Unit (ALU)*—Executes mathematical and logic calculations. Logic calculations make comparisons between values.
- *Floating Point Unit (FPU)*—Executes mathematical and logic calculations on non-integer values (values that may have a fractional portion after the decimal point).
- *Decode Unit*—Fetches machine language instructions from the instruction cache and translates them into binary code that the ALU processes.
- *Cache Memory*—Provides a staging area for instructions and the data. Because cache memory is faster than RAM, the processor can keep working without waiting on data.
- *Prefetch Unit*—Provides a small amount of memory that stores incoming instructions in a queue while awaiting execution, thereby reducing CPU waiting time.
- *Registers*—Small sections of memory that store data while the microprocessor needs it. A register address is expressed with a small number of bits, making it much faster to access than normal memory.
- *Clock*—A crystal that sits on the motherboard and vibrates regularly, many times per second. The clock speed refers to the number of cycles a CPU performs in the span of a tick of the computer's internal clock.

- *Bus*—A set of wires that transports data from one location to another. A CPU can have internal buses and address buses. Figure A.2 shows the bus as yellow lines.
- *Instruction Set*—A collection of machine language instructions that governs how the processor interprets and executes various tasks that it performs.

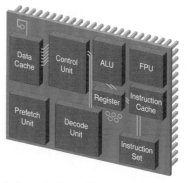

Figure A.3 shows how these components work together to execute instructions. Data and/or instructions are input into memory (initially RAM and then into data or instruction cache, or the prefetch unit). After fetching instructions, the control unit then directs the other components based on the instructions. For example, the control unit may direct data either to the ALU or FPU for processing. Memory stores the processed data, which are then available for further processing or output. These four functions—fetch, decode, execute, and store—provide the basic framework for this process.

FIGURE A.2 The CPU components, connected by the data bus.

The Instruction Set Each microprocessor has a permanently stored set of machine language instructions called the **instruction set**. The instruction set governs how the CPU interprets and executes the tasks that it performs to run computer software. There are two main types of instruction sets: *complex instruction set computer (CISC)* instructions and *reduced instruction set computer (RISC)* instructions. Usually, processors that use an RISC instruction set are faster than those using CISC, because an RISC processor needs to understand and execute fewer commands. RISC processors tend to be used in small electronic devices such as mobile phones or MP3 players. Modern chips like the Intel Core i5 combine the speed of the RISC approach with the power of CISC to provide increased speed.

Bandwidth The size of a CPU's buses determines its **bandwidth**, which is the number of bits the CPU can process in a single instruction. Recall that a **bus** is a set of wires over which data travel from one location to another. In a computer, the main bus is the *data* or *system bus*, which sends and receives data to and from the CPU to other components. However, the *internal buses* control the bandwidth. Internal buses carry data between the components that reside within the chip and *address buses*, which then connect them to main memory.

Bus capacity is expressed as the number of bits of data that can travel over the bus simultaneously. Higher bus capacities usually mean faster processing of instructions and data. For example, assume that a PC has a CPU with a 64-bit internal bus and uses a 32-bit system bus. The CPU internal bus would be about twice as fast as the system bus.

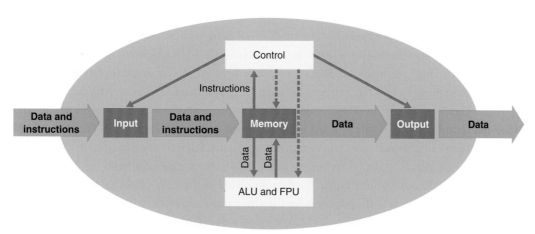

FIGURE A.3 How the CPU components work together to execute instructions.

Clock Speed The clock speed is probably the most common measure of CPU performance. Clock speeds are measured in *megahertz (MHz)*, millions of cycles per second, or *gigahertz (GHz)*, billions of cycles per second. In general, higher clock speeds translate to faster system performance. However, other considerations, such as internal memory and video speed, can also affect overall speed. As a result, clock speeds can be a little misleading. Different internal structure and instruction sets can cause two different models of processors with similar clock speeds to perform at different levels.

CPU Performance Characteristics Microprocessors are typically differentiated by their instruction set, their clock speed, and their bandwidth. As noted above, the clock speed is the most commonly used performance characteristic. All other things being equal, the faster the clock speed, the faster the capability of the CPU chip to process instructions. Many devices contain not only one CPU, but at least two. Dual core processor systems contain two complete processors, often on the same circuit board. The advantage of this configuration is the increased ability to multitask, which allows your computer to do more than one thing at a time.

Internal Memory

In addition to the CPU or microprocessor chip, all computers need internal memory to operate. Like humans, computers have both long-term memory (ROM) and short-term memory (RAM). However, the analogy falls short when we look at the physical implementation and the relative capacity of computer memory. For example, memory stores data and instructions on computer chips. Further, unlike humans, computers require a greater capacity of short-term, temporary memory than long-term memory (we're talking about memory, not storage). In IT devices, from MP3 players to digital cameras to computers, the main purpose of ROM is simply to hold instructions that control the device's start-up processes (booting up). This small set of instructions, known as the **BIOS (basic input/output system)**, activates the hardware components and loads the operating system.

Because ROM's instructions and data cannot be altered and ROM is usually not part of the decision when selecting IT, we focus our attention on RAM.

RAM The largest number of chips in your computer used for memory is in the form of *random access memory (RAM)*, so named because the CPU can access any item stored in RAM directly (randomly). Personal computers usually have two types of RAM: dynamic RAM (DRAM) and static RAM (SRAM). RAM can also be found in other components of your computer system, such as the printer and video and sound cards. This type of RAM is often referred to as peripheral RAM.

Main memory usually refers to the DRAM in your computer. Like the CPU, **dynamic RAM (DRAM)** has improved over the years to provide faster access and greater capacity. It turns out that one of the easiest and least expensive ways to upgrade an older system is to increase the amount of main memory (DRAM).

Static RAM (SRAM) is so called because it does not need to be constantly refreshed to maintain the data that it stores. This makes it faster and less volatile than DRAM, but it also makes it much more expensive. Due to its high cost, SRAM is typically used for smaller sections of memory known as *cache*. Cache memory typically contains the most recently accessed pieces of main memory.

RAM can also be found in other components of your computer system, such as the printer and video and sound cards. This type of RAM is often referred to as **peripheral RAM**. Peripheral RAM serves as a buffer area between the main system and a peripheral device. For example, the DRAM that exists in most printers is known as the *printer buffer*. This buffer temporarily holds the data until the item is printed. Without a printer buffer, the data processed by the CPU can begin to back up, since the CPU can send the data to the printer faster than the printer can print.

Video cards use another type of RAM, known as **video RAM (VRAM)**. The main difference between VRAM and DRAM is that two devices can access VRAM at the same time. This allows the card to simultaneously receive data from the CPU and transmit data to the monitor.

RAM Performance Two factors affect RAM performance: (1) capacity and (2) address bus bandwidth. Let's consider each factor, starting with memory capacity.

When you open multiple applications, such as a program to chat with your friends online while you write a report with a word processor and listen to some tunes, the main memory stores the software and data for these applications. Eventually, you reach your main memory's capacity. When you open your favourite game program (and who hasn't done this when they should be working), there is no room in main memory for its instructions. In this case, the CPU either leaves some of the game's instructions on secondary storage until needed, or it bumps instructions and data from other software out to secondary storage until needed again. Remember that accessing secondary storage is much slower than accessing main memory. As a result, your system may also noticeably slow down.

Thus, the memory capacity in a computer can profoundly affect the overall performance of the computer. Memory capacity is measured in terms of the number of bytes that it may store. Capacities of most types of memory are in the range of thousands (kilobytes, KB), millions (megabytes, MB), and in some cases billions (gigabytes, GB) of bytes. The memory in your computer is primarily a hands-off component. In most cases, once you make your initial purchase, you will not need to configure or troubleshoot the memory. What you mostly need to know is that the more main memory available to your system, the better. For example, Microsoft recommends that you have a *minimum* of 1GB for Windows 7. For two systems, with all other things equal, the one with the most RAM will be able to process more work.

While capacity is the most important consideration when measuring the performance of memory, there is another limiting factor on memory capacity: the bandwidth of the *address buses* that connect the CPU and other devices to main memory. An address is a number that a computer uses to specify the location of a particular piece of data within memory. The size of the address bus determines the maximum number of memory locations. Early address buses had an eight-bit bandwidth, which limited the amount of addressable memory to 2^8—256 locations. As it turns out, the address bus size is not much of a problem in today's computers. For example, core microprocessors use an address bus with a bandwidth of 64 bits. This means that the CPU can access up to 2^{64}—18,446,744,073,709,551,615 (18.45 extrabytes!) eight-bit locations of internal memory. Space and cost limitations with the average personal computer currently make a comparable amount of RAM impractical. But a 64-bit address bus can handle that much if needed.

Quick Test

1. The four functions of the CPU that provide the basic processing framework are the fetch, decode, _____, and store functions.

2. True or False. ROM instructions and data cannot be altered.

3. True or False. Because RAM is permanent memory, it is unnecessary to frequently save your work.

Answers: 1. execute; 2. True; 3. False

■ HARDWARE DEVICES

Input Devices

Any hardware device must have methods for inputting data. The primary input methods include the keyboard, pointing devices such as the mouse, scanning devices such as bar code readers, and the Internet or other network connection. We consider all of these in Table A.4 *except* the Internet/network connection, which we discuss separately in Tech Guide B.

Table A.4	Input Devices	
Device	**Description**	
Keyboard	A keyboard is generally recognized as the primary and most common input device for computers. When you press a key on a keyboard, a microprocessor in the keyboard determines the location of the button. It then sends the appropriate character in binary encoded digits to the computer. The primary value of a keyboard as an input device rests with its ability and versatility to input text data. Tactile response (how it feels) and ergonomics are considerations when purchasing a keyboard or laptop.	
Pointing Devices		
Mouse	A mouse is the most common pointing device. A *mechanical mouse* uses moving parts, such as a ball and rollers. An *optical mouse* does not require moving parts. An optical mouse, having no moving parts to detect motion, uses the light from an LED (light-emitting diode) reflected off a surface to measure the mouse movement. A *laser mouse* uses wireless technology and an infrared laser instead of LED, and can be more sensitive than other types.	
Touchpad	A commonly used pointing device on laptop computers, touchpads provide a small, flat surface that you slide your finger over using the same movements as you would a mouse. "Clicking" is accomplished by finger tapping, either directly on the pad or on nearby buttons.	
Joystick	A joystick is a pointing device often used to control games. It consists of a hand-held stick that pivots on one end and transmits its angle to a computer. A joystick usually has one or more buttons for entering instructions.	
Touch screen	A touch screen is a pointing device that allows the user to interact with a computer by touching the display screen. Using a combination of sensing technology and software, the computer interprets the location where the display is touched to perform the required operation. A touch screen is often used in public kiosks where a mouse would be a problem.	
Trackball	A trackball is basically a pointing device that resembles an upside-down mouse. It consists of a ball that rests in a socket containing sensors to detect the ball's rotation. Users roll the ball with their hand to move a cursor. It is used to replace a mouse in situations where physical movement is a problem, for example, when users have a physical disability.	

Device	Description	
Pen input	A pointing pen looks like a ballpoint pen, but it uses an electronic head instead of ink. Also called a *stylus*, you can use a pen with a digitizing tablet or touch screen. A stylus is often used with PDAs, which also incorporate a form of handwriting recognition that allows you to write directly on the screen.	
Light pen	A light pen is a pointing device that uses a light sensitive detector on a display screen. It allows you to move the pointer and select objects on the display screen by directly pointing it at the objects. A light pen works in a similar way as a mouse, except that you point directly at the objects on the screen.	
Wearable device	There are a number of pointing devices that a user can wear. For example, users can wear a data glove on their hand. The computer interprets hand movements to move the cursor. Buttons may be added on the sides of the fingers to provide command input. These are often used with virtual reality games. A Wii remote is a recent example of a wearable device.	
Tablet	A tablet is a pointing device that consists of an electronic tablet and, sometimes, a cursor that lets you input, draw, and sketch into a computer. A *cursor* is like a mouse, but it has a window with crosshairs and as many as 16 buttons (which may not be entirely visible, depending on the interface). The *tablet* contains electronics that enable it to detect movement of the cursor and translate the movements into signals to the computer. In the past, this device was most often used by graphic artists, engineers, and cartographers to convert drawings to digital form. Now tablets have become increasing popular as a recreational as well as a business device. Common uses of tablets today include point-of-sale devices where a screen captures the signature for your credit card and, of course, devices such as iPads and Playbooks. Many smartphones also include tablet-like functionality.	
Scanning devices		
Bar Code Reader	A bar code reader is a device that reads a printed horizontal strip of vertical bars. The bar widths and spaces between the bars vary in a standard way to represent a group of decimal digits. Most grocery stores use bar codes to encode product codes. Upon reading a bar code, the software then matches the resulting product code with the database records to retrieve such details as the product price, description, and inventory level. Companies number and code all consumer products to a worldwide standard called the Universal Product Code (UPC). A *laser scanner* is a type of bar code reader that projects an oscillating beam that appears as a red scan and senses when an object is placed in front of it. In comparison, a *wand*, or *pen-type scanner*, requires physical contact with a bar code.	

(continued)

Table A.4	Input Devices (Continued)	
Device	**Description**	
Biometric Scanner	Biometric scanners are devices that scan fingerprints or the patterns that exist in the retina of the eye. They can be used to uniquely identify a person and allow access to a facility, computer, or ATM bank account.	
Document Scanner	A document scanner is a peripheral device on which you scan a printed document. The scanner then uses reflected light to obtain the image, digitize it, and transmit it to the computer. *Flatbed scanners*, where you place the object to be scanned on a glass area, are often built in to other devices such as facsimile and copy machines. In addition to flatbed scanners, there are *hand-held scanners*, where the scanning device is dragged across the page; *sheetfed scanners*, which have a slot where a page is inserted and a motor draws the page across the scanner; and *drum scanners*, which use very sensitive sensors to read the document as it whirls around inside a cylinder.	
Magnetic Strip Reader	A magnetic strip reader is a device that reads the data stored on a small magnetic strip as the strip is swiped through the device. These strips are commonly found on the back of credit and library cards. This device could also be considered a form of secondary storage. Lately, strip readers are being replaced by smart card readers.	
MICR (magnetic ink character recognition)	A MICR system uses a special magnetized ink that can be read by a special scanner. It is primarily used in the banking industry to print information on cheques for efficient processing.	
OCR (optical character recognition)	Usually implemented as software, OCR converts scanned print documents directly to electronic text.	
OMR (optical mark reader)	OMR uses a special scanning device to read carefully placed pencil marks on specially designed forms, such as those used in standardized tests.	
Smart Card/Chip card Reader	Smart cards, sometimes known as chip cards, are plastic cards that have an integrated circuit embedded inside on which to store information. They are used for credit and debit cards, phone cards, and ID cards, for example. Smart cards can hold over 8 KB of data and are starting to replace magnetic strip cards for bank and credit cards.	

Other Input Devices With the increasingly popular use of multimedia information, audio/video input has become a major category. *Audio input* is primarily obtained through the use of a microphone. Applications range from simply storing audio comments within presentations or analysis files, to dictation of text input using specialized voice recognition software. For music, *musical instrument digital interface (MIDI)* devices allow note and effect information, like pitch and loudness, to be captured from a device and stored in a special format on a computer. MIDI devices include music keyboards, controllers, and other electronic music devices.

Video input is captured using a digital video camera, a webcam, video and DVD players, or from broadcast and cable emissions. A *webcam* is a video camera that delivers its output for viewing over the Internet. Typically, a webcam is a slow-scan video camera that captures images about every half-second. This slow rate of capture accounts for the choppiness of the picture relative to full-motion video cameras. This is improving with advances in technology, however. Input from cable and broadcast television antennas can allow the computer and its monitor to serve as a television.

Often, both audio and video input require equipping the computer with special cards. A microphone is connected to a port in the audio card, while a video card processes video input. These cards process the input into a form that the computer can use and store, and usually include their own processor and memory.

Finally, sensory input is another important category of input device. A *sensor* is an electronic device that measures a physical quantity like temperature or pressure, and then converts it into an electronic signal. There are two types of sensors—analog and digital. *Analog sensors* generally produce a voltage proportional to the measurement. The CPU then converts the signal to a digital form. A *digital sensor* captures the measurement digitally, which is then sent directly to the computer for processing. A multitude of applications rely on sensors, such as proximity sensors used in smoke alarms, temperature sensors that control office heating and air conditioning, and pressure sensors used in automatic garage doors. The popular video game system, Microsoft Kinect, uses motion sensors that detect movement using its webcam.

Selecting an Input Device Considering the extensive list of input devices, how do you select the appropriate input device to use? Ergonomically speaking, the workspace setup can be an important consideration in selecting a device. For example, if space is tight or a flat surface is unavailable, trackballs or touchpads present better choices than a mouse. Users should consider whether or not a device places undue stress on their arm, hand, or fingers, and if the buttons' location makes them easy to reach and use. Biometric scanners must be easily accessible, comfortable, and safe. Hand-held devices should fit neatly into the user's hand, and laser scanners should not be unsafe to the user's eyes.

Environmental conditions can be another important factor when choosing a device. Dust or moisture can make a standard mouse and trackball function erratically or require frequent cleaning or repair. A touchpad or optical mouse is sealed and contains few moving parts, which helps make it more suitable for harsh conditions. Because most scanners depend on the reflection of light off of a medium, surrounding light levels can affect them or the presence of particles in the air can impair their performance.

Performance is also a consideration. Compared with the keyboard, pointing devices are simple to use. Pointing is a natural human movement. Coupled with a good graphical user interface (GUI), controlling a computer with a pointing device can be intuitive and require little training. Pointing devices are most often used to point to items on the GUI, so they are typically more useful for entering commands than for entering data content. For example, you may click on a scroll bar and move it to page through a document on your screen, while you would most likely use a keyboard to enter text.

A way to measure performance is to determine the accuracy of the device being used. You can gauge the accuracy of a device by its resolution and tracking. **Resolution** refers to how precisely the device can pinpoint a location on a screen or the clarity and level of detail of an image rendered. **Tracking** refers to how close the screen cursor follows the movement of the device. For example, an optical mouse usually tracks better than a mechanical mouse, but can provide less resolution. If you are deciding on an input device for bar codes, for example, both resolution and tracking will be important.

Speed is another way to measure performance. All of us have personally experienced the speed of a bar code reader versus keyboard input in the grocery line. These are just some of the things to consider when selecting input devices. Think about your own technology. Do you prefer to text on a BlackBerry or use the touch screen of an iPhone? Do you prefer to use the PageUp and PageDown keys on your keyboard or your mouse to scroll through a document?

Display Devices

Output devices deliver the result of processing operations to the user. Output devices include display and printed output devices, storage devices, the Internet or other network connection, and a wide variety of other electronic devices. We will consider all but the Internet or other network connection here. Internet and other network connections are examined in Tech Guide B.

Because most of us prefer images, display devices continue to be, by far, the most common category of output device. When coupled with speakers, display devices deliver just about every data format to the user, ranging from plain text documents to movies with sound (of course, the sound itself is output by a speaker). Display devices are also a significant component for input. Using a display, mouse, and GUI-based operating system allows the user to interact with the computer by manipulating a pointer on the screen over graphic objects.

The display system is made up of two primary parts: the graphics card and the monitor, as shown in Figure A.4.

The Technology Behind LCD Monitors Display devices vary in shape, size, and underlying technology. Most monitors in use today are LCD monitors. At the heart of an LCD monitor is a piece of liquid crystal material placed between a pair of transparent electrodes. This combination of materials takes advantage of four facts from physics:

1. Light can be polarized.
2. Liquid crystals can transmit and change polarized light.
3. Electric current can change the structure of liquid crystals.
4. Transparent materials can conduct electricity.

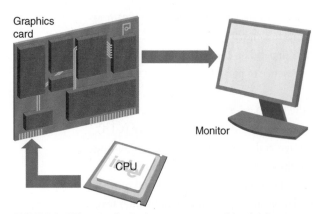

FIGURE A.4 This simple display system is capable of delivering just about every data format to the user, ranging from plain text documents to movies with sound.

A liquid crystal can change the phase of the light that passes through it. Moreover, applying a proper voltage controls the phase change. An LCD display consists of an array of cells (pixels) that can be controlled individually to create the image.

An LCD may be colour or monochrome. For colour LCDs, each pixel consists of three sub-pixels, one for each of the colours red, blue, and green. By carefully controlling the applied voltage, the intensity of each sub-pixel can range over 256 shades. Combining the sub-pixels produces a possible palette of 16.8 million colours. LCDs may also be either back-lit or reflective. Liquid crystals do not emit light; they can only change the phase of light as it passes through.

Small, inexpensive LCDs are often reflective, which means to display anything they need to reflect light from external light sources. However, most LCDs are backlit. Backlit displays have built-in fluorescent tubes above, beside, and sometimes behind the LCD. Combined with a white diffusion panel behind the LCD, this redirects and scatters light evenly through the display.

Display Device Performance Display device performance depends on the resolution; that is, the maximum number of pixels that the screen can show, typically measured by dot pitch. The *dot pitch* of a display is the distance between a pixel and the closest pixel of the same colour. For computer monitors, dot pitch is usually less than 0.30 mm. For a display screen of given physical width and height, a higher dot pitch results in a lower resolution.

For LCDs, the voltage to each pixel is refreshed many times a second. How often this occurs is called the *refresh rate*, measured in hertz (Hz). The monitor's horizontal scan rate and the vertical resolution limit the refresh rate, since a higher resolution means more vertical lines to scan. Higher refresh rates mean less flickering, thereby reducing eyestrain. Anything above 60–72 Hz is fine for most users.

The physical dimensions of the screen can also be an important consideration. For LCD displays, screen size is measured on the diagonal in inches. For example, a 20-inch monitor will measure approximately 20 inches from a lower corner to the opposite upper corner of the display. In addition, LCD monitors are generally rated in degrees for their visible *viewing angle* for both horizontal and vertical. A problem with LCD screens is that the colour in the image can only be accurately represented when viewed straight on. The farther away from a perpendicular viewing angle, the more the colour will tend to wash out. A higher viewing angle is usually preferred over a lower angle, unless you want to reduce the attempts of others to look over your shoulder.

An alternative to LCD display screens are LED (light-emitting diode) screens. The main difference between LED and LCD screens are that LED screens do not use florescent tubes and output directly to the screen by emitting light. This produces crisper, clearer images with bright and defined colours. An LED screen is more expensive than an LCD one, but is a good alternative if the screen is used often to view or create images and watch videos.

Touch Screens: The Future of Display Devices An interesting and increasingly useful twist on display technology is the touch screen monitor. A **touch screen monitor** is a computer display screen that is sensitive to human touch or a special pen. Kiosks (such as ATMs and self-service checkout lanes), PDAs, some phones, and tablet PCs use touch screens. Using a touch screen, the user can interact with the computer by touching images or words on the screen. Because of this interactivity, touch screens are both input and output devices. PDAs and tablet PCs can also include special software that allows the user to write using a special pen directly on the screen in "digital ink" or to simply use their finger.

There are currently four types of touch screen technology in use. A *resistive* touch screen panel uses a specially coated resistive layer. Touching this layer sends an electrical charge to the controller for processing. *Surface wave* technology uses ultrasonic waves that pass over the touch screen panel. Changes in the ultrasonic waves that result from touching the panel are registered and sent for processing. A *capacitive* touch screen panel is coated with a material that stores electrical charges. Touching this panel draws a small amount of charge to the point of contact. Circuits located at each corner of the panel measure the charge and send the information to the controller for processing. Finally, newer tablet PCs use an *electromagnetic digitizer* that accepts input only from a special pen containing an electromagnetic coil. Using the pen can prevent inadvertent movements of the cursor that can sometimes occur with other touch technologies. Figure A.5 shows a touch-sensitive display used for tablet PCs.

FIGURE A.5 LCD touch-sensitive displays respond to human touch or a special pen.

Printed Output Devices

The increasing use of PDAs and tablet PCs should reduce our dependency on paper. Think about the ease and lower cost of storing, editing, transmitting, and copying electronic information as opposed to paper documents. Yet we often need printed information. As Table A.5 indicates, a variety of printing devices provide a range of quality and options in outputting both text and graphics.

Printed Output Device Performance Printer performance is dependent on colour, resolution, speed, and memory. Colour is important for most users. In addition to needing colour pages for presentations or maps, colour printers can print near-photo quality, reducing the need to

Table A.5	Output Devices for Print	
Type	**Description**	
Inkjet	A popular type of printer for home use that prints by spraying dots from an ink cartridge. Capable of high-quality graphics and text printing at speeds over 80 characters per second.	
Laser	A popular type of printer for business and home use that prints by applying dots from a toner cartridge. Capable of very high-quality graphics and text printing at speeds as high as eight pages per minute.	
Multifunction device	A device that combines several types of input and output. Typically, a multifunction device will include a printer, fax, flatbed scanner, and copy machine—all in one device.	
Plotter	Prints very high quality graphics, although at slow speed, by manipulating a pen over a page. Unlike a regular printer, a plotter draws continuous lines. Plotters are typically used for architect blueprints, full-size engineering drawings, or very large printed items.	
Thermal	Uses heat to transfer an impression onto paper either by adhering a wax-based ink from a ribbon or by burning dots onto coated paper. Used in early fax machines and still used for printing receipts like those at pay-at-the-pump gas stations.	

pay for digital photo developing. However, colour printers are more expensive to operate because they require two or more different colour ink or toner cartridges.

Printer resolution is measured similarly to the resolution of display devices. The sharpness of text and images on paper is usually measured in dots per inch (dpi). Higher dpi means higher quality printing. Many inexpensive printers provide sufficient resolution at 600 dpi.

The more print jobs, the more important the speed of the printer. Printer speed is measured as the page rate in pages per minute (ppm). More expensive printers can print faster at about 20–30 ppm, while typical inexpensive printers print only about 8–10 ppm. Note that colour and extensive graphics can reduce these rates.

Most printers come with a small amount of memory called a *buffer*. With a large enough print buffer, the computer can download an entire job for printing and then process other items without having to wait for completion of the print job. As you might expect, higher capacity print buffers perform more efficiently.

Storage Hardware

Because of the limited amount of internal storage and the volatility of RAM, some form of storage external to RAM is necessary to permanently store data and programs. This **secondary storage** usually comes as magnetic storage media, optical disks, or chip-based flash memory. With all of these, stored information is accessed by internal memory when the control unit decides that this information is needed. Because the secondary storage unit must locate the information, read it, and then transfer it to internal memory, secondary storage is a much slower form of memory than internal memory. However, this slow transfer of information is balanced by the virtually unlimited storage capacity. Table A.6 lists the main types of storage used with personal computers.

Table A.6	Storage Devices		
Storage Technology	**Type**	**Description**	**Capacity Range (as of 2011)**
CD-ROM, R, RW	Optical	Capable of storing large amounts of data Some types can be recorded upon (R) or rewritten (RW) Becoming obsolete	Up to 1 GB; most common is 650 MB
DVD DVD-R DVD-RW DVD-HD DVD-Blu-ray	Optical	A faster, higher capacity type of optical disk than CD-ROM Some types can be recorded upon (R) or rewritten (RW)	4.7–100 GB
Hard disk drive	Magnetic	Very fast and with very high capacity Generally used for permanent but stationary storage of programs and data	Can be more than 2 TB
High capacity diskettes	Magnetic	Higher capacity diskettes such as Zip and Super disk Provide higher capacity while retaining the portability of a diskette	750 MB–3 TB
Tape	Magnetic	Magnetically coated strip of plastic used to store data Typically in the form of cassettes	Up to 5 TB
USB flash drives	Chip-based	Use a special type of ROM chip and plug into a USB port	Up to 32 GB and rising

Magnetic Disks Some secondary disk storage uses a *magnetic disk* to store information as a form of **direct-access storage** in which information may be accessed in any order, regardless of the order in which the information was stored. A magnetic disk is composed of metal or plastic covered with an iron oxide whose magnetic direction can be arranged to represent symbols. This magnetic arrangement is carried out on a *disk drive*, which spins the disk while reading and writing information onto it using a *read/write head*. Depending on the type of disk, the read/write head rides either directly on or immediately above the disk.

Almost all computer systems include a hard disk. *Hard disks* serve as the main storage device for programs and data. They have greater capacities and allow for faster access than most other storage technologies. Hard disks typically store anywhere from 10 MB to 500 GB; the latest drive options allow for up to 2 TB. A single hard disk usually consists of a stack of several platters. Each platter contains two read/write heads, one for each side. Each read/write head is attached to a single access arm so that they cannot move independently. Each platter has the same number of tracks, and a track location that cuts across all platters is called a cylinder. Each track is divided into sectors, the smallest unit accessible on the disk. Each sector has the same capacity, 512 bytes. When storing data to a disk, the data are divided into portions that can fit within a sector. The operating system and the drive list where data are stored by noting their track and sector numbers.

Hard disk drives are known for their access speed. High-speed disks have an access time of 9 milliseconds or less. Hard disks are generally considered to be stationary, but there are also removable hard disks.

Optical Disks Unlike diskettes and hard disks, which use electromagnetism to encode data, optical disk systems use a laser to read and write data. The two main categories of optical disk are *compact disk (CD)* and *digital versatile disk (DVD)*. Optical disks have very large storage capacity, but they are not as fast as hard disks. A compact disk is a small, portable plastic medium that includes a reflective surface in its makeup. To record bits of data, the surface of the disk is altered to affect how light is reflected when applying a laser. CDs are commonly used to store large files that need to be portable such as software, music, and video files. The original CDs were read-only memory (CD-ROM) that only the distributor wrote on, and that the user could only read. Now *CD-recordable (CD-R)* and *CD-read/write (CD-RW)* have become widely available, with most computers now coming with a CD drive that writes to CDs as well as reading them.

DVD is an optical technology that is rapidly replacing CD technology. Most commonly, one side of a DVD has a capacity of 4.7 GB, enough to hold an entire feature-length movie. With two layers on each of its sides, a DVD can hold up to 17 GB of data on a disk that is basically the same size as a CD. Because standards for recordable or rewritable DVDs (DVD-R or DVD-RW) have yet to be agreed on, several possible formats exist. More and more computers now come with a DVD drive that will write as well as read disks. Emerging types of DVD storage are high definition (HD) and Blu-ray, both driven by media producers and the need to store more high quality images such as movies.

Chip-Based Storage Flash memory is a special type of chip-based memory that can be written to as well as read into internal memory. This form of storage has quickly become a very popular way of transporting data between computers. These devices are known as *USB flash drives* and plug into the universal serial bus (USB), an external bus standard that supports transfer rates of 12 Mbps (megabits per second). All personal computer systems sold today contain several USB ports, so the use of flash drives is widespread as a portable form of memory.

USB flash drives have advantages over many other storage media, such as higher capacity, smaller dimensions, high reliability, and noiselessness.

Storage Performance Most personal computer systems include several types of storage devices, such as a hard disk, CD-RW drive, and DVD drive, as well as multiple USB ports that allow the attachment of additional units, including the flash memory modules. With all of these available, you should choose the format that is appropriate for the data you wish to store and the method you choose to use. Keep in mind that capacity, portability, and the ability to write to the media are important factors. Also, think about using networks for storage. The cloud provides storage services over the Internet, which allows you store your data at very little cost. Network storage could provide the ultimate in portability—even more than USB flash drives—as data is stored in the cloud, which can be accessed by any computer that has access to the Internet.

Quick Test

1. True or False. A scanning device works with GUI to provide data and instructions to the computer using physical movements.

2. For a display device, the _____ is the distance between a pixel and the closest pixel of the same colour.

3. True or False. Until recently, the most popular form of portable storage has been flash memory, but it is beginning to lose favour among computer users.

Answers: 1. False; 2. dot pitch; 3. True

■ OPERATING SOFTWARE

We introduced the concept of *software* in Chapter 2 as the set of instructions that direct the hardware. This is very much true when it comes to operating system software. Without it your hardware would be useless. Also true is that without application software, your operating system-enabled hardware would be much less interesting!

The **operating system (OS)** serves as the computer's "traffic cop," "office manager," and "chauffeur." As traffic cop, the OS manages all of the message traffic that flows from the user, to the application software, to the computer, and back again to the user. It is an office manager because it handles the allocation of resources and the assignment of tasks to various software programs. Finally, it is a chauffeur because the operating system enables users to get to their destination— that is, carry out needed tasks with application software—without worrying about the hardware interfaces.

For example, the OS monitors the keyboard and mouse to determine when users provide input to the computer. It also manages the video screen and printer to provide output from the computer. The operating system controls the operation of secondary storage to transfer data back and forth between secondary storage and main memory. Finally, the operating system controls the execution of application programs.

For desktop PCs and laptops, the most common operating systems include Microsoft's Windows family, the UNIX family (including Linux), and Macintosh operating systems (Mac OS X). In the next sections we look at operating systems in more detail, including how they work and what tasks they perform. We also compare these operating systems with those for mainframes, networks, and mobile devices such as smartphones.

Comparison of Operating Systems

The operating system functions apply to all computers, regardless of size. However, there are important differences between the operating systems for mainframes, networks, personal computers, and hand-held devices. The primary differences among the four operating systems are the number of users and the complexity of the peripheral devices that they manage. Mainframes and network operating systems manage multi-user systems, while most personal computer and hand-held device operating systems deal with only a single user.

Further, dealing with multiple users requires mainframe and network operating systems to have sophisticated security systems. For personal computers and hand-held devices, most users maintain a minimal security system, depending on their location and use. However, security is becoming more of an issue with hand-held devices due to additional wireless capabilities and storage of important data.

Mainframes must manage a large number of storage, input, and output devices. A network operating system must manage numerous hard drives, backup devices, and printers. On the other hand, a personal computer system usually has at most three or four storage devices: keyboard and mouse, printer, monitor, and set of speakers. Hand-held devices usually do not have peripheral devices. Because of these differences, mainframe operating systems are extremely large programs that require a staff of systems programmers to maintain them. Network operating systems may also be quite large, requiring support from individuals with special training and certification on the particular network operating system. On the other hand, operating systems for personal computers and hand-held devices are usually simple and need only periodic maintenance.

All four types of operating systems are multitasking systems, enabling the computer to work on more than one job or program concurrently. Table A.7 compares the mainframe, network, personal computer, and hand-held device operating systems in terms of number of users, security, number of peripherals, number of tasks performed, and support that each requires.

How the Operating System Works

The operating system is the foundation upon which all other software works. As such, the operating system is crucial to the operation of the computer. Yet, it is the computer's least visible form of software. The only direct outputs from an operating system, to either the screen or the printer, are login requests (when the system asks for your user ID and password), error messages, and configuration choices (the settings you can choose for your system).

Table A.7	Comparison of Operating Systems			
Feature	**Mainframe**	**Network**	**Personal Computer**	**Mobile Device**
Number of simultaneous users	Multiple	Multiple	One	One
Security	Sophisticated	Sophisticated	Minimal/ user-enabled	Minimal/ user-enabled
Peripherals	Complex	Numerous	Few	Few
Number of tasks	Many	Many	Many	Few
Support	Systems programmers	Networked-certified personnel	User	Provider
Example	OS390	Novell NOS	Windows XP	Windows Mobile

All operating systems consist of two parts: the kernel and the command interpreter. The **kernel** is the essential part of the operating system that internal memory must always include. It handles requests from either application programs or hardware (often printers or input devices) and then determines the processing order of the requests. Regardless of how fast something seems to happen from a user's perspective, most computers can accomplish only one task at a time (in actuality, this depends on the number of processors—one task per processor at a time). The kernel also handles demands for internal memory from competing applications by parceling out the limited amount of internal memory as needed.

The **command interpreter** (often referred to as the *shell* in UNIX operating systems) accepts commands from users and translates them into language that the kernel can understand. Users typically communicate with the command interpreter through a **graphical user interface (GUI)**, like that used in Windows or Macintosh operating systems. The GUI acts as a shell to interact with the command interpreter. For UNIX systems, the GUI converts the user's mouse clicks into the appropriate text commands that the operating system understands. The primary exception to this is the OS390 operating system used on most IBM mainframes and application servers. That OS command interpreter requires entering text commands that use a special syntax.

In addition to accepting commands from users through text commands or a GUI, the operating system also accepts commands from application programs through its **application program interface (API)**. The API is a specific process that allows the application program to make requests to the operating system or another application. For example, when you click the File|Print command or the Print icon on a Windows program, an API accepts this command and sends it to the operating system. The OS then communicates with the printer hardware to generate the desired output. Figure A.6 shows how the kernel, command interpreter, and API work together. Note that the user either communicates with the operating system kernel through an application program and API or through the command interpreter.

What Does the Operating System Do?

For any computer, regardless of whether it is a mainframe or other large server, a stand-alone or networked PC, or a stationary or hand-held device, the operating system is a collection of software programs that manages the following tasks:

- starting the computer
- managing hardware
- controlling access to the computer
- providing an interface for the user
- ensuring efficient use of the CPU
- providing services to application software

Starting the Computer Users must start, or *boot*, all computers. This start-up procedure relies on the use of the read-only memory (ROM) chip, which permanently stores the booting instructions. Because of its size and the number of hardware elements attached to it, booting a mainframe, termed the *initial program load (IPL)*, often takes many steps and some amount of time. On the other hand, to start a personal computer with a hard disk, users simply turn on

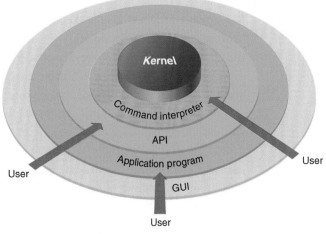

FIGURE A.6 Layers of an operating system.

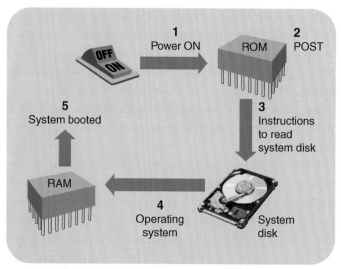

FIGURE A.7 The boot (start-up) process of a computer.

the computer. The time it takes to start a personal computer depends more on how many application programs will initially be started, rather than how long it takes the OS to boot up. The ROM chip and hard drive then take care of the following booting steps, as Figure A.7 shows.

1. Turning on the computer's main power sends a flow of electricity to ROM.
2. The flow of electricity to ROM causes the BIOS (basic input/output system) to provide instructions to the CPU to perform a *power-on self-test (POST)*, which checks the various components of the computer, including memory, to ensure that they are working correctly.
3. After the POST, ROM/BIOS tells the CPU to find the system disk (usually the hard disk) and read operating system programs from secondary storage.
4. The CPU loads operating system files into internal memory (RAM).
5. The CPU implements instructions in the operating system files and then displays the OS interface.

The hard disk stores the operating system (Microsoft says that your system needs 15 GB for Windows 7)[2] and your PC is instructed, via the BIOS, how to start up the operating system. The BIOS is specific to your PC and prepares it so that other software can load and execute. In the case of booting your computer, you can access the BIOS to change the boot instructions if you want to start your computer from a floppy disk, or more likely, from a CD. Why would you want to do this? This is a common cure for a system failure or when your PC has a virus.

Managing Hardware One of the most important tasks of the operating system is to act as a go-between for the user, software, and the hardware system. To do this, the operating system must control a large number of hardware elements. It must also manage the flow of data into the computer, as well as information out of it. Finally, the OS monitors the use of internal memory by tracking application and user memory space, and protecting one from encroaching on the other.

Hardware management includes **input/output (I/O) tasks**. For example, the OS accepts input data, such as commands from a keyboard, and coordinates its output, such as the printing of a document. Other I/O tasks include the transfer of data, instructions, and information between the CPU, internal memory, and secondary storage elements (e.g., CD-ROM drive, flash memory). I/O tasks also include the transfer of data and information over the telephone modem, cable modem, DSL connection, or LAN connection.

---

2. *www.microsoft.com/windows/windows-vista/get/system-requirements.aspx*, retrieved October 31, 2011.

Since mainframes serve multiple users, their operating systems must manage numerous hardware elements, including disk drives, tape drives, printers, communications equipment, and user workstations. Further, a mainframe OS must accomplish all this while minimizing delays for users and ensuring their access to the needed hardware elements. On the other hand, with only one user, the hardware control problem for a personal computer is much less complicated. However, it does involve many of the same elements as the mainframe system, plus such items as the mouse for GUI, speakers for audio output, and DVD players.

Finally, in addition to the devices a stand-alone PC operating system must control, a network operating system controls the communications between the local PCs on the network and other network resources, such as various printers and a tape backup for the file server. (We discuss networks in greater detail in Tech Guide B.)

Controlling Access Once the computer is up and running, unless it is a stand-alone PC, the OS must control access to it. For mainframe computers or networked PCs, the operating system must provide security to users' data, information, and programs against unwarranted intrusion. The most recent operating systems require users to enter a password to access the computer, limiting their access to specific areas.

Efficient Use of CPU In any computer system, the CPU always works much faster than the I/O operations. As a result, a key task of the operating system is to ensure that the slow I/O does not hold up the CPU. This is especially important for a mainframe, so that the processing for one user does not delay other users' I/O. Even on a personal computer, it would be inefficient for the CPU to wait on one task—for example, printing a job—before continuing its work.

To keep the I/O from interfering with processing, the OS directs the CPU to run programs concurrently. That is, the CPU processes part of one program, then part of another, then part of a third, and so on until the CPU has worked on all of them. The OS places the jobs in a queue (waiting line) to be executed according to their level of priority. It gives each job an extremely small amount of CPU time, called a time-slice, during which the CPU executes a portion of the job. Thus, the OS allows CPU *multitasking*, which mainframes have done for many years. Personal computers also widely use multitasking, due to the increase in CPU speed and amount of internal memory. Because a mainframe has multiple users as well as multiple tasks, it usually also has a secondary processor to handle I/O, while the CPU handles the multiple tasks and users. Network operating systems usually handle the problem of efficiently using the server's CPU by shifting a significant portion of the processing burden from the central file server CPU to the local PCs' CPUs.

Multitasking is often confused with *parallel processing*, but they are quite different. With multitasking, the CPU only handles a part of one task at a time. With parallel processing, the multiple CPUs in the same computer handle either multiple different jobs or multiple parts of the same job at the same time.

Think of the difference between multitasking and parallel processing as playing catch with yourself using five different balls. If you multitask, you pick up one ball, toss it, catch it, put it down, pick up the next ball, and repeat the toss-and-catch process. If you parallel process, you are juggling: tossing and catching all five balls at once. We all know that juggling is harder than catching one ball at a time. Similarly, this is why multitasking is much more widespread than true parallel processing. Newer microprocessors are being made as *dual-core* or *multi-core processors*; this is like having two or more processors on one chip. Having more than one processor enables PCs to parallel process, to some extent, and begins to address the need to multitask. Intel is introducing its Core i7 processor with multi-core technology to power demanding digital content creation, immersive games, and entertainment.[3]

---

3. *www.intel.com/pressroom/archive/releases/2008/20081117comp_sm.htm*, retrieved April 13, 2010.

Providing Services to Application Software While the operating system tasks just discussed are important to the operation of all computers, the main objective of an operating system is to provide services to application software. After all, the primary reason that most business professionals use a computer is to run application software to create business value. Operating systems provide a number of services to application software, including the following:

- running the application software and ensuring the availability of needed resources
- determining the processing order of concurrently running programs
- coordinating file/disk management
- providing memory management

Running Application Software The operating system must make it possible for the user to run application software. It does this by interpreting the instructions from the other software to the CPU and providing resources in the form of hardware devices when needed by the other software program. For example, when the user instructs a word processing program to print a document, the application software issues a command to the operating system, which handles the printing job. Network operating systems are not usually involved in running application software. Instead, the operating system on each individual PC handles this role. It is important to note that only certain applications run on certain operating systems. For example, you cannot run MS Office applications on the Linux operating system without special APIs. Even with the APIs, the full functionality of the application may not be available. Therefore, your choice of operating system may determine the application software you can use.

Determining the Processing Order Modern computers are multitasking machines running multiple programs concurrently. For example, you may create a document, work with a spreadsheet, query a database, and print a series of presentation slides, all *seemingly* at the same time. In most cases, one job runs in the foreground, with other jobs processed in the background. The Windows operating systems show programs running concurrently as buttons on the task bar, usually displayed at the bottom of the screen. Figure A.8 shows an example of this process for Windows, where the

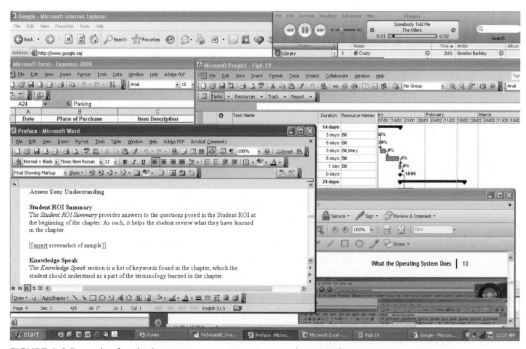

FIGURE A.8 Example of multiple programs running concurrently in Windows.

foreground application is Microsoft Word. Background programs include Excel, Microsoft Project, Internet Explorer, Adobe Acrobat, and iTunes.

The operating system must decide which task takes priority, not just between foreground and background jobs, but also between the various background jobs. Setting priorities depends on various criteria, some of which the user may set, others which the operating system defines.

Coordinating File/Disk Management The operating system must manage files on secondary storage (usually some form of hard disk) in such a way to make them available when needed, while also protecting them from unwarranted use or loss. A variety of file types are necessary to use application software, including data files, program files, and utility files. For example, program files execute application software, data files include specific information already entered by the user, and utility files provide assistance, such as spell-check ability.

For example, say you want to create a letter. To run a word processor in the Windows operating system, you click the appropriate icon. The operating system must know the location of the word processor program files, as well as the location of a variety of utility files, known as *dynamic link library (dll)* files. After you specify the location, the OS must also know where to save the result of your work (or where to find a previously saved document). On the other hand, if you click on a data file, the OS must detect the corresponding application software to launch. The file management element of the Windows operating system handles all of these operations. The same is true of the Mac OS X and Linux operating systems. It is important to note that files such as dlls are often not stored in the application folder on a PC; in the case of Windows, they are saved in the Windows folder. When you want to delete an application, you should always uninstall it, not delete the application folder directly; uninstalling ensures all of the application is removed from memory.

Mainframe and PC network systems have multiple users storing their files on centrally located disk and tape drives, so their operating system must track where files are stored and who may receive access to them. For this reason, security is an important element of a mainframe operating system. For networks, the operating system must also monitor software on the file server to restrict access to only those who have rights to use it.

On personal computers, the operating systems must accomplish the same file management tasks as mainframes and network servers, but usually for only one user. While security is slightly less important, file management continues to be crucial. Also, files on a personal computer hard disk are usually not stored as one contiguous unit. As a result, the operating system must be able to reassemble the parts of a file from many separate locations on the disk. The OS handles this via a table of the various file parts and their locations on the disk, called the *file allocation table (FAT)*. Because files are not contiguous, file fragmentation can occur. When this occurs, fragments of files are not stored efficiently, making it hard for your PC to recombine them and reducing system performance. To solve this problem, you can run a defragmentation utility on your PC. After you have *defragged*, you will usually notice an improvement in the speed of your PC.

The OS also provides file management tools to help users organize files for easy access and retrieval. Virtually all operating systems now use a *hierarchical* (tree) structure that divides a long list of files into several shorter lists, called folders. For example, assume that a company stores personnel files on disk for the employees in its 12 branches around the world. Each branch has between three and six departments. If the company has at least 10 employees in each department, the computer would store at least 360 ($12 \times 3 \times 10$) files. With a single folder on the hard disk, finding a particular employee's file might take time. However, as Figure A.9 illustrates, using the Windows Explorer utility to create a hierarchical structure to organize files resolves this issue.

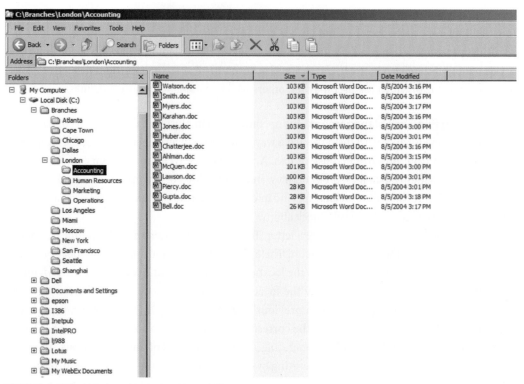

FIGURE A.9 The Windows hierarchical-based file structure.

Providing Memory Management Unlike the nearly unlimited secondary storage, internal memory continues to be a scarce resource and must be managed in several ways. First, because multiple programs often run concurrently, the operating system must ensure that these programs don't conflict when using memory or that there is even enough memory to run them. The operating system also tries to partition the various applications in such a way that an error in one does not cause the entire system to fail or lock up (commonly referred to as *crashing*).

Second, even with the large amounts of memory in modern computers, they still need more. One technique, which began with mainframe computers in the mid-1970s, provides the appearance of additional memory: virtual memory. **Virtual memory** divides the internal memory into pages, or sections, that match equal-sized sections of memory on disk. The process then exchanges, or swaps, internal memory with the disk or virtual memory when needed. As long as the processing needs only data or instructions that are currently in internal memory, it proceeds as usual. However, when the needed information is on disk, virtual memory swaps a page into main memory. The CPU tries to "think" ahead, to determine which pages from virtual memory will be needed next. As a result, the apparent memory exceeds the actual internal memory without great loss of processing speed. Virtual memory greatly enhances the ability of mainframes to run multiple jobs at high speeds. Personal computers also use virtual memory to expand their apparent memory capacity.

Has your PC ever been so slow that you could have grabbed a coffee before it finished saving your Word document? This could indicate that your PC is not managing memory well. Sometimes this occurs simply because you have too many applications open and your RAM is overloaded. Other times it could be because you have a memory leak or your hard drive needs to be defragged. In the case of a memory leak, you can use the task manager in Windows to identify applications and processes that are using a lot of memory and end them. Because RAM is constantly accessed to randomly write, read, and store to memory, it can get fragmented. You can use your PC's defragmentation utility to correct this. Of course, a reboot, which ends all processes, can also be effective in the short term.

Quick Test

1. Which of the following computer systems is designed to allow for multiple simultaneous users?
   a. mainframe and networks
   b. personal computers and hand-held devices
   c. all types of computers

2. True or False. The ROM chip is most important in the boot operating system function.

3. _____ uses disk storage to give the appearance of additional internal memory.

Answers: 1. a; 2. boot; 3. Virtual memory

■ APPLICATION SOFTWARE

You should now have a better understanding of how operating system software allows you to use hardware devices effectively. However, by far the largest amount of software available to the computer user is in the area of application software. Business professionals typically use either commercially-developed (also known as *commercial off-the-shelf [COTS] software*) or custom-developed application software.

Commercially-Developed Application Software

Commercially-developed application software is used for a wide variety of tasks and is often mass-marketed. The most widely used commercially-developed software categories used by business professionals include the following:

- word processing programs to create documents
- spreadsheets and accounting software to carry out financial and other quantitative analyses
- database programs to manage lists and tables of data
- presentation programs to create electronic slide shows
- Web browsers and other Internet-related software
- specialized software for specific industry needs

Many of these applications are often sold together in a bundle known as a **software application suite**, such as Microsoft Office. The major benefit of a software suite is that each application in the suite has similar functions (e.g., Copy/Paste) and these functions can be executed across applications (e.g., copy a table in MS Excel and paste in MS Word). In the next sections, we briefly discuss six common types of software.

Word Processing Software *Word processing software*, part of a larger category known as *document preparation software*, allows you to easily compose, edit, save, and print various types of documents. Because word processing software almost directly replaces handwritten documents, most business professionals often learn it first (other than games). Among other advantages, word processing software allows efficient creation and editing of text documents. *Desktop publishing software* takes word processing one step further. It combines word processing, graphics, and special page definition software to create documents that rival those available from professional typesetting companies.

Spreadsheets If you consider word processing as a replacement for handwritten documents, the spreadsheet is an even more powerful replacement for the calculator. Business professionals use this tool for almost any type of financial or quantitative analysis. To understand why, let's consider it in

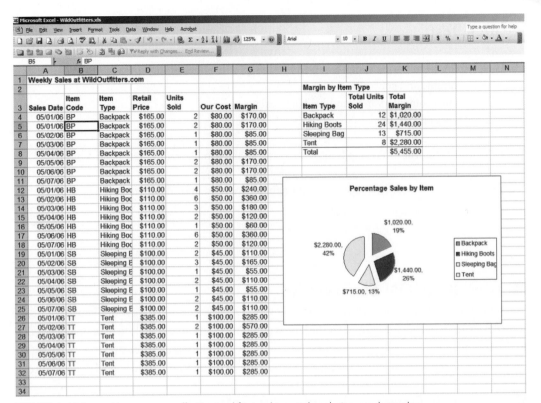

FIGURE A.10 Spreadsheets are an effective tool for tracking and analyzing product sales.

some depth. To start, a *spreadsheet* is an electronic table of rows and columns, with the intersection of a row and a column called a *cell*. The column letter and row number identifies each cell. For example, in Figure A.10, the highlighted cell, cell B5, is located in column B and row 5.

Business professionals enter column values, labels, and formulas into cells to create business models. The formulas typically use the addresses of other cells to create relationships between them. For example, Column G in Figure A.10 automatically calculates the margin for a given item, equal to the selling price (column D), times the number sold (column E), minus store cost (column F), times the number sold (column E). For backpacks (G4), the margin formula in G4 is: $= D4*E4 - (F4*E4)$. Note the use of the asterisk (*) for the multiplication operation in this formula. Note also that the spreadsheet performs mathematical operations in the same order that you do: multiplication first, then subtraction. The spreadsheet software uses the "mathematical horsepower" of your computer to efficiently determine the correct solution.

Spreadsheet software accomplishes other tasks to help business professionals. In the preceding example, the sales manager used the *Sort* tool in this spreadsheet software to automatically list the items according to item type. The manager also added a section to allow the spreadsheet to automatically calculate the total margin for each product type. Finally, the manager used the software to automatically generate a chart showing percentage sales by product type.

Another useful aspect of a spreadsheet is that, when a value changes in a cell that is involved in a formula cell, the value in the formula cell may change also, depending on the relationship. For example, say WildOutfitters (from Figure A.10) sells three backpacks instead of two and updates the value in the spreadsheet. The spreadsheet then automatically changes both the margin for backpacks and the margin for the seven-day period to reflect the increased number of backpacks sold. This capability enables business professionals to perform *what-if analyses* by changing the values in cells and quickly seeing the results.

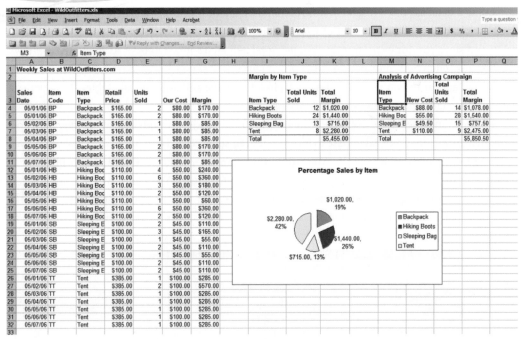

FIGURE A.11 Using existing spreadsheet information, such as that shown in Figure A.10, business professionals can perform a series of what-if analyses.

For example, assume the WildOutfitters marketing department suggests running an advertising campaign for the four products shown in Figure A.10 (that is, hiking boots, backpacks, sleeping bags, and tents). The marketing department believes this campaign will generate a 15 percent increase in unit sales for the four products. However, the cost of this campaign will result in a 10 percent increase in the cost to the company for each of the four items, which, due to competitive pressures, *cannot* be passed along to customers in the form of higher prices. The question is: Given these assumptions, should the campaign be run? On the face of it, it seems like a no-brainer. A 15 percent increase in unit sales should more than outweigh effects of a 10 percent increase in costs. Modifying the spreadsheet by inputting this revised information should back up this assumption.

Figure A.11, the revised spreadsheet, shows the new costs, the new units sold, and the margin figures (columns M through P). Note that the new total margin is $5,850.50, as compared with the existing total margin of $5,455. So, while there is a higher total margin using the assumptions for the advertising campaign given by the marketing department, the increase is far less than expected, with less than a 1 percent increase in total margin. Based on this what-if analysis, the company should study this issue further before initiating the advertising campaign.

Performing analyses requires the business professional to explore many different possibilities to determine the meaning of the raw data after the data have been transformed. As a business professional, you can expect that your early positions will require that you analyze a question or proposal, like the advertising proposal discussed in the preceding example.

Database Software Another popular way to transform data into a usable form is to organize them by entering the data into *database management software*. (We cover database management systems in greater detail in Chapter 3 and Tech Guide C.) Although the data are often input in a tabular form similar to that of a spreadsheet, the purpose differs. Spreadsheets assist in quantitative analysis, whereas a database locates information that matches some criteria. That is, it can be difficult to alter a database table to calculate margin as easily as you can change a spreadsheet, but you can use it to easily search for all sales of a particular item, say, the backpack.

Using a database often results in less redundancy than using a spreadsheet. Why? The data in a database can be spread over a series of *related* tables. While Figure A.10 shows the name, item code, price, and store cost for every transaction, using related tables in a database, as Figure A.12 shows, reduces this redundant information. Note how Figure A.12 shows the data on hiking item sales as they would appear in two related tables—a Transaction table and an ItemData table—for a popular database management system, Microsoft Access.

Further, databases allow users to locate information quickly, through queries. A *query* is a specially structured request to a database to locate a desired set of records. In our example, say you want to locate information on backpacks. You would therefore enter a query to find and display—or in database terminology, *return*—all records with the BP item code. You can indicate specific information as part of the query, such as the item name, price, and cost, the date of the transaction, the number sold, and even the calculated gross profit. Figure A.13 shows the result of this type of query.

TranNum	DateSold	Code	Number
5	5/1/2006	BP	2
6	5/2/2006	BP	1
10	5/3/2006	BP	1
15	5/4/2006	BP	1
18	5/5/2006	BP	2
22	5/6/2006	BP	2
26	5/7/2006	BP	1
4	5/1/2006	BP	2
1	5/1/2006	HB	4
7	5/2/2006	HB	6
11	5/3/2006	HB	3
17	5/4/2006	HB	2
19	5/5/2006	HB	1
23	5/6/2006	HB	6
27	5/7/2006	HB	2
3	5/1/2006	SB	2
9	5/2/2006	SB	3
13	5/3/2006	SB	1
14	5/4/2006	SB	2
21	5/5/2006	SB	1
25	5/6/2006	SB	2
29	5/7/2006	SB	2
2	5/1/2006	TT	1
8	5/2/2006	TT	2
12	5/3/2006	TT	1
16	5/4/2006	TT	1
20	5/5/2006	TT	1
24	5/6/2006	TT	1
28	5/7/2006	TT	1
0			

ItemCode	ItemName	ItemPrice	ItemCost
BP	Backpack	$165.00	$80.00
HB	Hiking Books	$110.00	$50.00
SB	Sleeping Bag	$100.00	$45.00
TT	Tent	$385.00	$100.00
		$0.00	$0.00

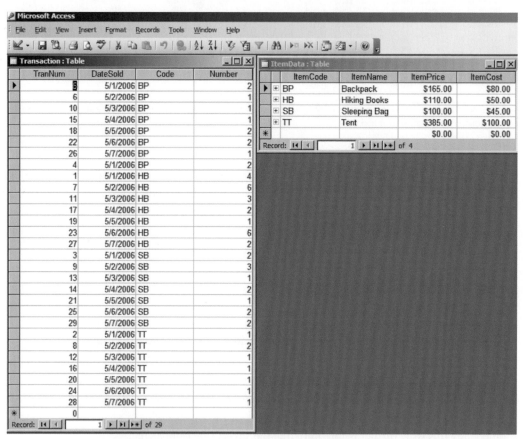

FIGURE A.12 Databases often result in less redundancy than spreadsheets.

ItemName	ItemPrice	ItemCost	DateSold	Number	Gross Profit
Backpack	$165.00	$80.00	5/1/2006	2	$170.00
Backpack	$165.00	$80.00	5/2/2006	1	$85.00
Backpack	$165.00	$80.00	5/3/2006	1	$85.00
Backpack	$165.00	$80.00	5/4/2006	1	$85.00
Backpack	$165.00	$80.00	5/5/2006	2	$170.00
Backpack	$165.00	$80.00	5/6/2006	2	$170.00
Backpack	$165.00	$80.00	5/7/2006	1	$85.00
Backpack	$165.00	$80.00	5/1/2006	2	$170.00

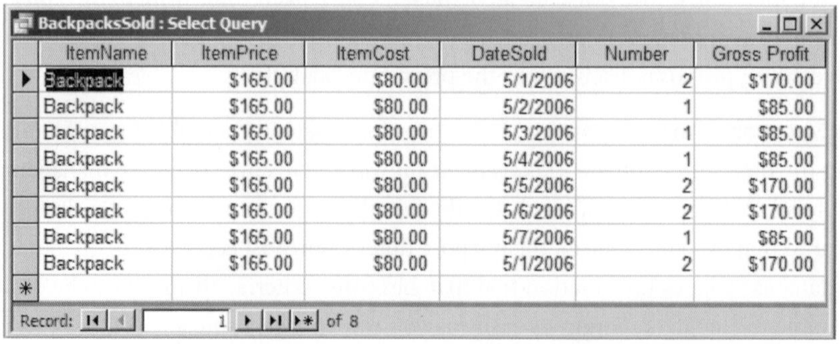

FIGURE A.13 A query can provide specific information as well as perform calculations.

Presentation Software *Presentation software* allows business professionals to use text in many sizes and fonts, graphics, photos, and even audio and video files, to inform an audience. Because of its ease of use, presentation software has become extremely popular for making business, academic, and instructional presentations. For example, Figure A.14 shows a slide from a presentation on teamwork. Presentation software can be used both to support a person giving a speech, and to present information on its own. For example, a product marketing manager may use presentation software to create a slide show that can display automatically at an information kiosk or at a conference booth.

FIGURE A.14 Presentation software allows business professionals to create slides to inform an audience.

Web Browser and Internet-Related Software

Since its widespread introduction in 1994, the Web browser has rapidly become one of the most popular (if not *the most* popular) type of software currently in use. The main reason for the popularity of the Web browser is its access to billions of pages of information available on the World Wide Web.

Browsers rely on point-and-click methodology to carry out desired operations. If you know the address of a web page, you simply enter it in the address box and press the Enter key to retrieve it. Once you have a web page on the screen, you can jump to other related pages by clicking on content that is either underlined or otherwise highlighted in some way, called a **hyperlink**. Of all the types of software that we discuss here, the Web browser is almost certainly the one that you have already used. Figure A.15 shows an example of a web page in a browser for the publisher of this book.

FIGURE A.15 It is possible to jump to other related pages to obtain additional information by clicking on hyperlinks.

Beyond simply accessing web pages, browsers have become the "jack of all trades" for Internet operations. Web browsers enable searches for web pages based on a word or term; communications with others through email, instant messaging, groups, and chat rooms; and downloading of files of all types, including audio and video files. The power and versatility of the Web result in its almost universal use by business professionals.

Using search engines from a Web browser enables you to search the Web and all of its billions of pages, as well as search discussion groups and even chat sessions. Many public and governmental agencies put their data on the Web in a form that can be searched and downloaded for use in problem solving. For example, in the WildOutfitters example shown earlier, a marketing analyst in the company could use a search engine to compare the company's prices and features with those of all possible competitors.

In addition, many organizations enable their employees to search for internal data and information using search engines on their intranet using a browser. In many cases, employees can send out questions to other employees using email to determine if a problem has already been solved within the organization. This makes it possible for an employee to access the accumulated organizational memory to answer questions and solve problems.

Specialized Software In many cases, business professionals rely on other developed software to handle specific situations. For example, while spreadsheets are the most general form of financial software, most organizations use other financial packages. These include accounting packages, real estate calculators, online stock and bond trading software, and retirement-planning software.

You can see how most knowledge work activities rely on commercially-available application software. However, specific tasks require specially-created software. Let's look next at developing customized software.

Developing Customized Software

Companies usually buy commercially-developed software, like word processing programs or spreadsheets, for routine business tasks. However, to achieve a competitive advantage, a company must often custom-develop software to meet its particular needs. As one analyst notes, "software needed to be competitively different is generally not available from off-the-shelf packages" and "building . . . systems for unique capability is often the single most important activity for an . . . organization."[4] As a result, there will always be a demand for programmers.

Computer programs are based on algorithms. An **algorithm** is a detailed sequence of actions that, when followed, will accomplish some task. For example, when making the bed, you may follow the steps in this algorithm:

1. Strip the covers and sheets from the bed.
2. Smooth out the fitted sheet.
3. Tuck the sheet under the mattress at the foot of the bed and spread to cover the mattress.
4. Tuck in the comforter and spread it over the top of the sheet.
5. Fluff the pillows and place them in their proper locations.
6. Crease comforter under the pillows and fold it over the top to cover the pillows.
7. Drop a quarter onto the bed to see if it bounces!

4. James Martin, *Cybercorp: The New Business Revolution*, New York: AMACOM Books, 1996, p. 104.

Table A.8	Commonly Used Computer Languages
Language	**Common Use**
C (including C++ and C#)	Writing a wide variety of applications for PCs or network servers
Java	Writing software for all types of computers; also, for writing browser and server-side Web software
PHP	Writing Web-based applications
SQL (Structured Query Language)	Writing queries to relational database management systems
VB.NET (Visual Basic .NET)	Writing software for PCs; also, for writing browser and server-side Web software

Defining an algorithm is just the first step in developing software. The next step is making a computer follow the algorithm; this is known as *programming*. A *computer programmer* takes the algorithm and translates it into instructions written in a programming language that the computer can understand. The set of instructions that follow the algorithm, written using the *programming language*, is known as a **program**.

Programming languages, like the machine language of the CPU, is a set of binary codes. With the first computers, programmers actually had to input binary instructions to their machines. As you can imagine, this was a difficult and error-prone process. Since the 1950s, there has been a trend toward abstracting the machine language instructions into a language that is more natural to human programmers. Unfortunately, the strict rules required for communicating instructions to the CPU confine programming languages to a formality that today is still far from natural and often difficult to master.

Programs are written in a number of computer languages. Table A.8 lists some of the more common languages and their uses.[5] Each computer language, like a human language, has its own vocabulary and grammatical rules. However, most share a similar logical approach to communication with the computer.

Of special interest is the **Java** language, originally developed to run on networks. Programmers now use it in many different ways, particularly in e-commerce applications. It actually runs differently than many other programming languages, in that it is platform independent. This means it can work on many different kinds of computers.

Java's main competitor is Microsoft's .Net platform of languages, including VB.NET, C++ .NET, and C# (pronounced "C-sharp") .NET. As an example of a .NET

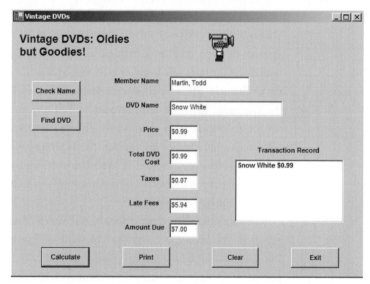

FIGURE A.16 A customized transaction form created using VB.NET.

---

5. *www.tiobe.com/index.php/content/paperinfo/tpci/index.html*, retrieved October 31, 2011.

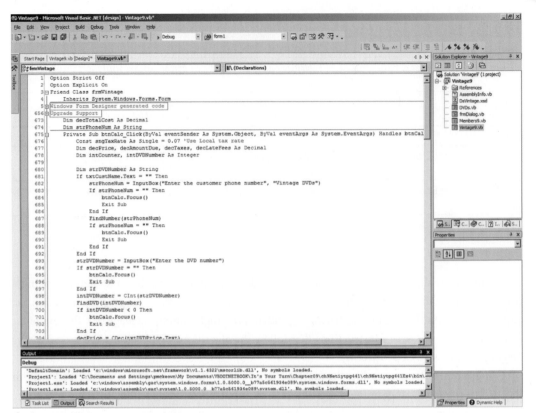

FIGURE A.17 Part of the VB.NET code written to produce the customized transaction form shown in Figure A.16.

language, consider Figures A.16 and A.17, which show an application in VB.NET for a video store. The figures show both the interface for this application and some of the corresponding programming instructions (code) necessary to implement the logic behind it.

Open-Source Software One ongoing argument in the world of software is the use and development of open-source vs. proprietary software. **Open-source software** refers to programs for which the authors allow anyone to view the *source code*—the programming instructions—and make changes. Many open-source software applications are freely available for downloading over the Internet. The only requirement is that any programmer who makes changes to the open-source code must also make those changes freely available to others. Examples of open-source software and languages are the Apache Web server software, the Linux operating system, MySQL database software, the Firefox Web browser, and the PHP Web development language. Open-source software is supported by a community of users who actively participate in newsgroups and websites, like *www.phpfreaks.com*.

On the other hand, **proprietary software** requires a purchased licence and typically restricts access to the source code to the company employees. Examples of proprietary software are the Microsoft Windows operating system and IBM's DB2 database software. Proprietary software is supported by the company that sells it through technical support centres and websites.

The trade-offs between open-source and proprietary software include cost and support. Open-source software is typically free, but often provides no centralized support centres. Proprietary software has a cost associated with it, but has a centralized support system.

There are cases where the software or language is free, but it requires the use of proprietary software to run. For example, it is possible to develop a website using a Microsoft language like ASP.NET using any text editor free of charge, but the website must run on the proprietary Microsoft Internet Information System Web server. An exception is Java, a proprietary language licensed by Sun Microsystems. Java is typically associated with the open-source movement because it will run on the Apache Web server software or under the Linux operating system, both of which are also open-source software.

As with hardware, software is changing rapidly to meet the needs of users. This is true for both application and operating system software. Further, the continuing contest between proprietary and open-source software will be one to watch. It may greatly influence both the software you use in the future and how much it will cost. If you use a mobile device or smartphone, this is an especially fluid area for software as companies vie to provide you with more ways to use your mobile device.

Quick Test

1. True or False. Spreadsheet software is not as good as database software for storing data records because it often includes redundant information.

2. A(n) _____ is a detailed sequence of actions that, when followed, will accomplish some task.

3. _____ software allows anyone to view the programming instructions and make changes.

Answers: 1. True; 2. algorithm; 3. Open-source

RO↑ | STUDENT RETURN ON INVESTMENT SUMMARY

1. Describe the elements that affect the processing capability of hardware.

The microprocessor contains the majority of the components that make up the central processing unit (CPU). The CPU works together with memory to control the execution of all instructions and the processing of all data. The CPU is located on the system's motherboard, the main circuit board in an electronic device. In a PC, the motherboard contains the bus, the microprocessor, and other chips and circuits. The CPU contains a number of components including the ALU, FPU, decode unit, cache memory, prefetch unit, registers, clock, one or more buses, and the instruction set, which enable it to carry out the required processing. Microprocessors are typically differentiated by their instruction set, their clock speed, and their bandwidth, which is the number of bits that the CPU can process in a single instruction. The CPU clock speed is the most commonly used performance characteristic.

2. Describe the various types of input, output, and storage hardware that business professionals should keep current with.

The primary types of input hardware are the keyboard; pointing devices such as the mouse; scanning devices such as bar code readers; and the Internet or other network connection. The keyboard is generally recognized as the primary and most common input device for computers. Pointing devices, which work along with a GUI, allow the user to provide data and instructions to the computer using physical movements such as *point* and *click*. Scanning devices read data and information stored on some form of non-connected media.

Output devices deliver the result of processing operations to the user. Output devices include display and printed output devices, storage devices, the Internet or other network connection, and a wide variety of other electronic devices. Display devices continue to be the most common category of output device. Display devices are also a significant component for input. Most display devices today use liquid crystal display (LCD) technology, which uses a piece of liquid crystal material placed between a pair of transparent electrodes. Display performance is a function of its dot pitch, refresh rate, and physical size. A variety of printing devices allow a range of quality and options in outputting both text and graphics. The most popular technologies for printers are inkjet, laser, and thermal.

Because of the limited amount of internal storage and the volatility of RAM, some form of external storage is necessary to permanently store data and programs. This secondary storage comes as magnetic storage media, optical disks, and chip-based flash memory. Stored information is accessed by internal memory when the control unit decides that this information is needed. Because the secondary storage unit must locate the information, read it, and then transfer it to internal memory, secondary storage is a slower form of memory than internal memory. However, this disadvantage is balanced by virtually unlimited storage capacity. Many individuals and business now use the cloud for data storage.

3. Explain why the operating system is so important to the use of all types of computers.

The operating system manages all of the message traffic that flows from the user to the application software to the computer and back again. It also handles the allocation of resources and the assignment of tasks to various software programs, and it carries out needed tasks with application software without worrying about the hardware interfaces. However, there are important differences between the operating systems for mainframes, networks, personal computers, and hand-held devices, depending on the numbers of users and the complexity of the peripheral devices that they manage.

All operating systems consist of two parts: the kernel and the command interpreter. The kernel is the essential part of the operating system that handles requests from application programs or from hardware and determines the processing order of the requests. The kernel may also handle demands for internal memory from competing applications by parceling out the limited amount of internal memory as needed. The command interpreter accepts commands from users and translates them into language that the kernel can understand.

4. Explain how business professionals obtain and use application software.

Business professionals rely on both commercially-developed and custom-developed application software. The most commonly used commercially-developed application software categories include word processing, spreadsheet, database, presentation, Web browsers and other Internet-related software, and specialized software.

Business professionals rely on custom-developed software, composed of multiple computer programs, to meet specific organizational needs. To develop each of these programs, an algorithm must first be defined. The next step is writing the program in a computer language that can be understood by the computer. Computer languages used for programming include SQL, C and C++, Java, PHP, and VB.NET. Of these, VB.NET is an example of a proprietary language from Microsoft, and PHP is an example of an open-source language that is not owned by any one company or organization. Java is a computer language that is proprietary but is often associated with open-source development.

KNOWLEDGE SPEAK

algorithm   368

application program interface (API)   357

bandwidth   343

binary   340

BIOS (basic input/output system)   344

bit   340

bus   343

byte   342

central processing unit (CPU)   342

character encoding   340

command interpreter   357

digital data   340

direct-access storage   354

dynamic RAM (DRAM)   344

graphical user interface (GUI)   357

hyperlink   367

input/output (I/O) tasks   358

instruction set   343

Java   369

kernel   357

machine instructions   341

memory chips   340

microprocessor chips   339

motherboard   342

open-source software   370

operating system (OS)   355

peripheral RAM   344

program   369

proprietary software   370

resolution   349

secondary storage   353

software application suite   363

Standard ASCII (American Standard Code for
    Information Interchange)   341

static RAM (SRAM)   344

system unit   342

touch screen monitor   351

tracking   350

transistor   339

Unicode   341

video RAM (VRAM)   344

virtual memory   362

TECH GUIDE

B | THE DETAILS OF NETWORKING

WHAT WE WILL COVER

- Network Architecture
- Network Layer Model
- Local Area Networks
- The Internet: A Network of Networks
- The World Wide Web

STUDENT RETURN ON INVESTMENT RO↑

Through your investment of time in reading and thinking about this Tech Guide, your return—or created value—is gaining knowledge. After reading this Tech Guide, you should be able to

1. Describe client/server architecture and explain how it works.

2. Explain how the network layer model describes a wide area network.

3. Describe how local area networks are configured, how the Internet works, and what makes the World Wide Web valuable to business professionals.

In Chapter 2, we briefly introduced the concept of computer networks and how they can benefit you as a business professional. We described the basic types of networks, network connections, and protocols, as well as network hardware and software. We discussed the Internet and World Wide Web. In this Tech Guide, we provide more details about these important topics.

We start with the topic of network architecture and its most common type, client/server networks. After that, we review the network software, protocols, and data component using a network layering model. Next we discuss local area networks in more detail, as this is likely the type of network you use at your university or college and are therefore somewhat familiar with. Finally, we take a closer look at the Internet and World Wide Web.

■ NETWORK ARCHITECTURE

Much like a building, **network architecture** refers to the design of a computer system or network. The term usually covers the overall combination of the hardware and software that makes up the network infrastructure. An *open architecture* is one where anyone can know the design, thus allowing anyone to develop software and hardware to work with it. A *closed architecture* network has a proprietary design, making it difficult for outsiders to design programs that work with the network. Most of today's computer systems are open to allow for easy growth.

In this section, we discuss the most common architecture for computer networks, the client/server network.

Client/Server Architecture

In the *client/server architecture*, each computer on the network is running either server software or client software, or both types of software simultaneously. *Server software* provides data or resources to other computers in the network. Computers running server software are typically referred to as **servers,** with each server typically focusing on a specific task. For example, a *file server* stores and delivers shared files. A *print server* manages one or more shared network printers. Other servers manage databases (*database server*), email (*email server*), and access to the World Wide Web (*Web server*).

Clients are network computers running client software that request services from the servers. The clients depend on servers for network resources like software, files, devices, processing power, and access to the Internet. Figure B.1 shows a client who is requesting database records from a server.

Note that while we use *client* and *server* to refer to hardware devices, it is actually the client software and server software running on the hardware that enable client/server processing to occur. In fact, it is possible to run several different types of client or server software on the same machine. For example, you probably have both Web browser and email client software simultaneously running on your computer.

How is the client/server architecture valuable to business professionals? Recall that in centralized computing, data are stored and processed on a central machine that is remote from the user, while PCs store and process data locally to the user. However, business professionals frequently need both

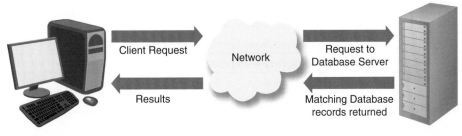

FIGURE B.1 Client/server architecture.

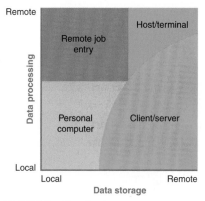

Data processing (vertical axis): Local to Remote
Data storage (horizontal axis): Local to Remote

Remote job entry
Host/terminal
Personal computer
Client/server

FIGURE B.2 Four basic computing architectures.[1]

the power of a central computer and the ease of use of a PC. Thus, the client/server architecture combines the best of central computers and PCs. This combination of local and remote data storage and processing leads to four basic computing architectures, shown in Figure B.2. Note that the client/server system overlaps both local and remote storage and processing.

The simplest form of client/server computing involves a file server, which controls access to the network, manages communications between PCs, and makes data and program files available to the individual PCs. The computing load, however, is still distributed among the individual PCs. This can actually pose a significant problem for many businesses. If a large number of clients attempt to access the server, the client/server performance declines. Therefore, to increase processing efficiency, many client/server networks involve a three-tiered architecture.

Three-Tiered Architecture In many cases, there is actually a series of clients and servers working to provide the data or application software that an end-user client requests. The most common form of series is the **three-tiered client/server architecture**, which uses a client, an application server, and a database server. In this client/server environment, a user working at a GUI-based client PC or workstation requests data or processing from an application server, which decides what data to supply. The application server then sends a query to the database server to retrieve those data. The database server processes the query and returns the matching data to the application server, which processes the data into the form required by the user. Figure B.3 illustrates this process.

One of the strengths of three-tiered client/server computing, therefore, is the capability to string together a series of servers to respond to a client's request while maintaining a single, central database. This allows an organization to maintain data in only one place, which avoids the difficulties of partitioning stored data. In the next section we discuss more advantages of client/server architecture.

Using Client/Server Systems to Increase Knowledge Work Efficiency

The client/server environment has a variety of purposes. Table B.1 shows the most commonly used servers, along with their purpose in a client/server network. For example, Web server

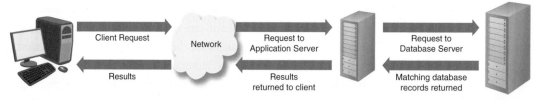

Client Request → Network → Request to Application Server → Request to Database Server

Results ← Results returned to client ← Matching database records returned

FIGURE B.3 Three-tiered client/server architecture.

Table B.1	Common Types of Servers
Server Type	**Purpose**
Application	Handles high-speed processing.
Database	Handles queries to a large database and returns matching records.
Fax	Sends and receives faxes for entire organization.
File	Provides both software and data files to users.
Mail	Sends and receives email for entire organization.
Web	Handles requests for web pages.

1. Based on R. T. Watson, *Organizational Memory,* 4th ed., New York: John Wiley, 2004, p. 354.

software handles requests for web pages, whereas email server software sends and receives email. In fact, many organizations now use the application server to replace centralized computers for handling large-scale processing tasks. For example, IBM refers to its large computers as *enterprise servers* to emphasize their use in client/server computing as application servers. Figure B.4 shows a typical client/server network that includes file, fax, mail, database, application, and Web servers, and a variety of clients.

Similar to the other types of computing, client/server computing has advantages and disadvantages, as listed in Table B.2. The primary advantage of client/server computing lies in its ability to share processing and data storage responsibilities among multiple machines and to use specialized servers to meet specific needs. The primary disadvantage is the complexity inherent in sharing responsibilities among multiple machines. Overall, however, the trend has been toward wider use of client/server computing because of its increased flexibility.

Peer-to-Peer Networks

As mentioned earlier, it is possible for computers on a network to run both server and client software at the same time. This enables organizations to set up a **peer-to-peer network**, where each computer in the network is on the same level as other computers and each computer is equally responsible for overseeing the functions of the network. Depending on the network connection, two computers in a peer-to-peer network may communicate directly with one another, or they may communicate through intermediate peer computers. In a pure peer-to-peer network, the two computers that are communicating with each other share the responsibility for carrying out the communication.

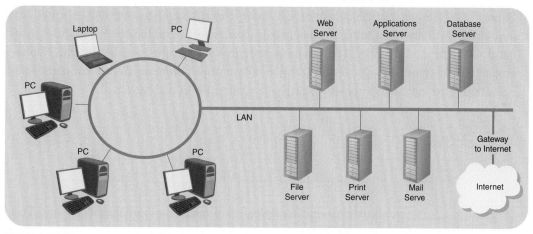

FIGURE B.4 Servers on a typical client/server network.

Table B.2	Advantages and Disadvantages of Client/Server Systems
Advantages	**Disadvantages**
The computing burden is shared among servers and clients.	There is a more complex programming relationship between clients and servers.
Specialized servers handle one particular type of task.	System upgrades require upgrading of all clients and servers, regardless of location.
The system can be upgraded in small steps.	There are more complex computer and network security issues due to increased numbers of users and client machines with access to networked resources, including data.
The loss of one client does not stop other clients from accessing the server.	

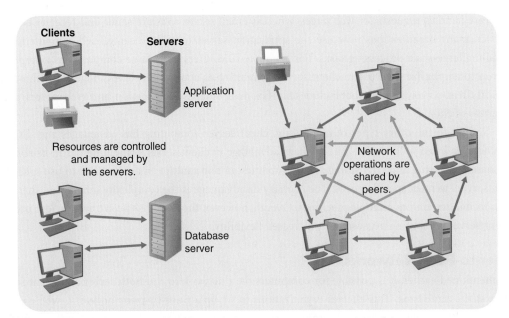

FIGURE B.5 Comparing client/server networks (left) with peer-to-peer networks (right).

There are no central computers or servers to manage the correct functioning of the network. Figure B.5 shows how peer-to-peer networks differ from client/server networks.

Prior to 1999, most business professionals primarily used peer-to-peer networks on small LANs. In June 1999, however, Napster, a famous service for sharing files, began operation. Napster demonstrated how to share files using a virtual peer-to-peer network over the Internet. Napster shared music files for free, with nearly 24 million users, and thus violated copyright laws. In 2001, Napster's original business model was shut down. Today, many companies, including Google, use peer-to-peer networks for the legitimate purposes of sharing data, information, and services.

Quick Test

1. The most common form of networking architecture is the _____ architecture.

2. A _____ architecture network has a proprietary design, making it difficult for outsiders to develop programs to use with the network.

3. In a _____ network, the computers are running both client and server software with no centralized server.

Answers: 1. client/server; 2. closed; 3. peer-to-peer

■ NETWORK LAYER MODEL

Now that you understand network architecture and how its design benefits business professionals, how does the network actually operate? Recall that networks include a data component, as well as network connections, which deliver messages between computers in a network. In addition, networks rely on a wide variety of application software to actually generate the message. A **network layer model** will help you understand how these three elements work together. In this model, each layer handles part of the communication between computers.

The International Organization for Standardization (ISO) created the original version of the network layer model. It consists of seven layers, where each layer of the standard defines a particular network functionality. Our simplified version of this model contains only three layers: the *application software layer*, the *network connections layer*, and the *data component layer*, as Figure B.6 shows. In this model, the application software generates the message, which the connections layer then relays to the data component of the network for transmission.

Looking at Figure B.6, note that at the sender end of the network, a message moves from the application layer to the network connections layer, and then to the data component layer. The reverse process occurs at the receiver end of the network, with the message first traversing the data component layer, then the network connections layer, and finally the application layer.

The postal system provides a good way to think about this model. In the postal system, you write a letter, put it in an envelope with a friend's address on it, and then place the envelope in a mail box. Think of this as the application layer. A postal worker picks up the envelope and takes it to the post office (the network connections layer), which decides how to send it to your friend (the data component layer). At the other end, your friend reverses this process to reply to your letter.

Application Software Layer

The application layer includes well-known software applications such as Web browsers and email. This software formats user data by adding information to make it conform to a specific standard or *protocol*, the specific set of rules for communicating. Protocols for the application layer of the Internet include *simple mail transfer protocol (SMTP)* for email, *hypertext transfer protocol (HTTP)* for web pages, and *electronic data interchange (EDI)* for large-scale exchange of data between organizations. The resulting message to the receiver thus combines the message generated by the application software and the protocol.

Application software may also encrypt the data (place the data in a secure, unreadable form) to protect it from unauthorized readers. For example, suppose a customer goes to an e-commerce website and fills out and submits a form to order a product. In this case, the application is a Web browser, the message is the contents of the form, and the protocol is HTTP. In addition, the message is encrypted. Figure B.7 shows the components of the application software layer for any message. For a product order, the message would include the message protocol (HTTP) and encrypted message and encrypted order data. Note that the contents of the message need to be decrypted on the receiving side as well.

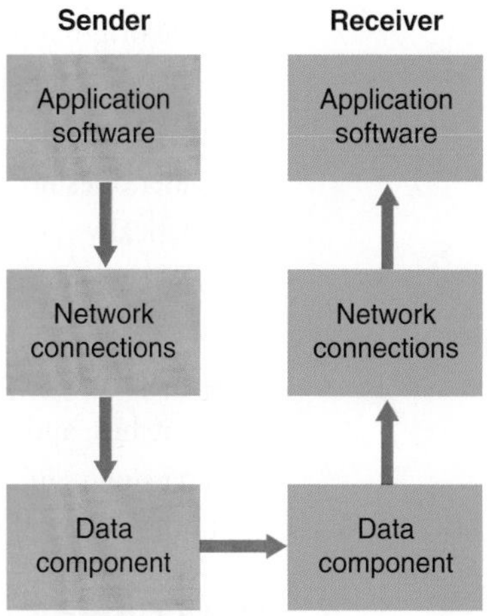

Network Connection Layer

In the network connection layer, the application software layer formats the message according to the network protocol. For example, the protocol for the Internet is the **transmission control protocol/Internet protocol (TCP/IP)**, as shown in Figure B.8.

With the TCP/IP Internet protocol, the network connection layer conducts a series of operations to prepare the message for sending across the Internet to a destination computer. It must first convert the address of the server at the destination from a text form (e.g., somecomputer.somewhere.org) to an *IP address*. The address is converted by using a conversion table stored either on the user's computer or on a computer with which the local computer can communicate. For example, say you want to send

FIGURE B.6 A simplified version of the network layer model.

FIGURE B.7 The components of the application software layer for a message.

FIGURE B.8 The components of the connection layer for a message.

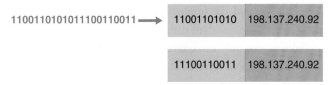

FIGURE B.9 Converting binary data into packets.

an email message to World Vision Canada, whose address is *info@worldvision.ca*. The domain name server (a client/server application) converts this to the IP address 205.189.149.31.

Next, the network connection divides the message into smaller digital units called **packets**, or *datagrams* in TCP/IP terminology, each of which contains a specific number of bytes. At this step, each packet receives a sequence number and a destination address. Figure B.9 shows this process of converting binary digits to packets and adding the IP address to them.

Because network computers send large amounts of data quickly and then do not send any data for a while, networks rely on a technology called packet switching. **Packet switching** routes individual packets through the network based on their destination addresses. It thus allows the sharing of the same data path among many computers in the network. Further, if a switching device on the network is inoperable, the packet finds another way to reach its destination. Packet switching is the key enabling technology that makes it possible to build large-scale, survivable networks like the Internet.

When sending a group of data packets—like product orders or email messages—to a computer with an IP address, software on the sending computer sends the packets to the nearest device that can switch network traffic for retransmission to other switching devices on the network. A common switching device is a *router*, which is a type of computer with the sole purpose of accepting packets and determining the best way to send them to the destination computer. That is, the router specializes in determining the best path for the packet and sending it there.

The original message packet is reconstructed using the sequence order that is attached to each packet. As a result, packets may follow different paths through the network, as well as arrive in a different order. As they arrive, the destination computer acknowledges received packets. If the sending computer does not get an acknowledgement that a packet has arrived within a certain time frame, it automatically resends the unacknowledged packets. This ensures the receipt of all packets.

Have you ever tried to make a phone call using voice over IP (VoIP)? Was it a little choppy and out of sequence at times if you were on a slow network connection? This occurs because a phone call using VoIP relies on packet switching. Voice is broken into packets (just like data), routed by routers and switches, and re-assembled at the destination. At times this results in poorer quality than calls placed using regular phone lines. Of course, providers of VoIP in Canada and elsewhere, like Skype, are finding ways of improving quality and offering their services at competitive prices.

Data Component Layer

You can share any data that can be converted to electronic signals over a computer network. The sending of data from one computer to another over a channel using electronic signals is known as *data transmission*. Data transmission is concerned with ensuring that the data are sent and received correctly and efficiently.

Data and information transmitted over networks travel over various media, including twisted pair wire, coaxial cable, fibre-optic cable, and microwave and satellite transmission. *Twisted pair*, which consists of twisted pairs of copper wires, is similar to the wiring used in much of the existing telephone system. Networks widely rely on it, both within and between locations.

Coaxial cable, which transmits cable television signals into your home, is also widely used in networks. Although television transmissions used to consist of only one-way signals, television cable across Canada has been converted to a type of cable capable of handling two-way signals. This two-way cable enables the connection of home computers to ISPs.

Fibre-optic cable is the newest medium and consists of glass fibre strands that can transmit a large number of signals at extremely high speeds. However, individual computers are not set up to

The details of networking 381

connect directly to fibre-optic cable, so it is often necessary to use twisted pair cable for the last few feet to the computer. Figure B.10 compares copper wire with fibre-optic cables for transmitting the same volume of information.

Microwaves are high-frequency radio transmissions that can be sent between two Earth stations or between Earth stations and communications satellites. This method is commonly used to transmit television signals. Direct broadcast *satellite transmission* uses microwaves for one-way downloads of data to homes and offices. It provides a way of carrying out transmission of data to a user, especially where traditional telephone lines do not exist or are difficult to install.

A variety of wireless technologies are also becoming popular as a way to provide mobile users with connections regardless of where they may be. The most popular wireless method of sending data relies on radio transmissions. Infrared light used to be a popular method, but is falling into disuse because it requires a line of sight. On the other hand, radio transmissions can pass through walls. However, security is a problem due to the radio waves going in all directions. (We discuss wireless networks in more detail in a later section.) Table B.3 compares the communication media used in the data component layer.

In addition to the media that transmit data, other aspects of the data component layer include the signal type and the data rate.

Signal Type The **signal type** is how data are sent over the network. A signal can be digital or analog. Digital transmission sends bits at different levels. A computer can therefore transmit over a digital communications link without changing the data (other than encoding it to make it suitable to the physical media). On the other hand, analog signals transmit bits as wave patterns, which requires modifying data before transmitting them. Because most telephone and cable systems are analog, *modems* convert digital signals from the computer into analog signals to transmit data over the communications link.

Telephone and cable modems convert between analog and digital forms of data using different methods. At the sender's end of a telephone modem, the modem modulates the digital computer data or information into an analog form that can travel over standard telephone lines. At the other end, a modem demodulates the analog signal back into a digital form that the receiver's computer can understand. Cable modems modulate and demodulate the cable signal into a stream of data. In addition, cable modems incorporate a variety of other functions to allow the PC to be linked to a network.

Both analog and digital data transmission are frequently used. Table B.4 lists some advantages and disadvantages of each form of transmission. The choice of signal usually rests on which of the two is more efficient for the given application.

Copper wire

Glass fibre

FIGURE B.10
Coaxial cable compared with glass fibre.

Table B.3	Comparison of Media[2]		
Media	**Cost**	**Error Rates**	**Speed**
Twisted pair	Low	Low	Low-high
Coaxial cable	Moderate	Low	Low-high
Fibre optics	High	Very low	High-very high
Radio	Low	Moderate	Low
Infrared	Low	Moderate	Low
Microwave	Moderate	Low-moderate	Moderate
Satellite	Moderate	Low-moderate	Moderate

2. Based on Jerry Fitzgerald and Alan Dennis, *Business Data Communications and Networking,* 8th ed., New York: John Wiley, 2005, p. 85.

Table B.4	Analog vs. Digital Data Transmission	
	Analog	**Digital**
Advantages	• Reflects natural phenomena; sound, light, and electricity are all analog • Low-cost, existing infrastructure for analog transmission	• Less susceptible to noise, resulting in a lower error rate • Allows transmission of multiple signals over one line at the same time (called *multiplexing*) • Faster rate of transmission • Less-complex and lower-cost circuits
Disadvantages	• More susceptible to noise, distortion, and interference	• Analog phenomena require conversion to digital signals

Data Rate and Bandwidth Issues The **data rate** is measured in bits per second (bps). For example, a telephone modem allows for a maximum data rate of 56 kbps. Even when using a 56-kbps modem, the actual data rate can vary depending on the quality of the telephone line. As a result, most business professionals increasingly use other methods of transferring data, including digital subscriber lines, television (TV) cable, and the various T-carrier circuits. A *digital subscriber line (DSL)* transmits computer data in a digital form along the same telephone line that analog voice communications uses. The *T-carrier circuits* are dedicated digital lines that a telecommunications company leases to users to carry data between specific points. Table B.5 lists the maximum data rates for various methods of transmitting data.

Transmission speed (often referred to as latency or propagation delay) relates to how fast a single message can be transmitted between two nodes. *Transmission capacity* relates to how many bits can be transmitted per second. While speed and capacity are not the same thing, they are highly related.

The term *bandwidth*, often used in relationship to data rate, measures how fast data flow on a transmission path. With the increasing demand from users for the capability to view high-quality photos, graphics, and full-motion video on their computers, the competition to provide higher bandwidth access is becoming keen among telecommunications providers.

The two extremes of bandwidth are baseband (which carries only a single digital signal) and broadband (which transmits in a variety of different analog signals). However, broadband is really

Table B.5	Maximum Data Rates[3]	
Transmission Method	**Maximum Data Rate**	**Comments**
Standard telephone service	56 Kbps	Available everywhere
Digital subscriber line (DSL)	6 Mbps in; 640 Kbps out	Becoming more available; does not slow down as more people sign up
Cable	As high as 55 Mbps but averages between 200 Kbps and 2 Mbps	Cable must support two-way communication; available in many locations but slows down as more people use it in a specific location
T-carrier circuits (T-1 to T-4)	1.544 Mbps–274 Mbps	Leased lines used for commercial telecommunication

3. Based on Jerry Fitzgerald and Alan Dennis, *Business Data Communications and Networking,* 8th ed., New York: John Wiley, 2005.

what makes Web-based services viable and attractive. To place orders on an e-commerce site, the data component layer must include the customer's modem and telephone line, or cable modem and cable. When the message reaches the customer's *Internet service provider (ISP)*, the ISP's modem and hardware connections then handle the data. Without a high-speed connection, popular applications like Facebook and Gmail would not work well. Certainly without broadband it is impossible to take advantage of software downloads and VoIP services like Skype.

Bandwidth is a consideration in any e-commerce venture. Not only do the technical aspects of the website have to take bandwidth into account, the bandwidth of the target customers also needs to be considered. It would be all well and good to have a fantastic video demonstrating your products on a website, but if a target customer does not have DSL or higher, they will not be able to view the video.

Until recently, Canada was a world leader in broadband adoption. Even though adoption rates are at a plateau, we continue to lead the United States in percentage terms.[4] Research on Canadian broadband usage and its social and economic impact is being conducted to answer questions such as: Does Canada's adoption of broadband enhance economic activities? Does it promote societal well-being or does it create a social divide between those who have high-speed access and those who do not?[5] It is certain that consumers will continue to move from baseband to broadband to access the increasing number of Web services offered by businesses and other organizations.

Now that you have a better understanding of how networks operate, let's look next at how business professionals use them.

Quick Test

Match the network layer with the appropriate hardware or software.

1. application software layer	a. TCP/IP
2. network connection layer	b. fibre optics
3. data component layer	c. email software

Answers: 1. c; 2. a; 3. b

■ DIFFERENT KINDS OF NETWORKS

Local Area Networks

Most organizations now use **local area networks (LANs)** to share information and resources among employees. Sharing information enables users to work with, and send, the same data or information files. Sharing resources involves the users' ability to share software and hardware.

Sharing software avoids the need for an organization to purchase a copy of a software package for every computer in the organization. Instead, the organization purchases *software licences* for their employees, which allow multiple people to simultaneously use a software package. Sharing hardware

---

4. Organisation for Economic Co-operation and Development, "Total Broadband Subscriptions per 100 Inhabitants in the OECD Area," *www.oecd.org/document/0,3746,en_2649_201185_46462759_1_1_1_1,00.html*, retrieved November 15, 2011.

5. Catherine A. Middleton and Christine Sorensen, "How Connected Are Canadians? Inequities in Canadian Households' Internet Access," *Canadian Journal of Communication,* 30(4), 2005, pp. 463–483.

allows the use of printers, disk storage, scanners, and so on through the network, rather than purchasing these devices for each user. Making hardware available through a LAN, especially highly specialized types of hardware, can significantly reduce an organization's costs.

The vast majority of LANs use the **Ethernet protocol** to connect computers and move information between computers on the network. With the Ethernet protocol, a computer on the network transmits a message that contains the address of the destination computer. Because all computers are free to transmit at any time, collision-detecting software must be in place. After detecting a collision, the software directs each computer to stop transmitting and wait a random length of time before re-transmitting its message. This system works well and is the basis for most LANs in operation today.

A client on a LAN can not only share information and software with other PCs on the same LAN, but also can communicate through gateways and bridges with other types of computers and with other LANs. A *gateway* is a combination of hardware and software that connects two dissimilar computer networks. The gateway allows LAN users to access a mainframe network without leaving their PC. Similarly, a gateway between a LAN and a WAN enables LAN users to send email over the WAN. In contrast, a *bridge* connects two different networks. For example, if a bridge connects two LANs, computers on each LAN can access the other network's file server without making any physical changes to the data.

Wireless LANs As its name implies, **wireless LANs (WLANs)** replace the usual LAN cabling between computers with wireless transmissions. They are becoming increasingly popular as mobile users need to connect to their local network and often from there to the Internet. WLANs eliminate the need for cable in remote areas, provide an inexpensive alternative to shared printing, and connect two networks separated by some obstacle, such as a highway or wall, through which cable cannot run.

Business professionals use WLANs to increase the efficiency of many activities in the workplace, including the following:

- Pricing, labelling, handling orders, and taking inventory from anywhere in a store, and then communicating that information directly to the back-office computer
- Connecting a wireless device to a bar code scanner to scan items in a warehouse and thereby produce a list of items and their locations
- Requesting medical tests, checking the results, and then entering the information into a patient's electronic record from the patient's room
- Checking email on laptops and handhelds from anywhere without having to be connected by wiring

Wireless networking hardware uses radio frequencies to transmit information between individual computers, each of which has a wireless network adapter. The individual computers do not communicate directly with each other. Instead, they communicate with a wireless network hub or router. The hub or router bridges the wireless network to a traditional Ethernet and provides a shared Internet connection. Figure B.11 shows how a wireless LAN connects a number of laptops to a hub, which, in turn, connects to the organizational LAN.

The current popular standard for wireless networking supports a data rate of 54 Mbps (or more), with a typical range through open air of about 200–1,000 m. *Wi-Fi (wireless fidelity)* typically uses the IEEE 802.11g standard for short-range radio transmissions. However, the 802.11n standard may surpass it, since 802.11n allows for faster data rates of up to 70 Mbps.

Any company or individual that uses a wireless LAN should be concerned about security. Access to a wireless LAN must be restricted by using passwords or allowing only certain computer IP addresses, or both. WLANs are even vulnerable internally between a laptop and the router; some form of encryption should be used to ensure that packets are not hacked.

Bluetooth and PANs One of the newest wireless technologies, developed by a consortium of companies including Nokia, Ericsson, and Motorola, is **Bluetooth**. Named after the tenth-century king who merged Denmark and Norway, Bluetooth is a form of **personal area network (PAN)**. PAN technology enables wireless devices, such as mobile telephones, computers, and PDAs, to communicate over a short distance—less than 10 m. By embedding a low-cost transceiver chip in each device, it allows total synchronization of wireless devices without the user having to initiate any operation. The chips communicate over a radio frequency at up to 2 Mbps.

As envisioned by its developers, a business professional would use a single device adhering to the Bluetooth protocol as a mobile telephone away from the office and as a portable telephone in the office. In addition, the device would work as a PDA and quickly synchronize information with a desktop computer (also containing a Bluetooth chip), or act as a remote control to initiate any number of other operations with other devices (with the appropriate chip). For example, a user could initiate sending or receiving a fax, or printing or copying a document, from anywhere in the office. Bluetooth thus enables pervasive connectivity between personal technology devices without the use of cabling.

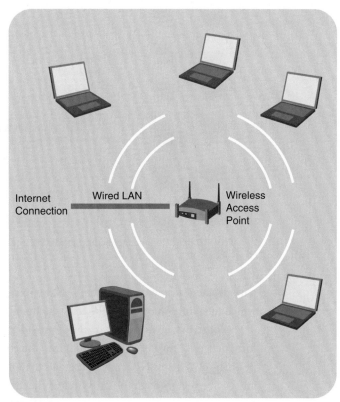

FIGURE B.11 Connection of laptops and PCs to the Internet through wireless LAN.

The Internet: A Network of Networks

Because of its tremendous growth over the last decade or so, the Internet is the subject of much discussion in newspapers, books, magazines, and movies. For many companies, the Internet is the basis for the widespread use of e-commerce. Without a doubt, the Internet is the most significant technology innovation to come along since the invention of the computer itself (over 60 years ago).

Originally developed in the 1960s and 1970s as a way of sharing information and resources among universities and research institutions, the Internet began its dramatic growth in 1991 when the United States government opened the Internet for commercial use. This growth further accelerated with the introduction of the World Wide Web in 1994. Today, the Internet is growing so fast that no one can say exactly how many people are using it. We do know that the number of users surpassed 1 billion sometime in 2005, and by March 2011, 2.09 billion people were online, representing over 30 percent of the world's population.[6]

How Does the Internet Work? The Internet is not a single network, but rather a network of networks. In fact, the name Internet is a shortened version of the term *internetworking* because it allows users to work among multiple networks. To connect to the Internet, as Figure B.12 shows, your computer will usually first connect to a LAN through a network interface card (NIC) or to an ISP through

---

6. Internet World Stats, "Internet Usage Statistics," *www.internetworldstats.com/stats.htm*, retrieved November 15, 2011.

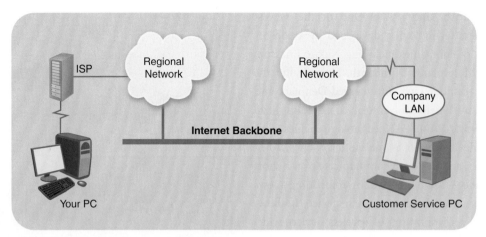

FIGURE B.12 Connecting a computer to the Internet through an ISP.

a modem and telephone line. The LAN, mainframe, or ISP, in turn, connects to a regional network, which then links into the backbone of the Internet.

A **network interface card (NIC)** provides the physical connection between a computer and a local network. Most NICs come built into the computer with a jack into which a network cable can be plugged. Wireless NICs convert signals to radio waves that conform to standard wireless protocols and can be sent through the air. Wireless client devices can communicate directly with each other or over the network through a wireless *access point (AP)*.

Within each network, there is at least one host computer that connects to the Internet, with full two-way access to other computers on the Internet and with a unique Internet address. In many cases, all computers in the network are host computers because all have Internet addresses, even if for only a short time, as with a dial-up system.

Each host computer that connects to the Internet uses the TCP/IP protocol for assigning addresses, and packet switching for forwarding information. By having all networks follow the same TCP/IP protocol, users on any network can exchange information with users on other networks, with little or no knowledge of their physical location or configuration.

TCP/IP rules also govern email and other Internet addresses. An email address consists of two parts: (1) the user name and (2) the server address. The user name is assigned to a person or organization that is connected to a server. The "at" symbol (@) separates the user name from the server address. The server address, also known as the *domain name*, consists of groups of letters separated by periods. Moving from right to left, this address goes from the most general (country name or organization type) to the most specific (computer name). The rightmost part of the address is known as the *top-level domain*. Note that these Internet addresses are easy-to-remember versions of the numeric IP addresses that actually identify computers on the Internet.

For example, Figure B.13 shows the email address of the sales department for a fictitious company (WildOutfitters). In this example, the user name is *sales*, the server name is *wildoutfitters.com*, and the top-level domain is *com*. Because the WildOutfitters example is the general email server, it has just the company name (*WildOutfitters.com*) as the server address. Other servers at WildOutfitters may have additional names to distinguish them from this server, say, *returns.wildoutfitters.com* for the email server for the returns department, or *www.wildoutfitters.com* for the Web server.

FIGURE B.13 Components of an email address.

The Internet Corporation for Assigned Names and Numbers (ICANN), a not-for-profit company set up over 10 years ago specifically to administer the domain name system, creates top-level domains for use

Table B.6	Top-Level Domain Names	
Type of Organization	**Designation**	**Example**
Canadian-based	.ca (approximately 556 million pages)	*www.chapters.indigo.ca* (Chapters and Indigo bookstores)
Educational institution	.edu	*www.athabasca.edu* (Athabasca University)
Commercial company	.com (approximately 25.3 billion pages)	*www.ebay.com* (eBay Auctions)
Not-for-profit organization	.org (approximately 4 billion pages)	*www.aiesec.org* (an international student organization)
Network services	.net	*www.bell.net* is the portal to several Bell applications
Government	.gc.ca	*www.cra-arc.gc.ca* (Canada Revenue Agency)
Businesses	.biz	*www.secor.biz* (a Canadian strategy consultancy)
Co-operatives	.coop	*www.ontario.coop* (a resource for co-operatives and credit unions in Ontario)
Various	.info	*www.cococay.info* (information about Coco Cay island in the Bahamas)
Museums	.museum	*www.annefrank.house.museum* (Anne Frank House museum)
Various	.name	*www.yourname.name*
Professionals	.pro	*www.broadway.pro* (Broadway theatre shows)

around the world. In June 2011, ICANN announced that it was removing restrictions on domain names and would allow custom domain names. For example Coca Cola could create its own domain .coke. These domains would be in addition to the 22 familiar Internet domain suffixes, such as .com and .org, and the 290 country domain designations (such as .ca and .uk).[7] Table B.6 lists several top-level domains and the types of organizations that might use them.

How do you know if an email or Web address is for a person or organization located outside Canada? For servers located in another country, a two-letter suffix may be used at the end of the server name as the top-level domain. For example, the server name for the University of Minho in Portugal is *minho.pt*. Further, businesses often use a second-level domain name of "co" prior to the top-level domain corresponding to their country. For example, the South African Tanda Tula game preserve's domain name is *tandatula.co.za* (where "za" is the top-level domain for South Africa). Many Canadian organizations prefer to distinguish themselves as Canadian by using the popular ".ca" top-level domain (e.g., *www.cbc.ca*).

Using the Internet to Perform Knowledge Work Activities

A number of software applications run on the Internet, such as the World Wide Web, email, and chat rooms. Many use the client/server approach, with each server on the network providing data and information to client computers connected to the network (although BitTorrent, Skype, and others use peer-to-peer networks). The client computer must run two types of software to take advantage

---

7. *www.theglobeandmail.com/news/technology/tech-news/internet-guardian-opens-up-naming-system/article2067783/*, retrieved November 16, 2011.

of the Internet: Internet conversion software and client software. The Internet conversion software enables the computer to work with Internet packets. Most operating systems, including Windows, come with this software built into the operating system.

Client software carries out the desired operation, such as sending email, downloading files from or uploading files to a server, participating in discussion groups, working on someone else's computer, or accessing the World Wide Web. For example, to send email, you would use an email client to generate the message, which then goes to the Internet conversion software that translates it into a form that can be sent over the Internet. The most widely used Internet operations are as follows:

- email (electronic mail)
- FTP (file transfer protocol)
- newsgroups
- telnet
- Internet relay chat
- World Wide Web

Email Poll after poll indicate that email over the Internet is the most popular web application (although email is quickly being overtaken by social media sites; see Chapter 8). In August 2011, Pew Research found that 92 percent of online adults use email, and that email has remained consistently popular for the last decade.[8] Email has fundamentally changed the amount of personal and business communication that occurs. So what exactly is email? Email is an asynchronous electronic method of exchanging information over a network. *Asynchronous* means that the sender and receiver are not communicating at the same time. Instead, one person sends a message, and the other person reads and replies to it at another time.

A special use of email is for listservs. A *listserv* is server software that can broadcast an email message from one member of a group to all other members. Group members simply subscribe to a listserv, and any messages sent to the listserv are automatically broadcast to the group members. Depending on how the listserv is set up, a member may be able to send messages to the listserv or may only be able to receive messages. Your instructor may have set up a listserv to which you subscribe. That way, he or she can communicate information to the entire class with one email rather than sending it to a large group of email addresses.

Email also has a number of commercial applications. Many companies use it as a powerful marketing tool. Incoming email can provide them with queries about their products, information about problems with products, or suggestions for better ways to serve their customers. Companies can combine emails with other contacts to create mailing lists for either email or postal mail (often referred to as *snail mail*) as a means of communicating with customers. On the other hand, customers expect companies to respond to email queries, complaints, or comments. Failure by a company to respond to these messages can result in very unhappy customers. Companies are finding it necessary to develop systems of responding to incoming email in addition to sending an automated response that acknowledges receiving the customer's email message.

Companies are also discovering that outbound email can generate revenue in ways never before considered. This includes sending special offers to customers who have purchased items online or who have sent a question via email. For example, airlines regularly send notices of special fares that users can only purchase online. This has resulted in a significant increase in ticket sales, with almost no additional cost to the airlines.

---

8. *http://pewinternet.org/Reports/2011/Search-and-email.aspx*, retrieved November 16, 2011.

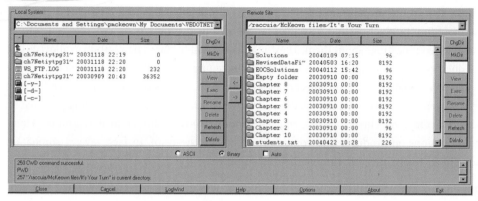

FIGURE B.14 Software for accessing an FTP server.

FTP Companies and individuals frequently need to make software, data, or document files available to a wide audience over the Internet. For example, a software company may want to distribute to current users an upgrade of a software package that it markets. Or it may make a utility software package or data files freely available. Distributing files to a large audience is done by placing them on a **file transfer protocol (FTP)** server and having the users download them over the Internet. Another protocol that is becoming increasingly popular is BitTorrent, *www.bittorrent.com*. BitTorrent provides an application that breaks files into pieces to send them more efficiently using less bandwidth.

Using an FTP site to download files is straightforward. You start FTP client software or a Web browser, enter the address of the FTP server that you want to use, and enter your user ID and password. At this point, you will see a list of directories or folders on the FTP server from which you can select files to download, as Figure B.14 shows. Downloading or uploading files with this client is a simple process of highlighting the file and clicking the upload or download arrow. Other systems allow you to drag-and-drop files between client and server windows.

Newsgroups The **newsgroups** Internet application is a vast number of discussion groups on a wide range of topics. A newsgroup consists of messages written on a series of news servers, each of which transfers messages to each other. This results in replicating all postings to one newsgroup on all the other news servers through the use of the *network news transfer protocol (NNTP)*. You typically use an email client to access the newsgroups.

A tree structure of discussion topics organizes the groups. The first few letters of each newsgroup name indicates the major subject category. For example, *rec* refers to recreation and hobbies, *sci* references topics in science, *alt* refers to alternative topics (anything that's not mainstream), and so on. Each major heading has many subgroups, separated from the major heading by a period (e.g., soc.culture.australia).

Newsgroup users can post questions or comments to existing newsgroups, respond to previous posts, and create new newsgroups. Messages on newsgroups are *threaded* so that answers to or comments about a newsgroup message appear beneath it in a list of messages, regardless of the data posted. This allows readers to easily follow a discussion.

Newcomers to newsgroups should become familiar with a newsgroup before posting to it by reading the newsgroup's *frequently asked questions (FAQ)* list. FAQ lists provide answers to the most frequently asked questions about a topic.

Many companies have begun to monitor newsgroups devoted to their products as a good source of customer feedback. Because bad news travels fast on the Internet, companies must quickly detect, and respond to, any emerging problems (see Chapter 8 for more on viral social interactions and brandstorms). In our example, WildOutfitters would probably want to monitor newsgroups dedicated to outdoor products to find new ideas for marketing its products, as well as to watch for negative or erroneous postings about them. They might also want to start a newsgroup to allow customers to ask questions and exchange information on hiking equipment with other customers.

Somewhat related to newsgroups are blogs. The word **blog** is derived from "Web log," a user-generated website written as a journal. Blogs can cover a variety of topics, including personal reflection, commentary on current affairs, movies, food, or games. Similar to newsgroups, blogs can contain opinions on products that companies should be aware of. In fact, several companies are creating blogs to discuss and promote their own products.

Telnet One of the original purposes of the Internet was to allow researchers at one university to use a computer at another university. To make it possible to use a computer at a remote location, the telnet protocol was made a part of the Internet from the beginning. With the *telnet protocol*, you actually log on to a computer at a remote location and run the application there, with your computer acting as a terminal.

The use of telnet has diminished greatly over the last few years as organizations have found ways to replace direct access to their computers with Web access, and because organizations have security concerns about telneting. Telneting does not provide any encryption or authentication capabilities and has been largely replaced by a system called *Secure Shell (SSH)*. This system provides all the functionality of telnet, with the addition of strong encryption to prevent sensitive data such as passwords from being intercepted, and public key authentication to ensure that the remote computer is actually what it claims to be. Furthermore, telnet is no longer a standard component of the Windows operating system since the introduction of Windows Vista in 2007.

However, telneting continues to be useful in locations where a slow Internet connection makes a typical email client or even Web-based email difficult to use. With telnet, or now more commonly SSH, a system administrator can log on to a remote system and perform any kind of maintenance or support required. This eliminates the need to be located at the same site as the system.

Internet Relay Chat Internet relay chat (IRC) is a *synchronous* way to use the Internet to communicate. That is, IRC allows users to communicate back and forth at the same time, similar to a telephone conversation. Chat rooms and instant messaging are two widespread uses of IRC. With *chat rooms*, many individuals can send and receive messages simultaneously regarding a subject of interest to all of them; it is a group conversation. **Instant messaging (IM)** provides a private link between two individuals over which they communicate. Although instant messaging requires a server to create the initial link between the two users, once the link is created it becomes automatic, it does not require the server any more, and it becomes a peer-to-peer network.

Note that chat rooms allow online discussions involving multiple persons, each adding their own comments. It is a very popular way of interacting online, and provides a way of meeting other people with similar interests. Meetings in a chat room have led to relationships, and even marriages. However, no one in the chat room has to provide evidence as to who they actually are. As a result, anyone using chat rooms should protect their own identity and be aware that others are doing the same. In same cases, individuals may be using chat rooms to lure unsuspecting people into dangerous situations.

The World Wide Web

Of the six Internet operations listed earlier, the most recent is the World Wide Web (WWW), more commonly known as simply the Web. The Web is a body of software and a set of protocols and conventions based on hypertext and multimedia that make the Internet easy to use and browse. *Hypertext* links relate information for which there is no hierarchy or menu system. *Multimedia* interactively combines text, graphics, animation, images, audio, and video displayed by and under the control of a computer.

Tim Berners-Lee, a computer scientist, developed the Web in 1989, at the European Laboratory for Particle Physics (CERN) in Geneva, Switzerland. He saw a need for physicists to be able to communicate with colleagues about their work while it was in progress, rather than waiting until a project was finished. To make this *real-time* communication possible, he wanted to create an interconnected web of documents that would allow a reader to jump between documents at will using hypertext links.

Although in use only since the early 1990s on most computers, hypertext actually predates the use of personal computers. U.S. President Franklin D. Roosevelt's science advisor, Vannevar Bush, originally proposed the idea in a 1945 *Atlantic* magazine article entitled "As We May Think." Twenty years later, computer visionary Ted Nelson coined the term *hypertext*. However, hypertext remained a largely hidden concept until Apple Computers released its Macintosh HyperCard software in 1987.

As you can see, the Internet, and especially the World Wide Web, provide valuable tools and resources to business professionals. So how do you access the Web? The client computer uses software called a *Web browser* (or simply, a *browser*) that initiates activity by sending a request to a Web server for certain information.

Using Browsers to Access the Web After using a browser to send a request to a Web server for information, the Web server responds by retrieving the information from its disk and then transmitting it to the client. Upon receiving the data, the browser formats the information for display. Web browsers use a graphical user interface (GUI) like that available on Microsoft Windows or the Apple Mac. With a GUI-based Web browser, you can perform various operations simply by pointing at menu selections or icons representing operations and clicking the mouse button; that is, point-and-click operations. For example, you can use a browser to navigate the Web by pointing at a hypertext link in the current document and clicking it. This operation causes the retrieval of the linked document, image file, or audio file from a distant computer and its display (or playing) on the local computer. You can also enter an address to retrieve a desired document or file.

When displaying information, the browser processes formatting instructions included in the text file retrieved from the server. For example, assume that the creator of a document stored on a Web server decides that a certain phrase should appear in italics when displayed. Instead of saving the file with an italics font, the server stores the text with tags of the form *and* that indicate the beginning and end of the text that will appear in italics when displayed.

The tags in World Wide Web documents are part of a special publishing language called **hypertext markup language (HTML)**. As such, the documents on the Web all have an.html (or .htm) extension. Documents on the Web are referred to as *web pages*, and their location is a *website*. Because HTML is standard for all computers, any Web browser can request an HTML document from any Web server. For instance, a browser running on a PC using Windows 7 can access files created on a Macintosh, which are stored on a Linux-based server.

Web servers can also store multimedia files, which include digitized text, images, animation, video, and audio. The browser retrieves these files and displays them using appropriate software. The transfer of multimedia files from the Web server to the client browser is one of the key operations that set the Web apart from the other Internet applications. Because multimedia enables us to view photographs, graphics, and videos and listen to music, it is a major reason for the phenomenal growth in the Web's popularity.

Figure B.15 shows a fairly simple web page. The underlined words indicate a hypertext link is beneath them. Also shown in this figure is the HTML source language, or source code, necessary to create the web page. Angle brackets (< >) enclose code tags, such as *title* to indicate the title of the

FIGURE B.15 HTML code (bottom of figure) determines a web page's appearance (top).

page, *center* to centre the text, and *b* to make the text appear in boldface. Today you can create web pages with word-processing-like software such as Microsoft Front Page and Netscape Composer, without knowing the details of HTML.

Browser Operations A Web browser retrieves web pages from Web servers and displays them on a client computer. In addition to being electronic rather than physical, web pages differ from pages in a book or magazine in other ways. For example, although the amount of information on a physical page is restricted to the size of the paper page, a web page can extend beyond the area shown on a screen and can also include audio and video.

Many individuals, companies, and organizations have created websites that contain information about themselves and their activities. They continue to add more web pages every day. A specific address identifies each web page. In Web terminology, the address of a web page is referred to as its **uniform resource locator (URL)**. A URL is a standard means of consistently locating web pages or other resources, regardless of where the Internet stores them. For example, the URL of the first page for the WildOutfitters website might be

http://www.wildoutfitters.com/welcome.htm

Like every URL, this one has three parts: (1) the protocol, (2) the Internet address of the server that contains the desired resource, and (3) the path of the resource (sometimes hidden). Figure B.16 shows the three parts of the WildOutfitters welcome page address.

http://www.wildoutfitters.com/welcome.htm

Protocol   Web server address   Path name

FIGURE B.16 The three parts of a URL.

Table B.7	Internet Protocols
Protocol	**Purpose**
http	Retrieve web pages
file	Retrieve files from local hard disk
telnet	Log on to a remote computer connected to the Internet
FTP	Download or upload files from an Internet FTP server
mailto	Send outgoing email
news	Display newsgroup

For Web resources, the protocol (also called the *service resource*) defines the type of resource being retrieved. The letters *http*, which, as we discussed earlier, stand for *hypertext transfer protocol*, identify a web page resource. Some of the other allowable protocols include file, telnet, FTP, mailto, and news. Table B.7 lists these protocols (service resources) and their purposes.

The second part of the URL names the Web server, in this case, *www.wildoutfitters.com*. The third part of the URL is the *path* of the Web resource, which includes the name of the web page file plus its location in any directories or folders. In our example, the path of the web page document is simply the file name, *welcome.htm*. In many cases, the path name will be much longer because it includes the folder(s) that stores the web page.

For example, the URL of the website for the Information Technology Management course offered at Ryerson University is

http://www.ryerson.ca/itm/Coursepdf/ITM700.pdf

In this URL, Coursepdf is a subfolder in the folder called "itm." Note also that this URL ends with a .pdf, indicating that this is a document. The complete path is interpreted as itm/Coursepdf/ITM700.pdf.

Many websites make use of index.html or default.html files to save people from having to type in URLs. This also helps you to guess the URL of an organization's web page. For example, you would guess correctly if you tried *www.dell.com* to access Dell Inc.'s web page. In fact, most browsers now have built-in search engines that will search for the *home* website if you simply enter the name. For example, entering *Dell* will result in finding and displaying matching websites, including the one shown above.

After entering a valid address for a resource, the next step is automatic: The browser software attempts to connect to the Web server at that address, find the page referenced in the address, and return it to the user's browser. If this operation is successful, then the Web browser displays the page on the screen; otherwise, it displays an error message.

The process of moving from one website or page to another one is known as *surfing* the Web. Web surfing can quickly become a time-consuming process as you follow links looking for information or a product to purchase. You can short-circuit this process to some extent by using one of the numerous Web search engines, into which you enter a query word or term and find pages or sites that match it. However, a problem with this approach is the large number of web pages that can be returned, many of which have nothing to do with the query you entered.

As you move from website to website, you may not be aware that something called a *cookie* is saved on your PC. A **cookie** is not an application or virus, but simply a data file that will be accessed by the related website the next time you visit it. This data file tells the website any preferences you have registered with them. Obviously there are privacy concerns associated with cookies, but they do make some websites very convenient to use since you do not have to re-register your information and preferences every time you visit. Every browser has the ability to reject cookies to prevent websites from installing them. However, if this function is enabled, many websites, especially those with shopping carts, will not work.

Wireless Connectivity to the Web and Internet

In the 1990s, a number of mobile telephone companies collaborated to create a special protocol, called *wireless application protocol (WAP)*, so their telephones could connect to the Internet. These companies—Ericsson, Nokia, Matsushita (Panasonic), Motorola, and Psion—also created a company named Symbian to develop and market an operating system named Symbian OS for their wireless devices. Symbian OS supports browsers and other software using WAP. Further, Symbian OS provides contact information, messaging, browsing, and wireless telephone calls.

WAP was transferred to some models of PDAs running the Palm operating system and GSM mobile phones, enabling them to take advantage of special WAP-based websites. WAP-based websites *cannot* normally be viewed with the most popular browsers, Firefox and Internet Explorer. Instead, they have been specially configured for WAP devices connected to a WAP server. A WAP server or WAP gateway supports the use of WML (wireless mark-up language), which allows content to be viewed on a mobile device, much like how HTML allows content to be viewed on a PC. This content viewed on a mobile device, however, is often stripped down to the bare minimum and may result in viewing pages in text only.

There are still mobile devices in use today that take advantage of WML and WAP, and websites that provide a WAP version of their site for easy viewing on a mobile device. Newer smartphones, like the Apple iPhone, however, use embedded mini-browsers to access the Internet just as a browser on a PC would. This allows all of the content—text and graphics—to be displayed. Smartphone technology (speed and graphics capability) and the 4G telecommunications infrastructure have laid the foundation for this new generation of mobile browsing. Of course, even more important than browsing the Web is being able to access mobile applications. There are thousands of applications available for every type of smartphone, ranging from games to personal productivity tools. Check out *www.apple.com/iphone/from-the-app-store/* for the latest iPhone applications, and *http://appworld.blackberry.com/webstore/?lang=en* for the latest BlackBerry applications.

Another popular use of connecting mobile telephones to a WAN is **short message service (SMS)**, which sends text messages of up to 160 characters to mobile telephones. SMS can send messages to a mobile telephone when it is not active and hold the message until it becomes active. The widest use of SMS is in systems that use the **global system for mobile communication (GSM) protocol**. It is also possible to send messages to GSM mobile telephone phones using a website. ITU (International Telecommunication Union) reported that in 2010, nearly 200,000 SMS messages were sent per second, globally.[9] A variant of SMS that allows images and audio to be sent via mobile devices is called *multimedia messaging service (MMS)*. Most mobile telephones now have the ability to take photos and send them via the mobile network. Even more popular is the ability to download ring tones for mobile telephones to personalize telephone rings.

Beyond personal applications, the business applications for wireless Internet, SMS, and MMS are numerous, such as:

- using SMS to notify a salesperson about a request for information, along with a number to call
- immediately sending a photo of a car accident to expedite an insurance claim

---

9. *www.statista.com/statistics/167048/number-of-sms-sent-per-second-worldwide-since-2007/*, retrieved November 15, 2011.

- providing a service person with the name and location of the next service call that includes a link to an Internet site with a map to the location
- using the company intranet via mobile phone to search for inventory while making a sale with a client

Quick Test

1. True or False. A gateway is another term used to describe a bridge.

2. True or False. A domain name is always included as a part of the server address.

3. The tags in World Wide Web documents are part of a special publishing language called
   _____.

RO↑ | STUDENT RETURN ON INVESTMENT SUMMARY

1. Describe client/server architecture and explain how it works.

The most common architecture for computer networks is client/server architecture, in which each computer on the network is running either server software or client software, or both types of software simultaneously. Server software provides data or resources to other computers in the network. Client software requests services from the servers. Clients and servers can work in series, with the most common form being the three-tiered client/server architecture that uses a client, an application server, and a database server. It is possible for computers on a network to be both servers and clients; this is known as a peer-to-peer network.

2. Explain how the network layer model describes a wide area network.

The network layer model is used to understand the way networks operate. The layers define the standards with which each network must comply. The simplified model presented in the text consists of three layers: the application software layer, networking software layer, and data component layer. The application software layer specifies the software on each computer on the network that the user uses to send and receive messages and data between computers, as well as the software necessary to encrypt the message or data streams. The networking software layer describes how the message from the application software layer is formatted according to whatever protocol will actually be used to send it over the network. For WANs, the Internet protocols (TCP/IP) and EDI protocols are important protocols in the network layer model. The data component layer describes the hardware and media (twisted pair, coaxial cable, and so on) over which a message is sent. Radio and infrared transmissions are now being used for wireless networks. Packets are transmitted over the Internet via a packet switching methodology that uses routers or switches. Two other key considerations are the signal type (analog or digital) and the data rate (the rate at which bits are transmitted through the network).

3. Describe how local area networks are configured, how the Internet works, and what makes the World Wide Web valuable to business professionals.

The parts of a local area network include the server, client computers, cabling and hubs, the network operating system, and network interface cards (NICs). The cabling and hubs tie the server and client computers together. The network operating system directs the operations of the LAN and resides on both the server and the clients. Finally, the network interface card handles the electronic interface between the servers or clients and the rest of the network. The Ethernet protocol is used in the vast majority of LANs. Wireless LANs (WLANs), in which the usual LAN cabling is replaced with wireless transmissions between computers, are becoming increasingly popular.

The Internet is a network of networks that have agreed to use the TCP/IP protocols for addressing computers and sending packets over the network. There is no governing authority or central computer. The six primary operations on the Internet are email, FTP, newsgroups, telnet, and Internet relay chat (IRC). Email uses the simple mail transfer protocol (SMTP) to send asynchronous messages over the Internet to individuals and groups. A listserv is a method of easily sending email messages to a group. FTP uses the file transfer protocol to transfer files between computers over the Internet. Telnet allows users to log on to a distant computer and to use software on that computer, although its use is quickly falling out of favour. Newsgroups enable users to engage in discussions on a global network of news servers. Finally, IRC enables users to communicate synchronously in chat rooms or through instant messaging.

The World Wide Web (WWW), often referred to as the Web, is a body of software and a set of protocols and conventions based on hypertext and multimedia that make the Internet easy to use and browse. It is a client/server network by which the client browser software requests web pages created in hypertext markup language (HTML) from a Web server. Multimedia files are retrieved separately from text pages. Hypertext allows the user to jump within pages or from page to page. The address of the website is called a uniform resource locator (URL) and consists of a protocol, a Web server address, and the path of a web page.

KNOWLEDGE SPEAK

blog   390

Bluetooth   385

clients   375

cookie   393

data rate   382

Ethernet protocol   384

file transfer protocol (FTP)   389

global system for mobile communication (GSM)
   protocol   394

hypertext markup language (HTML)   391

instant messaging (IM)   390

Internet relay chat (IRC)   390

local area networks (LANs)   383

network architecture   375

network interface card (NIC)   386

network layer model   378

newsgroups   389

packet switching   380

packets   380

peer-to-peer network   377

personal area network (PAN)   385

servers   375

short message service (SMS)   394

signal type   381

three-tiered client/server architecture   376

transmission control protocol/Internet protocol
   (TCP/IP)   379

uniform resource locator (URL)   392

wireless LANs (WLANs)   384

SelectSQL1 = " Select ;

QuerySQL1 = " where

QuerySQL2 = "

TECH GUIDE

C | THE DETAILS OF SQL, LOGICAL MODELLING, AND XML

WHAT WE WILL COVER

- Using SQL to Query Relational Databases
- Using Logical Modelling to Create a Relational Database and Querying Multitable Databases
- Using XML for Data Transfer

STUDENT RETURN ON INVESTMENT ROI

Through your investment of time in reading and thinking about this Tech Guide, your return—or created value—is gaining knowledge. After reading this Tech Guide, you should be able to

1. Explain how SQL is used to query a single-table database.

2. Explain how logical modelling is used to create effective relational database systems, and explain how SQL is used to query multiple-table databases.

3. Explain how XML is used to transfer data between software applications.

In Chapter 3, we discussed how relational database systems are used as a way of organizing and accessing data. In this Tech Guide, we provide you with more information on relational database systems and also discuss XML as a way of transferring data between software applications and for working with Web services.

■ USING SQL TO QUERY RELATIONAL DATABASES

The primary function of a database is to allow business professionals to obtain information from it in a usable form. You will recall from Chapter 3 that a *relational database* is a database structured with tables that are related to one another so data can be stored and retrieved efficiently. These relations allow a user to run *queries* (questions) on the database to retrieve specific data. To query a relational database, it is common practice to use **Structured Query Language (SQL)**, which is a computer language for manipulating data in a relational database. SQL queries also enable database users to add new records, or change or delete records in a database (instead of using commands from Microsoft Access or another software package). To demonstrate how to use SQL effectively, let's begin with a simple relational database example.

Relational Database Example

Recall the relational database that we used in Chapter 3 (WildOutfitters), shown in Figure C.1. The database tables, Product and Vendor, are related through the **primary key**, a field that holds a unique value for each record. The VendorID is the primary key for the Vendor table. The Product table includes VendorID as a **foreign key** to relate the two tables.

What types of queries would business professionals, such as marketing analysts, use for this database? They might use a query to display all WildOutfitters products that sell for more than $100. Once a query has been used to find matching rows, the marketing analyst could then update a row by making changes to the contents of one or more rows (e.g., modify prices), or to delete a row if it is no longer needed (e.g., discontinued products). It is also possible to add new rows to a table as WildOutfitters adds new products to its inventory.

Querying a Single-Table Database

A table is known more formally as an **entity**. All tables must be given an **identifier**, or a name, as must all fields in the database. In both cases, it is best to use descriptive names. Figure C.2 shows the Product entity with the fields shown in Figure C.1. Note that the table name is in upper-case to distinguish it from the field names. Note also that an asterisk denotes the primary key for this table, ItemCode.

ItemCode	ItemName	RetailPrice	ItemCost	VendorID
AM	Air Mattress	$100.00	$60.00	SFJ
BP	Backpack	$165.00	$80.00	BRU
CC	Child Carrier	$175.00	$85.00	SFJ
CK	Cookset	$50.00	$32.50	DOL
DP	Day Pack	$105.00	$60.00	WED
HB	Hiking Boots	$110.00	$50.00	DOL
PL	Propane Lantern	$35.00	$20.00	FEU
SB	Sleeping Bag	$100.00	$45.00	DOL
TT	Tent	$385.00	$110.00	WED
GC	Ground Cover	$20.00	$12.50	FEU

Product Table

VendorID	VendorName	Contact	PhoneNumber	Discount
BRU	Backpacks R' U	Nick Estelle	415-555-8328	5.00%
DOL	Doleman Manuf	George Burdell	770-555-4505	6.00%
FEU	Feuters Campin	Chris Patrick	406-555-2103	4.00%
SFJ	SFJ Enterprises	Ashley Hyatt	239-555-0308	5.00%
WED	Waters End	Todd Keegan	715-555-1212	7.00%

Vendor Table

FIGURE C.1 Related WildOutfitters database tables.

PRODUCT

ItemCode*
ItemName
RetailPrice
ItemCost
VendorID

FIGURE C.2 Single database table (in all capitals) with five fields.

How would SQL be used to query this database table? Let's look at the general form of an SQL query to search for matching records:

SELECT *fields* FROM *tables* WHERE *fields match query condition*

Here, the SELECT keyword designates which fields to display as a result of the query, the FROM keyword designates which tables to search, and the WHERE keyword specifies the search criteria, or **query condition**, to use in finding records. Note that we have used upper-case for keywords to make them stand out, but otherwise case is not important when using SQL.

To display the ItemCost for all records in the PRODUCT table that have an ItemCode of BP, the SQL query is

SELECT ItemCost FROM Product WHERE ItemCode = 'BP'

Enclose the BP ItemCode in single quotation marks to designate it as a character or text constant (you can also use double quotation marks). Numeric constants (such as the retail price or item cost) are not enclosed in such quotation marks. For this query, and assuming the entire product table is shown in Figure C.1, the result will show $80.

In addition to the SELECT keyword, you can use a number of other keywords to CREATE a table, to INSERT new records in a table, to DELETE records from a table, and to UPDATE one or more records in a table. You can also search for records that are *like* a specific condition, as well as calculate sums, averages, and so on for all records that match some criteria.

The next sections show how to use several SQL commands, which you should become familiar with to increase your productivity as a business professional.

Using SQL to Display Specific Information

You can use SQL to display the entire table; that is, all fields for all of the records. In this case, the form of the SQL command is quite simple:

SELECT * FROM *TableName*

Here, the asterisk is a placeholder for all fields in the table. Figure C.3 shows the result of this SQL command for the Product table.

ItemCode	ItemName	RetailPrice	ItemCost	VendorID
AM	Air Mattress	$100.00	$60.00	SFJ
BP	Backpack	$165.00	$80.00	BRU
CC	Child Carrier	$175.00	$85.00	SFJ
CK	Cookset	$50.00	$32.50	DOL
DP	Day Pack	$105.00	$60.00	WED
HB	Hiking Boots	$110.00	$50.00	DOL
PL	Propane Lantern	$35.00	$20.00	FEU
SB	Sleeping Bag	$100.00	$45.00	DOL
TT	Tent	$385.00	$110.00	WED
GC	Ground Cover	$20.00	$12.50	FEU

Product Table

FIGURE C.3 WildOutfitters Product table.

Displaying Selected Fields for All Records Instead of displaying all fields for all records, you may only want to display a subset of the fields. The standard form of this query is

SELECT *FieldName1, FieldName2, . . .* FROM *TableName*

Note that you can include one or more field names in the list. For example, if you want to display just the item names and retail prices for all products sold by WildOutfitters, the SQL command would be

SELECT ItemName, RetailPrice FROM Product

Figure C.4 shows the resulting output, which displays all the products along with their retail prices.

If you want to display these records in some order other than in increasing order of the primary key, you can add the *Order By* clause to the SQL statement. The standard form of this query is

SELECT *FieldName1, FieldName2, . . .* **FROM** *TableName*
ORDER BY *FieldName*

In this case, the results of the query will be ordered according to the last field name mentioned. For example, to show the same list of items as before but now in increasing order of retail price, the SQL statement is

SELECT ItemName, RetailPrice FROM Product
ORDER By RetailPrice

Displaying Selected Fields for Matching Records In many cases, you may only want to display selected fields for records that match some condition. To do this, you need to use the WHERE keyword followed by some query condition involving one of six comparison operators: equals ($=$), greater than ($>$), less than ($<$), greater than or equal to ($>=$), less than or equal to ($<=$), or not equal to ($<>$), plus a field name and a value. The general form is

SELECT *FieldName1, FieldName2, …* **FROM** *TableName*
WHERE *Query Condition*

For example, assume that the marketing department at WildOutfitters wants to know the names and wholesale costs of products with an item cost greater than $50. To display the item name and item cost, the SQL statement is

SELECT ItemName, ItemCost FROM Product
WHERE ItemCost > 50

Here, using the WHERE keyword restricts which rows to display; that is, only those that have an ItemCost value greater than $50. In this case, the query would display the item name and item cost for the five products with an item cost over $50: Air Mattress, Backpack, Child Carrier, Day Pack, and Tent.

It is also possible to combine conditions in a query by using the AND or OR operators, known as *compound operators*. The AND operator requires both conditions to be true, while the OR operator only requires that one or both of the conditions be true. For example, consider this query:

SELECT ItemName, ItemCost FROM product WHERE
ItemCost > 15 AND VendorID = "FEU"

The results of this query show the name, cost, and vendor ID for any product with a cost greater than $15 from the vendor whose ID is FEU.

ItemName	RetailPrice
Air Mattress	$100.00
Backpack	$165.00
Child Carrier	$175.00
Cookset	$50.00
Day Pack	$105.00
Ground Cover	$20.00
Hiking Boots	$110.00
Propane Lantern	$35.00
Sleeping Bag	$100.00
Tent	$385.00

FIGURE C.4 Result of query to display specific field names.

Using the LIKE Operator

Whenever you use the equals sign in a SELECT query, you are looking for an exact match. But what happens, for example, if you don't know the exact product name? Or if you're looking for information about a group of products? In that case, you should use the LIKE operator. The LIKE operator uses the **wildcard** character as a replacement for unknown or non-existing characters in an attempt to find matches to a group of characters (commonly referred to as a **character string**). The wildcard character is usually either the asterisk (*) in Microsoft Access or the percent sign (%) in other database management systems. The general form of this type of query is

SELECT *FieldName1, Fieldname2, . . .* **FROM** *TableName*
WHERE *FieldName* **LIKE** '*value*'

For example, to find the item names and retail prices of all types of backpacks offered by WildOutfitters, the query in Access is

SELECT ItemName, RetailPrice FROM Product
WHERE ItemName LIKE '*Pack*'

In this query, the wildcard character represents anything on either side of the word "Pack." The query results in this case will display records for the Backpack and the Day Pack.

Inserting or Deleting Records

As discussed earlier, you can use Microsoft Access or another relational database management package to add records to or delete records from a database table. It is also possible to carry out both of these operations using SQL. To insert a record into a table, you would use an SQL statement of the form

INSERT INTO *TableName* **Values** (*value1, value2, . . .*)

Note that, in this format, you must enter the values in the exact order as the fields in the record, separated by commas. If there are null or missing values, you must still enter the corresponding comma.

For example, to insert a new record for a heater with an item code of HH, a retail price of $75, and an item cost of $45 into the Product table of the WildOutfitters database, the SQL statement is

INSERT INTO Product Values ('HH', 'Heater', 75, 45)

As above, note that we use single quotation marks to set off the two character strings in this query.

To delete an existing record from a database table, you would use an SQL statement in the form

DELETE FROM *TableName* **WHERE** *FieldName* = *value*

This will delete all records that match the criteria. For example, assume that WildOutfitters no longer carries the Ground Cover product and needs to remove it from the database. To do this, the SQL command is

DELETE FROM Product WHERE ItemCode = 'GC'

Changing Values with SQL

To change values in a row of a database, you can use the UPDATE and SET keywords in the form

UPDATE *TableName* **SET** *FieldName1* = *value*
WHERE *FieldName2* = *value*

For example, assume the ItemCost for the tent has increased by 10 percent. To account for this increase in the database table, the SQL statement is

UPDATE Product SET ItemCost = ItemCost*1.1 WHERE
ItemCode = 'TT'

Executing this SQL statement will result in the ItemCost for the tent to increase from $110 to $121.

Using Aggregate Functions in SQL

Our final SQL operation is to use it to calculate certain values in the table using five different **aggregate functions**: COUNT, AVG, SUM, MIN, and MAX. As their names indicate, the purposes of these functions are to count the number of matching records, find their average value, sum the values, or find the minimum or maximum matching value, respectively. In each case, you must use a dummy field name for the result of the calculation. The form for the AVG function is

SELECT AVG(*fieldname*) AS *DummyName* FROM *TableName*
WHERE *Query condition*

In this SQL statement, the AVG function finds the average of the values of the field name in parentheses, subject to the query condition. It then stores that value in the dummy name variable, which is displayed after running the query.

For example, to find the average retail price for all items in the Product table, the query is

SELECT AVG(RetailPrice) AS AvgPrice FROM Product

Running this query on the PRODUCT table shown in Figure C.4 results in displaying the average retail price of $124.50.

The SUM, MAX, and MIN functions have the same form as the AVG function. The COUNT function, however, uses a different form, as the following shows:

SELECT COUNT(*) AS *DummyName* FROM *TableName*
WHERE *Query condition*

For example, to count the number of items in the table with a retail price of more than $75, the SQL statement is

SELECT COUNT(*) AS Over75Count FROM Product
WHERE RetailPrice > 75

The results of this query display the number of items with a retail price of more than $75.

So far in our discussion of relational databases we have been querying a single table using SQL. However, the real power of a relational database comes from the use of multiple tables. In the next section we discuss how creating a database with multiple tables usually increases the productivity of knowledge work activities.

Quick Test

For the Product table shown in Figure C.3, write queries to carry out the following operations.

1. Display the item name and retail price for all items with a retail price greater than $100.

2. Insert a new record for a product with ItemCode of 'CC,' an item name of 'Camp Chair,' an item cost of $95, and a retail price of $175.

3. Calculate the average item cost of all items in inventory.

Answers: 1. SELECT ItemName, RetailPrice FROM Product WHERE RetailPrice > 100;
2. INSERT INTO Product VALUES('CC', 'Camp Chair', 95, 175);
3. SELECT AVG(ItemCost) as AvgCost FROM Product

■ USING LOGICAL MODELLING TO CREATE A RELATIONAL DATABASE AND QUERYING MULTITABLE DATABASES

Most relational databases include many tables, not just one. Why? To help you understand the reasons for this, consider the expanded version of the PRODUCT table, shown in Figure C.5. Note that the table now includes information about the vendor that provides each product to WildOutfitters. Included in the vendor information are the vendor name, the contact name and telephone number, and the discount given by the vendor if WildOutfitters pays its bill within 30 days of delivery.

In looking at Figure C.5, you can now probably see a big reason for not using a single table: *redundancy*. Note that the Product table now lists each vendor's name, contact, phone number, and discount rate multiple times. This redundancy not only results in the database table taking up storage space (especially for a realistic-sized database table involving millions of records), but also causes problems, typically referred to as **anomalies**, when trying to insert new records, delete existing records, or update records. Therefore, to solve the problems associated with storing all the data in one table, relational databases are used.

As discussed in Chapter 3, reducing data redundancy is one advantage of using a relational database. Other advantages include improving data access and sharing by using database standards; maintaining the integrity of the data by having security and controls to prevent errors, duplication, and unauthorized entry; and allowing configurable views of the data to match the user needs.

Logical modelling is often used to create the appropriate relational tables. *Logical modelling* provides tools to help analyze and understand what data are important, and the relationships between the data.

Entity-Relationship Diagramming

The first step in logical modelling is to create an *entity-relationship diagram (ERD)*. The ERD is uncluttered by attributes so businesses can focus on the "big picture"; that is, the entities and the relationships. Businesses then use the ERD to build a *relational data model*, which adds the attributes and helps to organize them prior to creating the database.

For example, let's use the information from Figure C.5 (the Product-Vendor information), to pick out the entities and attributes to create the ERD. First, think about what entities you need to consider. In this case, you can easily identify two entities: PRODUCT and VENDOR. Now, using standard symbols, draw the entities and the relationships between the entities. Figure C.6 shows the standard symbols for an ERD. Note that 1:1 means one-to-one (a **one-to-one relationship**), and 1:M means one-to-many. These numbers are often replaced with vertical lines where one vertical line indicates a 1:1 relationship and two vertical lines indicate a 1:M relationship. This notation was used in our voting example in Chapter 3. The diamond indicates a relationship between two entities.

ItemCode	ItemName	RetailPrice	ItemCost	VendorID	VendorName	Contact	PhoneNumber	Discount
BP	Backpack	$165.00	$80.00	BRU	Backpacks R' U	Nick Estelle	415-555-8328	5.00%
CK	Cookset	$50.00	$32.50	DOL	Doleman Manuf	George Burdell	770-555-4505	6.00%
HB	Hiking Boots	$110.00	$50.00	DOL	Doleman Manuf	George Burdell	770-555-4505	6.00%
SB	Sleeping Bag	$100.00	$45.00	DOL	Doleman Manuf	George Burdell	770-555-4505	6.00%
PL	Propane Lantern	$35.00	$20.00	FEU	Feuters Campin	Chris Patrick	406-555-2103	4.00%
GC	Ground Cover	$20.00	$12.50	FEU	Feuters Campin	Chris Patrick	406-555-2103	4.00%
AM	Air Mattress	$100.00	$60.00	SFJ	SFJ Enterprises	Ashley Hyatt	239-555-0308	5.00%
CC	Child Carrier	$175.00	$85.00	SFJ	SFJ Enterprises	Ashley Hyatt	239-555-0308	5.00%
DP	Day Pack	$105.00	$60.00	WED	Waters End	Todd Keegan	715-555-1212	7.00%
TT	Tent	$385.00	$110.00	WED	Waters End	Todd Keegan	715-555-1212	7.00%

FIGURE C.5 Using a single table to store data often results in redundancy.

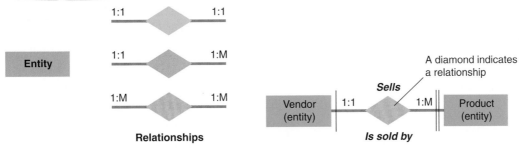

FIGURE C.6 Standard ERD symbols, where a diamond indicates a relationship.

FIGURE C.7 A one-to-many relationship.

Figure C.7 shows the ERD for this example. In reading from left to right, you can see the ERD indicates that *one* vendor sells *many* products, while each product is sold by only one vendor. Note that the 1:M is next to the Product entity, as it includes *many* products.

Think of another situation involving the Product table—one involving customers instead of vendors. If you think about

FIGURE C.8 A many-to-many relationship with no primary key–foreign key relationship.

it, a customer can purchase many products, and many customers can purchase the same product. As a result, the 1:M is next to both the Product and Customer entities. The ERD, shown in Figure C.8, includes what is known as a **many-to-many relationship** between the Customer and Product entities.

What happens when you have this type of relationship between entities? You have a problem, because many-to-many relationships violate logical modelling rules for creating a relational database. Specifically, it is not possible to create a primary key–foreign key relationship with a many-to-many relationship. As a result, you need to draw a new **relational entity** to lie between the original two entities. As Figure C.9 shows, the relational entity is connected to each original entity by a one-to-many relationship, thereby transforming the original many-to-many relationship into two one-to-many relationships.

This . . .

Many-to-many relationship (before transformation).

. . . Becomes this

Two one-to-many relationships with relational entity (after transformation)

FIGURE C.9 Converting a many-to-many (M:M) relationship into two one-to-many (1:M) relationships.

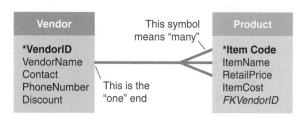

FIGURE C.10 Data model for a one-to-many (1:M) relationship.

CUSTOMER

*CustomerID
ShipAddress
ShipCity
ShipProvince
ShipPostal
EmailAddress

FIGURE C.11 CUSTOMER entity, where CustomerID is the primary key.

PURCHASE

*PurchaseID
FKCustomerID
FKItemCode
PurchaseDate
Number

FIGURE C.12 PURCHASE entity used to transform the M:M relationship into two 1:M relationships.

The Relational Data Model

After creating the ERD, the next step of logical modelling is to create the relational data model. Recall that this step fills in the details of the relationship between the entities. That is, a relational data model adds the attributes, as well as identifies primary and foreign keys. To see how to do this, convert the 1:M ERD (Figure C.7) into a data model.

As Figure C.10 shows, the symbols change when you convert the ERD to a data model. The relationship symbol changes from a "labelled diamond" to a "line with crow's foot." The "crow's foot" is placed on the "many" side of the relationship. The data model also adds more detail to the entities, including a listing of the attributes (fields) for the entities and indicators for the primary and foreign keys. A simple rule of thumb for determining foreign keys is that the primary key from the "one" side of the relationship is used as a foreign key on the "many" side of the relationship.

What about the data model for the ERD for the M:M customer–product situation discussed above? You can use the same PRODUCT table, but now you need a CUSTOMER table that includes a customer's ID number, shipping address, city, province, postal code, and email address. Figure C.11 shows the resulting entity, where the CustomerID field is the primary key.

Next, you need a PURCHASE table to convert the M:M relationship into two 1:M relationships. This entity will include the primary keys from both the CUSTOMER and PRODUCT tables (as foreign keys), as well as some unique identifier as its own primary key. The two foreign keys enable WildOutfitters to determine information on the buyer (customer) as well as information on the product purchased. Finally, you will also include the number of items purchased and the date of the purchase in this table. Figure C.12 shows the resulting entity.

Now, using the CUSTOMER, PRODUCT, and PURCHASE tables, you can create the data model that represents the purchase of a product by a customer. Note that the customer may purchase multiple products, and multiple customers can purchase the same product, by simply having one record in the PURCHASE table for each purchase. Figure C.13 shows the resulting data model, which matches the transformed M:M ERD shown in Figure C.8.

The VendorID foreign key is included in the PRODUCT table, since it is also related to the VENDOR table. You can now combine both of these entity-relationships into one complete data model, as shown in Figure C.14. As this shows, by using logical modelling, organizations can effectively expand their databases along with their businesses.

A final consideration in creating a data model is that of **referential integrity**, which enforces consistency between linked tables. To understand referential integrity, think of the values stored in a foreign key as a reference to a record in another table. If, for some reason, that record does not exist, then there are problems. For example, if you try to add a record to the PRODUCT table that tries to reference a VendorID for a vendor that does not exist in the VENDOR table, then a message will

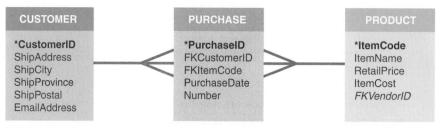

FIGURE C.13 Conversion of an M:M relationship into two 1:M relationships.

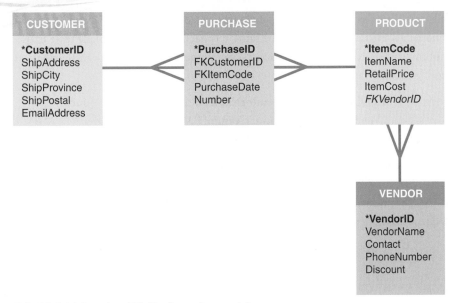

FIGURE C.14 Complete WildOutfitters data model.

warn you about it. Conversely, if you try to remove a vendor record from the VENDOR table and that vendor has products listed in the PRODUCT table, a warning message will also appear. This feature helps to maintain the overall integrity of databases.

After creating a relational database with two or more tables, use SQL to query it, in a manner similar to querying a single-table database.

Querying Multitable Databases

In this section, we look at the most common operation on a two-table database: the Join operation. We then discuss how to use views to save queried results.

The Join Operation The **Join operation** creates a single table from two (or more) tables, after which you can use it to perform calculations and carry out grouping of products. For our example, the SQL instruction to do this is as follows:

$$\text{SELECT * FROM Product, Vendor WHERE}$$
$$\text{Product.VendorID = Vendor.VendorID}$$

In looking at this query, note that because the field name for the foreign key in PRODUCT (VendorID) is the same as the primary key field name in VENDOR, we distinguish between them by combining the table name and the field name using a period; that is, Product.VendorID and Vendor.VendorID. Figure C.15 shows the result of this query.

	ItemCode	ItemName	RetailPrice	ItemCost	Product.VendorID	Vendor.VendorID	VendorName	Contact	PhoneNumber	Discount
▶	BP	Backpack	$165.00	$80.00	BRU	BRU	Backpacks R' Us	Nick Estelle	415-555-8328	5.00%
	HH	Heater	$75.00	$45.00	BRU	BRU	Backpacks R' Us	Nick Estelle	415-555-8328	5.00%
	CK	Cookset	$50.00	$32.50	DOL	DOL	Doleman Manufac	George Burdell	770-555-4505	6.00%
	HB	Hiking Boots	$110.00	$50.00	DOL	DOL	Doleman Manufac	George Burdell	770-555-4505	6.00%
	SB	Sleeping Bag	$100.00	$45.00	DOL	DOL	Doleman Manufac	George Burdell	770-555-4505	6.00%
	PL	Propane Lantern	$35.00	$20.00	FEU	FEU	Feuters Camping	Chris Patrick	406-555-2103	4.00%
	AM	Air Mattress	$100.00	$60.00	SFJ	SFJ	SFJ Enterprises	Ashley Hyatt	239-555-0308	5.00%
	CC	Child Carrier	$175.00	$85.00	SFJ	SFJ	SFJ Enterprises	Ashley Hyatt	239-555-0308	5.00%
	DP	Day Pack	$105.00	$60.00	WED	WED	Waters End	Todd Keegan	715-555-1212	7.00%
	TT	Tent	$385.00	$121.00	WED	WED	Waters End	Todd Keegan	715-555-1212	7.00%

Query1 : Select Query

Record: 14 ◀ 1 ▶ ▶I ▶* of 10

FIGURE C.15 Results of a Join query.

While this looks very much like the single table we decided earlier to avoid, it does help avoid update anomalies. Further, you can use the same approach as querying a single table to quickly do a number of things. For example, to list products, vendor name, and item cost in alphabetical order of item name, you could easily modify the previous query to the following:

> **SELECT ItemName, VendorName, ItemCost FROM Product,**
> **Vendor WHERE Product.VendorID = Vendor.VendorID**
> **ORDER BY ItemName**

It is also possible to carry out calculations and display them as the result of a join query. For example, each vendor offers a different discount to WildOutfitters for paying its bill within 30 days of receiving the merchandise. The net item cost then equals the item cost times (1 – discount). You can modify the previous SQL query to output the item name, vendor name, item cost, discount, and the net cost as follows:

> **SELECT ItemName, VendorName, ItemCost, Discount,**
> **ItemCost*(1-Discount) as NetCost FROM Product,**
> **Vendor WHERE Product.VendorID = Vendor.VendorID**
> **ORDER BY ItemName**

The results of this query will list the products in order of vendor, as well as create a new field, NetCost, that will indicate the discounted cost.

Creating Views With most relational database management systems, it is possible to save the queries you have created. Another name for a saved query is a **view**. However, note that these views are not actual tables, even though they might appear that way on the screen.

There are two main reasons for creating a view. First, it enables you to simplify query writing in the future. If you plan to reuse some aspect of a query, you can save it as a view and then use it by itself or as part of another query. For example, say you had saved a previous query as *TotalSold* and now only wanted to see the item names and revenue from this query. A new and simpler query to do this would be as follows:

> **SELECT ItemName, Revenue FROM TotalSold**

A second reason for using a view is for security. You can create a view only showing fields that you want others to see. That way, they cannot look at fields in the database, such as customer information, that may include confidential information.

Quick Test

Indicate whether the following statements are True or False.

1. Logical modelling helps to create anomalies in relational databases.

2. Referential integrity enforces consistency between linked tables.

3. The most common operation on a two-table database is the Intersection operation, which creates a single table from two (or more) tables.

4. You must include table names when creating a multitable query.

■ USING XML FOR DATA TRANSFER

Until now, we have limited our discussion to creating and using relational databases within an organization. However, most companies today require the ability to share data and resources over the Web. Although companies have been using a system known as *electronic data interchange (EDI)* for many years, EDI is expensive and is useful only to very large companies. With the rapid growth of the Internet, organizations have turned to XML as a way of carrying out the same processes. An XML file can be processed purely as data by a program, it can be stored with similar data on another computer, or, like an HTML file, it can be displayed.

XML vs. HTML

A good way to understand XML is to compare it with HTML, the markup language that is the basis for the Web. First, recall from Chapter 2 that HTML is a *formatting language* that is meant to display numbers and text in a predefined way on a Web browser. As such, it does not have the structure to impart meaning to items like part numbers or prices. Because it is not a good idea to have computers infer meanings from entries on web pages, HTML is not appropriate for transmitting large amounts of purchasing and shipping information over the Internet. HTML also has predetermined tags, which reduces its flexibility, and the only way you can retrieve information from it is to search for specific text.

XML solves these problems because it is a language that emphasizes the structure and meaning of data. This means that product information such as name, identifier, and price are easily transmitted using XML. XML is also flexible in that users can define their own tags. For example, a company could use XML to define tags that their trading partners can understand. This enables searches of the data using the meaning of the data instead of just using a text search. For example, the tag <PARTID> would indicate that the field that followed was a part number and it would be easy to find all part numbers by searching for this tag. An XML file can be processed purely as data by a program, it can be stored with similar data on another computer, or, like an HTML file, it can be displayed. For example, depending on how the application in the receiving computer wanted to handle the part number field, it could be stored or displayed, or some other operation could be performed on it, depending on the content of the field. Table C.1 compares XML with HTML.

Setting Up an XML Document

The first step to creating an XML file is to decide which tags to use to describe the data that are being transferred over the Internet. As with HTML, the tags are enclosed in angle brackets (< >). Each beginning tag *must* have an ending tag. For example, if using a <PARTID> tag to describe the part ID, then there *must* be a matching </PARTID> tag. These tags must come immediately before and after the data item to ensure that there is no ambiguity or inconsistency about the description.

While current browsers are usually capable of determining the matching tags for each data item in an XML file, it is a better practice to provide a formal definition of all the data elements in the XML file. This can be done in one of two ways: the **document type definition** method or the

Table C.1	Comparison of HTML and XML	
Feature	XML	HTML
Type of text	Structured with meaning defined	Formatted with meaning inferred
Definition of structure	User-defined	Predetermined
Retrieval	Context-sensitive	Limited
Searchability	Searchable by text or meaning	Searchable only by text or format
Hypertext linkage	Extensive	Limited

XML schema method. Both can be incorporated into the XML file or created as separate files with DTD or XSD extensions, respectively. These files are then referred to by the XML file to define the XML tags it uses to describe the data.

Using a DTD or XSD file, a program called a *parser* in a Web browser can work with the tags that the document contains. For example, Figure C.16 shows an XML schema (XSD) file for a list of WildOutfitters' vendors. Note that the first line of this XSD file with the "<?xml . . . >" tag defines it as also being an XML file. The tags that begin with *xsd*: make up the formal definition of the data elements to be used in the matching XML file. Note also that the schema defines the names of tag elements in the XML file and their data type. For instance, the schema defines an element called CompanyName, which will contain text (string) information.

Figure C.17 shows a portion of the XML file that uses this schema. Note that the file line defines it as an XML file, and the third line references the schema (XSD) file shown in Figure C.16 (companynew.xsd).

The second line refers to a stylesheet (XSL) file (which we will discuss shortly). You can see these elements used to describe actual data starting with the fourth line, which has a <company> tag. It is fairly easy to see that the first company is named ABC Metals, located at 550 Montgomery Street in Minneapolis, Minnesota, 55402. Note that a tag </company> terminates the data for the first company.

To display an XML file in a more readable form on a Web browser, you need to use an **XML stylesheet (XSL) file**. This file uses a combination of HTML and XML tags. In our example, the XML file references it in the second line. Figure C.18 shows the actual companynew.xsl stylesheet file. Note that it is also an XML file, and the *xsl*: tags reference the stylesheet elements along with HTML tags.

So what does the final result of these files look like on a Web browser? Figure C.19 shows the results.

```
<?xml version="1.0" encoding="UTF-8"?>
<xsd:schema xmlns:xsd="http://www.w3.org/2001/XMLSchema">
<!--Customer List-->
<xsd:element name="Customers">
 <xsd:complexType>
  <xsd:sequence>
   <xsd:element maxOccurs="unbounded" minOccurs="1" name="Company" type="companies"/>
  </xsd:sequence>
 </xsd:complexType>
</xsd:element>
<xsd:complexType name="companies">
 <xsd:sequence>
  <xsd:element name="CompanyName" type="xsd:string"/>
  <xsd:element name="Address" type="xsd:string"/>
  <xsd:element name="City" type="xsd:string"/>
  <xsd:element name="State" type="xsd:string"/>
  <xsd:element name="Zip" type="xsd:string"/>
 </xsd:sequence>
</xsd:complexType>
</xsd:schema>
```

FIGURE C.16 XML schema (XSD) file.

```
<?xml version="1.0" encoding="utf-8"?>
<?xml-stylesheet type="text/xsl" href="companynew.xsl" media="screen"?>
<NewDataSet xmlns:xsi="http://www.w3.org/2001/XMLSchema-instance" xsi:noNamespaceSchemaLocation="companynew.xsd">
    <Company>
        <CompanyName>ABC Metals</CompanyName>
        <Address>550 Montgomery Street</Address>
        <City>Minneapolis</City>
        <State>MN</State>
        <Zip>55402</Zip>
    </Company>
    <Company>
        <CompanyName>Backpacks R Us</CompanyName>
        <Address>122 Hilltop Avenue</Address>
        <City>Missoula</City>
        <State>MT</State>
        <Zip>59801</Zip>
    </Company>
    <Company>
        <CompanyName>Doleman Hiking Supplies</CompanyName>
        <Address>2532 Epson Blvd</Address>
        <City>Ocala</City>
        <State>FL</State>
        <Zip>34470</Zip>
    </Company>
    <Company>
```

FIGURE C.17 Portion of the XML file that uses the schema from Figure C.16.

```
<?xml version="1.0" encoding="UTF-8"?>
<xsl:stylesheet version="1.0"
xmlns:xsl="http://www.w3.org/1999/XSL/Transform">
    <xsl:output encoding="UTF-8" indent="yes" method="html" version="1.0" />
    <xsl:template match="/">
    <html>
        <head>
            <title> Complete List of Vendors </title>
        </head>
    <body>
        <h1> Complete List of Vendors| </h1>
        <xsl:apply-templates select="NewDataSet" />
        </body>
        </html>
    </xsl:template>
    <xsl:template match="NewDataSet">
        <table border = '1'>
        <xsl:for-each select="Company">
            <tr>
                <td><xsl:value-of select="CompanyName" /></td>
                <td><xsl:value-of select="Address" /></td>
                <td><xsl:value-of select="City" /></td>
                <td><xsl:value-of select="State" /></td>
                <td><xsl:value-of select="Zip" /></td>
            </tr>
        </xsl:for-each>
        </table>
    </xsl:template>
</xsl:stylesheet>
```

FIGURE C.18 This stylesheet (XSL) file uses a combination of HTML and XML tags.

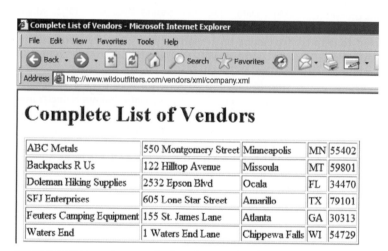

FIGURE C.19 How a browser displays the XML data from Figure C.18.

Quick Test

Fill in the blanks for the following statements.

1. XML files must include both beginning and _____ tags.

2. Unlike HTML, XML files provide _____ to the data.

3. A(n) _____ file is used to display an XML file in easily readable form.

RO↑ | STUDENT RETURN ON INVESTMENT SUMMARY

1. Explain how SQL is used to query a single-table database.

The primary function of a database is to enable users to obtain information from it in a usable form. Users obtain information from a database by constructing and running queries or questions to the database. For a relational database, the queries are written in Structured Query Language (SQL), which is a computer language for manipulating data in a relational database. The general form of SQL query to search for matching records is:

SELECT *fields* FROM *tables* WHERE *fields match query condition*

In the SQL statement, the SELECT keyword designates which fields to display as a result of the query, the FROM keyword designates which tables to search, and the WHERE keyword specifies the search criteria or query condition to use in finding records. In addition to finding data, you can use SQL to insert, delete, and update records in the database tables, as well as to carry out calculations on records.

2. Explain how logical modelling is used to create effective relational database systems, and explain how SQL is used to query multiple-table databases.

Logical modelling provides tools to help businesses analyze and understand what data are important and the relationships between the data by creating a picture of this world of data and relationships. An accurate logical model provides a business with a solid foundation upon which to build its database(s).

In logical modelling, the ERD focuses on the entities and the relationships. The Data Model adds the attributes and helps to organize them prior to creating the database.

Primary and foreign keys are identified as well. The Data Model is built after the ERD by adjusting some symbols and adding more detail.

The most common operation on a two-table database is the Join operation, which creates a single table from two (or more) tables. The general form of a two-table join is

SELECT*FROM *Table1, Table2* WHERE *Table1. PrimaryKey = Table2.ForeignKey*

The Join operation is not restricted to just two tables; it is possible to carry out a three, four, or even more table join as long as all of the tables are related.

3. Explain how XML is used to transfer data between software applications.

XML uses tags to mark up content and/or data so that software applications can recognize it. Using XML, companies can define their own tags, which their trading partners can then understand. An XML file can be processed purely as data by a program, it can be stored with similar data on another computer or, like an HTML file, it can be displayed. The first step to creating an XML file is to decide what tags you will use to describe the data that are being transferred over the Internet. While it can be left to the browser to determine the matching tags, the best way to do this is to use Document Type Definition or an XML schema, either in the XML file or as a separate file that is referenced by the XML file. To display an XML file, you can use a stylesheet (XSL) file that converts it into HTML.

KNOWLEDGE SPEAK

aggregate functions   403
anomalies   404
character string   402
document type definition   409
entity   399
foreign key   399
identifier   399
Join operation   407
many-to-many relationship   405
one-to-one relationship   404

primary key   399
query condition   400
referential integrity   406
relational entity   405
Structured Query Language (SQL)   399
view   408
wildcard   402
XML schema   410
XML stylesheet (XSL) file   410

GLOSSARY

adding value Ensuring that, as an organization moves through the value chain, value is added at each step, thereby increasing the value of the end product or service to the end customer. As such, if a step does not add value, it should be eliminated.

aggregate functions Functions that are used to work with and combine results from multiple records; for example, to count the number of matching records, to find their average value, to sum the values, or to find the minimum or maximum matching value.

agile development A methodology whereby the team develops software in short development cycles or increments to allow for continuously changing requirements.

algorithm A detailed sequence of actions that will accomplish some task when followed.

analysis The phase of problem solving that involves examining and looking at the details of available data. It can involve the use of mathematical models and the compilation of knowledge from various sources, depending on the kind of business the organization is involved in. Helps to answer questions and gain initial insight prior to doing more in-depth transformation and synthesis.

anomalies Database problems typically caused by redundancy in the system; they can harm the integrity of the database records.

application program interface (API) A specific process that allows the application program to make requests to the operating system or another application.

application service provider (ASP) An online technology company that develops and delivers software tools on the Internet.

application software A complete, self-contained program or set of programs for performing a specific job; for example, document preparation, electronic spreadsheet, presentation, and email clients.

automating Using technology instead of business professionals to perform tedious or repetitive tasks. By automating, a business may complete a task with more speed, economy, consistency, and possibly accuracy. It may provide additional benefits by allowing a business to perform work in different ways than before.

balanced scorecard A popular type of dashboard that includes both financial and non-financial performance measures in the context of financial, customer, internal business process, and learning and growth perspectives. Each of these has objectives, measures, targets, and initiatives associated with them, which are equally weighted. The purpose of the balanced scorecard is to measure an organization's actions against its strategic direction.

bandwidth The number of bits a central processing unit (CPU) can process in a single instruction.

Bill 198 An Ontario bill that amends the Securities Act and Commodity Futures Act. Bill 198 gives the Ontario Securities Commission (OSC) rule-making authority to require reporting issuers to appoint audit committees and to establish and maintain internal controls, disclosure controls, and procedures.

binary   The base 2 number system based on combinations of zero and one.

BIOS (basic input/output system)   The system that provides instruction to the computer on how to start up.

bit   The basic unit of measure in a computer; a contraction of BInary and digiT.

blog   A user-generated website written as a journal; derived from "web log."

Bluetooth   A type of personal area network (PAN).

brandstorm   A situation where a traditional brand faces an online storm of negative publicity that can quite literally damage its value overnight.

build-and-fix model   A methodology whereby developers create a system based on a set of requirements and then test and debug it with little attention to any pre-project analysis or developmental design.

bus   A set of wires over which data travels from one location to another.

business   An organization with one or more people who decide on one or more goals to pursue, work together to locate and organize resources, and create processes to achieve the desired goals. It involves producing goods and services and selling them to generate economic value. It includes financial, commercial, industrial, and human considerations.

business continuity plan   A plan put in place to address problem prevention, response to crises, resumption of business activities, recovery of losses, and restoration of systems and processes.

business environment   A company's complex collection of political, economic, social, and technological factors that organizational leaders must consider when making decisions regarding goals, organizational forms, and the creation of business value. Includes macroeconomic variables of the market the company operates in, the nature of the industry, competitors, customers, and suppliers.

business intelligence (BI)   A process that enables business leaders to make better decisions for gaining competitive advantage through the intelligent use of data and information in decision making.

business process   A series of steps that an organization needs to perform to transform inputs to their main outputs (products and services); for example, manufacturing of products or performing services.

business process reengineering (BPR)   The study of business processes with the objective of changing these processes to be more efficient and better support an organization's objectives and strategy.

business rule   A statement that defines or constrains some aspect of the business; it is intended to influence and, sometimes, enforce the behaviour of the business. Business rules are often found as part of policies and procedures, laws, or guidelines.

business strategy   A broad-based formula that lays out how a business is going to compete, what its goals should be, and what plans and policies will be needed to carry out those goals.

business-to-business (B2B) e-commerce   Electronic exchanges between companies.

business-to-consumer (B2C) e-commerce   The online equivalent of a retail store, as well as other services.

business-to-government (B2G) e-commerce   Online sales to government agencies, as well as electronic payments of business-related taxes (GST, PST, HST).

byte   A group of eight bits equivalent to a character of ASCII data.

central processing unit (CPU)   The brain of the computer made up of two components: an arithmetic logic unit (ALU) that performs calculations, and a control unit (CU) that controls the flow of operations. Takes instructions from the memory and runs them. Its speed is measured in GHz (gigahertz).

character encoding   The use of a specific combination of bits to represent each character.

character string   Data that is composed of a group of alphanumeric characters.

CIA triad CIA, which is an abbreviation for confidentiality, integrity, and availability, is a framework for Internet IT security policy development.

clients Computers connected to the file server on a network that is running client software. May request services from the file servers.

client/server network A network of computers that request services (clients) and computers that provide services (servers).

cloud computing Computing over the Internet; the term *cloud* is used as a synonym for the Internet.

code generation Allows a developer to use graphical diagrams to define a system's components and how they are related, and then to automatically create programming statements to implement the logic described by the diagrams.

code of conduct A social contract organizational members "sign" (sometimes literally) that outlines the organization's expectations of that individual's behaviour.

command interpreter The part of the operating system that accepts commands from users and translates them into a language that the operating system (OS) kernel can understand.

commerce The buying and selling of goods and services.

communication Sharing data, information, and knowledge with others using tools such as email, telephone, instant messaging, file sharing, central databases, and in-person meetings.

company-centric business model A model where a single company dominates the market, either when a company is a seller to many other companies (one-to-many) or is a buyer from many companies (many-to-one).

competitive advantage The advantage businesses obtain over their competitors by increasing the quality of insight, speed of execution, and cost competitiveness of the organization.

competitive necessity The need to keep up with competitors in order to stay in business.

compliance Reduces risk through policies and processes that ensure proper financial and accounting procedures, as well as protects employee and customer data that the corporate information system (IS) stores, processes, and transmits. Increases organizational stakeholders' ability to trust the integrity and accuracy of information reported by corporations.

compression technologies Technologies that help reduce the costs of storage and transmission of material on the Internet. With the rise of social computing sites, the demand for compression technologies (particularly of image and video-based formats) has increased substantially.

computer-aided software engineering (CASE) The use of computer-based support in the software development process.

computer hierarchy A means of categorizing computer technologies based on processing power. For example, supercomputers, which have the greatest processing power, are at the top of the hierarchy, and small, embedded processors are at the bottom.

consumer-to-consumer (C2C) e-commerce Use of online auctions like eBay or Yahoo! Auctions for consumers to sell to other consumers.

consumer-to-government (C2G) e-commerce Electronic interactions between consumers and the government, such as the payment of taxes or the purchase of various types of licences.

continuous improvement The ongoing effort to improve products, services, and/or processes. Improvements may involve increasing quality and/or reducing costs. Many believe that continuous improvement efforts lead to competitive advantage.

continuous learning Ensuring the continual upgrade of skills and knowledge to respond to an ever-changing competitive environment. This may involve re-examining assumptions, business practices or methods, and policies and creating new and innovative solutions. Can be in the context of the individual or a group/organization.

contract compliance   Adhering to the terms of a signed agreement; in the case of IS development, this means that vendors must do and provide what is expected of them or face penalties.

control advantage   The strengthening of internal controls and compliance through the application of IT-based controls to business processes, policies, and procedures.

controls   Specific actions, including policies and procedures, designed to ensure the achievement of business objectives.

cookie   A small text file that is placed on users' hard drives by an e-commerce website to store useful data between visits to the site.

co-operative website   Websites where owners of comparable assets (such as vacation properties) co-operate by advertising together.

co-opetition   A new term emerging in the business literature and practice of global commerce that implies that organizations can collaborate in one endeavour (for instance, a joint venture), while they compete in other areas. In other words, this is a business strategy that realizes the benefits of both co-operation and competition.

corporate governance   The leadership and management of a business are directly accountable to its owners (e.g., shareholders) for the proper operation and financial control of the organization.

customer relationship management (CRM)   A software system to help businesses connect with customers and their diverse and changing needs. Integrate data collection, transformation, storage, and analysis of customer transaction data, including purchases, service requests, and other forms of customer contact.

cyberterrorism   A large-scale form of Internet crime. The FBI has defined cyberterrorism as "The premeditated, politically motivated attack against information, computer systems, computer programs, and data which result in violence against noncombatant targets by sub-national groups or clandestine agents."

dashboard   A common way of organizing and presenting business intelligence or related information sources; the purpose of a dashboard is to provide critical information to business users at a glance.

data   Raw, unorganized facts, numbers, pictures, and so on that has to be organized in a way that business professionals can use to make sense.

database   A collection of data stored on a computer and organized based on one of several schemes designed to make the data collection easy to search and manage.

database management system (DBMS)   A collection of software that allows users to create, manage, and work with a database.

data flow diagram (DFD)   A traditional information systems (IS) model that depicts how data moves through a system: the external entities (boxes) that send input or receive output from the system; processes (boxes with rounded corners) that show activities that move or transform data; data stores (open-ended boxes) that usually correspond to tables in the data model; and data flows (arrows) that connect the components.

data hierarchy   Organizes stored data in increasing levels of complexity, from the bits used to store data (lowest level) up to the entire database structure (highest level).

data-information-knowledge continuum   The model of the evolution and hierarchy of data going to information, then to knowledge.

data mart   A data set, often a scaled-down data warehouse, that is usually tailored to the needs of a specific group within an organization.

data mining   A set of techniques for finding trends and patterns in large sets of data. Tools can incorporate advanced technologies such as artificial intelligence and provide aids for data visualization.

data modelling   The process of analyzing the data required by the processes of an organization to support it both operationally and strategically.

data rate   The rate at which data is sent over a network, measured in bits per second (bps).

data warehouse   A means of storing and managing large amounts of data for information access, typically composed of data from one or more transaction databases. Consists of data that have been cleaned and restructured to fit the model and to support queries, summary reports, and analyses.

decentralized structure   Decision-making authority is pushed down the organizational structure and shared with many lower-level employees. Decentralized organizations have fewer levels of management with wide spans of control, giving employees more freedom of action. Decentralized structures can be more efficient than centralized structures because they require fewer managers.

decision support system (DSS)   A software system that provides analytical and visualization tools to support and enhance decision making and planning. Data warehousing, mining, and reporting tools are important components of DSS.

denial of service (DoS)   Occurs when a network or networks are intentionally and maliciously overloaded to the extent that they can no longer function and users/customers cannot access the network(s).

digital data   Data that are stored as a sequence of discrete symbols from a finite set; for example, the set {0,1}.

digital divide   The social impact of technology intensification, creating both have and have-not parties (whether individuals, groups, or nations). Those that can afford technology have easy access and those that cannot are left behind.

direct marketing   Marketing messages that are sent directly from the company to the consumer.

direct-access storage   Storage in which information may be accessed in any order, regardless of the order in which the information was stored.

disaster recovery plan   A plan that allows an organization to resume operations after a major event that interrupts normal business processes.

disintermediation   When manufacturers sell and deliver products directly to consumers; the elimination of the so-called "middle man."

discovery   Finding data, information, and knowledge relevant to a task, problem, issue, opportunity, and so on. Usually the first step in problem solving/decision making.

document management system (DMS)   An information system (IS) for entering, tracking, routing, and processing the many documents used in an organization.

document type definition   One of two methods for providing a formal definition of all the data elements in the XML file.

dynamic content   Information on a web page that may change depending on a number of factors such as the time or date, user profile, or browser location.

dynamic RAM (DRAM)   Internal memory that must be refreshed several times per second.

e-commerce   The use of information systems, technologies, and computer networks by individuals and organizations to create business value.

e-commerce business model   A business model that combines a specific type of website with a successful revenue model that produces profits for the website owner.

e-commerce strategy   A general plan for how a business is going to use computer networks and information systems to compete in a global marketplace.

effectiveness   Pursuing the goal or task that is appropriate for the given situation (i.e., "doing the right thing").

efficiency   Getting the most output from a given input (i.e., "doing the thing right").

electronic data interchange (EDI)   A web-based, private sales channel through a private network or an extranet that links trading partners while keeping others out.

end-user development   IS development that is carried out by non-IT personnel; this is possible because IS development tools have become so advanced.

enterprise resource planning (ERP)   An information system that integrates and standardizes processes and centralizes the storage and management of a business' data with the goal of increasing operational efficiencies in business processes.

enterprise risk management (ERM)   A process started by an entity's board of directors, management, and other personnel, applied in a strategic setting and across the enterprise, to identify potential events that may affect the entity and to manage risk to be within its risk appetite. Designed to provide reasonable assurance regarding the achievement of entity objectives.

enterprise systems   Large-scale applications that support business units or functions.

entity   An object for which we want to store data. Usually corresponds to a table in a relational database.

entity-relationship diagram (ERD)   One of the two most commonly used models for designing the organization of a relational database. Indicates the entities, as well as how they are related, for which an information system (IS) will store data.

environmental scan   A survey of the internal or external environment of an organization in order to get a view of strengths, weaknesses, opportunities, and threats. In strategic planning, an environmental scan will also consider present and future organizational goals in the environmental context.

e-procurement   Using e-commerce for the sale and purchase of products or services that an organization needs to carry on its business.

Ethernet protocol   A network communications protocol in which all computers are allowed to transmit at any time; includes collision detection software to control possible collisions between transmissions.

evolutionary model   A model whereby developers first investigate, specify, and implement an important core part of the system with minimal functionality, and then the team tests and evaluates this version of the system to plan for the next version.

exchange model   A model where many companies use an exchange to buy and sell from each other though spot-buying transactions.

executive information system (EIS)   A system designed to provide summary information about business performance to those making higher-level strategic decisions.

explicit knowledge   Knowledge that is readily codified, such as the knowledge in a magazine or book.

eXtensible Markup Language (XML)   A standard format for marking up data according to its meaning. It is a primary technology that allows for the use of Web services.

extranet   A protected form of the Internet that is usually an extension of an intranet between business partners.

feasibility study   A detailed investigation and analysis of a proposed development project to determine whether it is technically and economically possible.

feedback   A special kind of output created by a business process that is then returned to the system ("fed back") to control the system's future inputs, processes, and outputs.

file transfer protocol (FTP)   A protocol that enables users to upload data to remote servers and download it as needed.

folksonomy   A collective cloud tag on social networking sites that is created by comparing and coalescing how other users tag the same or similar content to help users access information quickly and efficiently.

foreign key A field that is a primary key in one table and is included in a second table to relate or link the two.

functional information systems (FIS) An information system (IS) with a focus on the activities of a single functional department of an organization that is used to improve the efficiency and effectiveness of that department.

functional structure A business organized according to functional areas instead of product lines. Functionally organized businesses can be economically efficient but can lack flexibility, and it may be difficult to communicate between functional areas.

Gantt chart A graphical tool used to schedule and manage the tasks within a project.

globalization The phenomenon of modern businesses expanding into markets worldwide and distributing work across the globe to minimize costs and provide the convenience of doing business 24/7. Information technology and the Internet are significant enablers of globalization.

global system for mobile communication (GSM) protocol A global protocol for mobile phones.

graphical user interface (GUI) System software that allows users to communicate with the command interpreter through the use of graphics and icons.

grid computing Combining the processing power of several computers by networking them together.

groupware Collaborative software that enables communication between team members and helps them to share data, information, and knowledge.

hardware The electronic and mechanical components of a computer that can be seen and touched, such as the computer monitor.

hyperlink A link to another document or part of the current document, commonly highlighted in some way, such as through the use of underlining or colour.

hypertext markup language (HTML) A language for encoding information so that a variety of IT devices, mainly Web browsers, can display it.

hypertext transfer protocol (HTTP) A Web protocol that provides the rules used by browsers and servers as they communicate requests for data and responses between each other.

identifier A unique value that must be stored for each record in a database table.

IGOE model An abbreviation for inputs, guides, outputs, and enablers. A model for analyzing and better understanding processes.

indirect sources of information Communication about products that do not come directly from the company, such as product and ranking review sites, word of mouth, and so on.

informating Recognizing that executing business processes also creates new data and information. An organization may then use this new data to improve its decision making and to change or improve the process itself.

information Data that has been organized and is useful to a person.

information and communication technology (ICT) One of the measurable sectors of world economies upon which nations' GDPs are based. Data on the ICT sector includes sales figures for corporations in this sector, as well as job growth data. Individuals and corporations involved in the ICT sector are engaged in the creation, sale, and support of technology products and services.

Information and Communications Technology Council (ICTC) A program that works to establish, develop, and support national partnerships to address the pressing need for ICT workers.

information density   The quality and quantity of information about products and services of interest to the buyer.

information overload   The situation where people are overwhelmed by the amount of information available on the Web.

information system (IS)   An organized collection of people, information, business processes, and information technology designed to transform inputs into outputs to achieve a goal. Businesses use information systems to leverage the human ability to achieve business goals through the timely and appropriate application of technology, and the timely delivery of appropriate and useful data, information, and knowledge.

information technology (IT)   The branch of knowledge that deals with the uses of hardware, software, and networks to convert, store, protect, process, transmit, and retrieve information. It is especially relevant to organizations for increasing efficiency, cutting costs, and enabling closer customer/employee interactions, resulting in better profits.

in-house development   Using one's own staff to do the work required to develop a new system or product.

input/output (I/O) tasks   A variety of input and output of data, instructions, and information to and from the central processing unit (CPU) that is handled by the operating system.

in-sourcing   The strategic decision made by a business to bring various services or functions back in-house, or keep them in-house, rather than globally sourcing them.

instant messaging (IM)   A private link between two individuals over which they communicate.

instruction set   A collection of machine language instructions that governs how a processor interprets and executes various tasks that it performs.

integrated development environment (IDE)   Allows developers to complete several programming tasks within the same software application instead of using separate software packages.

internal control   A process started by an entity's board of directors, management, and other personnel designed to provide reasonable assurance regarding the achievement of objectives in the following categories: effectiveness and efficiency of operations, reliability of financial reporting, and compliance with applicable laws and regulations.

Internet   The global network of co-operating computer networks that use the same rules for sending and receiving information.

Internet relay chat (IRC)   A *synchronous* way to use the Internet to communicate that allows users to communicate back and forth at the same time, similar to a telephone conversation.

Internet service provider (ISP)   An organization that helps users connect with the Internet through its infrastructure in exchange for a fee. An ISP buys expensive equipment like routers and gateways needed to connect to the Internet and lets customers connect through dial up, cable, satellite, or ethernet. Connecting to the Internet through an ISP often entails the use of software utilities issued by the ISP.

interorganizational system (IOS)   A networked information system used by two or more separate organizations to perform a joint business function.

intranet   A private, organization-wide computer network that is typically based on Internet protocols.

invitational design   Most successful social networking sites use this method to allow users to welcome new people into the group and make it safe for them to learn and master the norms of the community.

IT governance   The distribution of decision-making rights and responsibilities among enterprise stakeholders, and the procedures and mechanisms for making and monitoring strategic decisions.

Java   A platform-independent, open-source computer language that is widely used for Internet applications.

Join operation   Creates a single table from two (or more) tables, after which it can be used to perform calculations and carry out the grouping of products.

kernel   The essential part of the operating system, which internal memory must always include.

knowledge   Created when a person combines information with judgment. Creating and adding economic value relies on the use of knowledge. It can be explicit or tacit.

knowledge management (KM)   The processes and systems by which an organization creates, manages, and shares knowledge. The purpose of knowledge management is to capture and sustain organizational knowledge and business intelligence.

knowledge management systems (KMS)   Systems that provide tools for working with both tacit and explicit knowledge.

knowledge work   The intellectual activity that people perform upon data, information, and knowledge to discover business options.

local area network (LAN)   A computer network confined to a relatively small geographic area; for example, school computing labs, private home wireless networks, and private networks over a few buildings of a corporate campus.

logical data model (LDM)   One of the two most commonly used models for designing the organization of a relational database. Translates the entity-relationship diagram (ERD) into a diagram of the tables in a database.

machine instructions   Computer instructions written as a sequence of binary strings.

management information system (MIS)   A software system that provides timely information to decision makers through processing and reporting. Timely reports enable managers to monitor critical processes and avoid costly mistakes.

many-to-many relationship   A relationship between entities where a record from each entity may be related to one or more records of the other entity.

mashup   An increasingly popular use of social media where users re-combine two or more ads, websites, or other digital marketing materials from a company to create a new ad, website, or marketing message.

mass customization   The ability to create custom products or services on demand.

matrix structure   A form of business organizational structure that blends the functional and decentralized organizational structures. Frequently uses teams of employees to accomplish work.

media transparency   Ensuring that your brand and advertising message are coherent and consistent.

memory chips   Digital electronic components that use transistors to store data within a computer.

methodology   A set of procedures that provides a framework for both the management and technical processes of an information systems (IS) project.

micro-markets   Purpose-built social media sites (or forums or groups) designed to meet a specific need that emerge as a market matures.

microprocessor chips   A digital electronic component with miniaturized transistors on a single semiconductor integrated circuit (IC). One or more typically serve as a central processing unit (CPU) in computer systems or handheld devices. Incorporates the arithmetic logic unit (ALU), the control unit (CU), and memory.

middleware   Software that links applications that use dissimilar software or hardware platforms.

mobile commerce   The use of laptops, mobile telephones, and personal digital assistants (PDAs) to connect to the Internet and Web to conduct many of the activities normally associated with e-commerce while on the go.

model   A simplified representation of something real, such as a building, weather pattern, or information system, that business professionals can manipulate to study the real item in more detail.

modem   A device that allows computers to connect to a remote network over a communications line by converting (modulating) the digital signals going out from the computer into an analog signal appropriate for the connection medium used. When receiving a signal, it converts (demodulates) the analog signal back into a digital signal that the computer can recognize. Modem speeds, measured in bits per second (bps), significantly affect knowledge work activities.

Moore's Law   A law that postulates computing power (as measured by the maximum number of transistors in an integrated circuit) roughly doubles every 18 months.

motherboard   The main circuit board in an electronic device.

network   A fundamental component of information technology (IT) that helps computers connect with one another. Increases the power of IT devices by allowing business professionals to share resources, including hardware, software, and information. Can be a local area network (LAN), a metropolitan area network (MAN), a wide area network (WAN), or even the Internet.

network architecture   The design of a computer system or network.

network interface card (NIC)   Provides the physical connection between a computer and a local network.

network layer model   A standard model of communication between computers in a network in which each layer handles part of the communications between computers.

newsgroups   An Internet application involving a large number of discussion groups on a wide range of topics.

niche markets   A market that serves the needs of a small group of consumers who are seeking very particular products or services. E-commerce has proven to be superior to almost any existing form of marketing in serving these markets.

one-to-one marketing model   When two companies collaborate to create a trading relationship that is good for both parties.

online social strategy   A strategy adopted by companies that are using social media to their advantage. Part of this strategy needs to address the risks of undertaking any kind of online social campaign that might backfire.

open source software   Program and software code (programming instructions) that is freely available for downloading over the Internet.

open systems model   A technique for viewing a business as an open system with a boundary, environment, inputs, outputs, processes, feedback, and decision makers. The model indicates that a business operates by transforming inputs into outputs and by constantly interacting with its environment.

operating system (OS) software   A piece of system software that coordinates and handles the details of working with the computer hardware. It frees the user from the responsibilities of input/output device management, memory management, file handling, multitasking, and process optimization. It also forms the base over which application software is run.

operational decisions   Decisions that affect the operations of a company. These are usually made by a manager of a department or unit.

organizational boundary   The separation between a business system and its environment. Business systems must keep an open boundary to their environment to allow for receiving inputs and to produce outputs.

outsourcing   Hiring another company to perform work that could otherwise be done in-house.

packets   Small digital units of data, each of which contains a specific number of bytes.

packet switching   A method of sending packets over the Internet that routes individual packets through the network based on their destination addresses.

participating identity   The identity social media users create that demonstrates their willingness to participate in the site and allows them to create and post content.

peer-to-peer network   A network in which each computer in the network is on the same level and each computer is equally responsible for overseeing the functions of the network.

peripheral RAM   A type of random access memory (RAM) found on components of a computer system such as the printer and video and sound cards.

personal area network (PAN)   A technology that enables wireless devices, such as mobile phones, computers, and PDAs, to communicate over a short distance—less than 10 metres.

Personal Information Protection and Electronic Documents Act (PIPEDA)   The federal act that sets ground rules for how private sector organizations may collect, use, or disclose personal information in the course of commercial activities. The law gives individuals the right to access and request correction of personal information these organizations may have collected about them.

personalization   A marketing message that a business customizes for each potential customer's interests based on his or her searching, browsing, or buying habits.

phishing   Occurs when criminals send fraudulent emails posing as legitimate organizations, typically governments or banks, for the purpose of obtaining account numbers, passwords, or other important information that can then be used for a variety of purposes, including identity theft.

platform   An IT platform consists of hardware, software, and network technology.

platform plays   General-purpose social media sites that attempt to appeal to very broad audiences.

primary key   A field that holds a unique value for each record.

problem   A state that exists when a person or organization faces an opportunity or fails to meet the desired goals, needs, or expectations.

problem solving   A series of steps or a process (logical sequence of activities) taken in response to some event or activity.

productivity   The ability of an organization to create the best business value at the least amount of cost.

productivity software   Software used by business professionals to work with data, information, and knowledge more effectively and efficiently; for example, document preparation software, electronic spreadsheet software, and database management systems.

program   The set of instructions in a computer language that follows an algorithm to carry out a desired task.

program evaluation review technique (PERT) chart   Used to schedule and manage the tasks within a project; it clearly shows the sequence and dependencies between tasks.

program management   Managing several related projects together. Essentially the same as managing a single project, but across multiple project teams.

project management   The application of knowledge skills, tools, and techniques to project activities to meet project requirements.

project management (PM) software   Software designed to support and automate the tasks of project management and decision making.

project portfolio management (PPM)   Selecting projects that are good strategic fits for the company (doing the right projects).

project steering committee (PSC)   A committee that oversees large and complicated IS projects. Its responsibility is to ensure the project and organizational goals are met, required resources are provided, contingencies are managed, and expected benefits are realized.

proprietary software   Software that requires a purchased licence and typically restricts access to the source code to company employees.

protocol   A standard set of rules that allow the communication of data between nodes on a network; for example, TCP/IP, HTTP, and FTP.

prototyping   The initial version of a system, which is continually revised to reach a final product.

query condition   A search criterion that may be added to a query to limit the query results.

random access memory (RAM)   Hardware that stores data only until it is no longer needed, or until the computer is shut down. The CPU can access any item stored in RAM directly (randomly).

rational decision   A choice that a person or group of people or organization makes about what actions to take (or not to take) in a given situation. Decision making usually occurs, however, as part of a larger problem-solving process.

read only memory (ROM)   Hardware that stores instructions and data that only special devices can alter. In a computer, it holds the instructions used to control the start-up processes (booting up). The data in ROM is permanently stored there.

referential integrity   Enforces consistency between linked tables by ensuring that all references to records (i.e., the foreign keys) are correct.

relational database management systems (RDBMS)   A software application that lets business professionals work with and manage relational databases.

relational data model   A model for organizing databases so that they store information about entities, such as suppliers and products for a retailer, and the relationships between those entities.

relational entity   An entity created to resolve reference problems between entities that share a many-to-many relationship.

request for information (RFI)   When an organization acquires an IS, it may issue an RFI to gather information about a product, service, and/or vendor capabilities. It is usually sent out to as broad a range of vendors as possible and is not as detailed as an RFP.

request for proposal (RFP)   A document that initiates a bidding process for potential vendors. An RFP provides very specific and detailed requirements for respondents to answer to determine the suitability of their proposed offering.

resolution   For a pointing device, refers to the preciseness with which a device can pinpoint its location on the screen. For a scanning device, refers to the clarity and level of detail of an image that it can capture. For a display device, refers to the maximum number of pixels that the screen can show, typically measured by distance between a pixel and the closest pixel of the same colour.

risk management   Recognizing, addressing, and eliminating sources of risk before they threaten the successful completion of a project.

roll-back strategy   A type of contingency plan that involves being able to reverse every action that took place to make a change happen such that everything is returned to its original state with no damage done.

schadenfreude   The psychological concept that implies people draw happiness from others' misfortunes; used to explain why negative stories go viral more readily than positive ones.

scripting language   A high-level computer language that another program (such as a browser) interprets when executed.

search engine   A tool used to search for information on the Internet. For most sites, users access an HTML form-based web page that allows them to enter their specific search criteria. The search criteria data are sent to the search engine Web server, which in turn passes it to the application server to search through the sites' databases.

secondary storage   A form of storage external to random access memory (RAM) that permanently stores data and programs.

secure gateway provider   A company that provides a network to process encrypted transactions from a merchant's website.

secure socket layer (SSL)   Protocol that allows a client and a server to communicate in a way that prevents eavesdropping, message forgery, or tampering.

selection criteria   Factors or measures that can be applied to solving a problem or making a decision that assist in rank-ordering alternatives and identifying the most desirable option.

self-regulating community   An online community where members report conduct they feel is outside the group norms to a moderator who is responsible for drawing the inappropriate behaviour to the attention of the member or removing or restricting the member's privileges.

semantic web   A next-generation (but not separate) web that makes information sharing and exchange easier by focusing on content, searchability, and interpretability at a technical level.

semi-structured decision   A decision that is not fully structured but still can be attained with the use of information, reasoning, and partly objective thinking to some extent.

servers   Computers on a network running server software that provide resources to other computers on the network.

server-side programming   Programs that run on the server in response to browser requests.

service-oriented architecture (SOA)   An infrastructure that supports the full-scale use of Web services.

short message service (SMS)   A wireless protocol that enables mobile phones to send and receive text messages up to 160 characters long.

signal type   A determination of how data are sent over the network as either digital or analog.

site audit   A strategy of search engine optimization where a site is reviewed to see if there are areas where the re-positioning of pages or content, changes in tagging consistency or weighting, or other types of changes can help increase your site's search engine ranking.

social transparency   The principle that states that a site should mimic real-life social interactions, be attractive, and be easy to use.

social utility   What people get out of social media sites, suggesting that people only spend time on sites that are *useful* to them by contributing to their happiness or social satisfaction, or creating social opportunities for them.

software   The set of instructions that direct information technology hardware.

software application suite   Commercially developed application software sold as a bundle.

software as a service (SaaS)   A way companies acquire enterprise systems without purchasing or building them; essentially, renting software.

software as an outsourced service   A way companies acquire software "on demand" from online vendors known as application service providers (ASPs) without having to build or purchase the software. Organizations rent the software at a fee and the software and data are delivered and hosted centrally by the vendor via the Internet/cloud.

spot buying Buying at market prices determined by supply and demand from someone that the consumer does not know.

stakeholder A person or entity (e.g., a government agency or a competitor) that has an interest in and an influence on how a business will function to succeed. May be external or internal relative to the organization.

stakeholder analysis The portion of the feasibility study that includes the evaluation of stakeholder opinions and attitudes about a project.

Standard ASCII (American Standard Code for Information Interchange) A type of character encoding that uses seven bits to represent the unaccented letters of the English language, a–z and A–Z; basic punctuation; numbers; space; and some control codes, such as the Enter key.

static content Fixed information, such as company information, online marketing, and electronic versions of company brochures.

static RAM (SRAM) A type of internal memory that does not need to be refreshed.

strategic decisions Decisions that affect the overall vision and direction of a company; usually made by executives.

strategic sourcing Forming a long-term relationship with another company and then setting prices through negotiation.

streaming Allows the transmission of multimedia (video, music, images, etc.) via the Internet without the need to download and save on a local device. Webcasts and programs delivered by Netflix are examples of content that is streamed.

structured decision A decision that can be programmed. It is routine or repetitive, and the necessary data are complete and certain.

Structured Query Language (SQL) A computer language for querying and manipulating data in a relational database.

subject matter experts (SMEs) A group of specialists working on a project who handle unique aspects of the project for which they are uniquely qualified.

supply chain A network of facilities and distribution options that perform the functions of procurement of materials, transformation of these materials into intermediate and finished products, and the distribution of these finished products to customers.

supply chain management (SCM) A set of methods that a business employs to manage the materials, information, and finances as they move in a process from supplier to manufacturer to wholesaler to retailer to consumer. Information systems (IS) are essential for efficient management of the supply chain.

synthesis Creating wholes from parts. In knowledge work activities, it facilitates the interpretation of trends and patterns leading to conclusions and recommendations. In problem solving, the results of analyses are typically synthesized to develop potential solutions for a problem.

system development life cycle (SDLC) The common term used for the stages and activities of system development.

system software Any software required to control the hardware components and to support the execution of application software. System software includes the operating system and utility software.

system unit The box containing the CPU, internal memory, secondary storage, and other electronic devices that we often think of as the computer when we look at it.

tacit knowledge Knowledge that people have gained through experience, insight, and discovery. Reading, movies, life experiences, and the experiences of others contribute to tacit knowledge.

tactical decisions   Decisions that are made every single hour of every single work day within organizations. They are usually made by the person doing the actual work, based on appropriate guidelines or policies.

tagging   A way to make content useful to other users that involves associating keywords with the content to make it searchable so other users can locate it and interact with it.

technical acquisition   Occurs when a company possessing a desired technology is purchased by another organization so that the acquiring company can own and use the technology of the acquired company. It is an alternative to build or lease/buy options when acquiring an IS.

Three Pillars of Sociability   A social psychology concept that humans have a need to affiliate, participate, and be validated by others. Social networking sites allow people to do this online.

three-tiered client/server architecture   A client/server architecture that incorporates a client, an application server, and a database server.

touch screen monitor   A computer display screen that is sensitive to human touch or a special pen.

tracking   For a pointing device, tracking refers to how close the screen cursor follows the movement of the device.

transaction   An exchange of goods or services (value) between two or more parties (businesses, individuals, or a combination of the two) that creates a relationship between the parties.

transaction processing system (TPS)   An information software system that enables transactions and captures and processes transaction data to make them available to the organization.

transformation   A knowledge work activity in which data and information are organized and manipulated to deepen understanding and further analyze the data prior to synthesizing a conclusion.

transforming   Using information technology (IT) to help a business acquire or continue a competitive advantage over its competitors by adjusting how the company does business.

transistor   An electronic switch that can be either on (represented by 1) or off (represented by 0). By combining several transistors, data can be represented as a combination of 1s and 0s; that is, in a binary format. Transistors can also be used to realize logic circuits. The logic circuits with binary input and binary output form the basic building blocks of all computing hardware.

transmission control protocol/Internet protocol (TCP/IP)   The network protocol used to transmit messages over the Internet.

Unicode   A character encoding system that adds an additional eight characters to the extended ASCII eight-bit character assignments to include the characters of the major modern written languages.

Unified Modelling Language (UML)   A modelling language designed for developing object-oriented systems; it consists of several graphical elements that, when combined, form a set of diagrams.

uniform resource locator (URL)   A unique address for each page that indicates the location of a document, either on the Internet or on a local network or machine.

unstructured decision   A decision that is characterized by uncertain data or information and for which there may be no known method of arriving at a solution.

user-generated content (UGC)   The content of most social media sites is provided by users, and thus is referred to as user-generated, in the form of blogs, conversation threads, videos, and so on.

utility computing services   An alternative to a company developing an information system from scratch. The goal is to provide computing resources when and where an organization needs them. Like electricity, clients pay for services only to the extent that they use them.

utility software   Provides additional tools that can be used to maintain and service the system; for example, antivirus software and disk partition tools, among others.

value chain   A view of a business organization as a connected series of activities, each of which adds value or supports the addition of value to the firm's goods or services. Every action that the organization takes is either a primary activity or a support activity.

vendor management   The management, control, and monitoring of third party providers or suppliers to the organization. It is the role of the *vendor manager* to keep vendors apprised of what is happening in the organization, including any new requirements for vendors.

video RAM (VRAM)   A type of random access memory (RAM) used on video cards.

view   A saved query.

viral social interactions   When something that is funny, unusual, shocking, interesting, or newsworthy almost instantly spreads online from its origins to nearly every corner of the world.

virtual memory   The use of hard disk space to give the appearance of additional internal memory.

visual analytics   An extension of a dashboard that enables a user to examine data in-depth, reorganize it dynamically, and change information parameters to do "what-if analysis."

voice over Internet protocol (VoIP)   Using the Internet's foundation technologies of packet switching and TCP/IP to carry voice instead of data to make calls anywhere in the world and bypass traditional switched telephone networks.

waterfall model   A model with a designed set of phases, where a new phase begins only after acceptably completing the preceding phase, causing development activities to move downstream through the phases in a formal, detailed manner.

Web 2.0   A term that represents what most people refer to as the interactive web—that is, moving from a passive site that basically displays information to a site that permits interaction with visitors or users.

Web browser   Software that can be used to view hypertext documents and browse (or surf) the Web.

Web service   An Internet application that obtains or processes data from a requesting application and then delivers the data back in XML format as a response.

Wi-Fi   The popular name for the 802.11 standards for wireless network access.

wildcard   A character used as a replacement for unknown or non-existing characters in attempting to find matches to a group of characters.

wireless LANs   LANs that don't have the usual cabling between computers; instead, the cables are replaced with wireless transmissions.

wisdom   An extension of the data-to-knowledge continuum that enables business leaders to perceive the underlying meaning and nuances of a business situation and ensures that knowledge from all relevant perspectives, disciplines, and sources is considered in the final decision.

workflow   The steps, organizational resources, input and output data, and tools needed to complete a business process.

workflow management systems (WMS)   Supports activities that several departments of the organization may carry out by supporting and automating workflows.

World Wide Web   A collection of Internet software applications and standards that allows the transfer of text, images, audio, and video. The Web makes it easy to publish information in a variety of ways so that it is accessible to business professionals and trading partners of a business.

XML schema   One of two methods for providing a formal definition of all the data elements in an XML file.

XML stylesheet (XSL) file   A file that uses a combination of HTML and XML tags to display an XML file in a more readable form on a Web browser.

PHOTO CREDITS

Logon
Page 1: Blend Images / Getty

Chapter 1
Page 6: © nyul / iStock; page 7: Courtesy of Ryan Chong; page 10: Monkey Business Images / Shutterstock.com; page 18: Huntstock.com / Shutterstock.com; page 19: Jolene Alexander / Associated Press; page 28: © Victor Martello / iStock; page 31: © Olena Timashova / iStock

Chapter 2
Page 46: © blackred / iStock; page 47: Courtesy of Derek Ball; page 51: © @ Studio City / eStock Photo; page 52 (left): Courtesy of Hewlett Packard; page 52 (right): © AlexGul / iStock; page 53 (top and bottom): Courtesy of Hewlett Packard; page 59: © zentilia / iStock; page 61: © Lee Pettet / iStock; page 62 (top): © SimonInns; page 62 (bottom): Hemera/ Thinkstock; page 68: Reproduced with permission of Yahoo! Inc. © 2007 by Yahoo! Inc. YAHOO! and the YAHOO! Logo are trademarks of Yahoo! Inc.; page 78: © Jennifer Byron / iStock

Chapter 3
Page 90: © Andrey Prokhorov; page 91: Courtesy of Diane Viveiros; page 92: © Rob Mattingley / iStock; page 94: © YanLev / iStock; page 100: Lisa F. Young / Shutterstock.com

Chapter 4
Page 130: © Ed Hidden / iStock; page 131: Courtesy of Dave Codack; page 138: © Gmosher / iStock; page 140: © ictor / iStock; page 143: © Kenneth Cheung / iStock; page 145 (left): Digital Vision / Getty; page 145 (right): © Corkbin, Inc.; page 147: © Levent Konuk / iStock; page 151: © hocus-focus / iStock; page 160: © Tarek El Sombati / iStock

Chapter 5
Page 176: © Steve Cole / iStock; page 177: Courtesy of Chris Moore; page 190: Photodisc / GettyImages; page 191: © Shane Shaw / iStock; page 193: THE CANADIAN PRESS/Chris Young; page 195: Ric Feld, Associated Press

Chapter 6
Page 210: © DaveBolton / iStock; page 211: Courtesy of Joey Peng; page 212: © Shawn Lowe / iStock; page 235: © Dean Mitchell / iStock; page 237: © narvikk / iStock

Chapter 7

Page 252: © Ingvald kaldhussaeter / iStock; page 253: Courtesy of Arti Davda; page 256: © Derek Latta / iStock; page 265 (top): © 2012 MINI Canada. All rights reserved. The MINI trademark and logo are registered trademarks. Reproduced with the permission of MINI Canada for educational and non-commercial purposes only; page 265 (bottom): Courtesy of Netflix; page 267: Courtesy of Canada Vacation Rentals; page 270: © Merve Karahan / iStock; page 273: © Edward Grajeda / iStock; page 284: Reproduced with permission of Yahoo! Inc. © 2007 by Yahoo! Inc. YAHOO! and the YAHOO! Logo are trademarks of Yahoo! Inc.; page 288: © Günay Mutlu / iStock

Chapter 8

Page 300: © Rich Legg / iStock; page 301: Courtesy of John Lennie; page 302: © hocus-focus / iStock; page 307: © Michael DeLeon / iStock; page 308: Annette Shaff / Shutterstock.com; page 309: © See-ming Lee; page 322: Stephen VanHorn / Shutterstock.com

Logoff

Page 335: © GYI NSEA / iStock

Tech Guide A

Page 338: © Kamil Krawczyk / iStock; page 342: © Lawrence Manning/Corbis; page 346 (top to bottom): Courtesy of Hewlett Packard, © AlexGul / iStock, Courtesy of Hewlett Packard, Images of Logitech Products are used with permission, © code6d / iStock, Courtesy of Hewlett Packard; page 347 (top to bottom): Images of Logitech Products are used with permission, © Photodisc / Media Bakery, © Alex Slobodkin / iStock, © Donald Gruener / iStock; Page 348 (top to bottom): © Mike Liu / iStock, TsR / Shutterstock.com, Andre Blais / Shutterstock.com, © VisualCommunications / iStock; page 352 (top to bottom): Courtesy of Wacom Technology Corporation, all printer images courtesy of Hewlett Packard, except for the thermal printer, which is courtesy of Epson America Inc. System Device Group; page 367: Courtesy of John Wiley & Sons Inc.

Tech Guide B

Page 374: © kjekol / iStock

Tech Guide C

Page 398: © Ermin Gutenberger / iStock

Common opening and end-of-chapter images

Page 46: © StockLib / iStock; page 80: © Skip Odonnell / iStock; page 81: © Eldad Carin / iStock; page 82: © DNY59 / iStock; page 83: © Mike Sonnenberg / iStock

INDEX

A

Access point (AP), 59
Accessing, internet, 61–62
Accountant, 18
ACID
  organizations, 138
  properties, 138
ActiveX, 283–284
ActiveX controls, 284
Adding value, 133
Address bus, 343, 345
Adobe Flash, 303
AdWords, Google, 264
Affiliation, 306
Aggregate functions, 403
Agile development, 239
AI. *See* Artificial intelligence
AJAX engine, 288
Alexa.com, 329
Algorithm, 368
Alpert, Jesse, 15
ALU. *See* Arithmetic logic unit
Amazon.ca, 255, 265, 272, 289
Amazon.com, 37
Analog sensors, 349
Analog signal, 54, 381–382
Analog *vs.* digital data transmission, 382
Analysis, 94
Analysis paralysis process, 101
AND operator, 401
Anomalies, 404
AP. *See* Access point
API. *See* Application program interface
Applet model, 259
Application program interface (API), 289, 357
Application protocol interfaces, 63, 303
Application server, 59
Application service provider (ASP), 64
Application software, 55–56
  commercially developed, 363–368
    database software, 365–366
    Internet-related software, 367–368
    presentation software, 367
    specialized software, 368
    spreadsheets, 363–365

    web browser, 367–368
    word processing software, 363
  customized software, 368
    database software, 365
    desktop publishing software, 363
    open-source software, 370–371
    presentation software, 367
    running, 360
    specialized software, 368
Application software layer, 379
Arithmetic logic unit (ALU), 342
Artificial intelligence (AI), 99
ASCII code, 341
ASP. *See* Application service provider
Association for Computing Machinery (ACM), 200
Association of Information Technology Professionals (AITP), 200
Asynchronous, 388
ATMs. *See* Automated teller machines
Attributes, 108
Audio content software, 242
Audio input, 349
Auditing and Assurance Standards Oversight Council (AASOC), 159
Authentication, 74
Authorization, 166
Authorization controls, 166
Automated bank machine (ABM), 8
Automated POS-TPS process, 139
Automated teller machines (ATMs), 106, 191
  transactions, 139
Automating, 153, 154, 190

B

Balanced scorecard, 119, 120
Ball, Derek, 47
Bandwidth, 343, 382
Bar code, 145
Bar code inventory systems, 190
Bar code reader, 347
Bar code scanners, 190, 384
Baseband, 382
Basel II Accord, 197

Basic input/output system (BIOS), 344, 358
B2B e-commerce
  extranet-enabled *vs.* EDI, 279
  supply chain efficiency, 277–280
B2B e-commerce exchange transactions, 275
B2B transactions
  BC Bid®, 280
  types, 275
BC Bid®, 280
B2C e-commerce
  advantages/disadvantages of, 271
  limitations of, 271
B2C websites, 259
Bell, 193
Benioff, Marc, 64
Berners-Lee, Tim, 68
B2G. *See* Business-to-government
BI system. *See* Business intelligence (BI) system
Bill 198, 197
Bill of lading (BOL), 277
BillPoint, 220
Binary, 340
Binary data, 340
Binary mathematics, 340–341
Biometric scanners, 348–349
BIOS. *See* Basic input/output system (BIOS)
Bit, 340
BlackBerrys, 17, 47
Blog, 390
Blogger.com, 306
Blogs, 322, 331, 390
Bluetooth, 385
BPM. *See* Business process management
BPO. *See* Business process outsourcing
Brandstorm, 316
Bridge, 59
Brin, Sergey, 103
Broadband, 382
Brochureware, 281
BS7799, 164
Build-and-fix model, 236
Bus, 343

Bush, Vannevar, 391
Business, 24
Business case, 213
Business continuity plan (BCP), 76
Business environment, 24–25
 stakeholders and boundaries, 179
Business ethics, 158
Business fundamentals
 automating, 190–191
 business process, 178–179
 competitive advantage, 188–189
 feedback, 187–188
 organizational boundary, 180
 value chain, 132–135
Business intelligence (BI) system,
  113–121, 330–331
 corporate information strategy, 113
 pyramid, 114
 stages of, 114
 tools, 117–121
 using IT, 114–117
Business models, 258–261
 website, 260
Business organizations, 178–181
Business partner goals, 4
Business process, 183–188
 customer service, 186
 feedback, role of, 187
 performance of automating, informating, and transforming, 213
Business process, 184
Business process management
  (BPM), 137
Business process outsourcing
  (BPO), 156
Business process reengineering (BPR),
  188
 goals, 188
Business processes, 178–181
Business professional, 101, 103, 106
Business rule, 138
Business strategy, 178, 268
Business-to-business (B2B), 256
Business-to-consumer (B2C), 256
Business-to-government
  (B2G), 256
Business value, creation, 182–183,
  189–194
 informating, 191
 IT automation, using, 190–191
 transforming, 191–194
Businesses
 as open system, 179–181
 values, creation, 179
Byte, 342

C
C, computer languages, 369
Cable modems, 381
Cache memory, 342, 344
Calgary, 30

Canada, top social sites in, 305
Canada's Charter of Rights and
  Freedoms, 311
Canadavacationrentals.ca, 267
Canadian Privacy Commission, 311
Canadian privacy laws, 311
Canadian Public Accountability Board
  (CPAB), 159
Canadian Securities Administrators
  (CSA), 159
Canadian Tire, 281
Capability maturity model integration
  (CMMI), 164
Capacitive touch screen, 351
Career, in ICT, 21, 23
Career centre, 41
Career management, 21
Case studies
 B2B e-commerce, 296
 Bluefin Labs, 208
 business administration, 43–44
 data everywhere, 129
 Dell Inc., 128
 Google Inc., 250
 iPads for enterprise, 88
 JEM Enterprises, 175
 Knitting for Dummies, 298
 marketing through social
  media, 333
 selecting computer, 87
 S2S stuff exchange, 251
 Transit Network, 209
 Walmart, 174
 WEB 2.0 applications, 330–332
 website building, 45
CASE tools, 242–243. See Computer-
  aided software engineering
  (CASE) tools
CBC Radio, 80
CD-read/write (CD-RW), 354
CD-recordable (CD-R), 354
Central processing unit (CPU), 49,
  342–343
Champy, James, 184
Character encoding, 340
Character string, 402
Chief executive officer (CEO), 25
Chief information officer (CIO), 21, 49,
  177, 194, 202, 204
Chip-based storage, 354
CIA triad, 73
Cisco systems, 23
Claudio, Cecilia, 162
Client/server network, 67–68,
  375, 378
Client-side scripting, 283
Client software, 396
Clients, 375
Clock speed, 49, 342, 344
Cloud computing, 63–64
 advantages of, 63

CMMI. See Capability maturity model
  integration
Coaxial cable, 380
COBIT, 164
Codd, E. F., 108
Code generation, 242
Codes of conduct, 200
Collaboration, 77, 192–194
Collaborative forecasting and
  replenishment (CFAR), 174
Collaborative management tools, 116
Collaborative software categories, 116
Command interpreter, 357
Commerce, 16
Commercial off-the-shelf (COTS)
  software, 363
Communication, 15, 97
Communications hardware, 53–54
Company-centric business model, 276
Competitive advantage, 154, 188
 cost, 192
 differentiation, 192
 resource-based model, 192
 ways, 192
Competitive intelligence, 29
Competitive necessity, 155, 188–189
Complementary skills, 81
Compliance, 159, 198
Compliance and Control Frameworks
  and Standards, 164
Compound operators, 401
Compression technologies, 312
Computer-aided design/computer-aided
  manufacturing (CAD/CAM)
  software, 136
Computer-aided software engineering
  (CASE) tools, 242
Computer-enabled marketing, 318
Computer hierarchy, 50
Computer languages uses, 372
Computer network technologies, 262
 business use of, 262
Computer networks, 57–58
Computer programs algorithm, 368
Computer Society of the IEEE
  (IEEE-CS), 200
Conferencing tools, 116
Connectivity, 11, 14, 27, 59, 394
Consumer information, 272
Consumer-to-consumer (C2C), 256
Consumer-to-government (C2G), 256
Continuous improvement, 188
Continuous learning, 188
Contract compliance, 219
Control advantage, 163
Control and controls, 163
Control totals, 166
Control unit (CU), 342
Controls, 163
 corrective, 165
 defined, 163

detective, 165
effective, 164
internal, 163
preventive, 163
Convergence technologies, 79
Cookie, 282, 393
Co-operative website, 267
Co-opetition, 193
Copyright, 27
Corporate governance, 194–196
laws and regulations, 196
Corrective controls, 165
Corruption, 76
COSO, 164
Cost-benefit analysis, 215–216
Cost management, 225
COTS software, 363
Council of Supply Chain Management
Professionals (CSCMP), 141
CPU. See Central processing unit
Crackberry, 66
Craigslist, 260
Credit card information, 272
Criteria, 103
scoring alternatives, 103
Criteria analysis, 216
CRM. See Customer relationship
management
Cross-functional team, 244
Customer relationship management
(CRM), 150
Customer relationship management
(CRM) systems, 20, 26, 56, 64,
150, 186, 211, 269
administration and finance systems, 151
human resources service, 152
procurement, 152–153
software, 56
technology development, 152
up-selling, 150
Customized software, developing
Apache Web server software, 370
computer languages, 369
computer programs, 368
languages, 369
Linux operating system, 371
open-source software, 370–371
programming languages, 369
Cyber-terrorism, 36

D
Dashboard, 118
Data, 12, 92
Data analysis, 114
Data bus, 343
Data component layer, 380
Data flow diagram (DFD), 110
Data hierarchy, 107
Data-information-knowledge
continuum, 12
Data integrity, 107

Data mart, 112
Data mining, 112
Data modelling, 109–110
Data rate
and bandwidth, 382–383
maximum, 382
Data redundancy, 404
Data transmission, 380
Data warehouse technology, 111–113, 142
businesses access and, 112, 113
database, comparison of, 111
multidimensional data, organizing, 112
Database administrators (DBA), 106
Database management system (DBMS),
55, 106
Database software, 365–366
Database system, 106
advantages, 107
Databases, 106–113
data flow diagram (DFD), 110, 111
data hierarchy, 107
data modelling, 109–110
data storage, 111–113
entity-relationship diagram (ERD), 110
logical data model, 110
relational data model, 108–109
Davda, Arti, 253
DBA. See Database administrators
DBMS. See Database management
system
Decentralized matrix organizational
structures, 182
advantages/disadvantages, 183
Decentralized structure, 182
Decision makers, 114
Decision-making process, 99–105
information in, 100–101
more informed, 101
and problem-solving tools, 102–105
rational, 99, 100, 102
types of, 100
Decision support systems (DSS), 25, 26,
114, 115
communications-driven, 115
data-driven, 115
document-driven, 115
financial models, 115
knowledge-driven, 115
model-driven, 115
optimization models, 115
simulation modelling, 115
statistical models, 115
Decisions classification
elements, 101
rational decision, 100–101
semi-structured decision, 100
structured decision, 100
unstructured decision, 100
Deferred payment, 286
Dell, 53, 255
Dell DataSafe product, 53

Denial of service (DoS), 36, 160
Detective controls, 165
Digital data, 340
Digital divide, 34
Digital products, 256
downloading, 256
ordering, 256
purchasing, 256
Digital sensor, 349
Digital signal processors (DSPs), 51
Digital subscriber line (DSL), 382
Direct-access storage, 354
Direct marketing, 318
Disaster recovery plan (DRP), 76
Discovery, 93
Disintermediation, 255
DMS. See Document management
systems
Document management systems
(DMS), 117
knowledge management systems,
115–116
Document preparation software,
55, 363
Document type definition, 409
Domain names, top-level, 386, 387
DoomJuice, 72
DoS. See Denial of service
Dots per inch (dpi), 353
Drive-by hackers, 75
DVD player, 2
DVD-RW, 353
Dynamic content, 282
Dynamic link library (dll) files, 361
Dynamic RAM (DRAM), 344

E
eBay, 260
Eclipse, 241
E-commerce, 16, 255
advantage, 261–266
benefits, 271–274
business models, 258–261
and business strategy, 268–269
co-operative website, 267
competitive difference, 266–268
credit card security codes, 272
definition, 254–255
first-generation technologies,
280–282
fourth-generation technologies,
288–289
generations of, 281
limitations of, 271–274
niche markets, 268
and organization strategy, 268–269
between organizations
B2B transactions, 275–277
business models, 275–277
procurement process, 277–280
and products, 255–258

E-commerce (continued)
  second-generation technologies, 282–285
  site, 286
  third-generation technologies, 285–288
  transaction, types of, 256
  vs. e-business, 255
E-commerce business model, 258–261
E-commerce software, 165
E-commerce strategy, 166
E-commerce system, 166
E-commerce technologies, 280
  on business, impact, 262
  e-tailer, 284
  first-generation, 280
  fourth-generation, 288
  HTML, 281–282
  HTTP, 281
  Internet2, 66
  order and payment systems, 286–288
  second-generation, 282–285
  third-generation, 285–288
  web services, 288–289
  XML, 288
Economy, Canadian, 33
Effective controls, 163
Effectiveness, 101
Efficiency, 101
E-info, 318
EIM systems, 78
Electromagnetic digitizer, 351
Electronic data files, 317
Electronic data interchange (EDI), 276, 278, 409
  extranet-enabled B2B e-commerce, comparison of, 279
Electronic directory, 25
Electronic product purchasing, 257
Electronic sensors, 270
Electronic spreadsheet software, 55
Electronics Magazine, 8
Email server, 59
E-marketing, 317
Embedded processors, 50, 51
Encryption/decryption, 273
Encryption systems, primary forms of, 273
End-user development, 243
Enterprise IM (EIM), 78
Enterprise resource planning (ERP) system, 25, 26, 142
  benefit of, 143
  disadvantage of, 143
  sales module, 142
Enterprise risk management (ERM), 157–165
  control and controls, 163–166
  COSO framework, 158
  definition of, 158
  risk acceptance, 161

risk avoidance, 161
risk deferral, 161
risk framework application, 160–161
risk reduction methods, 161–163
Enterprise servers, 377
Enterprise software, 153
Enterprise systems, 144
  strategic deployment of, 153–155
  value chain support
    administration and finance systems, 151–152
    human resource information systems (HRIS), 152
    inbound logistics, 144–147
    marketing and sales, 150
    operations, 147–149
    outbound logistics, 149–150
    procurement, 152–153
    service, 150–151
    technology development, 152
Entertainment, 320
Entity, 399
Entity-relationship diagram (ERD), 110, 404–405
Environmental scans, 181
E-procurement, 276, 278
  reverse auction, 276
EProcurement Scotland (ePS), 280
Equal opportunity, 29
Equity, 29
ERD. See Entity-relationship diagram
Ergonomics, 52, 346
Espionage, 36
E-tailer, 79
ETapestry, 168
Ethernet protocol, 384
Ethical dilemmas, in IT, 27
Ethical misconduct, in business, 29
Ethics, 27–29
  personal implications of, 28
Etsy, 263
Evolutionary model, 238
Exchange
  horizontal, 276
  vertical, 276
Exchange model, 276
Executive information systems (EIS), 117
Expert systems, 99
Explicit knowledge, 92, 115–116
eXtensible markup language (XML), 288
  for data transfer, 409–411
  document type definition, 409
  schema method, 410
  stylesheet, 411
  tags, 409
  vs. HTML, 409
Extortion, 36
Extranets, 276, 278

F
Facebook, 303–304
FAQ. See Frequently asked questions
Farmers Insurance Group, 162
Feasibility study, 213
Feature creep, 229
FedEx, 285
Feedback, 187
Fibre-optic cable, 380
Field, 107
File allocation table (FAT), 361
File/disk management, 361
File server, 59
File transfer protocol (FTP), 389
Files, 67, 107, 361
Finance systems, administration and, 151
Financial analysis, 19
Financial feasibility metrics, 214
Financial IS, 136
Financial models, 115
FIS. See Functional information systems
Flash, 303
Flash memory, 354
Flatbed scanners, 348
Flickr, 306, 320
Floating point unit (FPU), 342
Folders, 361
Folksonomy, 315
Foreign key, 109, 399
Form controls, 282
FPU. See Floating point unit
Freedom of Information and Privacy Protection Act (FIPPA), 311
Frequently asked questions (FAQ), 389
Frictionless economy, 261
Friedman, Thomas, 31
Friendster, 269
Frito-Lay, 150
FTP. See File transfer protocol
Functional information systems (FIS), 135–137
Functional matrix organizational structures, 183
  advantages/disadvantages, 183
Functional structure, 182

G
GAN. See Global area network
Gantt chart, 228
Garbage in, garbage out, 102
Gasoline, 3
Gates, Bill, 10
Gateway, 384
GDP, 33
General Motors, 174
GeoEye, 82
Geographic information systems (GIS), 115
Geographically dispersed team (GDT), 81
Gigahertz (GHz), 50

Global area network (GAN), 58
Global system for mobile communica-
    tion (GSM) protocol, 394
Globalization, 30
Gmail, 63–64, 383
Google, 63, 77, 82
Google Earth, 82
Google Toolbar, 284
GoToMeeting, 79
Governance- and compliance-
    related laws and regulations,
    197–198
Graphical user interface (GUI), 357
Graphics software, 55
Green IT, 29
Grid computing, 51
Groove, 15
Groupware, 77, 116
GSM mobile phones, 394

H
Hacker, 34, 73, 75
Haitian Earthquake Registry, 82
Hajaj, Nissan, 15
Hammer, Michael, 184
Handheld device, 145
Hard disk, 353–355, 357–358
Hard disks, 354
Hardware, 48, 49–54, 339
    communications, 53
    CPU
        devices, 339
        electronics of, 339–342
        performance, 344
        processing, 342–344
        speed, 350
        storage, 53
    display devices, 350–351
    embedded processors, 50
    input, 51
    input devices, 345–350
    memory, 51
    microprocessor, 49
    modern monitors, 52
    output, 52
    storage devices, 353–355
Hidemyass.com, 313
High capacity diskettes, 353
High level system requirements, 213
Hiring practices, 29
H1N1 infection statistics, 123
Horizontal exchanges, 276
Host computer, 386
HR management and policy, 134
Hub, 59
Human resources information systems
    (HRIS), 152
Hyperlink, 367
Hypertext, 68, 390
Hypertext markup language (HTML),
    68–69, 303, 391

form controls, 282
forms, 283
Hypertext transfer protocol (HTTP),
    68, 393
    request, 67–68
    response, 67–68

I
IAB. *See* Internet Architecture Board
IADD model, 104
    analyze stage, 104
    decide stage, 104
    do stage, 104
    investigate stage, 104
IBM Lotus Instant Messaging, 78
ICT careers, 21
ICT GDP, 33
ICT market, 34
ID codes, 165, 166
IDE. *See* Integrated development
    environments
Idea phase, 222
Identifier, 399
Identity theft, 34
IETF. *See* Internet Engineering
    Task Force
IGOE model, 184–186
IM. *See* Instant messaging
In-house development, 219
    vs. outsourcing, advantages and
        disadvantages of, 220
In-sourcing, 162
Inbound logistics, 132, 144–147
Inception phase, 237
Indirect sources of information, 318
Infomediaries, 259
Informating, 154, 191
Informating system benefits, 154
    enterprise resource planning, 142
Information, 12, 92
Information and communication
    technologies (ICT), 21
    sector, 33
Information and Communications
    Technology Council (ICTC), 22
    career clusters and work
        streams, 22
Information clutter
    online advertising, 264
    partnering and traffic trading,
        264–265
    search engine optimization, 264
    web usage and statistics, 265–266
Information density, 263
Information economy, 16
Information evaluation criteria, 102
Information overload, 15
Information security management
    systems (ISMS), 164
Information system (IS), 10
    in business, 26

business activities, 132–137
business value of, 26
components, 11–12
    of transaction processing system, 27
decision support systems, 115
document management systems, 117
functional information systems, 135
input-process-output (IPO) model, 11
knowledge management systems, 115
management information, 116
supply chain management, 141
transaction processing systems,
    138–140
types of, 38
vs IT, 14
workflow management systems,
    137–138
Information technology infrastructure
    library (ITIL), 164
Information technology (IT), 9
    applications, 191
    automation, 190
    in business, 5
    compliance, support, 159
    components of, 48–60
    and economy, 33–34
    ethics in, 27–29
    as fundamental for career, 18–21
    governance, 196
    hardware, 339
    key events in computing history, 37
    knowledge, 17
    manager, 21
    for organizations, 24–29
        business environment, 24–25
        business organizations, 24–25
    outsourcing, 156
    for personal productivity and enter-
        tainment, 17–18
    professionalism, 201
    professionals, 179
    roles, 151, 196
    for society, 30–36
    software, 363
    uses, 154
Initial program load (IPL), 357
Innovation, 188–189
Input devices, 51, 345–350
Input hardware, 51–52
Input/output (I/O) tasks, 358
Insourcing, 31
Instance, 108
Instant messaging (IM), 78–79, 390
Institute on Governance (IOG), 164
Instruction set, 343
Integrated development environments
    (IDE), 152, 241
Intel, 8, 339, 341, 343, 359
Intellectual property, 28
Internal bus, 343
Internal control, 163

Internal memory, 344–345
Internal rate of return (IRR), 214
International Telecommunications
    Union (ITU.int), 345
Internet, 15–16, 385–389
    accessing, 61–62
    applications, 62–65
    cloud computing, 63–64
    crime, 36
    internetworking, 385
    ISP, computer connection, 61, 383, 386
    next-generation, 65–66
    operations, 368
    security, 71–76
        ensuring, 73–76
        threats, 71–72
    Sophos, 71
    work activities, using
        email, 388
        file transfer protocol (FTP), 389
        internet relay chat (IRC), 390
        newsgroups, 389–390
        telnet protocol, 390
Internet2, 66
Internet Architecture Board (IAB), 61
Internet business models, 258
Internet cafes, 262
Internet Engineering Task Force (IETF), 61
Internet Explorer, 68, 282, 285, 361, 394
Internet fraud, 34–36
Internet protocol suite, 61
Internet Protocol Version 6 (IPv6), 65–66
Internet-related businesses, 258
Internet-related software, 367–368
Internet-related technologies, 31
Internet relay chat (IRC), 390
Internet search engines, 69–70
Internet security, 71–76
    threats, 72
Internet service provider (ISP), 20, 61, 383
Internet standards, 61
Internet technology, 278
    operating costs, reduction, 255
Internet TV, 320–321
Internet users, 262
Interorganizational system (IOS), 278
Interpersonal skills, 21
Intranet, 77–78, 94
Inventory management systems (IMS),
    144, 149
Invitational design, 308
IP address, 379–380, 384, 386
iPhone, 350
iPods, 31
IPv4, 65
IPv6, 65
IS. See Information system
IS development teams, 233–235
IS development tools
    authoring software categories, 242
    CASE tools, 242–243

code generators, 242
integrated development environments
    (IDEs), 241
modelling tools, 242
IS methodology, standard, 236–239
    evolutionary model, 238–239
    importance of, 236–237
    IS modelling, UML diagrams,
        240–241
    waterfall model, 236–238
IS project management, 223–230
    program, 230
    project management software,
        231–232
    project management tasks, 225–226
    project time management, 226–228
    risk management, 228–230
    triple constraint/iron triangle, 224
IS project team, 234–235
IS security, 185
ISO 17799, 164
IT. See Information technology
IT-enabled businesses, 134
IT governance, 196–198
IT governance and leadership, in
        sustainable business value,
        155–157
IT strategic tactics, 154

J
Java, 369
Java applet, 284
Java language, 369
Javascript, 303
Join operation, 407–408
Just-in-time (JIT) inventory concept, 150

K
Keller, Helen, 10
Kernel, 357
Keyboard, 346, 349, 358, 372
Knowledge, 12, 92
    analysis, 94–95
    communication, 97
    discovery, 93–94
    lifelong creation, 92–93
    synthesis, 96–97
    transformation, 95–96
    work activities, 93, 98
Knowledge-creation process, 92
Knowledge hierarchy, 13
Knowledge management (KM), 116
Knowledge management systems
        (KMS), 13, 114, 115–116
Knowledge work, 9
    activities, 93
    analysis, 94
    communication, 97
    discovery, 93
    synthesis, 96
    transformation, 95

L
LANs. See Local area networks
Lands' End, 78–79
Laser scanner, 347, 349
LCD monitors, technology, 350–351
Leasing, 217
Legal codes, 311
Lennie, John, 301
Light pen, 347
LIKE operator, 402
LinkedIn, 305
Links, 68
Liquid crystal display (LCD), 372
Listserv, 388
Local area networks (LANs), 58,
        383–384
    bridge, 384
    share information, 383
    software licences, 383
Logical data model (LDM), 110
Login IDs, 166
Logistics management systems (LMS),
        145
    marketing and sales, 144
    operations, 144
    outbound logistics, 144

M
Machine instructions, 341
Magnetic disks, 354
Magnetic ink character recognition
        (MICR), 348
Magnetic strip reader, 348
Mailto, 393
Mainframe, 50, 355
Malware, 72
MAN, 58
Management information systems
        (MIS), 26, 116–117
    demand reports, 117
    exception reports, 117
    periodic reports, 117
Manheim Auctions, 268
Many-to-many relationship, 405
Many-to-one model, 276
Marketing, 18
Marketing and sales, 133, 150
Marketing campaigns, 136, 318
Mashup, 289, 316
Mass customization, 265
Mass media, 320
MasterCard SecureCode, 273
Matrix, functional, and decentralized
        organizational structures,
        advantages and disadvantages
        of, 183
Matrix organizational structures,
        182
Matrix structure, 182
M-commerce, 269–270
Media transparency, 319

Medication Order Entry and Administration Record System (MOE/MAR), 212
Meetings, 390
Megahertz (MHz), 50
Memory, 51
Memory capacity, 345
Memory chips, 340
Memory management, 362
Merchant account, 286
Meta search engine, 70–71
Meta tags, 70
Methodology, 236
Micro-markets, 319
Microprocessor, 49
Microprocessor chips, 339
Microsoft Access, 399
Microsoft Visual Studio, 241
Microsoft Windows, 245
Microsoft.Net, 285
Microwaves, 381
Middleware, 56
MIDI devices. *See* Musical instrument digital interface
Mintzberg, Henry, 268
Mobile commerce. *See* M-commerce
Mobile phones, 32, 262
Model, 240
Modem, 53
MOE/MAR. *See* Medication Order Entry and Administration Record System
Moen, 272
Moore's Law, 8, 9
Moral code, 311
Motherboard, 342
MP3 player, 48, 80
MP3 technology, 80
MSN Messenger, 78
Multimedia, 390–391
Multimedia messaging service (MMS), 394
Multitaskers, 312
Multitasking, 359
Musical instrument digital interface (MIDI) devices, 349
MyDoom, 72
MySpace, 269
MySQL database software, 370

N

Net present value (NPV), 214
NetMeeting, 98
Netscape, 31
Network, 48
Network architecture
  centralized computing, 375
  client/server architecture, 375–376
  client/server systems
    advantage/disadvantage of, 377
    work efficiency, 376–377

four basic computing architectures, 376
  peer-to-peer networks, 377–378
  servers, types of, 376
  three-tiered architecture, 376
Network architecture, 375
Network connection layer, 379–380
Network interface card (NIC), 53, 386
Network layer model
  application software layer, 379
  bandwidth issues, 382–383
  data component layer, 380–381
  data rate, 382–383
  network connection layer, 379–380
  signal type, 381
  version of, 379
Network servers, 59
Network technology
  client/server architecture, 375–376
  local area network, 383–384
  network architecture, 375–376
  network layer model, 378–383
  peer-to-peer network, 377–378
  wireless LANs, 384
Network TV, 320
Networks, 57–60
  categories, 58
  hardware, 58–59
  software, 59–60
Newsgroups, 389
Next-Generation Internet, 65–66
Niche markets, 268
Nielsen Online survey, 305
Nokia, 385, 394
Non-IT professionals, 17
Non-value-added, 168

O

OCR, 348
Offshoring, 219
Oktoberfest, 324
OLAP. *See* Online analytic processing systems
OMR, 348
One-to-one marketing model, 275
One-to-one relationship, 404
Online advertising, 264
Online analytic processing (OLAP) systems, 114
Online banking, 34, 152, 190, 202
Online security, 311
Online social advertising, 321
Online social strategy, 315
Open-source software, 57, 370
Open systems model, 179, 180
Operating system (OS) software, 54
  application software, 360, 363–368
  boot process, 357
  comparison of, 356
  computer, starting, 357–358
  controlling access, 359
  CPU, efficient use of, 359

file/disk management, 361
hard disk, storage, 358
hardware, managing, 358–359
layers of, 357
mechanism of, 356–357
memory management, 362
parts, 357
processing order, 360–361
Operational decisions, 104
Operations, 132
Optical disks, 354
Optical mouse, 346, 349
Optimization models, 115
Oracle, 106, 136, 143, 242, 285
Organizational boundary, 180
Organizational database, IT, 122
Organizational stakeholders, 181
Organizational value chain, 133
Organizations
  ban social networking sites, 313
  business environment, 24
  buying/leasing/building, 217–219
  core processes, advantage, 134
  development teams, 221
  in-house development *vs.* outsourcing, 219–220
  needs, 219
  outsource, 219
  planning, 213
  strategy, 270
Outbound logistics, 132–133, 149–150
Output devices
  display devices, 350–351
    performance, 351
  for print, 352–353
    performance, 352
  touch screens, 351
Output hardware, 52–53
Outsource, 219
Outsourcing, 170
Outsourcing process, 31, 156

P

Packet, 380
Packet switching, 380
Page, Larry, 103
PageRank, 250
PAN, 58, 385
Parallel processing, 359
Parser, 410
Participating identity, 314
Partnerships, 28, 266
Password, 74–75
Patent violations, 28
Payback period, 214
Payment gateway, 286
PayPal, 220
PCMag.com, 263
PDA, 48, 50, 58, 341, 385
Peer-to-peer networks, 377
  client/server networks, comparing, 378

Pen input, 347
Pepsi, 150
Performance feedback, 188
Performance testing, 94
Periodic reports, 117
Peripheral RAM, 344
Persistent data, 282
Personal area network (PAN), 385
Personal computer (PC), 49–50, 339
Personal information management
    (PIM), 55
Personal Information Protection and
    Electronic Documents Act
    (PIPEDA), 197, 311
Personalization, 265
PERT chart. *See* Program evaluation
    review technique chart
Phishing, 34, 72, 271
Physical order, 256
Physical products, 256
    ordering, 256
Pickett, K. H. S., 165
Piracy, 27
Plain old telephone system (POTS)
    network, 59
Platform, 48
Platform independence, 78
Platform plays, 319
Plotters, 52
Plug-ins, 284
PM software. *See* Project management
    (PM) software
PO. *See* Purchase order
PodcastAlley.com, 280
Podcasting, 80, 92
Point of sale (POS) system, 140, 149
Portal, 25, 209, 259–260
Porter, Michael, 132, 179
Porter's five forces model, 179
Porter's value chain model, 155–156
Portfolio management, 199
POS system, 140, 149–150
Power-on self-test (POST), 358
PPM. *See* Project portfolio
    management
Presentation graphics software, 55
Presentation software, 98, 367
Primary key, 108, 399
Printer buffer, 344
Printers, 52
Privacy Act, 198
Privacy codes, 28, 311
Problem, 103
Problem solving, 99–105
Process mapping, 94
Processing hardware, 49–51
Procurement management, 225
Procurement process, 277
Productivity, 101
Productivity software, 55
Productivity zone, 14–15

Professional codes of conduct and
    practice, 200
Program, 230, 369
Program evaluation review technique
    (PERT) chart, 231–232
Program management, 230
Programming, 369
Programming languages, 57, 231, 369
Project feasibility, 213–217
Project governance, 198–200
Project management (PM), 198, 223–225
    integration, 226
    office, 230–231
    software, 231–232
Project Management Body of Knowledge
    (PMBOK®), 231
Project Management Institute
    (PMI), 200
Project portfolio management (PPM),
    199, 216–217
Project steering committee (PSC), 235
Project team, 31, 95, 102, 212
Project time management, 226–228
Proprietary software, 370
Protocol, 59
Prototype, 238
Prototyping, 239
Provincial privacy legislation, 198
Public IM, 78
Public key encryption, 273
Purchase order (PO), 277

Q
QR codes, 146
Quality assurance, 94
Quality control system, 148
Quality management, 148, 153,
    225–226
Query, 70, 109, 366, 399
Query condition, 400

R
Radio frequency identification
    (RFID), 145
    tags, 145
    type, 145
Radio transmissions, 381
Random access memory (RAM), 51, 344
    performance, 345
Rational decision, 99
Rational unified process (RUP), 239
RDBMS. *See* Relational database
    management systems
Read only memory (ROM), 51, 344
Records, 107
Reduced instruction set computer
    (RISC), 343
Referential integrity, 406
Refresh rate, 351, 372
Registers, 342, 372
Relational data model, 108, 406–407

Relational database
    logical modelling
        anomalies, 404
        entity-relationship diagram,
            404–405
        redundancy, 404
    multitable databases, querying,
        407–408
        creating views, 408
        join operation, 407–408
    relational data model, 406–407
Relational database management sys-
    tems (RDBMS), 108
Relational entity, 405
Religionnewsblog.com, 306
Rental websites, 267
Repeater, 59
Request for information (RFI), 218
Request for proposal (RFP), 218–219
Request for quote/request for tender, 218
Research In Motion (RIM), 32
Reservations system, 148
Resistive touch screen, 351
Resolution, 52, 349
Retail innovations, history of, 254
Retail Link, 174
Return on investment (ROI), 214, 234
Revenue model, 258
Reverse auction, 278
Reverse engineering, 28
RFID. *See* Radio frequency identification
Risk acceptance, 162–163
Risk appetite, 158
Risk assessment, 114, 158, 197, 231
Risk avoidance, 163
Risk deferral, 162
Risk management, 228–230
Risk reduction methods, 161–163
Risk response, 161
Risk response action, 230
Risk transfer, 161–162
Roll-back strategy, 170
Router, 59
Royal Bank of Canada (RBC), 111, 201
RSS feeds, 79

S
SaaS. *See* Software as a service
Sabotage, 36
Salesforce.com, 150
SAP, 136, 143
Sarbanes-Oxley Act of 2002, 159
SAS, 117
SAS® Dashboard, 118
Satellite transmission, 380–381
Scanning devices, 347
Schadenfreude, 315
Schedule control tool, 228
Schedule development, 228
Scope management, 225
Scripting language, 283

SDLC. *See* System development life cycle

Search criteria, 400

Search engine optimization, 264
  on social sites, 316–317

Search engines, 69–71

Secondary storage, 353

Secure electronic transaction (SET), 288

Secure gateway provider, 286

Secure server, 287

Secure Shell (SSH), 390

Secure socket layer (SSL), 287

Security, 166

Security breaches, 28–29

Segregation of duties, 165–166

SELECT query, 402

Selection criteria, 103

Self-regulating community, 314

Self-XSS attacks, 72

Semantic web, 302

Semi-structured decision, 100

Sensor, 349

Sequence diagram, 240–241

Server-side programming, 284

Server software, 285, 396

Servers, 375

Service level agreements (SLA), 161–162

Service marketing, 317

Service-oriented architecture (SOA), 289

ServiceOntario, 212

SharePoint, 77

Short message service (SMS), 394

Signal type, 381

Silver bullet syndrome, 243

Simple mail transfer protocol (SMTP), 379

Site audit, 317

Skype, 78, 387

Slicing and dicing, 112

Smart card reader, 348

SMEs. *See* Subject matter experts

Social business models, 322–323

Social computing, 260

Social media
  categories of, 304
  harnessing power of, 319–320
  legal and ethical framework for, 310–312
  limiting usage, 312–313
  tools, 317–319

Social media technologies, 319

Social networking
  banning sites of, 313
  sites, 305

Social patterns, 320

Social technologies
  business utility, 309–310
  design and usability, 309
  privacy and security, 310–311
  technology implications and costs, 312
  utility, 306–308

Social transparency, 309

Social website, 310–312

Software, 48, 54–57, 339
  application, 55–56
  middleware, 56
  open source, 57
  productivity, 55
  utility, 55

Software application suite, 363

Software as a service (SaaS), 64
  vs. application service provider (ASP), 65

Software as an outsourced service, 64

Sophos, 71

Spam, 28

Speechbobble.com, 319

Spiders, 70, 264

Spot buying, 188, 275

Spreadsheets, 41, 55, 95–96, 172–173, 363–365
  financial status, 172
  physical condition, 172

SQL. *See* Structured Query Language

SSL certificate, 287

Stakeholder, 180

Stakeholder analysis, 233

Stakeholders, importance of, 233

Standard ASCII (American Standard Code for Information Interchange), 340–341
  EBCDIC, comparison of, 341

Static content, 280

Static RAM (SRAM), 344

Storage hardware, 53

Storage hardware devices
  chip-based storage, 354
  magnetic disks, 354
  optical disks, 354
  performance, 355

Strategic decisions, 105

Strategic sourcing, 275

Streaming, 257

Structured decision, 100

Structured Query Language (SQL), 109
  aggregate functions in, 403
  changing values with, 402
  command, 399–402
  display specific information, 400–401
  inserting/deleting records, 402
  LIKE operator, 402
  for programming, 372
  queries, 109
  questions for database through, 105
  relational database, 399
  server, 285
  single-table database, querying, 399–400
  statement, 401–403
  uses, 402–403

Stylesheet (XSL) file, 410

Subject matter experts (SMEs), 234

Sun ONE Instant Messaging, 78

Supercomputer, 50

Supervisory review, 166

Supply chain, 170

Supply chain management (SCM), 140–141
  inventory management, 141
  logistics management, 141
  materials management, 141
  order management, 141

Supply chain system, 140

Surface wave technology, 351

Survey Monkey, 79

Switching devices on network, 380

Synthesis, 96

System design, 238–239

System development life cycle (SDLC), 221
  stages and importance of, 221–222
  waterfall presentation of, 221

System model, 240

System software, 54–55

System unit, 342

T

Tacit knowledge, 92, 116

Tactical decisions, 104

Tactile response, 346

Tagging, 315

T-carrier circuits, 382

TCP/IP protocol, 386

Technical acquisition, 220

Technical skills, 177

Telephone, 381

Text messaging, 245

Three Pillars of Sociability, 306

Three-tiered client/server architecture, 376

Ticoll, David, 21

Toner, 352

Top-level domain, 386–387

Touch screen monitor, 351

Touch screens, 351

Touchpad, 52, 346, 349

TPS. *See* Transaction processing systems

Trackball, 349

Tracking, 349, 350

Trading partners, 278

Traditional procurement method, 278

Transaction, 138

Transaction process characteristics, 138

Transaction processing systems (TPS), 26, 114, 138–140
  software applications, 139

Transformation, 95

Transforming, 192

Transistor, 49, 339

Transmission capacity, 382

Transmission control protocol/Internet packets/datagrams, 380
  protocol (TCP/IP), 379

Transmission speed, 382
Transport layer security (TLS), 288
Transportation management systems
(TMS), 149
Triple constraint, 224
Twisted pair wire, 380
Twitter, 11, 305

U
UCCnet, 164, 174
UHN. *See* University Health Network
UML. *See* Unified Modelling Language
Unicode, 341
Unified Modelling Language (UML),
240–241
Uniform resource locator (URL),
67, 392
Universal product code (UPC),
145, 347
Universal serial bus (USB), 354
University Health Network (UHN), 212
Unstructured decision, 100
URL. *See* Uniform resource locator
USB flash drives, 354
USB flash memory, 354
USB port, 353–354
User-generated content (UGC)
and brand risk, 315–316
creating content, 314
defined, 302
finding content, 315
Utility computing services, 64
Utility software, 55

V
Validation, 308
Value-added networks (VANs), 278
Value chain, 132–135
inbound logistics, 132
marketing and sales, 133
operations, 132
outbound logistics, 132
primary activities, 134
service activities, 133
support activities, 134
support of, 153, 154
VB.NET, 369, 370
Vendor management, 219

Verification controls, 166
Very large-scale integration (VLSI), 8
Video RAM (VRAM), 344
View, 408
Viral social interactions, 315
Virtual meetings, 79
Virtual memory, 362
Viruses, 72
Visa card security code, 273
Visual analytics, 119, 120
Voice over Internet protocol (VoIP),
62–63
VRBO.com, 267

W
Walmart, 263, 272
WAN, short message service (SMS), 394
Warchalking, 75
Waterfall model, 236
W3C. *See* World Wide Web Consortium
Web 3.0 technologies, 302
Web 1.1/1.2/3.0, 302
Web 2.0 technologies, 302
social and business impacts of,
320–322
social business models, 322–323
Web-based tool, 70
Web browser, 68, 367–368, 391
Web crawlers, 70
Web hosting, costs, 312
Web integration, 256
Web presence, 280–281
Web server, 59
Web services, 288–289
Web usage and statistics, 265–266
Webcam, 349
Websites
24/7/365 basis, business, 268
type, purpose, 259
WHERE keyword, 400
Wide area network (WAN), 58
Wi-Fi. *See* Wireless fidelity
Wikipedia, 30
Wikis, 304
Wildcard, 402
Wildcard character, 402
WildOutfitters, 392
WildOutfitters database tables, 399

WildOutfitters product table, 400
Windows hierarchical-based file
structure, 362
Windows Vista, 55, 390
Windows XP, 356
Wireless access point (AP), 59, 386
Wireless application protocol
(WAP), 394
Wireless connectivity, 394–395
Wireless fidelity (Wi-Fi), 61, 62, 384
Wireless LANs (WLANs), 384
Wireless mark-up language (WML), 394
Wireless networking hardware, 384
Wireless networks, use of mobile
devices, 269
Wireless transmissions, 384
Wisdom, 13
Word processing, 41, 363
software, 363
Workflow, 137
Workflow management system (WMS),
137–138
Workflow software, 31
World Wide Web Consortium (W3C), 61
World Wide Web (WWW), 15
browser operations, 392–394
browsers to access, 391–392
changing social trends on, 303
components of, 67–71
cookie, 282, 293
hypertext links, 390
Internet protocols, 393
multimedia, 390–391
surfing, 393
URLs, 393
WorldWideWebSize.com, 15
Worms, 72

X
XML. *See* eXtensible markup language
XML data, browser, 411
XML schema, 410
XML stylesheet (XSL) file, 410

Y
Yahoo! Messenger, 78
YouTube, 305
YouTube videos, 30

STUDYCARD

CHAPTER 1: IT for Business and Business Professionals

STUDENT RETURN ON INVESTMENT **ROI**

1. **Describe what an information system is and explain why IS is so important in today's world.** (pp. 8–16) An information system (IS) is an organized collection of people, information, business processes, and information technology, designed to transform inputs into outputs to achieve a goal. Information systems combine people, information, and technology to address business needs and to achieve business goals.

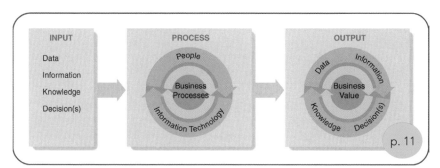

2. **Explain why the study of IT is so important to any future business professional.** (pp. 17–23) IT is an enabler; in every business discipline, whether finance, marketing, accounting, or other, IT provides essential tools for these business functions. IT can help make you more efficient and effective. By using IT, you can be more organized and faster. A knowledge of IT is also critical when you are working in an organization. You will be expected to understand the IT in use at the company, both standard and custom systems, as well as evaluate them for improvements.

3. **Describe some of the most common types of information systems used in businesses.** (pp. 24–30) Table 1.3 (p. 26) summarizes some key information systems used in business: TPS, MIS, DSS, ERP, and CRM. Each system supports key business processes, parts of the business's value chain, and ultimately the business strategy. Without these systems, businesses would have a more difficult time operating and significant challenges innovating and growing.

4. **Describe some of the ways that IT has changed society.** (pp. 30–37) It is clear that technology is so omnipresent that, from an early age, everyone becomes comfortable using it to manage all aspects of their lives. This includes using technologies to intermediate social interactions, which were formerly only done in person. We become used to technology not just as an aid to what we do, but as fundamental to what we do. In addition, we become used to thinking about technology as the "go-to" solution for anything—learning, researching, buying, travelling, etc. Most interactions with an organization can now likely be done through some form of technology assistance. This prevalence makes it incumbent on organizations, and particularly for-profit businesses, to ensure they are present and accounted for in those places where customers are.

KNOWLEDGE SPEAK

business (p. 24) An organization with one or more people who decide on one or more goals to pursue, work together to locate and organize resources, and create processes to achieve the desired goals. It involves producing goods and services and selling them to generate economic value. It includes financial, commercial, industrial, and human considerations.

business environment (p. 24) A company's complex collection of political, economic, social, and technological factors that organizational leaders must consider when making decisions regarding goals, organizational forms, and the creation of business value. Includes macroeconomic variables of the market the company operates in, the nature of the industry, competitors, customers, and suppliers.

commerce (p. 16) The buying and selling of goods and services.

communication (p. 15) Sharing data, information, and knowledge with others using tools such as email, telephone, instant messaging, file sharing, central databases, and in-person meetings.

data (p. 12) Raw, unorganized facts, numbers, pictures, and so on that has to be organized in a way that business professionals can use to make sense.

data-information-knowledge continuum (p. 12) The model of the evolution and hierarchy of data going to information, then to knowledge.

digital divide (p. 34) The social impact of technology intensification, creating both have and have-not parties (whether individuals, groups, or nations). Those that can afford technology have easy access and those that cannot are left behind.

e-commerce (p. 16) The use of information systems, technologies, and computer networks by individuals and organizations to create business value.

globalization (p. 30) The phenomenon of modern businesses expanding into markets worldwide and distributing work across the globe to minimize costs and provide the convenience of doing business 24/7. Information technology and the Internet are significant enablers of globalization.

information (p. 12) Data that has been organized and is useful to a person.

KNOWLEDGE SPEAK

information overload (p. 15) The situation where people are overwhelmed by the amount of information available on the Web.

information system (IS) (p. 10) An organized collection of people, information, business processes, and information technology designed to transform inputs into outputs to achieve a goal. Businesses use information systems to leverage the human ability to achieve business goals through the timely and appropriate application of technology, and the timely delivery of appropriate and useful data, information, and knowledge.

information technology (IT) (p. 9) The branch of knowledge that deals with the uses of hardware, software, and networks to convert, store, protect, process, transmit, and retrieve information. It is especially relevant to organizations for increasing efficiency, cutting costs, and enabling closer customer/employee interactions, resulting in better profits.

Internet (p. 15) The global network of co-operating computer networks that use the same rules for sending and receiving information.

knowledge (p. 12) Created when a person combines information with judgment. Creating and adding economic value relies on the use of knowledge. It can be explicit or tacit.

knowledge management systems (KMS) (p. 13) Systems that provide tools for working with both tacit and explicit knowledge.

knowledge work (p. 9) The intellectual activity that people perform upon data, information, and knowledge to discover business options.

Moore's Law (p. 8) A law that postulates computing power (as measured by the maximum number of transistors in an integrated circuit) roughly doubles every 18 months.

wisdom (p. 13) An extension of the data-to-knowledge continuum that enables business leaders to perceive the underlying meaning and nuances of a business situation and ensures that knowledge from all relevant perspectives, disciplines, and sources is considered in the final decision.

World Wide Web (p. 15) A collection of Internet software applications and standards that allows the transfer of text, images, audio, and video. The Web makes it easy to publish information in a variety of ways so that it is accessible to business professionals and trading partners of a business.

KEY FIGURES

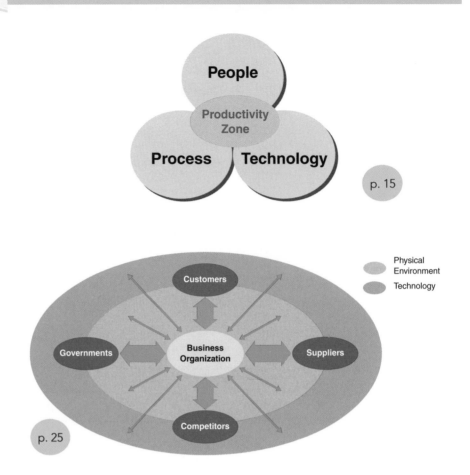

p. 15

p. 25

QUICK TEST

1. Which of the following sequences arranges the terms in order from least complex to most complex correctly?

   a. knowledge, information, data

   b. knowledge, data, information

   c. information, data, knowledge

   d. data, knowledge, information

   e. data, information, knowledge

2. Which of the following are included in Friedman's 10 forces that flattened the world *and* involve technology?

   a. inshoring, offshoring, insourcing

   b. the collapse of the Berlin wall, "the steroids," open sourcing

   c. Netscape, Nintendo, in-forming

   d. workflow software, supply-chaining, insourcing

3. For a manager, examples of _____ might include the names of clients, their phone numbers, and their email addresses in an address-book program in his or her smartphone.

STUDYCARD

CHAPTER 2: Technology Essentials

1. **Describe the fundamentals of information technology and how they come together to help increase your productivity as a business professional.** (pp. 48–60) An information technology (IT) device can accept and store information; perform mathematical calculations; apply logic (e.g., compare values of numbers to make decisions); and retrieve, display, and send information. As such, IT allows you, a business professional, to communicate your thoughts, ideas, and feelings with others. IT helps you obtain data and information that you can use. IT provides tools you can use to analyze data and information to help in your decision making. IT can help you organize and store data and information that is important to you. The meaningful application of this technology will achieve efficiencies, gain competitive advantage, and create business value.

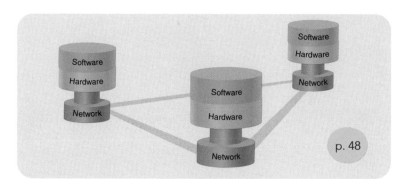

p. 48

2. **Explain why the Internet is so valuable to businesses, and outline some of the Internet applications available to businesses today.** (pp. 60–66) The Internet is arguably the most useful technological tool of the last few decades. The Internet uses the TCP/IP suite of packet switching protocols, a very general, non-proprietary set of communication rules. By adopting these rules and making use of software compatible with the TCP/IP standards, any computer, regardless of the platform (processor and OS), can connect and communicate over the Internet.

3. **Identify the basic components of the World Wide Web and describe how web pages are located on the Web.** (pp. 67–71) If the Internet is the technology platform, the World Wide Web is an application that works on that platform. The Web is the primary Internet application that supports many types of e-commerce. The Web basically provides a hypertext system that operates over the Internet. Hypertext provides an easy way to publish information on a network. Hypertext documents can include references (hyperlinks) to other information on the network. Using Web browser software, business professionals can view hypertext documents and use the hyperlinks to browse (or surf) other related documents.

4. **Outline important ways individuals and business can keep their data and information safe online.** (pp. 71–76) Both the CIA triad and the McCumber Cube provide effective outlines to ensuring data and information security for individuals and organizations. Some simple actions that anyone can take to minimize Internet security risks include installing and keeping up to date antivirus software and firewalls, patching security holes with system updates, or moving to less vulnerable systems, such as Linux. Avoiding simple human error is one of the most effective ways to ensure data and information safety.

5. **Explain how technology has made collaboration in the business world easier and more productive.** (pp. 77–79) Technological advancements in cloud computing have fostered collaboration over the Internet like never before. Users can now schedule meetings, monitor projects, share work files, and even conference online from any computer platform, regardless of its operating system. Through sophisticated new software and secure Internet connections, cloud computing is driving collaboration forward in the business world.

KNOWLEDGE SPEAK

application service provider (ASP) (p. 64) An online technology company that develops and delivers software tools on the Internet.

application software (p. 55) A complete, self-contained program or set of programs for performing a specific job; for example, document preparation, electronic spreadsheet, presentation, and email clients.

business continuity plan (p. 76) A plan put in place to address problem prevention, response to crises, resumption of business activities, recovery of losses, and restoration of systems and processes.

client/server network (p. 67) A network of computers that request services (clients) and computers that provide services (servers).

cloud computing (p. 63) Computing over the Internet; the term *cloud* is used as a synonym for the Internet.

computer hierarchy (p. 50) A means of categorizing computer technologies based on processing power. For example, supercomputers, which have the greatest processing power, are at the top of the hierarchy, and small, embedded processors are at the bottom.

groupware (p. 77) Collaborative software that enables communication between team members and helps them to share data, information, and knowledge.

hardware (p. 48) The electronic and mechanical components of a computer that can be seen and touched, such as the computer monitor.

hypertext markup language (HTML) (p. 68) A language for encoding information so that a variety of IT devices, mainly Web browsers, can display it.

hypertext transfer protocol (HTTP) (p. 68) A Web protocol that provides the rules used by browsers and servers as they communicate requests for data and responses between each other.

intranet (p. 77) A private, organization-wide computer network that is typically based on Internet protocols.

middleware (p. 56) Software that links applications that use dissimilar software or hardware platforms.

network (p. 48) A fundamental component of information technology (IT) that helps computers connect with one another. Increases the power of IT devices by allowing business professionals to share resources, including hardware, software, and information. Can be a local area network (LAN), a metropolitan area network (MAN), a wide area network (WAN), or even the Internet.

KNOWLEDGE SPEAK

open source software (p. 57) Program and software code (programming instructions) that is freely available for downloading over the Internet.

operating system (OS) software (p. 54) A piece of system software that coordinates and handles the details of working with the computer hardware. It frees the user from the responsibilities of input/output device management, memory management, file handling, multitasking, and process optimization. It also forms the base over which application software is run.

platform (p. 48) An IT platform consists of hardware, software, and network technology.

productivity software (p. 55) Software used by business professionals to work with data, information, and knowledge more effectively and efficiently; for example, document preparation software, electronic spreadsheet software, and database management systems.

protocol (p. 59) A standard set of rules that allow the communication of data between nodes on a network; for example, TCP/IP, HTTP, and FTP.

random access memory (RAM) (p. 51) Hardware that stores data only until it is no longer needed, or until the computer is shut down. The CPU can access any item stored in RAM directly (randomly).

read only memory (ROM) (p. 51) Hardware that stores instructions and data that only special devices can alter. In a computer, it holds the instructions used to control the start-up processes (booting up). The data in ROM is permanently stored there.

software (p. 48) The set of instructions that direct information technology hardware.

software as a service (SaaS) (p. 64) A way companies acquire enterprise systems without purchasing or building them; essentially, renting software.

system software (p. 54) Includes any software required to control the hardware components and to support the execution of application software. System software includes the operating system and utility software.

utility software (p. 55) Provides additional tools that can be used to maintain and service the system; for example, antivirus software and disk partition tools, among others.

Wi-Fi (p. 62) The popular name for the 802.11 standards for wireless network access.

KEY FIGURES

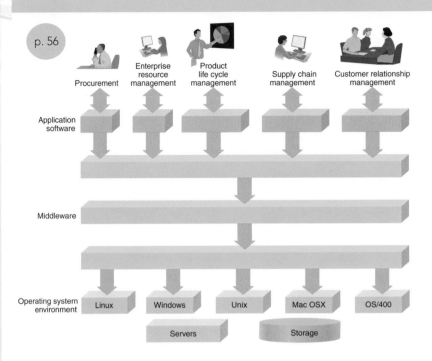

p. 56

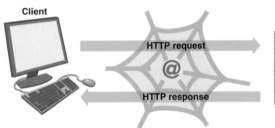

1. The **client (browser)** generates an **HTTP request** for a resource at a location indicated at a URL.

2. The **HTTP request** is sent over the **Web** to the server at the URL location.

3. The **server** receives that **HTTP request** and looks for the requested files.

p. 67

4. The **server** locates the requested resource.

7. The **client** receives the **HTTP response** and processes it. The response is displayed based on HTML.

6. The **HTTP response** is sent back over the Web to the client.

5. The **server** generates an **HTTP response**. The response will usually include the requested resource.

QUICK TEST

1. _____ software manages and controls the resources of a computer system.
   a. Application
   b. Operating system
   c. Productivity
   d. Utility

2. Which of the following is not a networking technology that allows connection to the Internet?
   a. DSL
   b. HTML
   c. Cable
   d. Plain old telephone system

3. A _____ allows members of an organization to share files, resources, servers, and other hardware with other members of an organization.

STUDYCARD

CHAPTER 3: Managing and Using Data

STUDENT RETURN ON INVESTMENT   ROI

1. **Define data, information, and knowledge and describe how business professionals engage in knowledge work activities.** (pp. 92–98) Data are the lifeblood of an organization. Organizations collect this raw information to begin to understand their operations and determine whether or not they are achieving their business objectives. Information takes data one step further by organizing it in a way that is useful, meaningful, and more easily accessible. Organizations attain knowledge through the knowledge work of the business professionals they employ. Knowledge work involves the discovery of data and information, its analysis, transformation, and synthesis, and finally the communication of conclusions, which may be solutions to problems or decisions. Throughout this process, individual and organizational experience is applied and value is added. It is with this knowledge that organizations can create competitive advantage.

2. **Explain how the structure, quality, and presentation of information influence the nature of the decisions made by business professionals.** (pp. 99–105) A decision is a choice you make about what actions you will take (or not take) in a given situation. Decisions can vary in the amount of structure and uncertainty, from structured and certain decisions (e.g., selecting prerequisite courses) to unstructured decisions that give little guidance about what to do, how to do it, and what the likely outcome will be. The amount of structure and the level of uncertainty can influence how much time business professionals will spend in different knowledge work activities, and how certain they might be about the outcomes of their decisions. Further, because the gathered data and information form the foundation for the analysis, the quality of data and information directly affects the quality of the decision.

3. **Describe how databases help businesses store and access their data, information, and knowledge.** (pp. 106–113) Through the use of databases, businesses can quickly and easily access interrelated data that are stored and organized in files. The ability to access and combine data enables businesses to understand and learn about the operations of the business. For example, this data helps businesses answer questions such as, How many sales were made in the last hour, day, week, month, quarter, year, decade, and for all time? What is our market share compared to our competitors? These data also support more advanced systems, such as decision support systems (DSS) and knowledge management systems (KMS), which are able to transform data to organization knowledge to inform strategic decision making, preserve knowledge beyond individuals, and improve efficiency.

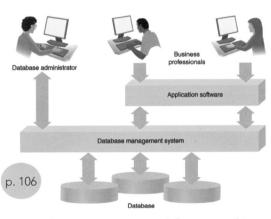

p. 106

4. **Explain how business intelligence enhances organizational decision making.** (pp. 113–121) Business intelligence (BI) is a process for gaining competitive advantage through the intelligent use of data and information in decision making. The goal of BI is to increase profitability by enabling business leaders to make better decisions. Decision support systems (DSS) provide computer-based tools designed to support business intelligence.

KNOWLEDGE SPEAK

analysis (p. 94) The phase of problem solving that involves examining and looking at the details of available data. Helps to answer questions and gain initial insight prior to doing more in-depth transformation and synthesis.

balanced scorecard (p. 119) A popular type of dashboard that includes both financial and non-financial performance measures in the context of financial, customer, internal business process, and learning and growth perspectives. Each of these has objectives, measures, targets, and initiatives associated with them, which are equally weighted. The purpose of the balanced scorecard is to measure an organization's actions against its strategic direction.

business intelligence (BI) (p. 113) A process that enables business leaders to make better decisions for gaining competitive advantage through the intelligent use of data and information in decision making.

dashboard (p. 118) A common way of organizing and presenting business intelligence or related information sources; the purpose of a dashboard is to provide critical information to business users at a glance.

data (p. 92) Raw, unorganized facts, numbers, pictures, and so on that has to be organized in a way that business professionals can use to make sense.

database management system (DBMS) (p. 106) A collection of software that allows users to create, manage, and work with a database.

data hierarchy (p. 107) Organizes stored data in increasing levels of complexity, from the bits used to store data (lowest level) up to the entire database structure (highest level).

data mining (p. 112) A set of techniques for finding trends and patterns in large sets of data.

data modelling (p. 109) The process of analyzing the data required by the processes of an organization to support it both operationally and strategically.

data warehouse (p. 111) A means of storing and managing large amounts of data for information access, typically composed of data from one or more transaction databases.

decision support system (DSS) (p. 115) A software system that provides analytical and visualization tools to support and enhance decision making and planning.

KNOWLEDGE SPEAK

discovery (p. 93) Finding data, information, and knowledge relevant to a task, problem, issue, opportunity, and so on.

document management system (DMS) (p. 117) An information system (IS) for entering, tracking, routing, and processing the many documents used in an organization.

executive information system (EIS) (p. 117) A system designed to provide summary information about business performance to those making higher-level strategic decisions.

information (p. 92) Data that has been organized and is useful to a person.

knowledge (p. 92) Created when a person combines information with judgment. It can be explicit or tacit.

management information system (MIS) (p. 116) A software system that provides timely information to decision makers through processing and reporting.

problem (p. 103) A state that exists when a person or organization faces an opportunity or fails to meet the desired goals, needs, or expectations.

problem solving (p. 103) A series of steps or a process (logical sequence of activities) taken in response to some event or activity.

rational decision (p. 99) A choice that a person or group of people or organization makes about what actions to take (or not to take) in a given situation. Decision making usually occurs, however, as part of a larger problem-solving process.

relational database management systems (RDBMS) (p. 108) A software application that lets business professionals work with and manage relational databases.

semi-structured decision (p. 100) A decision that is not fully structured but still can be attained with the use of information, reasoning, and partly objective thinking to some extent.

structured decision (p. 100) A decision that can be programmed. It is routine or repetitive, and the necessary data are complete and certain.

synthesis (p. 96) Creating wholes from parts. In knowledge work activities, it facilitates the interpretation of trends and patterns leading to conclusions and recommendations. In problem solving, the results of analyses are typically synthesized to develop potential solutions for a problem.

transformation (p. 95) A knowledge work activity in which data and information are organized and manipulated to deepen understanding and further analyze the data prior to synthesizing a conclusion.

unstructured decision (p. 100) A decision that is characterized by uncertain data or information and for which there may be no known method of arriving at a solution.

KEY FIGURES

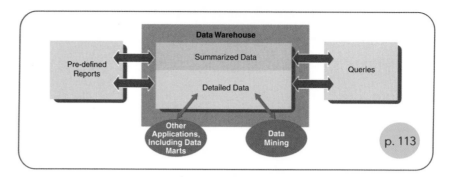

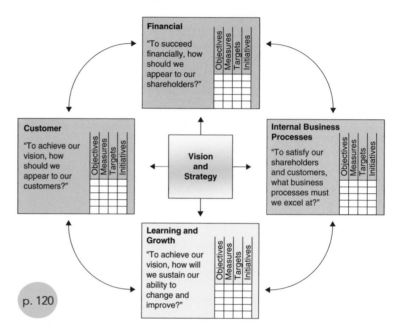

QUICK TEST

1. The knowledge activity where a business professional uses the results of analysis to gain a greater understanding of the data and information is called _____.

   a. analysis

   b. transformation

   c. communication

   d. discovery

2. At what level of decision making would data modelling technologies normally be applied?

   a. strategic

   b. operational

   c. tactical

   d. all of the above

3. Organizational _____ is created when you take base data and information and perform analysis and modelling to turn it into knowledge that can be applied to improve decision outcomes.

STUDENT RETURN ON INVESTMENT **ROI**

1. **Describe ways in which organizations can apply IT to build business value.** (pp. 132–142) Businesses can use IT to automate, inform, and transform organizational processes throughout the value chain to create a competitive advantage. Businesses use IT with a focus on automation to improve the execution of a process—simply doing it faster and more consistently. An IT-informating process recognizes the creation of new data and information about the business each time it executes a process. The business may then process the new data and use it to improve decision making in the organization and to change or improve the process itself. Finally, transforming organizational processes to gain competitive advantage may involve automating and informating, as well as innovation through application of new technologies like enterprise systems.

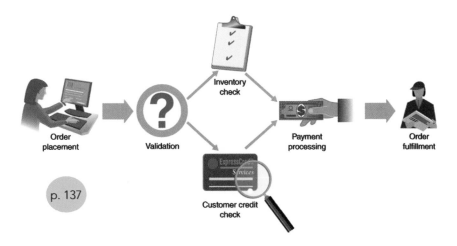

Order placement → Validation (?) → Inventory check → Payment processing → Order fulfillment

Customer credit check

p. 137

2. **Explain how businesses can use enterprise resource planning to strategically fit IT to the organization.** (pp. 142–157) Information systems, like the organizations they support, consist of more than IT. When applying IT, a business must consider the interaction of technology with the people who create and use it, the organizational structure and culture, the business processes, and the environment within which the organization resides. A business must consider the strategic fit of IT within the context of the organization as a system and what it is trying to accomplish. One specific way that IT supports business strategy is through the implementation of enterprise systems that support individual components of the value chain, like logistics management systems in the inbound logistics component, or across all value chain components in the case of ERP. These systems support business objectives and are measured by performance measures to ensure that they are creating the expected value.

3. **Describe IT's role in managing enterprise risk.** (pp. 157–167) IT plays an integral role in both identifying and managing risk. IT helps to identify risk by providing data to management that may help them recognize a threat. In managing risk, businesses turn to IT to implement technology and controls supported by technology to minimize or avoid risks, assist with outsourcing to transfer risk, undertake activities to defer risk, and assist with contingency plans to minimize the impact of unavoidable risks.

KNOWLEDGE SPEAK

adding value (p. 133) Ensuring that, as an organization moves through the value chain, value is added at each step, thereby increasing the value of the end product or service to the end customer. As such, if a step does not add value, it should be eliminated.

business rule (p. 138) A statement that defines or constrains some aspect of the business; it is intended to influence and, sometimes, enforce the behaviour of the business. Business rules are often found as part of policies and procedures, laws, or guidelines.

competitive necessity (p. 155) The need to keep up with competitors in order to stay in business.

control advantage (p. 163) The strengthening of internal controls and compliance through the application of IT-based controls to business processes, policies, and procedures.

controls (p. 163) Specific actions, including policies and procedures, designed to ensure the achievement of business objectives.

customer relationship management (CRM) (p. 150) A software system to help businesses connect with customers and their diverse and changing needs. Integrate data collection, transformation, storage, and analysis of customer transaction data, including purchases, service requests, and other forms of customer contact.

enterprise resource planning (ERP) (p. 142) An information system that integrates and standardizes processes and centralizes the storage and management of a business' data with the goal of increasing operational efficiencies in business processes.

enterprise risk management (ERM) (p. 158) A process started by an entity's board of directors, management, and other personnel, applied in a strategic setting and across the enterprise, to identify potential events that may affect the entity and to manage risk to be within its risk appetite.

functional information systems (FIS) (p. 135) An information system (IS) with a focus on the activities of a single functional department of an organization that is used to improve the efficiency and effectiveness of that department.

KNOWLEDGE SPEAK

in-sourcing (p. 162) The strategic decision made by a business to bring various services or functions back in-house, or keep them in-house, rather than globally sourcing them.

internal control (p. 163) A process started by an entity's board of directors, management, and other personnel designed to provide reasonable assurance regarding the achievement of objectives in the following categories: effectiveness and efficiency of operations, reliability of financial reporting, and compliance with applicable laws and regulations.

outsourcing (p. 156) Hiring another company to perform work that could otherwise be done in-house.

supply chain (p. 140) A network of facilities and distribution options that perform the functions of procurement of materials, transformation of these materials into intermediate and finished products, and the distribution of these finished products to customers.

supply chain management (SCM) (p. 141) A set of methods that a business employs to manage the materials, information, and finances as they move in a process from supplier to manufacturer to wholesaler to retailer to consumer. Information systems (IS) are essential for efficient management of the supply chain.

transaction (p. 138) An exchange of goods or services (value) between two or more parties (businesses, individuals, or a combination of the two) that creates a relationship between the parties.

transaction processing system (TPS) (p. 138) An information software system that enables transactions and captures and processes transaction data to make them available to the organization.

value chain (p. 132) A view of a business organization as a connected series of activities, each of which adds value or supports the addition of value to the firm's goods or services. Every action that the organization takes is either a primary activity or a support activity.

workflow (p. 137) The steps, organizational resources, input and output data, and tools needed to complete a business process.

workflow management systems (WMS) (p. 137) Supports activities that several departments of the organization may carry out by supporting and automating workflows.

KEY FIGURES

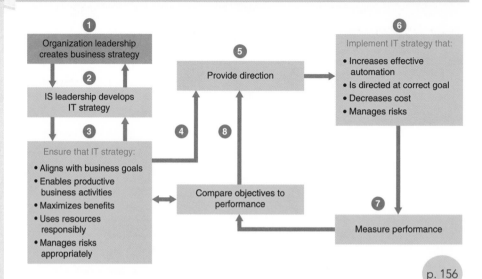

p. 156

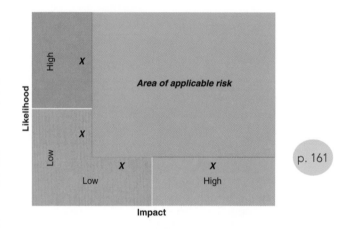

p. 161

QUICK TEST

1. Which of the following is NOT a system that supports the marketing and sales component of the value chain?

   a. CRM

   b. production scheduling

   c. salesforce automation

   d. ERP

2. A system that enables transactions and captures key data created by transactions is a(n) _____.

   a. WMS

   b. ACID

   c. DSS

   d. TPS

3. Organizations generally consider control as _____

   a. a process that runs through the organization

   b. being based around people and how they behave at work

   c. providing reasonable, not absolute, assurance that objectives will be achieved

   d. all of the above

CHAPTER 5: Creating Business Value

STUDENT RETURN ON INVESTMENT   **ROI**

1. **Explain how businesses organize and use business processes to achieve competitive advantage.** (pp. 178–189) Business organization dictates business growth. To get something done in an organization, you need to know where to go for the information and how to get to the authority required to accomplish the task. Too much business structure could create bureaucratic barriers that stunt the growth of a company, and too little structure can create chaos where employees are not held accountable for their actions. Team structures like the matrix structure play an important part in business because they facilitate the free flow of information between employees while holding members of the group accountable to one another. Competitive advantage is the result of creating more business value than competitors, and good business organization can be a key factor in maintaining or increasing advantage.

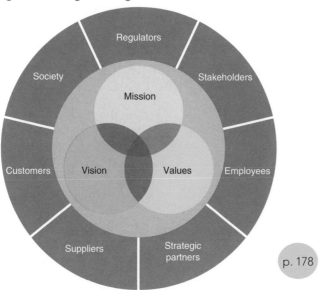

p. 178

2. **Describe how IT helps create business value.** (pp. 189–194) Businesses continually analyze their competitive position to, at minimum, maintain competitive advantage and hopefully increase advantage. In these endeavours, IT helps businesses to both identify and implement ways to increase business value and competitive advantage. First, IT enables businesses to more efficiently gather, process, and analyze data and information. Through these actions, business professionals can identify areas for improvement or opportunities that will lead to competitive advantage. Second, IT may be a crucial part of the business product or service that is offered to market. It certainly may be part of the way the product or service is produced. IT may assist by automating or informating processes to be more efficient and informative, or it may transform products to be highly successful in the marketplace.

3. **Explain the various types of organizational governance and state why governance is important in today's business world.** (pp. 194–201) Corporate governance involves basic questions of status, financial viability, strategy, and compliance within an organization. It ensures that the organization's efforts are all geared toward the organization's goals, mission, or purpose. IT governance is managed by a company's Chief Information Officer. The CIO must ensure proper and secure use of all the organization's information resources, and particularly the organization's compliance with privacy laws and regulations wherever it operates. By managing IT governance, CIOs are able to protect individuals who digitally communicate with the organization externally and internally, while protecting the company from unknowingly committing illegal actions in the global IT realm. Effective governance is a critical enabler for success in the global economy, for securing the enterprise's information resources, and for creating competitive advantage.

KNOWLEDGE SPEAK

automating (p. 190) Using technology instead of business professionals to perform tedious or repetitive tasks. By automating, a business may complete a task with more speed, economy, consistency, and possibly accuracy.

business process (p. 184) A series of steps that an organization needs to perform to transform inputs to their main outputs (products and services).

business process reengineering (BPR) (p. 188) The study of business processes with the objective of changing these processes to be more efficient and better support an organization's objectives and strategy.

business strategy (p. 178) A broad-based formula that lays out how a business is going to compete, what its goals should be, and what plans and policies will be needed to carry out those goals.

competitive advantage (p. 188) The advantage businesses obtain over their competitors by increasing the quality of insight, speed of execution, and cost competitiveness of the organization.

continuous improvement (p. 188) The ongoing effort to improve products, services, and/or processes. Improvements may involve increasing quality and/or reducing costs.

co-opetition (p. 193) A new term emerging in the business literature and practice of global commerce that implies that organizations can collaborate in one endeavour (for instance, a joint venture), while they compete in other areas. In other words, this is a business strategy that realizes the benefits of both co-operation and competition.

corporate governance (p. 194) The leadership and management of a business are directly accountable to its owners (e.g., shareholders) for the proper operation and financial control of the organization.

decentralized structure (p. 182) Decision-making authority is pushed down the organizational structure and shared with many lower-level employees. Decentralized organizations have fewer levels of management with wide spans of control, giving employees more freedom of action. Decentralized structures can be more efficient than centralized structures because they require fewer managers.

KNOWLEDGE SPEAK

feedback (p. 187) A special kind of output created by a business process that is then returned to the system ("fed back") to control the system's future inputs, processes, and outputs.

functional structure (p. 182) A business organized according to functional areas instead of product lines. Functionally organized businesses can be economically efficient but can lack flexibility, and it may be difficult to communicate between functional areas.

informating (p. 191) Recognizing that executing business processes also creates new data and information. An organization may then use this new data to improve its decision making and to change or improve the process itself.

IT governance (p. 196) The distribution of decision-making rights and responsibilities among enterprise stakeholders, and the procedures and mechanisms for making and monitoring strategic decisions.

matrix structure (p. 182) A form of business organizational structure that blends the functional and decentralized organizational structures. Frequently uses teams of employees to accomplish work.

open systems model (p. 179) A technique for viewing a business as an open system with a boundary, environment, inputs, outputs, processes, feedback, and decision makers. The model indicates that a business operates by transforming inputs into outputs and by constantly interacting with its environment.

organizational boundary (p. 180) The separation between a business system and its environment. Business systems must keep an open boundary to their environment to allow for receiving inputs and to produce outputs.

project management (p. 198) The application of knowledge skills, tools, and techniques to project activities to meet project requirements.

project portfolio management (PPM) (p. 199) Selecting projects that are good strategic fits for the company (doing the right projects).

stakeholder (p. 180) A person or entity that has an interest in and an influence on how a business will function to succeed. May be external or internal relative to the organization.

transforming (p. 192) Using information technology (IT) to help a business acquire or continue a competitive advantage over its competitors by adjusting how the company does business.

KEY FIGURES

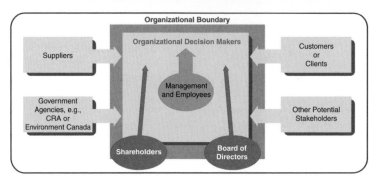

p. 181

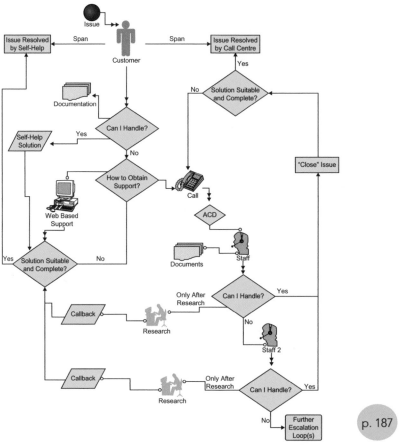

p. 187

QUICK TEST

1. Which is not a stakeholder in creating business strategy?
   a. society
   b. employees
   c. suppliers
   d. technology

2. When _____ a process, a business might apply technology to do the same things as before, but more efficiently.

3. A process is often shown as:
   a. Input → output → process
   b. Process → output → input
   c. Process → input → output
   d. Input → process → output

STUDYCARD

CHAPTER 6: Managing IS Projects and Creating IS Solutions

STUDENT RETURN ON INVESTMENT ROI

1. **Describe the major decisions organizations must address before developing an IS system.** (pp. 213–220) Organizations need to ask four major questions when considering obtaining an IS: (1) Do we need an IS? Business professionals in an organization are constantly looking for ways to improve their operations; (2) Is the project feasible? An organization needs to determine whether or not the project has a reasonable chance of success; (3) Should we build, buy, or lease the IS?; and (4) Do we build the IS ourselves (in-house), or do we contract with an outside firm (outsource) to build it?

2. **Explain the activities organizations must consider within each of the seven stages of the system development life cycle.** (pp. 221–223) The system development life cycle is a series of events viewed over time from the initial concept through to the retirement of an information system. We can divide the life cycle into seven main phases: concept, inception, elaboration, construction, transition, production, and retirement. The retirement of one system often means that an organization is about to transition to another system. Every project is unique in terms of the specific types of activities required to bring a system to life, but the SDLC provides a general guideline to the actions required in each of the seven stages.

3. **Describe the key tasks in managing an IS project.** (pp. 223–232) The key tasks in managing IS projects are related to time management, scope management, cost management, and quality management. It is these tasks that will have the biggest impact on the success of the project. As an IS project manager you want to be able to say that your project delivered on time, on budget, and at the expected scope and level of quality.

4. **Outline the importance of an IS development team and name some of the people who might be included on such a team.** (pp. 233–235) Without IS development teams, new systems would not be developed. Each IS development team may be composed of different members and will vary in size depending on the IS being developed. Most commonly, though, an IS development team involves a project manager, a business subject matter expert (SME), and at least one technical staff member. If the IS is being developed by an end user, it could be the SME doing the project alone as an end-user developer. If it is a multi-year, multi-functional ERP system being implemented, then the IS development team may number up to 50 members with various roles and responsibilities.

5. **Outline the methods organizations use to ensure that they obtain the best IS to help meet their strategic goals.** (pp. 236–241) The waterfall model is a well-known methodology that proceeds from concept through inception, elaboration, and construction, to transition and production. More modern methods involve a more evolutionary approach and use prototyping and agile development to complete IS projects.

6. **Describe some of the IS development tools available to businesses today.** (pp. 241–243) A popular tool is the integrated development environment (IDE). IDEs provide developers with everything they need to design, develop, de-bug, and document their programming code. Other development tools include modelling and CASE tools, which first provide a visual representation of the system to be developed and then can actually automatically generate code for developers.

KNOWLEDGE SPEAK

agile development (p. 239) A methodology whereby the team develops software in short development cycles or increments to allow for continuously changing requirements.

build-and-fix model (p. 236) A methodology whereby developers create a system based on a set of requirements and then test and debug it with little attention to any pre-project analysis or developmental design.

code generation (p. 242) Allows a developer to use graphical diagrams to define a system's components and how they are related, and then to automatically create programming statements to implement the logic described by the diagrams.

end-user development (p. 243) IS development that is carried out by non-IT personnel; this is possible because IS development tools have become so advanced.

evolutionary model (p. 238) A model whereby developers first investigate, specify, and implement an important core part of the system with minimal functionality, and then the team tests and evaluates this version of the system to plan for the next version.

feasibility study (p. 213) A detailed investigation and analysis of a proposed development project to determine whether it is technically and economically possible.

in-house development (p. 219) Using one's own staff to do the work required to develop a new system or product.

integrated development environment (IDE) (p. 241) Allows developers to complete several programming tasks within the same software application instead of using separate software packages.

methodology (p. 236) A set of procedures that provides a framework for both the management and technical processes of an information systems (IS) project.

model (p. 240) A simplified representation of something real, such as a building, weather pattern, or information system, that business professionals can manipulate to study the real item in more detail.

outsource (p. 219) Hiring another company to perform work that could otherwise be done in-house.

program (p. 230) The set of instructions in a computer language that follows an algorithm to carry out a desired task.

KNOWLEDGE SPEAK

program management (p. 230) Managing several related projects together. Essentially the same as managing a single project, but across multiple project teams.

project management (p. 223) The application of knowledge skills, tools, and techniques to project activities to meet project requirements.

project steering committee (PSC) (p. 235) A committee that oversees large and complicated IS projects. Its responsibility is to ensure the project and organizational goals are met, required resources are provided, contingencies are managed, and expected benefits are realized.

prototyping (p. 239) The initial version of a system, which is continually revised to reach a final product.

request for information (RFI) (p. 218) When an organization acquires an IS, it may issue an RFI to gather information about a product, service, and/or vendor capabilities.

request for proposal (RFP) (p. 218) A document that initiates a bidding process for potential vendors. An RFP provides very specific and detailed requirements for respondents to answer to determine the suitability of their proposed offering.

risk management (p. 228) Recognizing, addressing, and eliminating sources of risk before they threaten the successful completion of a project.

stakeholder analysis (p. 233) The portion of the feasibility study that includes the evaluation of stakeholder opinions and attitudes about a project.

subject matter experts (SMEs) (p. 234) A group of specialists working on a project who handle unique aspects of the project for which they are uniquely qualified.

technical acquisition (p. 220) Occurs when a company possessing a desired technology is purchased by another organization so that the acquiring company can own and use the technology of the acquired company. It is an alternative to build or lease/buy options when acquiring an IS.

vendor management (p. 219) The management, control, and monitoring of third party providers or suppliers to the organization. It is the role of the *vendor manager* to keep vendors apprised of what is happening in the organization, including any new requirements for vendors.

waterfall model (p. 236) A model with a designed set of phases, where a new phase begins only after acceptably completing the preceding phase, causing development activities to move downstream through the phases in a formal, detailed manner.

KEY FIGURES

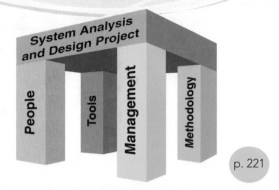

p. 221

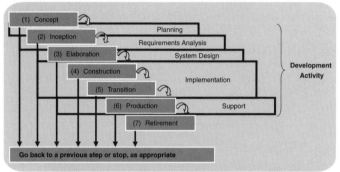

p. 221

PROJECT MANAGER AND PROJECT TEAM			
Scope Management	**Time Management**	**Cost Management**	**Quality Management**

Core Functions

PROJECT MANAGEMENT METHODS AND TECHNIQUES			
HR Management	**Risk Management**	**Procurement Management**	**Communications Management**

Facilitating Functions

IT-Based Tools

p. 225

Successful Project

QUICK TEST

1. In the _____ phase of the IS life cycle, the organization recognizes a need for an IS and defines the project.

   a. inception

   b. elaboration

   c. construction

   d. transition

2. Which of the following risk-mitigating tactics means that the project manager will act to eliminate the possibility of a risk occurring?

   a. risk reduction

   b. risk deferral

   c. risk acceptance

   d. risk avoidance

3. A(n) _____ consists of several graphical elements that, when combined, form a set of diagrams that provide multiple views of a system that highlight the system's purpose.